LONDON'S BEST BEER PUBS & BARS

Des de Moor

CAMRA BOOKS

Published by the Campaign for Real Ale Ltd
230 Hatfield Road, St Albans, Hertfordshire AL1 4LW
www.camra.org.uk/books

© Campaign for Real Ale Ltd. 2021
Text © Des de Moor
First published 2011 (Reprinted with corrections 2012)
Second Edition 2015
Third Edition 2021

ISBN 978-1-85249-360-8

A CIP catalogue record for this book is available from the British Library

Printed and bound in Slovenia by GPS Group

Commissioning Editor: Katie Button
Project Editors: Julie Hudson, Alan Murphy
Design/Typography: Dale Tomlinson
Typefaces: Guardian Sans family
Cover design: Jack Pemberton
Maps: Igloo
Sales & Marketing: Toby Langdon

Photo credits

The publisher would like to thank the pubs, bars,
shops, restaurants, breweries and individuals
who have kindly given permission for their
photography to be printed in this publication.

Specific thanks go to:
Ben Butler at Clapton Craft Brewery, p179;
Bel Shapiro, p62; Bob Steel, p104; Boak & Bailey
p240; Brewery History Society, 96(t), 114; Cath
Harries, p12, p15, p17(t), p32, p35; Claire-Michelle
Tavernier-Pearson p79; Matthew Black, p96(b);
Dan Breckwoldt/shutterstock.com, p11; Justinc,
115; Ewan Munro, 90, 163; Rev David Moore, 164;
Ross Cooper, p135; London Fields Brewery p143;
Matt Curtis, p155; Helen Cathcart, 175; Nic Crilly-
Hargrave, 187(b), 272; Emma Guscott, 221; Secret
Pilgrim, 276; Andrew Bowden, 272; Paul Winch
Furness, p61; pisaphotography/shutterstock.com,
p13; Rupert Marlow Photography, p33; Sambrooks
Brewery, p274; Geoff Brandwood, p106, p125, p306;
The Five Points Brewing Company, p45.

Contents

Celebrating London's beer renaissance

Despite the challenges of the Covid-19 pandemic in 2020 and 2021, London is still one of the best beer cities in the world, and this book sets out to provide the complete and indispensable guide to its beery treasures. Historically a brewing colossus and long renowned for its pubs, this great city has in a matter of years reclaimed its status as a world class centre for making beer as well as drinking it. These pages chronicle a brewing community that has grown tenfold in a decade, and direct both the beer beginner and the experienced connoisseur to the best places in which to experience this miraculous renaissance alongside the fruits of brewing excellence from the rest of the UK and the wider world.

Great local beer is now so easy to find in London that a time without it seems hard to imagine. But the first edition of this guide, published in July 2011, recorded only 14 breweries, several of them new arrivals: enough to generate a buzz but only a modest upturn after a century of seemingly unstoppable decline in a city that had once been the beer capital of the world. This book details 140 breweries and counting. It's an astonishing story that's told in more detail below.

The growth in brewing has been matched by an unprecedented surge in the range, variety and local provenance of quality beer in pubs, bars, restaurants and shops. London beers are now appearing on London bars with a ubiquity and frequency unseen since the 1970s, and the quality and variety on offer is almost certainly the best it's ever been. In certain parts of the city like Hackney or Deptford, it seems no-one would dream of bothering to apply for a new alcohol licence without at least some local beer to hand. I like to think this guide, appearing when it did, made a modest contribution to a truly remarkable renaissance.

The main part of the book is a directory listing not only all the breweries but several hundred other venues worthy of the thinking drinker's attention. In 2011, my task in selecting these was finding enough places besides the obvious specialists that genuinely offered quality, choice and interest. If I spotted two or three pumpclips from smaller independents and a Belgian bottle or two in the fridge, I'd flag the place for consideration. Today, the challenge is deciding what to leave out. The bar has been raised so much higher that many places featured in previous editions have been relegated to Try also status or left out entirely to keep the book within manageable proportions.

You can read more about how places were chosen on p63 but the main concerns are beer choice, quality, presentation and expertise, with priority treatment for brewery outlets or places offering something unusual or unique. The book has never been a simple pub guide and the venues in this edition are more diverse than ever, encompassing bars, restaurants, bottle shops, micropubs and taprooms as well as 'proper' pubs. It's also never focused exclusively on cask beer. Though for very good reasons explained on p34, I'm keen to celebrate great cask wherever I find it, there's no ignoring the fact that much of London's best beer is now in kegs, cans and bottles.

Besides brewers, beers and beer outlets, the book contains a wealth of other useful detail, with summaries of notable pub and bar chains, the main festivals and events, beer tour operators and beer styles brewed in London. I've included notes on beer with food, a pub and bar user guide for visitors, and an index of places to drink by theme. For additional depth you'll find material on the history and heritage of both pubs and brewing, and for breadth there are some alternative thoughts from some of the capital's beer movers and shakers. Finally, as excellent as London's beer is, it would be perverse to spend all your time here sitting at a bar. I've therefore included some context about the city, its history, geography and culture, and pointed out other features of interest in the areas surrounding the listed outlets. These notes are necessarily brief and selective, so I strongly recommend that to explore properly, you use this book in conjunction with a general guidebook (More information, p348). Beer is also a cultural phenomenon and putting it in context can only enrich your appreciation of London's zythological bounty.

If you're visiting London for the first time or have just moved here, or you know the city already but aren't yet familiar with its beer scene, I wish you a very warm welcome. I hope this book will provide an excellent starting point for what I promise will be a great beer journey. If you're a longstanding Londoner and beer connoisseur, the book can steer you to new discoveries and fill in the background to things you already know, or at least provide something to argue with. Together we can all help ensure London beer remains a cause for celebration for many years to come.

Taking stock

One of the many pleasures of researching this book is that every few years I get a unique snapshot of the London brewing scene through hundreds of conversations with people involved in the day-to-day business of brewing, selling and buying beer in the city. It might not be especially scientific, but it certainly helps you notice the trends. I've dealt with some of these in detail in the various history pieces, but I thought it would be interesting to summarise them here.

The most obvious one is the changing pattern of the industry's growth. On the one hand, the rate of increase of brewery numbers has slowed. 2019 saw the first single figure year-on-year increase since 2009, at only 5%. Previously, it had been at least 13%, sometimes much more. Several of the most recent new breweries are very small ones, as able home-brewers discover there's just enough in local sales to justify making 50 or 100 litre batches commercially on at least a part-time basis. Even before the Covid lockdowns, troubles at ambitious operations like Hop Stuff, Redchurch and Ubrew, detailed elsewhere, confirmed

there was no guarantee of constant expansion, especially given the large losses for enthusiastic individual supporters who had invested in these breweries via crowdfunding.

On the other hand, breweries have continued to open, even during the pandemic, and established and reputable producers have continued to expand, with businesses like Redemption, Sambrook's (both founded 2008), the Kernel (2009), Truman's (2011), BBNo, Partizan (2012), Brick, Five Points, Pressure Drop, Weird Beard (2013), Gipsy Hill, Signature and Wild Card (2014) now orders of magnitude bigger than when they started. The most extreme example of this is the more unsettling trend of multinationals buying their way in. The last edition in 2015 was hurriedly revised to report Meantime's sale to SABMiller, later succeeded by Asahi. All but one of the 70 other breweries listed were then independent. Today, the likes of AB InBev, Carlsberg, Heineken, Kirin and Molson Coors have joined Asahi as owners of sizeable chunks of London brewing, and their investment is financing several major expansions. In many ways, it's a vote of confidence in the industry, but it raises questions about access to market and fears for future diversity.

Perhaps the most shocking intervention by the big beer firms was Asahi's purchase of Fuller's brewing division early in 2019. London's oldest continuously operating commercial brewery, its biggest overall and its last surviving family independent, is no longer independent. Set against this, for those who appreciate brewing heritage, is the good news that commercial operations have at last been restored to the Ram Brewery site in Wandsworth, where John Hatch has heroically sustained regular brewing activities since Young's closed in 2006.

The emerging wedge between the appreciation of beer and traditional pub culture was already evident in the last edition but has grown rapidly since. Thanks in part to the prevalence of tied houses and chains, the old-school pub sector is lagging in terms of variety and quality, and beer aficionados are increasingly likely to find themselves in the rather different environment of a brewery taproom, an artisanal burger bar, a trendy market, a shopfront micropub or one of the new breed of bar-bottle shop hybrids. Purpose-built pubs no longer account for most places listed here. Bottle shop-bars were almost unheard of in 2015 but you'll hardly turn a page of this edition without finding one, while the number of micropubs listed has increased from five to 33, accounting for most of the Outer Southeast London section. Lockdown conditions have accentuated this trend, as the smaller, newer independent businesses have found it much easier to adapt to new ways of working, like home deliveries and click and collect, than traditional pubs tied to large companies.

The selection of beer you're likely to find on sale has also continued to evolve. I've said a bit more about the growth in both the quality and availability of lower alcohol beers on p41. Cans, a still-provocative novelty in 2015, are now the default for most 'small pack' (bottled or canned) beer and some London outlets are refusing to stock new UK-brewed lines in bottles. Specialist outlets are offering far fewer US imports, especially of hoppier styles, as UK brewers now provide fresher, cheaper alternatives that are just as good. London beers predominate in many outlets as localism continues to grow, so a few pubs and bars are now distinguishing themselves by focusing on brewers from *outside* the capital.

Technical quality has improved overall: fewer people in the industry raised the problem with me this time around. Some of this is likely down to investment in better equipment, but also increased knowledge and skills. A few notable breweries do amazing things with primitive brewhouses in the cramped conditions of railway arches. Good lager, a hard style to nail as the ideal flavour profile is so clean and unforgiving of flaws, is happily on the increase. Start-ups are increasingly aware of the high bar, but this is an area where there's always room for, as they say, continuous improvement. Some brewers need to pay more attention to recipe design, particularly when creating the ubiquitous 'hazy, juicy' New England-inspired pale ales that are currently the 'craft' style of choice, and when playing with fruits and other flavourings.

One major area of concern, raised by some of the commentators in this edition, is that while the diversity of styles overall has never been higher, cask ale, a format for which the

UK is uniquely renowned, is apparently struggling to retain its place on the bar, along with the subtle session styles in which it excels. Cask was still in growth across the UK at the time of the last edition, but recent studies have shown it's back in decline. While a handful of breweries still make significant amounts of what might be termed more traditional cask (Fuller's, of course, alongside Five Points, Portobello, Redemption, Sambrook's, Truman's, Twickenham, Wimbledon and others), several have stopped producing it and for others it's now a small proportion of their output. The rest is mainly in keg and can – well-made and usually naturally conditioned, but inevitably colder and more carbonated. As you'll note if you compare the numbers between this edition and the last, many places have cut back on their cask range – not itself a bad thing if it improves quality and reduces waste, but certainly indicative.

There are some small but encouraging signs, including a few breweries returning to cask and reviving traditional styles, for example Affinity, Boxcar and Anspach & Hobday. Most brewers love cask and would happily produce more if they could get a fair price for it and were confident it would reach the consumer at its best. And there's still a demand for local cask which some pubs find hard to satisfy. 'I started off with just kegs and bottles,' one very small brewer told me. 'But I've found myself doing more cask, partly because I've realised I really like it, but also because there's much more competition for the keg taps.' As a draught format for drinking in public, cask was particularly vulnerable during the lockdowns, and much was poured away when its short shelf life expired. But even then, some resourceful licensees found temporary work-rounds, with several micropubs doing a roaring local trade in takeaway containers of freshly poured beer, with new tappings promoted through social media.

I would love to see a healthier market for cask but achieving this will take creativity and lateral thinking. First and foremost, we need to confront the quality challenges of a product which requires careful handling and rapid turnover but doesn't always get them, and push for better trade and consumer education. We also need to confront a culture where significant numbers of customers expect the most specialist, fragile and labour-intensive product to be the cheapest on the bar. More appropriate sizes would help: while some draught keg beers are available in 10 litre kegs, the smallest quantity of cask that's generally sold is the traditional firkin containing nine gallons or 41 litres, and this for a beer that needs to be drunk in three days. There's a smaller traditional size, the 4½-gallon pin, which is surely ripe for a revival, and maybe there's an opportunity for an enterprising manufacturer to rethink the design and size of casks for our times. The old-fashioned image of cask detailed in recent research needs to be flipped to make the format relevant to a new generation of drinkers: events like Affinity's recently established and hugely popular CASK festival show what can be done. We certainly won't get anywhere by pretending that other beer formats don't exist or aren't worth drinking, one reason why this guide has never been cask-only.

One positive trend underlined by the pandemic was the strengthening link between breweries, retailers and the local community and the focus on ethical concerns. Many breweries and other beer-related businesses have formal links to charities and social organisations, many are living wage employers, nearly all strive to reduce their environmental footprint and to support their local community in various ways, from supporting local initiatives to simply being good neighbours. I've discussed the impacts of Covid-19 in more detail below but it was moving to hear how the concerns for the community were enthusiastically returned as people rallied round their local breweries, pubs and bars.

And both the industry and its customers are increasingly reflecting the diversity of those communities. These days I'm often the oldest person in the place, which can only be a good sign for the future, and if the scene is still more white and male than London at large, it's certainly much less so than it used to be. Women are making a vital impact as brewers, managers, communicators and customers, and the ethnic mix is getting richer too. More and more people are overtly pushing in the right direction with initiatives like CAMRA's ban on sexist marketing and Jaega Wise's work at SIBA. When in 2021 the much-lauded

Manchester brewery Cloudwater launched a four-pack of collaborations celebrating diversity, it included four London-based businesses: Lily Waite's Queer Brewing Project and two BAME-owned cuckoo brewers, Eko and Rock Leopard. Against some worrying trends in the wider world, London brewing, like London itself in the words of its mayor, remains open for business.

Keeping up to date

A disadvantage of guidebooks is that they soon slip out of date and given the dynamism of the current London beer scene, this one is likely to date more quickly than most. I've struggled in the past for an income stream to justify researching and publishing free updates, but I now have a Patreon page where you can support my work and receive exclusive updates and access to other material, tastings and events: sign up at patreon.com/ldnbestbeer. I continue to keep the breweries updated at desdemoor.co.uk/london.

Comments, updates, corrections, suggestions, Amazon reviews, compliments and criticisms are all very welcome. Feedback on previous editions helped shape this one. The book has a Facebook fan page at facebook.com/LondonsBestBeer where comments are welcome and news is periodically posted, as well as its own Twitter feed: @ldnbestbeer. You can contact me directly at des@desdemoor.com or follow me on Twitter: @desdemoor.

A note on the third edition

Readers familiar with the previous edition in 2015 will notice this one retains the same broad format, with one major change: all the breweries are now listed geographically alongside pubs, bars, shops and restaurants, with a themed brewery list at the back. Most breweries now have some public-facing facility like a taproom or shop, or at least organise occasional open days, and with so many to deal with, this seemed the best use of space. I've created several new geographical sections to reflect the increased proliferation of notable venues in certain areas and added a short Beer Tourism section to acknowledge the growth in beer-related holidays, walks and tours. All the entries have been reviewed

early 2020 took me to 767 places over 65 working days, travelling 3,306km (2,054 miles), including 644km (400 miles) on foot, the equivalent of walking from my flat in Deptford to Mugdock Country Park on the other side of Glasgow. But in March 2020, just as our designer Dale Tomlinson was assembling the last few pages for the printer, with tourism already affected by the growing Covid-19 pandemic and a hospitality industry lockdown looking increasingly inevitable, we took the galling but sensible decision to postpone publication. It wasn't until early 2021, as the rollout of the vaccination programme promised a sustainable return to something like normality, that we were confident enough to reschedule it, by which point all the details needed rechecking, several entries deleted and several more added in. So I've since clocked up another 37 visits over eight working days and 517km (323 miles), including 66 km (41 miles) on foot (which would take me on along the West Highland Way past Loch Lomond to Inverarnen).

As always, nearly all the entries, both main and Try also, are based on visits or revisits: the main exceptions are breweries closed to the public, particularly those in private homes. But as most of these visits took place before the pandemic, the majority of entries have been checked by additional desk research, including contacting nearly all the listed breweries and many non-brewing venues for updated information. I haven't been able to visit as many post-2019 new openings as I'd ideally have liked, and a few I missed but trust are worth looking at are shown as Try alsos. I'm aiming to correct this over the next year or so with online updates for Patreon supporters (see above).

and all the details checked and updated.

This edition has 316 main entries covering 343 individual venues, including 141 breweries and brewpubs. 134 of these had full listings in the previous edition, while 44 were also featured in the first edition in 2011, though some are under new management and perhaps new names and, in the case of breweries, at new locations. 62 places with full entries in 2015 appear here under Try also or Heritage pub.

The process of putting this edition together was more protracted and challenging than previously. We originally planned to publish it in May 2020, and the research in 2019 and

Weights and measures

Quantities are given either in metric measurements only, or both metric and non-metric measurements. The latter use the imperial system: remember that an imperial pint (568 ml) is 25% larger than a US pint (473ml), and a gallon is proportionately larger too.

For bulk liquid measurements such as for brewery equipment or annual output, I've used the international measure, the hectolitre (hl), equivalent to 100 litres, 22 gallons or 176 pints. Many British brewers still think in terms of the old

brewer's barrels, which hold 36 gallons (1.64hl, 164 litres, 288 pints). Note that British brewer's barrels are significantly more capacious than American ones: a US barrel holds only 31 US gallons (1.17hl, 117 litres, 198.5 imperial pints).

The city that invented itself

London wasn't meant to exist. Those ancient urbanists, the Romans, rarely built on greenfield sites, preferring to redevelop existing settlements. When the legions crossed the Thames in the year 43, they found nothing of note on the little rise of Cornhill, on the north bank just east of the Walbrook stream. Belgic and Celtic farmers populated the wider area, but the river then was much broader, shallower and marshier than today, so settlements clung to higher ground. There may have been a farm on or close to the place where London later grew, with a name later borrowed into Latin as *LONDINIVM*.

The Roman army originally used several crossing points, but sometime after the year 50, a decision was taken to build a permanent crossing between Southwark and Cornhill, a few metres downstream from the present London Bridge. No military emplacement was intended for the north end of the bridge, so the officer who signed off the plans couldn't have had any idea he was ushering one of the greatest cities in human history into existence.

Unsurprisingly given its strategic importance, the road junction over the bridge attracted service industries and a small settlement grew. In the year 60, the fledgling town was sacked by the Celtic Iceni tribe: their leader, Queen Boudica, is another inadvertent godparent as her actions prompted London's rebuilding as a proper planned city, with a defensive wall that can still be traced today. The centre of administration moved here from Colchester and by the end of the 1st century, it was the biggest city in and the *de facto* capital of the province of Britannia.

It's remarkable how the earliest development of London set so much of the tone for what was to follow, driven by entrepreneurs who saw the opportunities for hawking goods and services from the roadside. The importance of London as a port also goes back to Roman times: the sheltered estuary and good connections to a new road network making it a more favourable landing place than the old Celtic ports on the south coast. A complex of wharves soon projected into the river, the first of many such encroachments that eventually created the narrower, deeper Thames we know today.

Three centuries later, their empire crumbling around them, the Romans abandoned Britain and their grand city began to decay, although the Germanic invaders that filled the power vacuum continued to recognise it as a seat of power. The Guildhall is on the site of an Anglo-Saxon royal hall, and the Christian missionary Augustine established St Paul's cathedral nearby in 604. The Anglo-Saxons developed their own trading suburb, known as Lundenwic, along the Strand, in those days the actual riverfront, but the Roman site remained in defensive use and Alfred the Great had its walls restored.

Following the unification of England in 974, London's prosperity ensured its importance as a political centre and royal residence. The old city lost its political role in 1052 when Edward the Confessor moved his court upstream to Thorney Island, next to a tiny abbey which was rapidly bolstered with royal patronage. Though much altered, the palace and the abbey still stand at Westminster, and the split between economic and political centres remains a persistent feature of London's geography. This split is also behind the typographical subtlety that distinguishes the city of London – the totality of continuous development – from the City of London, occupying the original Roman site.

In 1066, William the Bastard, Duke of Normandy, conquered England, building what was to become the most powerful fortress in Britain, the Tower of London, in the southeast corner of the City. The Normans gradually

abandoned the old practice of peripatetic royal courts, and by the time Magna Carta was sealed in 1215, Westminster had emerged as the single administrative capital, its palace the meeting place of Parliament. The City remained the population centre and the economic powerhouse, home to the powerful guilds that controlled manufacturing and trade in the medieval world, exploiting this position to lever autonomy from cash-strapped monarchs. Today, the City of London retains a structure unique in English local government and still has its own police force.

London has long been the biggest city in Britain, but as the Middle Ages ended, it lagged behind Paris and even Bruges and Novgorod in the world league tables. Under the Tudors and Stuarts, it began to catch up, with the population spilling over the City walls into what became the East End. Southwark, to the south of the bridge, also fuelled its growth by providing services too disreputable for the City. The theatres for which it's best known signal London's emergence as a cultural crucible, a vibrant urban environment in which talents like William Shakespeare and Christopher Marlowe could flourish.

The river was central as both barrier and lifeline, now not only a conduit of trade but of England's growing sea power, with naval dockyards established at Deptford and Woolwich. As well as big ships, it was busy with watermen constantly ferrying commuters, and with royals who took to wafting in sumptuous flotillas between the string of riverside palaces from Greenwich to Windsor.

With the population rocketing, overtaking Paris by 1650, the aristocratic owners of adjoining rural estates realised the true extent of their good fortune. The Earl of Bedford got things started with the piazza at Covent Garden in the 1630s, but a pair of disasters interrupted developments. The Great Plague of 1665 killed at least 100,000 people, perhaps 20% of the population. Next year came the Great Fire, which destroyed 80% of the largely wooden buildings within the City walls over the course of four days. The wealth of London is evident from the grand rebuilding that followed, its centrepiece Christopher Wren's spectacular new home for St Paul's. But the funds didn't stretch to realising Wren's ambitious master plan for a new system of grand boulevards – something to ponder as you wander the streets and alleys that still thread between the City's high-rises on their Roman and medieval alignments.

After the Great Fire, the noxious industries were exiled east, while the west saw the onward march of property development through the 18th century. The now familiar pattern of streets, squares and terraces spread into the spaces between royal hunting grounds, themselves now remade into royal parks. New off-river docks boosted the city's trading capacity, and as the Industrial Revolution took hold, industry became bigger, more capital intensive and technologically advanced, feeding international markets secured by the country's growing naval might. London's famed cosmopolitan character grew as people flocked here from all over.

Better transport facilitated further expansion in the 19th century, with improved roads rapidly followed by railways that spawned commuter suburbs further out. 'Ribbon development' and sprawl swallowed scores of formerly separate villages and towns. Victorian London was the capital of a massive empire, dotted with sumptuous monuments to its own success, but at a cost. Beneath it was a sink of poverty, with millions packed into unhealthy slums of the sort that sparked Charles Dickens to righteous anger.

Amazingly, London had got this far without a single directing authority. It wasn't until 1855 that a Metropolitan Board of Works was set up to coordinate infrastructure such as sewers – just in time for the Great Stink of 1858 when the stench of raw sewage in the Thames even disrupted parliamentary proceedings. A multi-purpose London County Council followed in 1889, but the capital's boundaries had outgrown it before it even met.

As London entered the 20th century, political pressure built to contain this relentless growth, and to protect the remaining undeveloped areas. The city emerged relatively unscathed physically, though profoundly affected economically and socially, from World War I, but the outbreak of another war in 1939 marked a watershed. German bombs rained on London for 76 consecutive nights in the Blitz of 1940–41, destroying vast areas of the urban fabric, particularly around the docks and industrial areas. After the war, a new order took hold,

with an increased role for government. New planning controls locked the boundaries of the built-up area where they remain today, within a protected green belt. The slums the Luftwaffe had missed were cleared and many of their inhabitants deported to supposedly self-contained New Towns much further out.

London was now the capital of a humbler Britain, no longer a great imperial power. Its industry declined and by the 1970s, with its docks now too small for the new container ships, it had even lost its ancient role as a port. But the City clung to pre-eminence as a financial and business centre that is still only rivalled by New York City, handling most of the world's business in foreign exchange.

As the dowdy 1950s gave way to the 'swinging 60s', London's art and culture flourished. The evolution of British popular music from trad jazz, skiffle and rhythm and blues to the 'British invasion', psychedelia and prog can be traced through London's pubs, clubs and recording studios, and it was in London that provincial bands like the Beatles achieved their creative peak. A few years later, the city was the epicentre of punk. London has nurtured leading fashion designers, photographers, architects, artists and film makers, and provided the backdrop to countless novels from Martin Amis's *London Fields* to Monica Ali's *Brick Lane*. The rich heritage and contemporary cultural buzz have traditionally attracted more international visitors than any other world city, around 21 million in 2019.

London's creativity has been informed by its ever-changing complexion. From 1948, it became a new home to settlers from Britain's former colonies in the Caribbean and the Indian subcontinent, followed by significant groups from Cyprus, Vietnam, West Africa and, latterly, eastern Europe. Currently almost a third of Londoners were born outside the UK, and over 300 languages are spoken here. While new Londoners haven't always received the warmest of welcomes, historically they're only the most recent arrivals in the flow of humanity that's converged on the city over millennia. London has also been the scene of bitter struggles – it's inevitably a focus for political protest and occasionally violent conflict, from the anti-war demonstrations of the 1960s to the anti-globalisation and environmental protests and street riots of more recent years.

In 1964, it finally gained a local authority almost commensurate with its size, though still not quite matching its true boundaries, with the creation of the Greater London Council. By 1986, under its left-wing leader Ken Livingstone, this body became such a thorn in the side of Margaret Thatcher's Conservative government that they abolished it, leaving London balkanised between 33 boroughs. Livingstone ultimately became the first Mayor of London when a new system of governance was created in 2000, serving two terms before being ousted by future Conservative prime minister Boris Johnson. In 2016, Johnson was replaced in turn by current mayor Sadiq Khan who, despite a bitter and ugly campaign fought by his rivals, was returned with the highest number of votes ever for any politician in British history, and comfortably retained his majority in the 2021 election.

Recent decades have seen swathes of London transformed as former docks, ware-houses and industrial areas are regenerated, post-war social housing refurbished, and Victorian inner-city suburbs gentrified with new city and media wealth, driving up property prices to absurd and world-busting levels. The most obvious symbol of all this is the way the focus of the city has shifted eastwards, first to the new high-rise business district built around disused docks at Canary Wharf and on to other remodelled areas like the Queen Elizabeth Olympic Park at Stratford (a legacy of London's hosting the 2012 Olympic and Paralympic Games) and the Greenwich Millennium Village. Currently, upmarket flats seem to be sprouting on every patch of former industrial land close to a station. The city was the first part of the UK to bounce back from the recession of 2009, though the 'age of austerity' persists in local council spending, and the gap between rich and poor is widening again.

Unsurprisingly, London was one of the places that defied the narrow majority for 'Brexit' in the 2016 referendum, with 60% of Londoners voting to remain in the European Union. London also voted overwhelmingly against Johnson's Conservative party in the December 2019 general election, once again placing Westminster firmly at odds with its

surroundings. Mere weeks after officially leaving the EU on 31 January 2020, the capital, along with the rest of the UK and, indeed, the world, found itself coping with the Covid-19 emergency: by May 2021, the disease had claimed the lives of almost 20,000 Londoners, brought much of the economy to a halt and reduced tourism by 75%.

At the time of writing, it's still too early to assess the overall impact of both Brexit and Covid on a city that's now almost two millennia old. We can be certain, though, that London will continue to reinvent itself. The city's population, currently almost 9 million, continues to grow and, despite likely reductions in migration from the EU, is still expected to hit 10 million in the 2030s. As always, there's not much in the way of a grand plan: accommodating these incomers will simply add to the variegated patchwork of the city's haphazard growth.

This complex texture, although confusing to navigate, is one of London's principal delights, blissfully free of the sort of unofficial apartheid that afflicts so many US cities. When you set your sights on a great brewery taproom, pub or bar, don't forget to enjoy the process of reaching it. You're quite likely to pass a pompous Victorian pile, a gloomy 1960s estate, a hidden green space, a poshed-up terrace, some striking contemporary architecture and a world-famous landmark all within a few minutes' walk, and you'll undoubtedly hear snatches of some of those 300 languages along the way. Perhaps there's something to be said for unplanned cities after all.

City of brewing

On Chiswell Street on the very northern edge of the City is an events and conference venue known as the Brewery, which is used, according to its website, for everything 'from upscale state functions and company conferences to televised music events and discreet boardroom powwows.' The biggest available option to potential hirers is the Porter Tun Room, one of the largest unobstructed indoor spaces in London. Its name might sound like a piece of quaint nonsense dreamed up by the marketing team but is in fact an accurate reflection of the room's original purpose.

For well over a century, this room housed huge wooden vats known as 'tuns' in which thousands of barrels-worth of porter beer sleepily matured. Still more beer was kept in stone-lined cisterns in the basement, the largest of which held 625,000 litres – about 1.1 million pints. This was the heart of the Whitbread brewery, opened by Samuel Whitbread in 1750 as the first purpose-built mass production brewery in the world, and at its peak the most successful brewery in Britain.

London has many more such relics. The Truman brewery, now an entertainment, retail and business complex, is a little to the east, in Brick Lane. The Courage brewery by Tower Bridge fell early to the redevelopment of London's docklands, and is now offices and flats. The Anchor retail park in Mile End Road bears the name of Charrington's former Anchor brewery, of which a couple of key buildings survive. At Romford in London's far eastern suburbia, the Brewery shopping complex with its mattress superstores and multiplex cinema occupies the site of Ind & Smith, later Ind Coope. Between them these sites testify to London's former status as the world capital of beer.

Brewing almost certainly goes back to London's beginnings. The practice was well-established by the Middle Ages, though as elsewhere in Europe much of it took place alongside other activities in pubs and the domestic brewhouses of institutions and upper-class homes. The canons of St Paul's are said to have brewed 100 times in 1286, producing 67,800 gallons (3,082hl, 542,400 pints), the output of a small commercial brewery today.

The growing population created increasing opportunities for 'common brewers', standalone operations making a living from supplying beer. Southwark was particularly noted for such breweries (see Southwark Ale p90). The Worshipful Company of Brewers is one of the earliest of the city trade guilds, dating back to the end of the 12th century and granted a royal charter in 1437. It still maintains a hall north of the Guildhall, just within the old City walls, though most of the breweries were elsewhere. John Stow, whose 1598 *Survey of London* mentions 26 common brewers, notes they 'remaine neare to the friendly water of Thames'. This was principally for transport reasons: it's a misconception that the already sewage-laden river provided the main ingredient of London's beer. Brewers were banned in 1345 from using public water conduits, so sunk their own artesian wells, tapping the aquifers within the chalk underlying the Thames basin.

In terms of scale, these early common brewers were comparable to many of today's smaller microbreweries, producing 20–30 barrels (33–50hl, 5,760–8,640 pints) a week with a staff of four or five people. As the city grew, so did its demand for beer which back then was a truly everyday refreshment: water from public supplies, particularly in big cities, was often dangerously polluted and unpalatable, while beer, made with water from a protected source which was boiled as part of the brewing process, was a much safer and more pleasant drink. As the modern era approached,

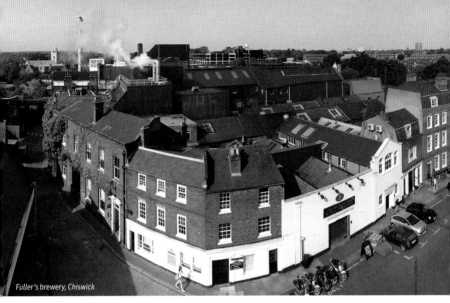

Fuller's brewery, Chiswick

the total number of brewers declined, with some of the smaller operations failing and the surviving breweries growing to fill the gaps. How some of these modest and labour-intensive businesses grew big enough to leave the impressive legacy visible today is partly answered by the story of porter.

There are various accounts of the 'invention' of porter which are now thought to be unreliable. The more realistic scenario is that it evolved and was refined over time by several brewers from an existing style of aged dark beer, probably in the 1710s. Most authorities agree that its name is best explained by its popularity with the porters who were then an important part of the busy city's workforce: there were 'fellowship porters' who carried bulk goods from ships and 'ticket porters' who transported a variety of goods around the streets.

Porter was a relatively strong beer of around 7% ABV, made with brown malt that had been roasted so ferociously it was 'blown' or popped like corn (the modern technical term is 'torrefied'). This gave the fresh beer a pronounced smoky tang, so it was aged to mellow the flavour. The long maturation in wooden vessels populated by numerous wild yeasts and other microflora produced a flat beer with distinctive sour, vinous flavours, as still found in some traditional Belgian as well as modern wood-aged beers. Beer in this condition was known as 'stale', meaning it had stood, with no negative connotations. Later recipes included pale malts and the stale quality was offset by blending aged beer with a fresher brew.

The process favoured better-resourced brewers who could afford to lock up cash and storage space with stock that might take two years to recoup its investment, sometimes accounting for over 10% of a brewery's assets. The increasing size of the porter breweries drove technological development and capital investment in mechanical equipment, steam power, coke firing and more accurate instruments like thermometers and hydrometers. Economies of scale increased profitability, and porter tuns swelled accordingly, with brewers competing to possess the biggest. Porter brewing made the most successful brewery owners into millionaires, and money bought honours and political influence for big names like the Whitbreads and the Trumans, creating a new British brewing elite punningly referred to as the 'beerage'.

In the 19th century, the porter brewers faced competition from a different style of beer that was ultimately to change the face of brewing, and once again it emerged from London. Pale ale first appeared in the 1650s, when the invention of coke made it possible to produce paler malts, but it really grabbed attention in the hoppy variant later known as India Pale Ale, famously exported to the sub-continent from East London. In the 1830s, the water of Burton upon Trent in Staffordshire was found to be particularly suited to pale ale brewing and some of the big London breweries set up branches there, though some abandoned the Midlands when they discovered 'Burtonising' London water with gypsum produced comparable results.

By the mid-19th century, London tastes were turning from stale porter to 'running ales': products which didn't require long ageing and could be served fresh in sparkling form using cask conditioning, made from paler malts with lower hop rates. The most basic of these were mild ales, which in their original form were pale rather than dark. Similarly fresh and light but more hoppy beers, known in the trade simply as pale ale but rapidly labelled 'bitter' by drinkers, had a growing more upmarket following. Breweries like Charrington, Courage and Watney proved adept at catering to these changing tastes. Porter brewers adopted similar methods, increasingly abandoning long maturation and making their beer as a running ale, using pale malt mixed with newly perfected, dark roasted malts to mimic the old colour and flavour.

Brewers also got more involved in retailing, first by providing cheap finance to would-be licensees in exchange for exclusive supply rights, then buying up their own pub estates by the end of the 19th century. Ultimately, this proved a mixed blessing for the industry, with pub estates benefitting from investment that really should have been spent on brewhouses. It was a contributing factor to the British brewers' retreat from the cutting edge of technology, with the centres of innovation shifting to countries like Denmark, Germany, the Netherlands and the US.

The expansion of London brewing continued for a while longer, reaching a peak around 1905 when the big brewers between them produced almost a billion pints. For two centuries, London had boasted the biggest brewers in the world, but after 1910 that distinction was lost. Limits on raw materials in World War I, economic challenges in the industry and increasing temperance-inspired regulation of alcohol began to drive down the strength of all British beer, which eventually became almost exclusively a low-strength product for drinking in quantity.

Mild and bitter dominated the interwar years, with porter now seen as an old man's drink. Its strength was much reduced – Whitbread's was down to 2.3% by 1930. Its cousin Irish stout, however, was growing in popularity and in 1933 Dublin brewer Guinness established a London plant. That same decade saw Watney's first experiments with filtered, pasteurised and artificially carbonated keg ales at the Stag brewery in Mortlake.

After World War II, the big brewers saw keg as a response to the challenge of rapidly changing markets and drinking habits, and through the 1950s and 1960s a wave of consolidation and rationalisation swept the industry as it invested in both the hardware and marketing muscle needed to launch first keg bitters, then keg lagers. Whitbread, for example, swallowed 27 smaller breweries across the country between 1948 and 1971, rapidly closing almost all of them. By the end of this period, London was home to just 11 breweries, all of them except Guinness dating back to the Victorian era, and most much older.

1971 is a significant year in the story of beer as it marks the foundation of the Campaign for the Revitalisation of Ale, shortly to be renamed the Campaign for Real Ale (CAMRA). In its early days, CAMRA faced a situation where seven big brewery groups brewed 75% of Britain's beer and owned half its pubs. Six of these – Allied (successor to Ind Coope), Bass Charrington, Courage, Guinness, Watney and Whitbread – had significant facilities in London. The seventh, Scottish & Newcastle, owned a significant number of London pubs. These groups enjoyed near-monopolies in certain areas and exploited them by brewing beer at the cheapest possible cost and selling it at the greatest possible profit with the support of glossy marketing. They viewed cask-conditioned ale as an unwelcome anachronism to be replaced by pasteurised, artificially carbonated keg beers of reliable consistency but minimal character, designed to be as inoffensive as possible to the maximum number of drinkers.

Two smallish London breweries, Fuller's

and Young's, retained their independence. Both became revered names among the growing number of dedicated real ale drinkers and grew substantially, though remained minnows compared to the big groups. The 'real ale revival' persuaded some of the big brewers to dabble with cask again, but their trajectory remained towards ever larger concentrations of production and greater efficiency. Sentiment was set aside as business logic questioned the need for capacity in a place with such high wages, property prices and traffic congestion as London.

Whitbread stopped brewing at Chiswell Street in 1976 although retained the site as a corporate headquarters until 2005. Watney's owners pulled out of brewing entirely in 1988 when its now-subsidiary Truman's closed. Courage left Southwark in 1981, Charrington shut up shop in 1985 and Allied quit Romford in 1993. Guinness, now part of global drinks combine Diageo, shut down Park Royal in 2005. Watney's Mortlake brewery, now in the hands of the world's biggest brewer, Anheuser-Busch InBev, was the last fragment of old-school big brewing left in London when it closed at the end of 2015.

Meanwhile, growing demand for character-ful beer in the wake of the real ale revival was spurring an upsurge of new UK microbreweries. London was home to one of the very first of these, Godson Freeman & Wilmot, founded in 1977. But Godson's mixed fortunes and short lifespan – it finally closed in 1986 after several suspensions of brewing – proved all too typical of similar initiatives that followed. All micro-brewers faced the challenge of reinventing an industry; London microbrewers faced all the

additional challenges of logistics and costs that were driving out their bigger rivals. Some of the more enduring new independent names, like Pitfield (1981), Freedom (1995) and O'Hanlon's (now Hanlon's, 1996) survived by moving out too. London also played a major role in the rebirth of the brewpub: David Bruce's Firkin chain was founded here in 1979, spreading across the country and beyond, but was shut down by new owners 20 years later.

The most significant brewery to buck the trend was Meantime, founded in 2000 by Alastair Hook (who was also involved with setting up the Freedom brewery), and still flourishing today though under multinational ownership. Significantly, it chose a different path to what was then typical for a micro-brewery, concentrating initially on quality lager and the bar and restaurant trade rather than pubs: a disappointment to some real ale fans, but also a demonstration that a successful modern micro could exist in the capital.

In 2006 came the grave news that Young's was abandoning six centuries of brewing history on its Wandsworth site and merging with Charles Wells in Bedford. As 2007 began, London had only nine working commercial breweries, its lowest number since 1979, and only three of these – Fuller's, Meantime and the Stag – were of any significant size. Three were small and sometimes struggling micros Battersea, Grand Union and Twickenham. The others were brewpubs: Brew Wharf, the Horseshoe and Zerodegrees. A century of relentless decline from world leadership to zero seemed near-complete. But events were about to take an unexpected turn.

The new city of beer

At the Great British Beer Festival at Earls Court in August 2006, Londoner Duncan Sambrook and two old friends were planning their evening's drinking when they noticed that, of all the many hundreds of breweries represented from Britain and across the world, only one, Fuller's, was from the same city in which the event took place. Mulling on this over a few pints, they concluded the only meaningful response was to start a brewery. It might just have been the beer talking, but the idea took root in Duncan's mind and, just over two years later, became reality with the opening of Sambrook's in Battersea, not far from the recently vacated site of Young's.

Sambrook's was then the most substantial dot on a line that had already begun to turn modestly upwards, despite the loss of two short-lived micros, Grand Union and Battersea (unrelated to the current brewery of the same name), in the intervening years. In March 2007, the Capital Pub Company included a small brewhouse in its refit of the Cock and Hen pub in Fulham; a couple of months later the experiment was repeated on a slightly larger scale at the Florence in Herne Hill. The Fulham pub was sold a year later without its brewery but brewing at its sister pub continued.

As Sambrook's was commissioning its kit, across the other side of London siblings James and Lizzie Brodie were busy restoring a brewery that had been abandoned for several years at the family's pub, the William IV in Leyton. An old farm building in east London's green belt became the part-time Ha'penny brewery in October 2009. What's in retrospect one of the most significant new openings took place a couple of months later, when former cheese-monger Evin O'Riordain began brewing and selling distinctively artisanal beers from a Bermondsey railway arch under the name of the Kernel.

Andy Moffat, struck by the pride communities in northern English cities had in their local ale, launched Redemption in Tottenham early in 2010. A few months later, the tiny vessel in the cellar of the Horseshoe at Hampstead metamorphosed into a substantial new automated brewhouse in Kentish Town railway arches under the name Camden Town. Like Meantime, it made flavoursome and unpasteurised bottled and keg beers from the start, and soon suspended regular cask production. Then there was the unexpected reappearance of the Truman's name, at first contract-brewed outside London by two young brewing heritage enthusiasts.

In March 2010, homebrewer and hop expert Phil Lowry and friends took over brewing at Borough Market brewpub Brew Wharf, junking its staid recipes in favour of internationally inspired experiments. It was Phil who, with Evin O'Riordain, invited all the other London brewers to dinner there in May 2010. That evening, fledgling newcomers and old hands discovered a shared passion and enthusiasm for London brewing and the London Brewers' Alliance (LBA) was born.

The brewers found selling their beer easier than perhaps expected. 'It's been a neglected market', Duncan Sambrook told me in 2011. 'My business partner David Welsh, who was once a director at Ringwood, was amazed at the contrast with Hampshire and Wiltshire where you're always bumping into reps from other breweries. When we started selling, we found there were more outlets than we originally thought – more free houses, and more opportunities to get guests in. The London market's so big, I think it could support all of us and more.'

Quite how much more nobody could have foreseen. The growing interest in brewing London beer dovetailed with the changing tastes of Londoners who were increasingly more sophisticated about what they ate and drank, more concerned with quality, authenticity, localism, provenance and green credentials. 'Craft beer', particularly if it was local, vibrantly flavoured and fetchingly branded, had suddenly and unexpectedly become trendy, an affordable luxury at a time when cash was tight. The trend was by no means limited to London of course – the craft phenomenon was already sweeping many other cities and countries, perhaps most notably the United States where brewery numbers have increased even more astonishingly from 89 in 1978 to almost 9,000 today. But given London's former brewing pre-eminence, this sudden reversal of the industry's fortunes seemed particularly significant.

When I submitted the manuscript of the first edition of this book in March 2011, Greater London had 14 operating commercial breweries including brewpubs, the highest figure since 1981. The total was up to 22 at the end of the year and by the next had risen to 36, already a higher tidemark than at the peak of the Firkin era in 1998. For the second edition in 2015, I found myself writing about 70 breweries, a five-fold increase over just four years. Since then, the number has continued to grow and now stands at 141, an extent unknown since the 1830s. Neighbourhoods that hadn't smelt a whiff of boiling hops for centuries are now swimming in beer, and the most localist of licensees are able to stock not just exclusively London beers, but the products of, say, the boroughs of Haringey or Southwark, while still offering an unprecedented variety of styles.

Brewery numbers don't equate to overall volume, of course, and the new breweries are minnows compared to the whales of the past. Veteran London brewer Derek Prentice, now at Wimbledon Brewery, estimated that while in the days of the Big Seven, nine or ten London breweries were producing 11.5 million hl a year between them, by 2015, seven times the number of breweries barely managed 1.5 million hl. A little counter-intuitively, the long-term decline in alcohol consumption due to health and lifestyle concerns may even have contributed to the upturn: if you're rationing yourself to the Chief Medical Officers' recommended maximum weekly consumption, you may be more inclined to spend your 14 units wisely on local beer of character instead of a ubiquitous industrial brand, even if the latter costs less per litre than mineral water in your local supermarket.

There have been some casualties. Brew Wharf, Brodies and Ha'penny are no longer with us and the Florence is mothballed, though brewing at Ha'penny's site was later revived by Solvay Society. Others have come and gone, often breweries too small to sustain themselves economically, or would-be brewpubs who discover that producing beer as consistently good as the stuff they could buy turns out to be more challenging than first thought. But many have survived, thrived and struggled to keep up with demand. This book records numerous instances of additional units and bigger sites, extended fermentation capacity and upgraded brewhouses, including among all the other founders of the LBA.

This expansion has inevitably begun to shift the economics of London beer. Though there have been some examples of organic growth from profits, small loans and personal investment from family and friends, much has been financed through crowdfunding. But it hasn't taken long for all this activity to attract the attention of rather bigger players. The most remarkable shift in the industry between the last edition and this one has been the return of big brewing to London, but in a rather different form than before.

At the beginning of 2015, every London brewery was independently owned except for the Stag, which AB InBev was in the process of closing. Then in May 2015, just in time to squeeze a last-minute amendment into the second edition, came the news that SABMiller had bought Meantime. The deal was met with some concern and dismay, but no great surprise as Meantime had long been one of the more commercially minded operators and its CEO was a former executive of the South African-US combine. What Meantime might not have been expecting, though, was that before the year was out, SABMiller itself would be swallowed by the world's biggest brewer, Brazilian-Belgian-US behemoth AB InBev (since rebranded as Budweiser Brewing Group in the UK). To assuage monopoly regulators, the combined group was obliged to shed some of its brands, so Meantime was packaged up with Grolsch and Peroni and sold on to Asahi, marking the first direct involvement of one of the big Japanese players in the UK market.

There was considerably more reaction to the news just before Christmas 2015 that Camden Town was also now the property of AB InBev. Those who had considered the brewery one of their own turned to social media to express their rage, including crowdfunders for whom an offer to buy back their shares at an impressive 70% return could not offset their feelings of betrayal. The prevailing culture of the resurgent London beer scene had made much of community, shared values and the idea of a brewery as a social institution with stakeholders beyond the directors and shareholders: here was the first painful example of that vision clashing with the reality of an ambitious business seeking to grow while continuing to pay salaries and dividends.

Much more was to come. Carlsberg bought London Fields in July 2017: the company hadn't brewed for some time thanks to the tangled affairs of its previous owner, but the Danish giant has since delivered on its promise to restore production. AB InBev's closest rival Heineken entered London brewing in November that year by buying a 49% stake in Brixton Brewing, financing a major expansion for what had been a relatively small outfit: it's since taken 100% ownership. But perhaps the biggest reaction was provoked in June 2018 when the Dutch brewer bought almost half of Beavertown. The brewery had already enjoyed a spectacular growth curve, from a corner of a Hackney pub kitchen to several well-equipped units on an industrial estate in little over six years, with quality beer and branding that seemed effortlessly to match the pulse of the

The new Truman's brew

burgeoning scene. The accusations of selling out were correspondingly loud and numerous independently minded stockists announced boycotts. But such gestures made only a tiny dent in the fortunes of an enterprise which has since opened the biggest purpose-built brewery in London for decades, just a short stroll up the Lea Valley from the already extensive facility AB InBev built for Camden Town in 2017.

Another Japanese brewer entered the London market in July 2018 when Kirin acquired Fourpure, in the craft heartland of Bermondsey, through its Australian-based subsidiary Lion Group. Reaction this time was relatively muted, perhaps because Fourpure, though producing excellent beers, had long positioned itself closer to the mainstream than some. The biggest bombshell dropped in January 2019, when London's last remaining historic brewery, Fuller's, announced it was splitting its brewing interests from its pubs and disposing of the former for £250 million. The same logic had already resulted in the demise of numerous traditional 'vertically-integrated' pub-owning breweries in the UK, including Fuller's former London rival Young's. The rationale was stark: 87% of the profits were generated by the pub side of the business. The new owner of the brewing operation was Meantime parent Asahi, which agreed to continue to supply Fuller's pubs.

The five biggest breweries in London – Fuller's, Meantime, Camden Town, Beavertown and Fourpure – are now owned or part-owned by multinationals. So far, all have kept their distinctive identities and their own management and brewing teams, who sincerely assure me that they've largely been left to get on with things as before. I've seen no clear signs yet of 'dumbing down' or reduction in quality: if anything, increased investment should raise quality and consistency, at least in the short term. Unlike in the post-war decades when big breweries swallowed smaller ones primarily for their pub estates, the multinationals are after credible brands and businesses that can respond more flexibly to the demands of a new generation of drinkers, and it's in their interests to limit the loss of customers who helped build those brands by changing too much too soon. Meanwhile, beers of the calibre of Beavertown Neck Oil and Camden Hells are much more widely available for more people to enjoy.

But there are genuine concerns about the power of big companies to restrict access to market. That bar with its colourful variety of taps may on closer inspection turn out to source everything from Heineken or AB InBev. The railway arch brewery down the road likely won't get a look-in. And ultimately, the top priority for the multinationals is their core brands, the industrial lagers that earn the bulk of their global profits. Big beer's interest in 'craft' is essentially a damage limitation exercise at a time when the mainstream brands are taking the biggest hit from declining consumption, and in ever-changing circumstances there's no guarantee that the cosy relationship between the multinationals and their new subsidiaries will last.

For the moment, though, most London breweries remain in independent hands, and the capital's beer culture is perhaps as healthy as it has ever been. One of the many positive innovations of the new wave is the direct relationship brewers now cultivate with drinkers. Once, breweries were industrial black boxes: today, nearly all welcome the public to taprooms, bottle shops, open days and tours. Establishing this practice is one of Evin O'Riordain's many achievements. The Kernel encouraged everyone to call in and buy beer from the start, and the string of nearby beer businesses it inspired have turned Bermondsey's railway arches into a zythophilic promenade. Since the last edition, smaller clusters of breweries and taprooms have emerged elsewhere, such as Bethnal Green, Hackney, Tottenham and, most recently, the Blackhorse area of Walthamstow.

Another very welcome recent develop-ment is the return of commercial brewing to one of London's (and indeed Britain's and the world's) most historic brewing sites. The closure of Young's in 2006 was one of the factors prodding Duncan Sambrook into action. So it's poetic that the brewery he founded in the early days of the current revival has relocated to the Ram in Wandsworth and taken on Young's former brewhouse manager John Hatch, who has heroically maintained the tradition by brewing privately on the site for 14 years. For more on this good news story, see p276.

People have been predicting the end of London's beer boom since soon after it started, but a new sense of caution unarguably emerged in 2019, prompted in part by two retail failures, Beer Boutique and the Bottle Shop. April saw the first major brewing casualty when staff at Woolwich's Hop Stuff found themselves locked out by the landlord: it was bought in a prepack administration deal by Molson Coors, but never reopened and is currently for sale. In May, Redchurch, which had expanded to a production site in Harlow just outside London while retaining a presence at its Bethnal Green birthplace, was sold to new owners in another prepack deal, while Bermondsey's shared brewing facility Ubrew was liquidated in September after a troubled year.

So far, the Covid-19 lockdowns which paralysed the trade in 2020 haven't resulted in the major cull some people were expecting: instead London's brewery count has continued to grow, though the most recent newcomers are mainly small operators and projects that were already advanced when the pandemic struck. As recounted under London under Lockdown below, many brewers turned their deep roots in the local community to advantage, surviving on home deliveries and pre-ordered doorstep pickups. It's always possible further closures will follow as the impact of accumulated debts plays itself out.

All the casualties of the recent past had raised significant sums through crowdfunding: £111,000 at Ubrew, £375,000 at Beer Boutique, £403,000 at the Bottle Shop, £500,000 at Crate, £900,000 at Redchurch and over £1.5 million at Hop Stuff. The losses, mainly to small investors, should have strengthened reservations about this method of financing growth. Contributors to crowdfunding rounds are typically what London-based beer writer Martyn Cornell terms 'fanboy investors', motivated by the satisfaction of owning a small slice of their favourite beer business and the perks that come with it, such as exclusive beers and merchandise and access to events and launches. Traditional investors, by contrast, are focused on cash returns, and take much more of a rigorous and risk-averse approach to business proposals.

Crowdfunding worked well in the early days of a growing and innovative market, with collectives of enthusiasts supporting inspirational projects traditional investors weren't prepared to gamble on. But as competition intensifies, matters that the fanboys might overlook, like a credible business plan and evidence of careful financial planning and monitoring, become progressively more important in determining a business's sustainability. The hard truth is that most start-up businesses fail. As the UK's financial watchdog the FCA warns would-be crowdfunders, 'it is very likely that you will lose all your money.' Yet, two years on from the 2019 failures, crowdfunding remains London brewing's favoured method of financing growth.

Veteran London beer and brewing history expert Peter Haydon, now retired, told me in 2015 that the capital won't re-enter the premier league of beer cities 'until Londoners at large think about their city and their beer in the same way as the citizens of Munich, Brussels, Denver and Bamberg do.' I doubt we're quite there yet, but we've certainly made further progress since the last edition of this guide. One of the best things you and I can do to ensure we keep moving in the right direction is to continue to enjoy the fruits of all this frenetic activity.

So raise your glasses, please, for a toast to London brewing. You've certainly got the widest choice ever of appropriately named libations – Bexley Black Prince, Brick Peckham Rye, Canopy Brockwell IPA, Five Points Railway Porter, Hammerton N7, Inkspot St Reatham, The Kernel London Export Stout, Muswell Hillbilly Down the Colney Hatch, Redemption Hopspur, Sambrook's Wandle, Southwark Bermondsey Best, Tap East End Mild, Wimbledon Common or Wrong Side of the Tracks Lewisham Pale Ale are all possibilities that spring to mind. And even if it's now owned by a multinational, there's still much to be said for toasting the health, long life and prosperity of London brewing with a pint of Fuller's London Pride.

LONDON UNDER LOCKDOWN

'It was uncharted territory, like being in a science fiction film,' says Marcus Grant of the Wenlock Arms in Hoxton, recalling the early days of the Covid-19 pandemic in the UK. The first cases here were reported at the end of January 2020, about the same time the World Health Organisation declared an international public health emergency, but nobody knew what the impact might be. Notoriously, the government initially favoured a laissez-faire policy of 'herd immunity', but by mid-March, with around 1,000 confirmed cases and panic buyers stripping the supermarket shelves, it was clear that 2020 wouldn't be a year of business as normal.

'We came back from a family visit to New Zealand via Singapore at the end of January,' recounts Jen Ferguson, co-founder of Hop Burns & Black bottle shops, 'and I took photos of pharmacies at the airport with notices saying they'd sold out of face masks and hand gel. We were already uneasy at the beginning of March and voluntarily suspended drinking in to protect our staff and customers, then closed completely a week before the first lockdowns. We already had the infrastructure to do mail order, so we switched to that.'

On 16 March the government advised the public to avoid pubs and other social gatherings and to work from home where possible, but without ordering closures or announcing any support measures. 'That was a very tricky period,' says Marcus. 'There weren't many customers around, and some were telling us it was our social responsibility to close, but we couldn't, there were too many commitments.

When they finally announced the formal lockdown, in many ways it was a load off your mind.' Compulsory closures of pubs and similar venues were introduced on 20 March, except for takeaway food, with non-essential shops and other businesses shutting a few days later.

Alison Taffs and Phil Cooke's Hornchurch micropub the Hop Inn had been open less than three months before the lockdowns. 'Those first weeks were some of the worst of my life,' says Alison. 'We closed before it became official, poured around £1,500 of beer down the drain, locked the doors and left.' But then they realised their license allowed for takeaway sales and confirmed with the council that they could reopen as a shop, which was soon doing a roaring trade in takeaways.

'Everywhere else was shut except for the supermarket and the pharmacy,' recalls Alison, 'so it was a treat for people to go out. We started a weekly delivery round: where people were self-isolating, I remember running down the path with a box, ringing the bell and running away again. But then they'd stop you to chat at a distance and it became a social thing. It created a different sort of relationship with customers: we now know their names, they're like old friends.'

Jen reports similar experiences. 'Before the lockdowns,' she says, 'our most regular mail order customers were all over the country. Now 90% of our biggest spenders are all within a few miles of our stores, and we know most of them by name. We were selling cases upon cases of local beer: people became very supportive and community

minded. That was the best of times among the worst of times.'

There are many other heart-warming stories highlighting both the resourcefulness of businesses and the way in which community relations were strengthened. London CAMRA's Lockdown Heroes scheme has recognised among others the Queen's Head in rural Downe, which not only sold takeaway but groceries and other essentials in a village otherwise without shops; the community-owned Antwerp Arms in Tottenham which ran a food bank and provided over 2,000 meals for the neediest locals; and the Railway Hotel in Greenford which crowdfunded a redistribution network for pub food that would otherwise have gone to waste. Enterprising businesses even found ways to support cask beer, a format principally for drinking in the pub, with delivery and click and collect facilities for minikegs, bag-in-box and freshly poured growlers. Small, flexible independents benefitted from the retreat of mainstream chain pubs, many of which simply shut down and furloughed all their staff.

Sambrook's brewery was previously dependent on cask sales to pubs, including the big chains. 'We went from 100% to almost 0% overnight,' says chief marketing officer Kieran Monteiro. 'So we switched to bottles, cans and minikegs for home delivery and found new bottle shop customers who were struggling with supplies. In the early days we all mucked in filling the minikegs and [founder and owner] Duncan Sambrook did the deliveries. We built it back up to 50% and made lots of new friends.' Other breweries

cont.

cont.

LONDON UNDER LOCKDOWN

adopted similar strategies, with long-planned online shops and canning lines rapidly bumped up the list of priorities.

Pubs and restaurants re-opened in July, with compulsory table service, social distancing and limits on groups. But in the autumn, with UK cases heading towards 1 million, a succession of new restrictions was imposed: a 10 o'clock curfew, a second lockdown, a confusing system of regional tiers when pubs were required to serve 'substantial meals' to open legally, and finally a third lockdown in January 2021.

'Our members appreciated the government financial support like the furlough scheme and loans,' says London Brewers Alliance secretary John Cryne, 'but struggled with the constant rapid changes of mind, poor communications and rules that didn't make much sense'. Andy Heyward, owner of Thames Side Brewery in Staines and regional chair of independent brewers' organisation SIBA, agrees. 'Of course, nobody really knew how to deal with it at first,' he says, 'but hospitality really shouldn't have been singled out when the virus was spreading in other ways. Personally, I'm sure some of the rules were inspired more by the anti-drink lobby than by the science: their voices were louder than ours.'

By February 2021, the on-going vaccination programme and a government timetable for a more sustainable reopening were promising a route back to normality. Outdoor areas of pubs and restaurants welcomed customers again in April and indoor areas followed in May. Compulsory requirements like table service, mask-wearing and

social distancing were lifted in July, though with caution still advised. As I write, 75% of UK adults have been fully vaccinated and there's a hope that further lockdowns can be avoided. But the long-term impact on the beer and pubs scene remains unclear, not just because of its financial effects but the way it may have changed work patterns and drinking habits permanently.

'I know of several pubs that aren't reopening,' says Marcus. 'We're a small place where you don't need much to have a successful day, but it's hard to do meals and table service, so we've been shut a lot of the time. We have another pub that's more food-led and we wouldn't have survived on the Wenlock alone. Most of our customers are now local residents and regular real ale drinkers: we've lost our after-work trade. The working landscape has totally changed and people don't want to go back to the office: several offices round here have closed.'

'We haven't yet seen the big drop-off we originally forecast now that pubs and restaurants are back open,' reports Jen 'I think there are several factors: people entertaining at home again, but also some nervous-ness and uncertainty about venturing out.' Several people I spoke to observed that more customers now prefer to sit out-side even in poor weather, and Alison speculates that the lock-downs have led people to discover other home-based activities. 'I think home delivery is part of the psyche now,' says Jen.

'Of course people will want to socialise in pubs like they used to, provided they feel safe,' says Geoff Strawbridge, chair of

CAMRA's London Liaison Committee and a longstanding campaigner. 'But this inculcated fear of going out could still be around for a couple of years yet.' And the willingness to socialise certainly hasn't declined: 'Micropubs like ours are designed for sharing tables with strangers,' says Phil, 'and plenty of customers seem really grateful to get back to doing that.'

The spring 2021 reopening brought a healthy rush of orders to many of the breweries, and some of them struggled to cope, a situation worsened as Covid itself is still affecting staffing levels, particularly as brewery staff are typically younger and less likely to be vaccinated. At least one was practically at a standstill because nearly all the staff either had the virus or were self-isolating, and one of my potential interviewees had to cancel due to a Covid infection.

This problem will pass with time, but there's more of a long-term concern about decreased orders from the mainstream trade, particularly of cask. 'Many LBA members previously sold guest beers to pub chains,' says John, 'but these pubs are now cautious of stocking up. Some haven't put cask back on, or they've cut back to a couple of discounted national brands.' But if habits are changing and customers are expecting more local distinctiveness when they do go out, such an approach may be self-defeating. 'The traditional model of chain pubs stocking global brands may be declining,' concludes Geoff, 'but the real story is the excitement of London's 140 local breweries, its taprooms and its independent pubs. That's something to celebrate.'

From alehouses to micropubs

The pub, or rather the idea of the pub, holds a privileged position in British culture. People rhapsodise about its virtues, citing authorities as diverse as Samuel Johnson and George Orwell; celebrate it as a uniquely British institution that expresses something profound about the national character (a puzzle to anyone who has ever open-mindedly enjoyed the superficially different but equally convivial drinking venues of many other countries); and, increasingly, fear and sometimes prematurely mourn its loss. But pubs are not some fixed and unchanging phenomenon that reconnects us with an idyllic Merrie England now lost in the mists of time. First and foremost, they are businesses that depend on attracting customers to thrive and prosper. As such, they have constantly reinvented themselves to achieve this more effectively, changing and evolving alongside the communities they serve.

The story of drinking houses in London stretches back to the *tabernae* of Roman times and most likely beyond, but the earliest we can usefully trace back the history of the modern London pub is the 16th century, when there were three clearly defined types of establishment. Inns offered accommodation as well as food and drink: a fine example, the George in Southwark (Heritage pubs p89), survives in inner London. Taverns concentrated on selling wine, though also stocked beer, and alehouses were simple places that sold only beer. During the 'gin craze' of the 1740s they were supplemented by numerous gin shops of the sort that promised to get you 'drunk for a penny, dead drunk for tuppence'.

It was the depredations of the gin craze, alongside growing industrialisation, that began to shift respectable public opinion against the social acceptance of drunkenness, eventually culminating in the temperance movement of Victorian times that gained increasing influence over public policy on the alcohol industry. Interestingly, the imperative to control alcohol sales was one of the factors that influenced the pub as we know it today, by using the licensing system to reduce the prevalence of 'public houses' — by then a catchall term for establishments where a member of the public could drink on the premises without having to eat, rent a room or become a member. Magistrates, then responsible for licensing the sale of alcohol, were discouraged from issuing new licences and prompted to find reasons to revoke existing ones, and temperance campaigners actively targeted local benches.

The other, linked, factor that shaped the modern pub was the emergence of the tied house system. Given the wealth of breweries and their obvious interest in the pub trade, it's not surprising that they began propping up landlords financially, usually through making free or low-interest loans on condition of exclusive supply rights, sometimes with the property as a guarantee. This eventually evolved into breweries taking on direct ownership of pubs. Interestingly, most London pubs remained

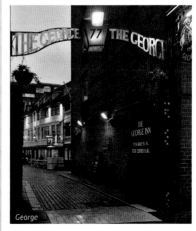

George

nominally independent later than those elsewhere, but in the late 19th century, at a time when the industry was awash with funds from stock exchange flotations, provincial brewers started buying into the capital. The London brewers had no choice but to respond in kind, creating the vertically integrated brewing industry that dominated most of the succeeding century. Often, the pubs were then leased back to licensees, who remained nominally independent, paying a reduced rent but obliged to source their beer and sometimes other stock from the brewery at a premium.

The combination of scarcity of licences and the drive towards tied houses had the effect of massively inflating the property value of pubs. And since they now needed to earn back the money spent on them, even more was invested to make them more attractive to customers, while simultaneously attempting to appease the temperance lobby. This spurred a flurry of redevelopment and refurbishment which came to a swift halt at the very end of the 19th century when the property market inevitably crashed.

This particular collision of historical circumstances accounts for why the vast majority of London pubs look like they do: they were pretty much all rebuilt, or extensively refitted, by a smallish handful of breweries in the 1880s and 1890s, mainly on existing sites as new licences were almost impossible to obtain. The breweries adopted a grandiose style intended both to attract a wide range of customers and to demonstrate respectability and broad social appeal. The result was a riot of coloured marble, Corinthian columns, pediments and porticos, mosaic floors, engraved and painted glass and mirrors, and massive back bars in complex classical stylings. Even small pubs were subdivided by elaborate screens and partitions, with each compartment aimed at a different demographic, both a reflection of the stratified society of the day and an advertisement for the fact that the pub set out to cater for all of it.

Very little recognisably survives from before this period, but significant examples endure from after it, as pub development continued in the early 20th century, but at a notably reduced rate. This was a period when London was rapidly expanding, despite the setbacks of a world war and a major recession, and all but the most ardent prohibitionists

conceded the need for new pubs to serve new developments. The result was a generation of large 'improved' pubs that justified their existence by incorporating restaurants, meeting rooms and ballrooms. The early 20th century also saw the emergence of self-conscious nostalgia for a more rural past in the worlds of art and design, as if to provide a comforting continuity to those whose lives were disrupted by urbanisation and change. Among pub architects, this expressed itself in the style known rather dismissively as 'Brewer's Tudor', with its mock half-timbered façades, interior wood panelling and fake ceiling beams.

'Brewer's Tudor'

The post-war period brought consolidation in the industry and a drive towards efficiency and integration that chimed well with the architectural modernism of the day. Segregation and fussy Victoriana fell out of fashion: during the 1960s and 1970s much pub heritage was lost as screens and partitions were unceremoniously ripped out to create more egalitarian, and more cheaply supervised, open spaces. The big brewery groups, and some of the smaller ones, subsumed their pub estates into the emerging doctrine of brand values, unsympathetically imposing standard decoration and, sometimes, cheesy ersatz themes. Branded chain pubs emerged, with more pubs managed directly by brewers rather than through leasehold arrangements.

There's a good argument that tied estates are one of the reasons why cask beer persisted in England, partly because they diverted investment that might otherwise have been spent on new brewing technology, partly as they gave brewers more control over the way the beer was treated after it left the brewery gates. And so long as drinkers were able to walk across the street to another brewery's pub, there was still an element of competition and consumer choice. But by the early 1970s, seven breweries produced most of the beer sold in the UK, and six of these between them owned over half the country's pubs, which, combined with restrictions on new licences, resulted in local monopolies in many areas. The breweries could now exploit their power by foisting inferior products on a captive audience at a premium price, a situation that gave rise to the consumer revolt led by CAMRA.

The real ale movement also spawned new microbreweries, including in London, but with the big players controlling most of the pub trade, the newcomers faced major challenges in reaching customers. CAMRA and others campaigned against this anti-competitive situation, advocating a limit on the size of estates across which the tie could be enforced. Following several official inquiries, in 1989 the government finally responded with regulations known as the Beer Orders, forcing breweries with large estates to release some of their pubs from the tie and allow the others to stock a guest beer.

The consequences of this seemingly modest intervention were extreme. Being obliged to allow their competitors' beer into their pubs prompted the breweries to question the very fundamentals of vertical integration. A few shed their pub estates and focused on their brewing businesses. Many more, including a poignant roll call of well-established independents, cashed in the property value of prime town centre brewing sites and focused on retail, contracting their production out to others.

Anyone who thought the outcome would be a nation of free houses with newly liberated landlords beaming a hearty welcome from behind an array of exotic pumpclips soon had those illusions shattered. A new wave of consolidation followed, and the old Big Seven have since been succeeded by five global giants, all but one of whom don't own pubs. A similar process swept the retailing side of the industry, with a handful of big pub owning companies or 'pubcos' eventually emerging, often streamlined around a limited range of beer.

Although they no longer brewed, pubcos retained their rights to enforce the tie on their leaseholders, placing the biggest ones in a powerful position. They negotiated aggressively for substantial discounts from the brewer, while selling on to the licensee at an eye-watering mark-up, as much as double the price the brewery would charge a free house, while progressively hiking up rents at the same time. Such practices have made it difficult for some leaseholders to stay competitive, and there are numerous stories of pubcos deliberately running down sites because they see more value in selling them off for non-pub use. A new law passed in 2014 aimed to give leaseholders of the bigger pubcos the right to move to a 'market rent only' option, paying a higher rent in exchange for freedom from the tie, with an independent Pubs Code Adjudicator to settle disputes. But the slow and piecemeal implementation of these arrangements has frustrated many licensees and campaigners, and further changes to the regulations are planned.

Today, about half the UK's pubs remain tied in one way or another, though in retrospect, the shake-up has resulted in an overall widening of choice and made the pub owners more susceptible to consumer demand. One effect has been a notable increase in the number of 'free houses' where the owners have no link to brewing interests. Historically, these were a small minority, including among their number several important specialist beer champions. Following the Beer Orders, chains of managed free houses emerged, again often with a limited range but more open to approaches from new brewers.

The opportunities for brewers were further boosted in 2002 with the introduction of Small Breweries' Relief, reducing the duty payable by the smallest breweries by as much as half. The number of British breweries has increased from around 100 in the early 1970s to around 1,800 today, with many newcomers selling significant quantities through big national pub estates that once would have been completely off-limits. Access to pubs has been increased by initiatives like small brewers' organisation SIBA's Direct Delivery Scheme, which enables breweries to supply beer direct to tied houses near them, though the pubs are still invoiced through the pubco at an inevitable mark-up.

Despite these improvements for drinkers, recent decades have seen an unprecedented wave of pub closures. The UK lost 25% of its pub stock between 1982 and 2015, and although the most recent figures suggest the decline has at least slowed and possibly modestly reversed, including in London, much damage has already been done. You don't have to spend long walking the capital's streets to spot ex-pubs: within a few minutes' walk of my flat there are a good 15 examples, now converted to flats, convenience stores or betting shops. The finger of blame is pointed in various directions – high taxation, greedy pubcos, undercutting by supermarkets, property inflation, the smoking ban, and the failure of licensees to offer a good enough service. But there are broader social changes at work too, including reduced overall alcohol consumption, increased home comforts and new home-based distractions, greater mobility and the heterogeneity of local communities, that have helped ensure pub-going is no longer the everyday habit it once was.

With pubs now having to work much harder to win customers, they've become more diverse. The phenomenon of gastropubs focusing on good food began in London in the early 1990s and continues apace. It's influenced not only pub menus but their interior decoration. Many now have a self-consciously casual stripped-back feel, with bare floorboards, clean pastel colours and mismatched reclaimed furniture including an obligatory corner with saggy old sofas and armchairs. Once-despised Victorian features are these days proudly exhibited, though our ancestors' taste for segregation is no longer honoured.

Another notable trend, sometimes little-remarked among pub campaigners, is the growth of communal drinking in buildings other than traditional purpose-built pubs. Chains like J D Wetherspoon and some breweries have been converting old department stores, banks, post offices, public halls, cinemas and the like into big town centre venues since the 1990s. Legal changes in 2005 simplified licensing regulations and transferred the main responsibility for granting licences from magistrates to local councils – in London, the boroughs. This has created further opportunities for selling alcohol in places that have never been and certainly don't look like pubs, like railway arches or small shops, so long as the council is satisfied there will be no negative impact on the local community.

The first beneficiaries of this have been the micropubs, small bars in shopfront sites which first appeared in Kent in 2005 and have now spread all over Britain: I've considered their proliferation in southeast London and beyond on p254. With their simple interiors and focus on cask beer and conviviality, many of them see themselves as a return to tradition, but in other respects they're thoroughly modern. In recent years, they've been followed by a wave of more explicitly contemporary places I've termed bottle shop-bars, also in smallish shop units, with a wide range of bottled and canned beers to take away, but at least some facilities for customers to drink in and likely a small handful of draught options. When these open in an area of dwindling beer choice, they tend to become social centres even if that wasn't the original intention, and some are quickly reconfigured to suit this unexpected role.

As mentioned in Taking stock, only a minority of the places now listed in this book are what most people would call pubs in the traditional sense of the word. One way of understanding what's going on is as a recon-figuration of space. With people drinking less overall and more at home, many big purpose-built Victorian pubs, whatever their charms, are now over-specified for current levels of demand. Micropubs and bottle shop-bars are much smaller and cheaper to run, with enough margin to provide an income for one or two people: indeed, some of them have such a small turnover they're not even obliged to register for VAT. Also in the mix are brewery taprooms, unheard of a decade or so ago but often providing a lively social space today.

The full impact of the Covid-19 pandemic on London's pub landscape remains to be seen. As reported in London under lockdown above, many of the newer, smaller, less traditional outlets found themselves able to adapt more easily to lockdown conditions and other restric-tions, while big, old-school pubs were hit parti-cularly hard. But even after this unprecedented challenge, reports of the death of the pub should not be taken at face value. The look and feel of the places we drink in are undoubtedly changing, as they have done throughout history, and those changes might not be to everyone's taste. But as recent innovations demonstrate, our desire to drink in a communal, social space certainly hasn't gone away.

From grain to glass

What is beer?

Technically speaking, beer is a fermented alcoholic drink made from cereals. Fermentation is a natural process involving a microorganism called yeast, which in the right circumstances will break down sugars dissolved in liquids in a way that leaves alcohol and carbon dioxide behind. The source of the sugars is a key factor determining the broad families of alcoholic drinks. Fruit sugars yield wine, cider and perry, while sugars derived from cereal starches yield beer. The alcohol in spirits like whisky, and some vodka and gin, is also derived from grains, but these drinks have gone through a second process of distillation to concentrate it.

Ingredients

Grains, malts and sugars

Grains in their raw state contain starches rather than sugars, alongside substances called enzymes which break down the starches during germination to provide sugar for the growing plant. Malting the grain by steeping it in water to encourage it to germinate and then rapidly heating and drying it to halt the process before too many roots and shoots appear results in a softer, sweeter ingredient with more readily available enzymes. One grain species, barley, has turned out to be ideally suited to malting and brewing. It's rich in enzymes and, because it has a husk, is less likely to turn to porridge and gum up the equipment. It also lends itself well to a range of different malting techniques, helping produce a wide range of flavours.

Most barley used in brewing is lightly kilned 'pale malt' or even lighter 'pilsner malt' but numerous 'speciality malts' can be used alongside these to add character to different styles. Varying kilning times, temperatures and techniques results in changes to colour and flavour comparable to toasting bread. Mild, Vienna, Munich and amber malts are progressively darker and toastier. Brown malt is darker still. Crystal and caramel malts ('caramalts')

Sacks of malted barley

have notable caramel and biscuit flavours. Chocolate and black ('patent') malts are highly kilned to give roasted and burnt character. Smoked and peated malts, the latter more normally used for whisky, lend distinctive notes to some beers. Roasted unmalted barley gives a classic bite to Irish stouts.

Malted barley is now so ubiquitous that you'll sometimes see it named as a defining ingredient of beer. Many beers derive their sugar from barley alone and the term 'malt' on its own usually means malted barley. Beer can also be made from a variety of other grains, though today they are normally used alongside rather than instead of barley. Wheat is the next most important brewers' grain, giving a unique character to wheat beers or added in small quantities to aid head retention in a range of other styles. Rye and oats are used in malted and unmalted form: rye adds spicy flavours and deeper colours while oats help achieve a creamy texture, or a fashionably cloudy appearance in certain contemporary styles. Maize and rice are most familiar from big name lagers where they're used to add strength and smoothness without too much additional flavour but can also lend character to speciality styles.

Using refined sugars alongside grains is a practice frowned upon in some traditions but almost a defining characteristic of others, such as Belgian monastic-style brewing where they boost strength while retaining drinkability. Special crystallised sugars like candy and brewing sugar, liquid 'invert sugar', caramel, molasses and honey all find their way into beer. Pre-prepared malt extract is also occasionally used. Lactose, extracted from milk, is an unfermentable sugar that lends a milk gum chewiness, traditionally used in sweet stouts but increasingly spreading to other styles too.

Water
By far the highest proportion of the liquid in a beer glass is likely to be water, known as 'liquor' in the industry, where 'water' is the stuff you use for cooling and cleaning. Once, most breweries had access to their own springs or wells, and the liquor lent a *goût de terroir* to the beers. London, sitting on its basin of chalk, has water with a high mineral content including calcium carbonate, which helps extract the colour from darker malts when brewing

porters and stouts (see Lavverly London Liquor p200). The local water in Burton upon Trent is naturally richer in sulphates, well-suited to hoppy pale ales as they aid the extraction of bitterness and preservatives from hops. Today, the chemistry is better understood, and most beer is made from the local mains, traditionally known as 'town's liquor', often purified and tweaked with additional minerals as required.

Hops and other flavourings
At tastings and workshops, when I ask participants to name the four main ingredients of most beers, the first one mentioned is invariably hops, even though technically they're the one inessential ingredient, and in terms of the millennia-old history of brewing, a relatively new arrival. Historically, brewers flavoured beer with other ingredients, or avoided additional flavours altogether. England was a late adopter of hopped beers: even in the 17th century some traditional 'ales' were still brewed from grains and water alone.

Hops are the cone-shaped fruiting bodies of an herbaceous climbing plant which grows wild in many parts of Europe including England. They originally won brewers' favour because they helped clarify and stabilise the product and acted as a natural preservative, substantially extending shelf life. But their floral, spicy and fruity aromas and bitter flavour proved popular with drinkers, complementing and balancing out the sweetness of the malt. Today hops have become brewing's equivalent of the wine industry's 'varietals', with a wide range of distinctive varieties grown around the world.

Classic British hops like East Kent Goldings and Fuggles have an earthy, smooth character that contributes to both aroma and bitterness. Challenger, Northdown, Northern Brewer and dwarf hop First Gold are more recent varieties. Bramling Cross, a hybrid of Goldings and wild Canadian hops, has a distinctive blackcurrant flavour.

Traditional mainland European hops lend their grassy, creamy, lightly spicy and sometimes lemony notes to classic German and Czech lagers. Five varieties – Hallertauer, Hersbrucker, Spalt and Tettnang from Germany and Žatec (Saaz), originally from Bohemia – are

p bines

tinged Pacific Gem. Australia produces notably fruity varieties like Galaxy, with a passion fruit scent, and the similar but rather pinier Vic Secret.

European hop growers have worked hard in recent years to develop new varieties capable of matching the expressiveness of their New World counterparts but in a less sunny climate. German growers lead the field with varieties like Mandarina Bavaria, Huell Melon and Hallertau Blanc, suggesting soft citrus, melon and grape-like flavours respectively. Kazbek from the Czech Republic is closer to a 'noble' hop but with some modern citrus character. New English hops include Jester, with delicate grapefruit and tropical fruit flavours, and mango-tinged Olicana. More beers featuring these and other, newer, varieties are likely to appear as costs of imported hops increase and breweries become more concerned about the environmental impact of transporting them long distances.

Hops are almost invariably used in dried form, though some brewers make a point of commemorating the harvest with fresh hops in annual 'wet hop' or 'green hop' beers. Some argue that the finest hop flavour is from whole dried cones, but hop pellets, which take up less space and have a longer shelf life, are in wide use. 'Cryo hops', introduced in 2017, use freezing technology to separate off the bitterest and most aromatic parts of the cone from the rest, resulting in a highly concentrated powder that has found favour in some modern hop-forward beers. Liquid hop extract is another more convenient but considerably less characterful alternative.

The use of other herbs, spices and flavourings has never entirely vanished and is once again on the increase, these days almost invariably alongside rather than instead of hops. London brewers have been known to use among others bay leaf, chamomile, chilli, chocolate, dried citrus peel, cinnamon, coffee, coriander, ginger, heather, juniper, lemongrass, passion berry, pepper, seaweed, tea, thyme and vanilla. Fruit is another addition with a long historical precedent, with evidence of ancient Egyptian beers made with dates. Apples, blood oranges, blueberries, cherries, raspberries, gooseberries, damsons, plums, rosehips, peaches, tomatoes and grapes are among the species in the brewer's fruit bowl.

sometimes known as 'noble hops'. Magnum and Perle are more recent German varieties, while Styrian Goldings is a Slovenian-grown substitute for English Goldings, though confusingly is derived from Fuggles. Poland, now the world's fifth biggest producer, offers sturdy Fuggles derivatives like Celeia as well as a growing range of delicate aroma hops.

North American hops are almost always more exotic and distinctive, with grapefruit and pine flavours and plentiful bitter acids. The classic example is Cascade, which along with Centennial and Columbus forms the 'Three C's' group of assertively citric hops. Amarillo, Citra and the piney Chinook are popular for their exotic fruit flavours, while Mosaic has berry and sometimes onion-like notes as well as tropical fruit. More reserved entrants include Crystal and Liberty, which are closer to German hops, and Willamette, a fruitier form of Fuggles.

Hops from Australasia enjoy increasing attention, led by New Zealand's Nelson Sauvin, its name referencing a resemblance in flavour to Sauvignon Blanc grapes, and blackberry-

Yeast and other microflora

Though we've been enjoying fermented alcoholic drinks for millennia, it wasn't until the 1860s and the ground-breaking work of Louis Pasteur that fermentation was fully explained as the work of a microorganism, a single-celled fungus known as yeast which grows wild on the skins of fruit and other organic matter. Brewing must have begun with wild yeast but by Pasteur's time brewers had been selecting the best strains for at least several centuries without really understanding what they were doing, by keeping back the residue of a particularly successful fermentation and adding it to the next. Today, nearly all yeast used in brewing is cultured in laboratories. Yeast can survive dormant for many years, and academic and commercial yeast 'libraries' retain thousands of cultures and strains, each with its own characteristics.

Yeast is what distinguishes the two great beer families – ales and lagers. Ales are the older style, fermented with yeasts that work at relatively high temperatures of around 20-25°C over a matter of days. Ale yeast cultures often contain a complex mix of different strains, producing correspondingly complex flavours with fruity and sometimes spicy notes.

Lagers developed from the practice in Bavaria of storing beer in cold caves over the summer – *lagern* means 'to store' in German. Yeast strains evolved which fermented more slowly, taking perhaps a fortnight at a lower temperature of around 12-15°C. 'Lagering' the

Pitching yeast into wort

results for several more weeks at just above freezing produces a clean-tasting beer with little flavour left over from fermentation. While big commercial producers have found ways to compress this process, often at the expense of character, several smaller London breweries have adopted traditional lagering techniques to help restore lager's reputation among connoisseurs.

Ale yeasts and lager yeasts are sometimes labelled 'top fermenting' and 'bottom fermenting' respectively after the tendency of the yeast residues to either collect at the top or sink to the bottom of a fermenting vessel, but yeasts are no longer so neatly classified. Old-fashioned ale yeasts used in modern closed fermenting vessels are more likely to sink to the bottom while still producing beers that are characteristically ales. A better distinction is between 'warm fermenting' and 'cold fermenting'.

Yeast can have a profound effect on the flavour of the finished beer – drinking two beers made to the same recipe but with different yeasts side-by-side is a revealing experience. Old-established breweries usually maintain house yeast cultures which help give their beers a characteristic flavour: Fuller's yeast, for example, is known for its spicy orange notes. Most smaller brewers buy their yeasts to order from a handful of international commercial suppliers, either dried or as live liquid yeast. These suppliers maintain extensive catalogues of yeasts optimised for different styles, but inevitably some are more popular than others, which helps explain why beers brewed on different continents can taste so remarkably similar.

Conventional brewers' yeasts are members of the genus *Saccharomyces* ('sugar fungus'), but there are other yeasts, most famously *Bretannomyces* ('British fungus', as the first strain isolated scientifically was from a British strong ale). 'Bret' ferments more thoroughly but more slowly, leaving behind distinctive funky, spicy notes which are sometimes pungent enough to remind tasters of farm animals: the old brewers' term was 'horse blanket'. Though undesirable in conventional styles, these yeasts can express themselves well in long-aged beers, mellowing with time to a complex fruitiness, and are part of the flavour characteristic of certain Belgian styles.

Mashing at Gipsy Hill brewery

While some adventurous new brewers have attempted to capture and manage the microflora in their local environment, commercial suppliers oblige with more predictable cultured strains of 'wild' yeast.

Other naturally occurring microflora which are decidedly unwelcome in most fermenting vessels but have benefitted from a revival of interest in specialist styles are numerous souring bacteria, particularly *Lactobacillus* and *Pediococcus*. These produce lactic acid from sugar, creating the signature flavour of 'sours', including a swathe of new beers inspired by traditional styles like Berliner Weisse, Gose and lambic.

The brewing process

Roughly milled malts and other cereals if used – the 'grist' – are mixed and then 'mashed': soaked in hot but not boiling water, releasing the enzymes that complete the conversion of starches into sugars. The sweet liquid, known as 'wort', is run off, usually with the help of additional hot water rinses ('sparging'), and boiled with hops and perhaps other flavourings. Hops are often added in stages, with those towards the start of the boil contributing more to bitterness, and the 'late hops' near the end towards aroma. The hopped wort is cooled and put in a fermentation vessel. Yeast is added, or 'pitched' as brewers say, and the mixture is left to ferment.

During fermentation, the yeast feeds on the sugar, converting it to alcohol and carbon dioxide, giving the beer both strength and sparkle. The strength is dependent on the ratio of fermentable sugar to water in the wort before fermentation – the 'original gravity' – and the 'attenuation', the extent to which the yeast converts this to alcohol. Highly attenuated beers are drier, with nearly all the sugar gone, while lower levels of attenuation leave more residual sugar to give a sweeter flavour. There are various ways of measuring alcohol content: the most common internationally is the percentage of Alcohol by Volume (ABV) which is used throughout this book.

After primary fermentation, the beer will likely undergo a further period of conditioning and maturation at a lower temperature to round off the rough edges. For the best lagers this could take up to three months at temperatures just above freezing. A few days may be adequate for many ales.

Additional hops can be added directly to the beer during both fermentation and conditioning, known as 'cold side hopping' or 'dry hopping', a practice that has increasingly predominated in recent years as fashions have shifted in favour of hop character. Some brewers are now pushing this further for particular recipes by boiling entirely without hops and adding them afterwards or even skipping the boiling stage entirely to make 'raw' beers.

There are also a few speciality styles that are fermented and conditioned in a rather different way, as explained under Wild, sour and barrel-aged beer below.

33

Packaging and dispense

By the end of conditioning, most yeast activity will have ceased but a few stray cells will still be nibbling away at the remaining sugars. Most large-scale commercial brewers seeking a uniform product now filter and pasteurise the beer, heating it rapidly to kill off any remaining microbiological activity. This knocks the sparkle out of it too, so it's 'force-carbonated' with additional carbon dioxide before packaging in sealed kegs, bottles or cans for distribution.

There are numerous alternatives. Some beer is filtered but left unpasteurised, or simply conditioned until it 'drops bright' with yeast sediment settling in the bottom of the vessel so clear beer can be drained from above. If the brewer considers the beer has lost too much carbonation this way, it will likely be force-carbonated using additional gas, perhaps captured from an earlier stage of the fermentation process.

Many connoisseurs argue that the freshest, most complex and characterful beers are those that continue to ferment in the vessels from which they're served. This is the secret of cask beer, but it also extends to bottle-conditioned beer, and, increasingly, live beer in other formats.

Cask beer

Cask conditioning at its best is a unique way of delivering complex and subtle flavour and character from comparatively low strength and supremely drinkable beers. Drinkers in parts of a few other countries, such as Germany, have also long enjoyed fresh unpressurised draught beer, and there's an increasing interest in cask techniques in the USA and elsewhere. But the format remains an everyday drink only in the UK, where it's sadly been in decline again in recent years. Cask beer outlets are highlighted in this guide, and I strongly recommend you take the opportunity to sample as much as you can responsibly drink.

A cask is a barrel-shaped container with a slightly bulging waist, once made from wood but now almost always from aluminium or plastic. Most are of a size known as a 'firkin' which holds nine gallons (41 litres), but there are also 'pins' of 4.5 gallons (20.5 litres), 'kilderkins' or 'kils' of 18 gallons (82 litres) and some rarely seen larger sizes. Crucially, casks have two openings: one near the rim of one of the heads, filled with a bung called a 'keystone', and the other at right angles to the first in the middle of the waist, filled with a bung called a 'shive'.

Casks are designed to host a continuing fermentation. Many brewers ensure this takes place by filling them with unfiltered and unpasteurised beer with just the right amount of residual sugar and active yeast left over from the initial fermentation, but casks can also be 'primed' with a little sugar or unfermented wort, and/or with additional yeast. Some breweries use a different strain of yeast in the cask and might filter the beer before packaging it, though this is rare especially among smaller brewers.

Depending on the yeast strain, most of the solids will eventually settle. Casks are designed to be kept on their sides in a cradle called a 'stillage', so the sediment accumulates in the waist, with the beer drawn off above it through the keystone opening, though there are now other techniques enabling them to be stood on end where space is limited. Many brewers boost clarification by using 'finings', a tasteless gelatinous substance usually derived from fish sources which slowly sinks through the liquid, taking suspended solid particles with it. Traditionally, British drinkers expected cask beer to be crystal-clear, or 'bright' in brewers' jargon, and most of it is still fined. But attitudes have shifted in recent years and unfined, naturally hazy cask beer is increasingly common. It's not only vegan-friendly but, according to

cking fresh beer into casks

still needs to be consumed within a few days before it becomes flat, oxidised and vinegary. Some pubs extend this a little by using 'cask breathers' which gradually fill the cask with sterile CO_2 at normal atmospheric pressure.

These methods allow cask beer to be served at a lower level of carbonation than pressurised beer from a keg, can or bottle, and therefore at a slightly higher temperature: as CO_2 dissolves into liquids more readily at lower temperatures, the more carbonated a beer is, the more it needs to be cooled to ensure a smooth pour without excess foaming. Cask is ideally served 'cellar-cooled' at around 10–12°C. At this temperature, the senses of taste and smell work more effectively, revealing subtleties of aroma and flavour not apparent at lower temperatures. The lower carbonation level emphasises flavour without too much of a gassy, bloating effect. But the beer should still be lively and cool enough to refresh, and certainly shouldn't resemble the warm, flat liquid of the popular stereotype.

Handpumped beer is typically a little livelier than beer direct from the cask, with more of a head, though in London and southern England in general, beer is traditionally served in glasses filled to the brim, with minimal head. Pubs in the north of England usually dispense via a nozzle called a 'sparkler' with multiple narrow holes, aerating the beer to emphasise the head. The use of sparklers has spread southwards and some London pubs use them indiscriminately, but they're arguably inappropriate for some beers, so the more conscientious places follow the brewer's recommendations.

Cask-conditioned beer at its best delivers a unique drinking experience particularly suited to the subtle, low-gravity session ales that became the norm in Britain in the 20th century. But achieving that best is complex and challenging, relying on factors outside the brewer's direct control. Unsurprisingly, the big brewing groups which emerged in the 1950s and 1960s were keen to jettison cask in favour of heavily promoted pasteurised and force-carbonated keg ales and lagers. Consumer resistance to this led to the formation of the Campaign for Real Ale, CAMRA, in 1971, and we largely have this organisation to thank for the fact that cask beer, even though long since outsold by industrial lager, retains a major presence on the

some, has more character and flavour too.

Prior to serving, a tap is driven through the keystone and the 'tut' which seals the hole in the shive is knocked out, replaced with a peg called a 'spile'. If the beer is too lively, a 'soft spile' of porous wood is used, enabling some CO_2 to escape without too much air getting in. Contact with oxygen rapidly spoils beer, not to mention the danger of infection from airborne organisms: the blanket of CO_2 generated by continuing fermentation will keep it at bay for a while. If there's too little carbonation, the cask is resealed with a 'hard spile' to let the fermentation develop further. All this takes time: a cask usually needs to spend at least a few days in a pub cellar before it's ready to serve.

Once in optimum condition, the beer can be poured direct from the cask, a method often used at beer festivals and at some pubs including most micropubs, with beer either fetched from the cellar or kept in a cooled stillage behind the bar. More commonly, the cask is hooked up via a tube to a hand-operated pump called a 'beer engine' and drawn into the glass using a distinctive pump handle on the bar, familiarly known as a 'handpump'.

The spile helps restrict the flow of air into the cask as the liquid runs out, but the beer

British scene. CAMRA coined the term 'real ale' for cask beer, though it's since been extended to beer conditioned in bottles, cans and even keykegs if served without additional gas. It isn't strictly accurate either, as these techniques can be applied to beers other than ales.

Though cask is still widespread in London and much of the rest of the UK, good cask is less easy to find. Too many pubs are prepared to serve it in less than optimum condition, continuing to sell beer once it's past its best, or tapping a cask too early while the beer is still 'green', with off flavours resulting from an incomplete fermentation. Other too-common complaints include serving the beer too warm, with too little carbonation or contaminated by dirty pipes and dispense equipment. Sticking to the recommendations in this book, you will hopefully avoid such problems.

Other formats

When CAMRA was founded and for some time afterwards, pretty much the only British beer worth drinking was cask beer, with very few exceptions. But this has changed dramatically in recent years, as speciality beers with great flavour and character proliferate in keg, bottle and can.

One thing all these formats have in common is that the resulting beer is almost invariably more carbonated than cask. Without a way of releasing it, carbon dioxide remains in the beer until it's poured, producing a vigorous sparkle and requiring additional cooling to serve successfully on draught. In my experience, the most common complaint dedicated cask drinkers have about other types of beer is that they're too 'fizzy', and, in the case of keg beer, too cold.

Secrets of the cellar

The cellar is the last link in the chain between the brewhouse and the glass on the bar, and what happens in it can radically affect the quality of that glass's contents, for better or worse. Yet, while most beer connoisseurs have visited a brewery or two, to almost all of us outside the licensed trade, the cellar remains a mystery. It's the place into which the bar staff annoyingly disappear when you're in a hurry to enjoy a last pint, muttering something about 'changing the barrel'.

The term 'cellar' implies an underground space, but licensees still use the term even if the beer is kept on the same level as or even above the bar. In the days before temperature control, cellars were often underground to benefit from natural coolness. These days, their temperature is usually artificially regulated, and draught systems might have their own integral cooling.

As is evident from the description above, a high level of cellar skills and best practice is vital in ensuring cask beer is served at its best. Casks must be treated gently, and their development carefully monitored with action taken accordingly. Good stock control is essential, and delivery, best before, spiling and tapping dates require conscientious noting and tracking. Temperature, too, must be monitored and regulated. Some cellars are subdivided, with different sections kept at different temperatures.

Hygiene must be scrupulously observed, to reduce the risk of infections. A common problem area is the 'lines', the tubes running to the bar, usually bundled together into a 'python'. Depending on its length, a line may contain several litres of beer vulnerable to going stale and sour when the bar is closed or turnover is low. Beer that's been sitting for too long in the lines needs to be pulled through as 'ullage' (the industry term for beer waste that must be discarded), and regular, thorough line cleaning is essential.

It's not just cask beer that needs looking after. Kegs are less prone to infection, but dirty lines and poor general hygiene can still compromise quality. The new generation of keg-conditioned beers all require well-informed treatment. Bottle and can-conditioned beers are ideally kept still and cool, and staff should keep an eye on the best before dates on all kegs, cans and bottles.

The venues listed in this book are reliable keepers of exemplary cellars. If you want to uncover more of the secrets of the cellar, the Hand in Hand (p282) offers public cellar workshops. Many micropubs keep their beer in glass-fronted cold rooms and if you ask nicely when it's not too busy, staff might oblige by pointing out the key features.

Some of this is a matter of taste, and of style. While the subtle flavours of low-gravity English ale styles are undoubtedly enhanced in cask, stronger and more robust styles, such as contemporary IPAs, may benefit from a different approach. I've found the bitter and piny notes of certain beers generously hopped with New World varieties, while overpowering and cloying in cask-conditioned format, sing out with the aid of the higher carbonation afforded by bottle or keg. Temperature is a genuine issue as cold liquids anaesthetise the senses: it's well worth letting some of the more complex keg beers warm up a little before tackling them.

Kegs and tanks

Kegs are metal or plastic containers in a variety of shapes and sizes, generally designed to be used upright, with one opening in the top. Mainstream pasteurised draught lager and stout are supplied in kegs, but today even artis-anal producers readily use them for specialist beers in more natural states, including 'keg-conditioned' beer which is still fermenting in the keg. Additional gas pressure is needed to force beer out, usually carbon dioxide or a mix of CO_2 and nitrogen ('nitrokeg').

It's possible to avoid contact between beer and gas by using a double-layered system, with the liquid sealed in a flexible inner layer protected by a rigid outer layer. By pressurising the space between them with gas or even compressed air, the contents are literally squeezed out. The most popular proprietary containers using this principle are 'keykegs', supplied in 10, 20 or 30 litre sizes and easily recognisable by their transparent plastic outer shell and inner metallic-coloured bag. Beer dispensed from these counts as 'real' by CAMRA's definition so long as it's still fermenting and served without additional gas dissolved into it.

There are some disadvantages to keykegs: they're expensive single-use products which many local authorities in the UK can't yet recycle. There are alternatives, such as 'Ecofass', which has a reusable outer shell and a disposable inner bag. But some breweries are moving back to conventional steel or plastic kegs, which are easily returnable and reusable even if they require additional gas.

Many 'tank beer' systems apply the keykeg principal on a grand scale using 1,000 litre polythene-lined and integrally cooled and insulated steel tanks, often displayed in the bar as a talking point. These count as 'real' if the beer is naturally conditioned, but you'll also find places using tanks that don't have liners and therefore must be filled up with additional CO_2 as the beer drains out.

Bottle and can

'Bottle-conditioned' beer which continues to ferment after packaging is classed by CAMRA as 'Real ale in a bottle'. Bottled beer from the smallest brewers often falls into this category as it's a good way of bottling successfully with the minimum of equipment. As with cask, beer may simply be packaged unfiltered and unpasteurised with enough yeast and residual sugars to continue fermentation or primed and perhaps repitched with fresh yeast.

Successful bottle conditioning requires care, skill and scrupulous hygiene. Too little fermen-tation and the beer will be dull, flat and prone to infection. Too much and you'll end up with a 'gusher' that bursts from the bottle on opening, or, worse, an exploding bottle. Infections that weren't apparent when the beer was bottled have plenty of chance to develop in the months spent on warehouse, shop and cellar shelves. By no means everyone always gets it right, though success rates are improving.

All bottle-conditioned beer will contain at least some sediment which tends to stick to the bottom. Certain styles like German and Belgian wheat beers and the new generation of hazy, fruity pale ales are intended to be served cloudy and brewers deliberately use yeasts that don't settle or even ask you to agitate the bottle gently before pouring. The sediment is harmless though will boost any yeasty flavour notes as well as affecting the appearance. Many brewers still recommend you pour their beer carefully, leaving the sediment behind: whether you follow their advice is a matter of personal taste.

Many more beers from specialist brewers are unpasteurised and unfiltered, though not technically 'real ale in a bottle' as no significant fermentation takes place after packaging. Either the brewer achieves the optimum carbonation level in a fermentation tank

Bottling at Five Points

before bottling or uses force-carbonation. Commercial mainstream beers are usually filtered, pasteurised and force carbonated.

Canned beer once had a poor reputation among connoisseurs, but this has changed dramatically. Can interiors have long been coated with neutral resin and beer from them should only taste metallic if you drink from the can rather than pouring the contents into a glass first, for obvious reasons. Compared to bottles, cans are more effective at protecting beer from damaging light and oxygen, cheaper, lighter and easier to transport and store. They take less energy to produce and are easily recyclable, although there is still some debate on their overall environmental impact. Like bottled beer, canned beer can be unpasteurised, unfiltered and even can-conditioned.

All bottled and canned beers – 'small pack' as brewers call them – tend to sit around longer than the draught equivalent, one reason why these formats work best with stronger, more robust styles (5% and up). While certain beers, usually stronger, bottle-conditioned ones, will develop increased complexity over many years when cellared like wine, most are intended to be drunk young. Contemporary hop-forward beers rapidly lose aroma with age, and some brewers mark them with a packaging date so you can identify the freshest supplies.

Draught beer at home

Bottle shops, brewery taprooms and even some pubs and bars increasingly offer 'growler fills', pouring draught beer into relatively large containers, around 1-2 litres, to take away. Customers normally pay a deposit on a reusable jug or bottle, but a few places have systems which can custom-fill a large single-use can. If the beer is simply poured from regular cask or keg taps, it's best drunk as quickly as possible before it suffers too much damage from oxygen. More hi-tech counter pressure systems, which only work with keg beer, purge the container of oxygen before filling: you should get away with keeping one of these unopened in the fridge for up to three days, but once opened treat as draught beer and drink quickly.

For larger quantities, 20 litre 'polypins' and 10 litre 'minipins' are cheap bag-in-box systems also regularly used for still cider and perry. They aren't ideal for beer that's still fermenting, so usually contain 'bright beer' with little residual yeast. More robust are 5 litre minicasks, which look much like a miniature version of a real cask turned on its end, and even have two openings: a tap at the bottom and a vent at the top. This suits them to cask-style beer, as the excess gas can be vented before serving. A minikeg also holds 5 litres but has only one opening and an integral

CO_2 capsule to force the beer out. All these formats have a relatively short shelf life: check the packaging or follow the supplier's advice.

For parties and other events, proper pub-style cask beer is usually impractical as you likely won't have the time, space, equipment and skills to condition it properly. Many brewers can supply firkins of 'bright' beer, essentially a giant 72-pint growler fill which needs to be drunk within a few hours once started. Keg beer lasts longer and doesn't usually require conditioning but does need special equipment to pour successfully: some suppliers lend or hire portable systems which are relatively easy to set up and use.

Cask or craft?

In the first edition of this book, I liberally splashed around the term 'craft brewer' as an internationally applicable way of identifying someone who approaches brewing as a craft, using quality ingredients, skill, experience and imagination to produce beers of character and distinctiveness. But since then, there's been such controversy and (sometimes deliberate) confusion around this innocent term in the UK beer community that in many places I've avoided it using at all, at least in connection with British brewing.

In the USA, the term has something like an official definition. The Brewers Association, the independent brewers' trade body, recognises a 'craft brewery' as one that's independently owned and produces no more than 6 million US barrels (7,154,000hl) per year. If a brewery is bought by a multinational, it loses its craft status even if there are no changes to the production process. Attempting to transplant this definition across the Atlantic is problematic: for one thing, breweries are much smaller on average and even most major industrial producers here fall within the limit.

For another, unlike the US, in the UK and certain other European countries like Belgium, Germany and the Czech Republic, we still have a significant indigenous traditional brewing industry using practices close to most people's understanding of the term 'craft' to produce distinctive local and regional beers. It's these cranky European styles and practices that largely inspired the US craft brewing movement in the first place, and even some of the most radical New World brewers still regard the most old-fashioned Old World beers with great reverence.

In the UK, the term seems to have been appropriated loosely to mean hoppy American-style beers in cans with graffiti art designs. Some even insist that craft beer specifically excludes cask beer, but if you push the self-declared craft drinkers on this, they usually make an exception for cask beers from brewers they approve of. Meanwhile, the established industry has scented a profitable trend, with companies dating from Victorian times or earlier scrambling to add trendily branded 'craft' ranges. In some cases, this has unleashed the long-inhibited creativity of some of Britain's most experienced brewers. In others, it's been faintly embarrassing in a grandad dancing sort of way. But none of it has helped in clarifying what we mean by 'craft'.

One useful aspect of the Brewers Association definition is the emphasis on independent ownership: you can't be a craft brewery if you're more than 25% owned by another alcohol industry concern which isn't itself a craft brewery. In London terms, this would exclude those producers wholly or partly owned by multinationals, including Beavertown, Fuller's and Fourpure. This doesn't necessarily mean their beers taste any better or worse, but many drinkers care about provenance, and might approach a beer differently if they knew it issued from a subsidiary of a big corporation despite its millennial-friendly packaging.

In 2016, SIBA, Britain's equivalent of the Brewers Association, launched the Assured British Independent Craft Brewer scheme, approving SIBA members to carry a special seal on their products if they're independently owned, meet basic quality standards and produce less than 200,000hl a year. So far around 50 London breweries are accredited: most of the others would qualify but aren't SIBA members. It's a valuable initiative, but without quite the authority yet to be used as an arbiter of what is or isn't 'craft'.

London beer styles

When the late great beer writer Michael Jackson wrote *The World Guide to Beer*, the book that's usually acknowledged as introducing the modern concept of beer styles, in 1977, he could hardly have guessed that, 40 years later, interpretations of nearly all the styles he wrote about and more would be brewed commercially in his home city. Back then, the *Good Beer Guide* needed only three symbols to describe the cask repertoire of English breweries: one for mild, another for bitter, and an occasional third for 'old ale or special'.

It wasn't always so. Beer historian Ronald Pattinson once told me that, at the beginning of the 20th century, 'you could walk into a London pub and have a choice of five or six draught beers such as bitter, mild, Burton and porter, all completely different in character and with strengths ranging from 3% to 7 or 8% ABV'. That diversity began to shrink just over a century ago, during World War I, not only through the shortage of ingredients but because of increasing taxation and regulation of the brewing industry – ostensibly in the name of the war effort but in reality largely driven by the same ideological objections to alcohol consumption that resulted in the USA's disastrous experiment with Prohibition from 1920–1933.

Besides increased regulation and the challenges of two wars, difficult economic conditions and consolidation in the industry contributed to a streamlining of production. By the time of the real ale revival in the 1970s, the idea that beer was all about low-strength session ales suitable for drinking in pints was firmly embedded in the British consciousness. The growth of microbreweries and the emergence of more discerning drinkers prompted a revival of interest in defunct styles like porter, and new developments like golden and summer ales, but almost always at session strengths.

The current abundance is partly the legacy of Jackson himself. His work directly and indirectly inspired would-be brewers in countries like the USA – where big brewing had almost entirely obliterated older and more locally distinctive techniques and styles – to start rebuilding their beer culture from a blank sheet. The resulting enthusiastic cosmopolitan eclecticism has now returned to the old European brewing heartlands. And nowhere is this more evident than London, a city with a long tradition of openness to exotic influences and new ideas.

All this makes it difficult to talk about specifically London styles. The beers with the deepest historical roots in the capital are porters and stouts, though, aside from a few wood-aged experiments, no contemporary London brewer makes them in a way comparable to the 18th century methods of maturing strong porter for years in wooden vats. By the end of the 19th century, mild was a more typical London style, originally in a paler form than drinkers normally expect today, and in the early 20th century, the related sweetish bottled brown ale style represented by Mann's Brown was regarded as an East End speciality. Today, only a tiny handful of London brewers offer a regular mild and none brews anything like Mann's Brown, which itself is still around but produced outside London.

Old-school real ale drinkers associate the capital with the revered cask bitters brewed by Fuller's and Young's, the two independents that survived into the 1970s. While Young's is no longer brewed here, Fuller's is still at its historic site under multinational ownership, though neither can be said to exhibit a distinctively London character. Instead, they reflect a general southeast English preference for relatively dry and hoppy cask bitters intended to be served with minimal head, doubtless influenced by the proximity of the Kentish hop gardens.

London can equally claim, alongside Wrexham and Glasgow, to be one of the UK's few historic lager-brewing cities. The first purpose-built British lager brewery, the Austro-Bavarian Lager Beer and Crystal Ice Company, opened in Tottenham in 1881, though it lasted a mere 14 years. In the 1930s, Barclay Perkins on Bankside became the first big brewer to commit to lager production. One of the UK's first 'craft lager' breweries, Freedom, now based in the West Midlands, originated in Fulham in 1995; one of its most successful, Meantime (p241), has been brewing in the London Borough of Greenwich since 2000. Several newer producers dedicated to quality lager have emerged in the past few years.

The city can also claim to be the UK's main centre for hop-forward US-inspired pale ales and IPAs. Though large numbers of new brewers don't bother with bitter and mild, nearly everyone offers at least one hoppy pale ale. Anyone regretting this as an apparent departure from tradition should remind themselves that London originally gave the world not only porter, but India Pale Ale too.

Below I've tried to provide some basic navigation through the bewildering variety of beers now brewed in the city, with a selection of suggested examples for each style. I've highlighted a few particularly excellent beers that I'd expect to find in my dream London beer case, limiting myself to one per brewery. The listings aren't exhaustive and certainly shouldn't discourage you from trying unlisted beers. The style categories, too, are pragmatic: beer styles are slippery things, and just when you think you have one pinned down, some pesky brewer insists on being creative and pushing the envelope.

Less alcohol, less gluten

When the last edition of this book was compiled, the choice of low-alcohol beer was still largely limited to artificially de-alcohol-ised industrial lager, tucked away in a remote corner of the pub fridge as an afterthought. Today, you can expect to find a range of characterful, good quality lower alcohol options proudly displayed at eye level in cutting-edge bottle shop-bars. Two London breweries specialise in such products, while quite a few others have launched sub-3% ABV brands. Many pubs and bars keep a small selection, and some venues are now using an extended range as a selling point.

There are various ways of producing a lower alcohol beer. The established method is to make a conventional beer then remove the alcohol. You can simply boil it off by heating, which also drives off much of the flavour and introduces a cooked note familiar from the industrial options of the past. Less damaging treatments including fine filtering and vacuum distillation.

Alternatively, with a careful choice of ingredients and strict control of mashing and fermenta-tion, you can brew a beer naturally lower in alcohol. This is the method adopted by many of the new arrivals. Properly brewed beers of under 3% ABV have a long history, though creating a balanced example that's not too thin and watery is still a stiff test of a brewer's skill. Recently, some brewers have achieved strengths as low as 0.5% by this method, and some claim to have reached 0%

The description 'low-alcohol' can only be used in the UK of beverages under 1.2% ABV, while anything below 0.5% is 'de-alcoholised' and anything below 0.05% is 'alcohol-free'. (However, 0.5% is the upper alcohol-free limit in the rest of Europe so, confusingly, some imported beers above 0.05% use this description.) Beers between 1.2% and 2.8% are officially referred to as 'reduced alcohol'.

Prospects have also improved for gluten-intolerant beer lovers.

Gluten-free beers have long been made using naturally gluten-free grains like maize, millet, rice and sorghum, but their resemblance to beers made with traditional malted barley can be partial to say the least. It turns out brewing and fermentation naturally break down at least some gluten in beers made to conventional recipes, and the thoroughness of this can be increased by using a proprietary enzyme known as Brewers Clarex, originally devel-oped to reduce haze. Tasting treated and untreated beers side by side reveals there is some impact on flavour, but the treated examples still taste better and more 'beer-like' overall than alternative grain examples. In the UK, a product can be described as gluten-free if its gluten content is less than 20 parts per million, though enzyme-treated beers might not be suitable for all forms of gluten intolerance and of course it's important to check all labelling carefully.

BITTER

The signature style of English cask beer, and by far the most common, bitter evolved from the hoppy pale ales developed in the late 18th century: brewers referred to it simply as 'pale ale' long after drinkers had taken to calling it 'bitter'. Thanks to the cost of paler malts and additional hops, bitter was once a little more expensive than styles like porter and mild, and therefore more upmarket and aspirational. Until very recently, pretty much all English brewers made at least one bitter, and most likely more.

Well-made cask bitter served in top condition packs immense subtlety and complexity into a low strength while remaining supremely refreshing and drinkable. Too much carbonation tends to mask this, so bottle, can and keg versions just aren't the same thing. Bitter had become so unhip among a certain stratum of drinkers that it was starting to look like an endangered style, but there's some evidence this is starting to turn, with several newer brewers introducing or reintroducing it to their range.

Strengths range from 3% to 5.5% or more, though most cluster between 3.5-4.8%, while the colour is classically amber but can run from golden to nut-brown. In the days when brewers produced each basic beer style in a range of strengths, it was the usual practice to offer an ordinary bitter at about 3.5%, a best at around 4.4% and perhaps a special at 4.8% or more. Relics of this can still be traced, for example in Fuller's trio of Chiswick (sadly now only an occasional seasonal), London Pride and ESB.

Classic bitters aim for a rounded flavour with a good balance between fruity, biscuity malt, often with crystal malt in the grist, sometimes giving a gently roasted crack in the finish, and a notable hop character achieved with earthy English varieties like Fuggles and Goldings. Some now include US hop varieties – not as novel as it might sound, as even in the 19th century British brewers used Oregon hops when domestic harvests were poor, though objected to their 'catty' flavours. Hop rates among the newer breed of bitters have notably increased, but remember the term 'bitter' is relative, and by current world craft brewing standards, these are polite beers.

Ordinary bitter

Anspach & Hobday The Ordinary Bitter (3.7%). Mid-amber, soft and earthy with a citrus-tinged English hop aroma and light notes of honey and toffee soothing a drying finish.

Sambrook's Wandle Ale (3.8%). Sambrook's first beer, this light but flavourful traditional amber bitter fitted into the London niche vacated by Young's 'Ordinary'. Maris Otter pale malt, Fuggles, Goldings and Boadicea hops result in a sweetish, earthy aroma with orange hints, a remarkably full-bodied, sweetish palate with toffee, biscuit and gently-spreading bitterness, and a firmly peppery finish. A straightforward beer but full of character, particularly on cask. Delightfully, its brewing location is in the process of moving to within a few metres of the like-named river.

Twickenham Grandstand (3.8%). Amber with hints of rum and liquorice on the aroma, leading to more liquorice and toffee on a gently bitter and autumnal palate and finish.

Volden Session (3.8%). Light amber house beer for Antic pubs. Pleasantly malty and toasty with a notably dry finish tinged with zesty grapefruit notes.

Best bitter

Brewhouse and Kitchen Islington Arcangel (4%). Deep amber with a caramel and hop aroma, a sweetish toasty palate with emerging bitterness, and a hint of brown sugar on an otherwise notably dry finish.

Five Points Best (4.1%). Foregrounding Fuggles hops with a gently honeyed, lightly earthy aroma, rosehip and citrus tartness across the palate, and a dry but lightly honeyed finish.

Macintosh Ales Best Bitter (4.6%). Solid English ingredients yield a light amber beer with a delicate orange-tinged hop aroma, notes of stewed fruit and currants and pithy bitterness over sweet chewy malt.

Southwark Bermondsey Best (4.4%). Amber with toffee, orange and hedgerow hints, caramel and autumn fruits on palate and a nettly, balanced finish.

Three Sods BoHo Bitter (4.1%). Golden with a tangerine jelly aroma, fruity palate with Bakewell tart and apricot, and a pleasant peppery finish with a contemporary twist.

Strong bitter

Fuller's ESB (Extra Special Bitter, 5.5%). Dark amber with a walnut and almond-tinged aroma, rich malt, pepper and orange zest, and a weighty finish with peppery hops. This was the beer that defined a whole style category in international competitions.

Dark bitter

Though this isn't a widely recognised beer style, enough London brewers offer notably dark beers broadly in the bitter category.

East London Nightwatchman (4.5%). Ruby brown with an earthy, slightly treacly aroma. Rye bread, caramel and orange on the palate, and a drying leafy, spicy finish.

Enefeld Speculation Ale (4.8%). Dark copper with a rich and grainy caramel body, earthy, spicy hop notes and a tart berry flourish on a hoppy finish.

Fuller's Gales HSB (Horndean Special Bitter, 4.8%). Brown with flavours of nuts and toffee, rich slightly syrupy malt and a mildly astringent finish with blackcurrant and roast notes.

Redemption Urban Dusk (4.6%). Chestnut-brown with fruit, chocolate and nutty, sappy malt, a bite of roast and a chewy finish with herbs and brown sugar.

MILD

Mild is usually assumed to be mild in terms of hop bitterness and/or strength, but originally 'mild' meant fresh and sweet, as opposed to matured acidic 'stale' beers like the first porters. Modern mild emerged in the early 19th century, originally as a pale beer, and gradually became the default style throughout much of England, with darker variants increasingly popular from the early 20th century. As a cheaper beer with a downmarket 'flat cap' image associated with its role in refreshing industrial workers, it later suffered in competition with bitter, particularly in upwardly mobile London. Mild retained a hold in the West Midlands and Northern England, where, by the 1970s, it was known as a low gravity, minimally hopped, malty, easy-drinking and usually dark beer. Today, it's regarded as a threatened style, and very little of it is made in London, although many brewers would love to make more. Given the growing interest in characterful reduced alcohol beers, I'm keeping my fingers crossed for a triumphal resurgence. Like bitter, it works best in cask, especially at lower strengths.

Boxcar Dark Mild (3.5%). Dark ruby with toasted nuts and light blackcurrant fruit on the aroma and orange zest and perfumed floral notes enlivening a rich chocolatey palate. There's charred toast and a dash of brown sugar on a crisp but still richly malty finish. A traditional delight from a brewery equally at home with contemporary brews, usually in can or keg at a lower carbonation than usual but keep an eye for it in cask.

Partizan X Ale (3.5-6%). An always-fascinating series of historical recreations that's ranged from mid-19th century strong pale milds to lower strength mid-20th century northern English dark examples, showcasing malt and English ale yeast. Almost exclusively bottle and keg rather than cask.

Spartan Son of Zeus (3.6%). This rare London light mild has a relatively complex recipe despite its simple golden colour, with five malts including rye and Bramling Cross among the hops. Blackcurrant and hedgerow notes, a gentle and sweetish but satisfying palate with hints of peach, and a dry malt finish with a light whiff of hops. It's widely available in cans, but unfiltered and unpasteurised with a lower carbonation to mimic the effect of cask, in which it also occasionally appears.

Tap East East End Mild (3.5%). Currently the only regularly brewed cask dark mild in London: richly malty with liquorice, blackberry and apple fruit hints and a chocolate note on the finish.

PALE ALE

Pale-coloured beers have been around since the invention of coke in the 1640s made it easier to control the kilning temperature of malt. The best-known pale ales are India Pale Ales, the robust, hoppy beers that dominated exports to India in the early 19th century. These originated in London though were later associated with Burton upon Trent. They became popular in the domestic market too, though their strength and hop character were gradually whittled down. Some longstanding cask beers labelled IPA are still around today, though now indistinguishable from standard bitter, itself the result of a parallel evolution from 18th century pale ales.

Inspired by accounts of early IPAs, pioneering US craft breweries tried to recreate them in the 1980s using the more assertive domestic hop varieties, resulting in a new wave of distinctive 'hop-forward' beers that subsequently spread across the world. The spectrum of hop flavours now encompasses not only US varieties but those from Australia and New

Zealand and an increasing number of new European cultivars. Rarer though not unknown are historical recreations using traditional English hops.

Given the long-ingrained British habit of drinking in pints, it's not surprising that London brewers have been at the forefront of delivering hop impact in lower-strength beers. Some of these are designated 'Session IPAs', indicating they're suitable for drinking in quantity over a 'session'.

Golden ale

Though the original pale ales were golden in colour, most of the draught bitters that developed from them preferred a deeper amber hue. A new generation of golden cask ales arrived in the 1990s as British microbrewers attempted to compete with mainstream lager. The trend to lighter colours has been further strengthened by US influence, and it's become increasingly difficult to distinguish golden ales and pale-coloured bitters from the new breed of American Pale Ales. The beers below are arguably more rooted in British beer culture and work well from the cask.

Signal Absolutely Fuggled (4%). Light amber with a creamy, grainy aroma, a sweetish palate turning lemony dry, and chewy Fuggles hops on a cheerful finish.

Southwark LPA (London Pale Ale, 4%). Light gold in colour, a gently malty-fruity aroma, a grainy palate with subtle grape and peach notes, and a generous malty finish with earthy hops.

Twickenham Naked Ladies (4.4%). This classic modern golden cask ale hopped with Celeia, Chinook and Hercules accounts for over a third of its brewery's sales. An inviting orange and pepper aroma heralds a creamy palate with a vanilla note at first, soon developing a peppery, earthy bitterness which persists through the fresh, smooth finish. It borrows the local name for the landmark late 19th century statues that form part of a water feature in nearby York House.

Wrong Side of the Tracks Lewisham Pale Ale (LewPA, 5.5%). Golden with a floral, fruity, spicy and grainy aroma, a honey-soft but complex estery palate with orange notes and a zesty peppery finish. Mainly bottled.

Contemporary light ale

'Light ale' was the 20th century term for the lowest strength pale ales, known in an earlier age as 'dinner ale' or 'table beer', the last indicating a tradition that has persisted in Belgium with reduced alcohol *tafelbier*. Today, a new wave of crisp, refreshing low-strength pale ales has reinvigorated the category. More commonly available in keg, bottle or can than cask, with some exceptions.

Battersea Session Pale (3.8%). Pale yellow with a tropical fruit ice cream aroma, a grainy, balanced and refreshing palate, and a peppery and lightly bitter finish.

Bullfinch Luna Ultra Pale Ale (3.8%). Pale straw in colour, a lightly lemony aroma, a light but interestingly estery palate, with lemon and spice on a refreshing, easy going finish.

Hackney Church Session Pale (3.8%). Golden-coloured, a delicately perfumed citrus aroma, lime marmalade zest on a substantial palate, and a lightly bitter grainy, chewy finish.

The Kernel Table Beer (3%). Hazy yellow with a gentle tropical fruit aroma, lemon and light mango fruit on a surprisingly full-bodied palate, and a zesty lightly bitter finish. Supremely refreshing.

Nirvana Hoppy Pale Ale (0.5%). Lightly piny and citric aroma, with good grain on a piny palate and a lemony-crisp, lightly bitter finish, very impressive at this strength.

Redemption Trinity (3%). The flagship beer of one of the earliest and still one of the best new London breweries. Three malts and three hops, including US varieties, are used to make a golden beer that's astoundingly flavoursome at such a modest strength. There's fresh grass, citrus and a hint of rose on the aroma, a chaffy palate with tropical fruit and even a note of smoke in a long, piny-bitter finish. Best on cask, it doesn't zing anywhere near as well from bottle or can.

Pale ale

These straightforward and refreshing session pale ales lean equally towards British cask traditions and a more eclectic contemporary sensibility.

Brick Peckham Pale (4.5%). Blond with a pineapple, peach and orange aroma, a chewy bitter note on a sweetly malty palate, with fruit and building pepper on the finish. Excellent from cask.

Five Points Pale (4%). The flagship beer of one of London's biggest independent breweries, made with Maris Otter pale, cara, Munich and wheat malt and hopped with Amarillo and Citra. This warm golden beer has a slightly spicy fruit salad aroma, notes of citrus and pine on a smooth palate and a complex pithy finish developing a peppery bitter note. It's also sold in keg, bottle and can but is particularly noteworthy from cask.

Ignition South of the River Pale Ale (4.2%). Golden with a creamy, vanilla-tinged aroma, delicate fruit on a full palate and a smooth, subtle orange-lemon finish. Mainly keg and bottled.

English-style India Pale Ale

Most British-brewed IPAs now use New World hops, but a few brewers have either revived home-grown recipes from times before the hop content was reduced or looked to new domestic hop varieties to add character without accumulating air miles. These beers tend to be bottled or canned.

Beerblefish 1892 IPA (6.9%). Amber with a lightly funky perfumed orange aroma from a *Brettanomyces* strain, leading to more orange with firm spicy, earthy hops over chewy toffee on both palate and finish.

Clarkshaws Hellhound IPA (5.5%). At a strength typical of interwar IPAs, this light amber beer has piny orange marmalade notes, a firm sweetish palate and a chewy, pleasant finish.

Meantime London IPA (7.4%). Made with strictly traditional Kent Fuggles and Goldings hops. Warm amber with a toffee and earthy hop aroma, a complex chewy palate with herbs, peach and pear drops, and a long, rounded and refined bitter finish.

Session IPA

These beers tend to be in keg, bottle or can.

Beavertown Neck Oil Session IPA (4.3%). Yellow in colour, stone fruit and pine on the aroma, a crisp but full palate with prickly hops and light citrus, and lingering pepper in a balanced moreish finish. Evolved from an attempt to clone Black Country ale Bathams Bitter.

Bianca Road Long Play IPA (3.6%). Hazy gold with a passion fruit and sweet orange aroma, leading to more tropical fruit in a firm but not too intense palate, and a crisp lightly bitter finish.

Fourpure Session IPA (4.2%). A modern London classic which I've found myself rating highly when judging it blind in competitions. It's a lightly hazy gold, with a slightly waxy mango and pine aroma, a very fresh and fruity palate with a hint of spice and plenty of grainy body. Citric notes persist into a lightly peppery, zesty finish. A great example of a modern beer with plenty of flavour and excellent drinkability at a relatively modest strength.

Signature Roadie All-Night IPA (4.3%). Yellow colour, a spicy tropical fruit and tangerine aroma, a slightly oily fruit palate, and a zesty grapefruit and lemon finish. Also sold on cask.

Two Tribes Metroland (3.8%). Mid-amber hue, a classic piny aroma with a toast and caramel, apricot jam palate with developing bitterness on a smooth finish.

American-style pale ale

It's sometimes difficult to place APAs, as they're often designated, with respect to session IPAs and standard American-style IPAs, though I'd expect them to fall between the two in both strength and hop character. These beers are usually keg, bottled or canned.

Beavertown Gamma Ray American Pale Ale (5.4%). Light copper, with a piny stone fruit and lightly woody aroma, sweet toasted malt with citric piny hops, and lingering fruit on a bitter finish.

Jawbone Bone Idle (4.6%). Pacifica and Simcoe hops yield an apricot aroma on a lightly hazy easy-drinking beer, with peachy citrus on the palate and very gentle zesty bitterness to finish.

Weird Beard Mariana Trench (5.3%). Light amber, a pineapple, pine and citrus aroma, a well-integrated peppery palate with chewy malt and a lasting spicy finish.

Wild Card Pale (4.3%). Formerly King of Hearts. Blond with citric and tropical fruit notes on a vivid aroma, then more fruit on a grainy, satisfying palate with a lightly bitter, pithy finish.

American-style India Pale Ale

These beers are usually keg, bottled or canned.

Brixton Electric IPA (6.5%). Warm orange in hue, a classic West Coast grapefruit and resin aroma, a substantial but balanced piny citric palate with a hint of sweet onion in a long, bittering finish.

Canopy Brockwell IPA (5.6%). Golden-amber, a lemon sherbet and grapefruit aroma, orangey tropical fruit on a firm palate, and a lingering spicy, earthy-bitter finish.

Crate IPA (6%). Golden, with a sticky citrus and tropical fruit aroma, some caramel on a creamy, grainy palate and autumn fruit on a persistent roundedly bitter finish.

Hammerton N7 IPA (5.2%). The name of this award-winning beer refers not just to the brewery's postcode but to the blend of seven US and New Zealand hop varieties used to create its complex character. A deep gold beer with grapefruit, orange and pine on the aroma, a silky palate with complex and tantalising citrus and pepper notes, and a pleasantly lingering finish with more fruit and salad-leaf bitterness. It's worth trying from both cask and keg, the latter yielding a slightly sweeter flavour.

Truman's Roller IPA (5.1%). Amber, a dark and richly perfumed aroma, sweetish orange and waxy piny hints on the palate, with a lingering dry and peppery finish.

Hazy, juicy pale ale

This is one of the most recent arrivals from the US, known to many drinkers as New England Pale Ale since a prominent early example originated in Vermont. I've preferred the designation used in competition guidelines. Its characteristic combination of an intensely fruity hop aroma and flavour with a relatively low level of bitterness is achieved by using hops sparingly, or even not at all, during the boil then dry hopping to extremes afterwards, thus 'DDH' for 'double dry-hopped'. This tends to leave a natural haze which fans associate with the style, prompting some brewers to cloud the issue still further with yeasts that settle less readily and/or additional wheat and oats, to the extent that some examples look like carton orange juice or liquidised vegetable soup. The results have been criticised as one-dimensional and lacking in balance but there's no doubting the intoxicating fruit aromas appeal to many. The approach is applied to a variety of strengths: expect New England IPA (NEIPA, pronounced 'neepa') to be above 5% and New England Double IPA (NEDIPA) stronger still. These are typically keg and canned beers, rather than cask.

Deviant and Dandy Dude Looks Like a Hazy (4.4%). Mango and lemon aroma, a lightly citric palate with a piny bitter edge and good fruit focus.

Gipsy Hill Carver Micro IPA (2.8%). Flavourful mix of tropical fruit, slight gooseberry and lemon tartness and strawberry yeast esters, with only a slight thinness revealing its low strength.

Gravity Well Cosmic Dust (3.8%). Very pale, with tropical fruit and balanced sulphur on the aroma, more fruit and delicate floral notes on the palate, and a lightly bitter finish.

Neckstamper To Lush (6.3%). Double dry-hopped with Mosaic, yielding characteristic tropical fruit, pine and sweet onion notes and a herbal orange finish.

Old Street Peely Wally (5.5%). Hazy gold. A citrus and tropical fruit aroma persists in a fresh, juicy palate over firm, bready malt. Short, crisp finish.

One Mile End Juicy 4PM (4.9%). Cloudy orange, a pineapple, papaya and green fruit aroma, a suggestion of banana on the smooth palate with a hint of mint, and a light finish.

Belgian pale ale

Outside Belgium, this usually refers to a pale ale fermented with Belgian yeast strains, which typically leave behind fruitier, more estery and sometimes spicier flavours than their British and American counterparts. Usually in keg or bottle.

Anspach & Hobday Patersbier (4.4%). Greenish gold with hints of grape and overripe apples, a dryish palate with yeasty and lemon notes, and a refreshing lightly bitter finish. Inspired by beers for internal consumption at Belgian monastic breweries.

Partizan Atomium Belgian Pale Ale (4.5%). Partizan's Andy Smith was one of several London brewers to tour Belgium just as the brewery was founded, and the influence still shows in several of his beers. This very drinkable golden ale is lightly spiced with coriander and orange peel, but just as important is the yeast which lends delicate spicy flavours and a fruity whiff. There are notes of lemongrass, clove and black pepper on the poised palate, and an orange-lemon finish with lingering spice and light sweetness.

Solvay Society Exotic Physics (6%). Gold, with pear and orange on the aroma, a juicy palate with a refined estery note and plenty of malt, and a perfumed finish with lingering hop spice. The bretted version adds complex waxy, woody and apricot notes.

Saison

Originally, *saison* was a term applied to golden ales brewed on farms in Wallonia, the French-speaking part of Belgium, for the refreshment of workers during the harvest. Without refrigeration, it was impossible to brew successfully in the summer, so beers were made in winter and laid down until early autumn – the term simply means 'season'. The style was commercialised from the end of the 19th century and during the 20th century, like Belgian beers in general, strengths went up to fill the gap when restrictions were placed on spirits. While some Belgian examples are quite straightforward strong pale ales, US brewers adopting the style were inspired by its more eccentric interpretations, often using flavourings and exhibiting 'funky' wild yeast characteristics. Internationally, saison has become a hard style to pin down – it's usually golden, it's usually made with a Belgian yeast, but there are numerous variations, including examples made entirely with wild yeast. For examples with additional flavourings, see below. Usually in keg, bottle or can.

Solvay Society Minimise Table Saison (3.2%). Very pale yellow, a lightly funky lemon-tinged aroma, a smooth perfumed palate with rose and citrus hints, and a quenching lightly bitter finish.

Bullfinch Milou Saison (4.6%). The earlier versions were stronger, but the current iteration of this cheerful golden beer reduces the alcohol to more English-friendly levels while retaining the profile of the classic style, using noble European hops and a dash of Vienna and Munich malts for sweetness. It has a bready and herbal aroma with light hints of clove and ginger, citrus, yeasty spice and fruit on a firm grain base and a refreshingly fruity, slightly sweet finish. It borrows the original French name of Tintin's dog, known as Snowy in English.

Mutineers Suffragette Saison (5.2%). Warm gold in colour, a rose and orange pith aroma, a lightly spicy palate with floral and toffee notes, and a full finish with pronounced herbal bitterness.

Three Hills Tank Fresh Saison (4.8%). Mixed fermentation beer with French saison yeast, a zesty golden delight with notes of lemon, Sauvignon Blanc, pepper and floral chamomile with a refreshingly bitterish finish.

Kölsch-style ale

The celebrated local beer of Cologne (Köln) in western Germany is a hybrid, fermented as an ale but then lagered at cold temperatures for an extended period. The result is a smooth, refreshing golden beer with just a subtle hint of yeast esters. In my experience, many brewers outside Cologne struggle to mimic it, but there are now some creditable London examples. The term Kölsch is a Protected Geographical Indication limited to the area in and around the city, so brewers elsewhere shouldn't be using it unqualified. Usually in keg, bottle or can.

40FT Larger (4.8%). Golden, a zesty, lightly fruity aroma with some grassy notes, a full herbal hoppy palate and a chewy, earthy finish nodding slightly to English bitter.

Distortion Inertia (4.8%). Perhaps more fruity than classic German versions, but crisp and characterful with light pear, banana and vanilla notes and a subtly grassy finish.

Orbit Nico (4.8%). Golden, a grassy, slightly waxy hop aroma, a simple, crisp palate with a suggestion of cucumber, and a dry, lightly peppery finish.

Park Phantom (4.2%). Delicate yellow, a grassy slightly honeyed aroma with red apple hints, a malty and honeyed but light palate, and a smooth lingering lightly drying finish.

Red ale

This is another style name without too specific a meaning other than to indicate a vaguely reddish colour and malty flavour, and some brewers add rye to the mix – see also Rye beer below. Several of the beers here are sold on cask and work very well in the format.

Bexley Red House (4.2%). Ruby-amber colour, a malty aroma with some dusty spice, fruity hops and toffee sweetness on the palate with a soft, chewy, lightly piny finish.

By the Horns Diamond Geezer (4.9%). Toasty, malty aroma with hop notes, a smooth and substantial palate with a tangy bite, and a lightly nutty finish.

Wimbledon Copper Leaf Red Ale (4%). Deep red-brown colour, piny toffee and blackcurrant fruit on the aroma, a juicy palate with caramel and raspberry, and a toasty bitter finish.

BARLEY WINE

'Barley wine' is used loosely as a general term for any ale, other than a porter or stout, with a strength approaching that of wine (around 8–12%). Strong beers have a long history in Britain, going back at least to the 16th century when the nobility cellared them in their homes. In the 19th century, the strongest beers, often matured in the brewery for a year before release, were known as 'stock ales', and the current term dates only from the 1950s. Beers at this strength, if left unfiltered and unpasteurised, can go on maturing for a long time, developing a variety of complex flavours like a fine wine. Typically a bottled style.

Fuller's Vintage Ale (8.5%). One of London's world class beers, this has been produced annually since 1997 in bottle-conditioned form, though it appears in cask for special occasions. The recipe changes slightly from year to year but is always simple and traditional and uses top quality ingredients, usually pale and crystal malts and English hops. Big and mouth-numbing when young, with earthy and peppery hop flavours and the characteristic orange tang of the Fuller's yeast, it mellows beautifully after a few years, developing sherry and port notes over a smooth but complex mix of olives, nuts, fruit and minerals, with a lingering orange dryness in the finish. Some vintages have been known to decline then improve again with age

One Mile End Pierre de Garde (10%). A strong northern French-style pale ale celebrating the family origins of brewer Pierre Warburton. Hazy amber with a woody, spiced apple aroma, firm malt and pastry on a honeyed palate, then blackcurrant and chewy, earthy hops on a long finish.

Partizan De Ronde Imperial Saison (8.7%). Hazy gold, a sweet orange peel and spice aroma, a rich boozy palate with orange and apricot fruit, lightly piny hops, drying wood and vanilla on the finish.

Sambrook's No 5 Barley Wine (8.2%). Originally a fifth anniversary beer, this will also age gracefully, with rich nutty malt, olive, cherry and orange notes and a lengthy chocolate truffle finish with rounded bitterness.

Truman's 1916 Barley Wine (9%). Hazy amber, a vanilla and wood aroma, more oak on a sweetish grainy finish with emerging bitter hops, luscious but surprisingly light.

Wimbledon XXXK Vintage Ale (10%). Boozy sweet malt, a marmalade and stone fruit aroma, more of the same on a spicy firm palate, and a drying, warming, woody and complex finish. Sometimes seen on cask.

PORTER AND STOUT

Porter was the first international beer style and the first industrial one, developed in London in the early 18th century. It spread worldwide, proving equally popular in the cold Baltic and the warmer climes of the Caribbean and sub-Saharan Africa. Most famously, it spread to Ireland, where the local variant flourished as its parent style declined towards the end of the 19th century, unable to meet the challenge from milds and bitters. The decline was slow, but porter brewing had ceased completely in Great Britain by 1958.

Like many other beer styles, porter was made in a variety of strengths, and the stronger examples were designated 'stout porter'. The stronger version resisted the decline longer and eventually the term 'stout' was used on its own, its original meaning forgotten as beer strengths declined overall. In 1978, partly inspired by Michael Jackson's musings on beer styles, a few British brewers started to experiment with approximations of old recipes, soon joined by colleagues in other countries. Porter has since comprehensively re-established itself as a modern specialist style.

Today, there's no consistent distinction between porters and stouts. Standard stouts are often inspired by the Irish variety – very dark brown, smooth, dry, with chocolate and coffee flavours, some of them with the distinctive ashy note of roasted barley. The term 'porter' tends to be used for beers that are broadly similar in character but where the brewer wants to avoid invoking a comparison with Irish stout. There's a growing fashion for adding raw or malted oats to the recipe, which lend a notably smooth texture. In this case, the resulting beer is usually known as oatmeal or oat malt stout rather than porter.

The most celebrated very strong, and notably hoppy, historic porter is imperial stout at 9–10% ABV or more, originally developed in the late 18th century for export to Russia and the Baltic. Its most famous exponent was Southwark brewer Barclay Perkins, whose successor Courage continued to brew it until 1993. Porters and stouts at slightly less daunting strengths of around 6–8% are sometimes labelled 'export', also derived from 19th century terminology.

At the other end of the scale, low strength (2–3%) sweet stouts, including milk stouts made with lactose, were popular in the early 20th century, and are now being reinvented by some adventurous brewers, though often with a higher alcohol content. Baltic porters are porter-like beers brewed using lager yeasts, following the example of Baltic countries that adopted the style. So-called Black IPA, a modern combination of dark malt and New World hops, is best thought of as a particularly hop-forward example of porter.

The thorough resuscitation of porter and stout is one of the great success stories of the brewing renaissance. Practically all London brewers have at least one example in their repertoire, often more, and the quality and diversity are remarkable. No-one has yet attempted staling porter in vats in 18th century fashion, though there have been some experiments with barrel ageing. Porter has not only been brought back from the dead, it's come home.

Session porter

This style works particularly well in cask.

Bexley Black Prince Porter (4.6%). Near-black, a piny note on a dark malt aroma, a rich foamy palate with complex chocolate and marmalade, and a chalky dry toasty finish.

Brockley Porter (4.3%). Very dark brown, a tarry aroma with coffee and berry fruit, a characterful dark palate and a drying finish with cherry and blackcurrant hints.

Five Points Railway Porter (4.8%). Very dark brown, with a sharply grainy chocolate aroma, a velvety dark malt palate with a roast edge, and a fine dark chocolate finish. The special edition Bret version, **Derailed Porter** (5.7%), adds spicy, meaty, perfumed notes.

Portobello Market Porter (4.6%). Dark ruby, a tarry dark malt and berry aroma, sweet but balanced with orange fruit, fine chocolate and light roast on a smooth finish.

Redemption Fellowship Porter (5.1%). Substantial but soft example with tangy notes balancing the sweetness, chocolate and fruit and a lingering coffee finish.

Strong porter

Beers in this category are more common in bottle and can but look out for cask releases.

Anspach & Hobday The Porter (6.7%). The descendant of a homebrew that excelled at numerous competitions, including a commercial one where it was sneakily entered, this is still the brewery's flagship and one of the great London beers. Very dark brown with a thick beige head, it has notes of burnt sugar, chocolate and leather on a dark and roasty aroma, an enveloping sweet-dry palate with hints of blackcurrant, smoke and bitter herbs, and a smooth and dry finish which lacks the harshness of some. At first it seems austere but turns out immensely rewarding. It's made with Maris Otter extra pale, chocolate, amber and black malts, Cascade and East Kent Goldings hops and an American pale ale yeast.

Beerblefish 1820 Porter (6.6%). Dark brown, with a cinder toffee and toast aroma, cola, chocolate and fruity yeast on the palate, and a blackcurrant-tinged finish with brown bread and chocolate.

The Cronx Entire Porter (5.2%). Near-black, with a spicy chocolate and coffee aroma, a smooth palate with brown sugar notes, coating chocolate, coffee and dark malt on the finish. Sold as both cask and nitrokeg.

Enefeld London Porter (5.5%). Very dark brown, a berry hop and coffee aroma, a slightly salty coffee palate with berry sweetness, grainy roast and chocolate later.

Stout

The Kernel Export Stout London 1890 (7.7%). Cakey malt aroma with notes of tobacco and sulphur, nettly, herbal flavours on a treacle and chocolate palate, and a beautiful roast dryness emerging in a long, rich and fruity finish. Bottled and keg.

Weird Beard Sharp Dressed Stout (6%). A lusciously chocolatey example made from a complex mix of grains, with plenty of tangy fruit, leady malt and almost a blue cheese note. Bottled, keg and sometimes cask.

Milk stout

Husk Milk Stout (4.4%). Near-black, a creamy coffee aroma, a slightly smoky sweetened black coffee palate, and a toothsome finish with vanilla hints. Cask and keg.

London Beer Factory Big Milk Stout (7.5%). With vanilla and cocoa nibs, a near-black colour and nutty chocolate aroma, luscious but not too sweet with creamy dark sugar and a suggestion of plum skins and dried apple. Keg and can.

Mad Yank Monaco Toasted Marshmallow Little Impy Stout (7.3%). Near-black with definite toasted marshmallow and almond notes, a sweetish raisin palate and a note of roast on the finish. Keg and bottle.

ORA Balsamic (6%). A London-brewed beer with a very Italian sensibility. The recipe infuses a British-inspired milk stout with balsamic vinegar from Modena, home city of the brewery's founders, made by the traditional method of maturing grape must for 12 years in wooden casks. It's accomplished with great subtlety, the vinegar lending fruit and wood notes with only a hint of acetic acid on the finish, cushioned by creamy dark malts and chewy lactose, with a touch of added vanilla and the berry flavours of Ekuanot hops. Keg and bottle, though has been seen on cask.

Three Sods Dark Magus Milk Stout (4.7%). Dark brown with an amber glow, a sticky chocolate and liquorice aroma, a toasty chocolate and coffee palate, and emerging bitterness on a milky, grainy finish. Cask and bottle.

Oatmeal stout

These styles work well in cask.

East London Quadrant (5.8%). Very dark brown, with coffee and apple fruit on a slightly savoury aroma, suggestions of bourbon and tobacco, and a lasting but not over-roasted finish.

Southey Ursus III Oatmeal Stout (5.5%). Very dark brown, a roasty chocolate aroma, whisky notes on a spicy, piny palate, and a dry but not too hoppy or roasty finish.

Black IPA

Another style that emerged from the US craft brewing scene in the 2000s, this is the result of using porter-style dark malts alongside IPA-style hops. The etymological dubiousness of labelling a beer style both pale and black has prompted the alternative name 'Cascadian dark ale', rarely seen outside style guidelines, and some commentators have observed the beer is essentially just a porter that's been heavily hopped with modern varieties. The challenge is to juggle the bitterness of both hops and roasted malts without ending up with something that's too astringently dry and bitter.

Beavertown Black Betty (7.4%). Ripe tangerine, dark honey and malted milk on the aroma, with grapefruit hops nested in a chocolate mousse palate and a suggestion of mint humbug to finish.

Dogs Grandad Black IPA (5.2%). Deep roast malts overlaid with tantalisingly complex floral tones: chocolate-coated Turkish delight, dried apricot, raspberry and a firmly peppery-bitter, coffeeish finish.

Speciality stout and porter

Anomaly Witch Doctor (4.6%). With added coffee, this near-black brew has a fine sappy chocolate aroma with a lightly burnt note, a very dry chocolate and black cherry palate, and lingering coffee on the smooth, dry finish. Bottled.

Bohem Raven Lagered Porter (4.3%). Made as a lager with porter-type ingredients, like a lighter version of the Baltic style. Near-black colour, roast coffee and chocolate, a little brown sugar on a clean palate, and a smooth coffee and cream finish. Keg or can.

Fearless Nomad Muscles from Brussels (9.5%). Added date syrup and muscovado sugar with a Belgian yeast yield a smooth and sticky delight, with toasty malt, rich black cherry and date fruit and a long slightly tannic finish.

Hammerton Oyster Stout (5.3%). Real Maldon oysters added to the boil are detectable but surprisingly successful in this jet-black briny, slightly fruity stout that still has plenty of chocolate and coffee character. Cask, keg and can.

Three Hills БЛАВК Marshmallow (10%). One of a series of luscious 'pastry stouts', dangerously mellow for strength with rich dark malt, hints of marshmallow and coconut and a light note of roast on spicy finish. Keg or can.

Weird Beard Black Perle (3.8%). Complex, nearly black but surprisingly light coffee stout, with coffee balanced against dark malt and brown sugar, then milk chocolate and charcoal on the finish. Cask, keg and bottle.

Imperial stout

Goose Island Brewpub Imperial Stout (8.8%). Very dark brown, an oaky bourbon, grape and blackcurrant aroma, spicy notes on a sweet boozy palate, leading to chocolate sauce and light fruit on the long finish. Cask and keg.

The Kernel Imperial Brown Stout London 1856 (10.1%). The deservedly high reputation of this Bermondsey pioneer was built on recreations of historic London stouts and porters as well as contemporary hoppy pales, and this one is arguably the crowning glory. It's a near-black beer with a thick beige head, a roast note on a chocolate truffle aroma, a sticky dark cake palate tinged with prune, herbal and liquorice notes and a roasty dry black bread finish with a subdued charred note, finally very dry and elegant. The recipe is complex, involving pale, brown, Munich, crystal, amber and black malts, brown sugar and hops including Apollo, Columbus and

SPECIALITY GRAINS

Wheat has played a role in brewing since prehistory, but historically its use has often been regulated or prohibited to protect stocks for baking, and brewers have found barley more versatile and easier to work with. Wheat beer was once common in England, particularly in the southwest, only finally disappearing in the 1870s. By the 1960s it seemed in terminal decline elsewhere, limited to a few shrinking enclaves in Belgium and Germany. Then an obsolete style was revived in the village of Hoegaarden near Brussels and suddenly wheat beer was a young drink again.

Wheat beer is an ale style that's typically served unfiltered, unpasteurised and cloudy with suspended yeast. Belgian witbier (white beer) is made with unmalted wheat and spiced, typically with coriander and dried orange peel, giving a smooth milky quality with an orange tang. Bavarian Weißbier or Weizenbier is made with malted wheat and no spices, but has bubblegum, banana and clove notes left behind by its characteristic yeast strains. Besides the standard version, there are dark and filtered variants. Brewers elsewhere, including in London, readily venture outside traditional boundaries, so you'll find wheat beers made with Bavarian yeast but with additional spicing, or hybrids with more traditional English ales. Wheat is also a key part of the grist for several traditional wild and sour beers, but I've dealt with these separately below.

Bavarian-style Weißbier

The examples below are typically in keg or tank.

German Kraft Edel Weiss (5.3%). Hazy deep gold, a perfumed citrus and spice aroma, a full lemon-orange palate with emerging clove, and firm hops on a lightly apply finish.

Block Vice (5.5%). Hazy blond, with a banana, grain and spice aroma, a tangy lemon-orange palate with emerging pepper and clove, and a drying spicy finish.

40FT Streetweiss (5%). 40FT was co-founded by a German brewer so it's unsurprisingly good at German styles, though with a contemporary twist seen here in the use

Nugget from the US and Magnum from Germany. Try cellaring a bottle for a couple of years, as the assertive flavours benefit still further from rounding out. Bottle and occasional keg, with limited quantities aged in barrels to approximate the mid-19th century 'stale' character.

Sambrook's Russian Imperial Stout (10.4%). Black, with a fruity caramel, black pepper and rum aroma, chocolate and coffee on a rich, smooth palate that hides its alcohol, and a very long roasty finish. Bottle, occasional cask.

Signature Anthology Imperial Stout (10%). Leathery blackcurrant aroma, smoky black treacle, herbs and chocolate truffle on the palate and a long, toasty, slightly savoury finish. Annual release in keg and can.

of a new hop variety, Hüll Melon. This hazy amber beer has the expected banana notes on the aroma and a full grainy palate with a deliciously frothy mouthfeel, plenty of clove flavours and a hint of lemon. The aromatics linger in a velvety finish with a developing sting of citrus peel bitterness.

Flavoured wheat beer

Affinity Breeze (3.8%). Marketed as a saison, this supremely refreshing, summery beer invokes the witbier style by its use of dried lime peel and coriander as well as a touch of wheat. A golden beer with a thick white head, it has an enticingly zesty, herbal and citric aroma, with more coriander emerging over sticky malt on a beautifully balanced palate. There's lime juice and a gentle hint of bitterness on the finish. Affinity work miracles in producing such consistently decent and drinkable session beers on a very basic setup. Keg and can.

Pressure Drop Wu Gang Chops the Tree (3.8%). At base a Bavarian-style wheat but flavoured with locally foraged bay leaves, this is a delightfully sessionable beer with notes of ginger, fennel, citrus and chamomile over a soft cereal backdrop with a delicate bitterness. It was the brewery's third beer and one of the cornerstones of its current success, though obtaining enough flavourings proved more of a challenge than expected. The name references the Chinese legend of an unfortunate man who was punished by being made repeatedly to chop down a tree on the moon which instantly regrew, a wry nod to the beer's moreishness. Keg and can.

Rye Beer

Alongside wheat, rye is one of several brewing grains eclipsed by the ubiquity of barley, though it continued in localised use, lending a distinctive spicy and oily note to Bavarian Roggenbier and Finnish sahti. More recently, brewers have discovered it works well with certain hops, particularly in combination with deeper-hued barley malts that give a supporting biscuit body. Some brewers add rye to beers labelled 'red', so there's some overlap with this category. These beers are typically in keg, can or bottle.

Beavertown 8-Ball Rye IPA (6.2%). Red-amber, a spicy overripe fruit aroma, and a cracker-dry palate with confectionery notes leading to a soft malt finish with spreading hop bitterness.

Brick Peckham Rye Red Ale (4.7%). Deep red-brown colour, a piny rye bread and spice aroma, a perfumed hop palate with chewy cereal and a light honey, crisp bittering finish.

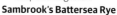

Sambrook's Battersea Rye (5.8%). Dark red, a pungently spicy aroma with banana toffee, a bold raisin fruit and rye bread palate, and a dry finish with light roast and spice.

Smoked beer

In the days when all malt was dried over wood fires, most beers tasted smoky, at least when fresh. Brewing with smoked malt persisted into the modern era in a few isolated pockets, notably Bamberg in Upper Franconia, a culturally distinct part of Bavaria which preserves several other idiosyncratic brewing styles and practices. Here, smoked malt is deployed in lager styles like amber Märzen and dark Bockbier, but it's re-entered the international craft brewing lexicon in a variety of contexts, including brown ale and porter – appropriately as historically these beers would have included a proportion of smoky, wood-fired malts.

Anspach & Hobday The Smoked Brown (6%). Roast nut and smoky toffee aroma, a full, rich and earthy palate with controlled smoke and a dry, toasty finish. Keg, can, sometimes cask.

Tap East Smokestack Porter (6.5%). Dark brown, a sweet aroma laced with wood-smoke, a chocolate and raisin palate with light smoke, and a dry tangy finish. Cask.

Muswell Hillbilly Down the Colney Hatch Smoked Porter (5.1%). Dark brown, with a blackcurrant and burnt toast aroma, coconut, whisky, chocolate, light smoke and spice on the palate, and a woodsmoke and fruit finish. Keg and bottle.

FLAVOURED BEER

Before hops became ubiquitous, brewers deployed a huge variety of flavourings. There are records of fruit beers from ancient Egypt, while whole fortunes were made in the medieval Low Countries from secret herb and spice blends known as *gruut* or *gruit*. The use of such ingredients persisted into the late 20th century in Belgium and a few other places, though invariably alongside rather than instead of hops. Many contemporary brewers have embraced the idea, sometimes to empha-sise a sense of place by using typically local or even foraged ingredients. The results can be variable: mastering the permutations achiev-able with just the four standard components of beer is a lifetime's study, and the complica-tions of adding further flavours to the mix are often underestimated. But in capable hands, judicious use of additional ingredients can open new dimensions of enjoyment. Spiced wheat beers are dealt with separately above, and I've considered flavoured 'sours' below.

Earth Ale Dandy Stout (7.3%), with dandelion root. Very dark brown, a lightly spicy aroma, cola notes on a sweetish but drying and tantalisingly spicy palate, and a little chocolate on the finish. Keg and bottle.

Friendship Adventure Tangent Grapefruit Saison (5.3%). Subtle but zesty grapefruit in this lightly hazy pale ale integrates well with cinnamon and ginger spice and a clovey Belgian yeast against a sweetish backdrop.

ORA Limoncello (6%). IPA with Sorrento lemons. Pale gold, a lemon and oregano aroma, a softly sweetish but spicy and herbal palate, and a spicy zesty lightly hoppy finish. Keg or bottle.

Partizan Saison Lemon and Thyme (3.8%). Very pale yellow colour, a lemon drop aroma with gentle thyme notes, a very fruity palate with integrated herbal flavour, and a zesty refreshing finish. Keg or bottle.

LAGER

To many British drinkers, lager is a golden beer usually sold under a familiar global brand, invariably pasteurised and highly carbonated, with a straightforward, clean, lightly malty, if not bland and boring, palate and a bit of grassy hop character. To brewers and informed connoisseurs, however, lagers are a whole family of beers initially perfected in Bavaria, Austria and the Czech lands, fermented slowly at low temperatures using specific strains of yeast and then tank-conditioned at even lower temperatures to achieve a smooth and clean-tasting result. Lagers can be gold, black, weak, strong and many other things, including unpasteurised, unfiltered and 'real'.

Although lager has been brewed in Britain since at least the 1870s, it lagged far behind ale in popularity until the late 1960s when the big brewing groups began to throw their massive marketing weight behind what we now recog-nise as the most familiar and least creditable examples of the style. Lager has outsold ale in Britain since 1989, but at the expense of besmirching its name among discriminating drinkers.

Commercial British lagers are derived very loosely from the Pils and Helles styles familiar to Bavarian drinkers. The former originated in Plzeň in western Bohemia, now the Czech Republic, as what was likely the first ever pale example of the style in 1842: previously, all lagers were darker in colour. The city is known as Pilsen in German, thus the adjective pilsener or pilsner. Czechs are loath to describe beers as Pils if they come from anywhere else, while in Germany the term usually indicates a hoppier alternative to Helles ('light'), which has a similar appearance but is more malt-forward in flavour.

Besides these, German brewers produce unfiltered and unpasteurised lagers known as Kellerbier and Zoigl; stronger and sometimes deeper-coloured Märzen and Oktoberfest beers; lightly toasty and caramelly dark lager or Dunkel; very dark and roasty though rarely bitter Schwarzbier ('black beer'); and strong, malty and usually dark seasonal beers called Bock. The Czech Republic has an equally fine-grained range.

The first modern 'craft lager' brewery in London opened in the 1990s (see Meantime p241), and one of the more pleasing developments of recent years is the growing number of producers keen to redeem the reputation of British lager by paying as much attention to quality ingredients and technique as a conscientious Czech or German brewer would. So far, most of the attention is on the pale side, though darker and stronger examples can be found. As with other styles, not all brewers feel bound by tradition, so don't be surprised to encounter newer hops alongside the established mainland European 'noble' varieties, with techniques such as dry hopping adding an extra aromatic flourish.

These beers are commonly served from keg, bottle or can.

Pale lager

Brick Peckham Helles (4.2%). A big grassy, honeyed noble hop aroma introduces this fresh grainy lager with hints of vanilla and meadowsweet and a lemon drop note on the finish. Gluten-free.

Exale Der Titan (4.8%). Inspired by the robust Dortmunder style but dry hopped, with a softly grassy and peppery aroma, plenty of grainy bitterness and a delightfully rounded but earthily drying finish.

Gipsy Hill Hunter (5%). Lemon and glucose notes on a grainy aroma, lightly perfumed hops on a clean malt palate, and a peppery, quite assertively hoppy finish.

Hackney Church Lazy Day Lager (4.8%). Gold, a delicate grainy and grassy aroma, a lightly chewy, hoppy and well-balanced palate, with a final flourish of peppery hops.

Meantime Brewery Fresh Lager (4.5%). Pale gold, a creamy lemon aroma with just a slight buttery hint, a tasty spicy palate and a lasting finish that bitters over creamy malt.

Pillars Helles (4.8%). This beer from the Walthamstow lager specialist twists the traditional Helles formula with New World hops, but subtly enough not to offend purists. The golden beer has light lemon and vanilla notes as well as some grassiness on the aroma, a creamy, grainy palate and a hint of fruit juice on a lightly bittering, gently hoppy finish. The recipe was perfected following customer feedback on several trial brews sold at the taproom.

Portobello Notting Helles (4%). Gold colour, a vanilla and grass-tinged grainy aroma with some toffee, lemon notes on a smooth lightly malty palate, and a drying grassy hop finish.

Signature Studio Lager (4%). Clean yellow colour, a soft grassy aroma with vanilla and lime, more lime on a nicely malty palate and a spicy bittering finish. Includes a hint of rye in the grist.

Wimbledon Gold Lager (4.8%). Pale gold, a spicy citrus and vanilla aroma, grape notes on a clean but full-bodied, zestily bittering palate, and a lingering finish. Dry-hopped.

Pilsner

Bohem Amos Pilsner (4.9%). Pale yellow, with a citrussy aroma from Kazbek hops, a crisp fruity palate with orange and apricot, and emerging pepper, leading to a nicely bittering finish.

Fourpure Lager (4.2%). Grainy, grassy, lightly honeyed aroma, a crisp palate with a fleeting suggestion of grape, and lightly spicy hops on the rounded finish.

Pretty Decent Pilsner (5%). Delicately pale with a traditional creamy vanilla and grass aroma, soft malt, hints of lime and a bite of hop bitterness on a clean finish.

Darker and stronger lagers

Bohem Sparta Amber (5.4%). In an unusual style for London, this is what Czechs call a *polotmavý ležák* or half-dark lager. It has a smooth malty aroma with hints of stone fruit and hop, plenty of malt on a creamy and satisfying palate with an emerging dry hop bitterness, and a lightly drying, hoppy finish. A superb beer from London's leading specialist lager brewery, made using Czech malt and hops with a traditional decoction mash that involves boiling some of the wort and returning it to the mash tun, creating subtle caramel notes. It changed minds about lager so effectively that it's credited with securing the initial investment in the brewery.

Inkspot Black Lager (4.6%). Very dark brown, with a chocolate and grassy hop aroma, a sweetish, easy drinking grainy chocolate palate, and a lingering crisp, dry finish.

Small Beer Dark Lager (1%). A standout beer from the Bermondsey lower alcohol specialists, this is made from pale and dark malts and a splash of oats for body. Dark ruby with a beige head, it has a coffee and chocolate aroma with a yoghurt or berry-like acidity, a full, grainy, slightly salty palate with plenty

of dark malt character, and a soft but refreshing finish with caramel, chocolate and very light hops. At regular strength it would be noteworthy; at this strength, it's a miracle.

Zerodegrees Beast of Blackheath Black Lager (4.6%). Near-black, a toasty blackcurrant aroma, dark but crisp and tangy with notes of fruit and treacle, leading to a soothing lightly roasty finish.

WILD, SOUR AND BARREL-AGED BEER

Beer likely originated when grain porridge or bread soaked in water or milk was fermented unintentionally by wild yeasts, perhaps drifting over from nearby fruit. Today, most brewers strive for close control of fermentation using cultivated yeast strains, but wild fermentation has been retained as a commercial brewing practice in the area around Brussels, Belgium, to create local speciality lambic. Wort made from a blend of malted barley and unmalted wheat is exposed overnight in a shallow vessel known as a *koelschip* or coolship to attract wild yeasts and souring bacteria, then fermented and matured for anything up to three years in wooden vats and casks in which still more microflora have established themselves. Such beers are rarely drunk in their native form: they're sweetened with sugar, or blended, or steeped with fruit such as sour cherries and raspberries. Other traditional entries in this broad category include Flemish old brown ale, a distant relative of the original vatted porters, and two German wheat beer styles which were near-extinct before being seized upon by international craft brewers: Berliner Weisse, once the default beer of the country's capital, and Gose, spiced with salt and coriander and once popular in Leipzig in the east. Both undergo an additional fermentation with lactic bacteria, imparting a mellow, yoghurt-like sourness.

Most contemporary 'sours' are descendants of Berliner Weisse or, less commonly, Gose, though now made by the process of 'kettle souring'. Lactic bacteria are introduced into the wort before the boiling stage and left to develop until the desired level of acidity is reached. The hop boil halts further bacterial activity while retaining the sour flavour, and the beer is then fermented normally, often with a final addition of fruit flavouring and/or dry hopping. The method is controlled and predictable, but the resulting beer can be a little one-dimensional.

A more adventurous option is to ferment with a 'mixed culture' containing both brewer's yeast and cultivated strains of the 'wild yeast' genus *Brettanomyces*, perhaps alongside lactic bacteria. Such cultures can be bought from yeast suppliers, though some brewers have cultivated their own from exposed wort, fruit skins or beers that became unintentionally infected, with interesting results. A handful of UK brewers are now experimenting with Belgian-style wild fermentation using coolships, including London Beer Factory.

Barrel-ageing is a closely related though distinct technique. As well as additional fermentations caused by the resident microflora, perhaps helped along with a dose of a prepared culture or ingredients like fruit, the wood itself adds flavour notes which progressively diminish as the barrel is reused, while previous occupants such as wine or whisky leave their own traces. Numerous London breweries have at least a few barrels on the go, some have extensive collections, and a couple – Beavertown and the Kernel – also have much more capacious tall wooden vats, today usually known by their Dutch name, foeders. Long and complex fermentations can also take place in steel tanks, or even ceramic vessels like the two amphorae kept at Beavertown.

Such processes are inherently unpredictable, so traditional styles made this way are often blended to achieve balanced and consistent results. Contemporary brewers are rediscovering these skills, as are others in the industry: one of the more intriguing current projects is the barrel-ageing programme at wholesalers and retailers Beer Merchants (p130), involving the maturation of coolship beers supplied by third parties for use in unique house blends.

Flavoured sours

Usually in keg, can or bottle.

Exale Krankie (4.2%). Developed with the help of an aroma specialist, this has the distinctive note of cult Scottish soft drink Irn Bru, working surprisingly well over a lightly sour base with notes of marshmallow, rose, orange, cardamom and tea.

Orbit White Label Tzatziki Sour (4.3%). Made with cucumber and mint, originally at now-closed Mad Hatter in Liverpool. Hazy gold with convincing tzatziki flavours, soft but refreshing tartness and a drying, lightly bitter finish.

Barrel-aged and blended beers

Beers in this category are typically limited editions and can show considerable variation from one batch to the next, so the following selection is only indicative. They are typically served from the bottle or can, sometimes on keg or cask.

Beavertown Tempus Project Birds of a Feather (6.2%). A *bière de coupage* blended from beer aged in Burgundy barrels and steel tanks. Hazy golden with immensely complex notes of grain, vanilla, wild yeast spice and aromatic grapes, then a long fruity finish. One of several intriguing, relatively light golden beers from the Tempus Project.

BBNo 12 Barrel-Aged Imperial Stout (11%). These beers regularly change: in 2019 they included a complex, surprisingly light-bodied Mexican Mole with a warming chilli finish.

London Beer Factory Barrel Project Oeno-Imperial Stout (9.8%). Near black, with a whisky and grape aroma, controlled dark malt and coffee on the palate, red fruit and a warming oaky bitter finish. Look out for wild fermentation coolship beer in the future.

Kernel Bière de saison barrel-aged (around 6%). This series of immensely complex fruited beers has included some stunners, like the crab apple version with estery, apple-tinged, vinous notes, pungent tartness, creamy nutty malt and a lingering fruity finish.

Solvay Society Mutual Attraction (6%). Blend of fresh saison and various barrel-aged beers. Golden, a lightly smoky, petrolly aroma, a complex fresh fruity palate with lemon, estery perfume and a coconut and oak note on the finish.

OTHER STYLES

Anspach and Hobday The Cream Ale (4.5%). Hybrid ale-lager style from the US, little made in London. Delicate yellow in colour, a fruit salad and sherbet aroma, a crisp but gentle palate with peach hints, and a lightly drying finish, very refreshing. Keg or can.

Battersea Scotch Ale (6.9%). A rare London strong and malty beer in the old-fashioned Scottish style, dark ruby with a spicy aroma and layers of rich malt and caramel on the palate. Keg or cask.

Belleville London Steam Lager (4.5%). An ale-lager hybrid in the California Common style. Light blond with a creamy, spicy aroma, a soft grassy palate with a hint of lemon, and a shortish grainy finish. Keg or can.

Ealing/Marko Paulo Burton Ale (5.5%). An example of a near-obsolete English style: dark amber, bready and malty with caramel and vine fruit, and a lightly hoppy finish. Cask.

Fuller's 1845 Celebration Strong Ale (6.3%). A pale ale adapted from a historic recipe to celebrate 150 years of the brewery in 1995, using amber malts characteristic of the period. Deep brown, toasty and substantial with an orange note, nuts, rooty hops and a suggestion of fine dark chocolate. Bottle-conditioned.

Mondo Figgie Smalls Belgian Strong Dark (8.9%). Brown ales have sadly almost disappeared from London: this Belgian abbey-inspired interpretation has a banana and chocolate aroma, a treacly, toasty, slightly smoky palate and a lingering burnt toffee finish. Keg or bottle.

Beer and food

While many places listed in this book serve decent homemade food in which they take great pride, and a few offer fine cuisine of quality and distinction (see the list under Exceptional food p355), only a handful seriously explore the gastronomic possibilities of serving beer with food. London is the birthplace of the gastropub, but the 'pub' bit of this designation is more about the informality than the beer, which is usually relegated to a couple of well-known cask ale brands and mass market lagers and stouts. Notable exceptions include the Pig and Butcher (p80) and its sister pub the Smokehouse (p181), alongside the award-winning Marksman (Try also p162) and the Bull and Last (Try also p177).

Beer advocates have been arguing for decades that beer is at least as worthy of a place on the dining table as wine. The grain offers a wider range of flavours than the grape — beer can be fruity, floral, rich, tannic and even sour just like wine, but it can also be biscuity, roasty and bitter in a way wine cannot. Even the most ardent oenophiles admit that wine struggles with certain foods, like chocolate and curries, while beer copes admirably. Diners usually agree too, if you can persuade them to experiment, but old habits and wine's sophisticated image go a long way, and progress in the trade has been slow. It's not helped by the fact that wine is generally pricier, and its retail mark-ups are more generously in favour of the restaurateur.

This is particularly true at the upper end of the market, where progress has been painfully slow. London now has one of the most interesting and varied fine dining scenes in the world, but you'll still struggle to find a serious gourmet restaurant with a good beer list, of the sort that are increasingly appearing in many US cities. I considered listing Michel Roux Jr's celebrated and dual Michelin-starred Gavroche

in a previous edition of this book, as it commissions its own beer and stocks several others, including aged Fuller's Vintage Ale. But I concluded that, given the beer list is a half-page at the end of a weighty tome that lists many hundreds of rare and fabulous wines, this was being thankful for very small mercies. A few Michelin-favoured fine dining establishments do better, including the Dysart (p281), Quilon (p123), and St John (Try also p100).

There's more promising news from the informal dining sector, though plenty of room for more. Last time around, I singled out the Byron gourmet burger chain for its then-innovative craft beer list. It's no longer so remarkable, as most modern independent burger flippers, pizza bakers, laptop-friendly avocado smashers and vegan jackfruit pullers now offer a small handful of local brews by default. Few make a serious effort with matching, though there are a few inspired exceptions reflecting the capital's cosmopolitan palate: both the excellent Nanban (p264) and the Tonkotsu chain (Try also p141) champion beer with ramen noodles while Booma (p257) promotes it alongside Indian street food.

Then there's the traditional combination of beer and shellfish. Belgian bars lubricating *moules frites* with tasty golden ales are well-established in London, though it's harder to find the more indigenous pairing of oysters with porter or stout. These were once everyday victuals in the capital and deserve to increase in popularity again. Wright Brothers Oyster and Porter House (p88), a branch of a Cornish oyster fishery at Borough Market, shows the way.

Even if matching isn't emphasised, there's the obvious opportunity to create your own combinations in a pub with a good range of both beer and food. British pub food has improved immeasurably in the past 25 years and London standards are generally high, especially in the

independent sector. Unfortunately, and inevitably, so are prices. 'Pub grub' has evolved under the influence of Modern British cookery, usually focusing on modern versions of comfort food classics — sausage and mash, fish and chips, pies, steaks, lamb chops, burgers — made with high quality ingredients. For fish, think ethical sourcing and beer batter, for sausage think free-range rare-breed organic, for herbs think the local allotment.

In 2015, I bemoaned the predictability of the vegetarian options emerging from pub kitchens. This is also starting to shift: the spread of vegetarian and, notably, vegan dishes through London food culture is one of the big culinary developments of recent years. There are even reports of vegetarians complaining that their favourite cheese and egg dishes have been replaced with vegan alternatives by chefs still lazy enough to offer only one meat-free main course option. Much of the effort has been around meat substitutes, matching the established millennial preference for 'dirty meat' — fat-dripping politically incorrect burger and sandwich horrors to make a dietician weep. There's some relief in the use of barbecued cauliflower as a substitute for ribs and curiously textured exotic jackfruit as a stand-

in for pulled pork, while more places are allowing other vegetables to shine. As much contemporary keg, bottled and canned beer is unfined and vegan-friendly, it sits well on the more ethically motivated menus.

With many of the better beer outlets now smaller and more specialised, licensees are rethinking the sort of the food that can be prepared without a proper kitchen. The scotch egg and the sausage roll, long debased by unappetising mass-market interpretations, now boast their own gourmet competitions, held, of course, in pubs. Now often available in both meat and veggie versions, they're a welcome companion to a pint. Cheese and charcuterie tasting plates have also become a mainstay — the former is particularly welcome, as contrary to received wisdom, beer easily trumps wine in getting friendly with fromage. While I'm yet to be entirely convinced by vegan 'cheese', it's improved in quality and variety sufficiently that some reputable bar managers are happy to offer tasting platters of the stuff. Even packet snacks have gone gourmet: meaty 'beer sticks' are everywhere, at least one bottle shop chain makes a point of offering specialist charcuterie, and you'll even find homemade roast nuts flavoured with spent yeast.

61

Beautiful beer, tremendous tapas

Taps and Tapas opened in Tooting in 2019 as an innovative collaboration between Brixton brewery London Beer Lab and Spanish wine and produce specialist the Tapas Room. I asked the team behind it for their favourite pairings with London beers, so manager Jenny Henriques got together with executive chef Paul Belcher and LBL brewer Slawomir Jasiewicz to come up with these suggestions. Sadly, the venue struggled to survive the lockdowns and closed in August 2021, but the matches were so mouth-watering that I couldn't leave them out.

Pale ale and cheese. Look for light to medium bitterness, floral and fruity aromas and flavours to match with a milder but still flavourful cheese. Try Bullfinch Luna (4%), Five Points Xtra Pale (4%) or our top choice **London Beer Lab QED** (4%) with **Murcia al Vino**, a hard goat milk cheese washed with red wine from southeast Spain. The cheese prolongs the bitterness in the beer and leaves you craving for more.

Pale lager and meat. It's common to match lager with shellfish but with its flowery,

bready and caramel notes and high carbonation, it can withstand richer, oilier foods too, even a meaty stew in winter. Our **mini hotdog with chistorra sausage, red onion and piquillo peppers** works well with Brick Peckham Pils (4.8%), Orbit Nico (4.8%) or our top choice **Gipsy Hill Hunter** (4.8%).

Mild and mushrooms. The dark, malty notes and sweetness of mild are a perfect pairing for earthy mushrooms, the darker the better. Some wild varieties like ceps develop a bitter flavour with cooking which provides a contrast too. We love our **truffled wild mushrooms with sherry glaze** alongside Redemption/The Kernel Victorian Mild (6%) though **Boxcar Dark Mild** (3.5%) has the bonus of low alcohol. For a different spin, try them with Tritium (6.9%), the pink peppercorn tripel from Solvay Society.

Sour beer and vegetables. The clean, tart and tangy notes of kettle sours need strong flavours alongside them, particularly with savoury umami for contrast. They'll overwhelm more delicate foods like simple salads but try with distinctive vegetables and strong cheese. Added fruit, and salt in Gose styles, provide extra dimensions. We've paired our **griddled artichoke with Asturian blue cheese and honey** with **Brick Kiwi and Lime Sour** (3.6%), but you could also try it with Mondo Slack Island Gose with cherries, blackberries and passion fruit (4.7%) or something like Partizan Saison Lemongrass (3.8%) which isn't a sour but has comparable tangy citric flavours.

Wheat beer and seafood. With their light but distinctive flavours and high carbonation, wheats are ideal food beers: think white fish with spiced Belgian styles or the banana notes in German Hefeweizen complementing everything from cakes to pork. We love **octopus with samphire and piquillo pepper sauce** alongside bay-spiced **Pressure Drop Wu Gang Chops the Tree** (3.8%), but it will also work with more Bavarian-inspired options like German Kraft Edel Weiss (5.2%) or Gipsy Hill Schunkeln (4.8%).

Porter or stout with dessert. The roasted malt in porters highlights chocolate, caramel and coffee flavours, making them a natural pairing for dessert, though they're also a wonderful contrast to the briny taste of oysters and the hoppier ones work well with rich, fatty meats too. **Churros with chocolate sauce and cinnamon sugar** are a classic companion to the **Kernel Export India Porter** (around 6%), though BBNo 08 Stout Chocolate and Hazelnut (4.8%) and Orbit Dead Wax London Porter (5.5%) can play a similar role.

How this guide works

In the following pages, you'll find details of almost 150 London breweries, most of whom sell their beer direct to the public, alongside around 170 non-brewing pubs, bars, restaurants and shops, with approaching 200 brief mentions of other places worth trying. All the breweries are listed by default, including those without public-facing facilities; of the other places, I aim to direct you to those most worthy of your time, money and attention.

With so many venues across London now stocking at least a small range of interesting beer by default, picking the final selection has become increasingly challenging. I've considered various factors, not only quality but variety and the representation of small and independent producers, particularly local ones. I've looked less favourably on places with ranks of handpumps all dispensing widely available mainstream bitters, or indeed with rows of keg taps pouring nothing but hoppy pale ales.

That doesn't mean everywhere listed is a beer exhibition with a lengthy list: there's no minimum threshold for numbers of beers, and a few places have a relatively small range but a long track record of choosing and looking after it extremely well. A few others have focused specialisms, for example matching beer with food, acting as a shop window for a notable brewery outside London or reflecting the beer culture of another country.

As explained in the Packaging and dispense section (above), cask-conditioned beer has a unique character that can't be duplicated any other way, and the persistence of the cask format is almost unique to Britain. Not every listed venue stocks cask, but those that do should offer it in reliably good condition, by no means always the case wherever you see a handpump on the bar.

I've also considered how the beer is presented, looking for places that encourage customers to experiment by offering information, tasters and good advice from knowledgeable and enthusiastic staff. All the listed venues, in their own way, should provide a welcoming and pleasant environment for the civilised customer. Some are small and informal, so don't always expect lightning-fast service and four-star attention, but you should at least be able to rely on a friendly welcome and pleasant company. If you find otherwise, I would very much like to hear about it (Updates and Feedback p8).

Beyond this, in several cases, the deciding factor has been my own personal taste, but I hope you wouldn't refer to a book like this without being prepared to trust the author's discrimination to some extent.

I can't stress enough that this isn't a pub guide. Of course, numerous pubs are included, but few of them conform to the traditional stereotype of horse brasses and Toby jugs. Even by stretching the definition widely to include more contemporary-styled venues, less than half the non-brewing venues with main entries are what most people would call 'proper pubs', a sign of quite how much the environments in which we enjoy beer have diversified in recent years (see From alehouses to micropubs above). The rest are mainly contemporary bars, brewery taprooms, micropubs and bottle shops with drink-in facilities, with a handful of restaurants and a few hybrids that defy categorisation.

Many of the places listed are also of interest for other reasons, among them food and other speciality drinks, history, architecture, location, views or activities like music or theatre, and where appropriate these are mentioned in the text. But such factors are insufficient on their own to qualify a venue for inclusion. Some of London's most famous pubs are absent, as I've judged their beer offer insufficiently interesting, although as explained below I've included brief mentions of a few unmissable heritage pubs.

All the information given can, and some of it certainly will, change during the currency of this book. See Updates and feedback p8 for more about how to keep up to date. While I've made every effort to ensure details are accurate at the time of going to press, I'm only human, and the aftermath of the Covid lockdowns may well affect the industry in unpredictable ways. I strongly advise that, if the success of your trip depends on a place being open at a certain time, or offering specific beers, food or services, you phone or email to check before setting out.

Navigation

The listings cover Greater London, as administrated by the Greater London Authority, the Mayor of London and the 33 London Boroughs. This area stretches out beyond the London postal district to include places like Barnet, Bromley, Croydon, Twickenham and Upminster which some people still insist are in Hertfordshire, Kent, Surrey, Middlesex and Essex even though they've been part of London since 1964. It covers a total of 1,572 square kilometres (607 square miles) and there's no universally

PUB AND BAR USER GUIDE

The following guidelines are aimed mainly at visitors and new arrivals to Britain but as the pace of innovation on the London beer scene has challenged several long-established aspects of drinking culture, even people who've lived here all their lives might find it useful. Special restrictions imposed during the Covid-19 pandemic should be lifted by the time you read this but look out for relevant announcements.

Traditionally in the UK, customers are expected to **order drinks at the bar** and pay for them immediately, except in restaurants, dining areas in pubs and a few swanky bars, where **table service** has long been the norm. But table service became temporarily obligatory during the pandemic and it's not yet clear how this might affect long-term practice. Many venues are keen to return to old informalities, but some who introduced ordering and payment apps found they worked well and plan to keep them once restrictions are lifted, usually alongside the reintroduction of bar service. Many places will also let you run a **drinks tab** on a credit or debit card, though may ask you to leave the card behind the bar as a deposit.

Most places still accept both **cash** and **debit and credit card** payments, but for the first time in this edition, a significant number of entries are shown as **cash-free**, mostly brewery taprooms and other small specialist places. Their numbers increased during the pandemic and are likely to grow further as more businesses try to avoid the increased hassle, crime risk and insurance premiums that follow from keeping cash on the premises. If you're visiting from abroad and your card issuer imposes heavy charges even on small transactions, it might be worth investing in a prepaid card with contactless chip and PIN suitable for use in the UK. At the other extreme, a handful of more traditional smaller places are still cash-only so it's always worth a check before ordering if necessary.

Quantities for serving draught beer (and cider and perry) are set by law and are still in imperial measurements. The legal measures are a third pint (197ml, 6.67fl oz), two-thirds (394ml, 13.33fl oz) or multiples of a half pint (284ml, 10fl oz). Only a minority of places offer the full range of legal measures. Half and full pints (567ml, 20fl oz) are the

most common, while thirds and two-thirds are more commonly found in specialist outlets.

Glasses have an official stamp showing the measure. Traditional half and pint glasses in London are designed to be filled to the brim, with almost no head, though specialist outlets use a variety of more attractive designs which are lined to show the correct measures. Licensees are legally allowed to fill brim glasses only 95% full, but if you're unhappy with the measure you've been served, you're within your rights to ask for a top-up, and all the places listed here should be happy to oblige.

Bottled and canned beer and all other drinks are sold in metric measures. British-brewed beers usually come in 330ml bottles and cans (11.2fl oz), 440ml cans (14.9fl oz, particularly popular for contemporary speciality styles) or 500ml bottles (16.9fl oz), and occasionally in bigger sizes like 750ml (25.4fl oz) or US-style 'bombers' (650ml, 22fl oz).

At the time of writing, a typical pint of draught cask beer in a London pub **costs** around £4.50 (€5.25, $6.40), but could vary by up to 50p either way. Specialist keg beers are usually at least £1 (€1.15, $1.40) per pint agreed way of subdividing it, so I've been pragmatic, taking account of postcodes, local authorities, local practice and the distribution of venues. The maps on the inside front cover and in the listings, and the introductions to each geographical section, should make things clear.

Markers on the maps use different colours to indicate different types of venue:

🔴 Breweries/brewpubs open to the public.

⚪ Breweries closed to the public.

⚫ Other non-brewing venues.

These colours correspond to those used in the entry headings.

The maps are intended to help plan a trip by showing the rough location of places listed and their relative distance from each other and from stations. They don't show all stations, roads or other features and aren't detailed enough for wayfinding on the ground so please use them alongside a mapping app or a street atlas.

more expensive, and can easily exceed £10 a pint if particularly strong and special: since 2011, a misguided duty regulation has disproportionately penalised beer that's stronger than 7.5% ABV. A decent 330ml can might cost £2 (€2.30, $2.80) in a super-market, but £4 (€4.60, $5.60) in a pub; again, stronger and rarer beers will cost more (currency conversions are approximate and the exchange rate is particularly volatile at the time of writing).

If you're unsure what to order, ask staff for advice: you may even be offered a free taster. If there's something genuinely **wrong with the beer** – and things do go wrong, especially with cask beer, even in the most scrupulous places – tell the bar staff before drinking a substantial amount. In anywhere decent, it should be changed without question.

Tipping isn't customary when ordering drinks at a bar. Tips jars are becoming more common but, though I certainly don't want to discourage generosity, it's not socially obligatory. If there's table service, particularly where you've also eaten, the bill may well include a 10–15% optional service charge, and the menu should forewarn

you of this. Otherwise, the bill will likely state prominently that service is not included, in which case 10–15% is the usual rate. You can refuse to pay a service charge if you think the service provided doesn't merit it, but this is a power to be used with discretion.

Once you've got your drink, you're free to occupy any unoccupied space, unless there's a **reserved** sign of or other indication you shouldn't be there (areas reserved for diners when you're only drinking, for example). Unlike in some countries, prices aren't cheaper at the bar. At busy times, it's fine to ask if you can share a table that's already partly occupied. Some pubs will reserve tables for large groups.

The **legal drinking age** in the UK is 18. The only exception is for 16–17-year-olds dining in the company of adults, who are permitted to drink, but not buy, beer, wine and cider with their meal. Most places now allow well-behaved under-16s to drink soft drinks and eat if accompanied by adults, though usually with an early evening curfew and sometimes only in certain parts of the premises (see Policy on children p68). Children are never allowed at

the bar itself. Some licensees have a policy of asking everyone who looks under 21, or even 25, to show proof of age, though evidence of identity is otherwise rarely required. Note they're under no obligation to serve you even if you are over 18, so long as they don't break equal opportunity laws by discriminating against you on the grounds of race, religion, gender, sexuality or disability.

Most venues listed here welcome well-behaved **dogs**, but not all, and as this is discretionary, it's best to check. I haven't had the space to note individual policies here. Dogs may be restricted to certain parts of the premises and are unlikely to be allowed in brewing and food preparation areas.

Smoking in enclosed public places has been banned since 2007. Some places have sheltered and heated outdoor smoking areas, but if one of these isn't available and you want to smoke in the street, check before taking your drink outside with you as local licensing rules sometimes prohibit this. The global ban doesn't apply to vaping (e-cigarettes) though many venues frown on it indoors so ask before switching on.

Names

Within each section, venue names are listed alphabetically, ignoring initial 'the' (and 'ye'). Punctuation of pub names is often inconsistent so in such cases has been regularised by dropping apostrophes. Heading colours distinguish different types of venue, corresponding to the map markers: see above.

⭐ indicates one of my top recommendations as listed under London's Very Best Beer (p72).

Venue category

Breweries

Brewery means somewhere with an active commercial brewhouse on the premises. If the brewery is owned or part-owned by a multinational company, this is shown in brackets. I've usually added a few more words to describe the public facilities or lack of them as explained below.

Taproom means some sort of regularly open bar in the same building (or occasionally very close by) selling the brewery's beer to drink in. This could be anything from an extensive dedicated area to a few tables put out on Saturdays in a corner otherwise used for production purposes. Sometimes, breweries and beer firms refer to an offsite bar as a taproom if it's their main outlet, but I've preferred to deal with these simply as bars or pubs.

Shop means you can buy the brewery's beer to take away. I've only used this if there's only a shop facility and no taproom, or the shop is open longer hours, or is clearly a separately operated unit, otherwise assume you can also buy takeaway from the taproom.

No visitors please applies to a small minority of breweries and means what it says. They're not being unfriendly: they simply don't have the facilities and aren't licensed or insured for the purpose. Some are on industrial estates that are locked outside working hours, and some of the smallest breweries are attached to private homes. In the last case, I've avoided giving a full address.

Brewpub indicates somewhere that's primarily a pub or bar but also makes and sells its own beer using brewing equipment on the premises. The brewhouse may not be visible from the public areas: some are hidden away in cellars. Otherwise, these places vary widely in appearance and facilities, so I've added a description like *traditional pub*, *contemporary pub* or *bar* (see below) to give a better idea of what to expect. It's becoming increasingly hard to distinguish between a brewpub and a brewery with a particularly well-appointed taproom, but I've done my best.

Beer firm means a company selling its own beer brands brewed on someone else's equipment, sometimes known as a 'cuckoo brewer' or 'contract brewer'. These are only shown in the main listings if they operate a bar of note: others are summarised under Brewers without breweries p320.

Brewery etiquette

Most brewers love meeting interested drinkers and getting feedback on their work. But remember that brewery staff don't always have time to deal with the public in between their main job of making and selling great beer, and that for practical, health and safety, legal and insurance reasons, not all sites are suitable for visitors.

Please don't turn up at a brewery unannounced outside its publicised hours, or at all at breweries closed to the public, expecting to get a look round and perhaps a few free tastings. It's always worth enquiring in advance about visits: some breweries can accommodate groups by arrangement if not individuals. It's also worth double-checking brewery websites and social media to see if they've added visitor facilities or extended their hours since this book was compiled.

Breweries are working environments where safety and hygiene are paramount, so when you do visit, stay in the designated public areas and make sure you follow the instructions of staff when on a tour.

Other venues

The term 'pub' is a contraction of 'public house', which historically meant somewhere licensed to sell alcohol for consumption on the premises to the public at large, rather than just diners, hotel residents or club members. Times and laws have changed, and multipurpose 'premises licences' now regulate alcohol sales. But describing somewhere as a pub still raises expectations of a certain kind of venue in terms of décor and atmosphere, so I've tried to reflect this in the listings, as well as identifying venues which meet different expectations.

A *traditional pub* is the closest thing to the romantic stereotype, usually in purpose-built premises with old-fashioned décor.

A *contemporary pub* may be in the same kind of building as a traditional pub, but has a more modern 21st century interior, often in a fashionable stripped-back style.

A *gastropub* looks like a traditional or contemporary pub but is primarily focused on food, with much of its floorspace likely dedicated to sit-down dining, while retaining some facilities for customers who just want to call in for a drink.

A *micropub* is a small bar established in the last decade, usually in a former shop or restaurant. Typically, they have simple but comfortable décor, a focus on cask beer and an absence of TV, music and games machines, but the model is a flexible one.

A *bar* is any other venue where you can call in just for a drink but doesn't really look or feel like a pub. Some provide a wide range of beer in unashamedly contemporary surroundings, other are inspired more by the drinking traditions of other countries.

A *club* is a bar reserved for members and their guests. The few included here welcome CAMRA and EBCU members, and sometimes people carrying CAMRA guides, as guests.

A *restaurant* primarily serves meals to sit-down diners, so assume you can only order drinks alongside a meal. If I've added the word *bar*, there's an area that just serves drinks, but it may prioritise people waiting for tables at busy times. If the word *bar* is first, you'll have no problem dropping in for a drink, but there will be a big restaurant area too.

A *shop* is somewhere that sells beer (and likely other drinks too) to take away, also sometimes known as an off-licence. The word on its own means they *only* do takeaway. Most of the specialist bottle shops listed here also have at least some facilities for people to drink in: I've described these as *Shop, bar*. Those that seem to place the focus on the drinking-in side while still offering a comprehensive range to take away are described as *Bar, shop*. It's not always easy to draw the line. In fact, many regular pubs and bars are also licensed for off-sales and may offer a discount on takeaway bottles and cans.

I've occasionally shown a venue owner in brackets after its category if this is of interest and not otherwise evident from the name or review.

Contact details

The street address includes a full postcode, useful for online mapping and journey planning. I've left out the word 'London' for places in the London Postal Districts (postcodes beginning E, EC, N, NW, SE, SW, W and WC). For breweries, I've shown the London borough in brackets.

T indicates a phone number where available. More and more places no longer publicise them, preferring to communicate electronically, though if a phone number is given, in my experience it's the most reliable way of contacting a venue.

Web addresses occasionally cover a group of venues but with an obvious way of searching for the correct place. I haven't listed emails as these can usually be found on websites, or there will be a contact form. Where there's no dedicated website, I show the most useful social media option: many more places regularly use Facebook, Instagram or Twitter but you'll need to search these for yourselves.

Brewery details

For breweries only, I've shown the month and year when they first sold their own beer brewed on their own kit. Many of them will have registered a company, obtained a licence and occupied premises long before this. They may have cuckoo-brewed somewhere else and even brewed trial batches, but to me the most meaningful date is the moment when the public can taste the product.

👣👣 indicates some sort of tour is available. This could range from well-drilled ticketed presentations and tastings to a chat in the brewhouse with a few drinks in hand. (Informal) means that if someone has a spare moment during taproom hours, they'll take you for a quick look round. Some breweries can't justify tours for individuals but may be willing to arrange something in advance for groups. Don't turn up on the expectation of a tour: check the website and/or contact the brewery to get more detail on what they offer, remembering that the more popular scheduled tours sell out well in advance. For health and safety as well as alcohol policy reasons, children aren't generally allowed on brewery tours. During the Covid crisis, all tours were cancelled for social distancing reasons.

Opening times

🕐 Shown using the 24-hour clock, with days indicated as *Mo, Tu, We, Th, Fr, Sa* and *Su*. Only days when the place is open are shown: for example *Mo-Sa* 12.00-23.00 implies a Sunday closure.

In this edition, hours are listed with an even heavier caveat than usual. They mostly reflect service patterns from before the Covid crisis, which was ongoing when we were checking the text. Those places that were able to open were keeping much shorter hours than previously and although most eventually hoped to return to normal trading, the situation was still fluid. Factors like the accelerated trend towards increased working from home may have long-term effects on local demand. Even at the best of times, hours are among the easiest of details to change at short notice, and places are occasionally closed for refurbishment, private parties or holidays or may of course go out of business, **so please make sure to check online or call ahead** if making a special trip.

Policy on children

'**Children welcome**' means a venue permits accompanied children indoors during opening hours with no specific restrictions other than trusting grownups to use their common sense (and see also the paragraph on legal drinking ages p38). If there's a curfew or other restriction, I've specified this here. 'Children very welcome' means the venue makes a special effort, for example offering a children's menu, play area or child-friendly activities (see the list on p354). If there's nothing about children, assume they're not permitted indoors: a few older licences have age restrictions and a few places prefer to maintain an adults-only environment.

Drink

The entries show how many different **cask**, **tank**, **keg** and **bottled/canned** beers you can expect to find on sale, ignoring mainstream industrial brands. Clearly, these details aren't set in stone, and some places vary them day by day, expanding the variety at weekends, particularly of cask beers. It's possible the number of cask lines mentioned in some listings will decrease: considerable quantities of cask had to poured away during the lockdowns and it will take time for confidence to build again.

Growlers means containers can be filled with takeaway draught beer. Besides the traditional big bottle, this could be anything from a two-pint paper carton to a custom-filled can (or 'crowler' if you insist).

I've highlighted notable selections of **other drinks**, though forgive me if I was so focused on the beer that I missed a few. References to **cider** and **perry** suggest the real versions, naturally fermented and served without gas pressure. Most venues now offer a handful of more interesting **spirits** and drinkable **wines**, so when I mention these it's because the range is more extensive than average. Take it as read that a selection of **soft drinks** will be on offer, and quite likely tea and coffee too, though they might not thank you for asking them to boil a kettle late on a busy weekend night. 🛒 Online mail order sales available.

Food

⚔ indicates the food on offer, beyond packets of crisps and nuts, with an indication of the style and price range and a little more detail usually given in the review. It's now very rare not to have at least one vegetarian option on the menu, and vegan options are becoming much more common. Chefs are more aware than they once were of how to deal with food allergies and other dietary requirements, but I strongly advise you contact a place in advance if you have specific needs.

As it's normal not to eat a formal three course meal in nearly all the places listed, I've based the price categories on the cost of a main course, or the most substantial items on the menu if the venue doesn't do conventional plated meals.

£ Mostly less than £8 (€9.20, $10.40)
££ Mostly £8–15 (€17.25, $19.50)
£££ Mostly above £15

This is a rough guide: different lunchtime and evening menus are common, with lunches often cheaper, and a few places serve cheaper and more limited dishes in the bar and more sophisticated and expensive meals in a separate restaurant.

Space precludes listing food service times so if you're relying on food, **always** contact in advance to check. Kitchens are normally open lunchtimes and evenings daily but could well be closed in the afternoon. I've tried to note when food is only sold at lunchtimes, or not on certain days of the week. On Sundays, everything can change: many places chuck out the regular menu in favour of a limited choice of roast dinners, usually with a veggie option, from midday until stocks run out, which might well be before dinnertime.

BYO stands for Bring Your Own, indicating a place without a substantial food offering where customers can bring in food bought elsewhere. Don't assume everywhere without its own kitchen is happy for you to bring your own food.

⚔ indicates somewhere offering outstandingly good food, to the extent you'd consider visiting it for this alone. For a list see p355.

For more on beer and food, see above.

Outdoor space

🌲 precedes a brief description of available outdoor space, from standing on the street to extensive gardens. If nothing is shown, assume licensing or space restrictions preclude you taking drinks outside. Smoking is legal outdoors, but some places have their own ban covering all or part of an outdoor area, particularly if it's used for dining.

🌸 indicates the venue has a particularly noteworthy outdoor area. This is a purely subjective judgement on my behalf: it could be because of extent, or facilities, or design, or seclusion, or obvious levels of pride and tender loving care, or other things that made me sigh with delight when I stepped outside.

Accessibility

♿ on its own indicates an accessible disabled toilet adapted for wheelchair users, and by implication level access to at least part of the venue itself, although it's always advisable to contact in advance, as this might be through a side door that's usually kept locked. In some cases, there's no properly adapted disabled toilet but the venue still has flat access for wheelchairs, in which case I've added 'Flat access only'. Other qualifying notes should be self-explanatory. If nothing is shown, assume there's no flat access and no adapted toilet. This is sadly one area in which London doesn't lead the world: most places in this book will be as helpful as they can, but facilities for wheelchair users are only obligatory with new builds and major refurbishments and retrofitting them to historic buildings can be a financial, design and heritage challenge.

Activities

These are listed in italics just before the reviews: they're mostly self-explanatory and include things like beer-related events, live entertainment and pub games, with regular days if applicable. *Functions* indicates that a separate room or a part of the venue can be set aside for private parties, meetings and other such activities.

Transport

Transport information is given as follows:

- ⇌ National Rail station
- ⊖ Station with services managed by TfL (see below)
- ⊖ London Trams stop
- 🚢 River pier or canal mooring with regular boat service
- 🚏 Bus stop
- 🚲 Principal cycling route
- 🚶 Principal walking trail

One advantage of London as a beer city is the extensive integrated public transport network overseen by **Transport for London** (TfL), which will take you safely and efficiently to within a few minutes' walk of anywhere in this book, and relatively comfortably too if you avoid peak hours. Londoners constantly moan about it, but they should try getting around some other cities without a car. It's not the world's cheapest but is affordable so long as you avoid buying individual cash fares, which is becoming increasingly difficult anyway as buses and many Tube station ticket machines no longer accept cash.

Likely the best option for users of this book who aren't already regular commuters is to use a **contactless** bank card (though not an overseas one that makes exorbitant charges) or a 'pay as you go' balance on TfL's own **Oyster** smartcard. These methods entitle you to discounted fares, with a daily and, on a contactless card, weekly cap so you never pay more than the equivalent multi-modal pass. For more see tfl.gov.uk which also has an excellent journey planner and the **TfL Go** app for smartphones.

I've shown the nearest rail station or tram stop for all listed venues except breweries closed to the public. TfL now oversees not only the famous **London Underground** (Tube) metro network but several other rail services under different brands: **London Overground**, **Docklands Light Railway** (DLR) and something called **TfL Rail** which at some point, perhaps in 2022, will be subsumed into the long-awaited and long-delayed **Elizabeth Line**, formerly known as Crossrail. As all are interchangeable in terms of fares structure, I haven't distinguished them, though a few sections of the Overground don't quite run to turn-up-and-go frequencies. **National Rail** stations in London are included in TfL's integrated ticketing system, but often with different fares: they may be rebranded Great British Railways during the currency of this guide.

The nearest **bus** stop for places more than 500m away from a station or tram stop is shown using TfL's official name. The nearest station isn't necessarily the most convenient interchange if you're completing your journey by bus, so it's best to check TfL's journey planner carefully.

Travelling by **boat** is not only a great way to see the city but also a reaffirmation of the Thames' historic role in the city's development, so I've shown river piers where they're convenient. **Thames Clippers** offer a fast, frequent and reasonably priced service on the central stretch of the river. The more touristy, summer-only services between Richmond and Kingston and on the Regent's Canal are referenced too.

Walking and cycling will help you work off the calories from all that beer, and facilities are improving all the time, though still some way behind international best practice. Note that while there's no specific blood alcohol limit for cyclists, it's illegal and highly irresponsible to cycle when drunk.

All venues are of course accessible by walking or cycling, but I've highlighted those close to principal **routes**. For cyclists, these are the Sustrans National Cycle Network (NCN) and TfL's routes. The latter used to be divided into Cycle Superhighways (CS), usually segregated routes alongside main roads, and Quietways (Q), following back streets and off-road paths and ideal for relaxed exploration of beer venues, but both are being combined into a single Cycleways (C) designation. For walkers, I've shown TfL's Walk London network of longer signed trails and some others. A route listed on its own is only a few minutes away; 'Link to' means a straightforward bit of extra legwork is required to reach it. If you can't find more information on the TfL site, try googling the route name/number.

TfL's own **Santander Cycles** docking stations are dotted over central London and some adjoining areas. You pay a minimal access fee for a period of at least a day and can then use any bike without further charge so long as you don't hang onto it for longer than half an hour. There are several competing private schemes using mobile technology with dockless bikes, including electric assisted ones, but these come and go and have patchy coverage: google for the latest situation.

There are two categories of **taxi**: Hackney Carriages, the traditional 'black cabs', which you can hail in the street for an exorbitant fare; and private hire vehicles, bookable in advance for a merely expensive one. Uber has had a troubled history in the capital and TfL withheld its operational license in 2019, though it was restored following a court case in 2020.

Beer notes

Most brewery entries end with brief notes on specific beers. The listings aren't comprehensive: if I've left something out, it's either because I haven't tasted it yet, or I have and don't feel able to recommend it. I consider every listed beer is a good example of its style, but I've highlighted those particularly worthy of your attention as follows:

*An excellent beer by London standards
**An exceptional beer by world standards

Though I hope these notes are helpful, please don't let my opinions dissuade you from trying unlisted beers. My evaluations are personal and subjective, if based on extensive tasting and judging experience. You may disagree with me, or one of the brewery's other beers may suit you or your mood better. Sometimes a brewer can have a particularly good day with a normally underperforming recipe, and sometimes a recipe is tweaked with significantly improved results. The reverse can be the case too. Brewery ranges are always subject to change for commercial reasons: a couple of years from now, some beers may have been dropped and perhaps replaced by even better options.

For more details on a representative selection of a variety of styles chosen from across the capital, see London Beer Styles.

Try also

There are now so many great beer places in London that this book could easily have run to several volumes. I've given many of them honourable mentions at the end of each geographical section. They include branches of chains with a similar offer to their more fully described stablemates; places that would have merited a full listing in previous editions but which I couldn't find room for in this one; and one or two clearly interesting very recent openings that I haven't had a chance to visit. I've given the full address and the website for each, so you can check online for opening times and other details.

Heritage pubs

London boasts a fine collection of historic pubs of great aesthetic and architectural note, many of which are listed on the Inventories of Historic Pub Interiors maintained by CAMRA and Historic England. These record pubs with significant interior features dating from before 1945 or, in some exceptional cases, before 1970. The most important venues are on the National Inventory, with a second rank on the Regional Inventory, and a supplementary list of those with 'some regional importance'. Most are owned by big pubcos and brewery chains, and only a handful have a beer offer that merits a full entry, but there are others anyone interested in brewing and pub heritage will want to see. My favourites of these are briefly detailed at the end of the relevant geographical section in the same style as the Try Alsos, and there's an alphabetical index including those with full entries on p353. You can search the complete inventories at pubheritage.camra.org.uk. There's also a book, *London Heritage Pubs: An inside story*, listed under More information (p349).

Pub exteriors are also often of architectural and historic interest and many of them are protected by Historic England's standard listings system, but they're more likely to have survived than interiors. It's not unknown for a pub with a magnificent late Victorian façade to have been completely stripped of all its original internal features. Places not on the inventories but otherwise of architectural interest, contemporary as well as historic, are indexed on p353. See From alehouses to micropubs (above) for context.

London's Very Best Beer

Visiting every main entry in this book on consecutive nights will take you about ten months and undoubtedly contravene the Chief Medical Officers' guidelines on alcohol consumption. Readers aiming to be more selective, or who have limited time, may find this list of my 30 top recommendations useful. Entries are subdivided according to broad categories of venues and listed in alphabetical order with no ranking intended. They're also highlighted with a rosette in the main body of the book.

Clapton Craft N4

Proper pubs

Black Dog TW8 p292
Cock Tavern E8 (see Howling Hops) p136
Craft Beer Co Clerkenwell EC1 p97
Dog and Bell SE8 p231
Harp WC2 p102
Hope SM5 p282
Old Fountain Brewhouse EC1 p111
Royal Oak SE1 p86
Star and Garter BR1 p251
Sussex Arms TW2 p312

Modern beer bars

Beer Merchants Tap E9 p130
Cask Pub and Kitchen SW1 p122
Euston Tap NW1 p78
Mother Kelly's Bethnal Green E2 p161
Rake SE1 p86

Bottle shop-bars

Clapton Craft N4 p179
Hop Burns and Black SE22 p222
Ghost Whale Putney SW15 p272
Indiebeer N7 p181
waterintobeer SE4 p238

Micropubs

Beer Shop London SE15 p217
Dodo W7 p293
Hop Inn RM11 p166
Little Green Dragon N21 p198
One Inn the Wood BR5 p249

Brewery experiences

Bermondsey Breweries SE1 and SE16 p207: self-guided tour, with option of formal brewery tour and tasting at Bianca Road, Fourpure or Southwark.
Blackhorse breweries E17 p144: self-guided tour, with option of formal brewery tour and tasting at Beerblefish, Hackney or Signature.
Five Points Brewing Co E8 p134: brewery tour and tasting.
Fuller's Griffin Brewery W4 p294: brewery and site tour and tasting.
Sambrook's Ram Brewery SW18 p274: brewery and heritage centre tour and tasting, also informal visits to Ram site, heritage centre and taproom.

CENTRAL LONDON

CENTRAL LONDON

My definition of Central London is based on Transport for London's Fare Zone 1, which includes all the mainline rail terminals and the area within the Circle Line, with extensions northeast to Angel and Hoxton, east to Shoreditch High Street and Aldgate East, southwest to Earl's Court and south to Vauxhall and Elephant & Castle. All the venues listed below are within a few minutes' walk of a Zone 1 station.

The 'square mile' of the City is the site of the original settlement that developed into the Roman provincial capital and gave the whole of London its name. The City is London's traditional financial district, buzzing during working hours and much quieter at other times. It's not as deathly as it once used to be at weekends, but many pubs are still closed, particularly on Sundays. There are numerous classic City pubs, though many serve a limited range of better-known brands. However, a few more specialist places have opened recently. My coverage of the area stretches a little east into Tower Hamlets to encompass the **City and Aldgate**.

To the northeast, **Shoreditch and Hoxton** were once refuges for less respectable activities not permitted in the City, including brewing and the performing arts: Samuel Whitbread started his career on Old Street and William Shakespeare worked in Shoreditch when he first moved to London. Once impoverished despite its proximity to a sizeable slice of the world's wealth, since the 1990s much of the district has become painfully fashionable, with former industrial units remade as galleries, restaurants and bars. Most places round here stock at least a few interesting, and frequently local, brews: I've picked the most noteworthy, including some along Brick Lane and around Old Street Tube station.

Clerkenwell and Farringdon, northwest of the City, were among London's first suburbs, once home to religious institutions like the Knights of St John, and later associated with printing, watchmaking and revolutionary socialism. This is a fascinating area to explore, with several fine beer outlets tucked away in historic streets and alleys, and a food culture shaped by the presence of the wholesale meat market at Smithfield.

The built-up area first spread west, across the now-covered River Fleet and along the Strand, in Saxon times. The Knights Templar had their London base, the Temple, here in the 12th century, with lawyers moving in

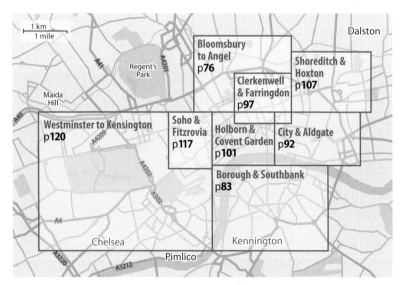

1 km
1 mile

Dalston

Regent's Park

Maida Hill

Bloomsbury to Angel p**76**

Shoreditch & Hoxton p**107**

Clerkenwell & Farringdon p**97**

Westminster to Kensington p**120**

Soho & Fitzrovia p**117**

Holborn & Covent Garden p**101**

City & Aldgate p**92**

Borough & Southbank p**83**

Chelsea

Kennington

Pimlico

when the Knights were suppressed. The area is still associated with the legal profession, as well as journalists, another vocation known to like a drink or two. Most of the latter are now gone but the area still boasts some classic backstreet pubs and interesting newcomers.

Covent Garden, west of Kingsway, became the site of London's first modern property development in 1630 when the Dukes of Bedford commissioned Inigo Jones to build a church and three terraces around an Italianate piazza. A fruit and vegetable market opened soon afterwards, redeveloped in 1980 as a successful leisure and retail destination, a model for many subsequent transformations of historic urban spaces. With its various theatres and other attractions, the neighbourhood is functionally an extension of the West End. I've dealt with all this easily walkable area, including the streets around Charing Cross, as **Holborn and Covent Garden**. Note that while the latter is lively every day, the former is quieter at weekends when the lawyers go home and some pubs close.

Northwards, the Georgian terraces and squares of Bloomsbury, with their early 20th century literary associations, stretch to Euston Road, originally known as the New Road when it was built in 1756 as London's first bypass. The area is noted for its educational institutions and a string of main line stations along the north side of Euston Road. A big brownfield site behind the easternmost of these, Kings Cross, has recently been transformed into a busy new residential and retail district, with several venues of interest.

From Kings Cross, the New Road continues eastwards as Pentonville Road to the Angel, a name originally from a now-vanished pub but more readily recognised by the nearby Tube station. The surrounding area of southern Islington was an early target of gentrifiers in the 1970s and the spiritual home of New Labour in the 1990s. It's still lively, even preserving remnants of its working-class roots in Chapel Market with its cluster of good beer outlets. I've grouped both these neighbourhoods together as **Bloomsbury to Angel**, while parts of Islington further north of Angel are under Islington to Stoke Newington (p178).

Venues in the main part of the West End are listed under **Soho and Fitzrovia**, which includes everywhere from Trafalgar Square through Soho north to Marylebone and Euston roads. This is the liveliest part of one of the world's liveliest cities, encompassing Chinatown, Piccadilly Circus, Theatreland, the shopping nexus of Oxford Circus, the 'gay village' around Old Compton Street, the media industry strip along Charlotte Street and the dwindling remains of a red light district in southern Soho. Property premiums here mean that most pubs are owned by big groups but there are a few noteworthy independents.

West of here, recommendable outlets are more sparsely distributed, so I've grouped together the rest of the central area north of the River Thames as **Westminster to Kensington**. It's a mix of royal parks and palaces, government offices around the Houses of Parliament and along Whitehall, grand 18th-century developments now occupied by embassies, hotels and very rich individuals in Mayfair and Belgravia, luxury shopping streets and more modest, but now largely gentrified, residential areas in eastern Kensington and Notting Hill. Places a little further west are covered in the West London section under Maida Vale to Dollis Hill (p304).

Things get more interesting on the other side of the river. Southwark, also known as the Borough, immediately south of London Bridge, is London's third historic core. The area was long associated with brewing, and the reinvention of Borough Market as a foodie honeypot has benefited the local beer scene. London's liveliest promenade stretches from Tower Bridge and City Hall upriver past Bankside, with Shakespeare's Globe and the Tate Modern, to the Southbank Centre with its concert halls, theatre and other arts venues, and on to overgrown ferris wheel the London Eye and Lambeth and Vauxhall bridges. There are several worthwhile venues not far from the riverside, and you'll find them all under **Borough and Southbank**. Though this section includes places on Tower Bridge Road itself, anything further east is dealt with under Southeast London (p201), including the celebrated Bermondsey 'mile' of railway arch breweries.

Bloomsbury to Angel

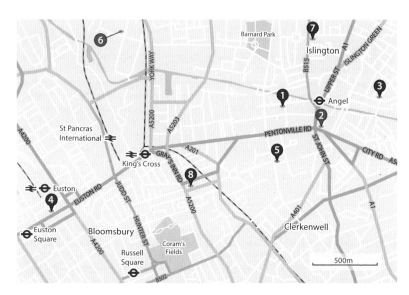

Alma   ❶

Traditional pub
77 Chapel Market N1 9ET
T (020) 7837 5430   **thealmalondon.com**
🕐 *Mo-Sa* 11.00-23.30, *Su* 11.00-21.30.
    Children until 19.00.
2–3 cask, 10 keg, 10 bottles/cans, gins, whiskies.
🍴 BYO, 🪑 Benches on street, ♿, 🛏
Meet the brewer, tap takeovers, big screen sport

⊖ Angel   🚲 link to C27, Q11   🚶 Jubliee Greenway

This small corner pub on Islington's historic
Chapel Market was bought and spruced up in
late 2014 by the owners of the One Mile End
brewery (p76) and is now the best place to
seek out its beers. You'll normally find several
from cask, keg and can, with draught beer in
flights for variety, alongside guests from breweries in and around London, like Hammerton,

Howling Hops and Mondo. It's an unpretentious
place that retains its old-school Irish feel,
with wooden tables, half height panelling
and racing often on the big screens. A single
booth at the back is sought after, and there
are boutique self-catering rooms upstairs.

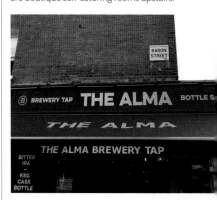

Brewhouse and Kitchen Islington ②

Brewpub, contemporary pub
Torrens Street EC1V 1NG (Islington)
T (020) 7837 9421
brewhouseandkitchen.com/islington
First sold beer: October 2014, ♛
🕐 *Mo-Th* 11.00-23.00, *Fr-Sa* 11.00-24.00,
Su 11.00-22.30. Children welcome.
3-4 cask, 18 keg, 40 bottles/cans, gins,
some other specialist spirits. ⌂.
🍴Sandwiches, enhanced pub grub **£-££**,
🎋Small front terrace, ♿
*Brewing sessions, tastings, meet the brewer, food
matching, seasonal beer launches, functions*

🚇 Angel   🚲C27   🚶Jubilee Greenway, New River Path

Pub entrepreneur Kris Gumbrell ventured into brewing from 2011 with former Convivial pubs the Botanist on Kew Green and later the Lamb in Chiswick; though these were later sold to M&B, they provided the template for small brewpub empire, Brewhouse and Kitchen, created in partnership with former Mitchells & Butlers executive Simon Bunn. This lively bar around the corner from Angel station was the first B&K to open in October 2014, with South African-born Pete Hughes, now the head brewer for the whole group, in charge of the former Botanist 4hl brewhouse. Branches at Highbury (p178) and Hoxton (p108) have since followed, with around 20 others elsewhere in the UK.

Islington, since upgraded to a new 5hl copper kit, still seems to offer the best beer of the London trio, with cask pumps and several keg taps dispensing house brews in good condition, also sold in tasting paddles. A wide range of guest beers offers few surprises, though some smart choices like London Beer Factory, Thornbridge and Vibrant Forest, bottled German and Belgian classics and the rare sight of low alcohol Big Drop IPA on keg. US-inspired beer-can chicken, stalwarts like pies and fish and chips, sharing boards with beer-laced dips and numerous vegetarian options like Cambodian curry and Buddha bowl salads appear on an extensive menu including beer style matching suggestions. The décor combines old-school polished wood and post-industrial bare brick and piping, cued by the copper brewhouse itself at the back, with numerous tucked-away cubby holes. In common with other branches, the brewing activities are pleasingly upfront: the equipment is clearly labelled, you can see which beer is in which fermenting vessel, and there's a busy programme of tours, tastings and 'brewer for a day' bookings.

BEERS in cask, keg and minikeg are brewed to site-specific recipes with locally themed names, though within a chain-wide template which leads on a quality cask best bitter, in this case the rather good **Arcangel*** (4%). Other Islington regulars are oatmeal stout **Hotblack Desiato** (5.4%), namechecking the estate agent immortalised by Douglas Adams, and American-style **IPA Chaplin** (6%). The monthly Project Cask challenge tasks B&K brewers with devising their own guest recipe within a specified style, while quarterly tapping parties launch keg seasonals. **Legend craft lager** (5%), sold in all branches, is outsourced to Shepherd Neame in Faversham, Kent.

Brewhouse and Kitchen Islington

Earl of Essex

Earl of Essex ❸

Contemporary pub (Graceland)
25 Danbury Street N1 8LE
T (020) 7424 5828   earlofessex.net
🕓 *Mo-Th 12.00-23.30, Fr-Sa 12.00-24.00,
Su 12.00-23.00*. Children until 21.00.
4 cask, 13 keg, 50 bottles/cans, 2 ciders,
specialist spirits.
🍴 Burgers, salads, cooked snacks **£-££**,
🎋 Rear garden ❀

⊖ Angel   🚉 Islington Green   🚲 C27
🏃 Jubilee Greenway, link to New River Path

Tucked away in terraced back streets east of
Upper Street and north of the canal, this pretty
pub, refurbished as a beer specialist in July
2012, recalls its past as a neighbourhood local
with a vintage back bar behind an island bar.
Otherwise this is a clean, modern space,
attractive enough for the general customer,
including guests of the various Airbnb lets
in the area, but with plenty to delight the
enthusiast. Handpumps with distinctive
wooden handles dispense beers from the
likes of Redemption, Burning Sky or Kirkstall.
Other options range widely: UK delights like
Partizan and Wander Beyond, classic Bavarians
like Andechs, exotic Scandinavians and big
sharing bottles from revered US specialists
like Blackberry Farm, Jester King and Logsdon.
Pumpclips are frowned upon so look at the list
on the wall for the draught choices. A simple

menu offers a range of burgers, beer battered
coley, superfood salads and small plates like
crispy squid. The former in-house brewery is
no longer operational.

Euston Tap ❹

Bar (Bloomsbury)
190 Euston Road NW1 2EF
T (020) 3137 8837   eustontap.com
🕓 *West Lodge: Mo-Sa 11.00-23.00, Su 12.00-22.00*.
Children until mid-evening.
4 cask, 18 keg, 80 bottles/cans.
🕓 *East Lodge: Usually open an hour later and
closed an hour earlier.*
2 cask, 10 keg, ciders/perries.
🎋 Side terrace

🚄 Euston   ⊖ Euston, Euston Square   🚲 Link to C6
🏃 Jubilee Walkway

One of the vanguard of a new wave of London
beer bars opened in 2010 in Euston station's
historic west lodge. The following year, the
same owners opened the east lodge as a dedicated cider bar, although this became a more
straightforward extension of its sister in 2016.
The original still offers the widest beer choice,
dispensed from taps mounted on a copper
back bar flanked by fridges; its neighbour still
has a few more ciders alongside additional
draught lines and less contested seating. Both
have precarious spiral staircases winding to
upstairs lounges, while terraces on Euston

Square Gardens provide attractive outdoor drinking even with all the construction work going on. Cask beers, served using a siphon method, are typically supplied by brewers like Anarchy, East London, Hawkshead, Howling Hops, Moor and Pig and Porter, while kegs include imported German lagers and beers from Kernel, in a notable range of styles. You might spot rare imports in the fridges like Azimut from France, Foolproof from Rhode Island and Oedipus from the Netherlands. An admirable offer in a unique and enviably convenient setting.

Visitor note. Dating from the 1830s, the lodges once flanked the largest Doric arch ever built, demolished in 1961 but potentially to be restored when the station is remodelled to accommodate the HS2 rail line. Originally they housed parcels and administrative offices, but were disused before being put to their current use.

Euston Tap

George and Monkey ❺

Contemporary pub
68 Amwell Street EC1R 1UU
T (020) 7278 6210
thegeorgeandmonkey.co.uk
🕐 Mo-Sa 12.00-23.00, Su 12.00-22.30.
   Children until 21.00.
1-2 cask, 12 keg, 25 bottles/cans, specialist spirits.
🍴 Pizzas **£-££**, 🪑 Tables on street, ♿
Tap takeovers, quiz (Tu)

🚇 Angel 🚌 Penton Street Chapel Market 🚲 C27
🥾 New River Path

George and Monkey

This attractive corner pub was given a sympathetic makeover in July 2018. The décor – floorboards and half-panelled walls decorated with mirrors and old maps – maintains a traditional pub feel alongside contemporary attractions. Beers range from cask Harvey's Sussex Best to kegs, bottles and cans from Londoners like Kernel, Partizan and Pressure Drop and Bristolians like Wild and Wiper & True, plus a few interesting imports. The kitchen turns out stonebaked pizzas with toppings like spicy sausage or bianco-style vegetables and pesto. The stuffed monkey above the bar is of course known as George.

Visitor note. The pub was originally named the Fountain, likely because of its proximity to the nearby terminus of the New River, a 17th-century water conduit, at Sadlers Wells.

Little Creatures Regents Canal ❻

Brewpub, bar (Lion/Kirin)
1 Lewis Cubitt Walk N1C 4DL (Camden)
T (020) 8161 4446   littlecreatures.co.uk
First sold beer: May 2019
🕐 Mo-We 16.00-23.00, Th 12.00-23.00,
   Fr-Sa 12.00-24.00, Su 12.00-22.00.
   Children until 20.00.
4 tank, 8+ keg, 5+ bottles/cans,
Australasian wines.
🍴 Brunch, sharing plates, pub grub, pizza **££**,
🪑 Front terrace, ♿
Occasional DJs and live music

🚈 Kings Cross, St Pancras 🚇 Kings Cross St Pancras
🚌 Copenhagen Street York Way 🥾 Jubilee Greenway

This substantial brewpub overlooking a green patch in the Kings Cross redevelopment area opened in May 2019 as the London outpost

Little Creatures

of Little Creatures. The parent began as a pioneering and influential craft brewery in Fremantle, Western Australia, in 2000, although it's been a subsidiary of Kirin-owned Lion Group since 2012. A neat 5hl steam-heated brewhouse is visible through glass in one corner. Imports and options from other Lion Little World breweries like Fourpure (p210) and Magic Rock are served alongside house-brewed beers, all of which can be explored with third-pint tasting flights. Though the space is unapologetically post-industrial with plenty of gleaming steel and exposed ducting, warm wood finishes and quieter corners provide a homely touch.

BEERS are fermented in and dispensed from the line of cylindro-conical vessels behind the bar under blanket carbon dioxide pressure, with numerous specials, collaborations and recreations of recipes from other locations in the group such as Singapore. Other Little Creatures beers, including the flagship **Pale Ale** (5.2%), are imported rather than replicated in-house.

Pig and Butcher ⑦

Gastropub (Noble Inns)
80 Liverpool Road N1 0QD
T (020) 7226 8304 thepigandbutcher.co.uk
🕐 *Mo-We* 12.00-23.00, *Th-Sa* 12.00-24.00,
   Su 12.00-23.00. Children until 21.00.
3 cask, 4 keg, 40 bottles/cans, wines, malts
   and specialist whiskies, liqueurs.
🍴 Gastro/Modern British menu **£££**,
🪑 Tables on street
Tastings, food themed events, private dining

🚇 Angel 🚌 Theberton Street 🚲 Link to C27

Gastropubs are rarely renowned for their beer lists, but this otherwise classic representative has been an exception since opening in 2011, with staff ready to offer pairing suggestions. Casks rotate but tend towards more traditional options from breweries like Bath Ales and Sambrook's, or local Hammerton. Bottles and cans range far and wide, with Londoners like Five Points, Hackney and Kernel alongside Belgian and German classics like Orval and Schlenkerla. A bright interior in white and muted grey is split into bar and dining sections: for the latter, expect to book well in advance or queue at all but the quietest of times. A daily changing menu features fish from Cornish day boats and meat butchered in-house: perhaps sea trout with globe artichoke, Tamworth pork or broad bean dumplings, with tempting puds like rice pudding brulée with Yorkshire rhubarb. It shares ownership with the Smokehouse (p181).

Queens Head   ⑧

Contemporary pub
66 Acton Street WC1X 9NB
T (020) 7713 5772   queensheadlondon.com
🕐 *Su-Mo* 12.00-23.00, *Tu-Sa* 12.00-24.00.
Children until 19.00.
3 cask, 13 keg, 60 bottles, 4-6 ciders/perries.
🍴 Ploughmans and cold sharing boards **£-££**,
🪑 Small rear yard
Tap takeovers, tastings, beer launches, beer book collection, jazz (Tu/Su), board games

🚆 Kings Cross, St Pancras   ⊖ Kings Cross St Pancras
🚲 Link to C6, C27   🚶 Link to Jubilee Walkway

On the one-way system at Kings Cross, this is a proper pub from the people who later brought you Mother Kelly's. It benefits from fine original features, preserved thanks to decades of underinvestment before its June 2010 refurbishment, including extensive ceramic tiling, engraved glass, mirrors and light fittings from the gaslight era. Redemption Trinity is the regular cask, alongside rotating guests from the likes of Revolutions, Tiny Rebel or Windsor and Eton, usually including a darker option. Most of the rest is from London and the UK – Kernel, One Mile End, Northern Monk, Three Hills, Wild Weather – with a good few interesting imports like Orval, Põhjala and Uiltje. Food is limited to cold plates and sharing boards of cheese and cold meat, some helpfully provided

with matching beer suggestions. A handsome, friendly place that hits the sweet spot of interesting dedicated beer geeks without scaring off everyone else. It was briefly a brewpub but brewing activity has since evolved into the standalone Old Street Brewing (p138). Hard hit by the lockdowns, it successfully crowdfunded to stay open, a measure of the affection regulars hold for it.

TRY ALSO

Beer + Burger Kings Cross 1a Arthouse, 1 York Way N1C 4AS beerandburgerstore.com: Top indie beer choice in the Kings Cross redevelopment area with 18 keg lines and around 200 bottles/cans including rarities, international classics and house brews sold by knowledgeable staff. A modern burger bar vibe like its Willesden parent (p304) but space for non-diners too.

Calthorpe Arms 252 Grays Inn Road WC1X 8JR calthorpearmswc1.co.uk: Longstanding local CAMRA favourite Young's pub in Grade II-listed early 19th century corner building, known for immaculately kept cask including London guests, plus a few Young's bottles, warm welcome and hearty grub.

Exmouth Arms 1 Starcross Street NW1 2HR publove.co.uk: Publove pub close to Euston station which narrowly escaped demolition for HS2 works. Decent local stuff from Belleville, Partizan and Sambrook's among five well-kept cask lines, 10 kegs and 15+ bottles and cans. Attracts a youthful cosmopolitan crowd from the hostel above.

Parcel Yard King's Cross Station N1C 4AH parcelyard.co.uk: Perhaps London's best station pub in the lavishly refurbished Grade I-listed parcels office with a glass-covered atrium, just upstairs from tourist photo-op Platform 9¾ at Kings Cross. Comprehensive range of Fuller's cask, immaculately served, plus bottles, several guest choices and an upmarket food menu.

Three Johns 73 White Lion Street N1 9PF three-johns.com: Corner pub near Chapel Market remade by Barworks in funky but civilised style with picture windows, a beaten copper ceiling and a customarily lengthy and well-picked beer list: one cask, 15 keg and 70+ bottles/cans including numerous US and Scandinavian imports besides UK high achievers.

HERITAGE PUB

Lamb 94 Lamb's Conduit Street WC1N 3LZ
thelamblondon.com: Comfortable Grade II-
listed pub likely dating from the 18th-century
development of Bloomsbury, close to Coram's
Fields and Great Ormond Street Children's
Hospital. Part-preserved late Victorian interior
features engraved glass, rare original snob
screens and a working Polyphon music box.
Good range of cask Young's beers and some
local guests.

HOP HISTORIES The great beer flood

One of the most notorious brewing disasters in history happened on 17 October 1814 at Meux's Horse Shoe brewery, at the junction of Tottenham Court Road and Oxford Street. At about 16.30 in the afternoon, one of the iron hoops fell from a giant 6.7m-high wooden vat containing 3,550 barrels (580,000 litres) of 10-month-old porter. Brewery staff thought little of the incident as this was a relatively common occurrence, usually easily fixed, but about an hour later, the whole vat collapsed, the force of its exploding staves knocking out several other vats and barrels nearby. A flood of porter and debris weighing several hundred tonnes poured out of the brewery in a wave at least 4.5m high, inundating cellars, knocking down walls and washing people from first floor rooms in the slum housing of St Giles 'rookery' opposite.

Eight people died, not, as is sometimes supposed, from drowning in beer or intoxication but from injuries caused by debris and the force of the flood. All were women and children: five from poor Irish families who were, tragically, holding a wake in a cellar, and three young children in the St Giles workhouse. The death toll would undoubtedly have been higher but for the time of day, as most people were out at work. And the vat that burst wasn't even the biggest in the brewery – it may have been one of the smallest. Astonishingly, the firm avoided paying compensation and even managed to reclaim the duty it had already paid on the lost beer, though the disaster made porter brewers rethink their policy of building ever-bigger vats.

Brewery owner Sir Henry Meux had been a partner in Meux Reid's Griffin brewery in Clerkenwell, built in 1763, which pioneered the use of giant vats in porter production. In 1807,

following a dispute, Meux set up on his own by buying the Horse Shoe, which had been around since (probably) before 1764. In 1914 Meux's took over Thorne Brothers' Nine Elms brewery in Vauxhall and transferred brewing there seven years later: the original Horse Shoe was demolished in 1922 and the Dominion Theatre (268 Tottenham Court Road W1T 7AQ) now occupies the site. Eventually merged as Friary Meux, the company became part of Ind Coope in 1961 and stopped brewing at Nine Elms in 1964.

Reid & Co, meanwhile, merged into Watney Combe Reid in 1898 (see Roll out the red barrel p126 and the Clerkenwell plant was closed a year later. Some of the brewery buildings still stand, including former tap the Griffin pub (125 Clerkenwell Road EC1R 5DB), which survives rather ignominiously as a strip club.

Borough and Southbank

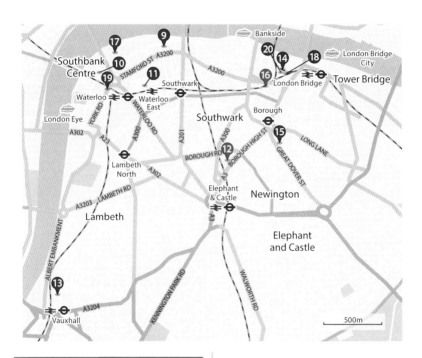

Beer Hawk ⑨

Bar, shop
6 The Gallery, South Bank Central SE1 9LQ
bars.beerhawk.co.uk
⊕ *Tu-Sa* 12.00-22.00. Children until 20.00.
 Cash-free.
11 keg, 120 bottles/cans, minikegs, specialist
whiskies and other spirits. 🍴
🍴 Toasties £, 🪑 Front terrace, ♿
Tastings, beer showcases, Tu quiz, running club,
board games

🚆 Blackfriars ⊖ Southwark 🚲 NCN4, link to C6, C10
🏃 Jubilee Greenway, Jubilee Walkway, Thames Path

Opened in May 2018 as a first bottle shop/bar
from the AB InBev-owned mail order business,
this is a modern but pleasant retreat on the
ground floor of a new development, its
entrance just off Upper Ground. Besides
'crafty' ABI brands on draught, there are
usually a few good Londoners, and the fridges
cover broader ground, with lots of fresh
hoppy stuff from the US as well as wild and
mixed fermentation beers in big bottles
(Alesmith, FiftyFifty, the Rare Barrel), a legacy
of Beer Hawk's acquisition of a cold chain
delivery network from the defunct Bottle
Shop, plus Goose Island rarities. You can also
order online from among 2,000+ items and
pick up here.

German Kraft
See Mercato Metropolitano

Hop Locker

Bar, shop
Royal Festival Hall (east side), Belvedere Road
SE1 8XX   twitter.com/thehoplocker
🕐 *Fr* 12.00-20.00, *Sa* 11.00-20.00, *Su (also bank
    holiday Mo)* 12.00-18.00 (may be closed for
    special events: check social media).
    Children welcome.
12 keg, 60+ bottles/cans.
🍴 Various from neighbouring traders,
🍷 All outdoor, ♿ (in Southbank Centre)
Occasional tap takeovers

🚆 Waterloo   ⛴ London Eye   🚲 NCN4, C10
🏃 Jubilee Greenway, Jubilee Walkway, Thames Path

A few years ago, a beer stall in the bustling
weekend food market behind the Royal Festival
Hall would have been a real surprise. Today,
the Hop Locker, which has been unlocking its
treasures here since April 2015, seems to fit
right in. Owner Joel Mellor and colleagues
evangelically provide helpful advice about
what to choose from a well-selected array of
London and other UK brewers, likely to include
Donzoko, Kernel, North, Pressure Drop and
Track, with occasional imports. You'll find it
on the northeast side of the market near the
Hayward Gallery stairs. In previous summers,
Joel has also operated a drink-in bar most days
on the RFH's riverside terrace, under the steps
to the downstream Golden Jubilee footbridge,
though the likelihood of this returning was
unknown at the time of writing.

Kings Arms

Traditional pub (Windmill)
25 Roupell Street SE1 8TB
☎ (020) 7207 0784
thekingsarmslondon.co.uk
🕐 *Daily* 12.00-23.00. Children until 19.00.
9 cask, 9 keg, some whiskies.
🍴 Thai menu ££, 🍷 Standing on street
Quiz (Su), major big screen sport, functions

🚆 Waterloo East, Waterloo   ⊖ Waterloo   ⛴ London Eye
🚲 C10, C14, link to NCN4   🏃 Link to Jubilee Greenway,
Jubilee Walkway, Thames Path

This delightful corner pub retains its smallish,
partitioned public and saloon bars, lettered in

an incongruous 1960s font that recalls a past
life as an Ind Coope house. A backyard converted to a conservatory operates as a Thai restaurant with a lengthy and veggie-friendly menu.
It's long been noted for well-kept cask in a
range of styles: Londoners Three Sods might be
on besides Kent suppliers like Caveman and
Pig and Porter or beers from the southwest
like Flying Monk, alongside regulars Adnams
bitter and a rebadged Sharp's Original. Kegs
are mainly from the Molson Coors stable but
with changing guests such as Wild Weather.
While it's often busy with informed Waterloo
commuters and visitors to nearby attractions
like the Southbank and the Old and New Vic
theatres, it stands sufficiently apart from all
of these to retain a community feel.

*Visitor note. The pub is part of the Roupell Street Conser-
vation Area, pleasingly breaking up one of several lengthy
terraces of workers' cottages developed between the 1820s
and 1840s, sympathetically framed by lamp standards in
Victorian style. If it looks like a set from a prestige BBC period
drama, that's because you've seen it featured in several
such productions.*

Mercato Metropolitano Elephant (German Kraft)

Brewpub, bars
42 Newington Causeway SE1 6DR (Southwark)
mercatometropolitano.com
German Kraft: germankraftbeer.com
First sold beer: October 2014, 🍻
🕐 *Mo-We* 12.00-22.45, *Th-Fr* 12.00-24.00,
    Sa 11.00-24.00, *Su* 11.00-21.45. Children very
    welcome until early evening.
6 tank, 4 keg, growlers.
🍴 Various from surrounding traders,
🍷 Tables and benches around market, ♿

🚆 ⊖ Elephant & Castle CS7, link to CS6, C10

This lively warren of a food market in a former
paper factory on an otherwise nondescript
street just off Elephant and Castle hosts an
on-site brewery which, in curious contrast to
its surroundings, leans to Bavaria rather than
Italy for inspiration. The first is the on-site
brewery German Kraft which, in curious
contrast to its surroundings, leans to Bavaria
rather than Italy for inspiration. It was opened
in December 2017 by Felix Bollen, Anton

German Kraft

Borkmann, Andrea Ferrario and Michele Tieghi, drawing on previous experience at Steinbach Bräu in Erlangen, Franconia. A 20hl brewhouse was in action a few months later, capable of making lagers in traditional Bavarian style with a three-step mash. Brewing on site is fundamental to the concept: according to the brewery, it not only guarantees freshness but cuts carbon emissions by 75% by reducing packaging and transport. The kit is shoehorned in behind the main bar within one of the market halls, while fermentation and conditioning tanks are just outside in the verdant semi-tropical garden. The full range is dispensed from tank both here and at six other bars on the site, alongside a few keg London guests. The team has since set up further breweries at a second Mercato in Mayfair (p123) and at Kraft Dalston (p136).

BEERS from German Kraft are sold only on the site, mainly from tank with some keg. They include unfiltered **Helles Heidi Blonde** (5.2%); an authentic cloudy wheat beer **Edel Weiss*** (5.3%); and a US-influenced 'Hopfenweisse', **Otto** (5.3%). Seasonals and specials have included a Vienna lager, dry-hopped pilsners, smoked beer and other German specialities.

Mother Kelly's Vauxhall ⓭

Bar, shop
76 Albert Embankment SE1 7TP
T (020) 7091 9779   motherkellys.co.uk
🕐 *Tu-Th* 16.00-23.00, *Fr-Su* 12.00-23.00. Children until 20.00.
30+ keg, 100+ bottles/cans, some specialist spirits. 🍶
🍴 Sandwiches and sharing boards **£-££**,
🪑 Benches at front, rear terrace overlooking park, ♿
Beer launches, tastings, beer books, DJs, board games

🚆🚇 Vauxhall   ⛴ St George Wharf   🚲 C5
🚶 Link to Thames Path

The biggest branch of one of London's leading beer specialists replicates the look of the Bethnal Green original, but in a much bigger railway arch in lively Vauxhall, almost next door to LGBT+ theatre Above the Stag and with a rear terrace overlooking Vauxhall Pleasure Gardens. The keg taps dispense a mix from Londoners like Bohem, Boxcar, Brick, Kernel, Three Hills and Orbit, other UK producers like Double Barrelled, and occasional imports like Alefarm and Põhjala. The contents of the fridges, in a segregated section at the front, aren't quite so wide-ranging or specialised as at some other branches but include a strong US selection (Firestone Walker, Jester King, Prairie) with plenty of UK options. It's a little cavernous but a colourful mural adds interest to the interior.

Rake ⑭

Bar
14 Winchester Walk SE1 9AG
T (020) 7407 0557 **utobeer.co.uk/the-rake**
🕐 *Mo-Th* 12.00-23.00, *Fr* 11.00-23.00,
　Sa 10.00-23.00, *Su* 12.00-22.00.
　Children on terrace only.
3-4 cask, 14 keg, 150+ bottles/cans, cider,
　some specialist spirits.
🍴 BYO, 🪑 Front terrace, ♿
Beer festivals, tap takeovers, tastings, beer launches

≠⊖ London Bridge　🚢 London Bridge City
🚲 NCN4, link to CS7, C14　🚶 Jubilee Greenway, Jubilee
Walkway, Thames Path

Richard Dinwoodie and Mike Hill of Utobeer (below) turned a greasy spoon café on the edge of Borough Market into one of London's earliest contemporary beer bars in 2006. Many other venues now compete, but the management's discerning palates and worldwide connections ensure the Rake retains its place as an essential stop on the international craft beer circuit, as attested by the various brewer autographs on the wall. The cask handpumps favour beers from Acorn, Crouch Vale, Hawkshead, Redemption, associated brewpub Tap East (p153) and many others, with over 20 different choices served in a week. Kegs and bottles stretch from London (Kernel, Solvay Society) across the world: US producers like Anderson Valley, Crooked Stave and Port City, a rich seam of Belgians and Germans and rarities from UK brewers like Burning Sky alongside numerous less recherché but impeccably rewarding beverages. 'We also want to stay faithful to beers that were good before craft became a thing,' says general manager George. Space is restricted ('the size of a mini-cab office' comments one reviewer) and basic but boosted by a pleasant wooden-decked and heated terrace.

Royal Oak ⑮

Traditional pub
44 Tabard Street SE1 4JU
T (020) 7357 7173 **harveys.org.uk**
🕐 *Mo-Sa* 11.00-23.00, *Su* 11.00-21.00.
　Children welcome.
7 cask, 3 keg, 20 bottles, cider.
🍴 Enhanced pub grub, pies **££**,
🪑 A few tables on street, ♿ Flat access only
Quiz (We), live music (Fr), functions

⊖ Borough　🚲 C10, link to C14

The Royal Oak is well-loved with good reason as it's pretty much the perfect traditional pub: clean, bright and civilised but unpretentious and friendly, with a genuine community feel, a

welcome lack of recorded music and bleeping machines, in a Victorian building with some surviving heritage features and a range of top quality beers. It's easily the best of three London pubs tied to Harvey's of Lewes, one of England's most respected surviving independent family brewers, and has improved still further since a change of management early in 2019 addressed a few weaknesses while keeping the basics intact. It stocks the full Harvey's range, with flawlessly-kept casks always including dark mild and, in season, Christmas Ale, alongside the famed Sussex Bitter and other options, with Imperial Russian Stout and several other old-school specialities among the bottles. The menu might include steak and kidney pudding, Thai-spiced quinoa burger and plates of Sussex cheeses. Two spaces divided by an island counter are still distinguished by the greater amounts of soft furnishings on the 'saloon' side, with a hatch in the lobby once used for takeaways.

Visitor note Tabard Street is the original route of Watling Street, the road to Canterbury used by Geoffrey Chaucer's fictitious pilgrims. Its modern name commemorates the now-vanished inn on Borough High Street where they assembled.

St Felix Place

Brewpub, bar, restaurant
45 Southwark Street SE1 9HP (Southwark)
stfelixplace.co.uk
First sold beer: May 2021
⏱ *Tu-Th* 16.00-22.00, *Fr-Sa* 12.00-22.00, *Su* 12.00-20.00. Children until early evening.
Keg, bottles, cans
🍴 Barbecue, pizza, 🪑 Large courtyard, ♿

🚉 ⊖ London Bridge 🚢 London Bridge City 🚴 CS7, Q14, link to NCN4 🚶 Link to Jubilee Greenway, Jubilee Walkway, Thames Path

In two historic railway arches close to Borough Market, this combined brewpub and food destination is a collaboration between musician Ben Lovett's Venue Group and Lagunitas, one of the US breweries owned by Heineken. There's a large outdoor courtyard and two resident restaurant partners as well as a bar stocking the products of the brewhouse behind it, other Lagunitas and other Heineken-linked brands and independents.

Understudy

Bar
National Theatre, Upper Ground SE1 9PX
T (020) 7452 3551   **nationaltheatre.org.uk**
⏱ *Mo-Sa* 12.00-22.30, *Su* 12.00-22.00. Children until early evening.
1 tank, 10 keg, 90+ bottles/cans; specialist spirits, cocktails.
🍴 Burgers, salads, summer changing food truck **£-££**, 🪑 Large riverside terrace, ♿
Tap takeovers, beer showcases, DJs (Sa), board games (Su), summer live music, performance and theatre on River Stage

🚉 ⊖ Waterloo 🚢 London Eye 🚴 NCN4, C10 🚶 Jubilee Greenway, Jubilee Walkway, Thames Path

Amazingly, the National Theatre didn't gain a proper riverside bar until October 2014 when this place opened in a former storage space in the northeast corner; even more unexpectedly, it turned out to be a beer specialist. There's no cask as cellar space is restricted, but there's unfiltered Meantime tank lager and plentiful keg, bottled and canned beer, including numerous sharing bottles, from Londoners like Anspach & Hobday, Gipsy Hill, Pressure Drop and Weird Beard, other UK big hitters like Burning Sky and Lost and Grounded, and well-chosen imports mainly from Belgium, the Netherlands and the USA. In summer, the satellite Otherstudy outside regularly plays host to tap takeovers. Clever interior design makes the best of the notorious *béton brut* architecture to create a cosy space that recycles theatre lighting and discarded wheels from the theatre's famous drum revolve, now serving as table bases.

Utobeer

Shop
24 Borough Market, Borough High Street SE1 1TL
T (020) 7378 6617   **utobeer.co.uk**
⏱ *Mo-Tu* 11.00-17.00, *We-Th* 11.00-18.00, *Fr* 10.00-18.00, *Sa* 09.00-17.00, *Su* 10.00-14.00. Cash-free
500+ bottles/cans. 🍾 (selection only)
🍴 Various from neighbouring traders **£-££**, ♿ (on market)

🚉 ⊖ London Bridge 🚢 London Bridge City 🚴 NCN4, link to CS7, C14 🚶 Link to Jubilee Greenway, Jubilee Walkway, Thames Path

Utobeer has flown the flag for fine beer among all the other fine food and drink traders at Borough Market since 1999, and by educating the taste buds of a generation of drinkers and brewers, it undoubtedly helped lay the foundations for London's current flourishing beer culture. It still has one of the biggest and best-chosen selections, often carrying stuff nobody else does despite selling off its distribution arm in 2016. London and UK brewers are well-represented, with a good showing from nearby Bermondsey, and rare sightings of beers from Left Handed Giant, St Mars of the Desert and Odyssey. You'll find quality US imports but their number has diminished in favour of closer sources in Scandinavia and the Netherlands (Kees, Nevel, Vandenbroek) and longstanding Belgian and German classics, including a solid lambic selection, rarely-seen Gruut and several smoked beers from Schlenkerla. Easily enough to forgive them their painfully punning name.

Waterloo Tap ⑲

Bar (Bloomsbury)
147 Sutton Walk SE1 7ND
T (020) 3455 7436 **waterlootap.com**
🕐 Mo-Th 15.00-23.00, Fr-Sa 12.00-24.00, Su 12.00-22.00. Children until 19.00.
5 cask, 19 keg, 5 bottles.
🎋 Small terraces both sides, ♿

⇌ ⊖ Waterloo 🚢 London Eye 🚲 NCN4, link to C10
🏃 Link to Jubilee Greenway, Jubilee Walkway, Thames Path

In a railway arch right on the busy main pedestrian route between the Southbank centre and Waterloo station, this little place has evolved into one of most highly rated members of its chain since opening in March 2016. The cask taps embedded in the smart copper back bar are usually supplied by locals like Five Points, Southwark or Twickenham, or the likes of Adnams, Gun or Siren. There's an even bigger spread among the kegs, which boasted stouts from Bristol Beer Factory and JW Lees when I last called. Optimised for thirsty commuters, it's not a place for rare bottles or food, but get there at quieter times and you might be able to nab one of the scallop-shaped booths at the back. It does a particularly good

job considering the cellar is inconveniently at the back of a neighbouring arch.

Wright Brothers Oyster and Porter House ⑳

Restaurant, bar
11 Stoney Street SE1 9AB
T (020) 7403 9554 **thewrightbrothers.co.uk**
🕐 Mo-Sa 12.00-22.00, Su 12.00-17.00. Children welcome.
3 keg, 10 bottles/cans, champagne, sparkling and other wines, sherry.
🍴 Oysters, seafood, fish **££-£££**,
🎋 A few stools on street

⇌ ⊖ London Bridge 🚢 London Bridge City
🚲 NCN4, link to CS7 🏃 Link to Jubilee Greenway, Jubilee Walkway, Thames Path

Pleasingly, this Borough Market shopfront for Cornish oyster fishery Wright Brothers foregrounds porter and stout as the ideal, and traditional, accompaniments to the company's principal product. Appropriately enough for an outlet a stone's throw from the former site of Barclay Perkins, one of the greatest porter brewers in the world, the beer list includes some of London's best examples of the dark stuff from BBNo, Five Points, Kernel and Partizan. Burning Sky and Mondo feature among paler choices, and then there's the more expensive but equally traditional

Wright Brothers

matching option of champagne. Depending on availability, at least six varieties of oysters are served, as well as mussels, shrimps, crab, fish from the Brixham day boats and even a vegetarian option or two. Non-diners might be able to squeeze onto a stool at the bar, but this is an intimate place with tables reserved for diners, so booking is advised. See website for other branches

TRY ALSO

Fountain and Ink 52 Stamford Street SE1 9LX fountainandink.co.uk: Impressively spacious, contemporary corner pub with ex-church furniture and indoor living walls not far from the National Theatre, with owner Barworks' customarily comprehensive international beer selection across one cask line, 13 kegs and 100 bottles/cans.

Hercules 2 Kennington Road SE1 7BL thehercules.co.uk: Handsome pub close to Lambeth North Tube station, the Imperial War Museum and numerous hotels, recently reopened with one of Fuller's biggest 'crafty' beer ranges: four cask, 14 keg and 200+ bottles/cans. Named after a Victorian strongman rather than a Classical hero.

Hide 39 Bermondsey Street SE1 3XF thehidebar.com: Longstanding smart but relaxed cocktail bar on trendy Bermondsey Street, close to London Bridge station, with an equally longstanding liking for good beer: 11 kegs in a range of styles, nearly all from London breweries like Crate and Partizan. Big brother of the Arbitrager (p92).

Hop Kingdom 16 Druid Street SE1 2EY hopking.org: Bar and indoor skatepark with tuition for beginners in two rail arches just up the line from the Bermondsey run. It's the home of Hop King beer (cuckoo brewed elsewhere), dispensed from keg taps mounted on an old skateboard. A few bottled/canned guests are also available.

Katzenjammers 24 Southwark Street SE1 1TY katzenjammers.co.uk: Bavarian-themed joint in the capacious cellars of the Borough's historic Hop Exchange, noted for an oompah band playing Queen covers. Go when it's quieter to enjoy 11 imported kegs (Kaltenberg, Paulaner) and 25 bottles (Früh, Schneider and sweetened Belgian fruit beers).

Miller 96 Snowsfields SE1 3SS themiller.co.uk: Big, funky pub and entertainment venue just south of Guy's Hospital with over 30 bottles/cans from reliable London names like BBNo, Kernel, Howling Hops, Partizan, Pressure Drop and Weird Beard, with a few cask and keg lines sourced mainly from larger local producers.

Simon the Tanner 231 Long Lane SE1 4PR simonthetanner.co.uk: 200-year-old pub with a name recalling the local leather industry in a biblical reference, now an attractive community local linked to Mother Kelly's, with up to four cask, nine keg and 25+ bottles/cans. Closed Mondays.

Spit and Sawdust 21 Bartholomew Street SE1 4AL spitandsawdust.pub: Backstreet pub near Bricklayers Arms road junction, now a youthful venue with shuffleboard and a back bar with taps sprouting from mocked-up kegs. Four cask, 15 keg, a few bottles/cans, wide selection from London and across the UK.

Tankard 111 Kennington Road SE11 6SF brewdog.com: Friendly, pleasantly pubby former Draft House, now a BrewDog pub, with an expansive roof terrace overlooking the Imperial War Museum and Geraldine Mary Harmsworth Park. Up to two cask, 13 keg including several from London brewers plus around 30 UK and international bottles/cans.

Tower Bridge Arms 206 Tower Bridge Road SE1 2UP brewdog.com: BrewDog pub and former Draft House with a slightly more restricted range than some, on the southern approach to Tower Bridge. Up to four cask, 12 kegs and 10 bottles/cans in a pleasantly pubby environment.

HERITAGE PUB

George 77 Borough High Street SE1 1NH greeneking-pubs.co.uk: One of London's few genuinely old pubs, the surviving wing of the last Southwark inn, a unique galleried 1676 building overlooking a yard off Borough High Street on a site used for hospitality since at least 1598. The Parliament Bar boasts an interior that's part 18th century, with some 17th-century woodwork; the adjacent glassed-in bar is also notable. Owned by the National Trust but leased to Greene King, with some local cask and other options.

HOP HISTORIES Southwark ale

SOUTHWARK owes its unique character to its strategic location, on the main road route to Kent and mainland Europe and at the foot of what was until 1750 the only bridge across the Thames in central London. In the past, the bridge was lined with houses and shops and was regularly congested, so transport terminated in Borough High Street. Travellers arriving outside daylight hours, when the crossing was closed, could take refuge in one of the numerous large inns on courtyards off the High Street, of which the George (Heritage pubs p89) is the only survivor. And Southwark escaped much of the City's regulation, making it a haven for more disreputable activities. Bankside, just upriver of the bridge, was famously the site of several theatres in Elizabethan and Jacobean times, as well as bull- and bear-baiting venues and London's largest concentration of brothels.

Courage Anchor Brewhouse, Horsleydown

All this created a healthy market for brewers. Southwark ale was famous enough by 1390 that the Miller in Geoffrey Chaucer's *Canterbury Tales* could apologise in advance for the potential effects of alcohol on his storytelling abilities with the words: 'and therfore if that I mysspeke or seye, / Wyte it [blame it on] the ale of southwerk, I you preye.' Originally, most brewing took place in inns, alehouses and institutions like nearby Bermondsey Abbey, but as standalone 'common brewers' emerged, Southwark remained a favoured location. The more cosmopolitan and liberal atmosphere would also have appealed to migrants who couldn't always rely on the warmest of welcomes. From the 15th century onwards, brewers from the Low Countries and Germany met an increasing demand for continental-style hopped beer in London, as opposed to old-fashioned English unhopped ale, from breweries in Southwark.

The district was also well-placed for the delivery of raw materials from Kent and other parts of southern England. Its role in the hop trade was confirmed by the building in 1867 of the magnificent Hop Exchange on Southwark Street, now the last surviving purpose-built trade exchange building in the capital. So important was this trade locally that when telephone exchanges were identified by three-letter mnemonics, the Borough was assigned HOP (407). And there was the activity on the river itself: London Bridge marked the upper limit of the stretch known as the Pool of London, once the busiest port in the world.

Brewing spread down the Pool to Bermondsey where the Anchor Brewhouse occupied the riverside at Horsleydown, immediately to the east of where Tower Bridge now stands, perhaps from the 16th century. It was once owned by a Flemish brewer, and in 1787 sold to a consortium led by John Courage, an ambitious shipping agent born in Aberdeen of French Huguenot descent. Most big London brewers back then specialised in porter, but Courage promoted fresher 'running ale' styles, and by 1895 when the now-expanded site was rebuilt, it was one of the most successful brewers in the capital.

Another Anchor, this time known as a brewery rather than a brewhouse, was built by James Monger in 1616 a little upriver on Park Street, on the site of William Shakespeare's Globe theatre, which had burned down three years previously (the current Globe, on the riverside 230m to the north, is a 1997 replica).

In the 18th century, the Thrale family turned this into one of London's best-known porter breweries, and in 1781, diarist Samuel Johnson helped sell it on behalf of his friend Henry Thrale's widow Hester, describing it as 'not just a parcel of boilers and vats, but the potentiality of growing rich beyond the dreams of avarice'. Bought by a member of a Quaker banking family in partnership with the incumbent head brewer, it became Barclay Perkins, the biggest and most technologically advanced brewery in the world by the mid-19th century when it was toured by VIPs from all over Europe. Its most famous beer was the potent Imperial Russian Stout, brewed originally for export from the end of the 18th century.

In 1921, Barclay became the first large and established British brewer to adopt lager brewing, which caught the attention of Courage, and in 1955 the latter bought out its near neighbour, soon turning it entirely over to lager production. By the beginning of the 1970s, brewing had ceased, though storage and distribution continued. Courage had by now expanded into one of Britain's Big Seven national brewers, and in 1981, it ceased all London production including at Horsleydown, selling off both sites. The Anchor Brewhouse still stands, now converted to luxury flats and offices, an early example of Docklands regeneration. There's a plaque on the wall at 50 Shad Thames SE1 2LY but the best view is from across the other side of Tower Bridge.

The Park Street site was almost entirely demolished and replaced by modern housing, though there are two plaques visible from Park Street (SE1 9DZ). One of these commemorates a curious incident in 1850 when General Julius Haynau, known as the 'Austrian butcher' for his brutal role in suppressing the 1848 revolutions, was recognised and beaten up by draymen while visiting the brewery. Both brewery taps survive: the Anchor Tap (20A Horsleydown Lane SE1 2LN) is now a Sam Smith pub which retains an unspoilt interior, while the Anchor Bankside (34 Park Street SE1 9EF) is a Greene King house popular with tourists. The brands are now owned by Marston's and some are still brewed at Wells in Bedford.

Brewing also spread upriver to Lambeth. The large Godings Brewery opened in 1837 between Belvedere Road and the river, surmounted by two large lion sculptures in artificial Coade stone, which became such familiar landmarks that the company later renamed itself the Lion brewery. Taken over by Hoare & Co (see Yeast Enders p163) in 1923, the Lion closed shortly afterwards, and lay derelict for years. It was demolished in 1949, and the Royal Festival Hall was built on the site for the 1951 Festival of Britain. One of the lions now stands a little further upriver, guarding the steps from the Thames Path to Westminster Bridge by County Hall.

The area immediately south of the river later played its part in the real ale revival. In 1979, unemployed young would-be entrepreneur David Bruce was out running when he spotted a large derelict former Truman's pub, the Duke of York, not far from Borough Tube station. Minimally renovated and renamed the Goose and Firkin, it became Britain's first modern brewpub, with an 8hl kit initially brewing from malt extract. The Goose provided the model for a whole chain of Firkin brewpubs across London, and ultimately the UK and abroad. Bruce sold the company in 1988, later founding several other pub chains, and eventual owner Bass closed all the breweries in 1995. The Goose is now a Shepherd Neame pub known once again as the Duke of York (47 Borough Road SE1 1DR).

Other early microbreweries in the area included Simon's Tower Bridge Brewery, set up with the help of investment from CAMRA in 1980, which brewed intermittently under several owners until 1983 at a site on the southern approach to Tower Bridge (218 Tower Bridge Road SE1 2UP); and a small brewhouse which operated between 1981-88 in the Market Porter on Borough Market, and again as the Bishop's Brewery between 1993-98 in the building opposite that now houses Monmouth Coffee (2 Park Street SE1 9AB): 'When we moved in,' recalls Monmouth's owner Anita Le Roy, 'the market trustees still called it "the brewery"'. The now-closed Brew Wharf brewpub around the corner hosted the inaugural meeting of the London Brewers Alliance in 2010. Though there are currently no commercial breweries in Southwark proper, the Bermondsey brewers (p207) are continuing a distinguished tradition nearby.

City and Aldgate

Arbitrager 21

Bar (Blood & Sand)
27a Throgmorton Street EC2N 2AN
T (020) 7374 6887 **thearbitrager.co.uk**
🕐 *Mo-Tu* 12.00-23.00, *We-Fr* 12.00-24.00.
   Children until early evening.
9 keg, occasional bottles/cans, growlers, 80 gins.
🛲 Standing on street
*Meet the brewer, tastings, food pairing, occasional
live music, functions*

θ Bank 🏃 Link to Jubilee Walkway

Developing the beery passion that its owners
first discovered at the Hide (Try also p89),
this narrow sliver of a place opened in March
2015 above a cocktail bar in the Drapers' Hall
complex, around the corner from the Dutch
church at Austin Friars. The simple but smart
interior, with its London beer and gin map
mural, has been optimised for vertical
drinking from what by today's standards is
a small but well-judged list of kegs in a range
of styles, exclusively from London brewers
like Hammerton, Mondo, Orbit and Partizan.

Visitor note: *An arbitrager is someone who exploits
unintentional discrepancies in the prices of the same
securities on different financial markets, buying them
on a market that lists them at a lower price and selling
them again on a market that lists them at a higher one.*

BrewDog Outpost Tower Hill 22

Brewpub, bar
21 Great Tower Street EC3R 5AR (City of London)
T (020) 7929 2545 **brewdog.com**
First sold beer: May 2018
🕐 *Mo-Th* 12.00-23.00, *Fr* 12.00-24.00, *Sa* 11.00-
   24.00, *Su* 11.00-23.00. Children until 20.00.
34 keg, 150 bottles/cans, growlers, some
   specialist spirits. 🍷
🍴 Burgers, pizzas, wings **££**, 🛲 Front terrace, ♿
*Beer launches, tastings, quiz (Tu), jam sessions,
shuffleboard, pinball, retro arcade games, functions*

🚆 Fenchurch Street θ Tower Gateway, Tower Hill
🚢 Tower Millennium 🚲 CS3 🏃 Jubilee Walkway, link to
Thames Path

London's biggest and the world's second biggest BrewDog bar, the chain's only brewpub in
the capital occupies a whole side of the ground
floor of the neo-Gothic Minster building. It's
fitted out in the usual post-industrial style,
with high tables, booths and a corner with
stepped wooden seating. At one end is a big
room with three shuffleboards, at the other a

Brewdog Outpost Tower Hill

shiny 10hl brewhouse surrounded by a hedge of keykegs. About two thirds of the long line of taps dispense the owner's core beers and specials, while the rest are allocated to guests like Fierce, Northern Monk or London's Pillars. Numerous bottles and cans, some from a vending machine, include Canopy and ORA, US imports from Crooked Stave and Hill Farmstead, and lots from BrewDog's own wild and mixed fermentation sub-brand OverWorks. The fast food menu is longer than in most branches, including numerous vegan options.

BEERS, including regular **Tower Hill Pale** (4.2%) and numerous specials and collaborations, are sold on keg in house and sometimes at other BrewDog bars.

Crosse Keys ㉓

Contemporary pub
9 Gracechurch Street EC3V 0DR
T (020) 7623 4824   jdwetherspoon.co.uk
🕑 *Su-Th* 08.00-24.00, *Fr-Sa* 08.00-01.00. Children until 21.00.
Up to 23 cask, 7 keg, 20 bottles/cans, 1-2 ciders/perries, gins, some wines.
🍴 Eclectic pub grub **£-££**, &
Beer festivals, functions

⊖ Monument, Bank   ♿ Link to CS7
🏃 Link to Jubilee Walkway

Though the low prices, corporate menu, canned music ban, densely packed and numbered standard wooden tables and curry nights are present and correct, the Crosse Keys is not your average local Wetherspoon.

The building is a palatial banking hall, once the London headquarters of HSBC, with massive pillars rising towards high skylights between green and grey marble walls, and a grand staircase climbing to a balcony with Chinese-style sculptures recalling the bank's origins. The big central bar offers one of the widest beer ranges in the chain: at least 16 cask choices and sometimes the full complement of 23, with a 24th handpump reserved for cider. On a midweek afternoon, I spotted Blindmans, Burton Bridge, Lacons, Grafton, Reedley Hallows and White Horse among others, with a good mix of styles including milds and porters. There are a few more bottles and kegs than usual, including Black Sheep, Portobello and Truman's.

Visitor note. *The pub revives the name of a coaching inn that once stood on the site, adopting the emblem of St Peter after neighbouring St Peter upon Cornhill church, a Wren rebuild which claims to stand on the site of the oldest church in Britain.*

Magpie

Traditional pub
12 New Street EC2M 4TP
T (020) 7929 3889   nicholsonspubs.co.uk
🕑 *Mo-Fr* 11.30-23.00. Children welcome.
9 cask, 3 keg, 8 bottles/cans, some specialist spirits.
🍴 Enhanced pub grub **£-££**,
🎋 Standing on street, &
Functions

⇌ ⊖ Liverpool Street

In a narrow alley just off Bishopsgate and on the site of a former ambulance station, the Magpie looks ordinary as Nicholson's pubs go but is favoured both for location and for beer choice, which has dwindled rather less than in other branches. The management makes enthusiastic use of the chain's seasonal guest list: I found Five Points, Rudgate, Stewart and Wild on a recent visit, though kegs, bottles and cans are mainly from bigger brewers. There's food from Nicholson's corporate pub grub menu: fish and chips, pies, toad in the hole and the like. Unsurprisingly given its location, it's very much a City boy haunt, but even if you're the only customer not power-dressing, you'll be made welcome enough.

Magpie

Williams Ale and Cider House ㉕

Contemporary pub
22 Artillery Lane E1 7LS
T (020) 7247 5163   williamsspitalfields.com
🕐 *Mo-We* 11.00-23.00, *Th-Sa* 11.00-24.00,
  Su 12.00-22.00.
🍴 7 cask, 8 keg, 45 bottles/cans, 7 ciders/perries.
🍴 Enhanced pub grub, cooked bar snacks **££**,
🌇 Standing on street
Meet the brewer, functions

⇌ ⊖ Liverpool Street

The Williams was an ordinary Greene King pub
until September 2013, when it relaunched as
the brewery's most centrally sited venture
into the craft beer category. Besides a remarkably small number of examples of its owners'
products, you might find By the Horns, Crouch
Hill, East London, Red Squirrel or Truman's on
the cask pumps, kegs from Gipsy Hill, Lost
and Grounded and Tiny Rebel and imported
bottles and cans from Belgium's Senne and
Verzet and Ireland's White Hag. An imaginative menu ranges from 'beer tapas' like
Taiwanese fried chicken and prawn tostada to
pies, burgers, teriyaki salmon with pak choi
and Mexican salad. If the brick arches and low
ceilings in the cavernous main space seem
claustrophobic, try to claim a diner-style
booth in the side room.

Williams Ale and Cider House

TRY ALSO

Bierschenke Beer Hall 4 London Wall Buildings, Blomfield Street EC2M 5NT bierschenke.co.uk: German-managed, British-owned, oompah-infested venue with enormous basement on genuinely Bavarian scale near Liverpool Street. Eight kegs include exclusive house beers commissioned from Mullerbräu in Neuötting near Munich, Krombacher and Paulaner, with bottled Altbier and Kölsch. Closed Sunday.

Craft Beer Co St Mary Axe 29 Mitre Street EC3A 5BU thecraftbeerco.com: Smallish branch close to landmarks the Gherkin, Lloyds building and Walkie-Talkie, largely used for post-work vertical drinking. Up to seven casks, 16 kegs and around 30 bottles/cans from UK and overseas. Closed weekends.

Hydrant 1 Monument Street EC3R 8BG thehydrant.co.uk: Fuller's contemporary 'crafty' bar next to the Monument, spinning the location into a light-hearted firefighting theme. Four casks sometimes include London guests, with 11 keg lines and over 30 bottles, mainly from London and UK heavy hitters with Scandinavian and US imports.

Mahogany Bar (Wiltons Music Hall) Graces Alley E1 8JB wiltons.org.uk: Cosy bar in the unique location of one of very few surviving complete Victorian music halls, hidden in an alley off Cable Street. You don't need a show ticket to enjoy three Adnams cask beers and a dozen bottles/cans including Canopy and Kernel, though check website for times.

Pelt Trader 3 Dowgate Hill EC4N 6AP pelttrader.co.uk: Bar linked to the Euston Tap (p78) group, using a spacious arch under Cannon Street station to evoke a vaulted German Bierkeller, with a range of beers to match, plus regularly changing good stuff from UK producers across five cask and 12 keg lines. Closed weekends.

Seething Lane Tap 14 Seething Lane EC3N 4AX brewdog.com: Modern, bright former Draft House, now a BrewDog pub, in a former post office at the foot of an office block close to the Tower of London and Fenchurch Street station, with Budvar tank beer alongside a good UK and international range of up to four casks, 14 kegs and 50 bottles/cans.

HERITAGE PUBS

Blackfriar 174 Queen Victoria Street EC4V 4EG nicholsonspubs.co.uk: Opposite Blackfriars station, this extraordinary 1905 remodelling of an 1875 building is a jaw-droppingly extravagant fusion of Arts and Crafts and art nouveau, light-heartedly inspired by the former Dominican friary nearby. Glittering mosaics, layers of multicoloured marble, stained glass, beaten copper, mirrors and bas-reliefs of jolly monks are a riposte to the British reputation for reserve, particularly in the vaulted dining area. Around 10 casks and some other beers from Nicholson's range, with extensive outdoor seating.

Blackfriar

Viaduct Tavern 126 Newgate Street EC1A 7AA viaducttavern.co.uk: 1870s Flemish Renaissance corner pub on the City side of Holborn viaduct opposite the Old Bailey, remodelled in elaborate style c1900, particularly notable for three giant Pre-Raphaelite paintings in marble surrounds and a rear manager's office, though the original partitions have gone. Now a Fuller's pub with cask and keg from the regular range. Closed Sunday.

HOP HISTORIES | The second biggest room in London

Bedfordshire-born Samuel Whitbread was only 16 when in 1736 he apprenticed himself to a Clerkenwell brewer. Six years later, he went into partnership with brothers Thomas and George Shewell at the Goat brewhouse in Old Street, at its junction with Whitecross Street. At first, they brewed porter here and ales at a brewhouse on the other side of Old Street in what's now Central Street. But it was porter that everyone wanted, prompting Whitbread to create, in partnership with Thomas Shewell, what was likely the world's first purpose-built porter brewery, a complete rebuild and expansion of a brewhouse called the Kings Head on Chiswell Street, a short walk south on the edge of the City.

Opened in 1750, the Chiswell Street brewery was by 1758 the biggest porter producer in Britain, with an output of 64,600 barrels (105,700hl) a year. By Whitbread's death in 1796, it was turning out 200,000 barrels (327,300hl). The famous Porter Tun Room was built between 1776-84, after fire destroyed its predecessor, at a scale sufficient to house the increasingly large vats used for maturing the beer. With a floor area of 778 square metres and the exposed timbers of a king-post roof over 18m above, it had the widest unsupported timber span in London after Westminster Hall. Even more remarkable were the vaults below, conceived by Whitbread as a more efficient and oxygen-proof alternative to the tuns: vast water-tight cisterns lined with a special cement capable of resisting the beer's acidity, applied by ship's caulkers, with a total capacity of 12,000 barrels (19,650hl or almost 3.4 million pints).

Inevitably tastes moved on and Whitbread diversified into other styles of beer. The last of the famous tuns was removed in 1900, though porter production, now by different methods and at declining strengths, continued into the 1950s. It was around this time that the brewery launched the so-called 'Whitbread Umbrella' in response to the wave of mergers then sweeping the industry, buying shares in smaller regional breweries and obtaining favourable trading agreements on the promise of protecting them from hostile takeover. The umbrella failed to shield them from Whitbread itself, as by the early 1970s, most of these regionals had been absorbed. The City brewer became a major national presence with an estate of around almost 8,000 pubs and a portfolio of nationally-marketed brands, including European lager brands brewed under licence in the UK, like Heineken and Stella Artois.

Brewing ceased at Chiswell Street in 1976, though the building continued in use as the corporate headquarters until 2005. By then, Whitbread had already sold its brewing interests to Stella brewer Interbrew in Belgium so it could concentrate on being a 'branded leisure retailer', operating among others the Premier Inn hotel chain. Interbrew is now part of the world's biggest brewing group, Anheuser Busch InBev. The brewery still stands, now converted into the luxury Montcalm hotel and the Brewery conference and events venue (52 Chiswell Street EC1Y 4SD). You can step inside the yard to admire the clock and other features. Whitbread tap the St Pauls Tavern is now a restaurant, the Chiswell Street Dining Rooms, but the Porter Tun Room still has one of the biggest uninterrupted roof spans in London.

Clerkenwell and Farringdon

Craft Beer Co **26**
Clerkenwell
Contemporary pub
82 Leather Lane EC1N 7TR
T (020) 7404 7049   **thecraftbeerco.com**
🕐 *Mo–Sa* 12.00–23.00. Children until 19.00.
8–12 cask, 19 keg, 90 bottles/cans, cider/perry, specialist spirits.
🍴 Pies, scotch eggs, snacks **£,**
🪑 Standing on street
Occasional meet the brewer, tap takeovers, tutored tastings, functions and private hire (Su)

≋ Farringdon   ⊖ Chancery Lane, Farringdon
🚌 Rosebery Avenue   🚲 Link to C6

This set the template for all the other Craft Beer Cos when it opened in June 2011: a previously failing pub spruced up and packed with a dazzling range of beer. It may no longer hold the record for the most draught lines in London but is still well worth a visit.' Though there are fewer handpumps in operation these days, cask remains a core feature, with house beers from Kent brewery, regular visits from Siren and Wylam and rotating features for breweries outside the capital rarely seen inside it, like Brewsmith and McColl's. Kegs include a regular Kernel line and some imports, often encompassing strong and unusual stuff: when draught Alesmith Speedway Stout from San Diego (12%) hit the taps in 2018, the press named it 'the most expensive pint in London'. Alesmith is more regularly found in the bottle fridges, alongside other US treats from Mystic and Prairie, lambics from 3 Fonteinen and Hanssens and contemporary Brits like Polly and Neptune. It's worth seeking advice from informed bar staff as not everything is on the list. Food is limited but like the beer is impeccably sourced.

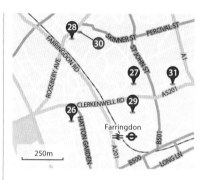

Visitor note. *The name of Leather Lane, the market where the pub stands, is derived from Le Vrunelane, a local merchant who obtained a market charter from a cash-strapped Charles II in lieu of payment for two horses. The first pub built on the site, around 1785, was called the Coach and Horses, later the Clock House. The current 1890s building preserves a few heritage elements: the wooden ceilings are original, but their mirror finishes are not.*

Dovetail **27**
Bar
9 Jerusalem Passage EC1V 4JP
T (020) 7490 7321   **dovepubs.com**
🕐 *Mo–Sa* 12.00–23.00. Children until 19.00.
14 keg, 100+ bottles.
🍴 Belgian bistro and British pub grub **££,**
🪑 A few tables on alley, ♿
Monthly tastings and quizzes

≋ ⊖ Farringdon   🚲 Link to CS6   🚶 Clerkenwell Historic Trail

The appealing little sister of the Dove in Hackney (p133) concentrates on Belgian beers: the smart pewter and marble bar counter is a rare outlet for draught Duchesse de Bourgogne, De Koninck and Westmalle Dubbel alongside Chimay Triple, Blanche de Bruxelles and a changing guest. A comprehensive Trappist selection, with the Netherlands' La Trappe and

Dovetail

the UK's Tynt Meadow joining the Belgians, leads a strong bottled list that stretches to Boon Mariage Parfait, Saison Dupont, Rodenbach Vintage, the odd younger name like Verzet and perhaps a few too many sweet and fruity options. Food has less of a Belgian twist but still includes mussels alongside 'the best vegan "fish" and chips in London'. Poster-sized reproductions of the covers of Hergé's Tintin graphic novels complete an attractive picture.

Visitor note. The name of this pretty alleyway just off Clerkenwell Green recalls the city where the order of St John was founded, and the building's foundations allegedly include stones brought back from Palestine.

Exmouth Arms

Contemporary pub (Barworks)
23 Exmouth Market EC1R 4QL
T (020) 3551 4772 exmoutharms.com
🕐 Mo-Th 11.00-24.00, Fr-Sa 11.00-01.30, Su 11.00-22.30. Children until 21.00.
2-3 cask, 13 keg, 80 bottles/cans, 1 cider, cocktails, mezcal, whiskies.
🍴 Burgers, hot sandwiches, cooked bar snacks **££**, 🪑 Tables on street, ♿ Functions

🚲🚇 Farringdon 🚌 Mount Pleasant 🚲 Link to CS6
🚶 Clerkenwell Historic Trail, link to New River Path

Incredibly, for many years the exquisite green Courage tiling on this corner pub with a sunny terrace on trendy Exmouth Market was hidden behind black cladding, until its glory was restored in a thorough 2011 refurbishment. Inside, dark green and maroon décor, simple

wooden furniture, bare brick and diner-style booths create a pleasant ambience, enlivened by some truly bizarre art. Cask beers are often sourced outside London, from the likes of Saltaire or Revolutions, and regularly include a traditional bitter. Elsewhere there are beers from excellent UK breweries like Burning Sky, Burnt Mill and Partizan, unusual Americans like Duck Rabbit and Uncommon and options from Belgium, Canada and Catalunya. An imaginative menu might include chargrilled chicken breast, spiced Neapolitan sausages and vegan green curry, with interesting cooked bar snacks.

Visitor note. Unexpectedly, the street took its name from the pub, already established when the market started in the 1890s.

Jerusalem Tavern 29

Traditional pub
55 Britton Street EC1M 5UQ
T (020) 7490 4281
stpetersbrewery.co.uk/london-pub
🕐 Mo-Fr 12.00-23.00. Children until 17.00.
4 cask, 7 keg, 22 bottles, minicasks, 2 ciders, some specialist spirits.
🍴 Home-cooked lunches, sandwiches, reduced evening menu (We-Fr) **£-££**,
🪑 Benches on street
Private hire (Sa-Su)

🚲🚇 Farringdon 🚲 Link to C6 🚶 Clerkenwell Historic Trail

This small and homely but hugely popular place has been the London outlet for Suffolk's St Peter's brewery since 1996. You'll need to time your visit carefully to be sure of grabbing one of the few tables in cubby holes or on a curious elevated platform in an interior that nods to 18th-century tavern style. Between the air pressure cask lines emerging through fake barrel heads behind the bar, the keg fonts and a good stock of the distinctively shaped bottles, there's comprehensive coverage of the owner's wide range of beers, from lagers and best bitter to cream stout and barrel-aged options. A seasonally changing menu might feature Cobb salad with bacon and chicken breast, ham egg and chips or lunchtime hot sandwiches and Ploughmans with bread from St John.

Visitor note. The original Jerusalem Tavern stood adjacent to the gateway of St John's Priory on Clerkenwell Green. This incarnation is in a building dating from 1720 that was once used as a coffee house but has also served as a watchmaker's. The glass partition that separated the shop from the workshop still stands, creating a small front drinking area decorated with tiles that are careful reproductions of examples uncovered during renovation.

Mikkeller Brewpub London

Brewpub, bar
37 Exmouth Market EC1R 4QL (Islington)
T (020) 3940 4991
mikkellerbrewpublondon.com
First sold beer: July 2020 🍺🍺
🕐 *Tu-Th* 12.00-22.30, *Fr-Sa* 12.00-23.30, *Su* 12.00-22.00. Children until 19.00. Cash-free.
7 tank, 12+ keg, 50 bottles/cans, growlers.
🍴 Nordic-influenced pub grub **£-££**,
🪑 Tables on street, ♿
DJs at weekends

🚅🚇 Farringdon   🚌 Mount Pleasant   🚲 Link to C6
🚶 Clerkenwell Historic Trail, link to New River Path

Danish nomad brewery Mikkeller opened its second London venue as a popup in a former menswear shop on the same street as the Exmouth Arms (above) in October 2019, converting it into a brewpub in 2020, with a bespoke 7.5hl brewhouse from Premier Stainless in San Diego in pride of place at the rear and fermenters downstairs. Up to half the draughts are house brews, supplemented by beers from elsewhere in the Mikkeller empire and UK and international guests in numerous styles and strengths, usually including an unblended lambic. Over half the bottle and can list falls into the 'Sour and funky' category, including contributions from UK producers like London Beer Factory and Pastore and Belgian classics. Scandinavian influences are evident in the smart but simple wood finishes and post-industrial piping of an interior with plenty of natural light, and in a short menu which could feature *pølse* hot dogs (including a vegan version), *smørrebrød* with gravadlax salmon, aubergine hummus and steaks.

BEERS are sold in-house from tank and sometimes kegged for export to Mikkeller outlets elsewhere. Brewers have autonomy to develop their own recipes, mainly producing rotating specials in a wide range of styles, though some recur more frequently than others, including summer ale **Sunsphere*** (4.3%) and hazy, juicy pale **Democracy Manifest** (5.6%). Following the success of dry stout **Can't Say No 2 U** (4.6%) in 2021, they're considering a regular beer for the nitrokeg line.

Sutton Arms

Traditional pub
16 Great Sutton Street EC1V 0DH
T (020) 7253 2462   **suttonarms.co.uk**
🕐 *Mo-Fr* 11.00-23.00. Children only when food served.
3 cask, 7 keg, 14 bottles/cans.
🍴 Imaginative pub grub *(Tu-Th)* **£-££**,
🪑 Front terrace
Tap takeovers, food pairing, functions

🚅 Farringdon   🚇 Barbican, Farringdon

This handsome and immaculately kept corner pub in a Clerkenwell backstreet has been a free house since 1991 under the guiding hand of licensee Mick. His son Jack was born in the building and has recently been instrumental in expanding the beer range. Besides some of the best cask Harvey's in London, you might find guests from Fierce, Moor, Redemption, Summer Wine or even Cloudwater on the handpumps, plus kegs, bottles and cans from the likes of Beatnikz Republic, Bohem, Burnt Mill, Siren and others with similar reputations, always covering a mix of styles. Food, not available every night, might include brie and beetroot tart or harissa lamb kebab alongside more familiar pub grub like burgers and scampi. With its carpets and old-school welcome, this is a rare combination of beer showcase and proper pub.

Visitor note. The name honours Thomas Sutton, who in 1611 turned the extensive former abbey and palace of Charterhouse nearby into a school (since moved) and almshouses.

BrewDog Clerkenwell 45 Clerkenwell Road EC1M 5RS brewdog.com/bars: Split-level bar close to Clerkenwell Green, one of London's smaller BrewDogs though with notably friendly staff. 18 keg, around 50 bottles/cans. Closed Sunday.

Farringdon Tap 41 Farringdon Street EC4A 4AN farringdontap.com: Opened early in 2020 in one of the imposing buildings housing the Holborn Viaduct stairwells as an unusually expansive branch of the 'Tap' chain (Euston Tap p78). Four cask and 16 keg of customary variety and interest, plus a gyoza kitchen.

Look Mum No Hands 49 Old Street EC1V 9HX lookmumnohands.com: Lively cyclists' café with verdant side terrace that's long sold decent beer alongside the coffee and smashed avocado. A well-advised choice of five kegs and 15+ bottles/cans mainly from UK producers. Check website for outdoor summer popups in alluring locations.

Smithfield Market Arms 55 Charterhouse Street EC1M 6HA brewdog.com: More of a party animal than some BrewDog pubs, and stocking fewer beers: up to three casks, 14 keg lines and 20 bottles/cans, sourced from London, the UK and internationally. Opposite Smithfield Market. Closed Sunday.

St John 26 St John Street EC1M 4AY stjohnrestaurant.com: Not-for-the-squeamish culinary institution serving good beer as well as wine with food since opening in 1994: currently three cask and three keg from well-chosen London and UK indie producers in both the airy bar and adjoining Michelin-starred restaurant.

LONDON DRINKERS Melissa Cole

Award-winning beer and food writer, beer educator and busy international beer judge Melissa has recently published her fourth book, *The Little Book of Lager*. She's lived in London for 20 years and has deeper connections with the city through her grandparents, 'proper Bow Bells Cockneys who were evacuated during the war but always brought me and my sister into town for visits'. Find her on Twitter @melissacole or Facebook and Instagram @melissacolebeer.

How do you rate London as a beer city, on a world scale?
I might be biased but I think it's right up there as one of the finest beer cities in the world, not only because of its world class brewers but because so many brewery taprooms are accessible via public transport, so often not the case in other places.

What's the single most exciting thing about beer in London right now?
Its wide availability. It's harder to find a place that doesn't do at least one decent beer. The canning revolution has made it easier for places like music venues and theatres to stock good choices, and with the growth of casual dining, there's better beer at good places to eat too.

What single thing would make things even better?
Better training for bar staff. There's a particular paucity of cask ale knowledge, which is deeply depressing as it's our national drink and we should be proud of it.

What are your top London beers right now?
Mondo ALL CAPS, Brick's sour beers, Gipsy Hill Carver, Fuller's London Porter, Fourpure Shapeshifter, Five Points Best Bitter, Orbit Tzatziki Sour, Wild Card Passionfruit Gose.

What's your top great beer night out?
Hanging out at the Rake (p86). There's always someone there I know, and you never know where the day or night will take you, but the beer will always be smashing.

Who's your London beer hero?
John Hatch at the Ram (Sambrook's p274): he really is the patron saint of London brewing and should be knighted for his services to the industry. He was recently acknowledged by the *Brewer's Journal* for his efforts and I'm not sure who was crying more, me or him.

Who will we be hearing a lot more from in future?
There's no doubt those that now have the might of big beer behind them will be making further waves. Otherwise it's hard to pick just one, though Gipsy Hill has been on an excellent trajectory of growth and improvement for quite some time.

Which are your other top beer cities?
Denver, though Leeds and Manchester vie for my affections within the UK, with Manchester just shading it. I have to say that because my mother-in-law wouldn't forgive me for choosing a Yorkshire town!

Holborn and Covent Garden

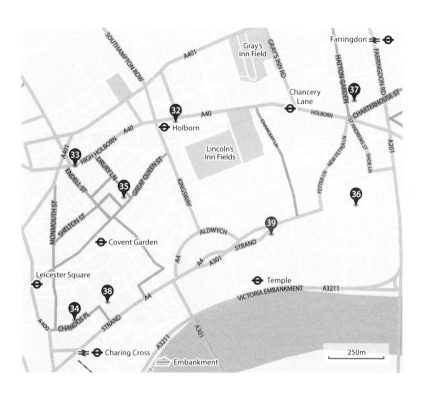

Bar Polski 32

Bar

11 Little Turnstile WC1V 7DX

T (020) 7831 9679 **barpolski.com**

🕐 *Mo* 16.00-23.00, *Tu-Fr* 12.30-23.00, *Sa* 18.00-23.00. Children welcome.

2 keg, 16 bottles/cans, Polish wodka and mead.

🍴 Polish pub grub **£-££**, 🪑 Table at front

🚇 Holborn 🚲 Link to Q1 🚶 Jubilee Walkway

This tiny café and drinking den in an alleyway behind Holborn station has been giving Polish expats a taste of home since 1998. It's long offered one or two more unusual imports besides the mainstream lagers like Lech, Tyskie and Żubr, earning it a 'Try also' mention in the last edition, and these have now expanded further. Bottles include Perła Miodowa honey lager, Tyskie's Vienna lager Książęce Czerwon and several specialist styles from Amber in Bielkówko. Polish cider, mead and of course plenty of wodka add further options for washing down national comfort food like *bigos* stew, *pierogi* dumplings, *gulasz* with potato pancakes and *śledź* herring with sour cream. It's a basic place enlivened by folk art murals with a warm welcome for all, Polish or otherwise.

Craft Beer Co
Covent Garden 33

Bar

168 High Holborn WC1V 7AA

T (020) 7240 0431   thecraftbeerco.com

🕐 *Su-We* 12.00-24.00, *Th-Sa* 12.00-01.00.
  Children until 18.00.

13 cask, 28 keg, 40+ bottles/cans, 2 ciders, whiskies, some gins and other specialist spirits.

🍴 Pork pies, snacks, BYO **£**, 🪑 Standing on street

Beer launches, themed beer events

⊖ Tottenham Court Road   🚲 Link to Q1
🚶 Link to Jubilee Walkway

Opened in May 2014, this is the most favourably located Craft Beer Co branch, in a prime position on the edge of Theatreland and Covent Garden, opposite the Shaftesbury Theatre and next door to the Oasis swimming pool. Though not the biggest in terms of floorspace, it boasts the widest range, ably curated by helpful staff. Besides the house bitter from Kent Brewery, casks from suppliers like Marble, Northern Monk, Roosters and Siren are featured, often with several beers from the same source. Kegs draw on imports (Alesmith, Cascade, Evil Twin) and UK producers, with Londoners like Kernel, Weird Beard and Wild Card often in evidence, stretching to at least two strong stouts. The bottled range has several good lambics and US imports from Hoppin' Frog and Westbrook besides UK options. Smartly turned out with wood finishes and gleaming pipe work, it's inevitably popular, though there's relief from the narrow ground floor bar in a more spacious, if windowless, basement in crimson and dark wood.

Essex Street Brewing
See Temple Brew House

Craft Beer Co Covent Garden

Harp   (34)

Traditional pub

47 Chandos Place WC2N 4HS

T (020) 7836 0291   harpcoventgarden.com

Mo-Th 10.30-23.30, Fr-Sa 10.30-24.00,
Su 12.00-22.30.

9 cask, 4 keg, 2 bottles, 4-6 ciders/perries, malts.
Sausage baps **£**, Standing at front and on rear alleyway

Functions

Charing Cross   Charing Cross, Leicester Square
Embankment   Link to CS3   Links to Jubilee Walkway, Thames Path

Built as the Welsh Harp in the 1830s, this longstanding real ale pub, still the only London venue to win CAMRA's National Pub of the Year, remains a magnet for beer lovers, though it's been in the hands of Fuller's since legendary licensee Binnie Walsh retired in 2014. Besides Dark Star Hophead, London Pride and Harvey's Best, expect a changing well-chosen selection of guest casks in flawless condition, including milds and stouts, from brewers like Bexley, Burning Sky, Hammerton, Oakham, Sambrook's, Siren and several from the north of England. An expanded range of mainly London kegs could include Gipsy Hill, Kernel and One Mile End, while the only hot food options are the much-admired sausage baps.

The smallish main bar with its chandeliers, mirrors and faded period portraits is often crowded, though there are usually seats in the elegant upstairs lounge. In an ideal location a minute or so from Leicester and Trafalgar Squares, Charing Cross station and Covent Garden market, such a fine pub is a rare find.

Lowlander Grand Café   (35)

Bar, restaurant

36 Drury Lane WC2B 5RR

T (020) 7379 7446   lowlander.com

Mo-Th 10.00-23.00, Fr-Sa 10.00-23.30,
Su 10.00-22.30. Children welcome.

15 keg, 250+ bottles/cans. .
Belgian and modern European **££**,
Standing on street

Tutored tastings for groups, beer launches, tap takeovers, major big screen sport, functions

Covent Garden   Q1   Jubilee Walkway

Opened in 2001 within sight of art deco Freemason's Hall, this place styles itself a grand café in the Belgian tradition. But though it's grand enough on welcome and enthusiasm, its dimensions are rather less so: best to visit off-peak if you want a premium seat on the little upstairs balcony or the big ground floor tables. A broad choice of Trappists includes aged Orval, with secular Belgians like Ellezelloise, De Koninck, Rodenbach, Troubadour and lambic from Boon, Cantillon, Hanssens and Tilquin. But the range broadens to encompass UK suppliers like Cloudwater, Gipsy Hill, Northern Monk or Lervig from Norway. Tasting paddles are offered, and manager Richard has various unlisted 'cellar secrets' stashed away so it's worth asking if you're looking to treat yourself. Food includes Belgian staples like mussels and *stoofvlees*, with veggie options like pumpkin gnocchi and sharing boards. All but the breakfasts listed with beer suggestions.

Olde Cheshire Cheese

Traditional pub
Wine Office Court, 145 Fleet Street EC4A 2BU
T (020) 7353 6170 **samuelsmithsbrewery.co.uk**
🕐 *Mo-Su* 12.00-23.00. Children welcome
except in ground floor bar.
1 cask, 7 keg, 12 bottles.
🍴 Pub grub and 'chop house' food **££-£££**,
🪑 Adjacent small public square
Functions

🚉 City Thameslink   🚇🚢 Blackfriars   🚲 Link to C6, CS3
🚶 Jubilee Walkway, link to Thames Path

Hidden down a gloomy alley off Fleet Street, this is one of London's few genuinely old pubs and one of the best places in the capital to sample the wares of Yorkshire brewer Samuel Smith. The single cask ale, Old Brewery Bitter, is well-kept and the brewery's wider beer range is present and correct, with keg wheat beer and organic lager and bottles including tastier stuff like Oatmeal Stout, Taddy Porter and Yorkshire Stingo. The old-school English menu is good value considering the pub is a fixture on the tourist trail: two elderly regulars enthusiastically sang the praises of the pies when I last called.

Visitor note. Though no-one can prove Samuel Johnson, who lived around the corner, ever drunk here, there's still much of historical interest, with parts of the building dating from the decades immediately following the Great Fire of 1666. The Chop Room at the front on the left, usually reserved for diners, recreates an 18th-century tavern, with some antique furniture. The small room opposite is the most characterful, preserving original wooden panelling, an impressive fireplace and a Victorian bar. Thankfully the house rule written up over the door, 'Gentlemen only served', is no longer enforced. The pub was extended in the 1990s and there's a warren of other rooms to explore, including the extensive cellar bar, where some of the vaulting is said to survive from a 13th-century Carmelite monastery.

Olde Mitre

Traditional pub
1 Ely Court EC1N 6SJ
T (020) 7405 4751 **yeoldemitreholborn.co.uk**
🕐 *Mo-Fr* 11.00-23.00. Over-11s until 19.00.
7 cask, 1 keg, 10 bottles/cans, 1 cider, whiskies.
🍴 Toasties, pies, snacks **£**, 🪑 Courtyard at side
Beer festivals, meet the brewer, functions

🚉 Farringdon   🚇 Chancery Lane   🚲 Link to C6

Look for the old-fashioned lamp standard at the south end of Hatton Garden to locate the tiny alley that leads to this photogenic gem, its three small rooms untroubled by piped music and machines. It's now a Fuller's house but managers have been keen to preserve its beer credentials, with guest casks that might be from Beerblefish, Three Sods, Wimbledon and Windsor & Eton alongside the Dark Star, Fuller's and Gale's brands. The choice extends further at the annual mini-festival coinciding with the Great British Beer Festival in August, the only weekend in the year the pub opens. At least one beer is regularly dispensed from a wooden cask, to the delight of the Society for the Protection of Beers from the Wood, which regularly meets here. A short menu featuring toasties, pies and scotch eggs hasn't changed since the 1970s, except for the prices of course.

Visitor note. Though the pub claims to date from 1546, its appearance today is a combination of a 1757 rebuild, a 1781 extension and a Tudor-style interior from around 1930. The lump of wood behind glass near the front entrance is from a cherry tree which once marked the boundary between Elizabethan politician Christopher Hatton's back garden and the precincts of the Bishop of Ely's palace: the pub was originally built within the latter for the benefit of palace staff. Some sources claim it's really in Cambridgeshire, which is clearly nonsense, though the diocese long denied London's authority over its property and the licence was issued in the county until the 1950s.

Olde Mitre

Porterhouse

Contemporary pub
21 Maiden Lane WC2E 7NA

T (020) 7379 7917   **porterhouse.london**

🕐 *Su-Th* 12.00-23.00, *Fr* 12.00-23.30,
  Sa 12.00-24.00. Over-21s only.

4 cask, 15 keg, 90+ bottles/cans, 150 whiskies, cocktails. 🍺.

🍴 Burgers, pizza, pub grub **££**, 🎏 Front patio, ♿
*Jazz (Mo), live music (Th-Sa and some We), big screen
rugby and Irish sport, functions*

🚆 Charing Cross   ⊖ Covent Garden   ⛴ Embankment
🚲 Link to CS3, Q1   🚶 Link to Jubilee Walkway

This brash and busy 'superpub' in a converted
warehouse has been operating since the dawn
of the millennium as the English outpost of
one of Ireland's most persistently successful
microbrewers, based in Dublin. The orange-lit
and labyrinthine multi-level interior is decked
out in spaceship-like post-industrial tubing
with a massive beer bottle collection
displayed on every spare surface, and it's
often heaving despite the size. Porterhouse's
own beers, from traditional stouts and red ale
to modern IPAs and strong ale An Brainblásta
account for most of the keg taps, with casks
from brewers like London Beer Factory, Purity
and Sambrook's and an improving bottle and
can list that includes newer Irish brewer White
Hag, UK stars like Titanic and Wild and even
some rare Mexican craft brews. Food is pizza,
burgers, mussels, steaks, fry-ups and salads.

Temple Brew House
(Essex Street Brewing)

Brewery, suspended brewpub
46 Essex Street WC2R 3JF (Westminster)
templebrewhouse.com/brewery
First sold beer: December 2014

⊖ Temple   🚲 Link to CS3   🚶 Link to Jubilee Walkway,
Thames Path

The City Pub Co already had brewpubs in Bath
and Cambridge when it added this London
branch near the Temple late in 2014. An 8hl kit
squeezed into a stairwell turned it into London's
most central brewery, with longstanding head
brewer Vanesa de Blas a keen participant in
London's brewing scene. The pub closed and

brewing ceased with the first lockdown in 2020:
it hadn't reopened at the time of going to press
and is likely to be used as a private hire venue
for the time being. But brewing should have
resumed by the time you read this, supplying
other pubs in the group.

BEERS in keg and cask, many of them gluten-
free, are sold throughout the City Pub Co
chain. Among the regulars are cask **Golden
Ale** (4%) and US-style bitterish **MAC Pale
Ale** (4.5%). Numerous collaborations have
included one with Toast Ale.

TRY ALSO

BrewDog Seven Dials 142 Shaftesbury
Avenue WC2H 8HJ **brewdog.com**: Big and
bustling BrewDog branch in the former
Marquis of Granby right on Cambridge Circus,
spreading onto three floors with 21 keg lines,
65 bottles/cans and the regular burgers and
wings menu.

Edgar Wallace 40 Essex Street WC2R 3JF.
Tucked away traditional corner pub popular
with local lawyers, long noted for well-kept
cask (5+, usually more traditional styles from
well-established independents), vintage ads
for decoration and a huge collection of Edgar
Wallace books and memorabilia upstairs.
Closed weekends, over-18s only.

HERITAGE PUBS

Cittie of Yorke 22 High Holborn WC1V 6BS
samuelsmithsbrewery.co.uk: Spectacular,
interwar, Tudorbethan theme pub near
Chancery Lane Tube, built in 1924 despite what
the notices say, with a lofty open half-timbered
ceiling, huge vats teetering precariously above
the bar, a Gothic-style stove and elaborate
carved booths along one side. Formerly the
Henekeys Long Bar, now a Samuel Smith with
variable beer quality.

Princess Louise 208 High Holborn WC1V 7BW
samuelsmithsbrewery.co.uk: Stunningly
elaborate 1891 interior in an 1872 building close
to Holborn Tube: mosaic tiles, mirrors, carved
wood, glass and moulded ceilings, subdivided
by timber and glass screens restored by
current owner Samuel Smith in 2008, plus the
second most sumptuous gents' pub toilets in

Princess Louise

the country. Similar beer range to the Olde Cheshire Cheese (above).

Salisbury 90 St Martins Lane WC2N 4AP **greeneking-pubs.co.uk**: Flamboyant and slightly camp 1899 confection of engraved mirrors, marble and polished brass surfaces, textured ceilings, pilaster-framed entrances and candelabras in human shape. Featuring in groundbreaking 1961 film *Victim*, it was a gay-friendly 'theatrical' pub from Oscar Wilde's day to the early 1990s when the then-management took a homophobic turn. Now a city centre Greene King house with a few better-known casks.

LONDON DRINKERS | Geoff Strawbridge

Geoff acquired a taste for Young's soon after moving to London in 1971. Based in Raynes Park, he's been active in CAMRA since the mid-1970s, taking on regional volunteer roles since the 1990s, including London regional director. 'I welcome the opening of so many new London breweries,' he says, 'but regret the closure of so many pubs that might have sold their beers.'

How do you rate London as a beer city, on a world scale?
London must be one of the best capital cities for beer, given the range of styles on offer, the quality of which many pubs can be proud and very reasonable pricing by some operators.

What's the single most exciting thing about beer in London right now?
The sour beers several London brewers have proved so capable of producing. They used to be a continental speciality, but not anymore.

What single thing would make things even better?
More local beers in local pubs. I can't see the consumer benefits of the ties operated by the property companies who own so many pubs and it seems wrong to me that such restrictive practices are still exempt from competition law.

What are your top London beers right now?
By the Horns Hopadelic, Wimbledon SW19 and Five Points Railway Porter, with some from Sambrook's and Twickenham also 'must-tries'. Wild Card's Lime Berliner Weisse and Brick's Winter Berry Sour were something else!

What's your top great beer night out?
Comedy night at the Railway

(2 Greyhound Lane SW16 5SD), with four or five London beers on handpump and many more available elsehow.

Who's your London beer hero?
Derek Prentice, our Olympian, advancing the state of the brewer's art over 51 years at Truman's, Young's, Fuller's and Wimbledon. A worthy winner of CAMRA's John Young Memorial Award in 2018.

Who will we be hearing a lot more from in future?
Jaega Wise at Wild Card, and Alex Leclere at SlyBeast, formerly at Partizan and Sambrook's.

Which are your other top beer cities?
I ought to get out more, but I could happily spend time drinking beer in Bristol, Derby, Nottingham, Sheffield or Kraków.

Shoreditch and Hoxton

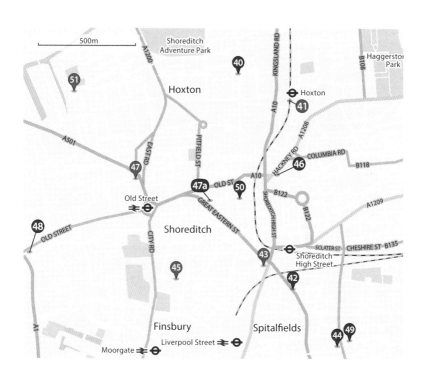

500m

Shoreditch Adventure Park

40

Hoxton

Haggersto Park

B108

KINGSLAND RD

A1200

A501

EAST RD

PITFIELD ST

A10

Hoxton **41**

A1208

HACKNEY RD

COLUMBIA RD

B118

46

A1209

47

47a OLD ST

A10

B122

Old Street

50

GREAT EASTERN ST

SHOREDITCH HIGH ST

B122

Shoreditch

CITY RD

OLD STREET **48**

45

43

SLATER ST CHESHIRE ST B135

Shoreditch High Street

42

A1

Finsbury

Liverpool Street

Spitalfields

44 **49**

Moorgate

---

7 Seasons **40**

Shop, bar

195 Hoxton Street N1 6RA

T (020) 7033 4560   sevenseasons.co.uk

Tu-We 12.00-21.00, Th-Sa 12.00-22.00,
Su 12.00-20.00. Children welcome.

2 keg, 350 bottles/cans, growlers, some
natural wines, ciders, mead.

Please check **££**, Tables on street

Tastings, beer launches, food pairing, board games

Hoxton   Geffrye Museum   Link to C51

This off-licence on historic Hoxton Market
upped its beer game by several notches when
brothers-in-law Tom Partridge and Matt Beard
took over in August 2018. A 'one case at a time'

ordering policy ensures rapid stock rotation
while café-style tables decorated with pot
plants encourage lingering. Beers include more
traditional British styles from Westerham
and Wye Valley besides newer arrivals like
Anspach & Hobday, Deya, Kernel, Pomona
Island, 6°North, Solvay Society, Track and
Weird Beard. Hoppy stuff is limited to Brits
and other Europeans for maximum freshness,
with US imports mainly comprising sours and
wild and mixed fermentation beers, shelved
alongside classic lambics: check Untappd for
the current list. One of the owners is a chef
who plans to expand substantially on the
food offer. A great example of its type,
combining thoughtful personal choice
with a hospitable welcome.

Block Brewery
See Wenlock Arms

Brewhouse and Kitchen Hoxton   ④①
Brewpub, bar
397 Geffrye Street E2 8HZ (Hackney)
T (020) 3861 8920 brewhouseandkitchen.com
First sold beer: December 2018, 🍴
🕐 *Su-Th* 11.00-23.00, *Fr-Sa* 11.00-23.30.
  Children welcome.
4 cask, 17 keg, 40 bottles/cans, minikegs,
  some wines and specialist spirits. 🍷
🍴 Sandwiches, enhanced pub grub **££**,
🪑 Front terrace, ♿
*Brewing sessions, tastings, meet the brewer,
seasonal beer launches, food matching, quiz (Tu),
live music, functions*

⊖ Hoxton

The most recent London branch of this now-extensive brewpub chain opened in June 2018 in a former cocktail bar under the London Overground right next to Hoxton station. Staff are friendly and helpful and the space itself is pleasant, with copper and wood breaking up the bare brick of three arches: one mainly for drinking, another for eating, and a third containing the 4hl copper kit, added a few months after opening. Food, drink and activities are broadly in line with other branches (see Islington p77).

BEERS in cask, keg and minikeg are site-specific within a common template, as at other branches. Regulars include US-style **Pennsylvania Pale** (4.8%).

Commercial Tavern   ④②
Contemporary pub
142 Commercial Street E1 6NU
T (020) 3137 9736   commercial-tavern.com
🕐 *Mo-Sa* 12.00-23.00, *Su* 12.00-22.30.
  Children welcome.
3-4 cask, 9 keg, 65 bottles/cans, some
  specialist spirits and cocktails.
🍴 Pizza, salads **£-££**, 🪑 Benches on street, ♿
Tap takeovers, functions

⊖ Shoreditch High Street

This landmark East End boozer close to both Brick Lane and Spitalfields markets is a jewel in the portfolio of owner Barworks, who bought the freehold in 2016 after selling its stake in Camden Town brewery. Locals Three Sods might join Harbour, Hawkshead or Roosters on the cask pumps, with guests like Kirkstall and Mikkeller on keg and a varied range of bottles and cans encompassing Londoners like Partizan and Pressure Drop, Europeans like Basqueland, Götlands and Rodenbach and imports from further afield like Australia's Nomad. Pizzas are topped with interesting combinations like aubergine and goat cheese or Italian fennel sausage. The interior is a curious mix of distressed post-modernism and Victoriana, dotted with angels' wings and painted cuckoo clocks, with a delightful upstairs room lit by large arched windows.

Visitor note. *The Grade II-listed 1865 building with its elaborate round-ended stucco façade claims once to have been home to 'elephant man' Joseph Merrick (1862-90).*

Fountain Tap
See Old Fountain

Goose Island Brewpub   ④③
Brewpub, bar (AB InBev)
221 Shoreditch High Street E1 6PJ (Hackney)
T (020) 3657 6555
gooseislandshoreditch.com
First sold beer: November 2018, 🍴
🕐 *Mo-Tu* 12.00-23.00, *We-Th* 12.00-24.00,
  Fr-Sa 12.00-00.30, *Su* 12.00-22.30.
  Children until early evening.
2 cask, 1 barrel-aged, 2 tank, 16 keg,
  60 bottles/cans.
🍴 Burgers **££**, 🪑 A few benches on street, ♿
*Beer launches, seasonal events, running club,
major big screen sport, functions*

⊖ Shoreditch High Street

Chicago brewery Goose Island, founded in 1988 and part of AB InBev since 2011, opened its first European brewpub in November 2018 in a former restaurant and cocktail bar on busy Shoreditch High Street. The long, narrow bar, its bare brick and black and white tiling inspired by the US original, stretches back to a brewhouse behind glass, a high-spec German-style 5hl installation. There's even a water filtration system and a grist mill, rare in a London brewery this size. The commitment to wood ageing is demonstrated by the only Rack Aeriale line in the UK, a nitrogen-based system developed by Dogfish Head brewery in Delaware allowing dispense direct from a refill barrel. As well as own brews, there are numerous imports otherwise hard to find, including the famous Bourbon County and other bottled specials, plus the likes of Harvey's and Siren joining house casks and guest kegs from UK independents. Guest chefs at the time of writing specialise in hand-pressed burgers and croquettes. There's very little to give away that this is a branch of the world's biggest brewer.

BEERS are currently only sold in the pub in tank, keg and from wooden barrels. Regulars include **Shoreditch Porter*** (5.1%), with numerous specials including a recurring **Imperial Stout*** (8.8%) and barrel-aged barley wine and Flemish red. Other Goose Island brands are imported from the US.

Kill the Cat

Shop, bar
43 Brick Lane E1 6PU
T (020) 3105 8194   killthecat.co.uk
Tu 16.00-22.00, We 12.00-22.00, Th-Sa 12.00-23.00, Su 12.00-21.00. Children welcome.
3 keg, 160 bottles/cans, growlers.
BYO
Beer festival, meet the brewer, tastings, beer launches

Aldgate East   Link to CS2

This little place among the Bangladeshi restaurants a little south along Brick Lane from the old Truman brewery is packed with a fascinating range of beer. Kegs, usually including a sour option, could be from UK outfits like Left Handed Giant, Neptune or Vibrant Forest, or imports from New Zealand. Londoners like Brick and Solvay Society line up in the fridges alongside Ale Apothecary and Jolly Pumpkin from the US, 3 Fonteinen lambics and Europeans like De Moersleutel

Kill the Cat

and Kees. There's limited table space – the big one at the back surrounded by rather disturbing cat portraits is often used for tastings and similar events – but it's well worth squeezing in. Further, more generously proportioned, branches are planned.

Visitor note. Owner Dan Sandy confides they've attracted heartfelt criticism from those who assume the name is an exhortation to violence against felines, but it's intended as reference to the old proverb about curiosity killing the cat, thus the strapline 'for the beer curious'.

Long Arm

Brewpub, bar
20 Worship Street EC2A 2DX (Islington)
T (020) 3873 4065   longarmpub.co.uk
First sold beer: March 2015 (at original site),
Mo-Sa 11.00-24.00, Su 12.00-23.00.
Children until 18.00.
6 tank, 1 keg, 15 bottles/cans.
Burgers, sharing platters ££,
Standing on street,
Tastings, big screen sport, functions

Moorgate, Old Street   Finsbury Square   CS1

The Long Arm is the brewing arm of the ETM pub group, which first reached out in 2015 from a 10hl brewhouse in a former hay store at the Ealing Park Tavern, a location that had seen brewing before but not since the 1850s. In July 2017, the company opened this second more central brewpub, with a smaller but more sophisticated 5hl kit and a tightly packed parade of fermentation vessels in a corner of the Montcalm Royal London House hotel. The original site was decommissioned and the equipment is now in use at Three Hills. With its high ceilings and tiled walls, the new home

Long Arm

has a post-industrial feel, with multiple big screens adding a sports bar twist, but there's also a comfy side room where stuffed animal heads preside. Tasting flights are available, while guest bottles and cans from breweries like Burning Sky, Harbour and Wild round out the beer offer. The menu includes burgers, sharing platters and numerous meat-free options including Kentucky-fried cauliflower.

BEERS are sold from tank in the pub and from keg at others in the group: regulars include **Tropical Thunder** fruity pale ale (4.5%), **Flying Flamingo** IPA (5.1%) and an unusual smoked brown ale, **Phoenix** (4.7%). The **Lager** (4%) is currently outsourced at Sambrook's but there are plans to bring it back in house.

Mikkeller Bar London 46

Bar
2 Hackney Road E2 7NS
mikkeller.com/locations
🕐 *Mo-Th* 12.00-22.30, *Fr-Sa* 12.00-23.30,
Su 12.00-22.00. Children until 20.00.
19 keg, 130 bottles/cans, Mikkeller spirits.
🍴 Unusual snacks, chocolate £,
🍸 Tables on street, ♿
Tap takeovers, beer showcases, running club

⊖ Shoreditch High Street, Hoxton   🚃 Shoreditch Church
🚲 Link to Q13

Prolific Danish nomad brewer Mikkel Borg Bjergsø established a London presence in October 2018 by teaming up with his unlikely childhood hero, 1980s pop idol Rick Astley. The pair have created a venue with the same unmistakably Scandinavian look as its siblings in Copenhagen, and elsewhere, in the shell of a solid old East End boozer, former gay pub the George and Dragon. A single airy space with pastel green and light wood finishes is dominated by a black-tiled back bar where taps dispense beers of strengths from under 3% to over 8% ABV, with Mikkellers's own brews,

Mikkeller Bar

including specials and rarities, supplemented by a few guests from the UK and elsewhere. A comprehensive bottled list covers London favourites, Bavarian and Belgian classics including various lambics and rare US imports like Tired Hands. Unusual snacks like Danish chocolate and homemade malted nuts flavoured with spent yeast substitute for a kitchen. Mikkel and Rick are planning to add a brewpub in 2020 at 37 Exmouth Market EC1R 4QL (Clerkenwell and Farringdon).

Old Fountain Brewhouse

Brewpub, traditional pub
3 Baldwin Street EC1V 9NU (Islington)
T (020) 7253 2970   oldfountain.co.uk
First sold beer: July 2016
⏰ *Mo-Fr 11.00-23.00, Sa 12.00-23.00,
Su 12.00-22.30. Children until 19.00.*
7-8 cask, 17 keg, 45+ bottles/cans, 1-2 ciders/
perries, 30+ whiskies, 20 gins.
🍴 Enhanced pub grub **££**, 🌲 Roof terrace, ♿
Flat access only
*Tap takeovers, beer launches, annual beer festival,
occasional live music, darts*

⇌ ⊖ Old Street   🚲 Link to Q13, C51

Fountain Tap   47a

Bar
14 Rivington Street EC2A 3DU
⏰ *Tu-Th 17.00-23.00, Fr 17.00-24.00,
Sa 14.00-24.00.*
2 cask, 12 keg, 8 bottles/cans, specialist ciders
🍴 Pizza **£-££**

⇌ ⊖ Old Street   🚲 C51, Q13

Between Baldwin Street and Peerless Street with entrances both sides, this enduring gem of a former Whitbread pub close to Moorfields Eye Hospital has been in the Durrant family since 1964 and a free house since 2002. It's a friendly place with padded benches, stained glass, a very pretty roof terrace and a tasty homecooked menu that could include 'our famous ham and eggs', smoked pork belly and apple sausages or stuffed squash heart, all with beer matching suggestions. Five Points XPA, London Pride, Oakham Citra and changing house beers

are regularly on cask, alongside guests from the likes of Anspach and Hobday, Siren and Tring. Kegs are often from locals like Bohem, Kernel or Solvay Society as well as Belgian and German suppliers: all guest draught lines are allocated by style, with dark and strong options. There's some serious stuff in the fridges too, including Boundary from Belfast and Behemoth from New Zealand when I looked. The choice has been intermittently enhanced by an in-house brewery, a 50 litre Braumeister kit in the cellar: its use was understandably disrupted during the lockdowns but it should be dusted off during the currency of this book. A smaller and more contemporary daughter venue, the Fountain Tap, opened on a quiet backstreet just on the other side of Old Street in May 2021, with a wide and changing range from reliable suppliers like Boxcar, Lost and Grounded, Pressure Drop and Verdant dispensed from a smart back bar.

BEERS (not tasted) are nearly all sold on cask through the pub, plus very occasional hand bottling, although may not always be available due to limited quantities. They've included a double dry hopped IPA, a New England IPA and a German-style altbier.

Pivo

Bar, shop
2 Old Street EC1V 9AA   pivohub.co.uk
⏰ *Su-Th 12.00-23.00, Fr-Sa 12.00-24.00.
Children until early evening.*
15 keg, 120+ bottles/cans, Czech wines,
spirits and soft drinks.
🍴 Czech pub grub **£-££**
*Beer school, tastings, major big screen sport,
functions*

⊖ Barbican

Given the proud beer culture of the Czech Republic, encompassing both old-established breweries and the proliferating microbrewing community, this central London showcase for Czech independents, opened in a former coffee shop at the western end of Old Street in May 2021, is a very welcome addition to this book. The draught range reaches far beyond the familiar golden lagers from big producers

Pivo

to names like Albrecht, Cvikov, Kanec, Kutná Hora, Matuška and styles that include amber and dark lagers as well as pale ones in a range of strengths and Czech takes on modern 'craft' styles like IPAs and sours. Beers are poured with a decent head, with three options for its proportion to the liquid, and if you want to learn how to create your own *hladinka* or *šnyt*, they provide courses. Still more variety is on display in the fridges, which also boast a few Belgian and German options. The offer is rounded out by what they claim is the biggest selection of slivovice in the UK and honest comfort food at reasonable prices for the area, like vegetarian *halušky* dumplings with sauerkraut, beer-roasted pork belly and beef *gulaš*. It's a stylishly designed place with three distinct spaces on street and basement level, and the fixtures and fittings are Czech-made too, including the handsome glass lampshades above the dramatically veneered bar.

Pride of Spitalfields ㊾

Traditional pub
3 Heneage Street E1 5LJ
T (020) 7247 8933
🕐 *Su-Th* 11.00-24.00, *Fr-Sa* 11.00-01.00.
Children until early evening.
5 cask, 2 keg, 3 bottles.
🍴 Sandwiches and hot specials,
Sunday lunch (prebooking only) **£-££**
Live piano (Tu), small functions

🚇 Aldgate East   🚲 Link to CS2

Just off the bustle of Brick Lane, this petite two-roomed free house is one of the few remaining traditional pubs for miles around. Vintage photos of docks and railways and ancient invoices in frames hang above red upholstery and a wood burning stove, and there's a panelled snug with a display of old bottles. The pumpclips rarely change – Crouch End Brewers Gold, Fuller's ESB and London Pride, Sharp's Doom Bar, various Truman seasonals and occasionally other guests – but the quality never disappoints.

Visitor note. *The pub was once the tap of a small brewery variously known as John Turner & Son and Best & Co that operated, in the long shadow of the old Truman's up the road, from the 1810s to 1893. The head brewer's house still stands on the other side of the gate to the former brewery yard.*

Strongroom ㊿

Bar
120 Curtain Road EC2A 3SQ
T (020) 7426 5103   strongroombar.com
🕐 *Mo* 10.00-23.00, *Tu-We* 10.00-24.00, *Th* 10.00-01.00, *Fr* 10.00-02.00, *Sa* 12.00-02.00, *Su* 12.00-22.00. Children until 21.00.
9 keg, 60 bottles/cans, whiskies, some other specialist spirits.
🍴 Burgers, tacos **£-££**, 🪑 Large yard 🐾, ♿
Beer festivals and launches, quiz (Mo), live music, DJs, spoken word, seasonal events, table football, arcade games, functions

🚆 🚇 Old Street   🚲 Q13, link to CS1

Shoreditch's current creativity owes much to the Strongroom, a recording studio established in 1985 in a former furniture warehouse on a courtyard off Curtain Road, originally sharing space with designers like punk iconographer Jamie Reid. A bar was added in 1997, originally as a facility for studio clients, becoming a friendly mainstay of a burgeoning local scene and a quietly persistent supporter of decent beer. Refurbished and extended with Reid murals and redundant items of studio equipment incorporated into the décor, it's additionally blessed with a leafy outdoor yard that intermittently hosts beer festivals. Kegs are supplied by the equally music-friendly Signature as well as the likes of Brighton Bier and Howling Hops, while cans and bottles include Belgian mainstays, Londoners like Wild Card and Scandinavians like Amundsen and Dugges. Food is suitable for hungry musicians, with good vegetarian options and an unusual range of tacos.

Visitor note. Clients of the adjacent studio have included John Cale, Nick Cave, Dido, Kasabian, Moby, Olivia Newton John, Orbital, Placebo, Santana, the Ting Tings and the Who. Imagine all that lot on stage at once.

Strongroom

Wenlock Arms
(Block Brewery)
Brewpub, traditional pub
26 Wenlock Road N1 7TA (Hackney)
T (020) 7608 3406   wenlockarms.com
First sold beer: December 2016
🕐 *Tu-Su 12.00-23.00.* Children until 19.00.
10 cask, 11 keg, 14 bottles/cans, 2+ ciders/
   perries, some malts and gins.
🍴 Pies, toasties **£**, 🪑 Standing on street
Occasional beer events, live piano, major big screen sports, darts

🚆 ⊖ Old Street   🚌 Windsor Terrace   🚶 Link to Jubilee Greenway

When I researched the first edition in 2011, the future of this legendary venue was uncertain: licensees Steve and Will, who had operated it as a real ale free house since 1994, were selling up to a property developer who aimed to demolish it and build flats. But following a local campaign, the council declared it part of a conservation area, and a less destructive conversion saw the ground floor retained for pub use. It reopened under the stewardship of current owners Marcus Grant and Heath Ball in 2013, with a sympathetic makeover preserving the essence of a place that still attracts beer pilgrims from across the country and the world. Further interest was added in 2017 when brewer Eugene started work on a 50 litre homebrew-style kit in the cellar. The horseshoe bar always boasts a good cask range, including milds and porters, from brewers like Crouch Vale, Five Points, Mighty Oak and Oakham. Hawkshead, Lost and Grounded, Moor, Tiny Rebel and Weird Beard might feature among the kegs and cans. The salt beef sandwiches have been replaced by pies, toasties and baked camembert, but the Wenlock remains an honest alehouse at heart, and one of London's best.

Visitor note. Despite the Wenlock brewery mirrors and the location opposite that brewery's former site, this was originally a Courage pub: both brewery and pub took their names from a local property-owning family. Look out for the floor mosaic in one of the porches, revealed in the recent restoration.

BEERS under the name **Block** are sold almost entirely at the pub in keg and occasionally cask. A Bavarian-style wheat beer, **Vice** (5.5%), is near-permanent and there are various specials.

HOP HISTORIES From Black Eagle to Dark Star

BRICK LANE was a country track through open fields in the mid-17th century when Thomas Bucknall chose it as the location of his small Black Eagle brewery. Sometime in the 1660s, one Joseph Truman joined the team, and by 1697 had bought Bucknall out. Truman's shrewd and ambitious grandson Benjamin took a seat on the board in 1722 and began the process of turning the brewery into one of London's biggest and most successful by concentrating on porter brewing.

Porter has a long association with this part of London. A widely repeated account dating from the early 19th century credits Ralph Harwood, of the Blue Last pub in Curtain Road, Shoreditch, with the invention of the style in 1730. The story that he devised it as a labour-saving single-cask replacement for 'three threads', a popular blend of mature, mild and pale ale that had to be mixed to order by bar staff, has now been discredited, but porter was certainly once hugely popular in the East End.

By the 1830s, Truman Hanbury & Buxton was producing 200,000 barrels (330,000hl) of porter a year. Its philanthropic links are mentioned by Charles Dickens in *David Copperfield*: partner Thomas Buxton, who joined in 1809, was an anti-slavery campaigner and prison reformer, and both he and his uncle and fellow partner, tobacco importer Sampson Hanbury, were Quakers, related to the Barclays who part-owned Barclay Perkins (see Southwark Ale, p90). The brewery was rebuilt extensively in 1929, with a new boiler house sprouting a 49m brick chimney that dominated the local roofscape. Truman clung doggedly to independence as consolidation swept the industry in the 1950s and 1960s, but finally fell in 1971 to the Grand Metropolitan hotel group who used it as leverage to buy out Watney the following year, creating Watney Mann Truman (see Roll out the red barrel, p126). It was finally closed in 1988 after years of neglect, but as we shall see was never quite forgotten.

Meanwhile, one of the UK's most influential early microbreweries was reaching its peak just up the road. In August 1981, beer fan Rob Jones became the manager of a pioneering specialist beer shop in Pitfield Street, Hoxton, then an impoverished and neglected backwater rather than the fashionable district of today. Jones began brewing in the basement in 1982 under the name Pitfield's, and soon afterwards got together with friend and customer Martin Kemp and others to buy the business, renaming it The Beer Shop.

In 1984, Pitfield's expanded to its own site around the corner in Hoxton Square, where a year later it brewed a new and unusual porter-inspired dark, strong ale called Dark Star. This proved a surprise success, becoming the first microbrew to win the title of CAMRA's Supreme Champion Beer of Britain. The brewery had to make way for redevelopment in 1989, and its owners disagreed on what to do next. Kemp hung onto the shop, while Jones and Canadian head brewer Andy Skene moved brewing to Staffordshire, merging with another micro which later collapsed.

The Beer Shop went on to introduce a generation of London drinkers to then-rare imports from Belgium and Germany as well as a variety of British brews. In 1996, it moved to bigger premises a few doors away at 14 Pitfield Street N1 6EY, where Kemp began brewing Pitfield's beers again, leaning towards organic beers

and historical recreations. Skene returned two years later as head brewer, but as the new millennium began, Hoxton's newfound desirability drove up rents to unaffordable levels, and in 2005 the shop and brewery relocated to rural Essex. Kemp went into semi-retirement in 2012 and Skene took over, adding his own Dominion brands to the range, though since 2018 it's operated only as a cuckoo.

Rob Jones, meanwhile, moved to Brighton where in 1994 he started brewing in the cellar of the Evening Star pub, adopting the name of his greatest previous success, Dark Star. This brewery went on to become one of the most lauded and loved in Britain, thanks in part to exceptional former head brewer Mark Tranter (who later set up Burning Sky), and now operates from a much bigger standalone site in Partridge Green, West Sussex. Fuller's bought the brewery in 2018, by which time Jones had already left, and at least one of its brands is now brewed in London at the Griffin, now under the stewardship of Asahi.

Back on Brick Lane, the original Black Eagle re-emerged as an arts, shopping and leisure complex in the late 1990s, the focus of an increasingly trendy local scene that gave yet another new face to one of London's most frequently reinvented streets. Head for that chimney and you'll find many of the original buildings still standing, giving a feel for the vastness of the site (91 Brick Lane E1 6QL).

Two beer and pub enthusiasts who fell for the place's sense of history were local workers James Morgan and Michael-George Hemus, who conceived

what seemed like the wild idea of resurrecting the beer. Truman had always retained its cachet, particularly in east London, and retained a visible presence thanks to the brewery's policy of building large, lavish, landmark pubs, many of which still proudly bore its name. After a year of persistent phone calls, current brand owners Heineken agreed first to license then to sell them the rights.

Lacking capital for new kit and premises, the pair initially opted to contract-brew outside London, originally at Nethergate in Suffolk and later at Everards in Leicester, starting in 2010 with some help from former Truman's brewer Derek Prentice.

The new owners were insistent that contracting

was only a means of helping make the case for returning the brand to its own plant in London. They'd considered, and dismissed, the romantic but expensive and impractical notion of a microbrewery at the Black Eagle itself but were determined to stay in the east.

The new Truman's opened at Fish Island in Hackney Wick in 2013 and soon found itself expanding: it's currently on another temporary site at Hackney Wick pending a relocation to Walthamstow (p140). Happily, and a little unexpectedly, the pleasure of sitting in a proper old East End Truman's boozer and drinking local Truman's beer now seems assured for the next generation of London drinkers.

TRY ALSO

BrewDog Old Street 211 Old Street EC1V 9NR brewdog.com: Split-level bar in the stylish Bower development right by Old Street Tube, converted in January 2020 from a Draft House. It was briefly London's only dedicated low- and no-alcohol bar and retains a wider range than usual of beers under 0.5% and less, plus stronger options and the usual house food menu.

BrewDog Shoreditch 51 Bethnal Green Road E1 6LA brewdog.com: BrewDog's second London bar, in a wedge-shaped, glass-walled space on Bethnal Green Road close to Shoreditch High Street overground and Brick Lane market. It has a funky vibe to match the area and stocks one cask, 24 keg and 75 bottles/cans.

Crown and Shuttle 226 Shoreditch High Street E1 6PJ crownandshuttle.com: Youthful, laid-back place with a magnificent back garden, a rarity for its location. Up to six rotating casks from London and elsewhere, Meantime tank lager, 15 kegs including Hackney and Howling Hops and a few bottled Belgian classics.

Griffin 93 Leonard Street EC2A 4RD the-griffin.com: Handsome Grade II-listed former Meux brewery pub, with some original interior features, in a Shoreditch back street, now a Barworks venue with two cask, 14 keg and 50+ bottles including aged lambics. Closed Sunday.

Howl at the Moon 178 Hoxton Street N1 5LH hoxtoncrafthouse.com: Friendly Irish-owned, rugby-loving contemporary Hoxton Market pub next to a community garden, with numerous keg and bottle/can choices from good Londoners and other UK brewers. No cask, cash-free.

Singer Tavern 1 City Road EC1Y 1AG singertavern.com: Large and handsome Barworks outlet in the Grade II-listed former UK HQ of the Singer sewing machine company, otherwise occupied by a Travelodge hotel. One cask, 18 keg and 120 bottles and cans, particularly focusing on pale ales and IPAs.

Well and Bucket 143 Bethnal Green Road E2 7DG wellandbucket.com: Main road pub that's now a Barworks, preserving some spectacular restored Victorian tilework, with an eclectic range of two cask, 14 keg and over 50 bottled and canned beers alongside oysters and traditional East End shellfish.

Crown and Shuttle

Soho and Fitzrovia

De Hems

Bar (Castle/M&B)
11 Macclesfield Street W1D 5BW
T (020) 7437 2494 **dehemspub.co.uk**
🕐 *Mo-Fr* 12.00-00.30, *Sa* 11.00-00.30,
   Su 12.00-22.30. Children until 20.00.
17 keg, 80+ bottles/cans, gin, whisky.
🍴 Dutch and British street food and pub grub
££, 🪑 Standing at front, ♿
*Occasional tap takeovers, weekly live music,
big screen Dutch football, functions*

⊖ Piccadilly Circus   🏃 Link to Jubilee Walkway

De Hems is what you'd expect if you crossed
a London pub with the more boisterous kind
of urban Dutch bruin café. Now surrounded
by London's Chinatown, it retains its bilingual
signing, unhealthy street food (*bitterballen*
meatballs, *patatje oorlog* or chips with mayon-
naise and satay sauce) and loyal expat customers given to occasional bouts of swaying and
singing in the guttural mother tongue. Since
the last edition it's happily expanded the
representation of the burgeoning Dutch
craft scene, and you'll find breweries like 't IJ,
De Molen, Oedipus and Uiltje among the kegs,
bottles and cans alongside well-established
imports like Lindeboom pils, Belgian lambics
and Trappists including aged Orval. UK
contributors include Tiny Rebel from Wales, a
nod to the nationality of the current manager.
There's usually more room upstairs, but if
you're after a quiet drink on Koningsdag
(King's Day) on 27 April, head somewhere else.

*Visitor note. Captain De Hem was a retired Dutch sailor
who ran the pub, then called the Macclesfield, as an oyster
bar in the early 1900s. During World War II, it was used as
an unofficial headquarters of the exiled Dutch resistance.
Renamed De Hems in 1959, it was soon attracting musos
like Georgie Fame and Alan Price.*

Lyric

Contemporary pub
37 Great Windmill Street W1D 7LU
T (020) 7434 0604 **lyricsoho.co.uk**
🕐 *Mo-Th* 11.00-23.30, *Fr-Sa* 11.00-24.00,
   Su 12.00-22.30. Children until 19.00.
9 cask, 18 keg, 10 bottles, 1 cider, wines, some
   whiskies and gins.
🍴 Enhanced pub grub **£-££**,
🪑 Standing on street
*Beer festivals, tap takeovers, major big screen
sport, functions*

⊖ Piccadilly Circus   🏃 Link to Jubilee Walkway

Within dazzling distance of Piccadilly Circus,
this popular free house with a genuinely
pubby atmosphere is easily one of the best

Lyric

beer options in the West End. Beyond the distinctively handsome bowed wood frontage with its etched windows and decorative tiles is a homely downstairs bar serving a wide range of cask options, traditional and contemporary, from Big Smoke, Harvey's and guests like Five Points, Moor, Southwark or Thornbridge. Kegs from the likes of Arbor, BBNo, Gipsy Hill, Hammerton and Wiper and True, usually including a strong stout or two, flow from taps on a brick back bar. An attractive room upstairs provides overspill for diners, who can choose from good value lunchtime specials, sausages, pie and mash and exotica like piri piri chicken or butternut squash curry. Rejigged in 2013, it's a far eastern outpost of the group that owns the Sussex Arms (p312).

Newman Arms 54

Contemporary pub
23 Rathbone Street W1T 1NG
T (020) 7436 9777   thenewmanarms.co.uk
🕐 *Mo-Sa* 12.00-23.30. Children welcome.
4 cask, 5 keg, 12 bottles, specialist spirits.
🍴 Pies, sharing boards, pub grub, sandwiches
££, 🪑 Standing on street
Functions

⊖ Tottenham Court Road   🚲 Link to Q1

This backstreet Fitzrovia pub was long a favourite of James Morgan, one of the founders of the new Truman's (p140), which

partly explains why, a year after it closed on the retirement of a longstanding landlady in 2017, it reopened as the brewery's smart central showcase, and one of a tiny handful of independent pubs in the West End. The small ground floor bar is done out in austere dark wood, but there's additional space in the gentlemen's club-style room above and a pair of more contemporary snugs below. Truman's has maintained the tradition of serving excellent pies, filled with everything from venison to veggies, alongside sandwiches and sharing plates. The brewery's beers are well-represented, including on cask, with a handful of well-chosen guests and Duvel and Kernel bottles in the fridge.

Visitor note *The image of a woman in a top-floor window is a reminder that the 1730 building was once used as a brothel. It became a beer house in 1830 and wasn't licensed to sell spirits until 1960. George Orwell used it as the model for the prole pub in* Nineteen Eighty-Four, *acknowledged in the names of the basement snugs, and along with adjoining alleyway Newman Passage it featured in Michael Powell's classic 1960 horror film* Peeping Tom.

TRY ALSO

BrewDog Soho 21 Poland Street W1F 8QG **brewdog.com**: Another West End BrewDog location in customary post-industrial style, with additional basement space. 21 keg lines, 45+ bottles/cans including unusual guests, with a burger and wings menu. Cash-free.
Queen Charlotte 43 Goodge Street W1T 1TA **brewdog.com**: Small corner BrewDog pub, formerly a Draft House, in the heart of Fitzrovia's media territory. Expect to stand at all but the quietest times to sample from three cared-for casks, 11 keg lines and over 40 bottles/cans.
Riding House Café 43 Great Titchfield Street W1W 7PQ **ridinghouse.cafe**: Bright and efficient restaurant-café-cocktail bar much loved by BBC staff and Fitzrovia creatives, offering 20 bottles/cans including Kernel, historical Shepherd Neame beers and Belgian classics alongside an imaginative seasonal Modern British menu.
Smugglers Tavern 28 Warren Street W1T 5ND **thesmugglerstavern.co.uk**: Recently modernised pub with refectory tables near Warren Street Tube, managing one or two cask and up

to five keg lines mainly from London brewers despite a Heineken tie, plus a balanced selection of 35+ bottles/cans mainly from contemporary UK breweries.

Whole Foods Market Piccadilly Circus 20 Glasshouse Street W1B 5AR wholefoodsmarket.co.uk: West End branch of US-based upscale supermarket chain with 120+ bottles/cans, largely from well-chosen London and UK producers, split between shelves and chiller cabinets.

HERITAGE PUBS

Argyll Arms 18 Argyll Street W1F 7TP nicholsonspubs.co.uk: Big pub just off Oxford Circus and opposite the London Palladium retaining a decorated lincrusta ceiling from 1868 and carved wood and glass partitions enhanced by ornate mirrors from an 1890s refit. The former manager's office is still visible at the back. Now a Nicholson's serving around seven cask and a few kegs and bottles from the regular group range.

Dog and Duck 18 Bateman Street W1D 3AJ nicholsonspubs.co.uk: Classic small, narrow Soho pub which became even more famous when Madonna named it her favourite in 2005. It features highly attractive preserved 1897 tiling and advertising mirrors, a 1930s wooden bar and exterior decorations of dogs and ducks to remind you of the area's hunting past. Now a Nicholson's with one or two more interesting casks than usual.

LONDON DRINKERS | Emma Inch

Based in Brighton, Emma is nevertheless out and about on the London beer scene most weeks pursuing her career as a beer writer and audio maker as well as socialising. Her award-winning podcast, Fermentation Beer & Brewing Radio (fermentationonline.com), is available on Apple Podcasts, Spotify and various other platforms. Follow her on Twitter @fermentradio.

How do you rate London as a beer city, on a world scale?

It's a great place to drink beer, with industrial heritage and brewing history as well as lots of contemporary breweries. It's also one of the most cosmopolitan cities in the world and I think that brings something special to the whole scene.

What's the single most exciting thing about beer in London right now?

The ongoing willingness to push the boundaries of innovation alongside the continued acknowledgement of tradition. There's also a vibrant home-brewing scene which feeds into commercial brewing in a really positive way.

What single thing would make things even better?

Even more collaborations that result in learning, development and innovation, like the recent Four Friends one between the Kernel, Burning Sky, Mills Brewing and Oliver's Cider or Derek Prentice and Ron Pattinson's Obadiah Poundage recreation at Goose Island.

What are your top London beers right now?

The Kernel's Imperial Brown Stout 1856 and pretty much anything by Anspach & Hobday.

What's your top great beer night out?

A quick whizz around Bermondsey – in particular the Kernel's new taproom, Anspach & Hobday and BBNo – then over to the Rake (p86), my most favourite pub in London.

Who's your London beer hero?

Jaega Wise. She has both raised the positive profile of beer outside the industry and effectively campaigned for equality and diversity within the industry. And she's done it with intelligence and dignity.

Who will we be hearing a lot more from in future?

I love what Five Points are doing to combine innovation and tradition and I'm looking forward to seeing how they continue to develop. I could drink their best bitter all day long.

Which are your other top beer cities?

Brighton, of course. It's a city built on the leisure industry, so we know how to do pubs well, and there's a growing brewing scene too with seven at the last count. Barcelona is a really exciting place to drink beer in: I was lucky enough to be there for the Beer Festival in March.

Westminster to Kensington

Bolton/Proeflokaal Rembrandt

Contemporary pub (Castle/M&B)
326 Earls Court Road SW5 9BQ
T (020) 7244 5921 **theboltonearlscourt.co.uk,
proeflokaalrembrandt.co.uk**
Pub ⏱: *Mo-Th* 12.00-23.00, *Fr-Sa* 12.00-24.00,
 Su 12.00-22.30. Children until mid-evening.
3 cask, 34 keg, 60+ bottles/cans.
🍴 Enhanced pub grub **£-££**, 🪑 Tables on
street, ♿ (ground floor only)
*Quiz (Mo), live blues/jazz (Th), DJs (Fr-Sa), seasonal
events*
Proeflokaal ⏱: *Sa-Su* 12.00-24.00.
12 keg, 130 bottles/cans, specialist spirits,
 jenevers.
🍴 Dutch menu **£-££**
*Tap takeovers, tastings, food matching, drawing
class (Mo), painting class (We), monthly quiz, films,
Dutch TV, Dutch seasonal events, functions*

⊖ Earls Court 🚲 Q15

This big Earls Court pub with its extravagant
late Victorian architecture is now looking
better than it's done in many years. The huge
downstairs bar has rotating casks from the
likes of Cotleigh, Laines and Little Critters,
and kegs, bottles and cans mixing renowned
UK names with more unusual Belgians like
Gruut and Troubadour and numerous Dutch
and Scandinavian imports. But venture
upstairs at the weekend to discover Dutch-
born manager Eric Bestebreur's real passion,
the Proeflokaal Rembrandt, a showcase for
the Netherlands' flourishing brewing scene.
It looks like a proper *bruin café*, though with
huge murals of its namesake's *Night Watch*
and, cheekily, Admiral de Ruyter chasing the
English navy up the Medway. Beers from
De Molen, La Trappe and, increasingly, Kees!,

Bolton/Proeflokaal Rembrandt

Oedipus and Uiltje, are relatively common in
London: less so those from Bax, 't IJ, Jopen,
Kompaan, Pelgrim, Oersoep, Oproer and
Prael, but you'll find them here, often thanks
to Eric's friendships with the brewers.
Downstairs food is upmarket pub grub like
mushroom risotto, pork belly or fish pie, while
upstairs continues the Dutch theme, with
smoked sausage, salmon and asparagus as
well as street food, cheese snacks and even
vegan *bitterballen*.

Buckingham Arms

Traditional pub
62 Petty France SW1H 9EU
T (020) 7222 3386 **youngs.co.uk**
⏱ *Mo-Fr* 10.00-23.00, *Sa* 11.00-21.00,
 Su 12.00-17.00. Children until 17.00.
5 cask, 3 keg, 9 bottles, 1 cider, some wines
 and gins.
🍴 Enhanced pub grub/gastroish menu,
sandwiches **£-££**, ♿
*Occasional tastings, quiz (Tu), major big screen
sport, private hire*

⊖ St James's Park 🚲 link to CS3 🚶 Link to Jubilee
Greenway, Jubilee Walkway

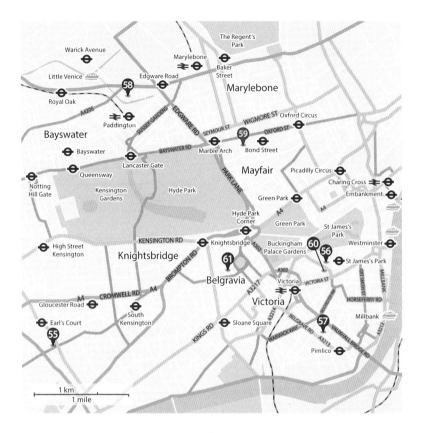

This fine Victorian Young's house not far from Buckingham Palace is one of only two London pubs listed in every edition of the *Good Beer Guide* (the other is the the Star below). It's still one of the top places to enjoy a pint of cask Original Bitter or Special, plus Winter Warmer in season, St Austell Proper Job and guests from Sambrook's or Truman's. Kegs from Beavertown and Camden Town and bottled Young's brands widen the choice. The menu might include salmon and prawn pie, honey-glazed gammon or sweet potato and leek burger alongside posh sandwiches and traditional stodgy puds. It's a handsome place with a skylight picking out stained glass and a mirrored bar back, while a former side corridor provides unusual additional drinking space.

Buckingham Arms

Cask Pub and Kitchen 57

Bar
6 Charlwood Street SW1V 2EE
T (020) 7630 7225   caskpubandkitchen.com
Mo-Sa 12.00-23.00, Su 12.00-22.30.
   Children until 17.00 (later on *Su*).
10 cask, 14 keg, 300+ bottles/cans, specialist spirits.
Burgers, pies **££**, Tables on street, Flat access only
Occasional tap takeovers and beer launches, acoustic music (Su)

Pimlico   Link to NCN4, C8   Link to Thames Path

Almost abandoned without hope by its owners Greene King, in 2009 the former Pimlico Tram was transformed by Martin Hayes into a ground-breaking beer bar that became the progenitor of the Craft Beer Co chain. It remains one of the very best places for London beer explorers, now looking less basic than it once did following a recent refurbishment but still modern, cheerful and functional. Bad Seed, Fyne, Hawkshead, Kirkstall, Roosters and Wiper & True are among the current favourites on the rotating cask pumps. Keg fixtures include Brick, Hackney and Mondo, with guests in a wide range of styles from UK breweries like Kernel, Pomona Island and Yonder or visiting Americans like Cascade and Prairie. A lengthy and thoughtful bottle and can list, best consulted on the website to ensure currency,

CHARLWOOD STREET SW1

CASK

REAL ALE · CRAFT BEER · LUNCH & DINNER 7 DAYS A WEEK

CASK

Cask Pub and Kitchen

includes wild and mixed fermentation beers in sharer sizes from Cantillon, Jester King, Tilquin and the like alongside Londoners and other UK entrants like Gun and Polly's: if there's a buzz about a small brewery in an obscure part of the country, its beers will likely pop up here. Food is gourmet burgers, including a vegan option.

Visitor note. *The pub forms part of a 1960s council housing block, Forsythe House, which is Grade II* listed for its distinctive architecture, the large, angled windows adding an attractively bright touch to the interior.*

Heist Bank 58

Bar
5 North Wharf W2 1LA
T (020) 7723 8080   heistbank.com
Mo-Th 08.00-23.30, *Fr* 08.00-24.00, *Sa* 12.00-24.00, *Su* 12.00-22.30. Children until 19.00, later in restaurant.
10 keg, 20+ bottles/cans, some wines and specialist spirits.
Gourmet pizzas **££**, Front terrace,
Pool, table football, karaoke, board games, functions

Paddington   Little Venice   Grand Union Canal Walk, Jubilee Greenway

The sign outside this big, bright designer bar in the Merchant Square development by Paddington Basin reads 'Beer – Pizza – Flowers' and indeed it incorporated a flower shop on opening in 2016. Though this has since closed, fresh flowers still brighten the contemporary interior with its naked concrete and granite bar top. Other venues owned by the Urban Leisure Group show a beer-friendly leaning and this leans further still, with Partizan Porter a regular feature on the kegs alongside Gipsy Hill, Harbour, Orbit and Wild and more from the same brewers and others, mainly from the UK, in the fridges. Buxton, six°north and Villages are particularly welcome inclusions, with helpful tasting notes on the printed list. The pizzas endure too, with toppings including wild boar and fennel salami or marinated courgettes with vegan 'cheese'.

Heist Bank

Mercato Metropolitano Mayfair (German Kraft) 59

Brewpub, bars

13A North Audley Street W1K 6ZA (Westminster)

mercatometropolitano.com

German Kraft: **germankraftbeer.com**

First sold beer: November 2020, ‼ Planned

🕐 *Mo-We* 12.00-22.45, *Th-Fr* 12.00-24.00, *Sa* 11.00-24.00, *Su* 11.00-21.45. Children welcome

4 tank, 1-2 keg, growlers.

🍴 Various from neighbouring traders **£-££**, 🪑, ♿

Music performances, music and cookery classes, community events.

⊖ Bond Street 🚲 Link to Hyde Park paths 🚶 Link to Princess Diana Memorial Walk

Following the success of its popular Elephant site (p84), the second Mercato Metropolitano opened in November 2019 as an indoor street market in the spectacular galleried surrounds of the former St Mark's Church, a Grade I-listed 1820s Greek Revival building in the upscale heart of Mayfair. A second German Kraft with a 2.5 hl brewhouse was installed in the crypt the following year. Opposite this, the main bar honours the architectural setting in spectacular style with over 1,000 golden glass bricks made by melting down broken glasses collected at Elephant. Some beers are served here in traditional Bavarian ceramic mugs. There's a second bar elsewhere in the building.

BEERS mainly in tank and sometimes keg, are sold only in-house. The core range is similar to the Elephant brewery, with exclusive specials which have included smoked Bockbier, Berliner Weisse and other more unusual German specialities.

Quilon 60

Restaurant, bar

41 Buckingham Gate SW1E 6AF

T (020) 7821 1899 **quilon.co.uk**

🕐 *Mo-Fr* 12.00-14.30, 17.45-23.00, *Sa* 12.30-15.30, 17.45-23.00, *Su* 12.30-15.30, 17.45-22.30. Children in restaurant only.

15+ bottles/cans, 180+ wines, 60 whiskies, specialist spirits and cocktails.

🍴 South Indian gourmet **£££**, ♿ (in hotel),

⊖ St James's Park 🚲 Link to CS3 🚶 Link to Jubilee Greenway, Jubilee Walkway

Stylish Quilon, opened in 1999 as part of the Indian-owned Taj 51 luxury hotel, is one of a pathetically tiny subset of London's fine dining restaurants to make any kind of effort with the beer list. Chef Sriram Aylur's Michelin-starred food is rooted in coastal southwest Indian cooking but with a contemporary twist including plenty of vegetarian options. And though oenophiles won't be disappointed, he's keen to promote beer as the ideal match for this delightful cuisine. Choices include Chimay, Innis & Gunn, Kernel, Little Creatures and Pietra, plus aged examples of Fuller's Vintage and Samuel Smith Yorkshire Stingo. There's even a tasting menu, matching beers to such delicacies as grilled scallop with papaya, Kerala chicken roast and vegetable dosas. Prices are high and you'll inevitably pay a premium on the beer, but the generous set lunches are some of the best bargains in London given the quality on offer.

Star Tavern

Traditional pub
6 Belgrave Mews West SW1X 8HT
T (020) 7235 3019
star-tavern-belgravia.co.uk
⏱ *Mo-Fr* 11.00-23.00, *Sa* 12.00-23.00, *Su* 12.00-22.30. Children until early evening.
5 cask, 2 keg, 20 bottles, 30+ whiskies, some gins.
🍴 Enhanced pub grub, lunchtime sandwiches
£-££
Beer festivals, board games, functions

⊖ Hyde Park Corner, Knightsbridge

Tucked away in elegant Belgravia, down an alley that runs between the Austrian and German embassies, the Star was probably intended for domestic staff working in the big houses. It's a relaxed and informal place centred on an old horseshoe bar, shabbily genteel but spotlessly clean. As you'd expect from one of only two London pubs to appear in every edition of the *Good Beer Guide* (see also Buckingham Arms above), the Fuller's cask here is in top nick. Guests are from the likes of Butcombe and Five Points, with more Fuller's in keg and bottle, including aged Vintage Ales and Brewer's Reserve specials. Food encompasses pies, steaks, smoked salmon and butternut squash and feta wellington.

Visitor note. *The Great Train Robbery was planned here, now commemorated by occasional events, and stars like Peter O'Toole and Diana Dors would come to rub shoulders with gang bosses.*

TRY ALSO

BrewDog Paddington 1 West End Quay W2 1JX brewdog.com: Waterside site in the recent development around Paddington Basin. 23 keg, 75 bottles/cans, hot-desking workspace and shuffleboard.
Jackalope 43 Weymouth Mews W1G 7EQ jackalopelondon.com: Picturesque mews pub close to BBC Broadcasting House, formerly the Dover Castle, smartened up and reopened in 2018 by the Euston Tap group. Up to four reliable guest casks, 13 kegs including US and German imports and a popup noodle bar. Closed weekends.

Mall Tavern 71 Palace Gardens Terrace W8 4RU themallw8.com: Lively, contemporary Notting Hill corner pub under the same ownership as Beer + Burger (p304) with two casks from Timothy Taylor, 18 keg and 12 bottles/cans including some from associated cuckoo Project 88.

Queens Arms 30 Queens Gate Mews SW7 5QL thequeensarmskensington.co.uk: Picturesque mews pub close to the Albert Hall, Hyde Park and the Kensington museums. A particularly beer-friendly M&B Castle outlet with up to eight reliable casks including a few unusual guests, plus 13 kegs mainly from bigger breweries and Belgian classics among the bottles.

Royal Exchange 26 Sale Place W2 1PU facebook.com/royalexchangew2: Corner pub near Paddington Basin and Edgware Road station reopened in May 2021 under same management as the excellent Priory Arms (p264), with a much-improved range of independently-sourced beers including two locally brewed casks.

Speaker 46 Great Peter Street SW1P 2HA bestcitypubs.co.uk: Tucked away within heckling distance of Parliament and named after the chair of the House of Commons, this longstanding traditional favourite has retained its cask appeal under new Stonegate management: up to five reliable beers usually from independents.

Thornbury Castle 29A Enford Street W1H 1DN thornburycastle.uk.com: Pleasantly traditional backstreet pub with a longstanding licensee serving six quality cask beers from Rebellion and others in the territory served by rail from nearby Marylebone station, plus Londoners and Glasgow's St Mungo lager on keg. Closed weekends, over-18s only.

Whole Foods Market Kensington 63 Kensington High Street W8 5SE wholefoodsmarket.co.uk: By far the biggest UK branch of the upmarket grocery chain, in Kensington's former Barkers department store. Around 200 bottles/cans: lots from London and the UK, a few Europeans and far fewer from the US than you might expect given the company's origins.

Windsor Castle 114 Campden Hill Road W8 7AR thewindsorcastlekensington.co.uk: Handsome heritage pub with a multi-roomed, wood-panelled 1930s interior in a sturdy 1830s hilltop building near Notting Hill. An M&B Castle outlet with up to six casks including sometimes unusual guests and a couple of rotating kegs from indie brewers too.

HERITAGE PUBS

Churchill Arms 119 Kensington Church Street W8 7LN churchillarmskensington.co.uk: Rambling local institution near Notting Hill Gate, festooned outside with spectacular floral displays and all manner of clutter indoors, much of it themed around the eponymous prime minister and the County Clare hurling team, with lepidoptery displays in the rear Thai restaurant. Regionally important 1930s panelling, stained glass and snob screens and selection of Fuller's beer including reliable cask.

Victoria 10A Strathearn Place W2 2NH victoriapaddington.co.uk: Beautiful round-fronted Bayswater pub not far from Hyde Park which unusually preserves mid rather than late Victorian features. The elegant mirrored back bar, Regency-style fireplace and extraordinary side wall with tiling and gilded mirrors likely date from 1864, as shown on the clock above the bar. The antique whisky water tap is still in use. Now a welcoming Fuller's pub with the regular range including decent cask.

Victoria

HOP HISTORIES — Roll out the red barrel

When James Watney bought the Stag brewery at the west end of Victoria Street in 1858, he couldn't have guessed his name would become one of brewing's most notorious brands. Back then, the Stag was a medium-sized ale brewery south of the royal parks and Buckingham Palace, which had only relatively recently become Queen Victoria's official residence. Before Victoria station opened in 1860, the neighbourhood was known as Pimlico, a label now usually restricted to the streets south of the station. Palaces once had their own domestic breweries, and it's likely the Stag originated as a brewhouse attached to St James's on the other side of the park. Commercial brewing started under William Greene in 1641.

Watney pursued a vigorous policy of expansion, eventually buying a second plant at Mortlake in 1889. The brewing tradition on this riverside site stretched back to a medieval monastery and a 15th-century domestic brewery. By 1765, there were two small commercial outfits that later merged as the Star brewery. In 1898, Watney became a major London force by taking on and closing Combe & Co in Covent Garden and Reid's Griffin brewery in Clerkenwell to form Watney Combe Reid. In 1931, it became one of the first UK brewers to experiment with pasteurised keg ale, producing a beer called Red Barrel at Mortlake. Through the 1950s and 1960s Watney grew into a national force through a ruthless programme of buying up and closing regional breweries, acquiring an estate of around 6,000 pubs through which it increasingly pushed its own generic keg products.

The company closed its historic Victoria site in 1959 to make way for a new traffic gyratory. It concentrated London production at Mann's brewery in Whitechapel (see Yeast Enders, p163), which it had bought the previous year, and at Mortlake, which inherited the Stag name. Red Barrel was originally promoted as a premium product sold aboard luxury liners like the Queen Elizabeth II. But it gradually came to symbolise all that had gone wrong with British brewing in the era of the Big Seven, especially the replacement of local distinctiveness and character with homogenous, bland, mass-produced, overpriced and heavily promoted national brands. The brewery reformulated and relaunched the beer in 1971 as Watneys Red, with an unlikely campaign exhorting drinkers to 'join the Red Revolution' under images of Fidel Castro and Mao Zedong. But the damage was done: Red Barrel was famously pilloried on television in *Monty Python's Flying Circus* in 1972, and Watney itself was written up in the first edition of CAMRA's *Good Beer Guide* in 1974 with the simple sentence 'Avoid like the plague', hastily amended to 'Avoid at all costs' at the insistence of the printer, who feared legal action. By the end of the 1970s, Red and other national keg bitters were fading from view as big brewers switched to promoting equally feeble lager-style beers.

By then Watney itself had fallen to bigger predators.

In the early 1970s, it was the subject of a bitterly fought hostile takeover bid by the Grand Metropolitan hotel group, and tried to strengthen and protect itself by attempting to buy London's last surviving major independent, Truman's. But instead, Grand Met took Truman's and, in 1972, Watney as well, merging them to create Watney Mann Truman. Mann was closed in 1979, Truman's in 1989, as Grand Met gradually withdrew from brewing, selling its remaining plants to Courage, which in turn was ultimately absorbed by Heineken.

In 1991, Courage leased the Stag to US giant Anheuser Busch as the main European production plant for Budweiser lager. It was later bought out by AB's successor AB InBev and finally made its last beer at the end of 2015. Redevelopment proposals for the site (Lower Richmond Road SW14 7ET) are currently grinding through the planning process. Back at Victoria, all trace of the original Stag has long since been obliterated. A new Stag pub in brutalist concrete was part of the late 1950s redevelopment scheme but has since been demolished as part of yet another regeneration. And with more than a hint of post-modern irony, the brand, once thought irredeemably toxic, was revived in 2014 by a startup beer firm who leased it from Heineken.

EAST LONDON

EAST LONDON

East London in this book covers all the E postcodes outside the central area, and the rest of London east of these and north of the Thames to the Essex boundary. While interest in **Outer East London** is limited to the occasional brewery or micropub, the inner districts are exciting territory for beer lovers. Everyone knows about Bermondsey, but over the past five years Bethnal Green, Hackney and Walthamstow have become new epicentres of London brewing.

My **Tower Hamlets** section covers much of the classic East End: all the Borough of Tower Hamlets except the central bits listed under the City (p92) and Shoreditch (p107), and the southern part of Hackney Wick which I've dealt with under Hackney below. This area was London's original industrial powerhouse, home to numerous prominent brewers of an earlier era (see Yeast Enders p163), so it's pleasing to find brewing returning to the area.

Hackney encompasses not only Hackney itself but the wider borough, including Clapton, Dalston and Homerton, though not Stoke Newington which has an N postcode and is dealt with under Islington to Stoke Newington (p178). I've included all of Hackney Wick too, though much of it is officially in Tower Hamlets. This is one of those neighbourhoods where it seems every new bar or trendy restaurant stocks at least some local beer

My **Stratford to Walthamstow** section covers the east side of the Lea Valley from Stratford and Wanstead in Newham borough northwards into Waltham Forest. A lengthy strip of 20th-century industrial estates along the western edge of Walthamstow, between the newly designated Walthamstow Wetlands nature area and Blackhorse Lane, is London's latest go-to destination for brewers, with at least four producers in operation by the time you read this. There's a smaller cluster around Lea Bridge station in Leyton.

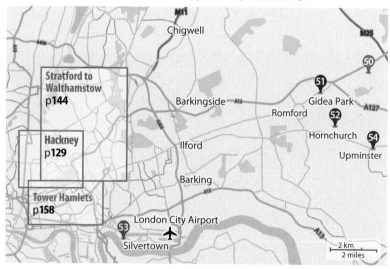

Hackney

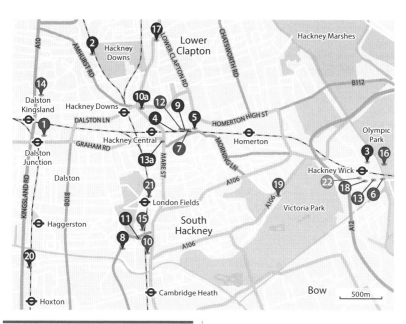

40FT

Brewery, taproom
Bootyard, Abbot Street E8 3DP (Hackney)
40ftbrewery.com
First sold beer: May 2015, 🍴
🕐 Mo-Th 16.00-23.00, Fr 16.00-24.00, Sa 12.00-24.00, Su 12.00-22.00. Children welcome.
10 keg, 5 bottles/cans. 🍷
🍴 Various from neighbouring traders (pizzas etc) **£-££**, 🪑 Tables at front
Occasional beer-related events and festivals

🔵 Dalston Junction, Dalston Kingsland   🚲 Link to CS1

The brainchild of German-born former London Fields and Truman's head brewer Ben Ott and three homebrewing business partners, including current chief executive Steve Ryan, 40FT was named after its home in a converted 40 foot (12.2m) shipping container. It's located in a former car park managed by the Bootstrap economic development charity behind Dalston's Arcola Theatre, where several other small businesses flourish, including a bakery and restaurant. Following several expansions and the addition of a smart taproom with upcycled veneers and a floor rescued from a school gym in two further containers in 2019, Steve jokes they should rename the business 160FT. The brewery uses a 10hl kit, old-fashioned open fermenters and horizontal conditioning tanks: most taproom beers are dispensed direct from these, alongside at least one keg guest. There's also a pilot kit for small runs. The site is ultimately due for redevelopment but that's at least four years away. The taproom deservedly won a regional SIBA award in 2020.

BEERS are brewed for tank and keg, with canning using a mobile line. Core beers include a contemporary-style **Pale** (4.1%); hazy, fruity pale ale **Dalston Sunrise** (4.4%), profits from which are shared with local charities; dry-hopped lagered ale **Disco Pils** (4.8%); flagship Kölsch-style **Larger** (sic, 4.8%); German-style Hefeweizen **Streetweiss*** (5%); **Deep*** (5%), the first guest dry stout poured at Guinness' Open Gate in Dublin; and numerous collaborations and specials.

All Good Beer

Bar, shop
Hackney Downs Studios, 17 Amhurst Terrace
E8 2BT
T 07964 243843   allgoodbeer.co.uk
⏰ *Mo-Tu* 15.00-21.00, *We-Fr* 12.00-22.30, *Sa* 10.00-22.30, *Su* 12.00-22.00. Children welcome.
5 keg, 70+ bottles/cans, natural and organic wines. 🍷
🍴 Ancient grain pasta from neighbouring trader **££**, 🪑 Tables at front, ♿
Tutored tastings, tap takeovers, beer launches

🚇 Hackney Downs, Hackney Central   🚉 Shacklewell Lane

Having started with a popup stall in 2016, Elliott Batchelor and Libby Elliott expanded in April 2019 to the small indoor market and food hall that replaced the Russet café at Hackney Downs Studios. This on-trend site in a former printworks is home to numerous artistic and other small businesses, attracting locals via a pedestrian tunnel under the railway direct from Hackney Downs park. The bar offers a well-chosen and changing range typically including Londoners like Brick, Kernel, Orbit and Pressure Drop, other Brits like Burning Sky, Odyssey, Wander Beyond and Wylam and

All Good Beer

global names like Alesong, Garage and Orval. You can take away or drink in at communal tables shared with a neighbouring café.

Beer Merchants Tap 🏅

Bar, shop, blending house
99 Wallis Road E9 5LN
T (020) 3222 5592   beermerchantstap.com
⏰ *Mo-We* 15.00-23.00, *Th-Sa* 12.00-23.00, *Su* 10.00-22.00. Children until 20.00.
2 cask, 19 keg, 600+ bottles/cans, speciality ciders, specialist spirits. 🍷
🍴 Toasties, cold plates, occasional food truck **£-££**, 🪑 Tables in yard, ♿
Tap takeovers, tastings, food pairing, DJs, quizzes, functions

🚇 Hackney Wick   🚲 NCN1   🚶 Capital Ring, Lea Valley Path, Olympic Park paths

The inflatable pink elephant, mascot of cult Belgian strong ale Delirium Tremens, presiding over the front yard of this warehouse-based bar barely hints at the delights within. Mail order retailer Beer Merchants and its parent, importer and distributor Cave Direct, have been introducing British drinkers to great beers from Belgium, Germany, the US and elsewhere since 1979, so expectations were high when the company opened its first bar in March 2018. They weren't disappointed, as this is a world-class venue that's massively boosted Hackney Wick's already considerable status as a beer destination. It's not often that a bar person apologises for only having a printed menu for the lambics right now, then hands you a list of over 90. Casks might be from Siren or Tiny Rebel; kegs include plentiful imports from the likes of Cascade, Lervig, Omnipollo, Verzet and White Hag alongside more familiar German lagers and top UK names. Well-stocked fridges are arranged in a drinking space featuring bare brick and repurposed wood. An obvious fondness for wild, sour and unusual stuff stretches beyond lambics to US imports from Half Acre and Rare Barrel. Even more excitingly, barrels displayed in a side room contain English wild fermentation coolship beers from Burning Sky, Harbour and Wild, destined for house blends which should appear during the currency of this guide. There's a current list on Untappd.

Brew Club

Bar

7 Bohemia Place E8 1DU **brewclub.uk.com**

🕐 *We* 15.00-20.00, *Th* 15.00-22.00,
Fr-Sa 12.00-23.30, *Su* 12.00-20.00.
Children until 19.00. Cash-free.

9 keg, 20 bottles/cans, homebrewing supplies.
🪑 Tables at front, ♿

*Brewing courses, shared brewing space,
tap takeovers, DJs (Sa)*

⊖ Hackney Central, Hackney Downs

Responding to the growing interest not only in drinking good beer but brewing it, this is both a bar and a neat and friendly shared facility for homebrewers, who as well as taking lessons can book a slot on one of six 20 litre Braumeister kits. They can then reward themselves with a drink in the adjoining taproom, which despite its name doesn't sell anything made on the premises as there's no commercial brewing licence, though you might be lucky to catch free samples. Instead, there's an eclectic range from local and wider UK brewers, sufficient to pique the interest of the keenest regular user – there were three stouts among the kegs when I last called – including offerings from breweries rare in London like Ampersand, Liquid Light, Runaway and UnBarred. The enterprise began in Clapton in 2016 but moved in 2019 to its current pair of arches in what's becoming Hackney's brewery row.

Chesham Arms

Traditional pub

15 Mehetabel Road E9 6DU

T (020) 8986 6717 **cheshamarms.com**

🕐 *Mo-Th* 16.00-23.00, *Fr-Sa* 12.00-23.00,
Su 12.00-22.30. Children until 20.00.

3-4 cask, 8 keg, 25+ bottles/cans, 2 ciders, some specialist spirits.

🍴 Order-in pizza **££**,
🪑 Rear terrace and garden ❀

Community events, board games

⊖ Hackney Central, Hackney Downs 🚌 City Academy, Homerton Terrace, Ponsford Street 🚲 C27

One of London's growing number of threatened pubs saved by being declared an Asset of Community Value, this charming backstreet local a few steps from central Hackney was reopened in July 2015 after being closed for almost 1,000 days. It soon challenged the previous owners' assertions of unviability by combining a traditional pub look, a welcoming community focus and a discerning beer offer. Casks from Londoners like East London and Redemption and others like Harbour or Salopian include more traditional styles, with keg lines dedicated to rotating beers from Five Points, Kernel and Mikkeller. Gipsy Hill and Tiny Rebel rub shoulders with Rochefort Trappist in the fridges. The interior has real fires and distinct 'public' and 'saloon' sides, the latter with an elegant art nouveau look. A rear terrace overlooks a splendid garden stretching back to a Victorian rail viaduct.

Cock Tavern

See Howling Hops

Crate Brewery

Brewpub, bar, restaurant

7 Queens Yard, White Post Lane E9 5EN
(Tower Hamlets)

T (020) 8533 3331 **cratebrewery.com**

First sold beer: July 2012, 🍺

🕐 *Su-Th* 12.00-23.00, *Fr-Sa* 12.00-01.00.
Children welcome until 19.00.

2-4 cask, 23 keg, 40+ bottles/cans, 1-2 ciders, bottled cider, cocktails on boat moored nearby. ♿

🍕 Gourmet pizzas in bar **££**, eclectic 'pre-industrial' menu in upstairs restaurant **££-£££**,
🪑 Canalside terrace, ♿

Occasional tap takeovers, DJs (Fr-Su), sustainable homeware shop

⊖ Hackney Wick 🚲 NCN1, link to Q6 🚶 Capital Ring, Jubilee Greenway, Lee Valley Path, Olympic Park paths

Opened just before the 2012 Olympic and Paralympic Games by New Zealanders Tom and Jess Seaton and friend and brewer Neil Hinchley, this funky brewpub with its cleverly hand-recycled wooden furniture and fittings was the first new beer initiative in the post-industrial arts and media colony of Hackney

Crate

Wick. It's in the White Building, a former sweet factory with a splendid terrace beside the River Lee Navigation, looking across to the Olympic stadium and Orbit sculpture. It expanded in 2014 by adding a production brewery across the yard, but loss of business during the lockdowns forced this into administration in July 2020 and it's now used by Truman's (below). Thankfully, the original brewpub survived, and production has since revived on the old 8hl AB-UK kit behind glass in the bar area. Besides house beers, there are numerous mainly London and UK guests like BBNo, Bohem, Burning Sky, Kernel and Wild Card, including a few classy sharing bottles. Bar food focuses on stone-baked pizzas of notable quality, deploying unconventional toppings like sweet potato, stilton and walnut, middle eastern lamb or Kashmiri dal. Since January 2020, diners have had the more upmarket option of Douglas McMaster's 'zero waste' Silo restaurant upstairs, with virtuous tasting menus that might include salted cucumber with sea lettuce and spruce or bavette steak with Tokyo turnip. An in-house pottery is also planned as part of a policy to encourage industrial use of the site.

BEERS are changing cask specials and sours, only available onsite. There's also a Crate core range, currently contract brewed for keg and can, which includes **Session IPA** (3.6%), **Citra and Yuzu Sour** (3.6%), a year-round **Stout** (5%) and **IPA⁺** (6%).

Deviant and Dandy 7

Brewery, taproom
185 Nursery Road E9 6PB (Hackney)
deviantanddandy.com
First sold beer: January 2018
⏱ *Th* 17.00-23.00, *Fr* 16.00-23.30, *Sa* 12.00-23.30
 Su 12.00-22.00. Children until 19.00. Cash-free.
10 keg, 6 cans.
☰ Large yard, mainly outdoor, ♿
Beer festivals and launches, live music

⊖ Hackney Central, Hackney Downs ⊘ Link to Q2

This intriguingly named outfit at one end of Hackney's 'beer row' is the second brewery co-founded by US exile Byron Knight, who previously helped set up Beavertown. He was the original 'deviant' while another founding partner, Rupert Selby, was the 'dandy'. Both have since moved on, with the project now led by another co-founder Ben Taub, who claims to be neither, with former Hackney head brewer Darren Walker. At first, beers were cuckoo brewed at Enefeld, starting in 2017, with the current railway arch site, equipped with a new 16hl brewhouse, launching the following year. In the warmer months, you'll walk through this to reach the sheltered seating and outdoor bar, in a converted container, in a yard on the south side of the railway; in winter the taproom sensibly moves indoors.

BEERS in keg and can are mainly specials and seasonals in contemporary styles, including pale ales and lagers. Hazy, fruity pale ale **Dude Looks Like a Hazy** (4.4%) is a near-regular.

Dove

Contemporary pub, bar
24 Broadway Market E8 4QJ
T (020) 7275 7617 **dovepubs.com**
🕐 *Su-Fr* 12.00-23.00, *Sa* 11.00-23.00.
Children until 18.00 or 20.00 if dining.
5 cask, 17 keg, 100 bottles/cans, some wines.
🍴 Eclectic pub grub **££**, 🪑 Tables on street, small balcony, ♿
Quiz (We), acoustic session (Su), monthly book club, board games, functions

⊖ London Fields 🚌 Ada Street, Broadway Market
🚲 Q13, link to C27 🚶 Jubilee Greenway

With its extensive food and drink selection and quirky but relaxed vibe, the Dove sits well on arty-crafty Broadway Market, though its makeover from Victorian boozer the Goring Arms dates from the 1990s, long before the street's recent facelift. The place is bigger inside than it looks outside, unfolding as a series of diversely decorated rooms, some with aged dark wood panelling and tiling. A pioneer in promoting Belgian imports alongside specialist UK beers, it still boasts a comprehensive list of Trappists and other classics from the likes of Boon, Dolle and Rodenbach, with newer Belgian entrants like Siphon alongside casks perhaps from Crouch

Vale, Timothy Taylor and East London, kegs from London Fields, Lost and Grounded, Tiny Rebel and Yonder, and bottles and cans that stretch to the Netherlands, Canada and the US, with all draughts offered in tasting planks of thirds. There are numerous meat-free dishes on the menu, including vegan lasagne and beer battered tofu and chips, besides Thai-inspired options and survivors of the original Belgian theme like mussels. Piped music and big screen TV are mercifully absent from this often-overlooked star performer.

Experiment ⑨

Bar
19 Bohemia Place E8 1DU
pressuredropbrewing.co.uk
🕐 *We-Th* 17.00-23.00, *Fr-Sa* 12.00-23.00, *Su* 12.00-21.00. Children until 19.00. Cash-free.
10 keg, 20+ bottles/cans.
🍴 Order-in pizza, nachos **£-££**,
🪑 Tables at front, ♿
Beer launches

⊖ Hackney Central, Hackney Downs 🚲 Link to C27

Pressure Drop's move to Tottenham in 2017 (p190) prompted the question of what to do with its former Hackney site. A chance

Dove

conversation with acclaimed Cornish brewery Verdant, based in Falmouth, resulted in its reopening in July 2018 as London's first collaborative brewery bar. The railway arch now seems much more spacious than when it was packed with brewing equipment, but retains a basic taproom feel, with a green wooden bar at one end and ex-German beer garden tables. Nearly all the beers are from the two partners, no bad thing given the quality and freshness on offer, though there are occasional guests including from US brewers rarely seen in London.

Five Points Brewing

Brewery, taproom: 61 Mare Street (Hackney)
T (020) 8533 7746 fivepointsbrewing.co.uk
First sold beer: March 2013, ❗❗
⏱ *Th-Fr* 17.00-22.00, *Sa* 12.00-22.00, *Su* 12.00-21.00. Children until early evening.
2 cask, 6 keg, 5+ bottles/cans, growlers, specialist ciders.
🍴 Gourmet pizza **£-££**, 🪑 Large partly covered yard, ♿.
Beer festivals, brewers' markets, tap takeovers, community events.

🚇 Cambridge Heath 🚲 Jubilee Greenway, link to Q13
🚶 Jubilee Greenway

Pembury Tavern **10a**

Contemporary pub: 90 Amhurst Road E8 1JH
T (020) 8986 8597 pemburytavern.co.uk
⏱ *Mo-Fr* 16.00-24.00, *Sa* 12.00-24.00,
Su 12.00-23.00. Children until 21.00.
5 cask, 10 keg, 10+ bottles/cans, 1 cider.
🍴 Gourmet pizza **£-££**, 🪑 Tables on street, ♿.
Tap takeovers, other beer events, tastings, quiz (Mo), comedy, board games, bar billiards, functions

🚇 Hackney Central, Hackney Downs 🚲 Link to C27

Five Points is one of the claimants to the title of London's biggest independent brewery. It was founded by pub operator Ed Mason with proceeds from the sale of pioneering craft beer bar Mason & Taylor, which became BrewDog Shoreditch. It began with a 16hl brewhouse in a railway arch under Hackney Downs station, taking its name from the busy five-way road

junction only metres away. A new 32hl brewhouse was commissioned in 2015, with the old kit sold to Signature Brewing. As well as taking on an adjoining arch, Five Points added warehousing and offices at a separate site on Mare Street, a little to the south, in 2016. Following several successful crowdfunding rounds, during 2021 the brewery vacated its birthplace, consolidating operations on an expanded Mare Street site with an annual capacity of over 15,000hl.

Long lacking a taproom because of its restricted accommodation, Five Points bought landmark pub the Pembury Tavern, located right on the eponymous junction, from Cambridgeshire's Milton brewery in 2018. This is now a splendid showcase, with smart wood finishes and a green-tiled bar that also dispenses guest beers, including traditional cask ales from family brewers, and kegs that might be from First Chop, Schneider or Yonder. A gourmet stone-baked pizza menu created in collaboration with Rachel Jones of Capish? includes white (without tomato) and green (vegan) options and various unusual toppings. The expanded brewery site now also has a taproom and pizza menu, originally just with outdoor seating but the interior should be completed by the time you read this. Regular lines here are restricted to house beers, except for festivals and special events.

BEERS still include a substantial amount of cask, though most beers are now also available in bottle or can – the brewery unusually maintains lines for both – and keg. The core range includes hoppy **XPA*** (Extra Pale Ale, 4%); **Best** (4.1%, cask only), a Fuggles-hopped bitter; contemporary-style **Pale*** (4.4%), the brewery's first and still its flagship and best-seller; **Pils** (4.8%); **Railway Porter*** (4.8%); juicy pale ale **JUPA** (5.5%); and West Coast-style **IPA** (6.1%, can only). More frequently recurring seasonals and specials include lower-strength **Micro Pale*** (3.3%); annual **Green Hop Bitter** (3.7%); rye ale **Hook Island Red*** (6%), formerly a core beer; **Derailed Porter*** (5.7%), a stronger version of the regular porter aged with *Brettanomyces* yeast; and **Old Greg's Barley Wine** (12.4%). A keg-only English-hopped lager (not tasted) was added in 2021.

Forest Road Tap Room ⑪

Bar

8 Netil Lane E8 3RL   forestroad.co.uk

⏱ *We-Th* 17.00-24.00, *Fr* 17.00-02.00,
   Sa 12.00-02.00, *Su* 12.00-22.00.
   Children until mid-evening.

13 keg, 2 bottles/cans, keg rentals, a few
bourbons

🍴 Occasional food trucks **£-££**, 🪑 Tables at
front, rear terrace, ♿. Flat access only
*Occasional beer events, running club, DJs,
occasional live music*

🚇 London Fields   🚲 Link to C27, Q13

This friendly, quirky railway arch taproom,
close to Netil Market and London Fields
brewery, opened in September 2016, predating
Forest Road gaining its own brewery (p231).
Expect to find a range of house beers served
in hop-draped surroundings that reveal the
owners' US roots. Recent expansion into a
neighbouring arch may presage the addition
of a pilot brewing kit.

Hackney Church ⑫

Brewpub, bar

16 Bohemia Place E8 1DU (Hackney)

T (020) 8986 2643 hackneychurchbrew.co
First sold beer: June 2018

⏱ *We-Th* 17.00-23.00, *Fr-Sa* 12.00-24.00,
   Su 12.00-22.00. Children very welcome
   until mid-evening. Cash-free

3-4 tank, 7-8 keg, 5+ bottles/cans.

🍴 Barbecued and smoked **£-££**,
🪑 Rear garden, ♿
Food matching, quiz (We), live music (Th)

🚇 Hackney Central, Hackney Downs   🚲 C27

The devil may not have all the best beers:
several board members of this impressive
railway arch brewpub are connected to nearby
St John's church, the premises are sometimes
used for religious events and elements of the
décor, like pew seating and ceiling beams,
evoke a church. Non-believers can relax,
though, as the higher purpose is the more
general one of providing community benefits
through apprenticeships and charitable work
around issues like local homelessness. Secular

co-founder and head brewer Ryan Robbins,
originally from Missouri, helms one of the
most serious recent startups in London,
with a bar, restaurant and kitchen in one arch
and a 20hl automated brewhouse in the other,
complete with its own water purifier and grain
mill. Guest kegs may be from Alphabet, Boxcar,
Kernel and Time & Tide, including sours and
dark options. Live-fire specialists Lagom occupy
the kitchen, producing dishes like smoked
aged beef burgers, smoked chicken and tasty
veggie options like beetroot carpaccio and
fried honey cauliflower. The pleasant garden
at the back is an unexpected extra pleasure.
The place was originally known as St John at
Hackney but changed its name to avoid confusion with the unrelated St John restaurant.

BEERS are served in house from tank and keg,
with kegs also sold elsewhere and there's
occasional mobile canning. Core beers include
Session Pale* (3.8%); rye-noted **Session
with Ry IPA** (4.3%); contemporary lager **Lazy
Day*** (4.8%); **Mare Street Mosaic Pale Ale**
(5.5%); and **Super Fly IPA** (5.5%). Regular
specials include beers in other lager styles: a
Pilsner* (5%) was particularly noteworthy.

Howling Hops Tank Bar ⑬

Brewery, taproom: 9 Queens Yard E9 5EN
(Tower Hamlets)

T (020) 3583 8262   howlinghops.co.uk
First sold beer: July 2012 (at original site)

⏱ *Su-Th* 12.00-23.00, *Fr-Sa* 12.00-01.00.
   Children welcome.

10 tank, 6+ cans, growlers, 2 ciders.

🍴 Changing popups **£-££**, 🪑 Tables in yard, ♿
DJs (Fr-Sa), community events

🚇 Hackney Wick   🚲 NCN1   🥾 Capital Ring, Jubilee
Greenway, Lee Valley Path, Olympic Park paths

THE U.K'S FIRST DEDICATED TANK BAR

Cock Tavern

Traditional pub, sometime brewpub:
315 Mare Street E8 1EJ (Hackney)
T (020) 8533 6369   **thecocktavern.co.uk**
⊕ *Mo-Th* 12.00-23.00, *Fr-Sa* 12.00-01.00,
  Su 12.00-22.00. Children welcome.
4-8 cask, up to 2 tank, 6-8 keg, 30+ bottles/
cans, ciders/perries, some specialist spirits.
⏗ Pickled eggs, order-in pizza **£-££**,
⅌ Tiny yard, ♿
Tap takeovers, weekly live piano

⊖ Hackney Central, Hackney Downs   ♿ Link to C27

The Cock, a classic corner boozer a few steps
from the famous Empire music hall and
Hackney's 'cultural quarter', was reopened
in 2012 by Pete Holt, owner of the renowned
Southampton Arms (p175), with a 6.5hl
house brewery in the cellar, previously used
by Camden Town at the Horseshoe pub in
Hampstead. Named Howling Hops as a nod
to blues musician Howlin' Wolf, this produced
over 100 different beers in its first two
years. In June 2015, operations relocated to
a new brewpub in an upcycled warehouse
at Hackney Wick billed as the UK's first 'tank
bar'. Here, a much bigger 25hl kit is used to
fill a battery of ten 1,100 litre conditioning
tanks lined up behind a bar decorated with
decidedly battered tiling, each one sprouting
a tap from which beer is poured directly, with
tasting flights available. The popup kitchen is
on long-term rotation, dishing up Colombian
street food for the past couple of years.

Beers at the Cock tick numerous style
categories including more traditional ones:
Holts Mild from Manchester was on cask when
I last looked in, and beers from Almasty,
Cloudwater, Deya, First Chop, Neckstamper,
Redemption and Wiper & True are also favoured. The kit in the cellar was rented for a while
by the Maregade brewery, which moved out
in 2017 and subsequently closed, then briefly
used by Howling Hops brewer Tim O'Rourke
under the name Short Stack: it's been mothballed since 2019 with no current plans to revive it. The solid, red brick building has Truman's
relief signing on one corner and a delightfully
old-fashioned public bar feel indoors, with
restored half-height dark panelling, ceramic

tiles and floorboards. It's at least as good as the
Southampton, and often less crowded too.

BEERS are sold from tank at Hackney Wick,
and in keg, can and sometimes cask outside
it, both at other outlets in the group and
elsewhere. Core beers include **Tropical
Deluxe** (4.6%) fruity session pale ale and East
Coast-style **House IPA** (6.9%), though much
of the output comprises changing specials
and one-offs.

Kraft Dalston (German Kraft)

Brewpub, bar
130A Kingsland High Street E8 2LQ (Hackney)
(020) 3877 0865   **kraftdalston.com**
First sold beer: December 2020
⊕ *Su-We* 12.00-23.00, *Th-Sa* 12.00-24.00.
  Children welcome.
6 tank, occasional keg, 2+ bottles/cans,
growlers, specialist spirits including from
in-house distillery.
⏗ Kebab and southeast Asian-inspired menu,
snacks, mezze **££**, ♿.   🍴

⊖ Dalston Kingsland, Dalston Junction   ♿ CS1

This ultra-modern brewpub-bar-restaurant is
a four-way collaboration between brewers
German Kraft; craft gin distiller Jim and Tonic,
their neighbours at their original Mercato
Metropolitano site at Elephant (p84); upmarket
reinvented kebab restaurant Le Bab; and
'aparthotel' operator Locke, which provides
accommodation on the upper floors of this
newly built Dalston site. A 5hl German-style
brewery operates in the basement, feeding
six serving tanks behind the upstairs bar, with
a handful of guests including quality British
contemporary beers and German classics.
There's plenty of seating on two levels,
beneath a skylight and dangling pink whales.

BEERS mainly in tank, sometimes keg, are sold
only in-house. The core range is similar to the
Elephant branch, supplemented by specials
that match German inspiration with the
adventurous tastes of the locals.

Laines Brew Lab
See People's Park Tavern

London Fields Brewery

Brewery, taproom (Carlsberg)
365 Warburton Street E8 3RR (Hackney)
T (020) 7241 5983 londonfieldsbrewery.co.uk
First sold beer: August 2011,
🕐 *Tu-Th* 17.00-23.00, *Fr-Sa* 12.00-23.00,
   Su 12.00-22.00. Children until 21.00.
12 keg, 25 bottles/cans.
🍴 Rotating street food popups **£-££**,
🪑 Some standing on street, ♿
Beer launches, food matching, dog day

🚇 London Fields 🚲 C27, Q13 🏃 Link to Jubilee Greenway

London Fields, around the corner from the historic open space of the same name, heralded the revival of brewing in Hackney. It began in railway arches in Helmsley Place with a 4hl kit, expanding to a 16hl kit in a bigger arch at the present address a few doors away in April 2012. There was much speculation about its future at the end of 2014 following publicity around founder Jules Whiteway, a convicted drug dealer overdue in repaying his criminal profits to the taxpayer, who was arrested again in December of that year for alleged tax avoidance. He was later acquitted, but by March 2015, the brewing equipment had been sold and many of the staff made redundant, with beers contract-brewed outside London.

When Copenhagen-based Carlsberg became the latest multinational to buy into London brewing in July 2017 by acquiring London Fields in a joint venture with Brooklyn Brewery of New York City, some beer commentators were unconvinced it could turn things around, but it's defied those expectations. Production returned to the capital with the help of Truman's, and following an eight-month closure for refurbishment, the taproom reopened in September 2019 with a new 15hl automated German-built kit. The facility boasts steam heating, a grist mill, a dedicated souring tank and a small canning line. The generously sized bar area has been refurbished and decorated with a 12-metre mural by local artist Luke McLean, also responsible for the beer labels. It's a funky place to enjoy the core house beers, specials and a low alcohol option, with guests from partners Brooklyn, perhaps on the Sunday 'dog day', when customers accompanied by canines are offered a discount.

BEERS are in tank, keg and can, with the more popular core brands currently contract brewed at Camerons in Hartlepool. Brands include flagship pale ale **Hackney Hopster** (4.2%), one of the earliest London beers to foreground New Zealand hops, and a modern pils, **Broadway Boss** (4.6/%). There are numerous specials including red ale **Love Not War** (4.2%), so named because it was first brewed while the August 2011 riots raged outside, various sours and fully fermented low alcohol beers.

Mammoth Beer ⑯

Brewery, shop, bar
1-28 Echo Building, East Bay Lane E15 2SJ (Hackney)
T 07970 927272 mammothbeer.com
First sold beer: January 2021
🕐 *Brewery*: For pre-arranged can collection only.
   Hackney Bridge Bar (under separate management):
   We-Fr 15.00-23.00, *Sa* 12.00-23.00, *Su* 12.00-22.00
4 cans at brewery; 1-2 keg at Hackney Bridge Bar, plus beers from other brewers.
♿ (on adjacent site).

🚇 Hackney Wick 🚌 The Copper Box 🚲 NCN1, C16
🏃 Capital Ring, Lee Valley Path, Olympic Park paths

London beer veteran Mark Pether bought the disued 16 hl brewhouse (now on its seventh owner) from his former employer Crate when they went into administration and took it across the River Lee Navigation to a new home at Hackney Bridge, a recently developed quarter of the Olympic Park. The brewery is a collaboration with music entrepreneur Vikram Gudi and takes its name from one of Vikram's companies. Currently there's no public-facing side other than a pre-booked can collection facility. An official taproom is planned for a separate site; meanwhile, the adjacent bar, under separate management, pours the brewery's keg beer alongside others, and there are street food stalls and a beer garden nearby.

BEERS in keg and can (not tasted) are in contemporary style, including **Primordial** (4%), a hazy, hoppy pale ale made with a kveik yeast; similar but slightly stronger 'double pale ale' **Sozonozo** (5%); and various flavoured sours.

Mermaid

Contemporary pub
181 Clarence Road E5 8EE
T (020) 8533 9677 themermaidclapton.com
🕐 *Mo-Th* 16.00-23.00, *Fr* 16.00-24.00, *Sa* 12.00-24.00, *Su* 12.00-22.30. Children until early evening.
1 cask, 20 keg, 60 bottles/cans, some specialist spirits.
🍴 Gastro-ish menu **££**, 🪑 Front terrace, ♿
Beer and food matching, monthly comedy and DJs, open decks night, board games, functions

🚇 Clapton 🚌 Clapton Pond 🚲 Link to C27

This handsome pub just off Lower Clapton Road has been through several hands in recent years, including Graceland, but since late 2018 it's been the domain of equally beer-friendly independent operators Alex and Conor, formerly of Meantime. Currently there's only one cask, often from a London brewer, but a thoughtful and varied range of kegs, including an exclusive house pale from Neckstamper, other Londoners like Mondo and Signature and guests from the rest of UK and abroad. The fridges show a Belgian bias, with plenty of good lambics and sour browns, smaller producers like De Ranke and Verzet, and Belgian-shaded big bottles from Burning Sky and Kernel. The mussels on the menu are dosed with Boon lambic, joining stalwarts like burgers, non-meat options like burrata salad and a weekly gourmet 'taco Tuesday'. It's a bright space with smart, dark green panelling and a leafy front terrace. The pub was closed for refurbishment following serious flood damage early in 2021 so it's worth checking opening times on social media.

Mermaid

Old Street Brewery 18

Brewery, taproom
1 Queens Yard, White Post Lane E9 5EN
(Tower Hamlets)
T 07491 990970 oldstreet.beer
First sold beer: January 2015 (at original site),
🍴 (informal)
🕐 *Tu-Th* 16.00-23.00, *Fr* 16.00-24.00, *Sa* 12.00-24.00, *Su* 14.00-23.00. Children until early evening.
Occasional cask, 14 keg, 40 bottles/ cans, growlers, some specialist spirits. 🍷.
🍴 'WestMex' barbecue and tacos **£-££**,
🪑 Tables at front, ♿
Tastings, food pairing, brewing days, fortnightly DJs, occasional films, monthly bingo, major big screen sport (including American football), board games, beer books

🚇 Hackney Wick 🚲 NCN1 🚶 Capital Ring, Jubilee Greenway, Lee Valley Path, Olympic Park paths

In 2013, staff at the Queens Head pub (p81) began brewing in the cellar. Initial experiments weren't successful but, following long delays and the installation of a new 1hl kit, the beers became good enough to sell over the bar, simply branded with the pub name. In October 2016, two keen staff members from related beer bar Mother Kelly's, Adam Green from Arizona and Andreas Wegelius from Finland, took over brewing duties. They renamed the operation Old Street Brewery after the location of the flat where they had begun homebrewing, rather confusingly as production was never based there. Following a temporary suspension, the kit, now resourcefully adapted to double its capacity, was relocated to a Bethnal Green railway arch in 2018, where it was replaced a year later by a much bigger 10hl brewhouse formerly at Pressure Drop. Further expansion followed with a move to this site in the cluster of breweries at happening Hackney Wick at the end of 2020, retaining the former arch as a bar (p162). The onsite taproom serves house brews alongside excellent guests, sometimes including draught lambics. Well-stocked fridges contain European classics, rarities and cult US lager Pabst Blue Ribbon: 'We sell the beers we want to drink,' explains Adam.

BEER is nearly all sold through the taprooms, from keg and sometimes cask, with occasional mobile canning runs. Most are changing specials in a wide range of styles with strengths a little higher than the London average, almost always worth trying, with a core juicy, hazy pale ale, **Peely Wally*** (5.5%). A berry sour, **Andy's Back** (7.5%), was particularly popular in 2019.

Pembury Tavern
See Five Points

People's Park Tavern
(Laine's Brew Lab)
Brewpub, contemporary pub
360 Victoria Park Road E9 7BT (Hackney)
T (020) 8533 0040   peoplesparktavern.pub,
laine.shop
First sold beer: February 2014
🕐 *Su-Th* 12.00-24.00, *Fr-Sa* 12.00-02.00.
   Children very welcome until 19.00.
2-3 cask, 7 keg, 25 bottles/cans. 🍶 (mainly from main brewery)
🍴 Burgers, salads, barbecue trays in summer
££-£££, 🪑 Terrace, side and rear garden ⚘, ♿
Life drawing class (Mo), quiz (We), DJs (Fr-Sa), pinball, vintage arcade games, functions

🚇 Homerton, Hackney Wick   🚌 Gascoyne Road
🚲 Link to NCN1, Q6, Q22   🚶 Link to Jubilee Greenway

This big pub with its large and verdant garden overlooking Victoria Park reopened in December 2013 as the second, and now the only surviving, of Laine's London brewpubs, with an 8hl brewhouse in its sprawling eastern wing. The extensive indoor space, in contemporary shabby-chic style but preserving an imposing carved wooden back bar and decorative ceilings, is a pleasant place to enjoy house brews and other options from Londoners like Beavertown, Brick, Brixton and Two Tribes. Food choices include barbecue trays with chicken, pork and halloumi options served with sweetcorn and pickles.

   The pubco first dabbled in brewing at the North Lane Bar in its home territory of Brighton in 2012. It reopened the Aeronaut in Acton as a brewpub in January 2014, just before the People's Park. Unfortunately, a major fire gutted the Aeronaut in January 2017, and although it's since been restored, the brewhouse wasn't replaced. The Four Thieves in Battersea became another brewpub in 2015 but brewing ceased here by the end of 2019. Laine was sold in May 2018 to a bigger pubco, Vine Acquisitions, which also owns Punch, but is still run as a separate unit with its brewing operations intact.

Visitor note. The pub, opened in 1865 as the Queens Hotel, stands beside the Queens Gate into Victoria Park. The 'People's Park', as it was nicknamed soon after opening in 1843, was London's first purpose-designed public green space, intended to improve the environment of the increasingly overcrowded and industrialised East End. The building has been a brewpub before: between 1986 and 1999, it was the Falcon and Firkin, the sixth branch of David Bruce's pioneering chain.

BEERS are normally in keg, sometimes cask, and labelled **Laine Beer Lab**: as this suggests, they tend towards the experimental, but among the more regular lines is **Beer Garden Pale** (4%). Other Laine beers are from elsewhere, and staff may not know what's brewed where. The lager and some other core beers are from the large production site the company now shares with Hepworth near Billingshurst, West Sussex.

Short Stack Brewing
See Howling Hops

Signature Brew Haggerston
Bar
340 Acton Mews E8 4EA
T (020) 7923 9417   signaturebrew.co.uk
🕐 *Mo-Th* 16.00-22.00, *Fr-Su* 12.00-22.00.
   Children until early evening.
10 keg, 30 bottles/cans.
🍴 Toasties **£**, 🪑 Side terrace, ♿
Live rock, jazz and acoustic music, quizzes, DJs, functions

🚇 Haggerston   🚲 Link to CS1, C27   🚶 Jubilee Greenway

Given Signature's links with the music scene, it's not surprising that this friendly, cosy railway arch bar has also functioned as a live venue since opening in September 2018.

Signature Brew

There's a proper stage, a small bar and a scattering of tables, one of them made from a flight case. Beers encompass the brewery's extensive range of core beers and specials, plus interesting guests in bottle and can.

Three Sods Brewery 21

Brewery, taproom
339 Mentmore Terrace E8 3PH (Hackney)
T 07554 457868   threesodsbrewery.com
First sold beer: January 2015 (at original site)
‼ informal
🕐 *Fr* 17.00-21.30, *Sa* 12.00-21.30, *Su* 12.00-21.00. May extend to *Th*: please check.
3 cask, 6 keg, 12+ cans, growlers. 🍺.

⊖ London Fields   🚲 C27, Q13   🚶 Link to Jubilee Greenway

Three business partners created this brewery late in 2014, adopting its apparently self-deprecatory name from the old Irish practice of displaying a sod of peat on houses selling illegal poitín. It began with a 5hl kit in a cramped and steamy space in the cellar of the historic Bethnal Green Working Men's Club. Two of the original founders are now less involved, but the business has continued to expand and during the 2020 lockdown relocated to a railway arch beneath London Fields station, expanding to a 10hl kit formerly at Wild Card. At the front of a smallish, well-filled arch there's a notably comfortable and attractive taproom which makes a point of offering cask.

BEERS are 80% cask, with some keg and canning. Regulars include **BoHo Bitter*** (4.1%); **Mon Chéri IPA** (4.5%), with a suggestion of cherry from the hops but no added fruit; **Old Normal Pale Ale** (4.5%), **Dark Magus*** milk stout (4.7%); and two regular US-style IPAs including **Maelstrom** (5.3%).

three SODS brewery

BoHo Bitter
4.1%

Brewed in the heart of East London

Truman's Beer 22

Brewery, no visitors please
The Brew Shed, 14A Queens Yard E9 5EN (Tower Hamlets)
T (020) 8533 3575   trumansbeer.co.uk
First sold beer: July 2013 🍺.

As explained elsewhere (p114), Truman's is one of the most important names in London brewing history, revived in recent years by James Morgan and Michael-George Hemus.

They began selling Truman's Runner, based on the spirit if not the letter of the old, in June 2010. After cuckoo-brewing in Suffolk and Leicester, they realised their ambition to return the brand to east London in July 2013 with a 33hl brewhouse on Fish Island in Hackney Wick, fermenting with the original yeast strain, a sample of which had been deposited at the National Collection of Yeast Cultures in 1958. The facility, known as the Eyrie, expanded in 2015 to a neighbouring unit previously occupied by Beavertown but had to relocate in 2020 due to redevelopment. The company secured a bigger site in the expanding brewing centre of Blackhorse Road, but the plans were disrupted by lockdowns. Since July 2020, Truman's has been brewing on an interim basis at the present address in Hackney Wick on the former Crate production brewhouse, vacated by its owners when financial difficulties necessitated downsizing (see above). The Blackhorse site is currently a large beer hall and events space, Truman's Social Club (p154), though production should relocate here eventually as originally planned. There's also a West End pub, the Newman Arms (p118).

BEERS are in cask, tank, keg and can. Cask was the mainstay in the early years, and despite the difficulties of Covid, the portfolio still includes cask ales like best bitter **Runner*** (4%), the inaugural beer, and Pacific pale ale **Zephyr** (4.4%). Keg regulars include **Pale Ale** (4.1%); the pils-style **Raw Lager** (4.5%), also in tank; cardamon-tinged **Social Porter** (4.5%); and **Roller IPA*** (5.1%). There are numerous specials and seasonals, sometimes including historical recreations.

TRY ALSO

BBNo Netil Market 13 Westgate Street E8 3RL bbno.co: Small outlet for this excellent southeast London brewery (p228) in an always-fascinating hip local market, with two keg lines and 10+ cans.

Beer + Burger Dalston 464 Kingsland Road E8 4AE beerandburgerstore.com. Long, narrow shopfront site in regular B&B format (p304): bar with 11 keg choices alongside burger kitchen at the back, fridges containing around 200 bottles/cans at the front. Staff picks are a nice touch.

Café OTO 18 Ashwin Street E8 3DL cafeoto. co.uk: Experimental and improvised music venue by night, pleasant café-bar by day, this Japanese-run Dalston institution (oto means sound) near 40FT and the Arcola Theatre is a longstanding stockist of Kernel, with various other UK and Belgian delights among five kegs and over 20 bottles.

Clapton Craft 97 Lower Clapton Road E5 0NP claptoncraft.co.uk: Original branch of this leading bottle shop chain, opened 2014. Four kegs, growlers, keg hire for events, 350 bottles/cans including some more traditional styles, especially in early December when CAMRA's Pigs Ear festival occupies the Round Chapel opposite. Takeaway only.

Crown and Castle 600 Kingsland Road E8 4AH thecrownandcastle.co.uk: Victorian street corner landmark in Dalston long used as a restaurant but rehabilitated as a pub by Barworks in 2020. No cask, eight keg and around 30 bottles/cans covering a wide range of styles.

E5 Bakehouse 395 Mentmore Terrace E8 3PH e5bakehouse.com: It's worth a look in this delightful bakery and café if visiting Three Sods a few doors down to see if they have any of their homemade kvass in stock, brewed at the Poplar branch (p159). A handful of good bottled and canned beers from other brewers too. Open daily but daytime hours only.

Hackney Tap 354 Mare Street E8 1HR hackneytap.com: The latest in the 'Tap' group (Euston Tap p78), opened April 2021 in landmark early 19th century Hackney Old Town Hall, on an attractive town centre square. Three cask, 15+ keg lines and a gyoza kitchen.

Off Broadway 63 Broadway Market E8 4PH offbroadway.org.uk: Friendly neighbourhood cocktail bar on Broadway Market close to the Dove (above). Co-owned by Deviant & Dandy founder Byron and serving three of its keg beers, plus 20+ bottles/cans including other Londoners like Five Points, Kernel and Solvay Society. Live music Th-Sa

Tonkotsu Mare Street 382 Mare Street E8 1HR tonkotsu.co.uk: Small informal restaurant chain serving up excellent, authentic Japanese ramen noodles with around eight inspired beer choices selected by experts, including an exclusive collaboration with Magic Rock. This branch has keg as well as bottles/cans; for other branches see website.

HACKNEY HOPSTERS

On August bank holiday Monday 2011, the first 21st century brewery in Hackney, and the first to open since the original edition of this book appeared, celebrated becoming the 15th London brewery with a public party. This was London Fields, under an arch of the rail viaduct which runs just to the east of the public space of the same name. I was a little surprised to be there: I'd expected Moncada in northwest London, which I'd just managed to squeeze into the book at the last moment, would be next in line. But I was glad to see at least something happening beer-wise in an area where I'd struggled to find listings for the book.

London Fields Brewery

I was one of a surprisingly large crowd of other guests crammed in among the vessels of a basic but serviceable brewhouse, a few of them familiar beer faces but mainly ordinary locals clearly excited at the prospect of a brewery on the doorstep. It was so busy the beer began to run out, and they started selling unfinished green beer from the fermentation tanks. Not the most promising sign for a brewery that was to have a troubled future (p137), but it was an early milestone in Hackney's ascendancy as one of the premier London brewing locations. Five more breweries opened in the borough over the following 12 months. Today there are 10 Hackney breweries, or 15 if you count the quartet in Hackney Wick that fall within Tower Hamlets and the shared homebrewing facilities at Brew Club.

It's a major change for one of London's most densely populated and vibrant neighbourhoods. In the mid-17th century, Hackney was a pretty village just outside London where Samuel Pepys went 'away into the fields to take the air'. Industry spread north from the East End along Roman Ermine Street and the River Lea in the early 19th century, and the railways rapidly followed. Though noted for products like paint, furniture, footwear and plastics, the borough was never home to the sort of big breweries found around Shoreditch and Bethnal Green to the south. Its last historic brewer, Michell Goodman and Young on Stamford Hill, was bought and closed by Mann's in 1919, though one of the biggest Firkin brewpubs, now the People's Park Tavern (p139), operated on the edge of Victoria Park between 1986 and 1999.

Why has Hackney proved such fertile ground for London's brewing resurgence? The borough has enjoyed a Bohemian reputation since the 1980s, as artists and alternative lifestylers moved in on what was already a lively mix of the old East End and postwar immigrant communities. Many were attracted to the Victorian housing, like the terraces between London Fields Brewery and the park. Originally built for the middle classes, these were now decaying but spacious and relatively cheap as the Tube didn't venture here despite the proximity to central London. The process of replacing this fabric with modern social housing estates hadn't got quite as far as in many comparable parts of the inner city thanks to local resistance, leaving some older houses in council hands but unoccupied and ripe for squatting and short-term occupation.

A grand souvenir of this period remains today right by Dalston Junction station: the fabulous peace carnival mural designed by Ray Walker in 1983. Across the road is the smart new development of Dalston Square with its upmarket restaurants, a sign of the borough's current attractiveness for well-heeled media and tech workers. They've arrived in the wake of the notorious Hackney hipsters, the more prosperous successors to those early Bohemians, who

HACKNEY HOPSTERS

have repurposed former industrial sites into studios and homes. And as in many other parts of London, contact between the various communities hasn't always been stress-free.

Car mechanic Mick Vallance, forced by rising rents to quit Mick's Garage in Hackney Wick after 23 years in favour of the expanding Crate brewery, hit out in the press in 2015 at 'arty types' colonising east London. Some taprooms have faced challenges to licences from resentful neighbours. While most readers of this book will rightly rejoice at the current health of the London scene, things might not seem so rosy if all the local pubs in the formerly deprived neighbourhood where you've spent your life have closed and the corner shops are struggling, while a nearby taproom does a roaring trade in craft sours at £6 a pint in the arch next door to the trendy bakery selling organic ancient grain sourdough loaves at £4 a throw.

There's no doubt of the link between craft beer and gentrification. A 2016 study found that the appearance of a new brewery in an area heralded a doubling of property prices. It's easy to see how this happens. Finding an ideal site for a brewery start-up is a delicate balancing act that often delays overoptimistic launch dates. The cheapest and most practical options from a production viewpoint are in traditionally remote industrial estates, but brewers are also seeking proximity to a customer base prepared to embrace them as a favoured local supplier. This will help reduce delivery costs and effort and ensure a busy taproom generating high margins, increasingly an essential part of the business plan. New breweries therefore gravitate towards up-and-coming areas where rents are still affordable but there's already enough of a community of thirsty regulars to provide the initial demand.

Ironically, many breweries are now becoming victims of the trends they originally exploited, struggling to remain economically viable and to expand in increasingly desirable and expensive locations. Five Points, founded in 2013 and now one of London's biggest independents, found itself inconveniently splitting operations between its original cramped arches close to central Hackney and a second unit a mile to the south. Thankfully, it was eventually able to stay in its native borough by increasing the space at its second site. In contrast, Hackney Brewery, despite its name, found itself having to move out of the borough, quitting its original arches for a bigger industrial unit in the burgeoning brewing centre of Blackhorse Road (Lure of the Lea, p157).

Clearly, gentrification is part of a wider social problem which is way beyond the scope of this book, but it's worth noting that many new breweries and similarly artisanal businesses are at least sensitive to the feelings of surrounding communities and do their best to mitigate problems. They get involved in supporting local charities and other community initiatives, advertise jobs locally and organise themselves to minimise disruption. During the recent lockdowns, those community links proved their worth, as residents returned the favour by rallying round their local breweries.

Stratford to Walthamstow

Visiting Blackhorse Breweries

When Wild Card expanded in spring 2018, it became the first brewery in a strip of post-war industrial estates in western Walthamstow. Just over three years later, the area has become a second Bermondsey, with six taprooms and perhaps more on the way, all within easy walking distance of each other and Blackhorse Road Tube and Overground station. Some of the venues open on weekdays but you'll need to visit on a weekend to find everything open. The area wasn't originally designed with promenading in mind and is a bit of a maze: when in doubt, return to Blackhorse Lane and look out for the signs marking access to specific estates. From the station heading north, you'll find Truman's on Forest Estate; Exale, Beerblefish and Signature Brew on Uplands C; and Wild Card and Hackney on Lockwood Way.

Or combine a brewery crawl with a visit to the Walthamstow Wetlands (**wildlondon.org. uk/walthamstow-wetlands-nature-reserve**), a collection of reservoirs that's now Europe's largest urban wetland nature reserve, immediately to the west. There are convenient entrances both at the end of Lockwood Way and on Forest Road/Ferry Lane so you could explore the reserve northwards and work your way south via the breweries. Note the station is called Blackhorse Road, after the southern part of the road, while the breweries are all off Blackhorse Lane, its northern extension.

Barrel Store

See Wild Card Brewery

Beerblefish ㉓

Brewery, taproom
2A-4 Uplands Business Park, Blackhorse Lane
E17 5QJ (Waltham Forest)
T 07594 383195   **beerblefish.co.uk**
First sold beer: October 2016, 🍴
🕐 *Th* 16.00-22.00, *Fr* 16.00-23.00, *Sa* 12.00-23.00,
  Su 12.00-22.00. Children until early evening.
  Cash-free.
4 cask, 2 keg, 15+ bottles. 🍷.
🍴 Occasional food truck, 'really nice crisps',
🪑 Tables at front, ♿
Tastings, live music, dance, DJs, library, pool table, board games

⊖ Blackhorse Road   🚌 Shakespeare Road Walthamstow
🚲 🚶 Link to Wetlands to Wetlands greenway

Homebrewers James Atherton and Australian-born Glenn Heinzel first brewed commercially at Ubrew late in 2015 under the names

blefish

Beerblefish and Tankleys respectively, but quickly decided they needed their own commercial-sized equipment. A year later, James and partner Bethany were producing beer in an industrial unit in the Lea Valley at Edmonton on a 1970s-vintage 8hl brewhouse made from converted Grundy tanks and sourced from a defunct Suffolk outfit. Struggling to balance this with their day jobs, they brought Glenn in full time to run the operations. A new site in the growing beer cluster off Blackhorse Lane, right next to Exale, opened as a taproom in July 2021, with production moving in September. One unusual and very welcome feature is the micropub-style coldroom visible behind the bar, where beer is poured straight from the cask, to be enjoyed on comfortable tables beneath an impressive mural depicting a Viking ship in space. The business aims to be ethical and socially useful, for example by helping retrain ex-forces personnel. The origin of the name will be obvious to anyone familiar with the babel fish in Douglas Adams' *Hitchhiker's Guide to the Galaxy*.

BEERS, sold in cask, keg and hand-bottled and all vegan-friendly, often nod towards historic recipes. Several use *Brettanomyces claussenii*, a different wild yeast species to the more familiar *B. bruxellensis*, isolated from English stock ale in the early 20th century. Signature beers are **1820 Porter*** (6.6%), **1853 ESB** (5.3%) and **1892 IPA*** (6.9%). **Impy Mild*** (7.1%) recurs as one of numerous specials and experiments which have included a mild of more modest strength, a rare London-brewed example of heritage German style Mumme and a wet hop beer with locally foraged wild hops. Some Tankleys beers are cuckoo-brewed here: see Brewers without breweries p322.

Collab
See Signature Brew

East London Brewing

Brewery, shop
45 Fairways Business Centre, Lammas Road
E10 7QB (Waltham Forest)
T (020) 8539 0805 eastlondonbrewing.com
First sold beer: September 2011, 🍴
🕐 Occasional open days, off sales *Mo-Fr*
     07.00-19.00, weekend by arrangement.
10 bottles/cans, bag in box. 🖐
Food matching, beer launches

🚆 Lea Bridge 🚲 Link to NCN1, C27 🥾 Link to Capital Ring, Lea Valley Path

Former research and development chemist Stu Lascelles switched career paths by setting up a brewery with his wife Claire Ashbridge-Thomlinson. The first in what's now a developing cluster of beer producers around Lea Bridge station, East London began with a 16hl plant and open fermenters in a single unit on an industrial estate between the railway and the Lee Valley Park. It's since expanded into two other adjacent units and in July 2019 upgraded to a 40hl kit and recruited a new head brewer, Adrian Morales-Maillo, formerly of Naparbier in Barcelona. The more traditional styles are made with a house yeast which originated at Thwaites. Due to site limitations, the brewery is open only occasionally but sells beer to take away during normal working hours. A taproom is planned by early 2022.

BEERS were initially mainly in cask and the format still accounts for 60% of its output: 'We won't ever leave cask,' says Claire, 'but commercially we're now in a different market so we've diversified.' Core beers include best-selling **ELB Pale** (4%); **Foundation** (4.2%) best bitter; a darker, stronger traditional bitter, **Nightwatchman*** (4.5%); oatmeal stout **Quadrant*** (5.8%); and a monthly special. Session IPA **Beyond the Tower*** (3.8%) and an unfiltered pils-style **East End Lager** (4.5%) lead the keg range. Most beers are available bottled or canned; some, including Quadrant, are bottle conditioned. A limited-edition **Imperial Stout*** (around 10%) appears occasionally in 750ml black ceramic flip-top bottles.

Exale Brewing

Brewery, taproom
2C Uplands Business Park E17 5QJ (Waltham Forest) **twitter.com/exalebrewing**
First sold beer: March 2018 (as Hale).
🕐 *Th-Fr* 16.00-24.00, *Fr* 16.00-02.00, *Sa* 12.00-02.00, *Su* 12.00-21.00. Children welcome. Cash-free.
9 keg, 12 bottles/cans, growlers, spirits and cocktails from Victory London in same unit.
🍴 Changing food truck **£**,
🪑 Tables at front, rear garden, ♿
Tastings, beer launches, DJs (Fr-Sa)

🚇 Blackhorse Road 🚌 Shakespeare Road Walthamstow
🚲🚶 Link to Wetlands to Wetlands greenway

With its pink and green décor, plentiful greenery, illuminated little fluffy clouds hanging from the ceiling and two mezzanines including an outdoor crow's nest rising above a sheltered beer garden, this is a friendly and suitably quirky home for the imaginative Exale brewery and one of the highlights of the Blackhorse cluster. The story begins when Affinity expanded from its original home in a collection of half-sized shipping containers outside the Five Miles bar and nightclub in Tottenham late in 2017. The bar's co-founder Mark Hislop (ex-Brewdog and Redchurch) created Hale Brewing with Daniel Vane (ex-Weird Beard and London Brewing), taking over the 4hl kit originally bought from Anspach & Hobday (and now at Muswell Hillbillies). In 2019 the operation, along with its neighbour at Five Miles, the Victory London Distillery, relocated to this unit with a new 20hl brewhouse, winding up the old company and creating a new one under the present multi-punning name. Daniel himself moved on late in 2020 but the great beer continues to flow. The enterprise also provides apprenticeships and takes care to reduce its environmental impact including turning waste beer into vinegar and soap. Beerblefish (above) is next door.

BEERS in keg and can are distinctive and sometimes unusually flavoured. Among the core beers are **Pale*** (4.2%), sometimes known to appear in cask; **Krankie*** (4.2%), an unusual Irn Bru-flavoured sour; and

Der Titan* (4.8%), a Dortmunder-style lager. There are numerous specials and collaborations, almost always worth trying, including mixed fermentation beers and recipes featuring home-grown or locally foraged botanicals.

Gravity Well Brewing Co 26

Brewery, taproom
Brewery: 142 Tilbury Road E10 6RE (Waltham Forest); **Taproom**: 155 Midland Road E10 6JT
gravitywellbrewing.co.uk
First sold beer: September 2018, 🍴 (informal)
🕐 *We-Th* 16.00-22.00, *Fr* 16.00-24.00, *Sa* 12.00-24.00, *Su* 12.00-18.00. Children welcome.
10 keg, local artisanal pre-mixed cocktails, low alcohol beer, soft drinks.
🍴 Delivery from local plant-based restaurants **£-££**, 🪑 Tables on street, ♿

🚇 Leyton Midland Road

Founder Ben Duck had already given up his career as a financial lawyer before deciding to turn the appealing mix of science and creativity he found in his homebrewing hobby into a day job. He spent a year perfecting recipes before moving into an arch below the Overground Gospel Oak to Barking line by Leyton Midland Road station. Ben did most of the conversion and installation work himself, including designing and commissioning a miniature 2hl brewhouse, soon upgraded to 6hl, and, unusually for a brewery this size, a reverse osmosis filter to purify mains water. An informal taproom added in the same arch in April 2019 expanded to its own arch across the main road during 2020, selling house beers and the occasional London guest: it's clean and compact, with extra tables looking excitingly precarious on a mezzanine above the bar. Further expansion is planned during the currency of this guide.

BEERS are mainly pale, hoppy and hazy to suit Ben's taste, with names drawn from astronomy, in keg with occasional hand-bottling. Core brands include **Cosmic Dust*** (3.8%), a hazy session IPA with Mosaic and Enigma, and **Galaxies Apart** (6%), a stronger hazy IPA, alongside various one-off and seasonal brews.

Greater Good Fresh Brewing Co (The) 27

Brewery (of sorts), no visitors please
11A Uplands Business Park E17 5QJ (Waltham Forest) thegreatergood.co.uk
First sold beer: September 2020. ⌂.

The brainchild of two former music festival promoters, Ralph Broadbent and Alex Dixon, this isn't a conventional brewery but supplies a hi-tech home beer-making gadget, the Pinter, billed as a 'Nespresso for beer', and ingredients packs to use with it. Technically, it's not a home-brewing system as there's no liquid to heat up: instead you use a special 'fresh press' concentrate, cold water and yeast in a single 10 litre vessel which took seven years to develop. This is cunningly designed to accommodate fermentation, conditioning and dispense, typically taking 4-5 days to produce drinkable beer. Ralph and Alex point to the environmental benefits of their system which they say reduces packaging by 70% and CO_2 emissions by 50% compared with bought-in beer.

BEERS, or rather Fresh Press packs, are created by ex-Camden Town brewer Evangelos Tsionos and are designed to fit through a letterbox. They encompass core brands including various pale ales, lagers and stouts as well as monthly changing recipes and ciders, and can be bought individually as well as on subscription. I couldn't get the one I tried to work but I've heard others have more luck.

Hackney Brewery (High Hill Taproom) 28

Brewery, taproom
10 Lockwood Way E17 5RB (Waltham Forest)
T (020) 3489 9595   hackneybrewery.co.uk
First sold beer: June 2012 (at original site). ‼
⏰ *Mo-Fr* 17.00-23:00, *Sa-Su* 12.00-23.00.
    Children until 21.00. Cash-free.
18 keg, 35 bottles/cans, growlers. ⌂.
‼Order-in pizza, ⊞Beer garden, ♿
Beer events and tastings, spoken word performances, comedy, big screen games

⊖ Blackhorse Road   🚌 Clarence Road Walthamstow
🚲 🚶 Wetlands to Wetlands greenway

Former homebrewers Peter Hills and Jon Swain both worked at an Islington pub when they decided to join the growing ranks of London brewers in 2011. They began with a small 8hl kit and a rapidly growing collection of fermenters squeezed into a railway arch under the Kingsland viaduct between Hoxton and Haggerston. The brewery expanded into a neighbouring arch in 2015 and upgraded to a bespoke 20hl kit the following year. With production approaching 5,000hl a year, in late 2020 they moved the kit to a bigger site in the new brewing hotspot near Blackhorse Road, Walthamstow, with plenty of room for a taproom at last. Besides a smart main bar with a row of 20 matched green tap handles and a beer hall-style space alongside the brewhouse itself, there's a fine garden with

Hackney Brewery

147

sheltered booths, a green wall and container bar. As well as a comprehensive range of Hackney core beers and specials, expect numerous UK and international guests: draught Oud Beersel lambic and Edinburgh's Newbarns on draught with sharing bottles from Burning Sky and Jopen when I last called. Along with Wild Card opposite (below), the brewery is set to benefit in the coming years from a council-sponsored plan to turn the street into a destination site.

BEERS are nearly all in keg, with increasing amounts in can. Regular cask beers were discontinued early in 2018, though a small amount is still sold to selected pubs and bars. Core beers include a craft-style **Lager** (4%); popular peach and basil sour **Millions of Peaches** (4%); flagship modern pale ale **Kapow!** (4.5%) and West Coast-style pale ale **Boogie Van*** (5.5%). There are regular specials and collaborations: Bourbon-barrel aged **Spirit of the Wood*** (8.5%), made with Against the Grain, was particularly noteworthy.

Leyton Orient Supporters Club

Club

Matchroom Stadium, Oliver Road E10 5NF

T (020) 8988 8288   orientsupporters.org

⏱ *See text below*. Children welcome though venue is often busy.

9 cask, 6-8 bottles/cans, 4 ciders/perries, 10 malts.

🍴 Filled rolls £, 🪑 Standing on terrace, ♿

Beer festivals, major big screen football, functions, football matches in adjoining stadium

⊖ Leyton   🚌 Buckingham Road

Leyton Orient may currently only play in League Two, in fact the fourth rung of English football, but its supporters' club has worked its way into the Premier League of beer venues. It all started in 1996 with one cask on the bar at the suggestion of a member, and when the Matchroom Stadium was redeveloped in 2006, the supporters gained their own purpose-built clubroom with a refrigerated cellar. A cask mild, usually Mighty Oak Oscar Wilde, is always on, served by gravity, with a wide range of other

styles on handpump from the likes of Arbor, Brew Buddies, East London and Iron Pier, all at keen prices, plus some interesting bottles and cans. Check online for exact dates and times: the bar is open immediately before and after matches as well as for beer festivals (where additional stillages are installed), brewery-themed nights, quizzes and screenings of away and major international games. It's a members' club but drinkers carrying CAMRA membership cards or guides are welcome, as are well-behaved away supporters on match days, for a modest day membership fee. Staffed by friendly volunteers, it's one of London's most delightfully unexpected beer venues

Leyton Technical

Contemporary pub

265B High Road E10 5QH

T (020) 8558 4759   leytontechnical.com

⏱ *Mo-We* 16.00-23.00, *Th* 16.00-24.00, *Fr-Sa* 12.00-01.00, *Su* 12.00-23.00. Children until 21.00.

8 cask, 8 keg, 10 bottles/cans, ciders, some specialist spirits.

🍴 Enhanced pub grub/gastroish menu ££, ♿

Quiz (We), monthly live music, functions

⊖ Leyton

This pub in a magnificent repurposed late Victorian building, originally a popup during the 2012 Olympics, has become one of the Antic chain's most consistent beer champions. Besides the group's own Volden beers, you'll likely find local guest casks from Crate, East London, Redemption and Signature. More locals like Five Points and Hackney are on keg, with Fourpure specials among the handful of bottles and cans. An imaginative food menu could include stuffed globe artichoke with wild mushrooms, ham hock and broad bean risotto or pints of prawns.

Visitor note*. The pub occupies part of Leyton's former town hall and technical institute, a fancifully neoclassical celebration of civic prosperity in red brick and Portland stone completed in 1896, with a grand porch and magnificent mosaic floors.*

Magic Spells

Brewery, taproom
Hare Wines, 24 Rigg Approach E10 7QN
(Waltham Forest)
magicspellsbrewery.co.uk
First sold beer: June 2017
⊕ Summer *Sa* 12.00-22.00, occasional other
days and special events: check social media.
Children very welcome until 20.00,
particularly on family days.
1 cask, 6 bottles/cans.
🍴Changing food truck **£**, 🪑Large front yard, ♿
*Brewing sessions and seminars, monthly family
days, graffiti workshops, classic car meets, DJs*

≋ Lea Bridge 🚲Link to NCN1, Q2
🚶Link to Capital Ring, Lea Valley Path

This brewing offshoot of drinks wholesaler
Hare Wines started when owner Jas Hare
noticed the booming popularity of the London-
brewed beers he was selling. Brewing began
in 2015 on a small scale in Epping, focusing
initially on own-label brews for restaurants and
similar businesses, with the brand launched in
2017. Initial commercial brews were made at
Red Fox in Coggeshall, but the brewer there,
Glenn Ackerman, later joined the Magic Spells
team, commissioning a 5hl kit in a space at
the back of the warehouse, on the site of the
now-demolished Lea Bridge speedway and
football stadium. This is mainly used for trial
brews and participatory activities, and as a
focus for a summer taproom (lack of heating
is a problem in winter) with a busy events
programme including graffiti workshops:
'We got fed up with all the tagging on our walls,'
says Jas, 'so we thought the best way to deal
with it was to make it a supervised activity
where the parents come as well'. More recent
commercial runs have been produced at
Firebrand in Cornwall. Note that though the
wholesale warehouse is open daily, it sells
only to the trade.

BEERS in cask, keg, botte and can include
the flagship **Hackney Hare** (4.2%) pale ale,
Unfiltered Lager (4.2%) and several other
core lines.

Neckstamper Brewing

Brewery, taproom
3 Cromwell Industrial Estate, Staffa Road E10
7QZ (Waltham Forest)
T (020) 7018 1760 **neckstamper.com**
First sold beer: January 2017, 🍴 (informal)
⊕ *Sa* 13.00-19.00.
6 keg, 15 cans. ♨
🍴 Occasional food truck, 🪑Tables on front yard,
♿ Flat access only
Board games, table football

≋ Lea Bridge 🚌 Staffa Road 🚲Link to NCN1, Q2
🚶Link to Capital Ring, Lea Valley Path

Another member of the Lea Bridge brewery
cluster, Neckstamper boasts a 16hl kit in a small
industrial unit, complete with a purpose-built
bar in a neat little taproom right next to the
brewing floor. Founder and long-time homebrewer Adam Jefferies began as a mechanical
engineer working in Formula 1 racing but
switched to banking before embarking on
professional brewing after a short course.

Visitor note *The curious brewery name is an obsolete
London term for 18th-century potboys who delivered beer
from pubs to private estates; the beer names make similar
use of archaic drink-related slang.*

BEERS are in keg and can. Core beers include
session IPA **Elbow Crooker** (4%); **Bonebox
Cooler** (4.4%) porter; and flagship **Squencher**
(5.4%) hazy IPA. Recurring specials include
To Lush (6.3%), a pale ale double dry-hopped
with a changing single hop, sometimes*; and
West Coast IPA **Supernaculum*** (6.6%).

Nirvana Brewery ㉝

Brewery, taproom
T6 Leyton Industrial Village, Argall Avenue
E10 7QP (Waltham Forest)
T (020) 3417 5580   **nirvanabrewery.com**
First sold beer: May 2017, 🍴 (informal)
⊕ Occasional pre-arranged events only.
Children welcome.
1 keg, 6 bottles. ♨ ♿
Yoga, occasional food pairing

≋ Lea Bridge 🚌 Staffa Road 🚲Link to NCN1, Q2
🚶Link to Capital Ring, Lea Valley Path

Founded by Steve Dass and Becky Kean, this operation in a modern industrial unit at Lea Bridge specialises in low alcohol beers. Everything is properly brewed and fermented from traditional ingredients but using reduced amounts of malt and controlling mashing temperatures and fermentation particularly carefully. Head brewer Chris Matthewman, formerly at Brixton Brewery, commands a 16hl brewhouse plus a pilot kit. The pleasant taproom on the mezzanine is open occasionally for events.

BEERS are mainly bottled, with some kegs and cans. Core beers include **Hoppy Pale Ale** and the more bitter **Classic IPA**, both a mere 0.5%. There's also a Soil Association-accredited Organic Pale Ale (not tasted) and seasonals

Pillars Brewery

Brewery, taproom: 2 Ravenswood Industrial Estate, Shernhall Street E17 9HQ (Waltham Forest)

T (020) 8521 5552   **pillarsbrewery.com**
First sold beer: October 2016, 🍴
🕐 *Fr* 17.00-23.00, *Sa* 12.00-23.00, *Su* 12.00-20.00. Children very welcome until early evening.
5 keg, 4+ bottles, growlers, beer cocktails. 🍷
🍴 Changing food truck **£**,
🪑 Tables on front yard, ♿
DJs, estate-based events, major big screen sports, functions

➔ Walthamstow Central, Wood Street   🚊 Addison Road

Untraditional Pub

Bar: 27 Crate Building, 35 St James Street E17 7FY
🕐 *Mo-Tu* 16.00-23.00, *We-Sa* 12.00-23.00, *Su* 12.00-20.00. Children until early evening.
6 keg, 30 bottles/cans.
🍴 Various from neighbouring traders **£-££**,
🪑 1st floor terrace, ♿

➔ St James Street

One of several welcome initiatives dedicated to improving London lager, Pillars (originally Four Pillars, though shortened just before launch) was founded by brothers Eamonn, Samie and Omar Razaq with their friend Gavin Litton. Their recipes were perfected over two years of test batches homebrewed in a garden shed belonging to the brothers' parents. Located in

a former car body shop alongside Trap (Try also below) and the Wild Card Barrel Store (below) in the buzzing surroundings of Walthamstow's Ravenswood Industrial Estate, the brewery boasts a water treatment plant and decoction brewhouse as well as an eye-catching mural on the outer wall. The expansive taproom was refurbished during the 2020 lockdowns in beer hall style, with plenty of natural wood and subdued lighting. In June 2019, Pillars added another outlet, the Untraditional Pub at Crate House, an attractive boxpark-style development of recycled shipping containers on the other side of Walthamstow, right by St James Street station. Here, customers queueing for beer at the front can admire kegs in the glass-fronted cold store, but make sure you check round the back too, where a well-stocked fridge offers numerous other London-brewed options as well as a few Belgian and German classics.

BEERS in the core range are brewed with only malt, hops and water in accordance with the Bavarian purity law, fermented using Czech lager yeasts and properly lagered, then sold unfined, unfiltered and unpasteurised in keg and bottle. They include traditionally-styled **Pilsner** (4.2%); flagship **Hop Lager** (4.5%), dry-hopped with US varieties and described as a Session IPL; and maltier but still modern **Helles*** (4.8%). Regularly changing specials have included hop varietals, decidedly un-Germanic fruit beers (a berry-infused Vienna was particularly popular) and the brewery's takes on lesser-known lager styles, including the UK's first traditional **Eisbock** (10%, not tasted), released annually

Pretty Decent Beer Co

Brewery, taproom: 338 Sheridan Road E7 9EF (Waltham Forest)

T 07825 381346   **prettydecentbeer.co**
First sold beer: May 2015, 🍴 (informal)
🕐 *Mo-Tu* 12.00-18.00, *We-Su* 12.00-23.00. Children welcome.
12 keg, 6+ cans, local spirits and soft drinks. 🍷
🍴 Small plates (*Fr-Sa* only), BYO,,
🪑 Benches at front, ♿
Occasional DJs

➔ Forest Gate, Wanstead Park   🚊 Wanstead Flats   🚲 Link to Q6, Redbridge Greenway   🚶 Link to Epping Forest Centenary Walk

When charity worker James Casey joined the swelling ranks of London brewers, he was determined that his enterprise would be about more than simply brewing good beer, so 15p from every pint sold goes to Pump Aid, providing reliable access to safe water in sub-Saharan Africa. Pretty Decent started in an arch under the Gospel Oak to Barking overground line in Forest Gate with an overgrown homebrew kit but has since upgraded to a 10hl brewhouse. The small taproom at the front was replaced in 2021 by a smart and shiny new dedicated space in the next-door arch which also stocks local guests.

BEERS are in keg or hand-bottled and bottle-conditioned. Core beers include **Oatmeal Stout** (4%); **Session IPA** (4.8%); **Pilsner** (5%); and flagship **American IPA** (5.5%). There are numerous specials.

Red Lion 36

Contemporary pub
640 High Road E11 3AA
T (020) 8988 2929
theredlionleytonstone.com
Su-We 12.00-23.00, *Th* 12.00-24.00, *Fr-Sa* 12.00-02.00. Children very welcome until 21.00.
9-10 cask, 6 keg, 30+ bottles/cans, 2-3 ciders, some wines.
Imaginative pub grub/gastro menu **££**, Sheltered rear garden, tables on street, &, 🚐 *Two annual beer festivals, quiz (Mo), DJs, live music, theatre, film, seasonal events, board games, vintage arcade games, functions*

⊖ Leytonstone   Link to Epping Forest Centenary Walk

The Antic group's beer showcase is a big street corner pub reopened in June 2011. Inside there's a single space with lounge furniture, standard lamps and iron pillars with peeling paint work ('it's meant to look that way,' bar staff once told me), with a big garden and outhouse at the back. A heritage floor mosaic in a bad state of disrepair is visible at the side. Besides the Volden and Sharp's regulars, the guest cask and keg taps offer an eclectic selection that might feature Bristolians Arbor and New Bristol, well-known names like Harbour and Thornbridge, Londoners Hackney and Twickenham or dark beer specialists Dark

Revolution. Bottles and cans have reduced a little but still feature plenty of London choices – BBNo, Kernel, Wimbledon – and unusual visitors like Funk Estate or To Øl from Denmark. Food from a shortish menu is imaginative with several seafood options – mussels and leeks, salmon and watercress fish cakes – alongside the likes of jerk chicken or spiced lentil and cauliflower fritters plus a British cheeseboard.

Visitor note. The 500-capacity ballroom above was a legendary rock venue in the 1960s and 1970s, hosting Led Zeppelin's first gig among others. Recently revived with a sympathetic restoration, it's now separately promoted as the Leytonstone Ballroom, hosting a busy programme of live music, club nights, theatre, film and comedy.

Signature Brew

Signature Brew Blackhorse Road
Brewery, taproom: 15 Uplands Business Park, Blackhorse Lane E17 5QJ (Waltham Forest)
T (020) 3397 8878   signaturebrew.co.uk
First sold beer: January 2014, 🍴
⊕ *Taproom*: *Fr* 18.00-23.00, *Sa-Su* 12.00-23.00. *Outdoor bar*: *Mo-Fr* 16.00-23.00, *Sa-Su* 12.00-23.00. Shop: *Mo-Th* 12.00-17.00, *Fr-Sa* 12.00-18.00, *Su* 12.00-17.00. Children welcome. Cash-free.
Occasional cask, 16 keg, 16 cans.
Weekend food trucks **£**, Tables at front, &
Live music, DJs, tastings

⊖ Blackhorse Road   🚌 Priestley Way
🚲 Link to Wetlands to Wetlands greenway

....

Collab 37a

Bar, restaurant: 198 Hoe Street E17 4QN
T (020) 8521 2948   thecollablondon.com
⊕ *Mo-Th* 12.00-22.00, *Fr-Sa* 12.00-23.00, *Su* 12.00-21.00. Children very welcome, children's menu.
16 keg, 24 bottles/cans.
Gourmet burgers and wings **£-££**, &
Live music, DJs

⊖ Walthamstow Central   🚲 Link to C27

....

Music fan Tom Bott and trombonist Sam McGregor conceived Signature out of frustration with the way multinational breweries dominated music venue bars. They collaborated with performers to create special edition brews, at first developing beers at a pilot brewery in Hackney which were then upscaled at Titanic in Stoke-on-Trent, owned by Tom's father and uncle, Dave and Keith Bott. Their first beer, created with the Rifles, was launched in September 2011. The brewery gained its own production site in Leyton late in 2013 and added a core range, some of it produced on the pilot kit, though with larger runs made at various host breweries. Brewing moved in house following a major upgrade in 2015 to a 16hl brewhouse previously used by Five Points. By 2018, the business had taken on two neighbouring units, with much-expanded fermentation capacity, but was once again struggling with space. A further crowdfunded expansion to the current address in the growing brewing hub off Walthamstow's Blackhorse Lane in 2019 has involved the installation of a 32hl brewhouse capable of lager-style step mashing and new kegging and canning lines. The ambition is to grow production to 20,000hl a year. As well as a large outdoor area, the site incorporates a smart taproom featuring a display on company history and a back bar made from musical equipment flight cases to match the brewery's distinctive tap handles, fashioned from the genuine casings of iconic Shure SM58 microphones. Signature was named Brewery of the Year by trade organisation SIBA in 2021.

There are two other outlets: a remote taproom in Haggerston (p139) and the Collab in central Walthamstow, opened in March 2019. The latter is a partnership with award-winning food popup We Serve Humans, which supplements its regular burger menu with exotica like a 'kimcheeseburger' and three veggie options, alongside Signature core beers and specials on tap and some interesting guests in bottle and can.

BEERS are in keg and can, with some cask. The core range includes noble-hopped **Studio Lager*** (4%); session pale ale **Roadie*** (4.3%), also in cask; **Backstage IPA** (5.6%); and coffee stout **Nightliner** (5.7%). There are various specials and seasonals including annual imperial stout **Anthology*** (10%), also in barrel-aged versions, and continuing collaborations with musicians, often sold at their gigs. The brewery has created beers with alt-J, Enter Shikari, Mastodon, Mogwai, Rodney P and Frank Turner among others.

Solvay Society 38

Brewery, taproom
223 Dyers Hall Railway Arches E11 4AF
(Waltham Forest)
First sold beer: July 2014 (on original site), ⚑
T (020) 8599 1338   solvaysociety.com
🕐 *Th-Fr* 16.00-23.00, *Sa* 12.00-23.00.
  Children until early evening.
5 keg, 20 bottles/cans. 🍴.
🍴Snacks, 🪑Bench at front, ♿Flat access only
Tastings, tap takeovers, homebrew club, quizzes

⊖ Leytonstone High Road, Leytonstone   🚌 Hampton Road

The Belgian leanings of this gem of a brewery are partly explained by co-founder Roman Hochuli's Brussels upbringing, while his background as a physicist explains the branding and the name, borrowed from a scientific research organisation begun by Belgian industrialist Ernest Solvay in the early 20th century. Commercial brewing began on a very small scale in 2014 when Roman and business partner J P Hussey installed a 50 litre homebrew kit in the cellar of the Warrant Officer in Walthamstow, moving later that year to a similar setup in the former Norfolk Arms, Canonbury. After a break for Roman to finish his PhD, in 2016 Solvay took on the site and 10hl kit of the mothballed Ha'penny

Solvey Society

brewery (operational between 2009 and 2014 and featured in the first edition of this book as one of the pioneers of the current London revival) in the Green Belt surrounds of Aldborough Hall Farm in Redbridge. Though idyllically rural, the site was too far off the beaten track for a regular taproom trade, so Solvay added an arch taproom beneath the Gospel Oak to Barking Overground in Leytonstone in 2019 and relocated the brewhouse to arch 224 next door in May 2021. The clean and bright space with its high stools and tables is an intimate showcase for house brews as well as draught guests from other local breweries (Essex's Leigh on Sea and Tottenham-based cuckoo Seven Sisters, for example) and imported bottled classics, including from Brasserie de la Senne in Brussels, one of the brewery's inspirations.

BEERS in keg, 440ml cans and 330ml bottles are Belgian-influenced but with a contemporary sensibility that favours session strength ABVs. Core beers include **Minimise*** table saison (3.2%); light unspiced wheat beer **Superposition** (4%); **Halmos** Brussels-style pale ale (4.2%); **Exotic Physics*** (6%) Belgian-style IPA; and **Tritium** (7.5%) tripel with pink peppercorns. Seasonal barrel-aged releases (some *–**) may be in 750ml bottles.

Stag and Lantern

well-stocked bottle fridge mainly focusing on London and other UK brewers (Bristol Beer Factory, Donzoko, Marble) with a few more Germans and the occasional Scandinavian rarity. Just down from the station and level crossing, it's in a single room shop unit with a mix of tables and a hop-draped bar, and soft-pedals on some of the stricter micropub requirements, with quiet background music.

Stag and Lantern 39

11 The Broadway E4 9LQ
thestagandlantern.co.uk
🕐 We-Fr 16.00-22.00, Fr 14.00-22.00, Sa 12.00-22.00, Su 13.00-19.00. Children until early evening. Cash-free.
3+ cask, 2 kegs, 45 bottles/cans, ciders
🍴BYO or order in, Tables on street
Tap takeovers, meet the brewer, live music, popup shops, drag bingo

➋ Highams Park

Opened in July 2020 as the first such outlet in a busy but underpubbed area, this very friendly micropub encompasses both classic bitters and more unusual options in a small but well-chosen cask range largely provided by brewers like One Mile End, New River and Redemption, with a decent German lager and a modern 'craft' on keg. The choice is widened by a

Tap East 40

Brewpub, bar
7 International Square, Westfield Stratford City E20 1EE (Newham)
T (020) 8555 4467   tapeast.co.uk
First sold beer: November 2011
🕐 Mo-Sa 11.00-23.00, Su 12.00-22.00.
    Children welcome.
6 cask, 10 keg, 150+ bottles/cans, some specialist spirits.
🍴 Hot dogs **£-££**, Front terrace, ♿
Tap takeovers, tastings, beer festivals, DJs (Fr)

⇄➋ Stratford International, Stratford   🚲Link to NCN1, Q6
🚶Olympic Park paths

When Westfield opened its massive Stratford City shopping mall adjoining the Queen Elizabeth Olympic Park in September 2011, at very short notice it invited the team at

Utobeer (p87) to create a brewpub for the Great Eastern Market, the requisite ghetto of specialists nestling amid the globalised brands. The result was an excellent beer venue in a space that's as comfy as it can be for an open-fronted shopping centre box, helped enormously by knowledgeable and enthusiastic staff. The handpumps dispense offerings crafted on the glass-fronted 4hl copper brewhouse, regularly including mild and stout, while Acorn, Bristol Beer Factory and Burning Sky often feature as guests. Kegs include local Pillars, solid UK producers like Brew York, Buxton, Nene Valley and perhaps Belgian, German or US imports. Renowned names from the same countries rub shoulders in the fridges with specials from Kernel and European upstarts like Basque and Kees! These are also sold to take away, alongside gift packs. Hot Dogs fill the food gap and there are several other grazing opportunities nearby. Much more than just a welcome break from retail therapy.

BEERS, sold in house and at sister pub the Rake, are in cask and keg, with occasional hand bottlings. They include currently the only regularly brewed cask mild in London, **East End Mild*** (3.5%); **APA** American pale ale (4.3%); recurring smoked porter **Smokestack*** (6.5%); and numerous seasonals, specials and collaborations.

Truman's Social Club

Bar

1 Priestley Way E17 6AL

T (020) 8533 3575   trumansbeer.co.uk

⏱ *Mo-We* 12.00-23.00, *Th* 12.00-24.00, *Fr-Sa* 12.00-01.00, *Su* 12.00-22.00.
Hours may extend to weekday mornings.
Children welcome. Cash-free.

4 cask, 1 tank, 15 keg, 20 bottles/cans, speciality coffee and spirits. ⏲.

🍴 Small plates, sharing boards, burgers, pizzas

££, 🪑 Large beer garden ♿

Beer festivals, music, films, big screen sport, markets, exhibitions, table games, shared workspace.

⊖ Blackhorse Road   🚌 Priestley Way   🚲 Link to NCN1, Q6
🚶 Olympic Park paths

This site in the burgeoning Blackhorse beer strip was intended as the new home of Truman's brewery (p140), though the pandemic ensured things didn't quite go to plan. Instead, it was opened in July 2020 as a purpose-designed socially distanced bar that could be reconfigured easily as conditions returned to normal. Easily the biggest destination in this book, it includes two vast but comfortable indoor spaces bedecked with murals and vintage Truman photos, one with table seating including some unusual booths, the other an events area. An extensive sunny beer garden has wooden decking, planters and its own container bar open at busy times. Expect a range of the brewery's core beers, specials and rarities plus guests sourced from independents in London and elsewhere, dispensed from a cellar visible behind glass on the way to the toilets. Food includes pizzas, brunches, rotisserie chicken, small plates like wings and spiced aubergine, burgers including vegan options and home-pickled quail eggs. The generous daily hours here are welcome in an area that's increasingly residential but has no proper pubs.

Untraditional Pub

See Pillars

Wild Card Brewery

Brewery, taproom: 2 Lockwood Way E17 5RB
(Waltham Forest)
T (020) 8935 5560   **wildcardbrewery.co.uk**
First sold beer: February 2014 (at original site),
🕐 *Fr* 16.00-23.00, *Sa* 14.00-23.00, *Su* 12.00-20.00.
   Children until 21.00. Cash-free.
10 keg, 10-12 cans. 🍷
🍴 Occasional food truck **£**, 🎍 Tables at front, ♿
*Occasional live music, DJs, films, games events,
functions*

⊖ Blackhorse Road   🚃 Clarence Road Walthamstow
🚲 🚶 Wetlands to Wetlands greenway

Barrel Store

Bar: 7 Ravenswood Industrial Estate,
Shernhall Street E17 9HQ
T (020) 8935 5560   **wildcardbrewery.co.uk**
🕐 *Fr* 17.00-24.00, *Sa* 12.00-24.00, *Su* 12.00-22.00.
   card only. Children welcome. Cash-free.
Occasional cask, 8-11 keg, 12 bottles/cans.
🍴 Pizzas **£**, 🎍 Tables at front, ♿
*Beer festivals, live music, DJs, art shows, films,
board games, major big screen sport*

⊖ Walthamstow Central   🚃 Addison Road

Wild Card is the creation of three university friends, Andrew Birkby, William John Harris and former chemical engineer and current head brewer Jaega Wise, originally from Nottingham. It began in January 2013 with amber ale Jack of Clubs, developed on homemade equipment in a garage and cuckoo-brewed just outside London. By the end of the year, the three friends had established themselves in a characterful unit close to Walthamstow Village, on an estate that was already a local attraction thanks to neon sign specialist God's Own Junkyard and Mother's Ruin, producer of fruit gin. Here, a modest 10hl brewhouse shared space with an increasingly popular taproom. In April 2018, Wild Card expanded to a bigger site, becoming the first of several breweries in industrial estates along Blackhorse Lane in the west of Walthamstow. At first, the old brewing kit was retained while fermentation capacity was substantially increased, with a small canning line and a new 20hl brewhouse added during 2019. The space includes a basic but pleasant taproom with a mezzanine overlooking the brewhouse. Twice-monthly brewery experiences here cram in basic food matching as well as a tutored tasting and brewhouse visit in expert company. Hackney Brewery

Jaega Wise, Wild Card Brewery

(above) moved into a unit opposite in early 2021 and over the next couple of years both are set to become mainstays of a new market destination area supported by the council. Meanwhile, the Ravenswood site, now with two other beer venues nearby, has become a bar named the Barrel Store, with a tiled back bar, verdant planters, extensive outdoor space on sunny days and a wall of gently maturing barrels. Jaega is now a brewing celebrity, not only for her great beers and extensive knowledge but for her tireless campaigning around inclusion and diversity in the industry.

BEERS are mainly in keg and in can, with some sold in major supermarkets. The core range includes **Pale*** (4.3%), **Lager** (4.4%) and **IPA** (5.5%), with a relatively regular **Table Beer*** (2.8%) and numerous specials, including changing sours. Cask was restored in 2019 with the addition of a best bitter and a pale ale.

TRY ALSO

Beer + Burger Walthamstow 368 Hoe Street E17 9AL beerandburgerstore.com: Small branch of reliable chain providing just what its name suggests (see Willesden branch p304). No cask.

Bell 6 Forest Road E17 4NE belle17.com: Comfortable and well-restored landmark early-20th-century pub with improving range despite tie: six casks including guests from Kent and northern England alongside 30+ bottles/cans. Handy for Lloyd Park.

Clapton Craft E17 76 Hoe Street E17 4PG claptoncraft.co.uk: Smallest branch of the chain (p129) well-stocked with four kegs and 250-300 bottles/cans including a strong London selection from lesser-seen breweries like Villages and Solvay. Takeaway only.

Clapton Craft Wood Street Unit 1, 147–151 Wood Street E17 3LX. Opened in April 2021 next to Clapton Craft's (p129) main warehouse and depot, this is their biggest site, with six keg lines and around 400 bottles/cans, all in fridges, and plenty of indoor and outdoor space for drinking onsite.

Eat17 24 Orford Road E17 9NJ eat17.co.uk: Upmarket and faintly hipsterish convenience store and deli, a Walthamstow Village fixture with 200 bottles/cans including lots of locals. Other branches (see website) have fewer beers but are still worth a look.

Froth and Rind 37 Orford Road E17 9NL eastlondoncheeseboard.co.uk: Pleasant Walthamstow Village coffee bar, specialist cheese shop and deli with encouragement to match from a choice of a dozen well-chosen cans from UK brewers and occasional local kegs.

Mother Kelly's Stratford/E20 27 Victory Parade E20 1FS motherkellys.co.uk: Overlooking Victory Park in the former London 2012 athletes' village, this ultramodern branch stocks 19 keg beers and 150 bottles/cans, also sold as growlers or to take away.

Northcote Arms 110 Grove Green Road E11 4EL thenorthcotee11.com: Rescued and comfortably refurbished independent community pub close to Leyton station with a busy event programme, including Sunday drag shows, with casks from Crate, East London, Signature and Wild Card on rotation and a few local kegs and bottles.

Olde Rose and Crown 53 Hoe Street E17 4SA yeolderoseandcrowntheatrepub.co.uk. This pretty and welcoming community local is now free of tie, with plenty of locals among the guests on six cared-for cask lines and independently sourced kegs. Also an in-house theatre, lots of interesting events and pub heritage relics.

Tavern on the Hill 318 Higham Hill Road E17 5RG tavernonthehill.co.uk: formerly the Warrant Officer, this neighbourhood pub on Higham Hill was refurbished by the team behind Wild Card in 2021 as an outlier of the Blackhorse brewery cluster with five cask, nine keg and a decent range of bottles and cans mainly from local brewers.

Trap Taproom 4 Ravenswood Industrial Estate, Shernall Street E17 9HQ therealalcompany.co.uk: Tempting shop window for indie distributor the Real Al Company, with six keg beers mainly from London and around 10 UK cans, plus 15 ciders and perries, on the same estate as Pillars and Wild Card Barrel Store (see above). The interior was largely created by a neighbouring furniture maker. Friday-Sunday only: check hours.

THE LURE OF THE LEA

It's easy to spot the River Lea (or Lee: both spellings are used) on maps of London, and not just because of its geographical prominence as the Thames's largest tributary. It's paralleled by successive lines of communication, from Roman Ermine Street to Victorian railways. In the much-reprinted series of silhouette maps illustrating the growth of urban sprawl in Patrick Abercrombie's *Greater London Plan* of 1944, the Lea Valley is already pointing up like a rude finger from London's fist in 1840. In 2021, as I soon noticed when mapping the locations in this book, it's picked out by a string of breweries.

As well as a creating a flat ribbon of land for roads and railways, the river provided a transport link between the capital and its rural hinterland, since the 1760s partly canalised as the River Lee Navigation. For centuries, this was the main route taken by grain from the fields of Hertfordshire and Essex to the bakers, brewers and distillers of London. Before its dissolution in the 1530s, Stratford Langthorne Abbey grew rich from its milling monopoly. The skein of waterways known as the Bow Back Rivers in the Queen Elizabeth Olympic Park was originally dug by the abbey's monks to service its mills. To the south of Stratford High Street, several historic 18th and 19th century mill buildings survive next to the busy film and TV studio at the aptly named Three Mills, though these mainly served gin distilleries rather than breweries. The lower Lea

also provided a convenient route for shipping beer, including the early India Pale Ales, from Bow Bridge to the East India Company's moorings at Millwall (see Yeast Enders p163).

With housing discouraged by flood risk, the valley became a patchwork of reservoirs, industrial estates, nurseries, gravel pits and remnant marshland. Following post-war neglect, much was transformed in the 1970s into a giant public open space, the Lee Valley Park, with another tranche becoming the Olympic Park following the 2012 Olympic and Paralympic Games, and even more industrial land is now undergoing redevelopment.

All this has proved fertile territory for new London brewers. A recent prime destination is the ribbon of industrial estates in western Walthamstow, between the new Walthamstow Wetlands wildlife area and Blackhorse Lane (Visiting Blackhorse Breweries above). The council's masterplan for this area envisages several thousand new homes, taking advantage of the nearby Victoria line Tube station. The new residents will be able to enjoy good beer at Beerblefish, Exale, Hackney, Signature, Truman's and Wild Card. There's

a further, smaller eastern cluster around Lea Bridge Road.

On the west bank, the fun begins at Hackney Wick: Crate, Howling Hops and Old Street are all on Queens Yard between the station and the Lee Navigation, while Mammoth is across the canal. Several more breweries are upstream at Tottenham (p184), where Beavertown and Pressure Drop are close to Hale Village, a new 'urban village' on the site of a former furniture factory. A short walk north through Tottenham Marshes will take you to Ora. Further on and a little west of the river, Bohem, One Mile End and Redemption are close together not far from the newly rebuilt Tottenham Hotspur stadium.

Though these breweries are more dispersed than in areas like Bermondsey, their proximity to the green spaces of the Lee Valley Park provides attractive opportunities for walks and cycle rides. The Lea Valley Path runs throughout on the Navigation towpath; National Cycle Network Route 1 either shares this route or runs on parallel paths. There are numerous connecting paths and trails, including the Capital Ring through Hackney Wick and a cycling route linking the Walthamstow Wetlands with the Woodberry Wetlands and Finsbury Park.

River Lee Navigation at Hackney Wick

Tower Hamlets

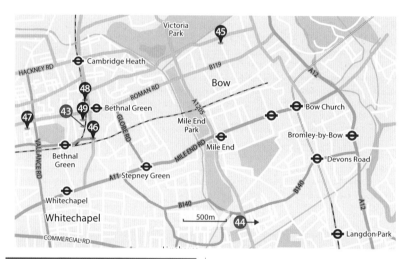

Boxcar Brewery 43

Brewery, taproom
1 Birkbeck Street E2 6JY (Tower Hamlets)
boxcarbrewery.co.uk
First sold beer: November 2017, 🍴: Please check
🕐 *We-Fr* 17.00-23.00, *Sa* 12.00-23.00, *Su* 12.00-
20.00. Children until mid-evening.
Cash-free.
8 keg, some bottles/cans. ⌾
🍴 Please check, 🪑 Partly covered front yard, ♿
Occasional special events

⊖ Bethnal Green

One of the more ambitious brewery projects
in the cluster around Bethnal Green, Boxcar
boasts a gleaming 20hl kit with automatic
mashing in one of a pair of arches under the
London Overground railway from Liverpool
Street. The other arch holds a taproom with a
smart white back bar dispensing fresh house
beers and the odd guest from like-minded
friends, a thoughtfully-stocked fridge, a sofa
corner and some welcome outdoor space.

It began much more modestly in late 2017
when head brewer Sam Dickison, formerly of
Moncada, Hammerton and Laine's, teamed
up with the founder of Vagabond Wines,
Stephen Finch, using a 200 litre kit in an
arch with no public facilities in Homerton.
Expansion to the current site was completed
in August 2019.

BEERS are in keg, with monthly mobile canning
runs, and occasional cask. Though much of the
range is keenly contemporary, Sam has a well-
publicised liking for mild and brews a regular
Dark Mild* (3. 6%) alongside other one-off,
experimental, seasonal and collaboration
brews including interpretations of traditional
styles. Notable successes have included
Table Beer* (3. 6%); a **Best Bitter*** (4.6%) in
collaboration with Mills; a Vegan **Milkshake
IPA** without lactose (6%); and a West Coast-
style IPA, **Power Cut** (6.4%). There's a changing
series of pale ales, IPAs and hazy DDH (Double
Dry Hopped) pales (usually over 5.5% *) with
varying hops.

Boxcar

E5 Poplar Bakehouse

Brewpub, restaurant, shop
2 Cotall Street E14 6TL (Tower Hamlets)
T (020) 8525 2890   e5bakehouse.com
First sold beer: December 2017 (at previous site)
🕐 *Daily* 08.30-16.30. Children welcome.
Occasional tank and keg, 12 bottles/cans,
coffee.
🍴 Breakfast, sandwiches, soups and stews,
takeaway bread and baked goods **£-££**,
🪑 Small terrace, ♿
Classes

⊖ Langdon Park   🚇 Broomfield Street   🏃 Lea Valley Path
(Limehouse Cut)

This excellent specialist bakery and coffee
roaster has a sideline in brewing its own kvass,
a low alcohol beer popular in eastern Europe,
in 50-60 litre batches using leftover rye and
spelt bread, sugar or honey and a sourdough
starter. It also offers workshops and courses
on fermented food and drink as well as baking
and sells a small selection of more conventional
bottles and cans from other brewers. Brewing
activities began in a railway arch at the London
Fields branch (Try also p141) but following a
suspension during the Covid crisis moved in
2021 to this recently refurbished site at the
foot of a new residential block overlooking
the Limehouse Cut canal.

BEERS (0.5-1.5%, not tasted) vary according
to the availability of leftovers and seasonal
foraged flavourings and brewer Simone's
experimental spirit. A couple of varieties should
be available in bottles, and sometimes from
keg or direct from the fermenter, but check
ahead if making a special trip as production
depends on the availability of leftovers.

Eleanor Arms

Traditional pub
460 Old Ford Road E3 5JP
T (020) 8980 6992   eleanorarms.co.uk
🕐 *Mo-Th* 16.00-23.00, *Fr* 12.00-24.00, *Sa* 12.00-
01.00, *Su* 12.00-22.30. Children until 19.00.
4 cask, 4 keg, 9 bottles/cans, 25+ malts.
🪑 Rear garden, ♿
*Monthly quiz, jazz (Su), major big screen sport,
board games, shove ha'penny, pool*

⊖ Bow Church, Bow Road   🚇 Alice Lane   🚲 NCN1
🏃 Jubilee Greenway

Only a few steps across the Hertford Union
Canal from Gunmaker's Gate on the southern
edge of Victoria Park, this is perhaps the most
inviting pub in the area. Once a Fuller's house,
it was one of several London properties
bought by Kent brewer Shepherd Neame in
the late 1980s and is a great showcase for its
beers. Master Brew and Whitstable Bay are
reliably well-kept cask regulars, with other core
beers and seasonals on rotation and guests
sourced nationally. A comprehensive range
of Shepherd Neame's bottled beers includes
historical recreations like IPA, and there are

several of the brewery's new keg lines too. Longstanding music-loving landlords Frankie and Lesley have decorated the place with classic rock posters, old advertising and quirky art and strewn it with a comfortable mix of tables and sofas to create a welcoming community space.

Fugitive Motel

Bar
199 Cambridge Heath Road E2 0EL
T (020) 3974 4455 fugitivemotel.bar
⏰ *Mo-Th* 10.00-23.00, *Fr-Sa* 10.00-24.00,
   Su 10.00-22.00. Children welcome.
12 keg, 40+ bottles/cans, kombucha, soft drinks.
🍴 Pizza, burgers, sharing plates **££**,
🎎 Tables at side, ♿
Community events, shuffleboard, cornhole, functions

⊖ Bethnal Green ♿ Link to CS3

David Burgess and Liam Tolan, both formerly musicians in indie bands, admit that the name of their bar just south of Bethnal Green Tube station has occasionally caused confusion since

Fugitive Motel

opening in June 2019. It's not in fact a motel, though the interior evokes the Californian freeways of the 1950s, with chequered floor tiles and booths that display illuminated vacancy signs when unoccupied. The beer selection is notable in showcasing the burgeoning lower alcohol sector: Adnams Ghost Ship 0.5% leads the kegs, and there's a wide selection of reduced and low options from Big Drop, Erdinger, Lucky Saint, Maisels, Mikkeller, Small Beer, Thornbridge and others in the fridges. Those seeking stronger stuff will find local draughts from Five Points and imports from Brooklyn and König. Besides beer, there's breakfast, brunch, good coffee and decent food.

Kings Arms

Contemporary pub
11A Buckfast Street E2 6EY
T (020) 7729 2627   thekingsarmspub.com
⏰ *Su-Th* 12.00-23.30, *Fr-Sa* 12.00-24.00.
   Children until 20.30.
3 cask, 13 keg, 60 bottles/cans, specialist spirits.
🍴 Cheese and meat boards, scotch eggs **£-££**,
🎎 Tables on street, ♿
Tap takeovers, beer launches

⊖ Bethnal Green 🚌 Barnet Grove

A rescued backstreet pub that was once a spirits house, this reopened in December 2013 as the second representative of Barworks offshoot Graceland, crewed by people as well-informed as at its predecessor the Earl of Essex (p78). Rotating casks might be from Five Points, Harvey's, Redemption, Siren or Tiny Rebel and always include a traditional bitter. Kegs stretch to Bavarian monastic brewer Andechs, Dutch newcomers like Kromme Haring and Nevel, and UK stars like Almasty and Kernel. Among the intelligently chosen bottle range are sharing options from Belgian and US names like Against the Grain, Ale Apothecary, Girardin, Jester King and Oud Beersel. The handsome pub a few steps from Weavers Fields has been tastefully done out with deep green padded benches round an island bar, an original porch that once led to a separate off-licence, and unexplained lepidopteran displays on the walls.

Kings Arms

Mother Kelly's
Bethnal Green/E2

Bar, shop

251 Paradise Row E2 9LE **motherkellys.co.uk**

🕐 *Tu-Th* 16.00-23.00, *Fr-Su* 12.00-23.00.
Children until 20.00.

18 keg, 350+ bottles/cans, 2 ciders/perries, specialist spirits.

🍴 Sharing boards, snacks, plus sushi tacos from food truck (not daily) **£-££**, 🍻 Front terrace, ♿
Beer launches, tap takeovers, beer festivals, tutored tastings, bottle share, occasional live music, beer books

⊖ Bethnal Green

Paradise Row, an alley parallel to Cambridge Heath Road, close to the Tube and the Bethnal Green Museum of Childhood, must long have seemed one of the most inappropriately named streets in London. But discerning drinkers can now imagine themselves in heaven thanks to Mother Kelly's, which opened its first branch here in April 2014 when London had seen nothing of the like before. Keg lines cover a wide range of styles, matching Brits like Bohem, Burning Sky, Burnt Mill, Kernel and Orbit with imports like Anchorage from Alaska, To Øl or

Pōhjala. A wall full of fridges contains bottles to take away at a discount or drink in: UK stars like Black Iris, Boundary, First Chop and Yonder; rare Italians like Lover Beer; shelves of fine lambics and newer Belgian and Dutch brewers like Senne and Uiltje. The late-May bank holiday Sour Power wild and sour beer festival began here in 2015 with what now seems like remarkable foresight. The space is basic, just a big brick railway arch decorated with graffiti art and equipped with communal tables, plus additional outdoor terrace seating. But who needs luxury when you've got heavenly beer?

Mother Kelly's

Old Street Taproom

Bar

11 Gales Gardens E2 0EJ

T (020) 3952 4926 **oldstreet.beer**

🕐 *Tu-Th* 16.00-23.00, *Fr* 16.00-24.00,
  Sa 12.00-24.00, *Su* 14.00-23.00.
  Children until early evening.

Occasional cask, 4 tank, 7 keg, 40 bottles/
cans, growlers, some specialist spirits.

🍴 'WestMex' barbecue and tacos **£-££**,
🎋 Tables at front, ♿

*Tastings, food pairing, brewing days, fortnightly DJs,
occasional films, monthly bingo, major big screen
sport (including American football), board games,
beer books*

⊖ Bethnal Green

Pick your way through the second-hand
furniture sold by the neighbours to find this
warmly woody and welcoming railway arch
space with a surprisingly verdant garden
terrace. Old Street beer was once brewed
here too but though production has since
located to a larger space at Hackney Wick
(p138), the place still reflects its owners'
knowledge and enthusiasm for beer in every
corner, with a similar list of house beers and
guests as at the brewery site. Prizes at the
regular bingo night have even included a beer
trip to Germany.

TRY ALSO

Angel of Bow 171 Devons Road E3 3QX
theangelofbow.co.uk: Shabbily elegant
gastro-tending pub with small leafy terrace
close to Devons Road DLR station, revamped
in partnership with Redemption. Though the
brewery is no longer involved, most of the five
cask and 15 keg lines are sourced locally, with
a largely Belgian bottle list. May close *Mo-Tu*.

Bethnal Green Tavern 456 Bethnal Green
Road E2 0EA **bethnalgreentavern.co.uk**: Old
Charrington pub close to Bethnal Green Tube,
converted to a Graceland venue March 2020
and maintaining the high standards set by the
Kings Arms nearby (above): three cask often
from Five Points and Moor, lots more in keg,
bottle and can.

Birdcage 80 Columbia Road E2 7QB
brewdog.com: Suitably pretty place at the
southern end of Columbia Road flower
market, a former Draft House that's now a
BrewDog pub with the usual wide choice
– two cask, 17 keg and 35 bottles – and more
of an old-school pub setting than some.

BrewDog Canary Wharf Unit 17, 2 Churchill
Place E14 5RB **brewdog.com**: Expansive glass-
walled bar by the Bellmouth Passage between
docks at the eastern end of the Canary Wharf
complex. Offers 20 keg, one of which is priced
according to the FTSE index, plus 40 bottles/
cans, some in an outdoor vending machine.

Craft Beer Co Limehouse 576 Commercial
Road E14 7JD **thecraftbeerco.com**: Friendly
branch in the former Railway Tavern, a smallish
pub with roof terrace, more like a proper local
right by Limehouse station. Six cask, 15 keg
and over 50+ bottles/cans matching the usual
standards.

Marksman 254 Hackney Road E2 7SJ
marksmanpublichouse.com: Handsomely
woody East End gastropub with pretty roof
garden, a previous Michelin Pub of the Year
winner, renowned for its food but also
managing three cask, eight keg and a handful
of bottled beers, mainly from east London.

Prospect of Whitby 57 Wapping Wall E1W
3SH **greeneking-pubs.co.uk**: Some of the
historic claims of this famous Grade II-listed
riverside pub are suspect as it was largely
rebuilt in the early 19th century and the interior
fittings are much more recent, but it's attractive
all the same and now stocks well-kept London
guest casks besides Greene King.

HOP HISTORIES Yeast Enders

ALONGSIDE Southwark, the industrial powerhouse of the East End was one of London's most important brewing centres, the home not only of Truman's (see From Black Eagle to Dark Star p114) but of several long-vanished businesses whose contributions to global beer culture still echo down the ages.

According to brewing historian Martyn Cornell, the mass production of porter was perfected in Lower East Smithfield, just downstream from the Tower of London. At the time of its closure in the 1930s, the Red Lion brewery, at the junction of what's now St Katharine's Way and Burr Close, was said to be the oldest brewery in Britain and one of the oldest businesses in London. A brewhouse on the site had Flemish owners in 1492 and by the 17th century the Parsons family were in control. Humphrey Parsons, who took over in 1705, was later twice Lord Mayor of London, a knight, a Tory MP and, allegedly, a hunting companion of Louis XV of France. Parsons likely first had the idea of maturing porter in tall vats rather than casks, installing several 1,500-barrel (2,450hl) vats in 1736. His investment paid off, and by 1748, seven years after his death, his brewery was the fourth biggest in London, its products toasted in verse by poet Oliver Goldsmith as 'Parsons' black Champagne'.

The brewery, later known as Hoare & Co, just escaped demolition during the construction of St Katharine Docks and was finally taken over and closed by Charrington in 1934, with the

new owners continuing to use its Toby jug logo. The Dickens Inn pub (Marble Quay E1W 1UH), an 18th-century timber-framed warehouse which was relocated 70m away from its original site when the docks were redeveloped in the 1970s, may be the only surviving remnant of this crucible of modern brewing.

George Hodgson began brewing further northeast in 1752, in what was probably an existing brewhouse on the western approach to Bow Bridge over the River Lea, then the boundary between Middlesex and Essex. Hodgson took advantage of good access by boat to the East India Company's moorings at Blackwall by offering preferential credit terms to the company's captains. Among the products he shipped to India was October beer, a strongish, long-maturing, well-hopped pale ale of a type popular among the landed gentry, who often laid it down in wooden casks in their own cellars.

As it turned out, the temperature changes and movement of an often-rough four-month sea voyage accelerated this beer's maturation so it arrived in India in top condition. Hodgson's was not the only such exporter but by the end of the 18th century its beers had built an enviable reputation among expatriates and in 1802 it was shipping 4,000 barrels (6,550hl) a year to the subcontinent.

In the 1820s, the brewery's management made a misjudged attempt to cut out the middleman by shipping the beer themselves, infuriating the East India Company so much it approached Allsopp, of Burton-upon-Trent in Staffordshire, to brew a similar beer in direct competition. Burton water turned out to be particularly suited to pale ale, and as the style's popularity grew in domestic and other markets in the 1830s, under the name India Pale Ale or East India Pale Ale, it became associated more with Burton than London.

The Bow Bridge brewery subsequently enjoyed mixed fortunes, though it survived until 1927 when, now known as Smith Garrett, it was taken over by Taylor Walker (see below). Council flats were built on the site in 1933, and still stand next to the modern replacement for historic Bow Bridge, the tangle of concrete known as the Bow Flyover.

Richard Ivory built the Albion brewery next door to his Whitechapel pub, the Blind Beggar, in 1808. In the early 20th century, the much-expanded firm, now known as Mann Crossman Paulin, developed a sweet bottled brown ale once

cont.

HOP HISTORIES — Yeast Enders *cont.*

regarded as something of an East End speciality. In 1958 Watney took over the brewery (see Roll out the red barrel p126), eventually closing it in 1979. Some of the buildings still stand, including the Blind Beggar itself, now notorious as the place where Ronnie Kray murdered George Cornell in 1966 (337 Whitechapel Road E1 1BU). Mann's Brown is still around though brewed some way outside London, at Banks's in Wolverhampton.

Other famous East End brewing names include Taylor Walker, which began as Hare & Salmon in Stepney in 1730 and relocated to Limehouse in 1823. It was bought by Ind Coope and demolished in the mid-1960s. Charrington originated in Bethnal Green in the 1750s, transferring to the purpose-built Anchor Brewery on Mile End Road in 1770. In 1963, it became a key component of the combine generally regarded as kicking off the 'merger mania' of the day, United Breweries, created by colourful Canadian entrepreneur Eddie Taylor. The Anchor ceased brewing in 1975 and most of the site became a retail park, but the offices were retained for a while by its successor, Big Seven brewer Bass Charrington, as its London HQ and still stand today (129 Mile End Road E1 4BF), as does Malplaquet House a few doors down, once home to Harry Charrington.

East London also played a role in more recent brewing history as home to arguably Britain's second-ever modern standalone microbrewery, and

Mann's Albion Brewery, Whitechapel, in the 1890s.

the first new brewing company launched in the capital since the beginning of the 20th century. In 1977, Patrick Fitzpatrick, who'd first become interested in beer by reading about London's remaining family brewers, began supplementing his real ale distribution business by brewing his own. He found a key collaborator in ex-Whitbread veteran John Wilmot, who went on to help set up several other microbreweries. The operation was first based in an old sweet factory in Clapton, relocating to Bow in 1978 and the following year to a former veneer factory near Victoria Park. On the basis that breweries should sound like solid Victorian partnerships, it was initially named Godson Freeman & Wilmot. At its peak it had a turnover of over £1 million a year and was even stocked by pioneering beer bar Café Gollem in Amsterdam.

Like many microbrewing pioneers, Fitzpatrick faced an uphill struggle with unsuitable premises, quality control and financial issues, and in 1982 production was suspended. It was briefly revived in 1982 under the name Godson Chudley following a merger with another struggling London start-up, but closed for good two years later. The building is now an art and performance studio and gallery complex known as Chisenhale Art Place (64 Chisenhale Road E3 5QZ). A disillusioned Fitzpatrick broke ties with the beer world: 'I was so devastated by what happened to the brewery,' he told beer writers Jessica Boak and Ray Bailey in 2013. It's about time he was better acknowledged as a modern hero of East End brewing heritage.

Outer East London

East Side Brewery

Brewery, no visitors please
5B Elms Industrial Estate, Church Road,
Romford RM3 0HU (Havering)
T (020) 3355 1197 **theeastsidebrewery.co.uk**
First sold beer: May 2021. 🖐.

Founded by lawyer and homebrewer
Rash Singh Mahal with the help of brewer
Thomas Newman on an industrial estate in
the Ingrebourne valley near Harold Wood,
this 8 hl setup was originally planned to
launch in 2020 but delayed by the pandemic.

BEERS in keg and bottle include an easy
drinking pils, **6PM** (?%).

Gidea Park Micropub

Micropub
236 Main Road, Romford RM2 5HA
T 01708 397290
🕐 *Mo-We* 16.00-23.00, *Th-Su* 12.00-23.00.
     Children until 19.00.
4-7 cask, 5 keg, 50+ bottles/cans, growlers,
     15+ ciders/perries, 40 gins.
🍴 Pork pies, snacks, ♿ Flat access only
Board games, darts

⊖ Gidea Park   🚌 Links Avenue, Balgores Lane

Suburban east London gained another much-
needed beacon of beer excellence in December
2017 when ex-Wetherspoon manager Trevor
Howard opened the second micropub in the
area. Occupying a former office in a neighbourhood shopping centre, it's a shade bigger than
some, equipped with smart high stools and
tables, a couple of saggy sofas and a stylish

flourish in the lighting festooned across the
ceiling. There's no bar counter: instead, rotating
cask beers in all legal measures are fetched
from a coolroom. Usually including a traditional
bitter, a dark beer and something stronger,
they're sourced from across the UK, with a
slight bias towards London and Essex: Wibblers
is a favourite and Bishop Nick and Crouch Vale
often return. Kegs, cans and bottles include
various Londoners (Pretty Decent, Wild Card)
and a couple of welcome Bavarians.

Hop Inn 52

Micropub, shop
122 North Street, Hornchurch RM11 1SU
hopinnhornchurch.co.uk
⏱ *Bar*: Tu-We 16.00-22.00, Th-Fr 14.00-22.30,
   Sa 12.00-22.30, Su 12.00-21.00.
   Shop: Tu 12.00-17.30, We-Th 12.00-18.00,
   Fr-Sa 12.00-20.00, Su 12.00-16.00. Cash-free.
5 cask, 2 keg, 180 bottles/cans, up to 10
draught ciders/perries, English wine, 70 gins.
other specialist spirits
🪑 A few tables at front, ♿ Flat access only
Tastings, tap takeovers

⊖ Emerson Park

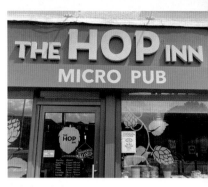

Opened in December 2019 a little north of
central Hornchurch as the second micropub
in Havering, this unexpected treasury of good
drinks is the brainchild of two drinks trade
veterans, Phil Cooke and keen beer and cider
educator Alison Taffs. It was planned just as a
micropub but switched to takeaway bottles
and cans during the lockdowns, which
worked so well that the next-door unit
became a permanent shop in April 2021.

Hop Inn

Casks largely from east London and Essex
breweries like Billericay, East London, Five
Points and Leigh-on-Sea cover a range of
styles, kegs are often from Kernel or Polly's,
and the bottle and can selection, all also
available to drink in, includes the very local
East Side, other Londoners like Exale and
Hammerton, British micros rare in London
like S43, Belgian classics (with several kept
correctly at cellar temperature to drink in)
and occasional US visitors like Allagash. It's a
clean and pleasant space furnished mainly
with high tables and stools, with thought
and care evident in every corner, right down
to the custom-designed hop motifs on the
wallpaper.

Husk Brewing 53

Brewery, taproom
58A Railway Arches, North Woolwich Road
E16 2AA (Newham)
T (020) 7474 3827   huskbrewing.com
First sold beer: January 2016, 🍺
⏱ Th-Fr 17.00-23.00, Sa 14.00-23.00. Children
   welcome.
10 keg, 3 bottles.
🍴 Burgers, toasties, **£-££**, 🪑 Benches at front,
♿ Flat access only
*Tastings, occasional live music and comedy,
functions, darts*

⊖ West Silvertown 🚲 NCN13

Despite its address, this small Docklands
brewery isn't under a railway but a road
viaduct, close to the Royal Victoria Docks and
Excel exhibition centre and within sight of the
Emirates Airline cable car and the Tate & Lyle

sugar factory. Founder Chris van der Vyver, originally from Pretoria, South Africa, is a former homebrewer and enthusiastic beer and food matcher who once worked for the Hawksmoor restaurant group. He's proudly named the business after the husk, one of the reasons why barley has proved an ideal grain for brewing. A taproom stocking own brews and occasional local guests overlooks the 4hl brewhouse from a pleasant mezzanine.

BEERS mainly sold through the taproom and local outlets, are almost entirely in keg with occasional cask and bottle conditioning. They include several with changing flavourings, like **Milk Stout** (4.4%) with coffee and vanilla or milkshake **IPA** (5.5%) with fruit or tea, and sour and mixed fermentation brews, alongside a best-selling more conventional **Pale Ale** (5.1%). There have also been collaborations with Mechanic (Standing by p328).

Chris van der Vyver

Upminster Tap 54

Micropub

1B Sunnyside Gardens, Upminster RM14 3DT

T 07841 676225

facebook.com/upminstertaproom

🕐 *Tu-Fr* 16.00-23.00, *Sa* 12.00-23.00,
  Su 12.00-22.00. Children outside only.

5-8 cask, 1 bottle, growlers, 17 ciders/perries,
  40 gins, some vodkas.

🍺 Front yard, ♿

*Annual beer festival, morris dancing, gin tastings,
animal blessing, carol singing*

⇌ ⊖ Upminster   🚲 NCN136

Permission for this rare refuge on the edge of Upminster town centre was initially refused by the council but persistent owners Bob Knowles and Caroline Sheldon finally rallied enough local support to open east London's first micropub in November 2015. The unevenly shaped space, originally offices attached to the adjacent house, is now resplendent in bare brick and half-panelling, draped with hops, decorated with classic album covers and fronted by a pleasantly sunny yard. It's a muzak-free place with beers fetched from a stillage visible through a window. Besides regular Dark Star Hophead, London and Essex brewers like Leigh on Sea and Mighty Oak

regularly feature on a changing list alongside other unusual visitors (Isle of Purbeck, Iron Pier from Kent), with at least one dark choice, a traditional bitter and a contemporary-style hoppy pale, presented as well as you'd expect from a serial local CAMRA Pub of the Year.

LONDON CITY AIRPORT

Brick Lane Brews London City Airport, Hartmann Road E16 2PX trumansbeer.co.uk: If you're past security at London City Airport and have time for a beer, your best option is this little Truman's bar by Gate 2, with four keg lines plus cans and bottles of London Keeper to take away.

HOP HISTORIES | Beyond the Marshes

Romford was a rural Essex market town in 1708 when George Cardon started brewing at the Star Inn. In 1799, the business was bought by Edward Ind in partnership with John Grosvenor, who later sold his share to John Smith. It was Smith's son Henry who, along with his brother-in-law, head brewer John Turner, quit the firm in 1845 to take over the Griffin brewery in Chiswick, creating Fuller Smith & Turner (p298). In 1856, like several other London breweries, Ind Coope, as it was now known, created a Burton-upon-Trent subsidiary, and in 1934 merged with Allsopp, the brewery responsible for bringing India Pale Ale to Burton in direct competition with Hodgson's in Bow (Yeast Enders p163).

In 1961, Ind Coope became the heart of one of the Big Seven breweries by merging with Tetley Walker in Leeds and Ansells in

Birmingham to create what was then the biggest drinks company in Europe, Allied Breweries. By now Burton was the main plant but Romford continued in use until 1993. Most of the brewery has been demolished and the site rebuilt as a shopping centre, but a chimney and façades are preserved and one of the buildings is now the Havering Museum (19 High Street RM1 1JU, haveringmuseum.org.uk). Displays about the brewery will interest heritage buffs but good beer options nearby are thin on the ground: the Gidea Park Micropub (above) isn't far away by bus or train. The rest of Ind Coope ended up in the hands of Carlsberg in 1997, and beers bearing the brand are occasionally commissioned from other brewers.

Tolly was a well-known brewing name in East Anglia into the early 21st century, but you may be puzzled why

some London pubs are also still nicknamed 'Tollys'. The answer lies in E17, where William Hawes opened the Walthamstow Brewery in St James's Street in 1859. In 1920, it was bought by Tollemache in Ipswich, later Tolly Cobbold, as a foothold in the London market. But Tolly's regional and national ambitions weren't realised and the London brewery closed in 1972. Tolly's subsequent history was chequered: the London pubs were eventually sold and, after passing through several different hands, the Ipswich parent, now reduced to microbrewery status, finally closed in 2003. The brand is now owned by Greene King and occasionally resurrected for seasonals. All trace of the Walthamstow brewery has vanished except the tap, which is still recognisable on Markhouse Road, though converted to flats in 2009.

NORTH LONDON

NORTH LONDON

North London in this book includes all the N and NW postcodes outside the central area, apart from a couple of places in Kensal Green and Queens Park which are further west than some of the W postcodes and can be found under Maida Vale to Dollis Hill (p304).

My **Camden** section includes the whole of Camden borough, except for the parts of it already dealt with in the central area. There are fewer good beer options than you might expect in major centres like Camden Town and Hampstead, with richer pickings to the east in Kentish Town.

Outlets in the southern part of Islington around Angel and Clerkenwell are listed under Central London but other locations in the borough like Archway, Barnsbury, Canonbury and Holloway, plus parts of Hackney with N postcodes, including western Dalston, are under **Islington to Stoke Newington**. Numerous fine new places to drink have opened around here recently including one or two brewery taprooms.

Perhaps the most dramatic changes to the beer landscape since the last edition are further north. The long-established presence of Beavertown and Redemption seems to have inspired numerous others to fire up the mash tuns, creating a brewery strip along the west side of the Lea Valley that mirrors Walthamstow to the east. And a rash of new and improved pubs and bars means Haringey is now one of the most beer-friendly boroughs in the capital, as described in **Tottenham and Haringey**.

Outer North London covers the rest, up to the Hertfordshire boundary, including a northern extension of the string of Lea Valley breweries into Enfield.

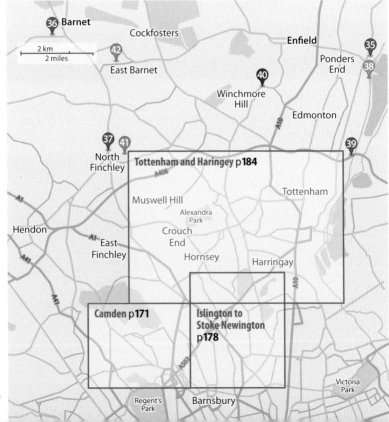

Camden

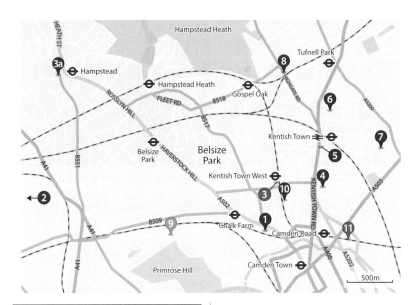

Baladin Camden ❶

Bar

724 North Yard, Stables Market,
  Chalk Farm Road NW1 8AH

baladin.it/en/baladin-camden

🕐 *We-Mo* 11.00-19.00. Children at discretion
of staff.

4 keg, 15 bottles, beer cocktails, Baladin spirits
and soft drinks

🍴 Focaccia, pasta, 🪑 Tables in yard

♿ (in market, stepped access to indoor bar).

⊖ Chalk Farm   🚢 Camden Lock   🚲 Link to C6   🏃 Link
to Jubilee Greenway

Founded in 1996 as one of the first modern
Italian craft breweries, Baladin has consistently
been one of the highest achieving, so the
appearance of a London outpost in May 2021
was particularly welcome. You'll need to brave
the hordes who descend on bustling Camden
Market to find this modestly proportioned site
in 'Italian alley', in the Stables Market right by
the Amy Winehouse statue. Despite its trattor-
ia-like layout, it's open to drinkers as well as
diners, either to sit in or from the takeaway
hatch in the curved façade of a former industrial building. Expect fresh core beers like
Belgian-style Nazionale on keg and a selection
of cans and bottles including the brewery's
renowned rare barrel-aged barley wines in
100ml sampling sizes. The kitchen serves up
Roman-style focaccia bread with a wide range
of toppings, with plenty of vegan options like
garlic and chilli as well as Italian sausage and pig
cheek, and more substantial pasta dishes too.

Bohemia House ②

Club
74 West End Lane NW6 2LX
T (020) 7372 1193 **czechandslovakclub.co.uk**
⏱ *Mo-Th* 17.00-22.00, *Fr* 17.00-23.00, *Sa* 12.00-
   23.00, *Su* 12.00-21.00. Children welcome.
4 keg, 3+ bottles/cans, Czech and Slovak
   aperitifs and spirits
🍴 Czech and Slovak meals and snacks **££**,
🌳 Rear terrace, large beer garden ♿
Czech TV, functions, pool, table football

⇌ ⊖ West Hampstead

This longstanding outpost of Czech and
Slovak culture, now open to all, is still much as
it was in the 1950s. Several rooms on the
ground floor include a small bar decorated
with posters of ice hockey heroes, a games
room and a restaurant where the typical pub
grub of the now divorced republics is the
order of the day – *halušky*, schnitzels, fritters,
gulaš and an unexpected but welcome
vegetarian selection. A big beer garden with
picnic benches at the back provides a further
authentic Central European touch. A 'try also'
last time around, it regained a main listing
early in 2020 with the delightful news that
Zdeněk Kudr, co-founder of Bohem (p185),
had taken over the bar, adding excellent
Tottenham-brewed beers, including Moric, a
house exclusive Slovak-style pale lager to
the longstanding immaculately kept draught
Pilsner Urquell and bottled Budvar.

Visitor note. *The venue traces its history to the beginning
of World War II when a club for exiled Czechoslovak service
personnel fighting with the British forces was founded in
Holborn. It moved to its present location in a substantial
villa after the war, attracting those fleeing the pro-Soviet
regime after 1948 and waves of migrants in recent decades.*

Camden Town Brewery ③

Camden Town Brewery Brew Hall
Brewery, taproom (AB InBev)
55 Wilkin Street Mews NW5 3NN (Camden)
T (020) 7485 1671
camdentownbrewery.com
First sold beer: May 2006 (at original site), 🍴
⏱ *Mo-Su* 12.00-23.00. Children until early evening.
13 keg, 10 bottles/cans, growlers.
🍴 Italian and Bavarian-inspired menu **££-£££**,
🌳 Front beer garden, ♿ Flat access only
Arcade games

⊖ Kentish Town West

Horseshoe ③a

Contemporary pub: 28 Heath Street NW3 6TE
T (020) 7431 6206
thehorseshoehampstead.com
⏱ *Mo-Th* 12.00-23.00, *Fr-Sa* 12.00-24.00,
   Su 12.00-22.00. Children welcome.
2 cask (cooler months only), 11 keg,
   10+ bottles/cans, wines.
🍴 Gastro menu **££-£££**, 🌳 Benches on street
Theatre upstairs

⊖ Hampstead 🚶 Belsize Walk, Hampstead Heath footpaths

Camden Town occupied a mere two arches
under the Overground at Kentish Town West
station when the first edition was published
in 2011. It's since taken over the whole street.
There's still a sizable working brewery here
and the well-appointed glass-fronted taproom
is a good place to sample its Arch 55 specials
as well as core brands from the much bigger
Lea Valley site, perhaps in the suntrap of a

courtyard. Acclaimed chef Theo Randall has overhauled the menu and the site is set to undergo refurbishment and expansion in 2021 to create a beer hall feel: check social media. The brewery also still retains the Hampstead pub where it all began, the Horseshoe, a cheerful bright space with large windows, stretches of whitewashed brickwork, refectory tables and an open kitchen. It stocks house beers alongside other London and UK guests like Lost and Grounded, Tiny Rebel and Wild alongside a short bottle/can list with classical leanings (Rochefort, Harviestoun Ola Dubh). Staff can recommend good matches for the short but stylish menu, which might include Korean fried chicken, native breed steaks, vegan burger and several fish and seafood offerings like butterflied sea bass. For more on Camden Town beers, see the larger site (p197).

Visitor note. Built as part of an 1880s redevelopment of central Hampstead, the pub was originally known as the Three Horseshoes and was once a Wetherspoon. The independently owned Pentameters theatre above dates from the heady days of 1968, when it was known for improvised poetry and jazz events.

Caps and Taps

Shop, bar
130 Kentish Town Road NW1 9QB
capsandtaps.co.uk
🕓 *Tu-Sa* 11.00-19.00, *Su* 11.00-17.00 (may open later at weekends, please check). Children welcome. Children until early evening.
2 keg, 350 bottles/cans, growlers, specialist ciders, natural wines. 🍷
Tastings, meet the brewer, bottle shares

🚉 Kentish Town ⊖ Kentish Town West, Kentish Town
🏃 Link to Regents Canal towpath

Partners Phil and Steph opened this well-informed bottle shop in April 2015 in a former florist on busy Kentish Town Road. An extensive but well-organised and lovingly picked range packs out the narrow unit: there are plenty of Londoners, including East London, Hammerton, Kernel and Redemption, and exemplary traditionalists like Harvey's beside UK newcomers like Cloudwater, Little Earth and Yonder. The strong imported selection includes excellent US picks from the likes of Great Divide and

Jester King, Scandinavian craft from Amundsen and Dugges and Belgian and German classics including fine lambics. There's space to drink in, a loyalty scheme, a bar service for private events and plenty of good advice on hand to help you choose.

Horseshoe
See Camden Town

Oxford Tavern 5

Traditional pub
256 Kentish Town Road NW5 2AA
T (020) 7485 3521   oxfordtavern.co.uk
🕓 *Mo-Th* 12.00-23.00, *Fr-Sa* 12.00-24.00,
   Su 12.00-22.00. Children until 19.00.
5 cask, 10 keg, 16 bottles/cans, specialist spirits.
🍴 Pizzas, burgers **£-££**, 🪑 Benches on street, ♿
Meet the brewer, beer pong, live jazz (Mo), monthly comedy, dog club (Th), acoustic music (Sa), role playing games and quiz (Su), board games, functions

🚉 ⊖ Kentish Town

This former Greene King house close to Kentish Town station underwent a bare-brick-and-sofas refurbishment in April 2018 to become perhaps the most welcoming of three London pubs owned by the West Berkshire brewery, now chaired by Firkin chain founder David Bruce. It's bigger than it looks, stretching from the main road to a handsome panelled area at the back and retaining an original long wooden bar and some floor mosaics. The owners' beers like Good Old Boy line up at the bar with locals from Gorgeous and Signature and great stuff from elsewhere like Burning Sky and Wiper & True. New York-style pizzas come with toppings like fennel sausage or vegetable antipasti, with meat and vegan jackfruit burger options too.

Oxford Tavern

Pineapple

Traditional pub (McGrath Davies)
51 Leverton Street NW5 2NX
T (020) 7284 4631 thepineapplepubnw5.com
🕐 *Mo-Th* 12.00-23.00, *Fr-Sa* 12.00-24.00,
   Su 12.00-22.30. Children until 19.00.
5 cask, 5 keg, 12 bottles, specialist spirits.
🍴 Thai menu **£-££**, 🪑 Tables at front, rear
garden ⌘
*2 annual beer festivals, tap takeovers, quiz (Mo),
cheese night (Th), board games, drink promotions,
functions*

🚆 ⊖ Kentish Town

Only a short stroll from Kentish Town Tube
station, this self-described 'beloved back
street boozer' seems a world away in its quiet
terraced street. It was saved from closure by
a CAMRA-backed campaign in the early 2000s
and the community remains keenly involved
in organising regular events like charity 'bring
your own cheese' nights. The front drinking
area is arranged around a small central bar
dominated by a Grade II-listed bar back with
etched glass mirrors, and at the back, beyond
an impressive red marble fireplace, an elegant
conservatory decorated with illustrations of
wild birds looks out onto a pleasant beer
garden. The window glass indicates this was
once an Ind Coope house, but today the house
cask is rebadged Marston's Pedigree, while the
other pumps rotate through Londoners like
Redemption and Southwark, or maybe Siren or
Stardust. Kegs include German König Pilsner
as well as Beavertown and Camden Town,
and you might spot bottles from Partizan. The

Thai menu includes plenty of veggie options,
sharing platters and £5 lunches. The name may
seem unlikely for a backstreet North London
pub but, as a traditional symbol of hospitality,
it's more than apt.

Rose and Crown ⑦

Contemporary pub (Carouse London)
71 Torriano Avenue NW5 2SG
T (020) 7267 4305
roseandcrownkentishtown.com
🕐 *Mo-Th* 16.00-23.00, *Fr* 16.00-24.00, *Sa* 12.00-
   24.00, *Su* 12.00-22.30. Children until 19.00.
1 cask, 9 keg, 30 bottles/cans, cider/perry,
   a few specialist spirits.
🍴 Changing popups **£-££**, 🪑 Sunken terrace
*Occasional meet the brewer and tap takeovers,
comedy, quiz, board games*

🚆 ⊖ Kentish Town

This smallish pub was threatened with closure
in 2014 when the longstanding licensees retired.
Ben Caudell and two business partners took it
on, strengthening its community role and
boosting the beer range by calling on mainly
UK independents. You'll find one rotating cask,
perhaps from Arbor, Hammerton or Marble,
and a noteworthy selection in keg, bottle and
can: Titanic stout, and others from breweries
like BBNo, Cloudwater, Duration, Kernel,
Oddysey, Track and Verdant. An artisanal
burger outfit occupied the kitchen when I last
looked. There's one room upstairs with high
tables around a simple central bar, a second
relaxed space downstairs, and a curious sunken

terrace garden at the back. Despite much love from the locals, the threat of redevelopment in this desirable residential area hasn't been entirely lifted. See also Brave Sir Robin (p178).

Visitor note. Built in 1937 for Watney's, the pub was long a noted music venue known as the Torriano: Amy Winehouse played the piano that's still in place downstairs.

Southampton Arms
Traditional pub
139 Highgate Road NW5 1LE
T 07958 780073
thesouthamptonarms.co.uk
🕐 *Su-Th* 12.00-23.00, *Fr-Sa* 12.00-24.00.
    Children welcome. Cash-free.
8 cask, 8 keg, 1 bottle, 6 ciders/perries.
🍴 Filled baps, scotch eggs, pork pies **£**,
🪑 Rear sheltered garden
Tap takeovers, live piano (Tu, We, Su), quiz

⊖ Gospel Oak   🚶 Link to Belsize Walk, Hampstead Heath paths

Transformed late in 2009 from a decaying old boozer into a perfectly judged purveyor of, as the sign says, 'Ale, Cider and Meat', the Southampton exerted a profound influence on London's subsequent beer renaissance. It's still one of the best, as proved by the crowds of everyone from local celebs to top-knotted geeks who pack the narrow space every night. The bare floorboards, old church furniture and white-tiled walls have a hint of the butcher's shop appropriate to the food offering: high quality pork pies, scotch eggs, sausage rolls and cheese baps. Though it's no longer, as claimed on its minimalist website, the only dedicated ale and cider house in London exclusively selling beers and ciders from small independent producers, you can still expect a well-chosen and varied range including bitters, milds and stouts. Casks from brewers like Beartown, East London, Northern Monk, Pig and Porter and Wilderness join associated brewery Howling Hops, with kegs perhaps from Kernel, Pressure Drop, Signature and Wylam, all to be enjoyed to the sounds of live piano or classic jazz on vinyl. Staff give great advice and customers are actively invited to request beers. Afternoons are recommended for quieter drinking.

St Mary's Brewery
Brewery, no visitors please
St Mary's Church, Elsworthy Road NW3 3DJ
(Camden)   stmarysbrewery.co.uk
First sold beer: November 2017

Stephen Reynolds, church warden at St Mary the Virgin, Primrose Hill, started this brewery as a way of raising money for the church's youth work. The first beer, cuckoo-brewed at Ubrew, was launched at an event in October 2016 when the Bishop of Edmonton blessed it and drank the first pint. A nano-sized kit was installed in the church crypt a year later, but larger runs are still cuckoo-brewed elsewhere.

BEERS in bottles (not tasted) are sold at Primrose Hill Farmers Market and by mail order via the website.

Southampton Arms

Tapping the Admiral

Contemporary pub
77 Castle Road NW1 8SU
T (020) 7267 6118   tappingtheadmiral.co.uk
🕐 *Su-Tu* 12.00-23.00, *We-Sa* 12.00-24.00.
   Children until 19.00.
8 cask, 6 keg, 10+ bottles/cans, 2 ciders/perries,
   specialist spirits.
🍴 Enhanced pub grub **££**, 🪑 Rear garden
*Occasional tap takeovers, poker night (Mo), quiz (We),
folk jam (Th), board games*

🚇 Kentish Town West

Pineapple (above) owner Kirk McGrath opened
this delightful place close to Kentish Town
West station in 2011, another characterful and
welcoming community pub with a strong beer
focus. Originally a Truman's house known as the
Trafalgar, the pub had been derelict for years
and at one point threatened with demolition
before its current rejuvenation. Now, pub cat
Nelson presides over a clean, modern and
woody interior. A rebadged Brakspear Oxford
Gold is permanent and the remaining casks
favour the likes of Adnams, Ilkley, Sambrook's
and Southwark, always including traditional
bitters. Big Smoke, One Mile End and Bavarian
abbey wheat beer Benediktiner add interest
to the kegs, with Anchor and Hammerton in
the fridge. Pies, including veggie variants, are
the focus of a menu that also includes sausage
and mash, white bean burgers and lunchtime
wraps.

*Visitor note. The name refers to a legend that Admiral
Nelson's body was returned from Trafalgar preserved in a
brandy barrel, from which sailors helped themselves by
drilling holes and inserting macaroni straws.*

Werewolf Beer ⑪

Brewery, taproom
87 Randolph Street NW1 0SR (Camden)
werewolfbeer.com
First sold beer: December 2020 (at Rose and
Crown), ‼
🕐 *Fr* 16.00-21.00, *Sa* 12.00-21.00.
   Well-behaved younger children welcome.
7-9 keg, 5+ cans, growlers. 🍷.
🍴 US snacks, changing food trucks **£**,
🪑 large yard, ♿

🚇 Camden Road   🚲 C6   🚶 Jubilee Greenway

This 'American brewery in London' is the
brainchild of US expat and former London
Brewing head brewer Rich White. Cuckoo
brewing started at Little Creatures early in
2020 but plans for a site were disrupted by
the lockdowns. The first commercial beers
flowed at the end of the year from a pilot kit
installed in the cellar of Kentish Town pub
the Rose and Crown, and in 2021 the project
successfully crowdfunded for a move to its
own arch under the London Overground
close to Camden Road, with its own haunted
train ride rescued from a derelict theme park.
This should be open by publication date but
I recommend you check times.

BEERS in keg and can will include pale ales,
an American brown ale (a rarity in London)
and a US-style rice lager.

Tapping the Admiral

TRY ALSO

BrewDog Camden 113 Bayham Street NW1 0AG brewdog.com/bars: Former pub which became London's first BrewDog bar in December 2011 when the brewery's founders rolled up true to style in a tank. It's a relatively cosy space spread across two levels offering 19 keg and around 100 bottles and cans, including rare US bottles.

Bull and Last 168 Highgate Road NW5 1QS thebullandlast.co.uk: This much-admired gastropub a short walk from the Southampton Arms (above) reopened in 2020 after a lengthy closure for refurbishment and the addition of boutique B&B rooms. A small but carefully chosen London-brewed beer selection, including two casks, accompanies an impressive modern British menu.

Camden Road Arms 102 Camden Road NW1 9EA brewdog.com: Expansive corner pub opposite Camden Road station, refurbished in rock 'n' roll style in 2017 though with a narrower range than some in the chain due to the Heineken tie. Two cask, 13 keg and 45+ bottles/cans including locals.

Clapton Craft NW5 326 Kentish Town Road NW5 2TH claptoncraft.co.uk: Branch of the specialist chain a few steps from Kentish Town station with four keg lines and 200+ well-categorised bottles/cans from UK and world brewers, including some exclusives. Takeaway only.

Magdala 2a South Hill Park NW3 2SB themagdala.co.uk: Pretty pub on a corner of Hampstead Heath that was almost lost but reopened in May 2021 as another excellent venue linked to Big Smoke (see Sussex Arms p312). Lots of London-brewed and other interesting choices among seven cask and 20 keg lines. Ruth Ellis, the last woman hanged in the UK, shot her lover on the street outside in 1955.

Stag 67 Fleet Road NW3 2QU thestaghampstead.com: Bulky, black-painted Victorian pub with pretty garden around the corner from the Royal Free Hospital, Hampstead, with a couple of cask options plus 20 kegs and 20 bottles/cans from mainly UK and European craft producers, under same ownership as the Beer + Burger chain.

LONDON DRINKERS **Jenn Merrick**

Brewing was at an all-time low in London when Jenn (@livebeerjenn) arrived from the US in 2006, keen to learn about British beer and brewing traditions. She studied in northern England before returning to the capital in 2010 just as the beer renaissance was heating up. Five years later, the British Guild of Beer Writers named her its Brewer of the Year for her work at Beavertown. Currently, she's a freelance brewing consultant and planning her own Earth Station HQ project. 'I have been very lucky to be involved in the early stages with a lot of interesting breweries over the past ten years,' says Jenn, 'in a city that many good brewers now make their home.'

How do you rate London as a beer city, on a world scale?
London is a world class beer city,

as it should be. It's a pleasure to see Londoners think of it as such.

What's the single most exciting thing about beer in London right now?
The enthusiasm and creativity coming from the breweries, and the cultural and social aspect surrounding them. There is a lot of power and potential there.

What single thing would make things even better?
The scene becoming more representative of London in all its glorious racial, social, ethnic, gender and sexual diversity. I'd love to see a broader range of drinkers being drawn to beer as well as different people joining us in roles right across the industry.

What are your top London beers right now?
Cold Spark by Big Smoke, Five Points XPA and any of Boxcar's pale ales.

What's your top great beer night out?
Bethnal Green is becoming an excellent beer destination these days and it's 20 minutes from my front door.

Who's your London beer hero?
Jaega Wise, of course. I don't know how she puts so much into the industry as well as her own brewery – there aren't enough hours in the day!

Who will we be hearing a lot more from in future?
I don't think we've seen the best that Sean Knight (ex-Fourpure and Sambrook's) has to offer yet. I'm hoping his new head brewer role at Siren really gives him the chance to shine.

Which are your other top beer cities?
Some ski town back home in the Rocky Mountains. Any of them are good, I don't mind which!

Brave Sir Robin 🅒

Bar

29 Crouch Hill N4 4AP

T (020) 7018 3830 **bravesirrobin.co.uk**

🕐 *Mo-Th* 16.00-23.00, *Fr* 15.00-24.00, *Sa* 12.00-24.00, *Su* 12.00-22.30. Children until 20.00.

4 cask, 12 keg, 20 bottles/cans, 2 ciders, some cocktails.

🍴 Changing popups **£-££**,

🪑 A few tables on street

Occasional tastings, food pairing, tap takeovers, DJs (Fr-Sa), jazz (Su pm), monthly quiz, board games

🚇 Crouch Hill 🚲 Link to Parkland Walk
🏃 Link to Capital Ring

Sharing ownership with the Rose and Crown NW5 (p175), this smallish wedge-shaped place offers a classy choice of beer from a corner bar overlooking the usual contemporary mix of upcycled tables and chairs, with banquettes creating some more intimate spaces. Supplies are from independents mainly outside London, though with appearances from BBNo, Kernel, Partizan and Pressure Drop. Rotating beers from Fyne, Moor, Oakham and Siren usually occupy the cask lines, while Flensburger and Titanic Stout are the only fixtures on keg. Also favoured are Deya, Verdant, Vibrant Forest, Boundary from Belfast and visiting Scandinavians, with a few Belgian and German classics too. Food was burgers and wings when I last called. Once a motorbike shop, the building went through various iterations as a bar, including under the now-defunct Late Knights brewery, before being relaunched by the current Monty Python-loving custodians in December 2017.

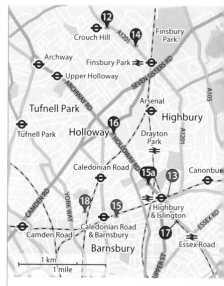

Brewhouse and Kitchen
Highbury 🅓

Brewpub, bar

2a Corsica Street N5 1JJ (Islington)

T (020) 7226 1026

brewhouseandkitchen.com/highbury

First sold beer: June 2015, 🍴

🕐 *Mo-Th* 11.00-23.00, *Fr-Sa* 11.00-24.00, *Su* 12.00-22.30. Children very welcome.

4 cask, 2 tank, 17 keg, 40+ bottles/cans, growlers, minikegs, specialist ciders, gins and other specialist spirits, cocktails, some wine. 🍷

🍴 Sandwiches, enhanced pub grub **£-££**,

🪑 Large front patio, outdoor balcony, ♿

Brewing sessions, tastings, meet the brewer, food matching, occasional DJs, board games, functions

🚆🚇 Highbury & Islington 🚲 NCN162

This former tramshed just off Highbury Corner was the second outlet in a still-expanding chain of smart brewpubs: see Brewhouse and Kitchen Islington (p77). The 8hl kit, originally at the Lamb in Chiswick, is at one end of a cavernous main bar with lots of nooks and crannies under high rafters. Guest beers, the food menu and brewhouse-focused activities are broadly in line with other branches.

BEERS are site-specific within a common template, as at other branches. Popular lines are dispensed direct from conditioning tanks, with others in cask, keg and minicask: **Goal Scorer Session IPA** (4%) can be compared in both cask and keg form.

Campfire
See Two Tribes Brewing.

Clapton Craft N4

Shop, bar
77 Stroud Green Road N4 3EG
claptoncraft.co.uk
🕐 *Mo-Th* 13.00-21.00, *Fr-Sa* 11.00-21.00,
   Su 12.00-20.00. Children until early evening.
6 keg, 250-400 bottles/cans, growlers, bottled
   ciders and perries, natural and organic
   wines, a few specialist spirits. 🍽
🍴 Order-in pizza **££**, ♿
Tastings, tap takeovers, food and beer pairing,
cookery and art courses

🚉 ⊖ Finsbury Park   ⊖ Crouch Hill   🚲 Link to Parkland
Walk   🚶 Link to Capital Ring

It now seems hard to believe that the first bottle shop in London with a hi-tech 'counter pressure' growler-filling system opened as recently as April 2014. This was the first branch of Clapton Craft in Hackney (Try also p141), founded by New Zealander and former Borough Wines staff member William Jack. The Crouch Hill shop was the fourth branch in what's now a small chain, and in 2019 became the first with a tasting room at the back, soothingly decorated with flowers in growlers. Kernel beers are regularly featured on the taps, alongside other Londoners,

wider UK brewers like Lost and Grounded and Time and Tide and occasional exotica. Bottles and cans, sourced from London and UK brewers with a scattering of imports including Belgian lambic, are helpfully categorised by theme, including an intriguing shelf of 'Bonkers Brews', and numerous low alcohol and gluten-free options. A loyalty scheme operating across all the branches provides further encouragement to patronise one of London's smartest and best-informed beer stockists.

Hammerton Brewery ⑮

Brewery, taproom: 8 Roman Way Industrial Estate, 149 Roman Way N7 8XH (Islington)
T (020) 3302 5880   **hammertonbrewery**
First sold beer: April 2014, ⑪
🕐 *Th* 16.00-22.30, *Fr-Sa* 12.00-22.30, *Su* 12.00-20.00. Children until 20.00. Cash-free.
19 keg, 10+ bottles/cans, bespoke can fills. ⚲
🍴 Pizza **££**, 🪑 Tables in yard, ♿
Tastings, food matching, yoga, major big screen sports

⊖ Caledonian Road & Barnsbury

House of Hammerton ⑮ₐ

Contemporary pub: 99 Holloway Road N7 8LT
T (020) 7607 2634
🕐 *Mo-Th* 16.00-23.00, *Fr* 16.00-24.00, *Sa* 14.00-24.00, *Su* 12.00-22.00. Children until 21.00.
2 cask, 19 keg, 50+ bottles/cans, 2 ciders/perries, specialist spirits.
🍴 Peruvian grilled chicken, burgers **£-££**,
♿ Flat access only
Beer tastings, food pairing, fortnightly quiz, board games

🚃 ⊖ Highbury & Islington   🚌 St Mary Magdalene Church

Former IT business analyst Lee Hammerton had already made plans to start an Islington brewery when he discovered he was distantly related to a defunct London brewing dynasty. The Stockwell Brewery was founded in 1730 on Stockwell Green, close to local springs. It was run by Lee's ancestor Charles Hammerton in the late 19th century and in 1938 became likely the first in the world to put real oysters into stout. Watney bought and closed it in 1951, although the site remained in use as a bottling plant for a while before being redeveloped as housing. The trademark passed to Heineken, but Lee got its claim revoked on the grounds of non-use. The new Hammerton, which has doubled capacity since opening, occupies several units alongside rather than underneath the overground railway at Caledonian Road & Barnsbury station, with a 25hl brewhouse. There's a taproom with plenty of foliage, a recycled wood bar, plentiful seating, an in-house pizza oven and unusual activities like beer and chocolate matching.

The brewery's first pub, the House of Hammerton, opened at Highbury in April 2017, with a single bar in modern distressed style, old pews and a front that opens entirely in good weather. This stocks the beers on cask as well as keg and can, alongside a good range of guests stretching to unusual UK entrants like Behemoth and Overtone and Belgian classics like Rodenbach. Peruvian-inspired food includes tapas like spicy potatoes, grilled free-range chicken and burgers including a veggie option.

Visitor note. In 1969, the House of Hammerton building became the Black House, a radical black power commune founded by controversial activist Michael X. John Lennon and Yoko Ono were keen supporters and they and Elton John and Bernie Taupin, who lived nearby, were among the visitors. The commune was destroyed in a suspicious fire in 1970, and its founder was hanged for murder in his native Trinidad in 1975, despite Lennon financing his defence.

BEERS are in keg, cask and can. Core beers include **N1** American pale ale (4.1%); **Panama Creature** gluten-free XPA (4.3%, not cask); properly lagered **Groll Pilsner** (4.7%, not

180

cask); contemporary **IPA N7*** (5.2%); an award-winning modern interpretation of the oyster stout, **Pentonville*** (5.3%); and popular speciality **Crunch Peanut Butter Milk Stout** (5.4%). There's a long-running series of small batch specials.

Indiebeer ⑯

Bar, shop
322 Holloway Road N7 6NJ
T (020) 7607 4760   indiebeer.co.uk
🕑 *Mo-Tu* 16.00-21.00, *We-Th* 12.00-21.00, *Fr-Sa* 12.00-23.00, *Su* 12.00-18.00. Children welcome.
4 keg, 300 bottles/cans, growlers. 🍺
🍴 Order-in pizzas **£-££**, 🪑 Tables on street
Meet the brewer, tap takeovers, food and beer pairing, games nights, functions

⊖ Holloway Road

One striking feature of this smart bottle shop-bar on busy Holloway Road, opened in September 2017, is the arrangement of the fridges at right angles, creating short aisles for specific beer categories. Owners Owen and Clare considered this less intimidating to the inexperienced than the usual batallions lining the walls. The same thoughtfulness is apparent in the selection, which encompasses a varied keg lineup, more unusual Europeans like Garage, Moersleutel and Stigbergets, serious US imports like barrel-aged Old Rasputin from North Coast, unusual Brits like Boutilliers from Kent, plenty of locals and a wide range of craft lagers. With more space than most venues of this type, it's also a pleasant place to drink in, with bare floorboards, flowers on the tables and even a miniature outdoor terrace.

Smokehouse ⑰

Gastropub
63 Canonbury Road N1 2DG
T (020) 7354 1144
smokehouseislington.co.uk
🕑 *Mo-Th* 16.30-22.30, *Fr-Sa* 12.00-22.30, *Su* 12.00-22.00. Children welcome.
1 cask, 17 keg, 25+ bottles/cans, wines, specialist spirits.
🍴 Gourmet home-smoked and barbecued **£££**,
🪑 Tables on street, side garden ⌖, ♿
Occasional tastings and food pairings, meet the brewer

⇌ Essex Road   ⊖ Highbury & Islington   🏃 New River Path

Noble Inns venues usually make a decent effort to offer beer with food, and this one has the advantage that its smoky specialities are particularly good beer matches. It indeed boasts its own smokehouse as well as a butchery, contributing to dishes like duck breast with peach hoisin, leg of lamb with cavolo nero or charred beetroot and goat cheese flatbread. Take your pick from a cask, often from Wild, and kegs, bottles and cans covering numerous styles including dark and sour, from producers like Hackney, Kernel, Kirkstall, Orval, Rochefort and Stiegl, with staff on hand to give advice. It's a crisp and elegant place, slotted into a triangular Canonbury road junction with a patch of maze-like topiary concealing al fresco dining tables. Booking is advisable, though you can take your chances on the unreserved 'pub' side where it's also possible just to drink. See also Pig & Butcher p80.

Two Tribes Brewing ⑱

Brewery, taproom
4 Tileyard Studios, Tileyard Road N7 9AH (Islington)
T (020) 3955 6782   twotribes.co.uk
First sold beer: April 2018 (May 2001 as WJ King), 🍴
🕑 *Mo-Fr* 08.30-22.00, *Sa-Su* 12.00-22.00. Children until 20.00. Cash-free.
10 keg, 10 cans, some specialist spirits. 🍺
🍴 Barbecue **££**, 🪑 large yard, ♿
Live music, DJs, major big screen sport, functions

⊖ Caledonian Road & Barnsbury, Caledonian Road
🚆 Vale Royal, Maiden Lane

This unashamedly modern brewery in the Tileyard, a complex of studios inhabited by hundreds of creative and high-tech businesses north of Kings Cross, traces its roots to the breakup of rather more traditional King & Barnes, founded in Horsham, Sussex, around 1800. After Dorset-based competitor Hall & Woodhouse bought and closed K&B in 2000, former director Bill King set up a micro, WJ King, nearby. This was sold on in 2010, first becoming King Beers, rebranding again to Two Tribes in 2015 and relocating to London in 2018, with a new 10hl steam-heated brewhouse and canning line. The taproom was originally in the brewhouse (4 Tileyard Studios) but was converted to additional production space during the lockdowns, housing additional tanks to triple capacity. Its replacement was a much larger and more unusual space across the yard, known as Campfire, which combines a container bar, sheltered and outdoor seating, a firepit for barbecue cooking and live music and DJs, many of them based onsite. Besides house beers, there are guests often from Manchester and further north (Beatnikz Republic, Fierce, Marble), with London and Belgian options in the fridges. It also acts as a daytime refuge for the neighbours, thus the unusually long hours, so you might rub shoulders with Antony Gormley, the Prodigy or Mark Ronson.

BEERS are in keg and can. Regulars include **Metroland Session IPA*** (3.8%); **Dream Factory Pale Ale** (4.5%); gluten-free lager **Power Plant** (4.5%), lagered for 42 days; and **Electric Circus American Pale Ale** (4.7%). There are regular specials and collaborations including sours.

TRY ALSO

Axe 18 Northwold Road N16 7JR theaxepub. com: Graceland pub overlooking Stoke Newington common, with an eclectic selection of two cask, 18 keg and 45 bottles/cans. Curiously, there's no sign, so look for the smart band of green tiling.

BrewDog Dalston 33 Stoke Newington Road N16 8BJ brewdog.com: Medium-sized high street branch, with particularly keen staff,

opposite the Red Hand (below). One cask, 21 keg, including locals, 60 bottles/cans and, uniquely, an all-vegan food menu in partnership with Biff's Jack Shack.

Charlotte Despard 17 Archway Road N19 3TX thecharlottedespard.co.uk: Comfortable local favourite with three cask, usually from London, and decent keg and bottled choices. Once one of the earliest Wetherspoon pubs, now a determinedly independent free house named after a novelist, socialist, feminist and Irish republican campaigner of the early 20th century. May close Mondays.

Duke of York 33 Downham Road N1 5AA thedukeofyorkpub.com: In De Beauvoir Town on the interface of Islington and Hackney, this is the pub where Beavertown Brewery began. Now a Barworks outlet offering a diverse range of 16 kegs and approaching 50 bottles/cans (but no cask) in handsomely pubby surroundings.

Foxglove 209 Liverpool Road N1 1LX thefoxglove.co.uk: Smallish contemporary Barnsbury pub listed in previous editions under two different names and once again beer-focused after another change of hands, with four casks, eight kegs and 30+ bottles/cans, mainly from London and the UK.

Highbury Vintners 71 Highbury Park N5 1UA highburyvintners.co.uk: Award-winning independent wine shop at Highbury Barn also stocking around 200 beers, mainly from London and the UK, including some more traditional choices. Deliveries and curated case subscriptions for locals.

Jack's 178A Stroud Green Road N4 3RS: Street corner off-licence open long hours right by a bus stop in Crouch Hill, stocking specialist beers since the mid-1980s thanks to the keen interest of a co-owner. 200 bottles/cans, both contemporary and traditional, from London, the UK, Belgium, Germany, the US and elsewhere.

Jolly Butchers 204 Stoke Newington High Street N16 7HU jollybutchers.co.uk: Stoke Newington stalwart, a pioneer when it reopened in 2010 though perhaps since eclipsed by newer arrivals. Good choice of three cask, 17 keg and over 40 bottles/cans in a pleasantly quirky makeover of a corner pub. See also the Crown and Anchor (p259).

Lamb 54 Holloway Road N7 8JL thelambn7.co.uk: Popular, handsome and friendly Highbury pub with a traditional feel but a modern beer list featuring numerous locals across three cask and 10 keg lines plus a few bottles/cans. Very busy when Arsenal play at home. Once the tap of the Highbury Brewery (1740–1912) and later Firkin brewpub the Flounder (1985–99).

Mother Kelly's Church Street Street/N16 92 Stoke Newington Church Street N16 0AP motherkellys.co.uk: A branch in one of the most chichi bits of Stoke Newington near Abney Park Cemetery, with more space and choice than is apparent at first glance. Six kegs and over 400 bottles/cans including lots of rarities, many in a walk-in coldroom. More shop than bar but comfortable enough to drink in.

Red Hand 36 Stoke Newington Road N16 7XJ red-hand.co.uk: Graceland venue opposite BrewDog Dalston (above), more post-industrial in style than others and with no cask, though 17 kegs and 40 bottles/cans including sharing bottles.

Shaftesbury Tavern 534 Hornsey Road N19 3QN theshaftesburytavern.co.uk: Handsome heritage pub in the Remarkable group opposite Elthorne Park: much dark wood, engraved glass and a massive elaborate bar back, plus a welcoming atmosphere, Thai menu, three local well-kept cask beers, interesting guest kegs and a few Belgian bottles.

Snooty Fox 75 Grosvenor Avenue N5 2NN snootyfoxlondon.co.uk: Not at all snooty place opposite Canonbury Overground station that regularly makes the best of a limiting tie to offer a small selection of well-kept cask and keg, expanding considerably during excellent regular beer festivals and tasting/matching events.

LONDON DRINKERS Peter Jackson

The founder of Southwark Brewing (p214), the only one of the Bermondsey breweries to produce substantial amounts of excellent cask, Peter has been in the industry for over 30 years including lengthy stints at Whitbread and Marston's. 'I've been fascinated at the rapid change in the London beer market over the past five years,' he says, 'and am pleased to be part of it.' Follow him on Twitter @englishbeerman.

How do you rate London as a beer city, on a world scale?
It's creeping into the top 10, but painfully slowly. The beer tie and the inertia of London publicans are holding it back.

What's the single most exciting thing about beer in London right now?
The changing demographic of craft and cask ale drinkers in London, with so many of them now under 35 and female. The pace of change and all the new pubs and bars are exciting too.

What single thing would make things even better?
A guarantee from the government that duty relief for small brewers will be with us forever!

What are your top London beers right now?
With so many new beers appearing, this is impossible to call.

What's your top great beer night out?
So many new venues are opening that it's difficult to choose, but you can't beat a good night at the Harp (p102 with beer quality guaranteed.

Who's your London beer hero?
I have no one hero, except perhaps the last person to open a great new pub, bar or brewery.

Who will we be hearing a lot more from in future?
Someone who we haven't heard of yet, who will expand the market in ways nobody was expecting.

Which are your other top beer cities?
Ghent. It has so many great bars with great beer menus, and they aren't quite overrun by tourists… yet.

Tottenham and Haringey

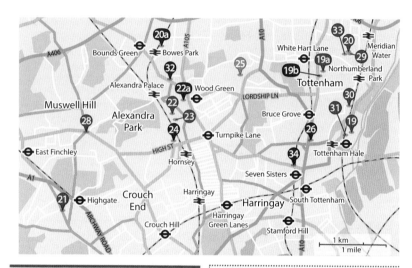

Beavertown Brewery  ❶⑲

Beavertown Tottenham Hale
Brewery, taproom (part-owned by Heineken):
17 Lockwood Industrial Park, Mill Mead Road
N17 9QP (Haringey)
T(020) 3696 1441 **beavertownbrewery.co.uk**
First sold beer: February 2012 (at original site)
🕐 *Sa* 14.00-20.00. Children welcome. Cash-free.
10 keg, 15 bottles, growlers.
🍴 Changing food truck **£**, 🪑 Benches at front
Occasional special events

⇌ ⊖ Tottenham Hale   🚲 NCN1   🏃 Lea Valley Path

Beavertown Tottenham Hotspur ⑲ₐ

Brewpub, bar (part-owned by Heineken)
Marketplace, Tottenham Hotspur Stadium,
782 High Road N17 0BX (Haringey)
First sold beer: April 2019
🕐 Match days only. Children welcome.
3 keg, 6 cans.
🍴 Various from neighbouring traders, ♿

⊖ White Hart Lane   🚲 CS1

Corner Pin ⑲ᵦ

Contemporary pub
732 High Road N17 0AG
🕐 To be confirmed

⊖ White Hart Lane   🚲 CS1

I've said much more about London's most
spectacularly expanded brewery under
Voyage to Beaverworld (below). The original
Tottenham taproom has simple seating and a
tiled back bar dispensing specials and one-offs
besides the core range and guests from like-
minded breweries. An extra outdoor bar has a
more limited selection on busy days. Regular
ticketed tastings among the barrels at the
Tempus Project unit across the yard offer a
more intimate and exclusive experience. The
brewpub in the rebuilt Tottenham Hotspur
stadium is in the Market Place in the southeast
of the site, with a view of the pitch. It's currently
only accessible on match days, when core
brand Neck Oil is sold on bars throughout the
stadium. Just outside the stadium, the Corner
Pin pub should be refurbished and reopened

as a promised 'fully immersive Beavertown pub experience' by the time you read this. Finally, there's the massive new brewery further up the Lea Valley (p196).

BEERS are in keg and can, with Tempus Project lines hand-bottled in distinctive 375ml bottles. Year-round core beers include **Neck Oil*** (3.3%) session IPA; flagship **Gamma Ray*** (5.4%) American pale ale; **Bloody 'Ell** (5.5%) blood orange IPA; and **Lupuloid** (6.7%) IPA. Recurring seasonals are saison-style **Quelle Farmhouse Pale*** (4.1%); **Smog Rocket*** (5.4%) smoked porter; rye IPA **8 Ball*** (6.2%); and a black IPA, **Black Betty*** (7.4%). **Tempus** beers vary widely but all are interesting, and some are exceptional: recent ones have included **Birds of a Feather**** (6.2%), a *bière de coupage* blended from old and new beer, some of it aged in burgundy and muscat barrels.

Bohem Brewery 20

Brewery, taproom: 5 Littleline House, 43 West Road N17 0RE (Haringey)
T 07999 0142943 **bohembrewery.com**
First sold beer: June 2016, ‼ (informal)
Tottenham Hotspur match days, check social media. Children welcome.
5-8 keg, 7 cans.
Occasional food truck, Small yard, Flat access only

Meridian Water | Scotswood Walk | Link to NCN1, Q18

Bohem Tap Room 20a

Bar: 120A Myddleton Road N22 8NQ
We-Su 16.30-23.00. Children until early evening.
8 keg, 3-4 cans, Czech wine, local gin.
Czech packet snacks and BYO,
Standing on street, (one step)
Live music (We), Czech and major UK big screen sports

Bounds Green | Bowes Park | Link to Q10
Link to New River Path

Bohem focuses on top quality craft lagers balancing Czech tradition and contemporary flair. Co-founder Petr Skoček, originally from Plzeň, began homebrewing when he moved to London from Prague, in response to the expensive and disappointing lagers then available locally. In 2015, he teamed up with a fellow expat enthusiast, businessman Zdeněk Kudr, to establish Bohem in Bounds Green, brewing four times daily on a tiny 160 litre kit to fill one fermenter. The business expanded to the current address on a Tottenham industrial estate in April 2018, using a 10hl Czech-built brewhouse capable of traditional decoction mashing, alongside cylindrical lagering tanks. Since April 2017, there's been a micropub-sized taproom close to the original site, on characterful Myddleton Road where the beers were once sold on a market stall. Despite being considerably smaller than the average Czech pub, this manages a delightfully woody Bohemian atmosphere, and manager Marek Průša, a Pilsner Urquell-certified master tapster, ensures a perfect pour, as explained in the informative menu. A simple taproom opens at the brewery itself on match days.

BEERS are in keg and can. Core beers include table lager **Slavia*** (2.7%); 'session pils' **Martina** (4%); **Raven*** (4.3%) 'lagered porter'; best-seller **Amos Pilsner*** (4.9%); and **Sparta**** (5.4%), a polotmavý amber lager. Specials include **Druid*** (5.7%) black lager and **Otakar** (6.4%), a brut lager that began as a collaboration with St Austell, using the same yeast as that brewery's **Korev**.

Bohem Tap Room

Bull (Gorgeous Brewery)

Brewpub, gastropub
13 North Hill N6 4BX (Haringey)
T (020) 8341 0510   thebullhighgate.co.uk,
gorgeousbrewery.com
First sold beer: September 2011 (as London
Brewing), 🍴
🕐 *Mo-Th* 12.00-22.00, *Fr* 12.00-23.00, *Sa* 10.00-
23.00, *Su* 12.00-22.30. Children very welcome.
4-6 cask, 8 keg, 20+ bottles, wines, local spirits.
🍴 Gastro menu **£££**, 🌴 Front terrace, rear
garden, ♿
*Quiz (Mo), food promotions, drawing lessons,
board games, functions*

🔁 Highgate   🚇 Hillcrest Estate   🚲 Link to Parkland Walk
🚶 Link to Capital Ring

Originally an inn beside the old Great North
Road, the Bull housed five different restaurants
over 15 years then spent almost two years
closed and squatted. It was then revitalised by
former White Horse (p302) manager Dan Fox
as the sort of food-led pub you'd expect in
select Highgate but favouring beer to the
extent of a 4hl brewhouse in the kitchen,
operating as London Brewing. Dan later expanded operations to the Bohemia, a bigger brewpub in North Finchley (p197), and in July 2016
sold the Bull to Rob Laub, who continued the
brewing tradition under the name Gorgeous.
Early in 2018, the brewhouse was sensibly
relocated to a purpose-built home in the
garden and increased to 8hl with an eye to
expanding external sales. Much of the elegantly
appointed space is dedicated to diners
enjoying a daily-changing menu that might
feature red onion tart tatin, flat iron steak,

Bull

roast cod fillet or roast lamb cutlets with
merguez sausages. But you can still call in for
a drink or, indeed, a takeaway, with keenly
priced wings a popular treat on Wednesdays.
The beer list has shortened but still includes
guests from breweries like Church Farm,
Lost and Grounded and Thornbridge.

*Visitor note. In June, like many Highgate pubs, the Bull parti-
cipates in Swearing on the Horns, a farcical annual ceremony
of obscure origins dating from at least the 18th century.*

BEERS in cask, keg and bottle all have names
beginning with G and tend towards pale and
contemporary in style. Regulars include **Glowfly**
Best Bitter (4%), session IPA **Gyrocopter** (4.1%)
and Pacific pale **Goofyhoof** (5%).

Earth Ale

Brewery: A007 The Chocolate Factory,
5 Clarendon Road N22 6XJ (Haringey)
earthale.com
First sold beer: July 2015 (at original site)
🕐 Only for pre-booked dinners and special
events

🚊 Alexandra Palace   🔁 Wood Green   🚇 Barratt Avenue

Earth Tap   **22a**

Bar: Blue House Yard, 5 River Park Road N22 7TB
🕐 *Su-We* 12.00-22.00, *Th-Sa* 12.00-24.00.
    Children welcome.
9 keg, 10+ bottles/cans, specialist tea and
    coffee, natural wine, specialist spirits.
🍴 Pizzas, gelato, snacks **£**,
🌴 Courtyard, ♿ (step access to bar)
*Comedy (Su), occasional tap takeovers, acoustic
music planned, huge selection of board games*

🔁 Wood Green   🚲 Link to C20   🚶 Better Haringey Trail,
link to New River Path

Not only is this one of London's most unusual
and specialist breweries, it also has one of
the capital's quirkiest and most charming
showcases: a converted double-decker bus
parked in sunny Blue House Yard, formerly
a derelict car park that's been ingeniously
repurposed as a workshop community close
to Wood Green station. It cohabits with
'board game café' Snakes and Ladders, but
the beers are sold even when the café is
officially in residence, alongside other locals

rth Tap

like Bohem and like-minded brewers from the UK and elsewhere like Duration, Tool and Yonder, with good value tasting paddles.

The project is the brainchild of Michelin-trained chef Alex Lewis, a specialist in foraged ingredients who began brewing commercially on a very small scale at home for a series of beer and food matching dinners he hosted at various south London venues in 2015. Following a period of cuckoo brewing, Earth Ale found space a short walk from the bus in July 2018, in the former Barratt's biscuit factory, now known as the Chocolate Factory. A 200 litre kit was used as a stopgap until April 2019 when beer began flowing from a more professional 10hl brewhouse. Although the brewery itself isn't regularly open, look out for a series of ticketed beer dinners at the site.

BEERS in keg and bottle-conditioned form usually contain foraged ingredients, including **Spicy Weiss** (4.5%) with hogweed, alexanders and coriander; **Pine Blond** (4.6%) with birch sap and spruce twigs; **Verbena Pale** (5.5%) with lemon verbena; and **Dandy Stout*** (8.4%) with dandelion root.

Goodness Brewing Company (The)

Brewery, taproom
5a Clarendon Yard, Coburg Road N22 6TZ
(Haringey)   thegoodnessbrew.co
First sold beer: September 2019 (at own site), 🍴
🕐 *Fr* 16.00-23.00, *Sa-Su* 12.00-23.00, card only.
   Children very welcome until early evening.
   Cash-free.
1 cask, 5 keg, 1 can.
🍴 Pizzas £, 🪑 Large rear yard, ♿
Cabaret, acoustic and other live music, art exhibitions, DJs, big screen

⊖ Wood Green   🚌 Barratt Avenue   🚲 Link to C20
🚶 Link to New River Path

The Goodness, as it styles itself, emerged out of the amusingly named Wood Green Hopping City, founded in 2016 as a collective of locals who grow hops in gardens and allotments and pool the harvest to create an annual special beer. At first the beers were cuckoo-brewed by Damien Legg and Mike Stirling with Zack Ahmed, including at the Prince (below) and in Sheffield, and sold through local markets. Production ramped up several notches in August 2019 with the commissioning of a substantial installation with a 15hl Chinese-built brewhouse. It's located in a large industrial unit in Clarendon Yards, an evolving hub of creative industries opposite Wood Green's similarly repurposed Chocolate Factory. A full-sized birch tree in a giant planter dominates an expansive taproom and is trucked outside in good weather to provide shade for a surprisingly attractive post-industrial patio.

BEERS are in cask, a format the founders are keen to support, as well as keg and can, with names that accentuate the positive. Regulars include flagship session IPA **Yes!** (4.5%) and red IPA **Sunset** (4.7%), both also available in cask, as is seasonal light-bodied oat stout **Shout Out** (4.1%). There's a recently added hazy IPA and various specials including the annual Hopping City brew.

Gorgeous Brewery
See Bull

187

Great Northern Railway Tavern

Contemporary pub
67 High Street N8 7QB
T (020) 8127 6632
thegreatnorthernrailway.co.uk
🕐 *Mo-Th* 12.00-23.00, *Fr-Sa* 12.00-01.00,
Su 12.00-22.30. Children until 19.00.
3-4 cask, 20 keg, 25+ bottles/cans, some
wines, home-infused gin.
🍴 Imaginative pub grub **££**, 🌳 Rear garden, ♿
Quiz (We), monthly tap takeover, flight club

🚊 Hornsey 🚶 New River Path

This sizeable heritage pub right by Hornsey's
New River Village, a big housing development
on the site of a former waterworks beside the
New River, was reopened in April 2017 after a
thorough restoration. The building provides
an impressive setting for one of Fuller's most
renowned contemporary-focused pubs, where
you might find exclusive one-offs from
Mikkeller besides the London Pride and Taylor
Landlord handpumps. Draught choices are
helpfully displayed on monitor screens:
favoured guests include Deya, North, Northern
Monk and Siren, with a line for local Bohem
and a fridge that stretches to Dugges and
Schneider Weisse. A regular 'flight club' presents
a selection of tasters picked by staff. A decent
menu combines staples like fish and chips and
pie and mash with Kentucky-fried seitan, London
Porter smoked salmon, pasta and noodles.

Visitor note *The Grade II-listed Flemish Renaissance
building was opened in 1897 in anticipation of a planned
underground line to Hornsey that was then abandoned.
Note the riot of ornamental ironwork on the exterior, the
original bar counter and bar back with its engraved mirrors,
and a beautiful stained glass skylight overlooking what was
once the music room at the back.*

Great Northern Railway Tavern

Greywood Brewery

Brewery, no visitors please
Wood Green N22 (Haringey)
greywoodbrewery.co.uk
First sold beer: March 2020

Designer and beekeeper Adam Armstrong
had been a keen homebrewer for several
years when the management at his local pub
suggested he make a commercial brew for
them. The result was this part-time home-
based brewery working in 1.5hl batches.
Following a successful first brew, activities
were suspended during the lockdown but
revived in 2021. Modest expansion is planned.

BEERS started with an English-style cask IPA,
The Longest Road (5.2%, not tasted). Other
styles and formats may be added: Adam is
keen to try a Scottish-style 'wee heavy'.

High Cross

Bar
350 High Road N17 9HT
T (020) 8292 8115
facebook.com/highcrosslondon
🕐 *Mo-Th* 16.00-23.00, *Fr* 16.00-23.30, *Sa* 12.00-
23.30, *Su* 12.00-22.30. Children until 19.30.
1 cask (weekends), 9 keg, 15 bottles, some
wines and specialist spirits.
🍴 Pub grub, pies **££**, 🌳 Benches outside, ♿
*Tap takeovers, tastings, occasional music and
charity events*

🚇 Bruce Grove, Seven Sisters 🚌 Tottenham Bus Garage
🚲 Link to CS1 🚶 Link to Better Haringey Trail

One of this book's most unusual venues, this
pleasant little bar occupies a 1920s former
public lavatory designed to resemble a Tudor
cottage. It was derelict for three decades before
Chris Johnson and Alex Beeson converted it in
May 2018. They've preserved the old signing
(which must confuse the occasional passer-by)
and tiling to create a cosy space with wood
panelling and flowers on the tables. A corner
bar offers a cask on stillage at weekends plus
kegs from London and further afield (Exale,
Kernel, Northern Monk, Siren), including strong
beers and sours, with Bristol Milk Stout as the
regular dark. You might find Põhjala from
Tallinn or Rodenbach Grand Cru in the fridges.

Remarkably, they've squeezed a kitchen in too, providing wholesome fare like pie and mash (including veggie options), fisherman's pie and Sunday roasts. And if you're caught short, the toilets are immaculate.

Visitor note. The name High Cross is from the pub's location at a junction on Roman Ermine Street that in medieval times was the nucleus of Tottenham village. A wayside wooden cross is first recorded here in 1409, replaced in the early 17th century by a brick monument that was subsequently remodelled in Gothic style in 1809 and still stands today.

Muswell Hillbilly

Brewery, taproom
24 Avenue Mews (taproom at 14) N10 3NP
(Haringey)   **muswellhillbillybrewers.co.uk**
First sold beer: April 2016, 🍴(informal)
🕐 Fr 16.30-22.30, Sa 13.00-23.00, Su 13.00-18.00.
   Children until early evening.
Occasional cask, 6 keg, 15+ bottles/cans.
🌲A few seats at the front
Occasional tastings, DJs, art/photography exhibitions

⇌Alexandra Palace ⊖Highgate 🚌Muswell Hill Broadway
🚶Link to Better Haringey Trail, Parkland Walk

Nodding in their name to local heroes the Kinks, the Hillbillies are also a quartet, though currently still holding their day jobs and working on the brewery part-time. Homebrewers Martin Hodgson and Pete Syratt began the project by experimenting at Ubrew. By late 2016, they were registered commercially, working on a small scale at Pete's home and selling very locally, including at the Alexandra Palace Farmers' Market. They moved up a notch in February 2017 with an upstairs space in Avenue Mews, a quiet back alley where a community of creative types works in an attractive terrace of former service buildings once linked to the big houses fronting Muswell Hill Broadway. Here they operated what was basically a big homebrew setup making 130 litre batches. A petite taproom opened a few doors down from the brewery in April 2018, serving mainly own-brews plus a few guests (bottles and cans from Canopy, Signature and Vocation when I called) in a pleasant space with a few tables and tasteful music on vinyl. In October 2018, the Hillbillies upgraded by

becoming the fourth owners of a 4hl kit previously used by Anspach & Hobday, Affinity and the predecessor of Exale.

BEERS are mainly cask and bottle-conditioned, with some kegging, and often use local ingredients: some of the hops are grown by the brewers and their friends in gardens and allotments. A surprisingly wide range of core beers includes **Down the Colney Hatch*** smoked porter (5.2%); **Fortis Green Breakfast Stout** (5.3%), with coffee from a well-established local roaster; a popular **IPA** (5.3%); and **Palace Sunset Red Ale** (5.5%).

One Mile End

Brewery
2 Compass West Estate, West Road N17 0XL
(Haringey)
📞 (020) 7998 0610   **onemileend.com**
First sold beer: June 2013 (at original site)
🍴Occasional
🕐 See social media. Children welcome.
Occasional cask, up to 7 keg. 🖐
🌲Front yard, ♿Flat access only

⇌Meridian Water 🚌Scotswood Walk
♿Link to NCN1

Named after the address of the White Hart pub in Whitechapel where it began, the brewery was briefly known as Mulligans when it commenced operations in June 2013 on a small 4hl kit in the cellar. When Redemption expanded to a bigger site in March 2016, One Mile End took over its former Tottenham premises and 20hl brewhouse. The pub brewery is still in place, but today production is focused at Tottenham which also has a small pilot kit. Currently the site isn't regularly open to the public but check social media as

there are plans for special events and a bar on Spurs match days when several other nearby breweries welcome visitors. Another good place to sample the beers is the company's second pub, the Alma (p76).

BEERS are in cask and keg, with canning on a mobile line and occasional bottle-conditioned specials. Regulars include **Salvation Pale Ale** (4.5%); hazy pale ale **Juicy 4PM*** (4.9%); **Snakecharmer IPA** (5.7%); and **Jazz Police DDH IPA** (6.3%). There are numerous specials, with recurring entries including **Hospital Porter*** (5.2%), a nod to the London Hospital which is close to the original pub; annual seasonal **Blood Orange Wheat Double IPA** (7.4%); and strong bière de garde **Pierre de Garde*** (10%).

ORA ③⓪

Brewery, taproom
16A Rosebery Industrial Park N17 9SR
(Haringey) orabeer.com
First sold beer: May 2017 (as Brewheadz),
!! (informal)
⏲ *Th-Fr* 16.00-21.00, *Sa* 12.00-21.00, *Su* 12.00-18.00. Children very welcome.
Occasional cask, 6 keg, 6+ bottles/cans. ⌁
!! Changing food truck **£**, 🎋 Seating at front, ♿ Flat access only
Brewing sessions, DJs, occasional live music

⇌ Northumberland Park, Tottenham Hale   ⊖ Tottenham Hale
🚌 Hanbury Road   ♿ Link to NCN1   🚶 Link to Lea Valley Path

An alluring fusion of northern Italian and London craft beer culture, ORA was founded in October 2016 in Modena, Emilia-Romagna, where two of its owners still live, but has mainly operated in London under the auspices of director Daniele Zaccarelli. It began as a cuckoo, one of the highest-achieving teams working at Bermondsey's ill-fated Ubrew. Meanwhile in April 2017, four other expatriate Italian homebrewing friends went professional under the name Brewheadz on a Tottenham industrial estate using a 14hl kit. This project ran into difficulties when one of its prime movers had to return to Italy for family reasons, so ORA took over in May 2019, gaining a much-needed brewhouse which it now plans to expand, as well as a taproom

operating from a neat bar in front of the brewing floor. The current head brewer, German-born and trained Julia Huber, once managed a brewery in Greenland. The location is right by the Lea Valley Park and conveniently midway between a cluster of breweries including Redemption to the north and Beavertown and Pressure Drop to the south.

BEERS are in keg, cans and occasionally cask. Core beers include **Panaro** (4.5%) West Coast pale ale; **Balsamic**** (6%), a strong milk stout with vanilla and wood-aged balsamic vinegar from the brewery's spiritual home; and **Limoncello** (6%) IPA with Sorrento lemons. There are numerous specials and collaborations with both UK and Italian brewers.

Pressure Drop Brewing ③①

Brewery, taproom
6 Lockwood Industrial Park, Mill Mead Road
N17 9QP (Haringey)
📞 (020) 8801 0616
pressuredropbrewing.co.uk
First sold beer: January 2013, **!!** (informal)
⏲ *Sa* 12.00-20.00. Children welcome.
10 keg, 12+ bottles/cans. ⌁
!! Summer changing food truck, 🎋 Front yard, ♿

⇌ ⊖ Tottenham Hale   ♿ NCN1   🚶 Lea Valley Path

Former Euston Tap cellarman Graham O'Brien and Sam Smith (no relation to the famous Yorkshire brewing family) are old school friends, and Graham met the third partner in Pressure Drop, Ben Freeman, on an internship at London Fields. They developed their first recipes on a Braumeister pilot kit in Graham's garden shed in Stoke Newington in the summer of 2012, but lack of space meant much of the work was done outside, not a viable option with winter on its way. The first commercial brews emerged from a small industrial unit nearby, but in March 2013 they moved to a Hackney railway arch using an 8hl kit. This eventually also proved too small, so over the course of 2017, production was transferred to a facility with a 32hl kit and canning line at Tottenham Hale, just opposite Beavertown on the same industrial estate. There's a generously proportioned taproom with a good view of the brewing floor: the fact that there's a separate glass collection and takeaway counter illustrates how buzzing the place can get. The Hackney arch has been restyled as The Experiment (p133).

BEERS in keg and can are mainly changing specials, with lots of contemporary hazy, juicy options. Regulars include **Wu Gang Chops the Tree**** (3.8%), a wheat beer flavoured with locally foraged herbs; and flagship **Pale Fire** (4.8%) pale ale.

Prince

Contemporary pub
1 Finsbury Road N22 8PA
T (020) 8888 6698　theprincen22.co.uk
Mo-We 12.00-23.00, Th 12.00-24.00, Fr-Sa 12.00-01.00, Su 12.00-22.30. Children very welcome.
6 cask, 10 keg, 4-5 cans, 2-4 ciders, some gins.
Pizzas plus popups £-££, Front terrace, public green opposite
Chess, board games, food and drink promotions, major big screen sport

Alexandra Palace　Park Avenue Wood Green
New River Path

A sizeable and solid pub set back from busy Bounds Green Road, the former Prince of Wales was threatened with redevelopment before being designated an Asset of Community Value. It reopened in July 2016 with a tasteful grey-painted interior, interesting art and an appropriately high quality, varied and changing range of beers, almost all sourced from UK-based independents. Cask Uley Bitter and keg Signature Studio local lager make for unusual permanent features: other favoured breweries include Almasty, Burnt Mill, Five Points, Gipsy Hill, Half Acre, Seven Sisters and Track, with a small number of changing hand-picked cans. Decent home-cooked food could include barley risotto, grilled sea bass or pulled pork

buns. When first reopened, it was a brewpub with a small brewhouse at the side, but this has since been removed.

Visitor note. *Customers are welcome to take their drinks onto the patch of grass and trees in front of the pub, a corner of Trinity Gardens which was once part of the common land of a now-vanished hamlet known as Woodleigh. The obelisk drinking fountain, made of Cornish granite, dates from 1879; it was originally at the junction of Bounds Green Road and Park Avenue but was moved here in 1904 to make way for trams.*

Redemption Brewing ③③

Brewery, taproom
16 Compass West Estate, West Road N17 0XL (Haringey)
T (020) 8885 5227
redemptionbrewing.co.uk
First sold beer: February 2010,
🕐 Tottenham Hotspur match days and some other days – check for hours – and at other times for pre-arranged collection. Children welcome.
3-4 cask, 4 keg, 3-4 bottles/cans, polypins. 🍺
🍴 Occasional food truck **£**, 🍴 Front yard, ♿
Tastings, functions

🚈 Meridian Water 🚌 Scotswood Walk 🚲 Link to NCN1

Redemption was one of the first of the current wave of new London breweries and the first in what's now the brewing hotbed of Tottenham. It was founded by Glaswegian-born former banker Andy Moffat, who studied at Brewlab in Sunderland after being inspired by Dogfish Head founder Sam Calagione's book *Brewing up a Business*. He began with a secondhand 20hl plant modified by brewing consultant

Andy Moffat of Redemption Brewery

Dave Smith, who also designed the early beers. Early in 2016, Redemption moved to a bigger unit on the same estate with a new 50hl German-built kit, while One Mile End (above) took over the original facility. The brewery maintains its own yeast culture, originally from Scottish & Newcastle in Edinburgh but since adapted to local conditions. It has never pursued aggressive expansion, remaining 'the right-sized brewery' as Andy puts it. 'You do need to grow,' he comments, 'but I wonder if for some it's been at the expense of getting the business right.' For visitors, there's a small improvised bar, benches and tables on the ground floor and a more comfortable, purpose-built space on a mezzanine above. Currently, opening is limited to match days at Tottenham Hotspur nearby, and for special events.

BEERS are 80% cask, including some in 18-gallon (82 litre) kilderkins, with the rest in keg, bottles and cans packaged unpasteurised and unfiltered at SEB in Broadstairs. Regulars include **Trinity** (** in cask, 3%), a modern light ale made with three malts and three hops; **Pale Ale** (3.8%); **Rock the Kazbek*** (4%) pale ale with Czech Kazbek hops; **Solar** (4.2%), a pale ale for keg and can; amber ale **Hopspur** (4.5%); unusual dark bitter **Urban Dusk*** (4.6%); **Fellowship Porter*** (5.1%); and **Big Chief IPA** (5.5%). **Victorian Mild**** (6%), an occasional collaboration with Kernel, is a special worth looking out for.

True Craft ③④

Contemporary pub
68 West Green Road N15 5NR
T (020) 8351 3397   **truecraftlondon.co.uk**
🕐 Su-We 12.00-23.00, Th-Sa 12.00-24.00.
    Children until early evening.
9-10 keg, 50+ bottles/cans.
🍴 Gourmet pizzas **££**,
🍴 Some benches on street, ♿
NCT charity family lunch (Mo), occasional meet the brewer, tap takeovers, live music

⊖ Seven Sisters   🚲 Link to CS1

The West Green Tavern not far from Seven Sisters station was considered a lost pub when it closed in 2015 for redevelopment into flats, but the ground floor was retained for

True Craft

commercial use. In August 2018, it reopened as a decent local craft beer bar, independently owned by a group of enthusiasts new to the industry. A smallish but pleasing café-like space retains restored Victorian pillars and floors. Kegs are dispensed from an impressive copper bar back installed by a local craftsman, favouring locals like One Mile End, ORA, Pressure Drop and Wild Card, though the Tottenham lager, despite referencing the locality's claim as home to the first purpose-built lager brewery in Britain, is from Huyghe in Belgium. A well-stocked fridge introduces beers from further afield, including German classics like Augustiner. Food centres on a pizza oven toasting up local mozzarella, with numerous vegetarian and vegan options.

TRY ALSO

Bottle Apostle Crouch End
49 Park Road N8 8SY bottleapostle.com: Smallish, colourfully decorated branch of the beer-friendly wine shop chain with over 100 mainly UK bottles/cans, including top small London breweries.
Salisbury Hotel 1 Grand Parade, Green Lanes N4 1JX thesalisburyhotelpub.co.uk: Magnificent early 20th-century heritage pub on Green Lanes: imposing porches with floor mosaics, art nouveau mirrors, carved wood booths and expanses of marble tiling plus up to six casks often including locals Redemption, imported Czech lager, German and Belgian bottles and 12+ eclectic rotating kegs.
Small Beer 22 Topsfield Parade N8 8PT smallbeern8.co.uk: Trendier younger sister of the Prince (above), with a notable range of up to six cask dispensed from handpumps resembling industrial bolts, 11 keg and a few bottles/cans all from independents. At Crouch End close to the Queens (below).

HERITAGE PUB

Queens 26 Broadway Parade N8 9DE brunningandprice.co.uk. Magnificent Grade II*-listed former hotel opened in 1902 by John Cathies Hill, also responsible for the Salisbury (above): the resemblance is obvious in the imposing turreted exterior, arched entrances with classical pillars, mosaic floors, art nouveau stained glass windows, huge circular bar and ornate alcoves. Now part of the upmarket Brunning & Prince group with a few cask and keg lines of note.

LONDON'S BREWING | Voyage to Beaverworld

Perhaps the most ambitious and restlessly expansive of new London breweries, Beavertown was founded by Logan Plant, son of Led Zeppelin singer Robert and himself a former musician. Logan's love of beer was first inspired by the celebrated cask ales of his native West Midlands, but he decided to brew after being astounded by the flavour combinations of barbecue food and craft beer while touring the US with his band. Developing recipes as a homebrewer from 2010, in February 2012 he opened Dukes Brew and Que in the Duke of York pub in De Beauvoir Town, Hackney, creating beers to match the food on an 8hl kit crammed into a corner of the kitchen, including light pale ale Neck Oil, which began as an attempt to clone Black Country legend Bathams Bitter. The brewery was branded Beavertown, from the local pronunciation of De Beauvoir Town, and demand for its products soon increased beyond the pub. The first expansion was to a lock-up some distance away used as a fermentation room, requiring the transport of hopped wort by car from the pub.

Logan Plant of Beavertown

In April 2013, the kit was transplanted to a bigger site in Hackney Wick, next door to the original site of the revived Truman's, with several more fermenters added. Once again demand outstripped capacity and the business relocated again the following year to a much bigger site on an industrial estate near the Lee Valley Park at Tottenham Hale, with a new 50hl kit fabricated in Bulgaria.

Here Beavertown became one of the early pioneers of 'craft cans', and soon ditched a parallel bottling line which was sold to Five Points. The packaging provided a perfect canvas for the distinctive style of designer Nick Dwyer, a former waiter at Dukes who is now creative director.

Early in 2015, the fermenters expanded into another unit opposite, also home to the brewery's Tempus side project (where beer is aged in a variety of wooden wine barrels, Belgian-style foeders and even ceramic amphorae),

Amphorae at Beavertown

and the original Dukes brewhouse, now used as a pilot kit. Dukes was quietly closed at the end of 2017 as it was 'no longer a natural fit for Beavertown's future' (it's since reopened under its original name the Duke of York: Try also p182). By now even the Tottenham plant was bursting at the seams despite occupying a fourth adjacent unit, with a team that ran to 115 people.

Surprise, shock and even anger greeted the announcement in June 2018 that Dutch-based multinational brewer Heineken had bought a minority stake in the company, subsequently confirmed as 49.1%. The reaction, which stretched to well-publicised delistings and calls for boycotts, was perhaps exacerbated by the brewery's previous championing of independence. Logan insists that the arrangement is a genuine partnership, intended to finance renewed growth, and he still considers the brewery independent by remaining in control of its own vision.

'When we first moved to Tottenham,' he says, 'I thought it would be our home for life.

But a couple of years on, we realised that if we wanted to put great beer on every street corner, it wasn't big enough after all. The more we planned, the bigger it got, and we ended up with this £40 million dream and had to ask ourselves who were were going to do it with. We spoke to various people, to bigger breweries, people we knew with personal wealth and venture capitalists. And all of them were enthusiastic. But the more I considered Heineken, the more I realised the support they could offer with marketing, people, resources and expertise was the best fit. We were insistent, though, that we wouldn't do it unless we owned that process on our terms. I wasn't going to give up my baby.'

Was breaking the news difficult? 'Yes,' he answers emphatically. 'But we knew we couldn't take everyone with us.' And drawing an apt metaphor from the music scene, he adds, 'There's a point where we had to say, look, we're not that little band in the basement anymore, we're on our second US tour.'

In 2020, with Heineken's support, the next phase of expansion unfolded with likely the biggest investment in a purpose-built brewery in London since Guinness's now-closed Park Royal site was developed in the 1930s. The new 2.5ha site by the River Lee Navigation at Ponders End, close to Camden Town's production brewery, includes a brewhouse from Krones in Germany which boosts the maximum potential capacity to 500,000hl a year, while the canning line can handle 30,000 330ml cans per hour. The Tottenham site, including taproom and Tempus Project,

Barrels at the Tempus Project

will be retained, and there's an ambition to offer a day out linking the two sites with a boat journey. Logan sees this as an extension of the approach taken at Dukes, which was successful not only because of the quality of the beer but its presentation as part of an overall experience. 'We want to create Beaver Believers,' he tells me with an evangelical look in his eye.

Even before the Heineken deal, the brewery was working on a brewpub at the rebuilt Tottenham Hotspur stadium not far away, using a 35hl German-built BrauKon kit – though Logan himself is a Wolverhampton Wanderers supporter, and quotes the team's slogan 'Out of darkness cometh light'. He's also, perhaps surprisingly given the brewery's current portfolio, still a fan of cask beer, while bemoaning the quality lottery of the format in London. 'Cask beer is a true art form,' he says, 'one of the most wonderful expressions of beer in its true state, which sadly you don't get very often. It's more reliable in some other parts of

the country: going back home to the Midlands is a pilgrimage in that respect. I think the future has to be in smaller breweries supplying their own estate of local outlets.'

Beavertown has also been something of a training ground for talented brewers. Two of the most notable are Jenn Merrick and James Rylance, the latter of whom moved from the Kernel to become the company's first full-time brewing employee at the Hackney Wick site, where he began developing what became the Tempus Project. He pursued his interest in wild and mixed fermentation further at Redchurch and, most recently, at Harbour in Cornwall. The original installation at Tottenham was overseen by Jenn Merrick, recruited from Meantime, who had the difficult job of ensuring the character of the beers survived as production was upscaled. Jenn has been freelancing since, while working on her long-awaited Earth Station project (Been, gone and standing by p328).

Outer North London

Barnet Brewery

See Black Horse

Beavertown Brewery Enfield (35)

Brewery, taproom (part-owned by Heineken)
102 East Duck Lees Lane, Enfield EN3 7SS
(Enfield) **beavertownbrewery.co.uk**
First sold beer: Due in 2020, ‼
⛩ Riverside terrace, ♿
Events likely to include tastings and markets

⇌ Ponders End   🚌 Duck Lees Lane/Lea Valley Road
🚲 Link to NC1   🏃 Link to Lea Valley Path

Beavertown's massively expanded Lea Valley
site is currently operating alongside the
existing Beavertown brewery and taproom
in Tottenham. The lockdowns interrupted
ambitious plans for a new taproom and visitor
centre, though the space has been used for
ticketed events and regular openings may follow. See p185 for beer notes and previous page
for the story of an extraordinary expansion.

*Visitor note. From 1886, the site housed the Edison Swan
Electric Light Company, where the first electronic valves
were developed. The factory later passed through several
hands including Philips, AEI and Thorn, before closure and
demolition in 1970.*

Black Horse (Barnet Brewery) (36)

Brewpub, contemporary pub
92 Wood Street, Barnet EN5 4HY (Barnet)
T (020) 8449 2230   **blackhorsebarnet.co.uk**
First sold beer: March 2013
🕐 *Su-Th* 12.00-24.00, *Fr-Sa* 12.00-01.00. Children
    until 19.30 in bar, later in restaurant.
7 cask, 2 keg, 2+ bottles, 1 cider.
🍴 Enhanced pub grub, lunchtime baguettes **££**,
⛩ Front terrace, front garden, ♿
Quiz (We), live music (most Sa)

⊖ High Barnet   🚌 Union Street   🏃 Link to Dollis Valley
Greenwalk, London Loop

This sprawling Victorian pub just outside
Barnet town centre was relaunched late in 2012
by Oak Taverns, a group with several brewpubs
outside London. Previously something of a
laddish big screen sport place, it has since
earned praise for being female-friendly and
providing a social centre. The 2.5hl kit, in an
outhouse at the side, was supplied by Iceni in
Norfolk, partly recycling vessels from the old
Federation brewery in Newcastle, and there's
a link to XT Brewing in Thame. Besides house
beers you'll likely find casks from Peerless
or Tring, sourced through SIBA. Outdoors is
a much-extended garden, while the interior
is part-pub, part-restaurant, serving dishes
like pan-fried chicken and chorizo, wholetail
scampi or halloumi and vegetables on
couscous. The division isn't enforced: 'Locals
wanted good food, but they also begged us
not to turn it into a restaurant,' staff told me.

BEERS in broadly traditional styles (not tasted)
are almost entirely sold on cask in the pub,
with very occasional bottlings. Check before
you travel as they're not always on.

Bohemia (London Brewing) ③⑦

Brewpub, contemporary pub
762 High Road N12 9QH (Barnet)
T (020) 8446 6661
thebohemia.co.uk, londonbrewing.com
First sold beer: September 2011 (at original site),
February 2015 (at Bohemia), ♦♦
🕐 *Mo-We* 12.00-23.00, *Th* 12.00-24.00, *Fr-Sa*
12.00-01.00, *Su* 12.00-22.30. Children very
welcome until 21.30, children's menu.
2-5 cask, 12 keg, 40+ bottles, growlers, 4-5
ciders/perries, some wines. ⌀
🍴 Enhanced pub grub, wings, burgers, salads **££**,
🎋 Front terrace, ♿
*Occasional beer tasting, quiz (Tu), live music, monthly
comedy, food promotions, table tennis, table football*

⊖ Woodside Park　🚌 Tally Ho Corner　🏃 Link to Dollis
Valley Greenwalk

This big North Finchley pub has been an
O'Neill's, a furniture shop and a supermarket
and was even squatted for a brief period
before reopening as a brewpub in May 2014
under Dan Fox, former manager of legendary
beer pub the White Horse (p302). It was Dan's
second such venture following the Bull (p186),
where the London Brewing Co began. The
Bohemia provided welcome extra space for a
new 10hl kit in a convenient lower-level area
at the back, in action from early 2015, and
brewing took place on both sites until July
2016 when the Bull was sold to new owners
who have rebranded the brewery as Gorgeous.
Dan moved on in summer 2017 (see Arnos
Arms, Try also below), leaving the Bohemia in
the hands of business partner Senan Sexton.
Beside house brews, the bar stocks keg guests
from Londoners like Pillars and Solvay Society
and a bottle and can list featuring the likes of
Howling Hops, Partizan, Roosters, various
Trappists, Schneider Weisse and Americans
like Ska and Stone. Dining is informal but
imaginative, including 'famous' chicken wings,
with a vegan cauliflower-based option, salads,
steaks and lunchtime sandwiches. Clever design
makes the best of the cavernous space and
prettily tiled floor. Despite its size and relatively
remote location, it's regularly buzzing throughout, and more than likely to send you into
rhapsodies.

Bohemia

BEERS are in cask, keg and can, sold both
through the pub and elsewhere. Core beers
include contemporary pale ale **London Lush**
(3.8%); **Beer Street Best Bitter** (4%), one
of the brewery's earliest recipes; **Upright**
session IPA (4%); **Chuckaboo** extra pale
ale (4.2%); and award-winning stout **100
Oysters*** (4.6%). There's an occasional dark
mild, **Flying the Mags** (3.8%).

Camden Town Brewery ③⑧

Brewery, no visitors please (AB InBev)
Morson Road, Enfield EN3 4TJ (Enfield)
T (020) 7485 1671 camdentownbrewery.com
First sold beer: June 2017 (May 2006 at original site)

Currently London's second biggest brewer,
Camden Town began with a single vessel in
the cellar of Hampstead pub the Horseshoe:
look carefully for the horseshoe in the logo.
The first brews bore the name McLaughlins,
from a long-closed brewery in Rockhampton,
Queensland, once owned by founder Jasper
Cuppaidge's family. Jasper found investment
to relaunch on a much bigger scale in June
2010 using a 20hl German-built automatic
brewhouse in two railway arches under
Kentish Town West station. The site has
subsequently expanded to a whole run of
arches. Just before Christmas 2015, the
brewery announced its sale to the world's
biggest brewer, Anheuser-Busch InBev, in a
deal thought to be worth £85 million, the

second such deal in London following the sale of Meantime. In June 2017, the company added a new 100hl brewhouse on a much bigger site in Enfield, providing a total eventual capacity of 350,000hl a year and removing the need to contract brew some beer in Belgium. Initially the operation was run autonomously but in 2021 it became fully integrated into ABI's Budweiser Brewing Group, with Jasper retained as a consultant. There are currently no visitors facilities here but you can sample the beers at the Kentish Town site (p197).

BEERS are 80% keg, the rest in can and bottle. Regulars include **Camden Pale** (4%), an American pale ale; **Hells*** (4.6%), the flagship and biggest seller, so named as it's halfway between a Helles and a Pils; and recently added IPA **Off Menu** (5.8%). Numerous specials brewed at the Kentish Town site under the Arch 55 brand.

Enefeld

Brewery
17A Eley Road N18 3BB (Enfield)
T (020) 8807 1533 **enefeld.com**
First sold beer: June 2015, 👣 (informal)
🕐 Occasional open days. Children welcome.
1+ cask, 4 keg, 6 bottles
🎋 Outside yard, ♿
Occasional live music

🚆 Meridian Water 🚇 Eley Trading Estate 🚲 NCN1, link to C1, C21 🥾 Lea Valley Path

Currently London's only brewery with its own well water, Enefeld was founded by Rahul Mulchandani on a site adjacent to his family's cash and carry warehouse just off the North Circular Road in Edmonton, adopting a spelling from the Domesday survey of 1086. Stuart Robson, founder of pioneer South African craft brewery Shongweni, was recruited as head brewer, working on a high-spec 32hl brewhouse. Stuart had left by 2018 when Rahul succeeded in tempting another brewing legend out of semi-retirement: Don Burgess, who had founded the influential Freeminer microbrewery in the Forest of Dean in 1993. Don has overhauled the recipes and helped oversee a rebrand. A smart bar right next to the inlet from the well is

currently open only intermittently, thanks partly to the industrial location, but this may change as the area is progressively redeveloped. For more about the water source, see panel p200.

BEERS are in cask, ecokeg and filtered, bottled form, with occasional bottle conditioning for specials. Core beers include **Enfield Bitter** (4%), based on a Freeminer beer; **London Porter*** (5.5%); **London Pilsner*** (4.8%), lagered for three months; dark bitter **Speculation Ale*** (4.8%), a revival of Freeminer's best-known brand; **London Pale** (5%); and **London IPA*** (6%).

Little Green Dragon

Micropub
928 Green Lanes N21 2AD
littlegreendragonenfield.com
🕐 *Tu-Th* 16.00-22.00, *Fr-Sa* 12.00-22.00, *Su* 12.00-19.00. Children until 18.00.
4-5 cask, 2 keg, 12 bottles/cans, 6-7 ciders/ perries, some gins.
🍴 Unusual snacks, pickled eggs, 🎋 Front terrace, small rear garden, ♿ Flat access only
Meet the brewer, tutored tastings, weekly acoustic music, seasonal events, table skittles, shove ha'penny, board games

🚆 Grange Park, Winchmore Hill 🚇 Green Dragon Lane 🚲 C20, link to C21 🥾 New River Path

Though opened as recently as August 2017 in a former hairdresser on a post-war parade of shops, this excellent micropub feels remarkably lived-in. A collection of clutter and artworks, some of them for sale, and various items of recycled furniture – deep sofas, a kitchen

corner bench and old casks with cushions – lend character, complemented by the warm welcome of owner Richard Reeve, who was inspired by visiting all 100 micropubs then in operation on a charity cycle ride in 2015. Cask is served from a stillage at the rear, alongside a few kegs, cans and bottles. Richard aims to balance locals like Beerblefish, Bohem, Enefeld, New River, Redemption and Wild Card half-and-half with renowned visitors like Mad Squirrel, Thornbridge and Tiny Rebel. Food is necessarily limited but they're proud of the pickled eggs. A comfortable space encouraging conversation with strangers, it's deservedly hoovered up local CAMRA awards.

Visitor note. The big Green Dragon looms over Green Lanes a few paces from the little one. There's been a pub of this name in Winchmore Hill since at least the 1720s, originally a modest alehouse opposite the current micropub site. It moved southwest in the 18th century and was subsequently rebuilt several times. Despite a vociferous local campaign, the building became a supermarket in 2014, though retains handsome tilework, mock-Tudor detailing and relief sculptures from a Courage rebuild in the 1930s. A series of paintings in the micropub depicts the successive incarnations.

London Brewing

See Bohemia

Oddly Beer

Brewery, no visitors please
Friern Barnet N11   facebook.com/oddlybeer
First sold beer: March 2017

Taking his brand name from expressions such as 'oddly delicious', Brian Watson began cuckoo-brewing in 2015 at Clouded Minds in Oxfordshire, itself a former cuckoo at London's Gipsy Hill. From 2017 he had his own brewery on Platts Eyot, a privately-owned island in the Thames at Hampton which is still home to Tiny Vessel, but the practical challenges of working somewhere only accessible by boat and footbridge prompted a relocation in December 2018. A move to a unit in Tottenham didn't work out and Brian subsequently found a new way of working. He now focuses on creating bespoke experimental beers for specific clients, events and bottle clubs, either on his own small kit or working as a cuckoo elsewhere. 'My dream was to brew beer as art,' he says, 'and I'm moving towards this. Who knows, one day perhaps I'll help create the world's first drinkable art gallery'.

BEERS vary widely and change frequently but are well worth trying if you find them: I particularly enjoyed **Poppy** (6%), a red ale with tomatoes and wild yeast.

Urban Alchemy Brewing Co

Brewery, no visitors please
New Barnet EN5 (Barnet)
urban-alchemy-brewing.co.uk
First sold beer: December 2019.

This 5hl brewery controlled by a bespoke Raspberry Pi computer system has been entirely designed and built in-house by four friends who had been homebrewing together for 10 years. Brewing waste is used as fertiliser on local allotments. While there are no visitor facilities at this home-based operation, the owners sell the beer from a mobile bar at local markets and organise charity fundraising beer events: check social media. Plans for a bigger site with taproom were delayed by Covid but may be implemented in 2022.

BEERS in cask, keg and bottle (not tasted) are naturally conditioned and vegan, combining both traditional and contemporary craft influences: they include amber ale **Crumbling Ghost** (5.1%), pale ale **Fat Labrador** (5.1%) and stout **Elephants' Graveyard** (5.4%).

TRY ALSO

Arnos Arms 338 Bowes Road N11 1AN **arnosarms.com**: Large mock-Tudor pub built by Charringtons in the 1930s right by Arnos Grove station, rejuvenated in 2017 by Dan Fox, founder of London Brewing, into a fine resource with up to three often-local cask beers, some interesting keg and bottles, good food and a busy events programme. **Old Wheatsheaf** 3 Windmill Hill, Enfield EN2 6SE **oldwheatsheaf.co.uk**: Victorian pub by Enfield Chase station renovated and reopened by Big Smoke in 2021: four cask, various kegs from owning brewery and other independents. Welcome addition in an area lacking in good beer venues.

LAVVERLY LONDON LIQUOR

As explained in the beer ingredients section, all London breweries once had their own water sources, usually artesian wells probing the chalk beneath the capital for water trapped in aquifers. Currently only one enjoys that privilege, and it's surprisingly new. When Rahul Mulchandani first conceived of brewing on a site adjacent to his family's cash and carry warehouse in Edmonton, he knew the neighbours, Coca-Cola, originally moved here partly for the water. So his Enefeld Brewery (above) was equipped with its own 55m borehole, tapping the same aquifer as the drinks giant.

The brewery is completely independent of the mains supply, using the well water for everything from brewing liquor to cleaning: 'We're the only brewery in London that flushes its toilets with mineral water,' quips Rahul. But he admits that in retrospect he wouldn't make the same decision again: they still have to pay Thames Water to deal with waste water, and as head brewer Don Burgess observes, if you exploit your own water supply commercially, legally you're treated as the equivalent of a water company, required to demonstrate you meet the same standards as the big utilities.

Still, it's a great story, and gives the beers a particular provenance as they've been partly designed around the very chalky and mineral-rich water profile. The liquid is lightly filtered to remove larger chalk particles and treated with ultra-violet light as a precaution against bugs, although analysis shows it's exceptionally clean already after years draining through the layers of chalk. It's pleasant as drinking water, tasting not only lightly chalky but also a little metallic from its high iron content. Used without further treatment in the brewery's London Porter, it performs as well as you'd expect for the type of water that once turned the city into the world centre of porter brewing. For the paler, hoppier beers, it's softened and 'Burtonised' with sulphates before brewing.

Meanwhile, on the other side of the city, another brewery has its eyes on a water source that played a major role in local history. In 1659, so the story goes, a farmer driving his cart across Streatham Common got a nasty shock when the ground collapsed beneath it to reveal a bubbling spring. By the beginning of the next century, Streatham Wells was a flourishing resort, with visitors eager to 'take the waters' of a chalybeate spring, rich in minerals including magnesium sulphate, calcium carbonate and iron. A flyer from 1878 claims Streatham water is beneficial for 'all obstinate Diseases of the Skin and Lymphatic Glands, especially in that afflicting disease called Scrofula... liver complaints, indigestion, especially in jaundice and bilious attacks... evacuating irritating matter from the intestines [and] a most valuable remedy for persons labouring under Nervous Debility.'

By then the original well had become contaminated and a new one was dug nearby, with a private house known as the Rookery occupying the old site. This was later demolished, but its former grounds, now owned by Lambeth council, have become one of the most beautiful public gardens in London. In 2018, the Inkspot brewery (p262) moved into an adjacent barn, and owners Bradley Ridge and Tom Talbot are intent on restoring Streatham's own water source as part of a programme of self-sufficiency that also includes using ingredients grown on the site. Liquor drawn from an 115m well will likely also be sold as mineral water, and nobody needs to fall into a hole to find it.

Well head at Enefeld

SOUTHEAST LONDON

SOUTHEAST LONDON

I live in southeast London, but I promise you I'm not biased: the area really does merit one of the longest sections in the book.

Bermondsey is now a famous name in international beer circles thanks to the string of breweries and other beer-related businesses in the arches of the railway line heading south-east from London Bridge, between Tower Bridge Road and South Bermondsey station. My section covers all these and one or two more in surrounding streets and industrial estates.

The rest of Southwark borough outside Bermondsey and the central area, including Camberwell, Dulwich and Peckham, is dealt with under **Central South London**, alongside parts of Lambeth with SE postcodes like Herne Hill and Kennington. This section also includes all the venues around Crystal Palace, some of which are just within Bromley and Croydon. There's plenty to enjoy round here, mostly brewery taprooms or new bars.

My **Greenwich and Lewisham** section covers not just the town centres but the wider boroughs, including locations like Blackheath, Brockley, Catford, Deptford, Eltham and Woolwich. With the Maritime Greenwich World Heritage Site, the royal park and numerous other attractions, Greenwich is London's most popular tourist destination outside the centre and is also home to its second-largest brewery, so you'd expect it to have a few good beer options. More surprising is quite how beer-friendly its dowdier neighbour Lewisham has become.

Even **Outer Southeast London** makes a good showing, thanks largely to the micropub phenomenon. In 2015, I noted three such places in the area; this edition lists 16 . This section also covers Bromley and Croydon boroughs, (except for a few around Crystal Palace as explained above), plus a couple of breweries just over the boundary in Sutton, though much more accessible from Croydon.

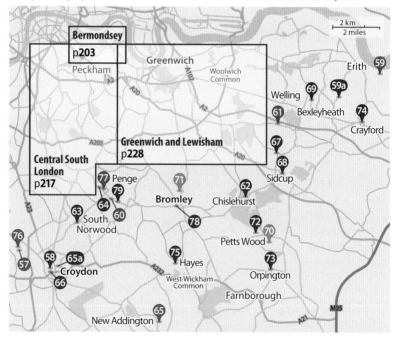

Bermondsey

Visiting Bermondsey

I still encounter people in Bermondsey trying to work their way through everything in a single day, but I'd strongly recommend you don't risk turning the experience into a joyless chore or a health and safety hazard. Instead, pick no more than four or five places and take time to do them justice, returning on other days if you can. You won't want to miss the Kernel, but all the other breweries have their strengths. For a bookable brewery tour and tasting, the top options are Southwark, where you may find yourself hosted by owner and expert raconteur Peter Jackson; Bianca Road, a friendly place with a pleasant taproom; and Fourpure, where you'll get to see the canning line as well as the expansive brewhouse. Remember too that, aside from Spartan which you should try to catch if you can, the Bermondsey phenomenon is no longer limited to Saturdays. Some third-party tour operators visit multiple sites on a single guided walk: see Beer tourism (p342).

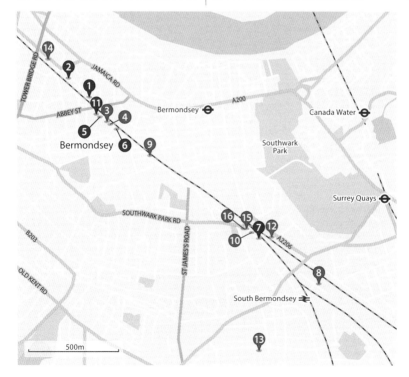

THE BERMONDSEY THREE

What sort of business might you expect to find in a railway arch? A car mechanic, miscellaneous storage, or perhaps an anonymous lockup where dodgy geezers are hung upside down from meat hooks in a British gangster film? These days, the average urban beer enthusiast thinks unhesitatingly of breweries, and quite likely of that symbol of the London beer renaissance, the string of arch-based beer businesses in Bermondsey detailed in this section. Appearing from scratch over a mere decade, they now flourish alongside numerous other food and drink firms: bakeries, coffee roasters, cheese and charcuterie specialists, street food kitchens, two distilleries, a cidery and many others.

Indeed, good food precedes good beer in the recent history of the arches, which begins at the end of the line at Borough Market. This ancient wholesale fruit and veg market was in decline by 1997, when artisanal coffee roaster Monmouth Coffee and its sister company, cheesemonger Neal's Yard Dairy, rented warehouse space there with no intention of a public-facing operation. 'But then people saw us working inside and started knocking on the windows asking if they could buy coffee,' says Monmouth founder Anita Le Roy. The two businesses got together with others to hold quarterly 'warehouse open days' on an informal basis, and following a successful one-off food fair, the market's trustees saw the potential for developing the venerable site into the foodie-friendly tourist attraction it is today.

As rents around the market rose, traders started looking elsewhere for storage space and found it along Druid Street to the southeast. The arches that support the world's first elevated railway and London's first steam-hauled line, built as the London and Greenwich Railway in 1836, were conveniently situated, cool, and cheap. Among Neal's Yard Dairy's staff at the time was Munster native Evin O'Riordain, whose interest in beer grew when his employers sent him to New York City on an extended business trip. On his return, Evin started homebrewing, and when he decided to turn professional, his colleagues alerted him to a vacant arch at 98 Druid Street, occupied today by baker and patissier Comptoir Gourmand.

The Kernel opened in September 2009 with a tiny 6.5hl brewing kit, sharing with a cheesemaker and a cheese and charcuterie importer. These arches opened at the other end onto a quiet passageway off Maltby Street, and a few months later Evin and his cohabitees began joining some of their neighbours in a repeat of the warehouse open days, selling informally from the passageway on Saturdays, an activity which later evolved into today's busy Ropewalk market. The licence allowed drinking on site, so they began pouring bottles for customers, occasionally adding keg. This was the beginning of today's vibrant Bermondsey taproom culture, although it was something of an unforeseen consequence. 'I think Evin wanted a market

stall rather than a taproom,' says Andy Smith of nearby Partizan.

Eventually, Monmouth and Neal's Yard began looking for a larger and more sustainable site for their continuing expansion. Network Rail offered them a long lease on a run of underused arches a little further down the line, at Spa Terminus, so-called because it was briefly the London terminal in 1836 before the line was extended to London Bridge. It was more space than they needed, but there was the obvious option of subletting to like-minded people. 'It took a lot of work and a lot of investment,' recalls Anita. 'Some of the arches hadn't been used before and still had dirt floors and no shutters or services. We had to put in drains and pay for two new electricity substations.'

Among the occupants when Spa Terminus opened early in 2012 was a much-expanded Kernel brewery, upscaled to a 32hl brewhouse in production by March of that year. This turned out to be good timing for Andy Smith, a homebrewer and former cellarman of the legendary White Horse pub at Parsons Green (p302), who first brewed professionally at another pioneer of London's new wave, Redemption in Tottenham, and was thinking about his next step. 'It felt like there was no way to progress there,' he recalls, 'and Andy Moffat, the owner, suggested I either go to a bigger brewery like Fuller's or Thornbridge, or start my own. I had the same conversation with Evin as I was down there every week and he just asked me flat out if I wanted to take his old brewing kit. I'd had

THE BERMONDSEY THREE

no aspirations to be a business owner, but I couldn't turn it down.'

Locating a friendly funder, Andy found an arch a little further down the line, at Almond Road in the area known as the Blue. 'I didn't want to be next door to the Kernel,' he recounts. 'I knew there would always be the association of starting with their old kit and I was concerned that we'd live under their shadow. But the rent was low for a central location, and in the end, it was common sense to be close to people we like a lot.' The new Partizan brewery opened in Bermondsey in November 2012 and was soon attracting excited attention from connoisseurs.

Also in the circle around the Kernel were Tom Hutchings and Dave Seymour, who first met on a climbing tour of southeast Asia. 'We loved what the Kernel were doing and sometimes helped out there,' says Tom, 'then we started homebrewing in August 2011 in the basement of a house on Southwark Bridge Road which a friend was renovating. We had a 50 litre setup, and we'd experiment by splitting a batch and doing different things. We used numbers to keep track of everything, which is how we ended up as Brew by Numbers.' Following feedback from Evin and others, Tom and Dave got a licence and first sold to the public at the Craft Beer Co in Clerkenwell in December 2012.

As well as drawing inspiration from the emerging craft brewing scene in Australia and New Zealand, where both spent time after moving on from Asia, Tom and Dave absorbed mainland European influences. They made

saison with a French yeast shared between several English brewers while still in their experimental phase and in June 2012 toured Belgium with Andy, then on the cusp of opening Partizan, and Toby Munn, head brewer at the Kernel. Their discoveries on that trip still echo in the products of all three breweries today.

Brew by Numbers (BBNo) became a fully-fledged Bermondsey brewery in May 2013 when it moved into an arch at 79 Enid Street, around the corner from the original Kernel site, with an 18hl kit hand-built from recycled stainless steel vessels. The expansion was partly thanks to investment from BrewDog, which has since sold its shares back at cost price. 'We were anxious not to tread on any toes,' says Tom, 'and originally we were planning on a site in Battersea, but that fell through, and it made sense to be part of this growing brewing community.'

Two breweries in the same railway arches might be dismissed as a coincidence but add a third and you have a phenomenon in the making. Fourpure was the next to open in the area, later in 2013, though in a traditional industrial unit rather than an arch. With the arrival of Anspach & Hobday and Southwark Brewing the following year, people began talking about the 'Bermondsey Beer Mile', a term not all the pioneers are comfort- able with, given its suggestion of a drinking challenge. But the influence of the original trio has stretched far beyond Bermond- sey. Evin co-founded the London Brewers Alliance in May 2010,

which provided an important support network for new arrivals. He's now regularly cited as an inspiration by brewers not only in London but across the world, closely followed by his two immediate successors. Their collective influence may not have been so pervasive if the beers hadn't been so good and so interesting, exploring styles then quite untypical of London brewing, like strong porters and stouts reviving historic recipes, hoppy US-inspired pale ales and Belgian styles, with an emphasis on bottled as well as draught beer.

At the Kernel, the emphasis has been on organic growth, quality, stability and a collabora- tive ethos. Though some of

cont.

THE BERMONDSEY THREE cont.

the staff specialise more than others, everyone is expected to take a turn at every task, which not only makes the work more interesting but builds in robustness to staff turnover and absence. More fermenters and a bottling line have been added, growing production to around 10,000hl a year. In late 2014, the brewery became the first to restore the practice of ageing in oak tuns to London brewing by buying several Belgian-style foeders. But it struggled to deal with the attention brought by its rapidly-rising reputation.

The decision in September 2015 to limit public facilities to a Saturday morning bottle shop provoked howls of anguish in some quarters, but as always at the Kernel, it was taken for the most principled of reasons. 'In the early days, the atmosphere was unparalleled,' recalls Evin. 'That sense of unplanned evolution is inherently infectious, it comes from the joy in what you're doing rather than purely business objectives. But once the critical mass had spread with four or five breweries, and we had people queuing down the street, it became untenable for us. It had become a place we wouldn't want to drink in, our hearts weren't in it, and the crowds were affecting our neighbours' businesses. We thought about ways of limiting the numbers, but we didn't want to become exclusive, so the only option was to stop.' Happily, in 2019, another Spa Terminus arch just a few doors down became a new dedicated taproom, spacious and comfortable enough to do the products justice.

Partizan expanded into the arch next door in Almond Street early in 2015, in preparation for a new brewhouse with a 25hl mash tun and a copper which the brewers converted themselves from a former power station water tank spotted rusting in a Yorkshire field. The old kit was gifted once again to Cyclic Beer Farm in Barcelona, co-founded by former head brewer Josh Wheeler. The brewery moved to its current site in a much bigger arch around the corner in Raymouth Road in November 2017, adding a parade of new fermentation vessels, all individually named after T S Eliot's Practical Cats, and a small bottling line as well as a more expansive taproom. 'I spent five years in fine dining, so hospitality is important to me,' says Andy. 'When you make something nice, you want to share it with people, and we're finally able to give them a quality experience.' The two arches he left behind were rapidly filled by two breweries, Affinity (since succeeded by Three Hills) and Spartan.

BBNo has subsequently expanded several times, leasing a second arch a few doors west, with a new bottling line, cold store, barrel vault and taproom in action by summer 2015. Dave stepped back from day-to-day involvement at the end of 2018 for a well-earned rest, leaving Tom to lead a further expansion to a bigger site in Greenwich in 2021. But the company, now better known by its acronym BBNo, is hanging onto its signature presence in Bermondsey with a pilot brewery and tank bar. 'The taproom model is

so important to us,' says Tom. 'Direct retail sales are financial gold, and that engagement in giving drinkers somewhere interesting to visit is so useful.'

In relocating its main production site, BBNo is following in the footsteps of neighbour Anspach & Hobday which has moved brewing to suburban south London, an indication of how the economics have changed. 'When we first moved into Druid Street,' says Evin O'Riordain, 'the rents on some of these arches were insignificant, partly because Network Rail were so inefficient, even forgetting about rent reviews.' Those times have changed, and Andy Smith tells me some tenants now pay ten times the rent charged for similar arches just five years ago. The shadows thickened when the rail infrastructure owner was forced by the government to sell a 990-year lease on all its arches to two big international property companies in 2018. A new partnership, the Arch Company, is now managing them, and some tenants are already complaining of hefty rent hikes. An investigation by the National Audit Office found the deal was completed without consideration of the impact on tenants' lives and livelihoods, and though the Arch Company has since made reassuring noises, many still fear rents will eventually rise beyond the means of the independent businesses that have made the arches attractive in the first place. The best advice, as with the whole London brewing scene, is to enjoy it while you can.

Parts of this piece originally appeared in BEER magazine Autumn 2018.

Arch House ❶
(Anspach and Hobday)
Bar
118 Druid Street SE1 2HH
T (020) 8617 9510 anspachandhobday.com
🕐 *Th* 15.00-21.00, *Fr* 15.00-22.00, *Sa* 10.30-22.00,
   Su 13.00-18.00. Children until 20.00. Cash-free.
1 cask, 12 keg, 20 bottles/cans.
🍴 BYO, 🪑 Standing area *(Sa)*,
♿ Flat access only.
Occasional beer events

⊖ Bermondsey 🚌 Maltby Street 🚲 Link to NCN4, C4, Q14
🚶 Link to Jubilee Greenway, Jubilee Walkway, Thames Path

This is the arch where one of London's most noteworthy breweries began in 2014, and still retains a couple of fermenters and a barrel vault, although the main production site is now in Sutton (p242). It's a pleasant place to enjoy the brewery's wide range of very good beers plus occasional guests, with bench seating and extra space on an upstairs mezzanine.

Barrel Project ❷
Bar
80 Druid Street SE1 2HQ
T (020) 7394 6763   thebarrelproject.co.uk
🕐 *We-Fr* 16.00-22.30, *Sa* 11.00-22.30, *Su* 12.00-
   18.30. Children welcome at quieter times.
23 keg, 15 bottles/cans.
🍴 Hot sandwiches, chips, salads **£-££**, ♿
Tastings, functions

⊖ Bermondsey 🚌 Druid Street, Tanner Street 🚲 Link to
NCN4, C4, Q14 🚶 Link to Jubilee Greenway, Jubilee Walkway,
Thames Path

An impressive gallery of over 200 oak barrels that previously held red wine from Bordeaux stretches along one wall of this railway arch, home since late 2017 to the wild and mixed fermentation and barrel-ageing side project of London Beer Factory (p223). Opposite the wall of wood is a smart green- and white-tiled bar which makes nifty use of a rear alcove, originally a connection between adjacent arches. It provides an atmospheric location for sampling its owner's wide range, including more conventional core beers, specials and

Barrel Project

collaborations alongside Barrel Project blends and limited editions. A corner kitchen serves up more substantial fare than the average taproom: salt pork sandwiches, grilled cheese and vegan rösti wraps among other delights.

BBNo (Brew by Numbers) ❸
Brewery, taproom
79 Enid Street SE16 3RA (Southwark)
T (020) 7237 9794   bbno.co
First sold beer: December 2012
🕐 *We-Fr* 17.00-22.00, *Sa* 12.00-22.00, *Su* 12.00-
   18.00. Children until 19.00. Cash-free.
Tank and keg beer, 15-20 cans.
🍴 changing food truck *(Fr-Sa)* **£**, 🪑 Standing at
front *(Sa only)*, ♿ Flat access only
Occasional beer launches and tastings

⊖ Bermondsey 🚌 Maltby Street 🚲 Link to NCN4, C4, Q14
🚶 Link to Jubilee Greenway, Jubilee Walkway, Thames Path

The third of the original 'Bermondsey Three' (above), Brew by Numbers had its main production brewery here until autumn 2021 when it expanded to a bigger site in Greenwich. But the company retains a lively presence in

BBNo

BBNo

Brew by Numbers

Bianca Road Brew Co ④

Brewery, taproom
83 Enid Street SE16 3RA (Southwark)
biancaroad.com
First sold beer: May 2016 (at original site), ‼
🕐 *We-Fr* 14.00-22.00, *Sa* 13.00-23.00,
    Su 12.00-18.00. Children welcome.
8 keg, 6-8 cans. 🍷
🍴 changing food truck *(Sa)* **£**, ♿
Tastings, functions

⊖ Bermondsey 🚃 Maltby Street 🚲 Link to NCN4, C4, Q14
🚶 Link to Jubilee Greenway, Jubilee Walkway, Thames Path

Engineer Reece Wood was inspired to brew during an epic cycle ride from San Francisco to Miami, discovering the local beers in each new town. The name is from the original location in a partly derelict industrial unit in North Peckham. The brewery moved in 2017 to a more practical space with a taproom in an 'off-Bermondsey' location near the Bricklayers Arms. When this was threatened with redevelopment, Reece snapped up the current pair of arches on the stretch between BBNo and the Kernel, completing the move in April 2019. The same PBC 25hl kit has been used throughout, though fermentation capacity has been increased. A bright taproom with a recycled wood bar and pot plants occupies a generous space in front of the brewhouse.

BEERS are in keg and can. Core beers include session IPA **Long Play*** (3.6%); **Blood Orange IPA** (4.5%); a relatively hoppy but traditional **Lager** (4.8%) and **Tropicali IPA** (5.3%) with fruity hops. **Red Rye IPA** (6%), one of the brewery's earliest beers, is now a seasonal, and there's a pale ale with changing hops.

Bermondsey with a stylish taproom and tank bar complete with pilot brewery, which should be in full operation by the time you read this (the main taproom was previously in nearby arch 79 but is due to move). House-brewed specials are on sale as well as regular beers and rarities brewed at the main production site.

BEERS brewed here are changing specials dispensed onsite direct from tanks. The more experimental are branded as the **π** series. For more about the wider range of BBNo beers, see the Greenwich entry (p228).

Bianca Road

Cloudwater Taproom 5

Bar, Shop
73 Enid Street SE16 3RA cloudwaterbrew.co
Bar 🕐 *We-Th* 14.00-21.00, *Fr-Sa* 12.00-21.00,
  Su 12.00-19.00. Children until 20.00.
Shop 🕐 As bar, plus *Mo-Tu* 12.00-19.00.
20 keg, 50 bottles/cans.
🍴 BYO, ♿
Beer showcases and launches

⊖ Bermondsey 🚆 Maltby Street ⛭ Link to NCN4, C4, Q14
🏃 Link to Jubilee Greenway, Jubilee Walkway, Thames Path

...water Taproom

The changing range of often excellent seasonally influenced beers flowing from Manchester's
Cloudwater since 2015 has defined it as one
of the most on-trend British breweries, and
this arch-based bar has been its London shop
window since September 2019. Besides the
house brews, including specials, there are
regularly rotating and impeccably selected
imported guests, usually all from the same
region – southern California or the Netherlands,
for example – with cans and bottles kept in the
walk-in coldroom. A Scandinavian-style designer
interior features diagonal tables, graphic
banners and a curious ambient soundtrack. It's
not the cosiest place to drink beer in London,
but the quality and commitment is indisputable.

Craft Beer Junction 6

Bar, shop
86 Enid Street SE16 5RA
📞 07916 126841 craftbeerjunction.co.uk
🕐 *We-Th* 16.00-23.00, *Fr* 15.00-23.00, *Sa* 12.00-
  23.00, *Su* 13.00-22.00. Children welcome.
  Cash-free.
9-10 keg, 15-20 bottles/cans.
🍴 Barbecue (*We only*), 🪑 a few tables at front, ♿
Tap takeovers, tastings

⊖ Bermondsey 🚆 Maltby Street ⛭ Link to NCN4, C4, C14
🏃 Link to Jubilee Greenway, Jubilee Walkway, Thames Path

This simple but comfortable bar opened in
May 2021 at the front of a white-lined arch a
couple of doors down from Bianca Road is the
public face of a beer importer and distributor
dealing mainly in US-brewed rarities. Owner
Marcin makes regular buying trips, often
concentrating on individual states and seeking
out personal contacts, including with very
small operations producing less than 1,000hl a
year, with consignments arriving by air freight.
Beers on sale regularly change – the last time
I looked there were numerous exclusive
delights from Escape, Hidden Springs and
Magnanimous, all in Florida, in keg as well as
bottle and can, alongside London and UK
beers from Little Earth and Overtone. In recent
years the burgeoning variety and quality of
local breweries has increasingly pushed US
imports from London shelves and bars, but
there's still much of interest off the beaten
track, so this is a welcome new specialist.

Craft Beer Junction

EeBria Taproom ❼

Bar, shop
15 Almond Road SE16 3LR **eebria.com**
🕐 *Sa* 12.30-20.00. Children Welcome.
8 keg, 120 bottles/cans. 🍺
🪑 Tables at front, small rear garden, ♿ Flat access only
Tap takeovers, retro arcade games, shuffleboard

⇌ South Bermondsey 🚌 Anchor Street 🚲 Link to C10

Online retailer and distributor EeBria, in an arch between Spartan and Partizan, operates this neat and funky little bar, with comfy seats as well as the obligatory benches and even a sunny little beer garden at the back. Beers are all from small independent brewers across the UK, some of them very good but hard to find in London, like Cross Borders from Midlothian, Torrside from the Peak District or Twisted Barrel from Coventry, with some imports like Belgian's Alvinne and regular tap takeovers. Well worth calling in for a tasting flight or two.

Fourpure Brewing ❽

Brewery, taproom (Lion/Kirin)
25 Bermondsey Trading Estate, Rotherhithe New Road SE16 3LL (Southwark)
T (020) 3744 2141 **fourpure.com**
First sold beer: October 2013, 🍴
🕐 *Fr* 16.00-22.00, *Sa* 12.00-20.00, *Su* 12.00-20.00. Children until 20.00. Cash-free.
19 keg, 15-20 cans, growlers. 🍺
🍴 Burgers, hot dogs **£-££**, 🪑 Tables at front, ♿
Tastings, beer launches, functions

⇌ South Bermondsey 🚌 Beamish House 🚲 Link to C10

Always one of London's most ambitious new beer makers, Fourpure is now one of the biggest. Founded as the fourth Bermondsey brewery by former City technology firm executive and homebrewer Dan Lowe and his brother Tom, it rejected the railway arch model in favour of a conventional industrial unit with more elbow room between the lines at the southeast end of the strip, near Millwall FC's New Den stadium. The name refers to the four traditional ingredients of beer. The Lowes recruited John Driebergen, formerly of

Fourpure Taproom

Meantime, as head brewer and installed a 30hl kit bought second-hand from Purity in Warwickshire. The early addition of a canning line in a nearby unit was a brave move at the time. The site has since expanded greatly: a 2017 enlargement into an adjacent unit accommodated a new 50hl German-built brewhouse and three outdoor silos for base malts and spent grain. In July 2018, Fourpure became the sixth London craft brewer acquired by a multinational, Kirin of Japan, becoming part of its Australian-based Lion Little World subsidiary, though with the same management as before. Further expansion into two more adjacent units followed in summer 2019, one of them now entirely occupied by an expansive taproom. This boasts a big island bar, also stocking guests from other breweries in the group, surrounded by a mix of seating: booths, stools, a few swing seats and sofas, and more tables on a mezzanine with a glass-walled private room in the corner, used for tastings and included on the popular regular tours of the brewhouse and canning line. A dedicated shop area near the front sells takeaway cans.

BEERS are in keg and can, with much sold through supermarket chains. Core beers include **Citrus Session IPA** with added citrus (4%); **Session IPA*** (4.2%); **Lager*** (4.7%); **Oatmeal Stout** (5.1%); **Citrus IPA** (5.9%); **IPA** (5.9%), a West Coast style; and **Lost at Sea*** (9%) imperial stout with maple syrup, oak chips and lactose.

Kernel Brewery (The)

Brewery, taproom
7 Dockley Road Industrial Estate SE16 3SF
(Southwark)
T (020) 7231 4516   thekernelbrewery.com
First sold beer: December 2009
Taproom ⏰ Th-Fr 15.00-22.00, Sa 11.00-21.00,
   Su 12.00-20.00. Children very welcome.
15 keg, 20+ bottles.
🍴 Cheese, charcuterie and vegan boards,
🌲 A few tables at front, ♿
Tastings, beer showcases
Shop ⏰ Mo-We 09.00-17.00, Th-Fr 09.00-22.00,
   Sa 09.00-21.00, Su 10.00-20.00.
20+ bottles, mixed cases. 🍷

🚌 Bermondsey   🚲 Link to C4

As explained in much more detail under The Bermondsey Three (above), the Kernel is the founder of the current Bermondsey scene and still one of the best and most influential breweries in London. Connoisseurs were delighted in November 2019 when, after more than two years of providing limited takeaway sales only, it opened a new taproom in another arch a few doors away from its brewing site at Spa Terminus. This basic but stylish space, with additional seating in a mezzanine, serves mainly house beers, with a takeaway shop that's open longer hours. Food is supplied by near neighbours including the bakery next door. The brewery is in Arch 11 but the two are linked behind the scenes. Taproom hours may extend to Wednesdays: please check.

BEERS are in keg and 330ml, 500ml and 750ml bottles, often variants on several basic recipes, notably the various pale ales and saisons which frequently rotate through hop varieties, though almost everything is worth trying. A brief summary would include light blond and delicately hoppy **Table Beer*** (2.5-3%); **Dry Stout*** (around 4.5%); Belgian-style wood-aged golden ale **Foeder Beer*** (4.6%); **Bière de Saison*-**** (around 4.5-5.5%), either conventionally made with varying hops or barrel-aged and blended with added fruit (a crab apple version was particularly well-received); a newly-added changing range of **Lagers***, including foeder-aged versions (4.5-5%); **Pale Ale** (often *, around 5.5%); **Brown Ale** with changing hops (often *, around 5.6%); **Export India Porter*** (6.5%); **India Pale Ale*-**** (around 7%); red rye ale **London Brick*** (7%); **Export Stout London 1890**** (7.8%); and **Imperial Brown Stout London 1856**** (9-10%).

Kernel Brewery

Mash Paddle Brewery

Brewery, taproom
Almond Road SE16 (Southwark)
mashpaddlebrewery.com
First sold beer: End 2021.
🕐 Please check.
Occasional cask, regular keg, bottles/cans.
🍴 Rotating food trucks, 🪑 Tables at front.
Brewing facilities, brewing courses, tastings, functions.

🚆 South Bermondsey   Ⓔ Surrey Quays   🚌 Anchor Street
🚲 Link to C10

Nick Harkin, a passionate homebrewer with a background in financial services, plans to open this crowdfunded communal members' brewery in the heart of Bermondsey by the end of 2021. The idea is to offer anyone from homebrewing beginners to commercial cuckoo start-ups the opportunity to use professional-grade equipment with help and advice on tap, with a commercial license and its own onsite taproom. Importantly it will also be a social enterprise, working to support people with criminal convictions.

BEERS will depend on what members brew but are likely to be mainly in keg: there are currently no plans for a commercial-scale bottling or canning facility.

Moor Vaults ⑪

Bar
71 Enid Street SE16 3RA
T (020) 3952 5456   **moorvaults.co.uk**
🕐 We-Th 16.00-22.00, Fr 15.00-22.30, Sa 12.00-22.30, Su 12.00-21.00. Children welcome.
2-6 cask, 12-15 keg, 150+ bottles/cans.
🍴 Pies, pickled eggs, snacks, cheeseboards £, 🪑 Tables on street, ♿ Flat access only
Beer showcases, tastings, functions

Ⓔ Bermondsey   🚌 Maltby Street   🚲 Link to NCN4, C4, C14
🚶 Link to Jubilee Greenway, Jubilee Walkway, Thames Path

Now one of the UK's very best beer producers since being bought and overhauled by Californian Justin Hawke in 2007, Moor was the first non-London brewery to establish a bridgehead in Bermondsey in December

2017. The initial ambition for a distribution depot evolved into a bar and barrel vault, so although the beer is brewed at the Bristol base, some of it claims local provenance by being aged and blended here. The brewery is laudably committed to cask and a range of its unfined offerings is always on sale, alongside various kegs and packaged beers. But that's before you get to one of the best lists of sour, wild and mixed fermentation beers in London, courtesy of Moor's involvement in the annual Arrogant Sour Fest back home, including a changing draught lambic and bottled rarities from producers like Baladin (Italy), Agullons (Catalunya), Eik & Tid (Norway) and Sour Cellars (US). Aside from intriguing decorations and a window to the coldroom behind the bar, the surroundings are taproom-basic, with stools, benches and repurposed barrels, but always hospitable.

Partizan Brewing ⑫

Brewery, taproom
34 Raymouth Road SE16 2DB (Southwark)
T (020) 8127 5053   **partizanbrewing.co.uk**
First sold beer: November 2012, 🍴
🕐 Fr 17.00-21.00, Sa 12.00-21.00, extended for events. Children until 20.30.
8 keg, 20+ bottles/cans.
🍴 Gourmet pizzas, cheese boards, occasional food truck £-££, 🪑 Tables in yard, ♿ Flat access only
Occasional music and other events

🚆 South Bermondsey   Ⓔ Surrey Quays   🚌 Corbetts Lane, Anchor Street   🚲 Link to C10

Partizan Brewing

Partizan, the second of the Bermondsey Three (above), has moved since the last edition of this book into two much bigger arches around the corner. It boasts a decent-sized taproom with wooden seating and a bar with unique fonts designed by regular graphic artist Alec Doherty. These almost exclusively dispense the excellent house beers, with occasional guests as the result of collaborations and the like.

BEERS are in keg, bottle and, rarely, can, the last using a mobile line. A wide range of styles embraces Belgian and contemporary US influences and English brewing heritage. Reflecting founder Andy Smith's background, restaurants make up a significant proportion of customers. The range regularly changes but usually includes light modern pale ale **Table Juice** (3%); flavoured saisons (around 4%), with **Lemon and Thyme***, **Lemongrass** and **Raspberry and Lemon** regularly recurring; a modern **Pale Ale** with changing hops (some *, 4.5%); a distinctive pale **Lager*** (4.6%); Belgian pale ale **Atomium*** (5%); **X Ale*·****, a series of milds made to various historic recipes, both light and dark and of varing strength; a **Porter*** (6%) which is sometimes flavoured; **IPA**s with varying hops (some *, 6.5%); and a **Stout*** (around 7.5%). There are numerous specials, one-offs and collaborations, including 'imperial saison' **La Ronde**** (8%) and **Imperial Stout*·**** (around 10%).

Small Beer Brew Co ⑬

Brewery
70 Verney Road SE16 3DH (Southwark)
theoriginalsmallbeer.com
First sold beer: November 2017, 🍻
Shop 🕐 Mo-Fr 09.00-18.00
Bar 🕐 Occasional taproom and special events: check website. Children only for daytime events.
5 keg, 5 bottles.
🍴 Varies for special events, 🌲 Small smokers' yard, ♿
Monthly comedy, tastings, food events, yoga, baby sensory classes, functions

🚆 South Bermondsey 🚲 NCN425, link to C10

In the 17th century, small beer was the lowest-strength entry in a brewery's portfolio, consumed daily by people of all ages in preference to water. James Grundy and Felix James have given the idea a contemporary twist in response to the growing interest in lower-alcohol drinks with a brewery that produces nothing over 2.7% ABV. Its beers are properly mashed and fermented with no artificial alcohol extraction, just careful control of recipes and processes. Felix, a homebrewer previously at AB InBev and Fuller's, though on the packaging side, met James when both worked at pioneering craft distillery Sipsmith. The idea for Small

Beer followed from their mutual frustration at the lack of flavourful beers compatible with their busy professional and social lives. They moved into a former laundry in an industrial area of South Bermondsey, just off the main 'beer mile', in summer 2017, installing a sizeable 50hl steam-heated bespoke brewhouse. It's not only optimised for brewing to lower ABVs but for minimum environmental impact, with low water consumption and 100% renewable energy. There's plenty of space beside this for a taproom, a stage for bands and the diverting addition of a mobile bar built into a Mini Cooper, but public opening is currently only on an occasional basis.

BEERS are in keg and distinctive stubby 350ml bottles, filled off site: Felix is unconvinced by the environmental arguments for cans, and chose the shape as it takes up less space and weighs less than a traditional long neck. The core range includes a remarkable **Dark Lager*** (1%), officially classified as low alcohol. The others, classified as reduced strength, are best seller **Lager*** (2.1%); hop-forward **Session Pale*** (2.5%); and California common-style **Steam** (2.7%).

Southwark Brewing

Southwark Brewing ⑭
Brewery, taproom
46 Druid Street SE1 2EZ (Southwark)
T (020) 3302 4190 southwarkbrewing.co.uk
First sold beer: October 2014, ⑪
🕐 *Tu,Th, Fr* 17.00-22.00, *Sa* 12.00-18.00,
  Su 12.00-17.00. Children welcome.
3-6 cask, 5 keg, 8 bottles/cans, growlers,
  some specialist spirits.
🪑 Tables at front, ♿
Functions

🚆 ⊖ London Bridge 🚌 Druid Street 🚲 Link to NCN4, C4, C14

Unusually for the owner of a new London brewery, Southwark co-founder Peter Jackson is an industry veteran, with many years at Whitbread and Marston's on his CV, including as marketing director at the latter. He created this brewery, the fifth in Bermondsey and the closest to central London, with the help of another long-serving industry figure, Rooster's founder Sean Franklin, a key early UK champion of New World hops. It's rather smaller than Peter's former employers, with a 13.5hl brewhouse in a single arch, just behind a lively, recently refurbished taproom which boasts displays on the brewing process and local brewery history. This holds the welcome distinction of offering the widest choice of house-brewed cask beer on the 'beer mile', in reliably great condition. Friendly brewery tours are often hosted by Peter himself, a mine of information and anecdote.

BEERS are largely in cask and often sold in major pub chains, with an increasing proportion of keg and some cans and bottles. Among the core casks are US-hopped red ale **Routemaster Red** (3.8%); flagship **LPA*** (London Pale Ale, 4%), with a contemporary twist; **Potter's Fields Porter** (4%); traditional English bitter **Bermondsey Best*** (4.4%); and **Harvard American Pale Ale** (5.5%), commemorating university founder John Harvard's birthplace in Southwark. Kegs include a session IPA, pale ale and a craft lager. Among less frequent brews, look for a series of single hop pale ales (5%); occasional appearances by **Maltby Street Mild** (3.8%); an annually brewed **Double Stout*** (7.5%) which is also barrel-aged; and an imperial, **Peter's Stout** (8.9%).

Spartan Brewery

Brewery, taproom
8 Almond Road SE16 3LR (Southwark)
T 07920 032565   spartanbrewery.com
First sold beer: June 2018, 🍴 (informal)
🕐 *Sa* 13.00-20.00. Children until early
    evening.
1-2 cask, 4 keg, 3 cans. ⌀
🍴 Snacks, 🪑 Tables at front, ♿

⇌ South Bermondsey   ⊖ Surrey Quays   🚌 Anchor Street
🚲 Link to C10

In the original Partizan railway arch at the Bermondsey Blue, Spartan is a relatively substantial undertaking considering its founders and sole employees, Colin Brooks and Mike Willetts, still have full-time day jobs as a software engineer and a financial risk analyst respectively. They were homebrewing for over five years before making their first commercial beers at Ubrew in November 2016. Moving into the arch a year later, they initially sold existing stock at an improvised taproom while installing a new 16hl kit complete with an auger to transport the grist into the mash tun. The taproom has since been overhauled: as well as keg taps, the small ground floor bar has a handpump and often a second cask on stillage, and there's more seating with traditional pub stools and tables on a mezzanine. Given their work commitments, we can forgive them for only opening on Saturdays.

BEERS are in cask and keg, with some can conditioning offsite at Bottled in Cumbria. Styles lean towards the traditional with a contemporary twist, using nearly all UK ingredients, with branding using ancient Greek references, reflecting one of Mike's personal interests. Regulars include **River Styx*** (3.7%) porter; **Achilles Heel** (4.2%), a contemporary English-style pale ale; and another pale ale with a rotating English hop, **Hoplite** (3.8%). Among the notable seasonals are light mild **Son of Zeus*** (3.6%); dark mild **Phalanx** (5%); and English IPA **Polemarch** (5.5%).

Three Hills Brewing The Outpost

Brewery, taproom
7 Almond Road SE16 3LR (Southwark)
threehillsbrewing.com
First sold beer: September 2020 (at this site,
October 2016 at Northamptonshire site) 🍴
🕐 *Fr* 16.00-22.00, *Sa* 13.00-22.00, *Su* 14.00-22.00,
    occasional *Th* for special events. Children
    welcome.
Occasional cask, 1+ tank, 16 keg, 10+ bottles/cans
🍴 Changing popups **£-££**, 🪑 Tables at front, ♿
Tap takeovers, meet the brewer, homebrew club, spoken word, possible live music, vintage chess, pianos

⇌ South Bermondsey   ⊖ Surrey Quays   🚌 Anchor Street
🚲 Link to C10

Andrew Catherall worked as a brewer in China before founding Three Hills as a small batch nanobrewery in a rural setting at Woodford, Northamptonshire. A longstanding aspiration for a London outlet was realised in 2020 when Affinity moved from a Bermondsey arch to the cellar of the Grosvenor Arms in Brixton (p261), leaving its old kit behind. Indeed, the arch is now on its third brewing tenant since 2015 when it was first occupied by Partizan, founded next door. Three Hills retains its original site, though 75% of production is currently at Bermondsey, using the old Affinity brewhouse, originally at Long Arm in Ealing, and a new set of fermenters. There are also plans for a third, much bigger brewery back home. An attractive mezzanine taproom includes three pianos, one of them converted into a tap mount, vintage chess sets and much greenery. Half the beers are produced in-house including the brewery's celebrated big stouts, the remainder are guests from other independents plus bottled lambics and other wild fermentation beers. The logo consists of the Chinese characters for 'three hills' (三山).

Threer Hills

BEERS are in keg, tank, can, bottle and occasional cask. They include **Happy Hour DDH Table Beer** (3.5%); **Tank Fresh Saison*** (4.8%), a taproom exclusive mixed fermentation beer; several variants on hazy, juicy pale ale **Heidrun** (strength varies) including a raw (unboiled) version; and equally varying expressions of imperial pastry stout **BPAVK** (10%, sometimes labelled in Cyrillic as **БЛАВК**) – a marshmallow version* was particularly noteworthy. There are several other changing specials and seasonals.

TRY ALSO

Billy Franks Craft Beer and Snack Shack 104 Druid Street SE1 2HQ billyfranks.co.uk: Selling their gourmet jerky (including vegan options) and occasional beers since 2015, this friendly bunch rejigged their arch just northwest of Anspach & Hobday into a small but welcoming bar and shop in spring 2021. Only two keg but around 200 bottles/cans mainly from contemporary London/UK brewers including own label collabs. Thursday to Sunday only, cash-free.

Hiver Beers 55 Stanworth Street SE1 3NY madeofengland.co.uk: Friendly arch-based bar next door to Jensen's Gin, a showcase for Hiver honey beers and sister brand Fabal in keg and bottle, with bookable tutored tastings in an upstairs room. Weekend daytimes, cash-free.

Marquis of Wellington 21 Druid Street SE1 2HH craft-pubs.co.uk: The only actual pub right by the Bermondsey arches, a red brick estate boozer refurbished in contemporary style in 2016. Four cask (though quality varies), 12 keg and around 15 bottles/cans including Anspach & Hobday exclusives and lots from other smaller London brewers.

Secret Goldmine Yeastie Boys Taproom 19 Old Jamaica Business Estate SE16 4AW secretgoldmine.co.uk: A collab between the noted New Zealand-based cuckoo brewer (p324) and a railway arch café noted for pies, scotch eggs and croquettes, currently *Sa-Su* 12.00-20.00 only but may expand. Around 16 bottles/cans, including numerous Yeastie Boysand other New Zealand brands like Speights and Tua, supplemented on Saturdays by four keg taps dispensing YB and Bermondsey beers.

HERITAGE PUB

Mayflower 117 Rotherhithe Street SE16 4NF mayflowerpub.co.uk: Riverside pub in Rotherhithe village, close to the Brunel Museum and overground railway, best known for its association with the ship that took the Pilgrim Fathers to Massachusetts, which set out from the adjacent steps in 1620. The current building is late Victorian and the cluttered 'olde worlde' interior an effective and atmospheric 1957 fake. Now independently managed with some local cask among the beers.

Founder Peter Jackson hosts the brewery tour at Southwark Brewing

Central South London

Affinity Brewing Co Shop ⑰

Shop, bar
22 Church Road SE19 2E
T 07904 391807   affinitybrewco.com
🕐 *We-Th* 13.00-19.00, *Fr-Sa* 12.00-20.00,
  Su 12.00-18.00
4 keg, 8 cans, growlers
Tastings

⇌ ⊖ Crystal Palace   🚌 Westow Hill   🏃 Link to Capital
Ring, Green Chain Walk

Affinity's Crystal Palace outlet opened in 2020 in connection with the brewery's move to Stockwell: see Grosvenor Arms p261. It mainly stocks its owner's excellent beers, with occasional guests. Limited to takeaways during lockdown, it has since added modest drink-in facilities.

Beer Shop London 🌹 ⑱

Micropub, shop
42 Nunhead Green SE15 3QF
T (020) 7723 5555   thebeershoplondon.co.uk
🕐 *We-Fr* 16.00-23.00, *Sa* 12.00-23.00, *Su* 12.00-20.00. Children until 19.00. Cash-free.
2-4 cask, 8 keg, 100 bottles/cans, growlers, bag-in-box, 8-10 ciders/perries.
🍴 Pork pies, sausage rolls £, 🌳 Small rear garden
Meet the brewer, beer and cheese, tastings, occasional acoustic music, open mic, board games

⇌ Nunhead   🚌 Nunhead Green   🏃 Link to Green Chain Walk

In an old haberdasher's shop on Nunhead Green, this unusual and delightful place is more a contemporary take on a micropub despite its name. The living room-sized space is scattered with cushions and decorated with a primary-coloured mountain landscape mural.

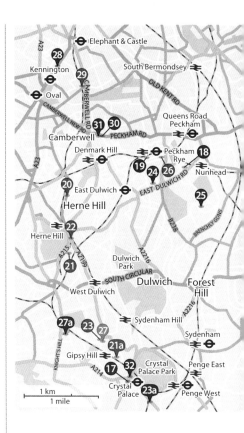

Casks, poured from stillage in the coldroom, often include locals like Anspach & Hobday, Brockley or Canopy alongside visitors like Brighton Bier, Burning Sky or Fyne. A similar policy applies to the mainly UK-sourced kegs, while an excellent bottle and can list stretches to the US, Belgium and Scandinavia, with Kent's Boutilliers, Cigar City, Solvay Society and Tilquin among the highlights when I last looked. Ex-Antic manager Lee Gentry and partner Lauren Willis, who opened the place

Beer Shop London

in December 2014, are effusive with advice and recommendations, and to justify the name there's a takeaway trade in bottles and cans, gift packs, bag-in-box and cartons filled from cask.

Brick Tap Room (19)

Bar
209 Blenheim Grove SE15 4QL
T (020) 3583 9640 **brickbrewery.co.uk**
Tu-Th 17.00-22.00, *Fr* 17.00-24.00, *Sa* 12.00-24.00, Su 13.00-22.00. Children welcome.
2 cask, 16 keg, 40+ bottles/cans.
Greek-style gyros **£-££**, Front and rear gardens, ♿
Beer launches, occasional tastings, film screenings, art exhibitions, craft fairs, community events

Peckham Rye C35 Link to Surrey Canal path

Brick has since moved production to a much bigger site in Deptford (p229) but the arch under Peckham Rye station where it began, previously an evangelical church, remains its taproom and spiritual home. Behind a sheltered south-facing yard is a basic but comfortable space dominated by a mural of Britain's Three Peaks, commemorating the time brewery staff took on the challenge of climbing them. An impressive range happily includes cask options, a comprehensive selection of house brews and numerous guests including Londoners like Weird Beard and visitors from as far as the US (KCBC) and New Zealand (8 Wired). An imaginative events programme has included conker and salsa competitions, and this, alongside strong community links, doubtless helped win the place the Best UK Watering Hole award at the 2019 London Craft Beer Festival. The area is due for redevelopment but the taproom is secure.

Brixton Brewery (20)

Brewery (Heineken)
1 Dylan Road SE24 0HL (Lambeth)
T (020) 3609 8880 **brixtonbrewery.com**
First sold beer: October 2013 (at original site), !!
Occasional open daysand events only
Beer range varies.
Changing food truck **£**, Tables on yard, ♿

Loughborough Junction Lowden Road Carnegie Library

Conceived in 2011 by four homebrewing neighbours Jez and Libby Galaun, Xochitl Benjamin and Mike Ross, Brixton eventually opened two years later with a 10hl brewhouse in an arch not far from Brixton station, subsequently expanding into a neighbouring arch. Many were surprised when this still-small outfit became the fourth new London brewery to attract the attention of a multinational group, with Heineken buying a 49% stake in November 2017, though the strong brand and association with an iconic neighbourhood was doubtless part of the attraction. The Dutch brewer's resources enabled a major expansion to the current site, under a kilometre from the brewery's birthplace, where a 50hl automated brewhouse and a canning line installed on a hi-tech floor provide a potential capacity of 30,000hl a year. Heineken acquired full ownership in February 2021, though the existing management remains in place. The Brixton arches have been retained as a secondary brewery and taproom (p258).

BEERS are in keg and can, with small amounts of cask and some bottling at the original site. The names are nearly all local references. Core beers include **Reliance Pale Ale** (4.2%); **Low Voltage Session IPA** (4.3%); **Coldharbour Lager*** (4.5%); **Windrush Stout** (5%, bottled and sometimes in cask); **Atlantic APA** (American pale ale, 5.4%); and West Coast-style **Electric IPA*** (6.5%); plus numerous specials and collaborations.

Bullfinch Brewery 21

Brewery, taproom: 886 Rosendale Road SE24 9EH (Lambeth)
T 07899 795823 **thebullfinchbrewery.co.uk**
First sold beer: February 2014 (when brewing at Anspach & Hobday), ‼ (informal)
🕐 *Tu-Fr* 16.00-22.00, *Sa-Su* 12.00-22.00, Children until 19.00. Cash-free.
2 cask, 7 keg, 20 cans, minicasks, growlers.
🍴 Street food stall, snacks, BYO, 🪑 Tables in yard, ♿ Flat access only
Craft workshops, monthly book club, board games, shove ha'penny

🚆 Herne Hill   🚌 Rosendale Road   🚲 Link to C17

Bullfinch Brewery

Bull and Finch 21a

Brewpub, Bar: 126 Gipsy Hill SE19 1PL (Southwark)
First sold beer: August 2021, ‼ (informal)
🕐 *Tu-Fr* 16.00-23.00, *Sa* 14.00-23.00, *Su* 14.00-22.00. Children until 20.00. Cash free.
2 cask, 14 keg, 4 cans, growlers, some whiskies.
🍴 Order in from local suppliers **£-££**
🪑 Tables at front
Tastings, tap takeovers

🚆 Gipsy Hill   🚲 C17

Ryan McLean, originally from Ballymena, discovered international craft beer as a much-travelled live sound engineer. He began brewing commercially as a cuckoo at Anspach & Hobday in February 2014, but soon outgrew the arrangement. In December 2015, Ryan and his wife and business partner Carly resumed production in two smallish railway arches a few steps from Brockwell Park and a short walk from Canopy (below). One arch just squeezes in an 8hl brewhouse that began its life as a pilot kit at Charles Wells in Bedford, alongside numerous fermenters, some of them added after a 2016 crowdfunding round. The other arch houses a pretty taproom draped in dried hops, with cable hubs recycled as tables, atmospheric lighting and a mural of the titular finch. Since May 2019 there's been a second outlet, the Bull and Finch opposite Gipsy Hill station, previously Beer Rebellion, refitted in soothingly woody style: in 2021 this gained its own 1.5hl nanobrewery, visible behind a window in the cellar. Rows of taps between brick pillars on the back bar are cunningly staggered to make best use of space, dispensing interesting British brewers like Hairy Dog and imports including excellent Franconian bottles from small producers as well as house beers. Pleasingly, both bars stock cask.

BEERS, usually named with astronomical references, are currently in keg, can and cask. Regulars include reduced alcohol **Juno Pint-Sized IPA** (2.8%); the very pale-coloured **Luna Light Pale Ale*** (3.8%); a traditional **Special Bitter** (4.2%); **Rascal** session IPA (4.4%); **Dark Side of the Moon** (4.5%) porter; **Laika** (4.8%) craft lager; and American pale ale **Wolf** (5%). Notable seasonals include spring **Born to be Mild*** (3.3%); summer saison **Milou*** (4.6%) and winter **South Eastern Bloc*** (5.2%) stout. Single hop beers appear as the Apollo series. Since the lockdown, many of the more popular brands have been cuckoo-brewed at larger scale, most recently at Belleville, and this is likely to continue, with Herne Hill used for seasonals. The nanobrewery produces specials branded **Bullfinch @ The Bull and Finch**, only sold onsite, and mixed fermentation brews as part of lead brewer Jon Griffiths's side project **So What Brewing Co**.

Canopy Beer Co

Brewery, taproom
Arch 1127 Bath Factory Estate, 41 Norwood Road SE24 9AJ (Southwark)
T (020) 8671 9496   canopybeer.com
First sold beer: October 2014, ⚑For pre-arranged groups only
🕐 We-Fr 17.00-23.00, Sa 12.00-23.00, Su 12.00-22.30. Children welcome. Cash free.
1 cask (cooler months only), 10 keg, 10 cans, minicasks, growlers, 1 cider. 🍺
🍴Sausage rolls, snacks **£**, 🎋Tables in yard
DJs, live music, occasional film nights, functions

🚉Herne Hill   🚲Link to C17

Canopy is now an established local fixture alongside various mechanics in a railway arch near Herne Hill station, close to Bullfinch (above) and Brockwell Park. It was founded

by Estelle and Matt Theobalds after the birth of their first child triggered a lifestyle change, beginning with 6.5hl kit from a brewery in Wakefield that never got off the ground. In the tradition of the 'backyard tinkerers, garden shed inventors, do-ers and make-ers' celebrated in brewery publicity, the installation evolved through various often home-built additions and can now manage 18hl batches, with a canning line added to coincide with a rebrand in autumn 2018. The taproom, with its flag-draped yard, make-and-mend aesthetic and brightly painted brewing vessels, concentrates on selling house beers, in tasting flights if required, and sends out cans locally via Deliveroo. There's a cool feature on the website which generates customised misfit characters based on the can labels. See also Sympathetic Ear (p265).

Canopy Beer Co

BEERS are mainly in keg (60%) and can, with a small amount of cask and minikeg. Core beers include flagship **Sunray Pale Ale** (4.2%), also in cask; **Champion Kölsch** (4.5%); **Llopper Everyday Oyster Stout** (5%) made with real oysters; and US-style **Brockwell IPA*** (5.6%). There are four specials a month, including a sporadic ruby mild, decent Belgian styles and an annual wet hop beer in collaboration with the local hop growing collective.

Douglas Fir
See Gipsy Hill Brewing

Gipsy Hill Brewing

Gipsy Hill Brewing ㉓

Brewery, taproom: Unit 5, 160 Hamilton Road
SE27 9SF (Lambeth)
T (020) 8761 9061 **gipsyhillbrew.com**
First sold beer: July 2014,
⏲ Th 16.00-21.00, Fr 18.00-22.00, Sa 12.00-23.00,
  Su 12.00-18.00. Children welcome. Cash-free.
18 keg, 30+ bottles/cans, 1 cider, some
  specialist spirits. ⌂
🍴 Order-in pizza, weekend changing food
truck **£-££**, 🪑 Tables at front, ♿
*Tastings, quiz (Th), live music (Fr), monthly retro
gaming, art nights, board games, ping pong*

≋ Gipsy Hill   🚌 Oaks Avenue   ♿ Q7

Douglas Fir ㉓ₐ
Contemporary pub: 144 Anerley Road SE20 8DL
T (020) 3583 3130
⏲ Th 18.00-22.00, Fr 16.00-23.00, Sa 12.00-23.00,
  Su 12.00-20.00. Children welcome. Cash-free.
2 cask, 7 keg, 35 bottles/cans, some specialist
  spirits.
🍴 Various order-in nights **££**, 🪑 Tables on street
Tap takeovers, beer launches, art shows, board games

≋ Crystal Palace   ⊖ Crystal Palace, Anerley
🚶 Link to Capital Ring, Green Chain Walk

Already one of London's biggest independent
breweries, Gipsy Hill has a target to grow output to 24,000hl in the next few years. Its footprint on the industrial estate in the like-named
neighbourhood it calls home has expanded
from one to six units. The credit lies with the
three sturdy-looking chaps on the logo:
founders Charlie Shaw (ex-Five Points), former
City worker Sam McMeekin and head brewer
Simon Wood, recruited from Dorset's Piddle
brewery. The first kit was a relatively generous
25hl and the company was soon adding extra
fermenters and warehousing. Disaster struck in
2016 when the brewing floor began to collapse,
but this proved a turning point. The brewery
not only invested in a new high-quality floor
but upgraded the following year to a 60hl
brewhouse with a pilot kit and a canning line.
A dedicated taproom opened in 2018 across
the yard, providing an expansive and comfortable drinking environment, with a polished
wood bar and the cellar visible behind glass.
As well as house beers, you'll find guests from
other Londoners, UK brewers like Bristol Beer
Factory and Up Front and some rare imports
like Piggy in France. The fridges hold well-chosen
sharers from around the world: I spotted
Cloudwater, Glazen Toren and Scandinavians
Kinn and Frejdahl. Gipsy Hill's pub the Douglas
Fir, on the other side of Crystal Palace Park at
Anerley, opened as a popup in a former shop
in 2016 but soon became permanent: its dark
green single room, with a bar made from
recycled pallets, is regularly busy. It stocks at
least as many guests as beers from its owners,
mainly from reliable contemporary London and
wider UK producers, with less exotica than at
the brewery but a smattering of good Belgians.

BEERS are in keg and can, with hand bottling
for barrel-aged specials and occasional one-off
casks. The core range, featuring portraits of
brewery staff on the branding, includes hazy,

juicy 'Micro IPA' **Carver*** (2.8%); **Bandit** (3.8%), a gluten-free version of long-established pale ale Beatnik; **Hepcat*** (4.6%) session IPA; Helles-style lager **Hunter*** (4.8%); and IPA **Baller** (5.4%). There's a busy programme of specials and collaborations, including sours and hazy, juicy pale ales. Barrel-aged releases have included several versions of an English IPA.

Hop Burns and Black ㉔
Shop, bar
38 East Dulwich Road SE22 9AX
T (020) 7450 0284 hopburnsblack.co.uk
🕐 *Tu-We* 13.00-19.00, *Th-Fr* 13.00-20.00, *Sa* 11.00-21.00, *Su* 12.00-18.00. Children welcome. Cash-free.
4 keg, 350+ bottles, natural wines, specialist cider. 🍽
🍴 100+ hot sauces, fresh popcorn, tinned fish **£**,
🎋 Tables at front
Meet the brewer, tap takeovers, food pairing, tastings, chilli karaoke at other venues

🚆 East Dulwich   ➔ Peckham Rye   🚌 Oakhurst Grove

Just inside this stylish bottle shop is a set of shelves proudly labelled Southeast London. When the first edition of this book was published, there were only two breweries that would qualify; today, there's not room for all the potential candidates, but the section still has the highest turnover in the shop. Brick, Canopy, Gipsy Hill, Kernel, Small Beer and Villages are among the highlights, with numerous other Londoners too, alongside other UK brewers like Braybrooke, Cloudwater and Northern Monk, Europeans like Demoersleutel, a few Belgian and German classics and New Zealanders 8 Wired and Yeastie Boys. These last two are a nod to the origins of proprietors Jen Ferguson

Hop Burns & Black

and Glenn Williams, who took on this former launderette in 2014 aiming to stock affordable independents and have since become some of London's most admired beer traders, with a second branch in Deptford (Try also p240). Their other passions are hot chilli sauces and vinyl records, thus the name and the additional merchandise on sale. It's a welcoming place with a few drink-in seats and a miniature front terrace close to Peckham Rye Common.

Ivy House ㉕
Traditional pub
40 Stuart Road SE15 3BE
T (020) 7277 8233 ivyhousenunhead.com
🕐 *Mo-Th* 12.00-23.00, *Fr-Sa* 12.00-24.00, *Su* 12.00-22.30. Children very welcome until 20.00, children's menu.
7 cask, 9 keg, 25+ bottles/cans, 1 cider.
🍴 Quality pub grub, sharing plates **££**,
🎋 Tables at front, rear garden
Annual beer festival, live music, community events, children's classes, Lindy Hop, yoga, veg box pickup, functions

🚆 ➔ Brockley, Peckham Rye   🚌 Stuart Road
🚶 Link to Green Chain Walk

In a backstreet location in Nunhead, close to the 'Magnificent Seven' cemetery and Peckham Rye Common, this big wood-panelled pub hosts everything from gigs to children's theatre classes and yoga in a large performance space at the back. The handsome and more compact left-hand bar provides the main drinking area, with a second, bigger room on the other side. Excellent casks are from people like Big Smoke, Blackjack, Five Points and Truman's, with keg guests that extend to Kernel and Siren and lots more local brewers among the bottles and cans. Sadly, the prices on a 1960s list displayed on the wall no longer apply. A short menu offers pub grub like chargrilled chicken, quinoa and lentil burgers and sharing plates, perhaps enjoyed al fresco in the ferny garden. A great night out that's also a case study in how to run a heritage pub.

Visitor note. *The Grade II-listed building was rebuilt by Truman's in vaguely Tudor style in 1937 when its street was a lively local centre. The adjoining shops were destroyed*

House

by a V1 during World War II and never replaced, so the pub now seems out of proportion to its surroundings. In the 1970s, as the Newlands Tavern, it was a famous pub rock venue, hosting performances by Ian Dury, Dr Feelgood and Joe Strummer's pre-Clash band the 101ers. Threatened with development in 2012, it became England's first pub listed as an Asset of Community Value and the first building in the country bought under the community right to buy provisions of the 2011 Localism Act. It's now owned and run by a community interest company with 371 local shareholders.

Kanpai London Craft Sake 26
Brewery, taproom
2A-2 Copeland Park, 133 Copeland Road SE15 3SN (Southwark)   kanpai.london
First sold beer: June 2017, ♨♨
🕐 *We-Th* 17.00-22.00, *Fr* 17.00-23.00, *Sa* 12.00-23.00, *Su* 12.00-19.00. Children welcome.
10 keg, 10-15 bottles, cocktails, Japanese spirits and tea. 🍴
♨♨ Seasonal open-flame Japanese-style menu ££,
🎍 Tables at front, ♿ Flat access only
Tastings, supper clubs, workshops, food pairing, brewing sessions, karaoke, film nights

🚆 ⊖ Peckham Rye

Though sometimes called 'rice wine', sake, or *nihonshu* (literally 'Japanese alcoholic drink'), is technically beer as its alcohol is derived from grain. Thus, the inclusion here of the UK's first sake brewery, one of only seven in Europe, founded by Tom and Lucy Wilson. Tom was a homebrewer who got interested in sake when he worked in financial marketing in New York City. He started making his own, setting aside plans for a conventional brewery in favour of something more unusual, for which he prepared

with study trips to Japan. Despite a challenging taxation regime – sake is in a higher duty category and isn't eligible for small breweries' relief – the initiative, named with the Japanese word for 'cheers' and originally at a smaller site elsewhere in Peckham, has prospered. In August 2018, Kanpai expanded to an old industrial building in Peckham's 'cultural quarter' of Copeland Park, a community of creative businesses and other specialists. There's an attractive taproom on a mezzanine above the rice cookers and fermentation tanks, with a collection of empty bottles that identifies the Wilsons as true enthusiasts. House sake is sold in keg – unusual even in its homeland – and bottle, alongside examples from other producers and western beers from locals like Brick as well as some Japanese craft lines. But perhaps the most authentic touch is the toilet, which, much to the delight of the Japanese customers who provide 20% of the trade, is equipped with a heated electronic bidet seat.

Technical note. The process differs from western brewing in that there's no malting and mashing: the polished rice is steamed before undergoing a lengthy and complex fermentation which as well as yeast involves a mould called koji *capable of converting starches into sugars.*

BEERS are in keg and bottle: all are high grade *junmai* sake made entirely from rice and water. Core brands are **Fizu*** (11.5%), a sparkling version dry hopped with Mosaic; flagship clear **Sumi*** (15%), using a prized rice variety from Toyama prefecture; and **Kumo**** (15%), a cloudy version of Sumi aged on lees. There are occasional ultra-premium releases in 375ml and 750ml bottles, plus regular collaborations with with more conventional brewers like By the Horns and other producers like Peckham meadery Gosnells. Beavertown collaboration **Onna Bugeisha**** (7.1%), a lager fermented with sake yeast and aged in red burgundy barrels, was particularly noteworthy.

London Beer Factory 27
Brewery, no visitors please
160 Hamilton Road SE27 9SF (Lambeth)
T (020) 8670 7054
thelondonbeerfactory.com
First sold beer: August 2014. 🍴

Warehouse Taproom 27a

13 Beadman Street SE27 0DJ
⏱ Tu-Fr 17.00-23.00, Sa 12.00-23.00, Su 12.00-19.00.
Keg, bottles/cans.
🍴 Rotating food truck, 🪑 Tables at front

🚉 West Norwood

With its distinctive sawtooth roof echoed on its logo, the other brewery on the industrial estate now dominated by Gipsy Hill indeed resembles a no-nonsense factory. It was founded by Ed Cotton, a veteran of Australian vineyards, and his homebrewing brother Sim, initially with brewer Archie Village, later of Villages. The original 35hl kit is still in use, alongside additional fermenters and a canning line which have necessitated expansion to a neighbouring unit. Noted for decent conventional beers with wide appeal, the brewery unexpectedly branched out into wild and mixed fermentation and barrel ageing in summer 2017 with the Barrel Project in Bermondsey (p207). In 2019, it crowdfunded the construction of a bespoke mobile coolship, a shallow rectangular stainless steel vessel with a capacity of 750 litres and a similar geometry to those used in lambic breweries to attract wild yeast. This is now touring the UK, collecting the local microflora and visiting other breweries for collaborations. With space restrictions at the brewery itself ruling out a taproom, the company added a bar to its offsite warehouse, not too far away at West Norwood, in December 2020. Former Fuller's brewing director John Keeling has joined to assist in a planned expansion to a larger site during 2022.

London Beer Factory's Barrel Project Beers

BEERS are mainly in keg and can: the brewery was the first in the UK to package in '360' cans with entirely removeable ends, though it sticks to distinctive 375ml bottles for the specials. Core beers include **Hazy Daze** (4.6%) session IPA; **Sour Solstice** (4.8%), a kettle sour with blood orange and cranberry; West Coast-style **Paxton IPA** (5.5%), a nod to the architect of the Crystal Palace, which once stood nearby; hazy, juicy IPA **Dance Juice** (7.5%); and **Big Milk Stout*** (7.5%) with vanilla, cocoa and lactose. Irish-style **Sayers Stout** (4.5%) regularly recurs, and there are various other specials and seasonals. **Barrel Project** limited editions have included **Kamoni*** (5.7%) barrel-aged Brett IPA with Citra; Belgian IPA **The Brux of It*** (6%); and **Oeno-Imperial Stout*** (9.8%) aged in wine barrels.

Oaka (Mansion House) 28

Restaurant, bar
46 Kennington Park Road SE11 4RS
☎ (020) 7582 5599   oakalondon.com
⏱ Mo-Th 12.00-24.00, Fr-Sa 12.00-01.00,
      Su 12.00-23.00. Older children until 19.00.
5 cask, 7 keg, 6 bottles/cans, wines, cocktails.
🍴 Pan-asian menu ££, 🪑 Tables on street, ♿
Functions

🚇 Kennington   🚲 CS7

Peterborough's excellent Oakham brewery, one of the UK pioneers of modern hop-forward beers, established a London presence in March 2013 with the conversion of Kennington's Mansion House pub into a branch of its Oaka pub-restaurant chain. Two thirds of the smart modern space with its Thai-style carved wood is given over to sit-down dining. Food is pan-Asian fusion, with dishes including tamarind duck, sambal pork belly, 'big bang' tofu or miso aubergine, with plentiful set menus and veggie options. It's still possible to go just for a drink, perhaps alongside one of the unusual cooked bar snacks, though the atmosphere doesn't quite encourage you to settle down for the evening. Oakham core beers like JHB and the ever-popular Citra are well-served on cask, with more house options under the Craftworks brand in keg alongside a few from bigger breweries.

Orbit Beers

Brewery, taproom
233 Fielding Street SE17 3HD (Southwark)
T (020) 7703 9092   orbitbeers.com
First sold beer: August 2014, 🍴(informal)
🕐 We-Fr 16.30-23.00, Sa 12.00-23.00, Su 12.00-22.00. Children welcome.
9-10 keg, 8-10 bottles, craft kombucha. 🍷
🍴Weekend food trucks, snacks, 🪑Tables at front, ♿

🚆 Elephant & Castle   ⊖ Kennington, Elephant & Castle
🚌 Westmoreland Road   🚲 Link to NCN425, C17, C36
🚶 Link to Surrey Canal path

Robert Middleton worked in occupational pensions until deciding to take a career break travelling round his native Scotland and visiting breweries. The results included a book, *The Tea Leaf Paradox: Discovering Beer in the Land of Whisky*, and a keen interest in brewing. With the help of Stuart Medcalf of Twickenham Fine Ales, he set up a16hl plant in a railway arch under the Thameslink Sutton branch, with branding that reflected his love of music and vinyl records. There have been two expansions since, most recently a doubling in 2021 to the current four-arch footprint, with an expanded but still cosy and attractive taproom and a new 25 hl brewhouse due in 2022. The location off an unpromising stretch of Walworth Road is better than it looks, with the pretty Grosvenor Park conservation area on one side and rapidly regenerating Elephant & Castle only a short walk away.

BEERS are in keg or bottled on the brewery's own line. In the early days, Orbit distinguished itself by focusing on traditional European styles, notably adding a few then-rare German styles to the London repertoire. The approach has since broadened a little, though the musical influence remains, with graphics based on amplifier controls illustrating label tasting notes. Core beers are Belgian-style pale **Peel** (4.3%); **Ivo** (4.5%) contemporary pale ale; Kölsch-style **Nico*** (4.8%), named after iconic Andy Warhol and Velvet Underground associate Christa 'Nico' Päffgen, who was born into a brewing family in Cologne; and London porter **Dead Wax*** (5.5%). **White Label** beers are experimental brews in a variety of styles, including a welcome revival of **Tzatziki Sour** (4.3%), which head brewer Paul Spraget used to make at now-defunct Liverpool brewery Mad Hatter. Let's hope Orbit's own discontinued German-style Altbier **Neu** (4.7%) returns too. Barrel-aged beers form part of the **Diggers Series**.

Pigeon

Bar
41 Camberwell Church Street SE5 8TR
anspachandhobday.com
🕐 Tu-Fr 17.00-23.00, Sa 12.00-24.00, Su 13.00-23.00 (may be closed for private parties Sa eve). Children until 20.00. Cash-free
9 keg, 25 bottles/cans.
🍴 BYO, ♿Flat access only
Darts, board games, computer games, functions

🚆⊖ Denmark Hill   🚌 Camberwell Green, St Giles Church

Anspach & Hobday (p242) originally opened this now-permanent bar in a former bike shop as a popup in November 2018. A few doors down from the excellent Stormbird (below), it's a good source not only of its owner's outstanding products but plenty from other well-chosen suppliers like Brew York and Wiper & True from the UK and Cantillon and De La Senne from Brussels. The narrow, cleanly-decorated space stretches back from the street with more room than is at first evident, enlivened by changing art and photography and numerous attractions for games lovers.

Stormbird

Contemporary pub
25 Camberwell Church Street SE5 8TR
T (020) 7277 1806 stormbirdcamberwell.com
⏰ *Mo* 16.00-23.00, *Tu-Th* 16.00-24.00, *Fr* 16.00-
01.00, *Sa* 12.00-01.00, *Su* 12.00-23.00.
Children until 18.00.
3-4 cask, 18 keg, up to 200 bottles/cans, 1 cider,
some specialist spirits.
🍴 BYO, 🪑 A few benches on street

≷ ⊖ Denmark Hill   🚌 Camberwell Green   🚲 Link to C17

Publican Maura Gannon, of well-loved but tied
Camberwell local the Hermits Cave, gave free
rein to her passion for beer in 2011 by opening
Stormbird in a previously average bar across
the road. Serious beer geeks now rub shoulders
with local art students in this neat, smallish and
friendly venue. Bristol Beer Factory, Five Points,
Fyne, Pig and Porter and Siren are regulars on
the cask pumps, while a good range of styles
on keg is mainly drawn from locals and other
Brits like BBNo, Gipsy Hill, Neon Raptor and
Wander Beyond. You'll need to consult the
bar staff to appreciate the full breadth of the
bottles and cans: rarities from 3 Fonteinen,
Crooked Stave, Kernel, De Molen, Tilquin and
Westbrook jostle for space in the fridges,
some hidden behind others. The one thing
that would most improve this treasure trove
is an up-to-date list. Maura has since
expanded operations to the similarly
outstanding Star and Garter (p251).

Westow House

Contemporary pub
79 Westow Hill SE19 1TX
T (020) 8670 0654 westowhouse.co.uk
⏰ *Mo-Th* 12.00-23.00, *Fr* 12.00-24.00, *Sa* 10.00-
24.00, *Su* 12.00-22.30. Children very
welcome until 21.00 (kids corner).
5 cask, 9 keg, 35+ bottles, 2-3 ciders/perries,
some specialist spirits.
🍴 Gastroish menu **££**, 🪑 Front terrace, ♿, 🛋
*Beer festivals, meet the brewer, tap takeovers, quiz
(Tu), DJ (Fr), live music (Sa), pinball, table football,
board games, functions, ballroom under construction*

≷ Crystal Palace   ⊖ Crystal Palace   🏃 Link to Capital
Ring, Green Chain Walk

Looking rather forbidding behind its busy
terrace near the southwestern corner of
Crystal Palace Park, this big pub reveals a
playful interior with comfy old Chesterfields,
well-used games tables and a clued-up beer
selection established under previous operators
Antic though slanted more towards London
by current incumbents Portobello. Besides
house beers, cask guests might be from Five
Points, Southwark or Woodforde's in Norfolk.
Gipsy Hill and London Beer Factory are the
most local of the keg suppliers, alongside
Portobello's lagers, Paulaner and a rotating
range from London independents. An imaginative daily changing food menu could include
spicy chickpea stew, chicken Caesar salad and
pub grub staples like Cumberland sausages.
A recent restoration project has reinstated
the upper storeys, previously demolished
following bomb damage during World War II,
and added B&B rooms and additional drinking
and function space.

TRY ALSO

Beer Rebellion Peckham 129 Queens Road
SE15 2ND beerrebellion.org: Lively, quirkily
decorated bar with jam jar lampshades in a
former bookmaker's near Queens Road
Peckham station, linked to skateboarding
cuckoo Hop King and serving its beers alongside
Fourpure, other Londoners and UK top names.
Up to three cask, nine keg, 20+ bottles/cans.
Craft and Courage 28 Westow Hill SE19 1RX
craftandcourage.co.uk: Long, narrow bar with
small beer garden, a Crystal Palace offshoot of
Craft Tooting (p270), with five rotating kegs and
150+ bottles/cans mainly from contemporary
UK brewers including lots of locals, plus gins.
Local deliveries via Uber Eats. Cash-free.
Dulwich Beer Dispensary 481 Lordship Lane
SE22 8JY southeybrewing.co.uk: Southey's
third outlet, in a shop unit close to Dulwich
Park, run on the same lines as the London Beer
Dispensary (p233) with three cask and various
keg and bottled beers from the owning brewery
and other local suppliers, plus a pizza menu.
East Dulwich Tavern (**EDT**) 1 Lordship Lane
SE22 8EW eastdulwichtavern.com: Antic's
first pub and still one of its best, with a mix of
traditional and offbeat lounge décor, rare cask
Brick Peckham Pale regularly on one of eight

handpumps and some decent kegs and bottles, on a good site overlooking Goose Green.

Tap In 2 Sayer Street SE17 1FG tapin.london: Football-themed sports bar and bottle shop in newly redeveloped Elephant Park, just south of Elephant and Castle, with outdoor space overspilling into an adjoining designer pocket park. Up to 20 keg, some from better-known brands, and a good range of over 200 bottles/cans.

Watsons General Telegraph 108 Forest Hill Road SE22 0RS watsonstelegraph.pub: Big roadside pub between Honor Oak and Peckham Rye, preserving elements of grand Truman

style though much refurbished. Now one of the best Laines for beer: four cask, 11 keg and 35 bottles/cans from good locals and other UK independents as well as the owner, sold by keen staff.

Wild and Lees 2 Half Moon Lane SE24 9HU wildandlees.com: Charming, well-run shop and tasting room near Herne Hill station with over 100 beers, some from Canopy around the corner, alongside other locals (Kanpai, Orbit, Small Beer), wider UK producers and a few imports, plus a wide range of natural and organic wines. Local deliveries.

LONDON DRINKERS | Mauritz Borg

Now manager of the Kernel Arch 7 taproom, Mauritz has been working in beer-focused pubs and bars since 2013. 'I started with zero experience,' he recalls, 'but worked hard, was open to learning any and every task, listened to those with more experience and devoted myself to becoming the best possible publican that I can possibly be. If you hire the right team, pay them well and respect them, then any venue has the potential for greatness.' Follow him on Instagram @Mauritzborg.

How do you rate London as a beer city, on a world scale?
It's one of the best in Europe. You can still get top quality cask ale if you know the right places, and we also have all kinds of modern, innovative beer establishments. At last more restaurants are educating themselves and stocking a good range of beer.

What's the single most exciting thing about beer in London right now?
Average drinkers are getting much more educated about what they want to drink, thanks

to my peers in pubs, bars, bottle shops and breweries sharing their knowledge and passion.

What single thing would make things even better?
Much higher standards for cask beer. The state of cask is sad, especially in the south of England. There's a renewed buzz for it but walk into a random pub and you're rolling the dice on getting a stale and vinegary pint.

What are your top London beers right now?
Cask Five Points Best, particularly at the Pembury Tavern (p134), always in perfect condition, a blend of traditional and contemporary with a lovely blackcurrant and grassy aroma, refreshing with every sip.

What's your top great beer night out?
I have a tour of excellence for friends who haven't been to London before: grab some food at Borough Market, pop into Utobeer (p87) to buy bottles and cans for later, walk along the Southbank to the Hop Locker (p84), across the river to the Harp (p102), then over to Hackney for the Pembury Tavern, the Experiment (p133) and the

Cock Tavern (p136). Then a cocktail at Satan's Whiskers (343 Cambridge Heath Road E2 9RA) if we still have steam left.

Who's your London beer hero?
Oh, that's a hard one. Chandru Lekraj at the Great Northern Railway Tavern (p188), the most hardworking bartender I've ever met. I hired him as one of the bar staff at the Axe (Try Also p182) and he was general manager within two years. An efficient, expert cellarman, great with customers, loyal and always looks after his staff.

Who will we be hearing a lot more from in future?
Court Mooney, here at Arch 7. She astonishes me on every shift: quick, efficient, polite, great with every type of customer, learns instantly and is constantly hungry for knowledge.

Which are your other top beer cities?
New York City, especially Brooklyn, for level of service, quality and innovation in bar and cellar design. Manchester is incredible as the home of so many great breweries, bars and pubs and my favourite beer festival, Indyman.

Greenwich and Lewisham

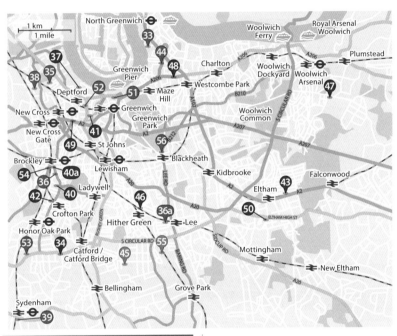

Map labels: North Greenwich, 33, 44, 48, 37, 35, 38, Greenwich Pier, Charlton, Woolwich Ferry, Royal Arsenal Woolwich, Plumstead, Woolwich Dockyard, Woolwich Arsenal, 47, Deptford, 52, 51, Maze Hill, Westcombe Park, New Cross, Greenwich, Greenwich Park, Woolwich Common, New Cross Gate, 41, St Johns, 56, 49, Blackheath, Brockley, 54, 40a, Lewisham, Kidbrooke, Falconwood, 36, 42, 40, Ladywell, 46, Eltham, 43, Crofton Park, 36a, 50, Honor Oak Park, Hither Green, Lee, 53, 34, Catford / Catford Bridge, 55, Mottingham, 45, New Eltham, Bellingham, Grove Park, Sydenham, 39

BBNo (Brew by Numbers) 33

Brewery, taproom
South Warehouse, Greenwich Beach,
Morden Wharf Road SE10 0PA (Greenwich)
T (020) 7237 9794 bbno.co
First sold beer (at original site): December 2012
🕐 *We-Th* 17.00-23.00, *Fr* 17.00-24.00, *Sa* 12.00-
24.00, *Su* 12.00-23.00 (TBC). Cash-free.
30 keg, 25+ cans. 🍺
🍴 Full menu TBC, 🪑 Riverside terrace, ♿
Beer festivals, tastings, beer launches, food events

⊖ 🚆 North Greenwich 🚌 Morden Wharf Road, Dread-
nought Street 🚲 NCN1 🚶 Jubilee Greenway, Thames Path

BBNo should have opened one of London's
most impressive taprooms by the time you
read this, on their new brewing site in a former
glucose refinery beside the Thames in the
redevelopment area of Morden Wharf on the
west side of the Greenwich peninsula. Expect
a comprehensive range of the brewery's regular
beers, specials and rarities plus numerous
guests, in comfortable surroundings with
spectacular river views. Meantime (below) is
a relatively short walk away.

The new BBNo

Visitor note. Developed into a hive of industry in the early 19th century with investment from Morden College in Blackheath, Morden Wharf was particularly associated with submarine cables: the first transatlantic cable was made nearby in the 1860s. Part of BBNo's site was once home to an evocatively named riverside pub, the Sea Witch, demolished following bomb damage in World War II.

BEERS are almost entirely in keg and can, with some specials in 750 ml bottles. They're hard to summarise as there are so many and they change frequently. As the name suggests, there's a numbering system, originally with a two-digit number indicating a broad style and another designating a specific recipe, though today only the first number is used. Among the most notable are the **05** India Pale Ales (around 6.5%) with varying hops; **10** coffee porters with varying beans (around 9.5%); **11** session IPAs, including a core beer with Mosaic hops* (4.2%) and some other variants; **30** lagers (sometimes *, around 5%); the recurring **42 Morden Wharf DDH Pale Ale*** (5.5%) marking the move to Greenwich; and **55** double IPAs (around 8.5%, some *). The original Belgian and French-inspired examples are less seen today, though look out for **01** saisons, **07** witbiers and **18** farmhouse ales, often flavoured. Nearly all are worth trying, so dip in and find your lucky number.

example of the best sort of old-school local. It's relaxed but respectable, with staff in shirts and ties, a heritage interior decorated with sporting and Irish themes and a selection of flawlessly-kept cask beers with traditional leanings. Courage Best, Dark Star Hophead and Harvey's Best are mainstays but you'll also find the very local Brockley and perhaps Crouch Vale, Franklins or Sambrook's, sometimes fetched from the cellar. Beavertown and Kernel line up beside retro Mann's Brown in the fridges, and the cider selection has earned multiple awards.

Visitor note. The former Courage pub preserves a multi-room layout and décor little changed since a refit in the 1920s, including fake wood panelling, nailed-on ceiling beams and fine tiled fireplaces.

Blythe Hill Tavern (34)
Traditional pub
319 Stansted Road SE23 1JB
T (020) 8690 5176   blythehilltavern.co.uk
🕑 *Su-We* 11.00-23.00, *Th-Sa* 11.00-24.00.
    Children very welcome until 19.00.
5-6 cask, 12 bottles/cans, up to 12 ciders/
    perries, some whiskies and gins.
🪑 Large garden, tables at front
Quiz (Mo), Irish music session (Th), big screen sport, board games

🚆 Catford, Catford Bridge   ⊖ Forest Hill   🚌 Blythe Vale
🚲 Link to NCN21   🚶 Link to Waterlink Way

'Perhaps I've been here too long, it just looks old to me,' Con Riordan, leaseholder of 32 years standing, once told me. 'But everyone else loves it.' And quite rightly too, as this obscurely sited pub on the South Circular between Catford and Forest Hill is a rare surviving

Brick Brewery (35)
Brewery
13 Deptford Industrial Estate, Blackhorse Road SE8 5HY (Lewisham)
T (020) 3903 9441   brickbrewery.co.uk
First sold beer: November 2013 (at original site)
🕑 Occasional open days: see social media.
    Children very welcome.
4-6 keg, 5 cans.
🍴 Food truck **£**, 🪑 Tables at front,
♿ Flat access only

🚆 Deptford   ⊖ Surrey Quays   🚌 Deptford Fire Station
🚲 C10, link to NCN4   🚶 Link to Jubilee Greenway, Thames Path

Like countless others, the beer epiphany for York-born Ian Stewart was a bottle from the Kernel. He began developing his own beers in a Peckham shed, and opened commercially in an arch under Peckham Rye station while still holding down his marketing job. Starting with a 9hl brewhouse, Brick extended fermentation capacity several times and expanded into a neighbouring arch in 2015, but still struggled with space. By the end of 2017, production had moved to the current much bigger facility on a Deptford industrial estate beside the route of the old Grand Surrey Canal. Here, head brewer Tom Dixon and his team work on a 32hl brewhouse, with plenty of fermenters, a souring tank, barrel ageing facilities, a keg filler and canning line. The site is only occasionally open to the public; the regular taproom remains in the original Peckham arch (p218).

BEERS are in keg and can, with some cask mainly for local outlets. Core beers include gluten-free **Peckham Helles*** lager (4.2%); flagship **Peckham Pale** (4.5%), also in cask*; red rye ale **Peckham Rye*** (4.7%); Czech-style **Peckham Pils** (4.8%); and West Coast-noted **Peckham IPA*** (6%). There's a regular succession of specials, collaborations and experimental brews, including the recurring **Blackhorse Milk Stout** (4.7%), various hazy, juicy pales and IPAs and a monthly sour release. Some exclusives are brewed for specific outlets, such as **Golborne Helles*** (4.2%) lager for Real Drinks.

Brockley Brewery

Brockley Brewery (Brockley) 36

Small brewery, taproom
31 Harcourt Road SE4 2AJ (Lewisham)
T 07814 584338   brockleybrewery.co.uk
First sold beer: March 2013
🕐 *We-Fr* 17.00-21.00, *Sa* 13.00-21.00, *Su* 13.00-19.00. Children welcome.
4 cask, 3 keg, 4-5 bottles/cans, growlers, bag-in-box. 🍺
🍴 Pies, BYO £
Occasional beer events, brewing school, quiz, music, films, board games night

🚆🚇 Brockley   🚶 Link to Green Chain Walk

Brockley Brewery (Hither Green) 36a

Production brewery, taproom
28 Chiltonian Industrial Estate SE12 0TX (Lewisham)
First sold beer: November 2019, 🍴
Taproom 🕐 *Th* 18.00-21.00, *Fr* 18.00-23.00, *Sa* 13.00-23.00, *Su* 13.00-19.00. Children very welcome.
Shop 🕐 Taproom hours plus *Mo-Fr* from 13.00.
4 cask, 3 keg, 4-5 bottles/cans, growlers, bag-in-box. 🍺
🍴 Popup curries £, 🪑Tables at front
Children's activities

🚆 Hither Green, Lee   🚌 Manor Lane

Missing decent locally brewed beer, Andy Rowland and five of his neighbours founded a brewery. They installed an 8hl kit in a small and characterful backstreet industrial building close to Brockley station, previously a builder's workshop, and soon established a following in a neighbourhood with a strong sense of community. The initial takeaway counter evolved into a particularly attractive taproom with a bar making good use of the obligatory recycled wood, a shocking pink toilet and tables between the mash tun and fermenters. A second, larger facility on an industrial estate between Hither Green and Lee was added in November 2019, with a 30hl brewhouse formerly at Fourpure (and originally at Purity in Warwickshire). This welcomes visitors to relatively frequent open days where you can sometimes meet the horses who eat the spent grain in a small petting zoo. The brewery's original home remains active, used for specials, additional capacity and an extended programme of events and activities including brewing schools hosted by head brewer Craig Vernon, formerly at Camden Town.

BEERS tend towards the more traditional, with cask still a major product, though with significant amounts of keg and bottled beers, bag-in-box and occasional canning on a mobile line. Regular cask beers include **Porter*** (4.3%), **Red Ale** (4.7%) and a changing seasonal. Red is also in keg alongside Kölsch-style **Lager** (4.1%) and **Session IPA** (4.6%).

Dog and Bell
Traditional pub
116 Prince Street SE8 3JD
T (020) 8692 5664
facebook.com/thedogandbell
⏲ *Mo-Fr* 12.00-24.00, *Sa-Su* 11.00-24.00. Children until 20.00.
5-6 cask, 5 keg, 60 bottles/cans, whiskies.
🍴 Pub grub, sandwiches **£-££**,
🪑 Rear garden, tables on street 🐾, ♿
3 annual beer festivals, folk music (We), quiz (Su), annual pickle festival, bar billiards, board games

🚃 Deptford 🚆 Deptford High Street 🚲 NCN4, C4, link to NCN21, C10 🚶 Jubilee Greenway, Thames Path, link to Waterlink Way

An era ended in December 2016 when Eileen and Charlie Gallagher retired as licensees of the pub they'd turned into one of the very best in London since taking it on in 1988. It was a particularly noteworthy achievement given the unpromising location in a Deptford backstreet near the river, once bustling with commercial wharves but now quietly residential. Thankfully, the new tenants have built on that foundation, giving the old place a lick of bright red paint and freshening up the homely interior but maintaining the policy of serving great beer in a proper community pub. Cask guests in a range of styles roam far and wide but retain a local slant, with Brockley and beers from Kent like Larkins and Old Dairy often on. Brockley also has a keg line beside guests from the likes of Iron Pier, Park and Siren. The mainly Belgian bottle range has been maintained and

expanded, with top choices like Oud Beersel and St Bernardus. The wholesome pub grub has moved up a gear and might include salmon and haddock fishcakes, hunter's chicken or falafel and spinach burger. The annual pickles festival in late autumn must be unique in the capital.

Visitor note. Opened in 1823 and rebuilt in the late 1860s, the Dog once belonged to the now-closed Wenlock brewery of Islington, later passing to Bass and briefly to Fuller's in the late 1970s. Its unique name may derive from Dock Street, the old name of Prince Street. Convoys Wharf opposite is the site of the first and most significant of London's Royal Naval Dockyards, founded by Henry VIII in 1513. Most of its historic structures are lost but what remains may become easier to appreciate when the derelict site undergoes a long-delayed and controversial redevelopment over the next few years.

Forest Road Brewing Co 🟢38
Brewery, taproom
1A Elizabeth Industrial Estate, Juno Way SE14 5RW (Lewisham)
T (020) 7249 7033   forestroad.co.uk
First sold beer: September 2021 (at own site) 💈
⏲ *Fr* 16.00-22.00, *Sa-Su* 12.00-22.00. Children until 18.00. Cash-free.
8-10 keg, 5+ bottles/cans, keg rentals. 🍶
🍴 Rotating food truck, 🪑 Tables at front, ♿ (planned – please check).
Tastings, live music, DJs, arcade games

🚃 South Bermondsey 🚆 Surrey Canal Road, Grinstead Road 🚲 C10, link to NCN425

Pete Brown (not to be confused with the like-named beer writer), originally from Massachusetts, worked at Siren and Camden Town before launching his own brand in February 2016, named after the Hackney street where he was then living. The path from cuckoo brewing in Belgium and northern England to owning his own kit proved unusually tortuous – three potential sites fell through, the last when a second-hand brewhouse bought from Russian River in Santa Rosa, California, was already on the ship through the Panama Canal. Lockdown then struck and the build on the current site was beset by flooring and utilities problems and a distributor going into administration. Thanks in part to investment from a friendly diner owner back home, everything should be up and running under head brewer

James Garstang by the time you read this, and on a substantial scale, with the 60hl brewhouse joined by a kegging line from Austrian brewery Schloss Eggenberg. The site, just off the southern end of the Bermondsey 'mile' in a characterful early Edwardian industrial building, includes a decent-sized taproom with an old van suspended above the bar and other intriguing bric-a-brac. The longstanding taproom near London Fields continues to operate (p135).

Visitor note. Dating from 1901, the building was part of a complex originally housing the Mazawattee Tea Company, sited to take advantage of the Grand Surrey Canal which until the 1960s flowed along what's now Surrey Canal Road. Several relics are on display, including the bricks of the back bar which were recycled from masonry found on site.

BEERS in keg, bottle and can are in contemporary easy-drinking style. Core brands include **Ride** session pale ale (4%); best-selling **Posh** lager (4.1%); and the latest iteration of the inaugural beer, the West Coast-leaning IPA **Work** (5.4%).

Greenwich Brewery
See Up the Creek

Ignition Brewery
Brewery, taproom
44A Sydenham Road SE26 5QF (Lewisham)
ignition.beer
First sold beer: May 2017, 🍴
🕐 *Th* 17.00-21.00, *Fr* 17.00-22.00, *Sa* 14.00-22.00, (may change: check social media). Children until 20.00. Cash-free.
5 keg, 3 bottles.
🍴 Snacks, 🪑 A few tables at front, ♿
Art exhibitions, occasional live music, community events, functions

🚆 ⊖ Sydenham   🚶 Link to Green Chain Walk

Not just a brewery, this is a social enterprise employing and training people with learning disabilities, founded by economist Nick O'Shea, an energetic and passionate man who has also been heavily involved with human rights charity Liberty. The 4hl kit began its career at short-lived brewpub the Botanist on Kew Green, then saw service at Brewhouse and Kitchen

Islington before being donated to the project. It's installed in the back room of a 1960s council community centre. The main room at the front, as well as hosting everything from yoga and pilates to art exhibitions, serves as an unusual and very welcoming taproom, with a colourful mural and picture windows under eye-catching exterior mosaics as well as the full range of house beers.

BEERS are all keg- and bottle-conditioned, with regulars including contemporary pale ale **South of the River*** (4.2%) and **Jump Start IPA** (4.6%), plus changing specials including an annual collaboration with local hop growing collective Palace Pints.

Joyce/Salthouse Bottles

Joyce *Bar*: 294 Brockley Road SE4 2RA
joycebrockley.com
🕐 *Tu-Th* 16.00-23.00, *Fr* 16.00-24.00, *Sa* 12.00-24.00, *Su* 12.00-23.00. Children welcome. Cash-free.
7 keg, 4 bottles/cans, growlers, natural wines, some specialist cider and spirits.
🍴 Pork pies, cheese, snacks **£**, 🪑 Front terrace, ♿ Planned, please check
Occasional tastings, natural wine club, book club

🚆 Crofton Park

Salthouse Bottles *Shop*:
12 Coulgate Street SE4 2RW
T (020) 8691 1578   salthousebottles.com
🕐 *Tu-Sa* 10.00-21.00, *Su* 11.00-17.00. Cash-free.
200+ bottles/cans, natural wines.
Occasional tastings, wine club

🚆 ⊖ Brockley   🚶 Link to Green Chain Walk

Richard Salthouse opened a small but smart bottle shop in an oddly wedge-shaped site near Brockley station in September 2016, adding an inviting bar two bus stops away late in 2019. The latter, bigger than it looks from outside but still pleasantly intimate and with a sunny terrace, is named Joyce after Richard's grandmother. You'll find photos of her on the wall in a delightful corner with armchairs, a fireplace and a plaque recalling the building's former function as a funeral parlour. The draught range here is mainly from locals like Anspach & Hobday, the Kernel, Macintosh and Villages: there's always a lager, a table beer and a bitter, and though the last is on keg, it's on a special line avoiding the cooler so is served at cellar temperature. Drinks are complemented by quality gourmet grazing options like sardines or marinated soft cheese served with sourdough bread. Bottles and cans here are limited to gluten-free, low alcohol and special sharers, but there are many more at the shop, with a particularly good showing for rare big bottles from people like Brekeriet, De Cam, Fantôme, Jester King and Little Earth. There's a local delivery service too.

Little Faith 41

Beer firm, taproom
Artworks Creekside, 3 Creekside SE8 4SA
T (020) 8692 7612   littlefaithbeer.com
🕐 *We:* please check. *Th* 17.00-23.00, *Fr* 17.00-
    23.00, *Sa* 13.00-23.00, *Su* 11.00-18.00.
    Children until 21.00.
12 keg, 20 bottles/cans, growlers.
🍴 Indian-inspired street food **£-££**,
🌳 Large nearby courtyard, ♿
Tastings, live music, comedy, table football, board games

🚇 Deftford Bridge   🚲 NCN21, link to C10   🚶 Waterlink Way

A little smarter and bigger than the average post-industrial taproom and with sturdier wooden furniture, this is the home of Little Faith beer, a side project of Kernel and ex-Beavertown brewer Alex Woods. He plans to open his own London brewery eventually, but for the moment, the house beers poured from the black-tiled back bar are made elsewhere. Almost exclusively sold here, they include some admirable examples of contemporary styles. The leafy outdoor courtyard is shared with the Bread and Butler sourdough bakery and JerkOff BBQ and operates as a café during the day.

Little Faith

Visitor note: *Creekside runs parallel to Deptford Creek, the tidal section of the River Ravensbourne where it joins the Thames: it's home to numerous other creative and specialist businesses, as well as the Laban conservatoire and environmental project the Creekside Discovery Centre.*

London Beer Dispensary 42

Bar
389 Brockley Road SE4 2PH
T (020) 8692 1550   southeybrewing.co.uk
🕐 *Mo-Th* 12.00-23.00, *Fr-Sa* 12.00-24.00,
    Su 12.00-22.30. Children until 20.00.
3 cask, 6 keg, 40 bottles/cans, 1 cider.
🍴 Burgers, wraps **£-££**, 🌳 Rear patio
Tastings, quizzes, board games

🚆 Crofton Park   🚲 Link to C35   🚶 Link to Green Chain Walk

Graham Lawrence's longstanding Crofton Park wine bar and bottle shop Mr Lawrence was already a beer-friendly destination, earning it a listing in the first edition of this book. One side was then recast as the original London Beer Dispensary following Graham's involvement in the Late Knights brewery. That company is no more, and the wine bar has closed, but little has changed at the Dispensary except that there's now a proper bar counter and the house beers are from LK's successor Southey. With its wood panelling, tiles and rear snug equipped with sofas and a stuffed stag's head, the place has an old-fashioned feel though the range is bang up-to-date. Draught guests might be from Bad Seed, Five Points, Fyne, Thornbridge or Wiper & True. Bottles and cans are particularly well-chosen with treats like Burning Sky Stock Ale alongside Behemoth from New Zealand, First Chop, Marble and Orval.

Long Pond ㊶

Micropub

110 Westmount Road SE9 1UT

T (020) 8331 6767

thelongpond.co.uk

🕐 *Mo* 17.00-22.00, *Tu-We* 11.30-14.30, 17.00-22.00,
Th-Fr 11.30-14.30, 17.00-23.00, *Sa* 11.00-15.00,
18.30-23.00, *Su* 12.00-14.30.

6 cask, 5 ciders.

🍴 Ploughmans, cheese and meat platters **£-££**,
♿

Acoustic music, quizzes, trips for regulars

≋ Eltham   🚌 Eltham Park Gardens   🚲 C10
🚶 Link to Capital Ring, Green Chain Walk

A former plumbers' merchant became London's
fourth micropub in mid-December 2014 thanks
to ex-money broker Mike Wren. It's a friendly,
chatty place that's just a little bigger than
average, with a plain but comfortable main
drinking area of the half-panelled and high
stools variety, collections of framed music-
themed beermats and a partitioned snug with
tables and chairs. Eltham hasn't been in Kent
since 1889 but the sourcing policy displays
regional loyalties, with a house beer supplied by
Tonbridge brewery and guests from the likes
of Bexley, Goachers, Hop Fuzz, Musket and Old
Dairy. The range always encompasses traditional bitters and dark options, poured directly
from cask in a cool room behind the bar.
Minikegs are available for local delivery.

Visitor note. *Named after a landmark in nearby Eltham
Park South, this was the first pub ever in the Eltham Park
estate, thanks to the covenants preventing alcohol sales
placed on the properties by the Scottish teetotaller who
built them in the early 20th century.*

Long Pond

Meantime Brewing ㊹

Brewery, taproom (Asahi)

1 Lawrence Trading Estate, Blackwall Lane
SE10 0AR (Greenwich)

T (020) 8293 1111   meantimebrewing.com

First sold beer: April 2000, 🍴

Taproom: 🕐 *Tu-Th* 15.00-21.00, *Fr-Sa* 12.00-21.00.
Children until 20.00.

2 tank, 9 keg, 8 bottles/cans. ⌖

🍴 Burgers, small plates **£-££**, 🌳Terrace on
street, side yard at weekends, ♿

Tastings, food matching, beer launches

Shop: 🕐 *Tu-Sa* 12.00-21.00.

10+ bottles/cans, growlers, glasses, merchandise.

≋ Westcombe Park   🚌 Tunnel Avenue   🚲 NCN1
🚶 Link to Thames Path

Meantime's comfortable taproom, its hexagonal floor echoing the wet floor in the brewery
itself, serves up simple but well-cooked food
alongside beers which include limited editions.
The adjoining shop has London's first public
walk-in fridge. Entertaining and informative
tours include a tasting session amid exhibits
from the Michael Jackson Collection in the
seminar room next to the main brewhouse.
Sadly, during the 2020 lockdown the brewery
decided to sell its longstanding showcase pub
the Greenwich Union (on Royal Hill close to
Greenwich town centre) to Young's, which
already owns the popular Richard I next door.
For more about London's second oldest continuously operating brewery, see panel below.

BEERS are in tank, keg, bottle and can: the
bottles are filled on site but canned beer,
though brewed in Greenwich, is packaged at
Grolsch in the Netherlands. The tank beer is
Kellerfresh Tank Lager* (formerly Brewery
Fresh Lager, 4.5%), known as London Lager in
other formats. Other core beers in keg and can
or bottle, tagged 'Full-Time' by the brewery,
include US-style red ale **Yakima Red** (4.1%);
Anytime Session IPA (4.7%); **Chocolate
Porter** (6.5%); and English-style **London
IPA**** (7.4%). Quarterly seasonals form the
'Part-Time' series, while 'Off-the-Clock' small
batch specials, often in experimental styles,
have included collaborations with Record
Store Day and the Greenwich Royal
Observatory and a beer to mark the autumn
clock change back to GMT. Let's hope the

long-overdue anniversary brew of the first Meantime beer, Vienna Lager **Union*** (4.9%) in 2019 will be repeated.

Old Kent Road Brewery

Brewery, no visitors please
Catford SE6 (Lewisham)
instagram.com/oldkentrdbrewery
First sold beer: December 2019

Will O'Neale and David Clack's beers inspired by the history of the Old Kent Road first appeared early in 2016, cuckoo brewed at Ubrew and, later, various other facilities. They're now working from their own 50 litre installation at a private address some way south of the like-named road, though some longer runs are still outsourced. All brewing takes place outside, so this is likely London's only weather-dependent brewery.

BEERS (not tasted) include contemporary keg-conditioned pale ales and wild and mixed fermentation beers in 750ml bottles, one of which used grapes grown on site.

Park Fever 46

Bar, shop
21A Staplehurst Road SE13 5ND (Lewisham)
T 07775 841270   **parkfever.co.uk**
🕐 *Mo-Tu* 16.00-20.00, *We-Fr* 13.00-21.00, *Sa* 11.00-21.00, *Su* 12.00-18.00. Children welcome.
200 bottles/cans.
🍴 Specialist chocolate and snacks **£**,
🪑 A few tables on street, ♿ Flat access only
Tastings, book club, board games, functions

🚆 Hither Green

In food matching terms, beer has a particular affinity with chocolate, so the concept behind this little place in a pretty shopping parade near Hither Green station makes a lot of sense. Opened in March 2017 by Adrian Varley, who previously worked for chocolatier Paul A Young, it offers a shelf or two of handmade chocolate bars from small artisanal producers and rather more shelves of beer, mainly from London and UK independents – Bohem, Brick, Kernel, Little Earth, Polly's, Villages – with a small handful of Belgians and Germans. Everything

is available to drink in as well as take away, among soothing surroundings in pastel colours and fittings made from OSB board. It's become a popular community hangout – appropriately, as Adrian's first thought was to open a pub.

Plum Tree 47

Micropub, planned brewpub
154 Plumstead Common Road SE18 2UL (Greenwich)
facebook.com/theplumtreebeershop
🕐 *Tu-Th* 15.00-21.00, *Fr-Sa* 14.00-22.00, *Su* 14.00-20.30. Children very welcome.
3-4 cask, 5 kegs, 30 bottles/cans, 4 ciders/perries, local spirits, a few wines.
Beer events, occasional acoustic music, board games

🚆 Plumstead   🚌 Plumstead Common The Ship   🚶 Green Chain Walk

Garrulous Nick Turner opened this welcoming Plumstead bar in July 2019 out of frustration with the existing beer options in the London neighbourhood where he'd always lived. Occupying a former builder's merchant that had been derelict for years, it's nominally a micropub with casks on stillage, containing a range of styles from brewers like Brew Buddies, Clouded Minds and Hawkshead, but pushes the format further than most. There are good kegs, some from less frequently seen breweries like Liquid Light and Manual, and a bottle and can range including top London names like Anspach & Hobday, Brick, ORA and Small Beer. These may soon be joined by house beers once a planned brewhouse at the back is online. The relatively compact interior, all

self-built, combines bold yellow and dark blue with polished wood finishes, including a solid oak bar top: 'Unfortunately, plum trees are too thin,' apologises Nick.

River Ale House

Micropub
131 Woolwich Road SE10 0RJ
T 07963 127595
theriveralehouse.com
⊕ *Mo-Th* 16.00-23.00, *Fr-Sa* 12.00-23.00,
  Su 13.00-23.00. Children until 18.00.
6-10 cask, 24 bottles/cans, growlers, cider,
  some gin.
⫴ Filled rolls, pickled eggs, snacks **£**,
⟐ Ambulant toilet
Tastings, organised trips, board games

⇌ Westcombe Park 🚌 Marlton Street ⌾ Link to C14

Trevor Puddifoot went from brassières to *brasseries* in the original sense when he converted the offices of his lingerie business into this impressive micropub in September 2017. In recycled wood and bare brick, with a Greenwich Observatory-style 24-hour clock on the wall, it's a little bigger than it seems, with a proper bar counter and extra space at the back. Casks often includes rare examples from Anspach & Hobday, alongside Redemption, Southwark and less familiar names from outside London like 360 Degree, Framework, Nene Valley and Phipps. Harviestoun, St Bernardus and Westerham are among the varied selection in the fridges, and a regularly updated list of all the beers on sale, complete with tasting notes, is particularly welcome. The site in east Greenwich, on the way to Charlton, isn't *that* close to the river, but it's a beacon in an area otherwise bereft of good beer options.

Royal Albert

Contemporary pub
460 New Cross Road SE14 6TJ
T (020) 8692 3737 royalalbertpub.co.uk
⊕ *Su-Th* 12.00-23.00, *Fr-Sa* 12.00-01.00.
7 cask, 5 keg, 14 bottles/cans, some wines and
  specialist spirits.
⫴ Gastroish menu, cooked bar snacks **£-££**,
⊞ Front terrace, ⟐
*Beer festival, quiz (Mo), live music (Su), bar billiards,
board games*

⇌ New Cross ⬤ New Cross, Deptford Bridge
⌾ Link to NCN21 🚶 Link to Waterlink Way

This medium-sized roadside pub spent years hiding much of its Victorian splendour under the guise of a music venue. In 2007, then-fledgling pubco Antic jettisoned the entertainment but restored much else, including its original name, some chunky carved wood and a splendid skylight. More recently, a delightful art nouveau-styled 'secret room' has been added at the back. The pub, taken over by Portobello late in 2020, still celebrates the day it doubled its handpump count with its Octopump festival in September; for the rest of the year, expect well-kept beers from the owning brewery and guests from By the Horns, Southwark and Norfolk's Woodforde among others. Five Points and locals Villages are regularly on keg, with Bristol, Kernel and Wiper & True among the bottles and cans. An imaginative daily changing menu includes small plates like mussels and whitebait, a charcuterie board, asparagus and mushroom pappardelle, hake fillet with samphire or Cumberland sausages.

Rusty Bucket

Contemporary pub
11 Court Yard SE9 5PR
T (020) 3260 1051 therustybucket.pub
⊕ *Mo-Tu* 16.00-22.00, *We-Th* 16.00-23.00, *Fr*
  14.00-24.00, *Sa* 12.00-24.00, *Su* 12.00-22.00.
  Children until 18.00.
3-4 cask, 18 keg, 40+ bottles/cans, 5 ciders.
⫴ Pork pies only **£**, ⊞ A few tables on street, ⟐
*Tutored tastings, meet the brewer, quizzes, live music
(Su), major big screen sport, board games, beer books*

⇌ Eltham 🚌 Eltham Church ⌾ Link to C10
🚶 Link to Capital Ring, Green Chain Walk

'We like to think of it just as a small pub rather than a micropub,' says Stuart Gyles of the venue he opened with Rachel Lagzda in April 2018. Casks fetched from the coldroom include traditional and darker styles from breweries like Kent, Kirkstall, Siren or Wylam: they had a fine best bitter from Beatnikz Republic in Manchester when I last called. Kegs include locals (Bohem, Boxcar, Kernel, Villages), others like Polly's and Tempest and occasional imports, with tasting paddles available. Well-stocked fridges might yield Mikkeller or Northern Monk, with Belgian and German classics and sharing bottles. This neat but comfortable single space with half-panelling and stools fashioned from recycled keykegs was once a bigger pub called the Crown which had a rather less inviting reputation and was eventually closed by the police. The building was gutted and its upper floors converted to flats, but happily space was reserved for what's now one of the best beer venues in southeast London. There's a local delivery service too.

Salthouse Bottles

See Joyce.

Up the Creek 51

Brewpub, bar
302 Creek Road SE10 9SW (Greenwich)
T (020) 8858 4581 **up-the-creek.com**
First sold beer: October 2018
We-Th 17.00-23.00, *Fr* 17.00-02.00,
Sa 13.00-02.00, *Su* 13.00-23.00.
Children until early evening.
3 cask, 5 keg, 1 bottle (mainly UK), growlers.
Burgers **£-££**, A few tables on street,
Comedy in adjoining venue

Greenwich Cutty Sark NCN1, NCN4, NCN21, C4, C10, Jubilee Greenway, Thames Path, Waterlink Way

Perhaps not the most obvious place you'd expect to find an in-house brewery, Greenwich institution Up the Creek is a comedy club in a former church hall, founded by the late comedian Malcolm Hardee in 1991. But the present owner is a keen beer fan, and a neat 4hl brewhouse, clearly visible from the street, has been at work since October 2018, though with some gaps when brewers moved on. The comfortable chalet-like bar, also open to guests without comedy tickets, stocks a few keg and bottled options too, though mainly from Molson Coors subsidiaries.

BEERS (not tasted) are currently nearly all in cask, with small scale hand-bottling, and sold exclusively in house except for the occasional festival. They include a session IPA, **Truth Serum** (3.8%) and a red ale, **The Creek Copper Red** (4.7%). Originally they were branded Greenwich Brewery but now simply carry the club name.

Villages Brewery 52

Brewery, taproom
21 Resolution Way SE8 4NT (Lewisham)
villagesbrewery.com
First sold beer: December 2016
Th 18.00-23.00, *Fr* 17.00-23.00, *Sa* 12.00-23.00, *Su* 14.00-22.00. Children welcome. Cash-free
7 keg, 6 cans.
Occasional weekend food truck, BYO,
Tables in yard,
Quiz (Th), DJs (Sa), folk music (Su), board games

Deptford C10, link to NCN21, C4 Link to Waterlink Way

Currently the only actual brewery in a cluster of beer-friendly venues around Deptford station, Villages occupies two arches, with space extending into a lean-to at the back, under the same historic railway as in Bermondsey but a little further southeast. Its rustic-sounding name refers to the founders, Heriot-Watt-trained brothers Archie and Louis Village. Archie once worked at London Beer Factory and Fourpure, Louis at Gipsy Hill, and the latter brewery helped get the brothers started by selling them its old 25hl Malrex kit, since replaced with a bespoke 15 hl kit. The basic but stylish and relatively spacious taproom in the arch

Villages Brewery

adjacent to the brewhouse is enlivened with banners depicting Deptford scenes.

BEERS are in keg and can. The core range includes **Rafiki** (4.3%) session IPA and **Rodeo** (4.6%) pale ale, plus changing specials including a variety of IPAs and lagers.

Volden Brewing

Brewery, taproom
72 Malham Road SE23 1AG (Lewisham)
volden.co.uk
First sold beer: March 2015, 😃
🕐 To be confirmed

🚆 ⊖ Forest Hill 🚌 Forest Hill Fire Station

The supplier of the Antic pub group's own brands can trace its slightly complex history back to October 2012, when Victoria Barlow and Duncan Woodhead founded Clarence & Fredericks as the second contemporary brewery in Croydon (after Cronx). Meanwhile, the growing pub chain was planning to set up its own brewery in Camberwell, and when that fell through, took over the C&F site with its 16 hl kit as a stopgap when Victoria and Duncan decided to retire in March 2015. Following a break during the 2020 lockdowns, production relocated to the current site during 2021: a taproom may be open by the time you read this. Head brewer Stephen Lawson is a London brewing veteran who worked at the Firkin chain and briefly at the old Pitfield brewery

in the 1980s: he's likely the only 20th century London microbrewer who is still brewing at micro scale in the 21st, though with a gap when he did other jobs before being introduced to Antic at the relaunch event for Truman's in 2010. Pubco founder Anthony Thomas is a fan of vintage vehicles and the brewery name and logo are an homage to the 1950s Vulcan lorry.

BEERS made almost entirely with English ingredients and a house yeast strain are currently in cask only and sold exclusively in the pubs: 'I'm an old-school production brewer,' says Stephen, 'making core session beers of good consistent quality at a reasonable price. There's not much room for experiment with the current setup. My happiness is in seeing people drink and enjoy what I make.' Regulars are **Session** (3.8%), a light amber bitter originally known as Vim, and **Pale Ale** (4.2%), plus seasonals including an autumn/winter **Porter*** (5.2%).

waterintobeer

Shop, bar
2 Mantle Court, 209 Mantle Road SE4 2EW
waterintobeer.co.uk
🕐 *Mo-Tu* 16.00-20.00, *We-Th* 14.00-21.00, *Fr* 14.00-22.00, *Sa* 12.00-22.00, *Su* 12.00-18.00. Children until 20.00.
2 keg, 250 bottles/cans, homebrewing supplies, secondhand records. 🍺
🍴 BYO, 🪑 Tables on street, ♿ Flat access only
Tastings, homebrew club and workshops, quiz, acoustic music, beer books

🚆 ⊖ Brockley 🚶 Link to Green Chain Walk

In contrast to the slick contemporary neon and pine style of most bottle shop-bars, owner Tim Livesey has bestowed his with a homely feel, dotted with old kitchen tables and a generous scattering of breweriana. Combined with a friendly welcome, it encourages lingering to explore a range of mainly independent beers, with around 50 new ones arriving every week. Leodian Tim favours Yorkshire beers on the kegs, perhaps from Abbeydale, Crooked or Ilkley, but the bottles and cans range far and wide: locals like Brockley, Villages and Wrong Side of the Tracks; other UK brewers like Salt;

more traditional options from Coniston, Titanic and various well-established German and Belgian names; and on-trend Europeans like Basqueland. Opened in August 2016 on the western side of the Overground close to Brockley station, it's also a centre of the local homebrewing community, selling ingredients and equipment and hosting a club.

Visitor note. The name wasn't devised for the shop: it was originally given to a punk fanzine Dave and friends ran in Leeds in the early 2000s, and later transferred to a Sunday League football team.

Wrong Side of the Tracks 55

Brewery, no visitors please
Hither Green SE6 (Lewisham)
wrongsideofthetracks.beer
First sold beer: August 2019.

Daniel Jackson is a frustrated IT professional and homebrewer, currently working commercially on a small scale using a 1hl kit in a garage on the edge of the Corbett Estate, Hither Green. He's studying brewing science in his spare time with the ambition of upscaling to a bigger brewery with taproom, but likely not for a few years.

BEERS are hand-bottled and in keg. The flagship is modern but not too hoppy **Lewisham Pale Ale*** (LewPA, 5.5%), with varying specials sold through a handful of local outlets.

Zerodegrees Blackheath 56

Brewpub, bar, restaurant
29 Montpelier Vale SE3 0TJ (Lewisham)
T (020) 8852 5619   zerodegrees.co.uk
First sold beer: August 2000
⏰ Su-Th 12.00-24.00, Fr-Sa 12.00-00.30.
    Children in restaurant only.
6-7 tank, minicasks, wines, cocktails..
🍴 Pizzas, mussels, salads, pasta **££-£££**,
⛲ Front and rear terraces, ♿
Tastings, occasional DJs, functions

🚉 Blackheath   🚲 Link to C10

Remarkably, this popular local beer and pizza venue is now the capital's oldest-established independent brewery as well as its longest-

Zerodegrees

serving brewpub. It was one of the first in the UK to draw inspiration from the US craft brewing scene, following a trip across the Atlantic by a member of a family of local restaurateurs. An automated 10hl kit was sourced in Germany and the first beers were devised by a head brewer from the US. The company went on to open further brewpubs in Bristol, Cardiff and Reading, sharing the same name even though, unlike the original, they're considerably further from the prime meridian. Behind an unassuming frontage is a spaceship-like warren of mezzanine floors wrapped around the gleaming brewhouse, all decorated in smart contemporary style. Besides pizzas with unusual toppings like caramelised pear and gorgonzola or Jamaican chicken, the menu expands to mussels, risotto and vegetarian parmigiana.

BEERS rarely travel beyond the premises, which is perhaps why they're often overlooked among London's current proliferation. They're served by air pressure from polythene-lined maturation tanks, with some minikegs and very occasional kegs for special events. Regulars include American pale ale **Downtown** (4.6%); **Beast of Blackheath*** (4.6%) black lager; and pils-style **The Bavarian** (4.8%). Two changing specials are usually on sale: **Tea Party*** (4.2%) English amber ale with tea was an impressive recent example.

TRY ALSO

Beer + Burger O₂ Street Food Market, The O₂, Peninsular Square SE10 0DX beerandburgerstore.com: A welcome refuge from macro lager between the Cineworld and arena entrance E in the massive North Greenwich venue, this brash branch of a lively chain offers 18 varied kegs mainly from interesting London and UK brewers, though in deference to the location there are no stronger beers, bottles or cans.

Berry and Barrel 18 Well Hall Parade SE9 6SP berryandbarrel.com: Micropub just off the main road near Eltham station, bigger and smarter than some with a sizeable rear garden. Up to four casks usually from local and Kent breweries, four 'craft' keg including bigger brands, plus gins, cocktails and locally made pies. Closed Mondays, draught list on Untappd.

Bottle Cave 22 Sydenham Road SE26 5QW bottlecave.co.uk: Longstanding wine shop with an expanding range of over 250 beers, including lots of locals and some imports. Takeaway only.

Clapton Craft SE23 10 Perry Vale SE23 2LD claptoncraft.co.uk: One of the smaller branches in the chain and the only one in south London, reflected by the local representation among five keg lines and 150+ bottles/cans covering a customarily impressive range. Situated on the east side of Forest Hill station. Takeaway only.

Cloud Nine The O₂, Peninsula Square SE10 0DX signalbeerco.com: Another alternative beer option at the O₂, this small bar usually has a cask beer on stillage and four others on keg from operators Signal.

Green Goddess (Common Rioters Beer) 43A Vanburgh Park SE3 7AB commonriotersbeer.co.uk: This brewpub should be open in a former bank building at the Blackheath Standard by the end of 2021. Check website for details: see also Standing by p328.

Hare and Billet 1a Hare and Billet Road SE3 0QJ hareandbillet.com: Well-situated over-looking the pond named after it on Blackheath, this landmark is now a Greene King Metropolitan outlet. At least six well-kept casks include unusual and local options in a range of styles, with a scattering of interesting kegs too.

Hop Burns and Black Deptford Arch 1 Deptford Station, Deptford High Street SE8 4NS hopburnsblack.co.uk: Smaller satellite branch of the outstanding East Dulwich original (p222) in a Deptford station arch close to other good venues. No draught, though 250+ bottles/cans from independents, also sold to drink in, with outside tables on the handsomely redeveloped Market Yard. Card only. Closed Mondays, cash-free.

Park Tavern 45 Passey Place SE9 5DA parktaverneltham.co.uk: Up to eight well-kept casks, sometimes from unusual independents, plus some quality kegs in a handsome former Truman's pub with a civilised, almost tea shop-like interior close to historic Eltham Palace.

Dog and Bell (see p.231)

240

LONDON'S BREWING | Meantime

It's not too fanciful to suggest that Alastair Hook changed the face of British brewing. Back in the early 1990s, he already had a much more international background than the typical aspirant microbrewer. Born in Greenwich, he trained at Heriot-Watt in Edinburgh, but regularly spent summers in California witnessing and modestly assisting in the early days of the craft beer movement. Then he learned German so he could pursue postgraduate studies at the famous Weihenstephan brewing school near Munich. Despite an early love of good real ale, he wasn't about to start brewing best bitters, but in Britain back then there wasn't really a model for much else, and 'quality lager' was almost a contradiction in terms.

In 1991, Alastair became the brewer at a pioneering brewpub, the Packhorse, in Ashford, Kent, specialising in German-style beers. Four years later he was back in London as the major force in the creation of Freedom in Fulham, which turned out to be the first successful UK craft lager brewery, still in operation today, although in Staffordshire under different ownership. He then helped set up two of Britain's earliest US-style upmarket brewpub-restaurants, before launching Meantime in 2000, in Charlton near the Thames Barrier, named for its location near Greenwich and its commitment to properly matured beers.

The brewery originally earned its keep by contract brewing and marketing to restaurants and bars rather than the pub trade, but soon gained confidence to launch its own brands. And ultimately, public tastes caught up with

Alastair's vision. In 2010, he finally achieved his ambition to relocate to Greenwich itself, with an automated 100hl German-built Rolec brewhouse on a new site on the approach to the Blackwall Tunnel not far from the O_2, where the brewery grew to become the second-biggest in London.

The first modern UK-brewed unpasteurised and unfiltered beer for dispense from 1,000 litre tanks, inspired by the Czech model, launched from here in 2013. A new tasting room opened at the front of the site in 2015, next to a 10hl pilot kit visible from the road and a shop with the first walk-in beer fridge in London, with a cluster of nine outdoor 100hl tanks further back. There's also a third brewhouse, a 20 litre homebrew kit used internally for tests and experiments.

Meantime became a pioneer in another, perhaps more problematic, way in May 2015 as the first 21st century London brewery sold to a multinational. Its new owner was US-South African group SABMiller, former employer of the brewery's then-Chief Executive Nick Miller. A round of corporate pass-the-parcel followed as SABMiller was

bought out in turn in October 2016 by the world's biggest brewing group, Anheuser-Busch InBev. To comply with monopoly regulation, ABI sold on the Greenwich business along with Grolsch and Peroni to Asahi, marking the first direct involvement of one of the big Japanese-based groups in the UK industry.

Meantime retains its own identity and management, and Alastair remains involved, though no longer on a day-to-day basis. In 2019, the operation finally occupied two units formerly used as an archive by the National Maritime Museum which had previously separated the tasting room from the main brewery. It's a mark of the respect Alastair commands among beer experts that legendary beer writer Michael Jackson bequeathed his collection of bottles, glasses and breweriana to Meantime: part of this is on display in a sampling room used on the highly rated tastings and tours, and there are plans for a small museum to present it better as the site is reconfigured around the additional floorspace.

Outer Southeast London

Anspach and Hobday 57

Brewery, taproom
11 Valley Point Industrial Estate, Beddington
Farm Road, Croydon CR0 4WP (Sutton)
T (020) 8617 9510 anspachandhobday.com
First sold beer: February 2014 (at original site), 💬
🕐 Please check. Children welcome.
   Check for beers and other facilities.

🚋 Therapia Road   🚲 NCN232

When childhood friends and former musicians
Paul Anspach and Jack Hobday won a homebrew competition, one of the judges, TV pres-
enter and wine writer Oz Clarke, suggested
they turn professional. They were further
encouraged when a homebrew sneakily
entered in a commercial competition won a
medal. Tasting samples were available under
the name Alements in summer 2012 but it
wasn't until March 2014 that Jack and Paul
opened in the Bermondsey arches, restoring
brewing to Druid Street after the Kernel's
relocation. The initial 1hl installation was also
used by Bullfinch in its early days. It was
replaced a few months later with a 4hl PBC kit,
then a new 14hl brewhouse in 2016: its
predecessor was sold to Affinity. With no room
for further expansion in the arch, production
was moved to an industrial unit just across
from Signal (below) in 2019, in Sutton borough
but closer to Croydon by tram, with Drop
Project only two stops away. The existing
brewhouse is still in use, though with much-
increased fermentation capacity and a canning
line. The original site is now a bar and barrel
vault, with fermentation and wood-ageing
space for specials (p207), and the brewery has
a separate pub, the Pigeon (p225).

BEERS are mainly keg and canned, with some
specials hand-bottled in 750ml and a small but
increasing amount of cask. Core beers include
lower alcohol choice **The Table Beer** (2.7%),
The Pale (4.4%), in contemporary style; **The
Cream Ale*** (4.5%), a rare London-brewed
example of the style; **The Lager** (4.7%), in
German style; **The Sour Dry Hop** (4.9%);
The Smoked Brown* (5.5%); and **The IPA**
(6%), in West Coast style. **The Porter**** (6.7%),
the descendant of the original competition
winner, is also available in several variants at
different strengths, like regular **The Stout
Porter*** (8.5%) and **Brother Sean*** (8.4%),
an annual release with Belgian yeast. Various
seasonals, specials and collaborations include
a number in German styles which appear in
the autumn around Oktoberfest: Bavarian-
style **The Wheat Beer** (4%) is sold at other
times too. Others worth looking out for are
casks of **The Ordinary Bitter*** (3.7%), **The
Belgian Pale*** (4%) and **The London ESB**
(5.5%), and a Belgian-style **Patersbier*** (3.9%)
in keg and can, and mixed fermentation
specials emerging from the Bermondsey site.

Art and Craft CR0 58

Bar, shop
46 Surrey Street, Croydon CR0 1RJ
T (020) 8686 3014   artandcraft.london
🕐 *Tu-We* 12.00-22.00, *Th* 12.00-23.00,
   Fr-Sa 12.00-01.00, *Su* 12.00-20.00.
   Children until early evening.
6 keg, 50+ bottles/cans, growlers, a few
   mainly local specialist spirits.
🍴 Snacks, 🪑 Tables at front, side terrace
Acoustic music, DJs

🚆 🚇 West Croydon   🚋 George Street, Church Street

Inkspot is behind a handful of nifty little
outlets combining the functions of bottle shop,
bar and urban art gallery – the last thanks to

brewery partner Bradley Ridge, an art dealer and collector. This Croydon branch, opened in April 2018 in a corner of the old Croydon Advertiser building boarded up for 30 years, is the most bar-like, and a welcome addition to a busy shopping district short on beer choice. Beside a little square with outdoor seating on historic Surrey Street market, the petite split-level interior has banquettes and a pewter-topped bar dispensing house beers alongside constantly changing guests in a range of styles: Londoners like Pressure Drop and Two Tribes and other good UK options like Kirkstall and Marble. There's more of the same among the bottles and cans, which might include Cloudwater, Overtone or Vocation. Artwork, meanwhile, might be by Banksy or Lucus Price.

Bexley Brewery

Brewery, taproom: 18 Manford Industrial Estate, Manor Road, Erith DA8 2AJ (Bexley)
T 01322 337368   bexleybrewery.co.uk
First sold beer: August 2014, **‼**(informal)
🕐 *Sa* 11.00-15.00. Children welcome.
2-3 cask, 10 bottles, growlers, minicasks, bag-in-box, cider.
‼ Special events only, 🍴 Tables at front, ♿ Flat access only
Occasional special events

🚃 Erith   🚌 Slade Green Road Manor Road   🚲 NCN1
🚶 London Loop

Bird and Barrel 59a

Micropub: 100 Barnehurst Road, Bexleyheath DA7 6HG
🕐 *Fr-Sa* 14.00-22.00, *Su* 14.00-18.00. Children until 19.00.
3 cask, 3 keg, 20+ bottles/cans, growlers, minicasks, ciders, some specialist spirits.
‼ Sausage rolls *(Sa)*, 🍴 Garden at rear ♨
Tastings, beer festivals, occasional quiz

🚃 Barnehurst

On an industrial estate beside the River Thames, by Crayford Marshes on the edge of Erith, this is the first standalone brewery in Bexley since Reffell's was closed by Courage in 1956. It's run by former IT manager Cliff Murphy, his wife Jane, once a teacher, and their son Cameron. The local focus is evident from the logo depicting a ring-necked parakeet: there are now feral colonies of these exotic birds all over London but they were first noted in Bexley. The unit is the smallest suitable and affordable space the founders could find, and though fermentation capacity has been expanded several times, it's still less cramped than many. All bittering hops are from Hukins in Tenterden, Kent, though some aroma hops are imported. The Murphys always planned a micropub and in April 2018 opened the Bird and Barrel not far away, in a former tropical fish shop close to Barnehurst station. The parakeets pop up here too on a mural of a tree which overlooks a small space furnished with pews and tables. Besides a good range of house beers, there are guests from other small breweries and some bottled Belgian classics. The sheltered garden is a treat, particularly when in full bloom.

BEERS are in cask, still accounting for 80% of sales, with some keg and bottle-conditioned. Core beers include English-style golden ale **Golden Acre** (4%); flagship best-selling best bitter **Bexley's Own Beer** (BOB, 4.2%), originally developed by Cliff in his homebrewing days; **Red House*** (4.2%) ruby ale; porter **Black Prince*** (4.6%); and US-influenced IPA **Anchor Bay** (4.8%). Seasonals and specials include the **Howbury** range of one-off experimental beers, a wet hop beer made with Hukins hops and a winter beer, **Crook Log** (5.3%).

Br3wery 60

Brewpub, bar
253 Beckenham Road, Beckenham BR3 4RP
(Bromley)   br3wery.com
First sold beer: February 2019 (at original site).
🍴 (informal)
🕐 *Mo-Fr* 16.00-21.00, *Sa* 14.00-21.00, *Su* 14.00-
   18.00. Children welcome. Cash-free.
8 keg, growlers
🍴 BYO (numerous takeaways nearby),
🪑 Tables on street.
Tastings

🚋 Clock House   🚌 Beckenham Road   🚲 NCN21
🚶 Waterlink Way, link to Capital Ring, Green Chain Walk

You can't get much more up close and personal
with a London brewery than at this little brewpub right by Beckenham Road tram stop: the
indoor seating is in arm's reach of an 8.5hl
Hoplex brewhouse shoehorned into a small
shop unit and you can relax to the gentle
bubbling of carbon dioxide from a fermenter
as you sip your pint. Founder Cadú Gomes
began on an even smaller scale at his nearby
home, creating the current site during the
2020 lockdowns and opening in December.
Besides a couple of house beers, the small bar
dispenses guests from local friends like Brick,
Bullfinch, Canopy and Gipsy Hill. A canopy-
covered pavement terrace provides welcome
additional seating. The brand stresses the local
focus by punning on the Beckenham postcode.

BEERS are mainly changing specials, currently
in keg only, sold from the taproom and
through selected local outlets. Pale ale **XPA**
(4%) regularly recurs; when I called, there was
an unusual **BEL Belgian Lager*** (4.2%), with
a black cherry sour and a Bavarian wheat beer
in the fermenters.

Br3wery

Broken Drum 61

Brewpub, micropub
308 Westwood Lane, Sidcup DA15 9PT (Bexley)
thebrokendrum.co.uk
First sold beer: October 2018
🕐 *Mo-Fr* 15.00-22.00, *Sa* 12.00-22.00,
   Su 13.00-16.00. Children until 20.00.
3 cask, 2 ciders/perries.
🍴 Scotch eggs, sausage rolls, pork pies **£**,
🪑 Benches at front
*Cheese and whisky nights, beer tours, occasional
quizzes, board games*

🚋 Welling   🚌 Westwood Lane

Former ICT professional and CAMRA volunteer
Andy Wheeler tapped the first cask in this
former nail bar at Blackfen in April 2015,
between Welling and Sidcup in the shadow of
the A2 Rochester Way flyover. It's a simple,
smallish space furnished with plain but neat
and clean tables and chairs, with the obligatory
cooled stillage at the back and quiet policy. In
2018, Andy began brewing commercially at his
home in Belvedere, not far away, on a small
scale using a 2hl kit, so you might well find
one of his beers, alongside some from local
and Kent breweries like Bexley, Canterbury,
Tonbridge or Wantsum, or from further afield
like Salopian or Titanic. There's only room
for three at once, though they'll vary in style
and strength.

Visitor note. *The pub is named after a fictional one in
Ankh-Morpork, the city created by the late fantasy author
Terry Pratchett for his* Discworld *cycle of novels.*

BEERS (not tasted) are almost entirely sold
from cask in the pub.

Cockpit 62

Micropub
4 Royal Parade, Chislehurst BR7 6NR
facebook.com/cockpitchislehurst
🕐 *Su-Th* 12.00-21.30, *Fr-Sa* 12.00-22.00.
   Children welcome.
6 cask, 20+ cans, growlers, cider, gins.
🍴 Cheese boards, pork pies, scotch eggs,
🪑 Front terrace 🐾
Tap takeovers, monthly quiz

🚋 Chislehurst   🚌 Chislehurst War Memorial   🚶 Green
Chain Walk

Cockpit

Like most micropubs, this operation, opened in December 2020, is in a former shop unit – the difference is that the previous occupant, a florist, has downsized rather than moved out. Her floral displays at the front and dazzling planters around the outdoor terrace, coupled with the setting on a handsome parade right by Chislehurst common, make this a picturesque as well as a friendly place to drink. The section with chairs and tables by the flower counter is almost like a tea shop; up a step at the back are stools and a pleasantly woody bar area decorated with vintage photos. Co-owner Paul Steadman presides over the cask range, dispensed from a rear stillage: there's a house beer from Brithop and guests in a range of styles, including a best bitter and a porter, from local and Kent breweries like Bexley, Iron Pier or Mutineers, or from further afield like Moor, supplemented by a changing range of cans from smaller and often rare UK outlets. Simple food like pies and scotch eggs is beautifully presented on boards with homemade coleslaw.

Visitor note. When looking for the Cockpit using online mapping, make sure you're heading for the pub, not the remains of a genuine historic cockpit on the village green nearby, which may date from the mediaeval period.

Craft Beer Cabin

Shop, bar
210A Selhurst Road SE25 6XU (Croydon)
craftbeercab.com
🕐 *Mo-Tu* 17.00-22.00, *We-Su* 12.00-22.00.
   Children welcome. Cash-free
5 keg, 50+ bottles/cans, some natural wines,
   specialist gins.
🍴 Sausage rolls, 🪑 A few tables on street
Occasional food and beer matching, beer launches

⇌ ⊖ Norwood Junction

This former bric-a-brac shop on a shopping street in South Norwood became a stationary home for Craft Beer Cab, a mobile bar in an adapted black taxi, in August 2018. Owner Nick Thomas has a hand in cuckoo brewery Roaring Four, so you'll likely find its beers on sale beside kegs in a range of styles from the likes of Burnt Mill, Deya or Gipsy Hill. Bottles and cans are of similar repute, mainly British but with occasional imports like Oedipus from the Netherlands. Functioning equally well as bottle shop and bar, the place is small but comfortable and well-designed, with a bit more space up a few steps in an elegant room complete with pot plants and pictures.

Craft Metropolis ⑥⑷

Bar, shop
47 High Street SE20 7HW
T (020) 8659 2678   craftmetropolis.co.uk
🕐 Tu-Fr 16.00-22.00, Sa 12.00-23.00, Su 12.00-18.00. Children welcome.
10 keg, 300-350 bottles/cans, gift boxes, specialist and natural wines, rum. 🖰
🍴 BYO (numerous takeaways nearby)
Beer tastings and launches.

🚆 Penge West, Penge East   ⊖ Penge West   🚶 Capital Ring, Green Chain Walk

Former ITV producer Oli Meade first turned his passion for beer into a profession with a mail order and subscription box business focusing on London brewers, followed by this neat shop and bar in Penge, opened in December 2019. It's a smallish but atmospheric place with black walls, high tables and stools. Knowledgeable staff will steer you through a range that still features plenty of Londoners, including smaller outfits like Dogs Grandad, Jeffersons and Three Hills, as well as other UK producers like Deya, Utopian and Vault City and interesting imports from Europe and the USA, like Equilibrium and Sloop. Draughts cover a good range, usually including stronger and darker options. Bottles and cans are mainly in fridges but look above these to find an impressive parade of wild and mixed fermentation beers from producers like the UK's Little Earth Project and Pastore or Grimm from New York City. A second bar and shop at the company's warehouse in Battersea is planned by 2022.

Cronx Brewery (The) ⑥⑸

Brewery: 6 Vulcan Business Centre, Vulcan Way, New Addington, Croydon CR0 9UG (Croydon)
T (020) 3475 8848   thecronx.com
First sold beer: August 2012
🕐 Mo-Fr 09.00-15.00 for pre-arranged takeaway
10+ bottles/cans, gift packs, minikegs, bag-in-box. 🖰

🚍 Addiscombe   🚌 Vulcan Way   🚲 Link to NCN21

Cronx Bar ⑥⑸a

Bar: RO3-04 Boxpark Croydon, 99 George Street, Croydon CR0 1LD
T (020) 8688 4912
🕐 Mo-Sa 12.00-23.00, Su 12.00-22.00. Children until 19.00.
4-5 cask, 9 keg, 15 bottles/cans, gift packs, 5 ciders/perries, some local gins.
🍴 Various from neighbouring traders £-££,
🌳 Terrace in boxpark, ♿ (in boxpark)
Occasional meet the brewer, live music, quiz

🚆 ⊖ East Croydon   🚲 Links to NCN212, NCN232
🚶 Vanguard Way

Drinks wholesaler Mark Russell and City worker-turned-brewer Simon Dale founded the Cronx as the first standalone brewery in Croydon since Page and Overton closed in 1954, operating from a 20hl plant in an industrial estate in New Addington. Fermentation capacity has increased several times and Simon has moved on, but Mark remains as managing director. The name jokingly blends the name of an equally outlying New York City borough with Croydon's postcode. Though there's no regular onsite taproom, the Cronx became one of the first businesses to open at the Boxpark next door to East Croydon station in October 2016. The brewery bar is a particularly neat conversion of a shipping container with light fittings made from old T-bar tap mounts, more seating than you might expect and a cartoon mural of the brewing process. Besides a comprehensive range of house beers, including Entire Porter on both cask and nitrokeg, it stocks London and other UK guests like Hammerton, Pig and Porter and Redemption.

BEERS are mainly keg, alongside cask, cans and bottles. The core range includes the recently introduced **Lockdown Lager**

(4.2%); **Nektar** (4.5%) pale ale; IPA **Pop Up!** (5%), with a mix of New Zealand and US hops; and **Entire*** (5.2%) porter. There's a changing range of specials, usually in keg and can.

Green Dragon

Contemporary pub
58 High Street, Croydon CR0 1NA
T (020) 8667 0684
craft-pubs.co.uk
🕐 *Mo-We* 11.00-23.00, *Th* 11.00-24.00, *Fr-Sa* 11.00-01.00, *Su* 12.00-23.00. Children until 20.00.
8 cask, 9 keg, 14 bottles/cans, 6 ciders/perries, 50 gins.
🍴 Breakfasts, pizzas, burgers, enhanced pub grub ££, ♿
Quiz (Mo), poker (Tu), games night (We), open mic (Th), DJs (Sa-Su), occasional live music, food promotions, book swap, pool, board games, functions

🚆 East Croydon, West Croydon ⊖ West Croydon
🚌 George Street 🚶 Links to Vanguard Way, Wandle Trail

Afforded exceptional freedom by its owning pubco Stonegate, this big central Croydon pub has long combined a strong beer offer with a lively, youthful vibe. Casks might be from East London, Elgoods, Gloucester or Southwark, all with a 'specimen jar' display for colour. Besides more familiar brands like BrewDog and Tiny Rebel among the keg, bottle and can selection is local Signal plus rarer entries from the likes of Anarchy, Angels and Demons and Mad Squirrel. A comprehensive menu starts with breakfast, moving on to sandwiches and pub grub like cheese and potato pie, fish and chips and lemon and herb chicken.

Green Dragon

Hackney Carriage

Micropub
165 Station Road, Sidcup DA15 7AA
T (020) 3637 9096
thehackneycarriagemicropub.com
🕐 *Mo-Th* 15.00-22.00, *Fr-Sa* 12.00-23.00, *Su* 12.00-20.00. Children until 20.00.
6-10 cask, 4 keg, 3 cans, up to 20 ciders/perries, gins.
🍴 BYO, 🪑 Tables at front, ♿ Flat access only
Occasional meet the brewer, quiz and live music, board games

🚆 Sidcup

This micropub of character opened in a former school uniform shop a short walk from Sidcup station in August 2016. Wide front windows illuminate a space equipped with high tables and benches. Cask beers fetched from the coldroom behind the zinc-topped bar often include locals and unusual names: Arbor, Bad Seed, Gyle 59, Parkway, Twickenham or XT might be represented. Beerblefish supplies a house brew, with a keg lager from Westerham and a few local cans. The range is given an extra twist on Strong Beer Thursdays when the 6%+ options hit the bar. Owner Liz Twort's husband is a black cab driver, thus the name.

Hoppers Hut  ⑱

Micropub

1 Invicta Parade, High Street, Sidcup DA14 6ER

hoppershut.weebly.com

🕓 *Mo-We* 14.00-22.00, *Th* 14.00-23.00, *Fr-Sa* 12.00-23.00, *Su* 12.00-20.00. Children welcome.

4-5 cask, 9 keg, 4 bottles, 20 ciders/perries, 60+ gins, other specialist spirits.

🍴 Lunch from local tearoom, cheese and charcuterie platters **£-££**

Tap takeovers/tastings, quiz (Tu), afternoon teas, live music, vinyl night, seasonal events, board games

🚆 Sidcup　🚌 Church Road　🏃 Link to London Loop

This micropub in a former fancy dress shop was originally linked to Brew Buddies brewery in Swanley, Kent: the founders have since relocated to France, which explains the intriguing presence of bottles from P'tit Brasseur d'Argentonnay in Nouvelle-Aquitaine on Sidcup's main shopping street. Casks and kegs, dispensed from the back bar, are mainly sourced from contemporary-leaning UK brewers, including locals: Arbor, BBNo, Howling Hops, Kernel, North and Vibrant Forest are often favoured with repeat orders. An attractive interior in bold deep green and red, with art posters and plenty of cushions, creates a comfortable experience. The rural surroundings which persisted here until the late 19th century included hop gardens, thus the name.

Kentish Belle ⑲

Micropub

8 Pickford Lane, Bexleyheath DA7 4QW

thekentishbelle.co.uk

🕓 *Mo-We* 16.00-22.00, *Th-Sa* 12.00-23.00, *Su* 12.00-20.00. Children until 19.00.

4-12 cask, 70+ bottles/cans, 12 ciders, gins, whiskies.

🪑 Tables at front (weekends only)

Tap takeovers, beer festivals, monthly quiz, charity events, board games

🚆 Bexleyheath

Much thought has gone into both the appearance and the range of this excellent 'micropub plus' close to Bexleyheath station. The décor

behind the unassuming shopfront is a modern twist on Arts and Crafts style, with proper tables and hand-made walnut banquettes. The expertly marshalled cask choice can reach a dozen on a good day, often including Beerblefish, Bexley, Brightside, Five Points, Tiny Rebel and Tonbridge, in a truly eclectic range of styles with stronger and flavoured options. Cask beer is sold in thirds if required, and nothing is left on for longer than 72 hours. Then there's the excellent bottle and can list, which boasts admired names like Burnt Mill, Buxton, Deya, Moor and Partizan with good Belgians (Tilquin, Rodenbach) and some other interesting imports (Garage, Half Acre). Since opening in March 2018, the Belle has quickly established itself as a must-visit.

Visitor note *Owner Nick Hair is a former train driver, which explains the name, borrowed from a luxury Pullman train running between London Victoria and Ramsgate in the 1950s. The distinctive William Morris wallpaper recalls the designer himself, who built the Red House nearby for his family in 1860: it's now a National Trust property with limited opening.*

Marlix Brewing Co ⑳

Brewery, visits by appointment only

Petts Wood BR5

marlix.co.uk

First sold beer: December 2020.　🍴 Informal

🕓 By appointment

🚆 Petts Wood　🚌 St Johns Road St Georges Road

Old friends Mark Irwin and Alex Mears had been homebrewing together for 20 years before starting this part-time, home-based brewery, currently in action once a month at the weekend. 'We are very happy to have people come and watch,' they say, 'but realise it might be a bit boring.'

BEERS (not tasted) in small batches vary in style: they've included a Christmas ale and vanilla milkshake porter **SPG** (4.2%).

Mutineers Brewery ㉑

Brewery, no visitors please

Bromley BR1 (Bromley)　mutineers.beer

First sold beer: October 2018

Inspired by an 'experience day' at London Fields, engineer Rob Vote began homebrewing with three friends, later graduating to small-scale commercial brewing with a 1hl three-tier kit at a private address.

BEERS in cask and bottle are mainly at session strengths, sold through local outlets. Regular beers include session bitter **Filibuster** (3.4%), hazy pale **You Don't Know Jack** (3.4%) and a hoppy saison, **Suffragette*** (5.2%).

One Inn the Wood 72
Micropub

209 Petts Wood Road, Petts Wood BR5 1LA
T 07799 535982   oneinnthewood.co.uk
⏰ *Tu-Th* 12.00-15.00, 17.00-22.00, *Fr* 12.00-15.00, 17.00-23.00, *Sa* 11.30-23.00, *Su* 12.00-20.00. Children until 19.00.
5-7 cask, 7 bottles/cans, growlers, minikegs, 9 draught and bottled ciders, Kent wine, gins.
🍴 Pork pies, sausage rolls, cheese plates **£**,
🪑 Tables on street
Occasional live music and quizzes

🚂 Petts Wood   🥾 Link to London Loop

Former money broker Barry Bridge's friendly and popular micropub, opened in May 2014 in a quiet cul-de-sac close to Petts Wood station, reclaims southeast London's Kentish heritage by featuring beers, ciders, wines, pies and cheeses from within the traditional county boundaries. Gadds, Goachers and Tonbridge products often appear among casks served from a stillage in the rear coldroom, alongside Bromley nanobrewery Mutineers and a few

interlopers like Signature or Vibrant Forest. At least one dark beer is usually on, alongside a handful of bottles and cans including gluten-free options. A bright, simple design with high stools and bare floorboards makes good use of the limited space in this former wine bar. Highly recommendable for quality, welcome and thoughtful choice.

Visitor note. The mural-sized photo shows the nearby National Trust woodland which gives the town its name, noted for its monument to daylight saving time inventor Wiliam Willett, who allegedly thought of the idea while riding through the woods.

Orpington Liberal Club 73
Club

7 Station Road, Orpington BR6 0RZ
orpingtonliberalclub.co.uk
⏰ *Mo-Th* 20.00-23.00, *Fr* 18.00-23.00, *Sa* 12.00-15.00, 19.00-23.00, *Su* 12.00-15.00, 20.00-22.30. Children until at least 20.00.
4 cask, 2-3 keg, around 20 bottles/cans, growlers, 9 ciders.
🍴 Cheese and ham plates *(Sa)* **£**,
🪑 Patio and back garden
2 annual beer festivals, monthly meet the brewer, tap takeovers, blues/folk (Tu), jam session (We), live music (Fr-Sa), ukelele night, quiz, darts, functions

🚂 Orpington   🥾 Link to Cray Riverway

You don't have to be a Liberal Democrat to appreciate this little place in a domestic-looking detached house on the edge of Orpington town centre. Indeed, some of the keen volunteers who run the bar have put their own politicial loyalties aside to celebrate a common interest in great beer which has won the club regional awards. Beer sourcing has broadened, lining up Bexley, Five Points or Twickenham with northerners like Great Oakley or Settle. All are announced in an email newsletter and sold at keen prices, in thirds or takeaway cartons if required. Bottles and cans tend towards local or low alcohol. The regular drinking space is a homely bar with pub furniture and sofas, expanding to the adjoining hall and the extensive garden during regular beer festivals. For licensing reasons, you'll need to show a CAMRA membership card or similar to be admitted as a guest.

ONE INN THE WOOD

Penny Farthing   74

Micropub
3 Waterside, Crayford DA1 4JJ
T 07772 866645
pennyfarthingcrayford.co.uk
🕓 *Tu-Th* 12.00-15.00, 17.00-21.30, *Fr-Sa* 12.00-22.30, *Su* 12.00-15.00. Children until 21.00.
4-6 cask, 1 bottle, 8 ciders/perries.
🍴 Pies, scotch eggs **£**, ⅌ Tables on street
Occasional tap takeovers, morris dancers and quiz

🚆 Crayford   🚶 Cray Riverway, London Loop

London's third micropub, opened in September 2014 by Bob Baldwin, overlooks a little park beside the River Cray near the ford that gives Crayford its name. Although the last tenant sold pottery, for many years this was a cycle shop, thus the name. The room is painted in relaxing pastel shades, festooned with hops and equipped with tall benches and tables. Casks, dispensed into oversized glasses or takeaway cartons from a glass-fronted stillage in one corner, change rapidly, with around 1,600 different ones served in the first five years. Locals and Kent brewers like Bexley, Iron Pier, Gadds, Mad Cat and Westerham often appear alongside the likes of Arbor, Harbour and Oakham, with half the range usually in darker styles. It scooped the local CAMRA Pub of the Year award in four of its first five years of operation: 'We must be doing something right,' observes the website modestly.

Real Ale Way   75

Micropub
55 Station Approach, Hayes BR2 7EB
therealaleway.com
🕓 *Mo-Th* 14.00-22.00, *Fr-Sa* 14.00-23.00, *Su* 14.00-20.00.
6-9 cask, 12 bottles/cans, growlers, ciders/perries, wines, spirits.
Tastings, meet the brewer, bimonthly quiz, live music, board games

🚆 Hayes   🚶 London Loop, Bromley circular walks

Right opposite the station in the heart of a Tudorbethan suburb, this micropub in a former accountant's office, opened in July 2018, is bigger than average. It's a bright, irregularly

shaped space with a proper bar and plenty of tables at regular height as well as the usual high stools. There's a generous range of cask beers too, fetched from the coldroom in traditional micropub style and with even more of a Kentish slant than customary in this part of London. Tonbridge provides the only regular beer and other favoured suppliers include Goody, Larkins, Mad Cat and Pig and Porter. Cider, wine and gin display the same county loyalties. It's a friendly spot, ideally sited for people-watching and admiring the local Christmas tree in season.

Signal Brewery   76

Brewery, taproom
8 Stirling Way, Beddington Farm Road, Croydon CR0 4XN (Sutton)
T (020) 8684 6111   signalbeerco.com
First sold beer: January 2016, 🍴
🕓 *Sa* 12.00-19.00. Children welcome.
3 cask, 4 keg, 4 cans. 🍺
🍴 Food truck, ⅌ Tables at front, ♿ Flat access only
DJs, beer launches, seasonal events

🚌 Therapia Road   🚲 NCN232

The origins of Signal go back to the day when South African-born chemical engineer Murray Roos's children claimed the garden shed, previously home to his homebrewing setup, as a play space, and his wife said this was his signal to find commercial premises. He teamed up with a fellow parent at his children's school, Charlie Luckin, who had a background in wine and hospitality, on a Beddington industrial estate, just in Sutton but with a Croydon postcode. The original 12hl brewhouse is still in use, alongside several extra fermenters and

a canning line. The initial intention was to specialise in craft lagers but, interestingly, these were soon supplemented by ale styles and cask: 'We saw there was a demand from our pub customers,' says Charlie. Signal opened a bar at the O$_2$ in July 2017 (Try also, p240) and has an onsite taproom, with a smart bar displaying the streamlined retro branding. Anspach & Hobday (above) has since moved in across the yard.

BEERS are in keg, cask and can. Casks include English-style pale ale **Absolutely Fuggled*** (4%), **Solo Porter** (4.6%) and changing seasonals. Keg and canned beers include flagship European-style **Lager** (4.8%) and an **American Pale Ale*** (4.9%).

Southey Brewing Co
Brewery, taproom
21 Southey Street SE20 7JD (Bromley)
southeybrewing.co.uk
First sold beer: May 2013 (as Late Knights)
🕒 *We* special events only, *Th-Fr* 17.00-23.00, *Sa* 12.00-23.00, *Su* 12.00-20.00. Children until 21.00.
2 cask, 7 keg, 5-8 cans, some wines, specialist spirits. 🍴
🌳 Tables in yard
Quiz, films

🚃 Penge East 🚇 Penge West 🚌 Penge High Street

Southey is a successor to Late Knights, founded by former licensee and cuckoo brewer Steve Keegan, who helped devise Fuller's early 'crafty' pubs. He formed a partnership with Graham Lawrence, longstanding owner of Brockley wine bar and importer Mr Lawrence, to found a brewery and small pub chain based in a Victorian building just off Penge High Street that had once served as a slaughterhouse and a candle factory but had latterly been Graham's warehouse. In September 2013, Sam Barber became head brewer after approaching Steve for feedback on his homebrews. The rapid expansion contributed to both financial and beer quality problems and the company folded in August 2016. Sam and Graham then set up a new business and following a few months of closure and £20,000 of improvements,

restarted brewing as Southey in December 2016 on a 10hl kit formerly belonging to Clarkshaws. An atmospheric taproom opened in March 2018, with a mix of tables and armchairs, a window onto the brewhouse and outdoor seating on a side passage decorated with graffiti art. There are two other London outlets, the London Beer Dispensary (p233 and Dulwich Beer Dispensary (Try also p226), plus a third in Brighton.

Visitor note. The name is from the brewery's street address, in turn named after the Romantic poet Robert Southey, so the vowel in the first syllable is pronounced like the one in 'tough' rather than 'south'.

BEERS are in cask, keg and can, mainly sold through the taproom and bars. Regulars include reduced alcohol **Low Pils** (2.3%); session IPA **Lazy Jesus** (4.1%) and best bitter **Best** (4.5%). Oatmeal stout **Ursus III*** (5.5%) is a semi-regular. Changing specials include Belgian-style beers and IPAs with various hop recipes.

Star and Garter
Contemporary pub
227 High Street, Bromley BR1 1NZ
T (020) 3730 9458
starandgarterbromley.com
🕒 *Mo-Th* 16.00-23.00, *Fr-Sa* 12.30-24.00, *Su* 12.30-21.00. Children until 18.00.
6-7 cask, 17 keg, 70+ bottles/cans, specialist spirits especially brewery-linked, single malts.
🍴 BYO, 🌳 Rear garden ♿, &
Board games, beer books

🚃 Bromley North 🚌 Bromley High Street Market Square

Bromley beer enthusiasts celebrated in November 2016 when licensee Maura Gannon upped the standards established at Camberwell's Stormbird (p226) by creating that elusive

Star and Garter

combination of a great beer range in a proper pub, in this case a magnificent late Victorian town centre edifice that had been closed for over two years. The ground floor drinking area is centred on an expansive horseshoe bar, brightly refreshed with a mix of seating, intimate corners and beer enamels on the walls. Siren Broken Dream is the only cask regular; other suppliers have included Brew Buddies, Cloudwater, Deya, Five Points and Salopian, all at keen prices, with cask and keg taps usually assigned to ensure a range of styles, including 'the silly line', about which you can draw your own conclusions. Some of the most mouth-watering bottles and cans are hidden away behind others in the fridge and staff have been known to let customers behind the bar to dig through: you may be rewarded with rare Burning Sky specials, premium lambics from Boon and vintage Rodenbachs. Sunflowers brighten the rear garden and there's more space in a smart upstairs room. It was named local CAMRA pub of the year three years running, and also offers a local delivery service.

Visitor note *The Grade II-listed building, dating from 1898 and originally a hotel, has one of the most impressive pub frontages in London, in elaborate timber-framed Vernacular Revival style with a large projecting sign, entrance floor mosaic and exquisite etched glass incorporating the star and garter motif, as originally used for the royal Order of the Garter. Most of the interior is new, but the bar, fireplace, pillars and lincrusta ceiling are original.*

Three Hounds
Bar, shop, beer firm, planned brewpub
57 Beckenham Road, Beckenham BR3 4PR
threehoundsbeerco.com
🕐 *Daily* 12.00-22.00
1 cask, 9 keg, 100-150 bottles/cans, some wines, cider and spirits.
🪑 Tables at front and rear
Beer festivals, tap takeovers, live music, poetry, art, participation in local events

🚆 Clock House 🚲 Link to NCN21
🚶 Link to Capital Ring, Waterlink Way

This neat local beer café and bottle shop a few steps from Clock House station is run by the enthusiastic and well-informed Matt Walden, who started with a market stall before creating a permanent outlet in October 2017. Two years later, the business moved a few doors along to this bigger shop unit, given a smart but informal makeover, with much dark wood and a homely downstairs space boasting beer enamels, candles in recycled cans and plenty of natural light. Besides own brands (currently cuckoo-brewed but with plans for an onsite kit: see Brewers without breweries p323), you'll find numerous locals and personal favourites, all ordered in small quantities to ensure turnover, with over 1,500 beers on sale just in the first year. Expect to see Affinity, Bexley, Brick, Brockley, Dogs Grandad, Drop Project, Gipsy Hill, Kernel, ORA, Park, Partizan and Villages alongside the likes of Vibrant Forest, plus mainly Belgian imports like 3 Fonteinen, Dochter van de Korenaar and De Ranke. The varied draught range always includes a Belgian beer, a sour and a gluten-free option.

Three Hounds

TRY ALSO

Barrel and Horn 206 High Street, Bromley BR1 1PW barrelandhorn.com: The original Fuller's 'crafty' pub in central Bromley, recently recovering some of its mojo with 13 keg, 50+ bottles/cans from all over and regular tap takeover events. One cask line, usually Siren.

Bolthole 12 Falconwood Parade, Welling DA16 2PL bolthole-micropub.co.uk: 2019 micropub in a Falconwood Green shopping parade, stocking four unusual changing cask beers and also open as a coffee shop on weekday daytimes. Over-21s only.

Claret and Ale 4a Bingham Corner CR0 7AA: Mock-Tudor shopfront pub by Addiscombe tram stop freshened up in 2016 by the new owner, former airline pilot Charles. Long a real ale rendezvous with six cask lines always including Palmers from Bridport, Dorset, which is rare in London, alongside changing, traditional-leaning guests.

Door Hinge 11 High Street, Welling DA16 1TR thedoorhinge.co.uk: Opened in March 2013 as London's first permanent micropub, this is now one of the smaller entrants in the category, in a former electrical shop refitted in traditional but basic pub style. Under new owners since 2019, it stocks at least three casks on gravity dispense, often from Kent breweries. Closed Mondays.

Freshfields Market 86 Church Street, Croydon CR0 1RB freshfieldsmarket.co.uk: Specialist Croydon food shop with 150-200 bottles/cans, lots from south London and other UK brewers, with a tram stop right outside. The Wine Cellar, 9 Sanderstead Parade, South Croydon CR2 0PH, near Sanderstead station, has the same owners and a similar range. Both are takeaway only.

Golden Ark 186 Addington Road, Selsdon CR2 8LB thegoldenark.co.uk: Comfortable micropub not far from Selsdon Wood nature reserve. Four rotating casks, four kegs and 30 bottles/cans from good local and other UK breweries, including a cuckoo-brewed house beer. Why the name? 'Sounds better than the Woolwich Ferry,' says landlord Matt.

Halfway House 188C Halfway Street, Sidcup DA15 8DJ thehalfwayhousepub.com: Small micropub with faintly 80s décor deep in suburban Sidcup with three handpumped cask and six keg options, in tasting flights if required, plus 25 bottles/cans, mainly from solid London and other UK producers, plus plenty of cider.

Lock and Barrel 18 London Road, Bromley BR1 3QR: Micropub in a former locksmith's on the edge of Bromley town centre, a little bigger than some. Three casks on stillage, often from Kent brewers, six kegs and four bottles/cans from London and elsewhere in the UK.

Long Haul 149 Long Lane, Bexleyheath DA7 5AE thelonghaul.co.uk: Micropub in a former tattoo parlour in suburban Bexleyheath, with three beers direct from the cask, often from local breweries, plus cider and Kent gins. Closed Monday.

Next Door 3 Mill Row, Bexley High Street, Bexley DA5 1LA nextdoorbexley.com: Micropub-style bar in a Bexley Village railway arch right by the London Loop walking trail, with five cask beers from local and Kent breweries as well as better-known brands. Check hours: may be closed early in the week.

Red Lion 10 North Road, Bromley BR1 3LG redlionbromley.co.uk: Longstanding friendly real ale favourite in Victorian backstreets northeast of the town centre. Despite branding from now-defunct Beards, it's a Greene King house with five tiptop casks including unusual, though traditional-leaning, guests.

Robin Hood and Little John 78 Lion Road, Bexleyheath DA6 8PF robinhoodbexleyheath.co.uk: Both beers and building are immaculately kept at this longstanding local CAMRA favourite traditional backstreet pub, with local representation from Bexley and Westerham alongside well-known brands across eight cask lines.

BROMLEY PUB WALKS

Bromley is the capital's greenest borough, with expanses of both suburban green space and genuine countryside on the edge of the North Downs, crossed by numerous footpaths. In 2019, Bromley CAMRA launched an excellent new resource at bromley.camra.org.uk/pub-walks, highlighting opportunities for combining fresh air, exercise and a decent beer or two along the way by describing a network of walking routes between pubs. Two of the venues listed above – One Inn the Wood and Real Ale Way – are on the network, as are various country pubs that don't quite make it into this guide but are well worth a look if you're exploring the rather untypical attractions of this beautiful part of London on foot.

MICROPUBS GO MACRO

Before retired cabbie Ray Hurley opened the Door Hinge in Welling in March 2013, London had no micropubs. Today, there are 30, with 21 in the boroughs of Bexley, Bromley and Greenwich. The remainder are in similarly suburban outlying areas like Gidea Park, Ruislip, Selsdon, Upminster and Winchmore Hill, where they're often the only good beer option for miles around. There are now so many I haven't found room for them all.

Nailing the category isn't easy, particularly as its trendier relative, the bottle shop-bar, has also proliferated. Both types of outlet tend to occupy smallish former shop units, replacing businesses like hairdressers, plumbers' merchants, tattoo parlours, nailbars and even a mail order lingerie supplier. The Micropub Association defines a micropub as 'a small freehouse which listens to its customers, mainly serves cask ales, promotes conversation, shuns all forms of electronic entertainment and dabbles in traditional pub snacks'.

The first example, the Butchers Arms, was opened by

Martyn Hillier in Herne, Kent, in 2006, and venues based on his model soon began springing up across the county and beyond, with over 350 recognised by the association today. The link to Kent explains their concentration in boroughs like Bexley and Bromley: these were officially part of Kent until 1965 and in the view of many locals they still are.

The pioneers followed the classic model: a varied handful of beers usually from smaller and often local brewers, poured direct from the cask in a cold room and brought to your table, with simple décor encompassing a vestigial bar counter, or none, and old mobile phones nailed emphatically to the wall. Some newer arrivals have started to stretch the format, adding proper bars, comfier furniture and beer in keg, can and bottle. Some take a less prescriptive approach to encouraging conversation than shaming customers who dare to communicate telephonically indoors, and one or two even play quiet background music.

But the focus on good beer,

conversation and community persists, and many have become busy social centres, taking on the niche once occupied by bigger, purpose-built pubs, but at a fraction of the space and cost and with more flexibility. Significantly, they appear largely to have survived the lockdowns by tweaking the business model, many of them offering growlers of freshly poured cask for doorstep collection or local home delivery and providing much needed social contact in the process. There's no more eloquent symbol of their place in the changing retail landscape than the Little Green Dragon (p198), a delightful example in outer north London. A few paces up the road is the original Green Dragon, a substantial, and very attractive, interwar roadhouse pub that's now a Waitrose supermarket.

The Micropub Buses

Bus 51 links Woolwich and Orpington, passing or stopping close to the Plum Tree (p235), Door Hinge (Try also p253), Bolthole (Try also p253), Broken Drum (p244), Halfway House (Try also p253), Hackney Carriage (p247), Hoppers Hut (p248) and Orpington Liberal Club (p249).

Bus 286 links Sidcup (Queen Mary's Hospital) and Greenwich, passing or stopping close to the Hackney Carriage, Halfway House, Long Pond (p234), Rusty Bucket (p236), Berry and Barrel (Try also p240), Green Goddess (Try also p240) and River Ale House (p236).

Both routes operate daily to a frequent timetable.

Casks on stillage at the Kentish Belle

SOUTHWEST LONDON

SOUTHWEST LONDON

In this book, Southwest London covers all the SW postcodes outside the central area and south of the Thames, and further out to the boroughs of Kingston upon Thames and Sutton. This is potentially slightly confusing as there are also SW postcodes to the north of the Thames, but these are included under West London.

Unsurprisingly, there's a good concentration of recommendable venues in the bustling and vibrant inner-city neighbourhoods of **Brixton, Clapham and Streatham**. This section includes everywhere with SW postcodes in the London Borough of Lambeth, outside the central area, stretching to Stockwell.

Further west is **Wandsworth**, renowned in brewery history circles as home to the Ram Brewery. Happily, 15 years after the closure of Young's and following a heroic one-man

effort to maintain a working, if private, brewhouse, brewing on a commercial scale has been restored to the Ram. My coverage extends to cover the wider borough, taking in Balham, Battersea (including Clapham Junction which despite its name isn't in Clapham), Putney and Tooting.

Outer Southwest London mops up the rest, including Wimbledon in Merton borough, which has a notable brewery and several good pubs and bars, and the leafy suburban riverside centres of Kingston and Richmond. Note that although Twickenham and Teddington are in Richmond borough, I've listed them as Outer West London (p308) as they're on the opposite bank of the Thames. See also Outer Southeast London (p242) for a couple of breweries in an area on the very edge of Sutton that everyone thinks of as Croydon.

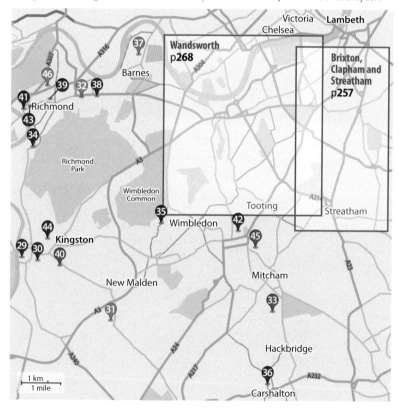

Brixton, Clapham and Streatham

Art and Craft

See Inkspot

Booma ❶

Restaurant

244 Brixton Road SW9 6AH

T (020) 7737 4999 **booma-brixton.co.uk**

🕐 *Mo-Th* 17.00-23.00, *Fr* 17.00-23.30, *Sa* 12.30-23.30, *Su* 12.30-22.00. Children welcome.
9 keg, 12 bottles/cans.

🍴 Modern Indian small plates, tasting menu

££-£££, 🎋 Front terrace

🚆 Brixton ⊖ Brixton, Stockwell 🚌 Loughborough Road
🚲 Link to CS7

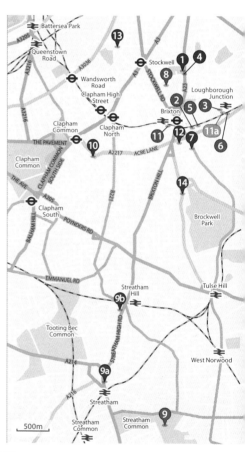

Opened in August 2016, this informal restaurant is one of the few in London to take beer and food matching seriously. Tasty and imaginative northern Indian-inspired food is in small portions for mixing and sharing, including plenty of veggie options, with a choice of well-made dals and curries, potato patties, tandoori tiger prawns, duck kathi roll and crab with asparagus. Draught beers like Bristol Milk Stout, Camden Wit, Oakham Green Devil and Rodenbach Grand Cru all have good affinity with such flavours. You'll need to ask staff about the changing selection of bottles and cans. A cheerful place decorated with colourful umbrellas, it's linked to the Crown and Anchor opposite (below), and the concept has been extended to sister pub the Jolly Butchers. I'd hazard it was partly inspired by the excellent Leeds-based Bundobust, and although falling a little short of that standard, it's nonetheless a welcome development.

Brixton Brewery Taproom ❷

Brewery, taproom (Heineken)
548 Brixton Station Road SW9 8PF (Lambeth)
T (020) 3609 8880 brixtonbrewery.com
First sold beer: October 2013, 🍺🍺
🕐 *We-Th* 17.00-22.00, *Fr* 17.00-23.00, *Sa* 12.00-23.00, *Su* 14.00-18.00. Children welcome.
Cash-free
10 cans, minikegs. 🖐
🍴 BYO, 🎏 Tables on street, ♿
Tastings

🚆 ⊖ Brixton

Brixton Brewery began in these arches just east of Brixton station and close to the famous markets. A gleaming new plant has since opened at Herne Hill, but the older site still brews, producing core brands as well as short run specials, bottles and occasional cask. Arch 547 is the original one and still houses the brewery, while 548 has been converted into a simple but attractive taproom, now a popular local bolthole. You'll find well-tended planters outside, a bar surround made from OSB board and a back bar that looks suspiciously like leftover hexagonal floor tiling from the new brewery. The selection concentrates on house beers, including specials. See the main brewery entry for more on the beers (p218).

Clarkshaws Brewing ❸

Brewery, taproom
497 Ridgway Road SW9 7EX (Lambeth)
T 07989 402687 clarkshaws.co.uk
First sold beer: September 2013, 🍺🍺
🕐 *Fr-Sa* 12.00-20.00, *Su* 14.00-20.00 (may be reduced in winter: check website). Children welcome.
1 cask, 3 keg, 7 bottles, 7 minicasks. 🖐
🍴 BYO, 🎏 Tables on street
Brewer days

🚆 Loughborough Junction

Self-styled 'beer imps' Ian Clark and Lucy Grimshaw are two of the most charming people in London brewing, but their enterprise has something of a tortuous history. It began in a small industrial unit in East Dulwich, then expanded in early 2015 to a Brixton railway arch in partnership with the London Beer Lab (below), with the intention of sharing the 8hl kit with other small brewers. This ended unhappily, and Lucy and Ian decided to down-scale rather than attempt to expand, figuring this would suit them better both financially and in lifestyle terms. They completed the move to another arch close to Loughborough Junction station in October 2017, installing a compact 1.5hl brewhouse and three small but high-spec fermenters, with the old kit going to Southey. A cool little taproom is resourcefully shoehorned into the Brixton site, with a tiny bar that can be forklifted away when production space is needed. The brewery works hard to reduce its environmental impact and makes a point of using UK ingredients even for its hop-forward beers.

BEERS are all unfined and vegan friendly, packaged in cask, keg and minikeg and hand bottled. They're mainly sold directly through the taproom and on market stalls. Regulars include **Gorgon's Alive** (4.3%) pale ale; lager **Hell Yeah!** (5.3%); amber lager **Darker Hell** (4.5%); and **Hell Hound**, a more English-styled IPA (5.5%). Specials have included pale ale **Four Freedoms** (4.3%), which unusually contained some mainland European ingredients as it was brewed for a local anti-Brexit campaign.

Crown and Anchor 4

Contemporary pub (London Village Inns)
246 Brixton Road SW9 6AQ
T (020) 7737 0060
crownandanchorbrixton.co.uk
🕐 *Mo-Th* 16.30-24.00, *Fr* 16.30-01.00, *Sa* 12.00-01.00, *Su* 12.00-23.00. Children until 21.00. Cash-free.
6-7 cask, 11 keg, 60+ bottles, 3-4 ciders/perries.
🍴 Sharing plates, burgers, salads, pub grub **££**,
🎋 Tables at side
Quiz (Tu)

🚆 Brixton   ⊖ Brixton, Stockwell   🚌 Loughborough Road
🚲 Link to CS7

This big Victorian main road boozer on the edge of Brixton claims amongst other things to be the home of London's first rock'n'roll club in the 1950s, but its original interior is largely gone. Plain glass windows illuminate bare brick and pillars offset by arty light fittings, though the old bar counter has been restored and there are some unusual arches at the back. Opened in April 2012 as a sister to Stoke Newington's pioneering Jolly Butchers (Try also p182), its beery attraction remains undimmed, always serving cask Oakham Citra, perhaps alongside By the Horns or Wild. Locals Mondo are among the kegs beside other high-achieving UK breweries, some less familiar, and draught Rodenbach. Several other good Belgians are in the fridges alongside Buxton and Cloudwater. Food includes burgers, wings, sharing plates and main courses like lamb köfte or Cambodian curry. The pedestrianised street next to the pub leads to Slade Gardens, providing al fresco opportunities.

Dogs Grandad Brewery 5

Brewery, taproom
550 Brixton Station Road SW9 8PF (Lambeth)
dogsgrandadbrewery.co.uk
First sold beer: March 2021
🕐 *We-Fr* 17.00-23.00, *Sa* 12.00-23.00, *Su* 12.00-18.00. Children until 19.00.
5 keg, 3 cans, growlers, local and specialist spirits 🍶.
🎋 A few tables at front, standing space opposite.
Fortnightly DJs (Fr), acoustic music (Su), arcade games, major big screen sport.

🚆 ⊖ Brixton

Passionate homebrewer and hardcore metal singer Alex Hill speculates that he may have set up this railway arch brewery 'for the cheapest price ever' as he installed and built much of it himself. A 10hl brewhouse from Latimer Ales, Chinese-built fermenters, a canning line and even a reverse osmosis filter are carefully shoehorned into a small arch a few doors down from Brixton Brewery (above), with the kit proudly bearing the house colour and brand. Somehow there's room for a basic but lively taproom at the front, enlivened further every Friday by an arcade game tournament. Beers on sale are mainly house-brewed, with a guest craft lager.

BEERS in keg and can are mainly easy-drinking hazy, juicy pale ales in contemporary style and all vegan friendly. Simply-named regulars include **Session IPA** (4.2%); **Pale Ale** (5%); and **Black IPA*** (5.2%).

Alex Hill of Dogs Grandad

Friendship Adventure ⑥

Brewery, taproom
Unit G1 Coldharbour Works, 245A
Coldharbour Lane SW9 8RR (Lambeth)
friendship-adventure.com
First sold beer: April 2021. ‼ By arrangement.
🕐 *We-Th* 17.00-23.00, *Fr* 14.00-23.00, *Sa* 12.00-
23.00, *Su* 12.00-22.00. Children until early
evening. Cash-free.
11 keg, 6+ cans, growlers. ⌂.
‼ Order in from neighbouring restaurants, ♿
Comedy nights

≥ Loughborough Junction

Homebrewer Ed Pragnell and friends Toby
Ejsmond-Frey and Neil Wates began working
together in 2017, subsequently cuckoo
brewing at Reunion, Signal and elsewhere
and developing a joyful sideline promoting
comedy events. They added their own 16
hl facility in 2021, appropriately enough in
an old grain mill right by the railway near
Loughborough Junction station and close to
Clarkshaws. The generous taproom boasts
plenty of tables, greenery, and upcycled
timber bar and bold murals, with proudly
branded brewing vessels visible behind a
railing. Around half the draughts are house

Friendship Adventure

brews, with sours, low alcohol beers and
other options from local guests like Mondo
and Signature. Partnerships with local
caterers provide order-in food, an interesting
range of *bánh mì* and other Vietnamese
snacks when I last looked. A percentage
of sales is donated to the Baytree Centre,
a nearby charity promoting social inclusion
for women and girls.

BEERS in keg and can are brewed mainly to
session strength. The core range includes
Helles-style 'modern lager' **Caper** (4.5%) and
a grapefruit saison, **Tangent*** (5.3%), developed
for a local restaurant, as well as modern table
beers and pale ales.

Ghost Whale

Shop, bar
70 Atlantic Road SW9 8PX
T (020) 7207 1641   **ghostwhalelondon.com**
🕐 *Tu-We* 14.00-23.00, *Th* 12.00-23.00, *Fr-Sa*
11.00-23.00, *Su* 12.00-22.00. Children
welcome. Cash-free.
6 keg, 350+ bottles/cans, growlers, some
cider and mead. ⌂.
‼ Snacks, ⛱ Rear garden
*Meet the brewer, tap takeovers, beer launches,
bottle shares, beer and food pairing, occasional
summer barbecues*

≥ ⊖ Brixton

With so many good bottle shop-bars in London,
the bar for new entrants is high, but Ghost
Whale effortlessly vaulted it in December 2016.
Described by its owners as 'a passion that got
a little out of hand', with an odd but memorable
name that's meant to evoke rarity, it occupies
a former hairdresser's just off Brixton's tangle
of markets. The list ventures further than many
in finding excellent independent producers
rarely seen in the capital: alongside well-known
locals and others you may find less-familiar
names like Brass Castle, Liquid Light, Padstow
and Pilot. A strong US selection focuses mainly
on Belgian and dark styles rather than hoppy
stuff, with Blackberry Farms, Jolly Pumpkin,
Laughing Monk and Logsdon among its stars.
Cyclic Beer Farm from Catalunya and Garden
from Croatia show up too. Staff are particularly
well-informed; thoughtful touches include gift

Ghost Whale

vouchers and a willingness to pour keg beers in all the legal measures. The good-looking interior is done out in clean wood with a well-lit central tasting table and there's even a beer garden. A second branch in Putney is if anything even better (p272).

Grosvenor Arms ⑧
(Affinity Brewing Co)
Brewpub, bar
17 Sidney Road SW9 0TP (Lambeth)
thegrosvenorarmsbrixton.com
affinitybrewco.com
First sold beer: December 2016 (at original site).
🍴 Planned
🕐 Mo-Fr 16.00-23.00, Sa-Su 12.00-23.00.
   Children until early evening.
2-3 cask, 19 keg, 30 bottles/cans, cider,
   some specialist spirits. 🍷.
🍴 Pizzas **££**, 🪑 Terrace at front, ♿
Occasional beer festivals, quiz, board games, private hire

⊖ Stockwell 🚇 Irving Grove 🚲 Link to CS7

The owners of the well-regarded Priory Arms (below) opened this modern beer bar in a former backstreet pub between Brixton and Stockwell in March 2019. Its extensive cellar has since become the home of Affinity Brewing and, though pub and brewery are separate companies, both parties agree it's almost a perfect match. Plain windows light an interior softened by dark wood tables, floorboards and beer enamels. Both cask and keg beers are dispensed from a row of taps behind the smart white-tiled bar: casks include a house golden ale alongside guests like Anspach & Hobday and Kent. There's more Affinity, including a house lager, on the kegs besides choices typically sourced from Mondo, Siren or Wild with imports from de la Senne or Põhjala. Bottle fridges provide solid Belgian and German choices, while a corner kitchen makes gourmet pizzas to soak it all up.

Affinity was started by Steve Grae (ex-BBNo) and Ben Duckworth on Anspach & Hobday's old 4hl kit in two half-sized shipping containers outside a Tottenham bar. The socially conscious operation expanded in October 2017 to one of two adjacent Bermondsey arches previously occupied by Partizan, upgrading to a few months later to a 10hl kit from the original Long Arm in Ealing. When the loss of a busy taproom in the 2020 lockdowns put pressure on finances, the brewery moved to its current location, leaving the arch and the old kit to Three Hills. The current brewhouse, formerly at Ryedale, is the same size but makes use of unusual square-shaped vessels in more cellar-friendly dimensions. Affinity is also behind the remarkably successful annual Cask festival (Festivals and events p338) and operates a small shop in Crystal Palace (p217).

Visitor note: Dating from 1898, the pub was once famous for regular punk gigs in a large ballroom at the back, but all that ended when its historic interior was ripped out in preparation for redevelopment into flats and a convenience store in 2014. A campaign to protect it as an Asset of

Community Value only partly succeeded when the Planning Inspectorate overruled Lambeth council in restricting the designation to the ground floor only, allowing flats above. This at least means there's still a pub, albeit a rather smaller one. Look out indoors for the old pub sign, rescued from a skip.

BEERS from Affinity are in keg, with some cask as well as 440ml cans filled by hand and sealed using a self-built seamer. Core lines include **Breeze*** (3.8%) saison with lime peel and coriander; session IPA **Broadstairs Pale*** (4.2%); West Coast-style **Grosvenor Pale*** (5.2%); and two modern-style IPAs, **Paper Mountains** (5.9%) and **Crystal Palace IPA** (6%). Cask **Grosvenor Gold** (3.8%) and a modern lager are brewed exclusively for the pub. There are numerous seasonals, specials and collaborations, often with additional flavourings: two recurring entries are gingerbread amber ale **Maid of More** (5.5%) and **Toowoomba** (6.2%) raspberry and coconut stout, also produced in a stronger variant, **2woomba** (9.4%).

Inkspot Brewery 9

Brewery: Rookery Barn, 40 Streatham Common South Road SW16 3BX (Lambeth)
T (020) 8679 7322 theinkspotbrewery.com
First sold beer: Feburary 2012 (at original site), ♨
🕐 Monthly *Sa* (check social media) 12.00-20.00. Children welcome.
5 keg, 5 cans, growlers
🍴Changing food truck **£-££**, Yard at front,
♿ Flat access only
Occasional live music, DJs, films

⮞Streatham 🚃The Rookery 🚶Capital Ring

Inkspot Brewery

Art and Craft Streatham 9a
Shop, bar: 308 Streatham High Road SW16 6HG
T (020) 8769 2557   artandcraft.london
🕐 *Tu-We* 15.00-21.00, *Th* 12.00-21.00, *Fr* 12.00-22.00, *Sa* 11.00-22.00, *Su* 11.00-19.00.
 Children until early evening.
4 keg, 200 bottles/cans, growlers.
Art displays

⮞Streatham

Art and Craft Streatham Hill 9b
Shop, bar: 2A Streatham High Road SW16 1DB
T (020) 8696 7590   artandcraft.london
🕐 *Mo* 16.00-20.00, *Tu-We* 15.00-21.00,
 Th 12.00-21.00, *Fr* 12.00-22.00, *Sa* 11.00-22.00,
 Su 11.00-19.00. Children until early evening.
4 keg, 150 bottles/cans, growlers.
Art displays

⮞Streatham Hill

Ex-Army officer Tom Talbot and restaurateur and art dealer Bradley Ridge began working together by cuckoo-brewing a beer endorsed by charity Help for Heroes at Tunnel in Nuneaton, then they started producing on a homebrew kit for Bradley's Streatham restaurant Perfect Blend. Plans for a proper site in Beckenham fell through when they discovered a 1920s covenant blocked alcohol production, but their luck changed when the head gardener at the Rookery on Streatham Common approached them to brew with hops grown by a local collective and alerted them to a vacant building.

It's taken a lot of work since, including 350m of new power line, but Inkspot now has one of the most idyllic sites of any London brewery, in a barn right next to one of the capital's most beautiful public gardens. A 12hl brewhouse has been in action since December 2018, with waste hops used on site as fertiliser and botanicals from the herb garden or honey from the apiary occasionally added to the beers. Monthly 'Shutters Up' events reveal a stylish taproom and some seriously good urban art. Future plans include tapping the local well water (see panel p200). The name, recalling Tom's past career, references a military strategy for occupying a hostile region by establishing several separate safe areas that are then enlarged until they overlap.

Inkspot also owns the Art and Craft minichain combining bottle shop, bar and art gallery. The nearest one, near Streatham station, has a few tables and a wide selection of mainly UK guests. Further north is the original branch in a former greengrocer's around the corner from Streatham Hill station: smaller, more characterful and particularly well-stocked, with some tasty rarities. The biggest branch is in Croydon (p242).

BEERS are in keg and canned using a mobile line. Core beers include a rare **Black Lager*** (4.6%); flagship **St Reatham*** (4.6%) Munich-style lager, originally devised for the restaurant; **DDH American Pale** (5%); and **556 IPA*** (5.6%), a West Coast style named after a rifle calibre. An annual local wet hop brew is still a part of the calendar.

King and Co

Contemporary pub
100 Clapham Park Road SW4 7BZ
T (020) 7498 1971 thekingandco.uk
🕐 *Mo-We* 16.00-23.00, *Th* 16.00-24.00, *Fr* 14.00-01.00, *Sa* 12.00-01.00, *Su* 12.00-23.00. Children until 20.00.
3-5 cask, 15 keg, 40+ bottles/cans, ciders, some specialist spirits.
🍴 Changing popups **£-££**, 🪑 Front terrace
Tap takeovers, tastings, quiz (Mo), occasional live music, board games, functions

🚇 Clapham Common 🚲 C5, CS7

Formerly known as the Kings Head and briefly an Antic pub, this prominently sited local with a raised front terrace not far from Clapham Common continued its beer-friendly turn under new ownership in 2014. It's since changed hands yet again, and in September 2019 became Portobello's (p305) first pub and a good source of the brewery's beers. Guest lines favour other Londoners, perhaps with Five Points, Sambrook's or Southwark on cask and Fourpure and Mothership on keg, though with Bavarian BHB lagers an unusual addition. The bottle and can list was still to be decided when I last asked but expect a similar mix. An island bar dominates a room fitted out in modern but homely style, and a popup kitchen has touched bases as diverse as Ghana and Taiwan.

London Beer Lab

Nano Brews and Tap brewery, taproom, shop:
41 Nursery Road SW9 8BP (Lambeth)
Production brewery, no visitors please:
283 Belinda Road SW9 7DT (Lambeth) **11a**
T (020) 8396 6517 londonbeerlab.com
First sold beer: December 2013
Nano: 🕐 *Th* 17.00-21.00, *Fr* 17.00-22.00,
  Sa 11.00-22.00, *Su* 12.00-18.00. Children welcome. Cash-free.
24-30 keg, 100+ bottles/cans, growlers, homebrewing supplies.
🍴BYO, 🪑 Tables at front,
♿Flat access only
Brewing course (Sa, Su), beer tastings, homebrew club

🚆 🚇 Brixton

This interesting combination of a brewing school, brewery and taproom is the brainchild of French-born Bruno Alajouanine and Irishman Karl Durand O'Connor, who met playing football when they both had jobs in the City. It opened in 2013 with an assortment of homebrew kits in an arch tucked away behind Brixton town centre on Nursery Road. Much to the confusion of HMRC, the owners also brewed for sale from an on-site shop and a few local outlets. Early in 2015, LBL launched

a partnership with Clarkshaws (above) to share the latter's bigger kit and rent it out to others in a second arch on Belinda Road near Loughborough Junction, dubbed the Beer Hive. This didn't work out and in 2017 Clarkshaws downsized to its present location around the corner. LBL has continued at both sites, using Belinda Road as a production facility closed to the public, with a 24hl brewhouse which also hosts occasional cuckoos and a 5hl pilot kit added in 2021. Nursery Road continues to offer brewing tuition on an upstairs mezzanine, with several 20 litre homebrew kits and a 2hl pilot kit for specials and experiments. Downstairs is a very pleasant bar and shop serving up beer in lab-style glassware to enjoy on a scattering of tables decorated with malt and hop samples. There are guests from the likes of Brick, Buxton and Pressure Drop on keg and an impressive list of UK and international bottles and cans, particularly featuring sours and farmhouse ales.

BEERS are mainly in keg and can, with occasional cask and bottles. Core beers include contemporary-style **QED Southwest Pale Ale*** (4%) and **Session IPA** (4.2%). Changing specials brewed as short runs at the Nursery Road site are usually identified as 'nano' on lists and packaging, and further specials are due from the new pilot kit. Various cuckoo brews and commissioned beers are also produced.

Nanban 🄬

Restaurant, bar
426 Coldharbour Lane SW9 8LF
T (020) 7346 0098   nanban.co.uk
🕐 *Mo-Th* 17.00-23.00, *Fr* 17.00-01.00, *Sa* 12.00-01.00, *Su* 12.00-22.00. Children welcome.
1 keg, 8+ bottles/cans, 6 sake, Japanese whisky, shochu, tea.
🍴 Japanese fusion **££**
Occasional beer launches and tastings, private dining

🚆 ⊖ Brixton

Youngest-ever MasterChef winner Tim Anderson's fusion of authentic south Japanese ramen soup noodles, the *izakaya* pub tradition and Caribbean and west African ideas and ingredients from nearby Brixton market has resulted in some of the most unusual casual dining in London. More importantly for our

purposes, customers are encouraged to match the complexity of the food with beer. It's a personal passion for Tim, who collaborates with the likes of Pressure Drop and Wild to create exclusive brews. The list is short but well-chosen: Brixton Reliance on draught and various pale ales, sweet stouts, yuzu-flavoured sours and mixed fermentation rarities from brewers like Burning Sky, Ignition, Lost and Grounded and Japan's Hitachino Nest, plus sake from Peckham's Kanpai. Ramen bowls include Tim's signature dish with curried goat and a veggie option with spiced aubergine, courgette and parmesan cheese, alongside various small plates, distinctive takes on chicken wings and bananas in miso and butterscotch sauce for dessert. The space preserves the brown marble floors and arched windows of the pie and mash shop that once stood here, with a marble-topped bar and an upstairs room equipped with dining booths on wheels. There's now a second branch in Covent Garden (see website).

Visitor note. The name means 'southern barbarian', a term once applied to European traders.

Priory Arms

Contemporary pub
83 Lansdowne Way SW8 2PB
T (020) 7622 1884   theprioryarms.com
🕐 *Mo-Fr* 16.00-23.00, *Sa* 12.00-23.00, *Su* 12.00-22.30. Children until early evening.
4+ cask, 13 keg, 30 bottles/cans, 8+ ciders, some specialist spirits.
🍴 Burgers, burritos **££**, 🪑 Front terrace
At least three annual beer festivals, quiz (Su), board games, functions

⊖ Stockwell   🚌 Stockwell Bus Garage   🚲 Link to C57

This modest gem, just down the road from Stockwell's impressive and architecturally important 1950s bus garage and the Playhouse theatre, was likely the first UK pub offering draught imported wheat beer in the 1990s. Under the stewardship of ex-Craft Beer Co manager Tom Power since 2013, it's flowered into a contemporary champion while retaining its agreeable community pub feel. The place has a tasteful, slightly continental vibe with big

windows illuminating a raised seating area. Casks in a range of styles could be from Anspach & Hobday, Five Points or Kent while kegs represent locals Mondo alongside Lost and Grounded and Verdant. The mainland European slant persists with draught Paulaner Helles and bottles from illon, Rochefort, Schlenkerla and Tilquin. The kitchen offers burgers alongside Tex-Mex-inspired burritos and quesadillas, with ample vegetarian options. Tom also now runs the Grosvenor Arms not far away (above).

Sympathetic Ear   ⑭

Bar, shop

37 Tulse Hill SW2 2TJ

T (020) 8671 8458 **thesympatheticear.co.uk**

🕐 *Tu-Fr* 16.00-23.00, *Sa* 12.00-23.00, *Su* 14.00-22.00. Children until early evening. Cash-free.

7 keg, 130+ bottles/cans, growlers, natural wines, a few gins.

🍴 Sausage rolls, beer cheese, occasional popups **£**, 🪑 Benches on street, ♿

Meet the brewer, tap takeovers, beer and food pairing, art exhibitions, monthly quiz, DJs, film screenings, board games, retro video games, functions

🚆 Brixton, Herne Hill   ⊖ Brixton   🚌 Brixton Water Lane Effra Road

This cheerful bar in a shop unit near the bottom of Tulse Hill opened in November 2017 as an offshoot of Canopy (p220). The owner's products account for around half the kegs, with guests from breweries like Boundary and Siren allocated to ensure a variety of styles. Bottles and cans, also sold to take away, extend the range considerably: locals including Villages and Wild Card, other UK suppliers like Duration and Moor, more Americans than usual (Barrelhouse, Mason Ale Works, Great Divide) and even Italians like Ducato. Changing art and sculpture, comfy sofas and a stylish neon depicting the titular ear all contribute to an appealing package, and you can indulge your inner child downstairs by playing Super Mario on the big screen.

TRY ALSO

Bottle Apostle Clapham 59 Abbeville Road SW4 9JW **bottleapostle.com**: Branch of the small indie off-licence chain on a parade of boutique shops in desirable Abbeville Village, with even more beer wisdom than usual. 100 bottles/cans including plenty of locals and a few unusual imports. Takeaway only.

BrewDog Brixton 419 Coldharbour Lane SW9 8LH brewdog.com: Friendly branch in central Brixton with plenty of booth seating. Up to 22 draught lines with the usual selection and around 60 bottles/cans, mainly BrewDog or Belgian.

Earl Ferrers 22 Ellora Road SW16 6JF facebook.com/earlferrersstreatham: Local gem of a single-room backstreet corner pub not far from Streatham Common, stocking four consistently well-kept casks from Sambrook's and other local brewers. Closed Mondays.

Craft Beer Co Brixton 11 Brixton Station Road SW9 8PD thecraftbeerco.com: Lively branch in central Brixton by the markets. It's smaller and more bar-like than some, though with more room upstairs. Seven cask, 17 keg and 70+ bottles and cans of reliable quality and variety.

Railway 2 Greyhound Lane SW16 5SD therailwaysw16.co.uk: Large, lively local CAMRA award-winner right by Streatham Common station. At least four cared-for casks and 20 bottles/cans from London brewers. Briefly housed a brewery which is now closed.

Taproom by Brixton Village 43 Brixton Village Market, Coldharbour Lane SW9 8PS wearetaproom.co.uk: Tiny bar in one of Brixton's famous covered market arcades with 12 kegs and a range of bottles/cans all from south London brewers. Closed Mondays and Tuesdays, cash-free.

LONDON DRINKERS · Lotte Peplow

Lotte is Craft Beer Ambassador for Europe for the Brewers Association, a not-for-profit trade association representing American craft breweries. She works to promote US independent brewers in London, the UK and Europe, and as a member of CAMRA's London Tasting Panel, regularly evaluates London-brewed beers in pubs across the capital. Follow her @LottePeplow.

How do you rate London as a beer city, on a world scale?
Pretty high! Five years ago, my answer would have been very different, but it's come on in leaps and bounds and now boasts a plethora of exciting new breweries.

What's the single most exciting thing about beer in London right now?
The growing awareness of quality and the need to deliver a perfect pint every time. It might not sound that exciting but it's so important.

What single thing would make things even better?
Even more awareness about quality.

What are your top London beers right now?
Difficult question! I'll go with Wimbledon Quartermaine IPA, Tap East East End Mild and anything from the Kernel.

What's your top great beer night out?
The monthly bottle share night at the Mitre in Richmond (p283), sharing amazing beers from far and wide with my beer geek friends and sampling the fine array of casks on offer.

Who's your London beer hero?
Jaega Wise for helping to diversify the image of beer and growing its appeal amongst a wider audience, and Roger Protz for building awareness about beer over many decades.

Who will we be hearing a lot more from in future?
Natalya Watson, an inspirational new beer communicator with a fantastic podcast, Beer with Nat (beerwithnat.com) and a book on beer styles published in 2020.

Which are your other top beer cities?
Denver, Colorado. Portland, Maine and Portland, Oregon are next on my bucket list.

Wandsworth.

Battersea Brewery

Brewpub, bar
12 Arches Lane, Battersea Power Station SW11
8AB (Wandsworth)
T (020) 8161 2366   batterseabrew.co.uk
First sold beer: November 2018, 🍴
🕐 *Su-Th* 12.00-23.00, *Fr-Sa* 12.00-24.00.
    Children until early evening.
Occasional cask, 4 tank, 5 keg, 25+ bottles/cans,
    some wines.
🍴 Toasties **£**, 🪑 Tables at front, ♿
*Beer classes and tastings, local festivals, major big
screen sport*

🚆 Battersea Park, Queenstown Road Battersea 🚇 Battersea
Power Station 🚌 Battersea Park Chelsea Gate 🚲 C8
🏃 Thames Path

One of London's smarter railway arch breweries,
this occupies two arches on the southern
approach to Grosvenor railway bridge. Alongside
other businesses facing Battersea Power Station,
it's a few steps from the Thames, with Battersea
Park on the other side of the line. It's the
brainchild of former Draft House and Young's
manager Steve Kelly, created in partnership
with the Mosaic pub group. The arch closer to
the river holds an 8hl brewhouse and fermentation tanks, overseen by ex-Brodie's (Brewers
without breweries p321) and Hopcraft Pixie
Spring brewer Tom Barlow, while the other is a
post-industrial bar and mezzanine in brick,
concrete, steel piping and mottled copper.
Besides the brewery's beers, mostly dispensed
from tank, you'll find guests that might be from
Brixton, Harviestoun or Tiny Rebel, imported
German lagers and interesting entries like
Bosteels Deus, Lervig and six°north among the
bottles and cans. Several of the neighbours
have lengthier menus if food options prove
too limited.

BEERS are in tank, keg and canned using a
mobile line, with occasional cask, mainly sold
through the taproom. Regulars include
Session Pale (3.8%); a cask **Best Bitter**
(4.2%) with changing UK hops; Kölsch-style
House (4.2%); US-style **IPA** (5.8%); and
Scotch Ale* (6.9%), a style rare in London.
Specials have included **Russian Imperial
Stout*** (12%). Battersea brands sold in other
Mosaic pubs are usually contract-brewed due
to capacity constraints at the brewpub.

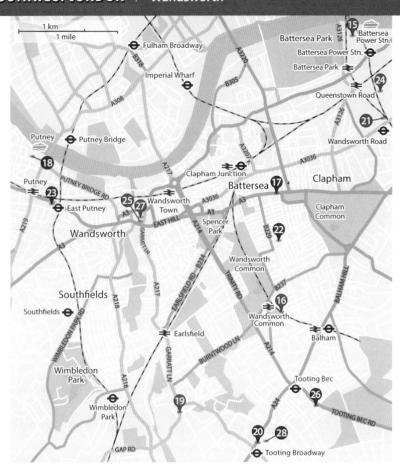

Belleville Brewing

Brewery, taproom
36 Jaggard Way (taproom 44 Jaggard Way)
SW12 8SG (Wandsworth)
T (020) 8675 4768 bellevillebrewing.co.uk
First sold beer: March 2013, 🍴
🕐 *We-Th* 17.00-22.00, *Fr* 16.00-22.00, *Sa* 12.00-22.00, *Su* 13.00-20.00. Children welcome.
9 keg, 12 bottles/cans. ⬦
🍴 Pork pies and snacks, usually food truck £,
🪑 Tables at front
Beer festivals, tastings, major big screen sports, functions

🚉 Wandsworth Common

Musician Adrian Thomas was prompted to become a homebrewer when he organised a beer festival as a fundraiser for his son's school,

Belleville Primary. He then got together with nine other Belleville dads to set up a brewery on a small industrial estate alongside the railway at Wandsworth Common station. It began with an 8hl kit, selling mainly through local outlets. After successfully fighting off a misjudged legal threat from AB InBev in 2013, alleging infringement of its trademark for sweetened lambic Belle Vue, the brewery expanded in the summer of 2016 with a canning line and a new 24hl brewhouse from the US. Continue a few doors past the brewery unit to find the tap-room, opened in January 2017. It's a pleasant and welcoming space on two levels, with an upstairs mezzanine fitted out with repurposed pallets and scattered with cushions. A comprehensive range of house beers, including specials, is supplemented here with a few guests which are usually either local or from the US.

BEERS are mainly in keg and can, with a few casks for selected outlets. The US slant is acknowledged in the longstanding strapline 'Beers from over there, brewed over here'. Core beers include **Picnic Session IPA** (4.4%); **London Steam Lager*** (4.5%), a California common; contemporary-styled **Commonside Pale Ale** (5%); and West Coast-style **Thames Surfer IPA** (5.6%). There are numerous specials, experiments and seasonals, including a dark lager, **Balham Black** (4.6%).

BrewDog Clapham Junction

Bar
11 Battersea Rise SW11 1HG
T (020) 7223 6346   brewdog.com
🕐 *Mo-Th* 15.00–24.00, *Fr-Sa* 12.00–24.00, *Su* 12.00–23.30. Children until mid-evening.
25 keg, 70 bottles/cans, growlers, specialist spirits.
🍴 Pizzas, sharing boards, salads **££**,
🌳 Sheltered front terrace, ♿
Beer launches, tap takeovers, art shows, quiz, board games

🚆 ⊖ Clapham Junction   🚍 Eccles Road

BrewDog bars now follow such a formula it's difficult to rank them, but this one has long had an edge for me, with particularly friendly staff and an interior that seems more soothing and intimate than usual. It opened in August 2014 just off the northwest corner of Clapham Common and has been refurbished since but not at the expense of its charm, with plenty of booth seating and a small terrace. Two thirds of the draughts are from the owner, the rest widely sourced guests: perhaps Affinity from Brixton, Jackie O's from Ohio and Whiplash from County Kildare, covering a wide range of styles and ABVs including some stronger stuff. Cloudwater specials might join Estonia's Pühaste and BrewDog's own OverWorks rarities in the fridges. Lack of a kitchen means cheese and charcuterie plates prepared by bar staff were long the only food option, but these have since been supplemented by sourdough pizzas, including vegetarian and vegan choices.

Bricklayers Arms

Traditional pub
32 Waterman Street SW15 1DD
T (020) 8789 0222   bricklayers-arms.co.uk
🕐 *Mo-We* 16.00–23.00, *Th-Sa* 12.00–23.00, *Su* 12.00–22.30. Children until 21.00.
10 cask, 2 keg, 4 bottles, 1 cider/perry.
🍴 Only for prebooked functions, 🌳
Occasional beer festivals, monthly live folk music, morris dancing, major big screen sport, skittles, shove ha'penny, board games, functions

🚆 Putney   ⊖ Putney Bridge   🚢🚍 Putney Pier
🚲 NCN4   🥾 Thames Path, link to Beverley Brook Walk

This pretty little pub within cheering distance of the start of the annual Oxford–Cambridge University Boat Race has been a real ale champion since former actor Becky Newman took it on in 2005. It has long showcased the work of admired Yorkshire family brewery Timothy Taylor and stocks several other examples of its cask beers besides the ubiquitous Landlord, alongside guests in cask, keg and bottle/can often from London brewers like 40FT, By the Horns, Five Points, Portobello and Twickenham. A long-planned refurbishment, largely preserving the basic but comfortable interior, was completed during the lockdowns, and the pub celebrated reopening in May 2021 with a collaboration beer brewed at SlyBeast in Wandsworth.

Visitor note. Dating from 1826, this is likely the oldest pub in Putney and was listed as 'a compact Victorian gem' among the Top 10 traditional English pubs by National Geographic magazine in 2012. Look out for fragments of a snob screen incorporated into the bar counter.

By the Horns Brewing ⑲

Brewery, taproom
25 Summerstown SW17 0BQ
T (020) 3417 7338 bythehorns.co.uk
First sold beer: October 2011, 🍺
🕐 *Tu-Th 16.00-22.30, Fr 16.00-23.00, Sa 12.00-23.00, Su 14.00-22.30.* Children until early evening.
3 cask, 10 keg, 12-15 cans, 1 cider/perry. 🍷
🍴 Pizzas (not every day) **£-££**, 🪑 Tables at front, ♿ Flat access only
Tastings, live music, seasonal events, big screen sport, darts, board games, functions

🚆 Earlsfield 🚌 Summerstown 🚲 Link to Avenue Verte, NCN20 🚶 Link to Wandle Trail

Alex Bull and Chris Mills, then only three years out of university, started brewing on an industrial estate between Earlsfield and Wimbledon in September 2011, using a bespoke 9hl kit. A new 18hl brewhouse was installed in 2015 when operations began expanding into adjacent units, eventually occupying a whole row. Even this wasn't enough, and in 2021 the main production facility was transferred to Salfords, near Redhill, Surrey, just outside London. A pilot brewery remains at the old place, where the taproom is being expanded alongside the installation of a craft distillery and improvements to the longstanding cider-making facility. The range concentrates on house products, with a few guests from other locals like Belleville, Canopy and Mondo. A pizza kitchen operated by a separate company, Dough Shack, provides the food.

Visitor note*. Opposite is the site of Wimbledon Greyhound Stadium, closed in 2017 and since demolished. A new development in its place will change the face of the area, providing homes and shops as well as a new ground for League One football team AFC Wimbledon.*

BEERS are in keg, can and cask, the last mainly pale ale **Stiff Upper Lip** (3.8%). Other regulars include award-winning **West End Pils** (4%); **Old Smoke** (4%, also in cask), an unusual smoked tea bitter; **Hopadelic Session IPA** (4.3%, also in cask); and **Cosmic Warrior Pale Ale** (4.8%). Among various seasonals and specials are red ale **Diamond Geezer*** (4.9%); red IPA **Wolfie Smith*** (5.2%), which had to be rebranded when actor Robert Lindsay, who played the eponymous 1970s TV sitcom character, objected to the use of his image; **Lambeth Walk** (5.1%) porter and **Russian Imperial Stout**** (10.5%), a collaboration with Russian brewery Crazy Brew.

Craft Tooting ⑳

Bar, shop
1 Broadway Market, 29 High Street SW17 0RJ
crafttooting.co.uk
🕐 *Tu-We 17.00-23.00, Th 16.00-23.00, Fr 12.00-24.00, Sa 11.00-24.00, Su 13.00-18.30.* Children until early evening.
3 keg, 100+ bottles/cans
🍴 Various from neighbouring traders,
♿ (in market)

🚇 Tooting Broadway

Trendy restaurants and Sicilian *cannoli* (pastry) sellers now mix with haberdashers and Gujarati greengrocers in Tooting Broadway Market, an indoor market opened in 1936. One of the new arrivals is Craft, just inside the entrance. Not much more than a booth, it crams a lot in, with both session beers and 'something more unusual' on the keg lines and shelves packed with bottles and cans to take away or drink in at 50p corkage. Seating opportunities are mainly limited to a few cheerful orange bar stools, but there are communal tables elsewhere in the market. Expect a mix of Londoners, contemporary Brits (Burnt Mill, Duration, Wylam) and interesting imports (Modern Times, Naparbier, Westmalle). There's now a bigger branch at Crystal Palace, Craft and Courage (Try also p226). Not to be confused with Tooting Market a few steps further north, where We Brought Beer (below) has a stall.

Distortion Brewing ㉑

Brewery, taproom
647 Portslade Road SW8 3DH (Wandsworth)
T 07765 328900   distortionbrewing.co.uk
First sold beer: December 2020. ‼ Planned.
🕐 *Fr* 17.00-23.00, *Sa-Su* 12.00-23.00, Children
   until 18.00.
Up to 6 tank, some keg and cans
🪑 A few tables on street, ♿
Tastings, beer launches

🚆 ⊖ Wandsworth Road   🚲 Link to C5

Inspired by a road trip to the US West Coast in
2007, Andy North began developing recipes
in his garage, eventually taking on an arch
under Wandsworth Road station in his native
Battersea in 2020, with a scattering of
outdoor seating overlooking an open green.
The indoor drinking area, equipped simply
but comfortably with school-style tables and
stools, takes up about half the space, with the
10hl Chinese brewhouse and fermenters
behind a parade of serving tanks. The choice
focuses on house beers, available in third-pint
tasting flights, with some guests from local
brewers in styles not brewed here, like
Belgian styles and sours. A friendly, quality
option in an area with few breweries.

BEERS in tank and keg include **Kozmic IPA**
(5.3%); Kölsch-style **Inertia*** (4.8%); hazy IPA
Quantum (5.5%); and a more traditional
porter, **Decibel** (4.8%), with rotating specials.
Most is currently sold in house with some kegs
sold elsewhere and future plans for canning.

Eagle Ale House ㉒

Traditional pub
104 Chatham Road SW11 6HG
T (020) 7228 2328
facebook.com/eaglealehouse
🕐 *Mo-Fr* 15.00-23.00, *Sa* 12.00-23.00, *Su* 12.00-
   22.30. Children until early evening.
6-8 cask, 10 keg, cider, malts, wines.
🍴 Pies, barbecues to order in summer **£**,
🪑 Rear garden with sliding roof, front terrace
*Occasional live music, piano singalongs, summer
barbecues, major big screen sport, Toad in a Hole
(game), board games*

🚆 ⊖ Clapham Junction   🚌 Darley Road
🚲 Link to Q4   🚶 Link to Capital Ring

A long-established real ale stalwart just off
Northcote Road, the Eagle defiantly remains
the best kind of traditional pub in an area over-
burdened by gastro makeovers and informal
dining chains. The exterior is modestly
handsome, with a fine terracotta frieze above
the entrance. The well-worn interior is a
pleasingly jumbled mix of benches, saggy sofas
and high tables for vertical drinking. Licensees
and pub campaigners Simon Clarke and Dave
Law, now approaching their third decade here,
finally managed to free themselves from a
pubco tie in 2020, increasing still further the
range of independently sourced beer. Downton,
Pilgrim and Surrey Hills are regulars, joined by
the likes of Bedlam, Dorking, Redemption or
Wimbledon in a cask range that usually includes
mild or another dark beer, while kegs include
several from locals Belleville.

*Visitor note. Originally two 1860 cottages, the pub was
remodelled 30 years later by the same architects who
designed the fountains in Trafalgar Square. The man
thought to be the model for Sherlock Holmes' fictitious
nemesis Moriarty was a regular and you can just about
imagine the arch fiend plotting his misdeeds among the
worn armchairs and dusty books of the snug.*

Ghost Whale Putney 23

Bar, shop
134 Upper Richmond Road SW15 2SP
T (020) 8780 3168 ghostwhalelondon.com
⏲ *Mo* 16.00-20.00, *Tu-Th* 13.00-22.00,
Fr-Sa 11.00-23.00, *Su* 12.00-20.00.
Children until 19.00. Cash-free.
8 keg, 500+ bottles/cans, growlers, bag-in-box.
🍴Snacks
Meet the brewer, tap takeovers, tastings

⇌ Putney ⊖ East Putney 🚲 Link to NCN4
🏃 Link to Thames Path

After setting new standards of excellence at its original Brixton outlet (p260), Ghost Whale opened a second branch close to East Putney Tube station in August 2019, happily retaining the beer connections of a site that formerly housed now-defunct Beer Boutique. The long space has been smartly refurbished with small tables and cushions by the front windows, a big central tasting table, a tiled back bar surmounted by the company logo in neon and fridges along both sides. It arguably pips the Brixton branch as a place to hang out and drink (£1 corkage on bottles and cans), while offering a similarly breath-taking and well-researched range, encompassing a long list of locals, top contemporary UK producers, new Europeans (Alvinne, Beerbliotek, Garden, Mont Salève) and rarities in big bottles and cans, often from the US (Bruery, Laughing Monk). There's an extensive choice of lower alcohol options and, at the other end of the scale, one keg line is dedicated to imperial stouts and barley wines. Oud Beersel lambic in a box, aged Fuller's Vintage Ale and mixed fermentation specials from Burning Sky and Harbour complete the picture. There's a current list on Untappd.

Mondo Brewing 24

Brewery, taproom
86 Stewarts Road SW8 4UG (Wandsworth)
T (020) 7720 0782 mondobeer.com
First sold beer: March 2015, 🍴
⏲ *Th-Fr* 17.00-23.00, *Sa* 14.00-23.00.
Children until early evening. Cash-free.
15 keg, 12+ cans, some wines and cider. 🍴
🍴Pizza slices or order in, 🪑Tables on street, ♿
Beer launches, occasional tap takeovers, live music, board games, major big screen sport

⊖ Wandsworth Road 🚌 Linford Street

In a distinctive industrial building on a quiet street between Battersea Power Station and Clapham, Mondo is the work of two US expat homebrewers, Todd Matteson and Thomas Palmer. Starting with a 10hl kit, they upgraded to a 20hl brewhouse in 2017, followed by additional fermentation capacity and a new canning line in 2019. The site has long boasted a dedicated and comfortable taproom in wood and brick, with plenty of seating, views of the brewhouse through big windows and a help-yourself popcorn machine. The bar concentrates on showcasing the brewery's core range, specials and collaborations in a wide range of styles that lives up to the internationalism suggested in its name.

BEERS are in keg, can and bottle. The core range includes **Little Victories** (4.3%) session IPA; a hazy, juicy pale called **Road Soda** (4.8%); and flagship West Coast-style IPA **Dennis Hopp'r** (5.3%). Among the specials and seasonals are strong, dark abbey-style ale, **Figgie Smalls*** (8.9%) and various hazy, juicy 'mountain-style' IPAs.

Mondo Brewing

Ram Brewery

See Sambrook's Brewery.

Ram Inn (SlyBeast Brewing) 25

Brewpub, contemporary pub
68 Wandsworth High Street SW18 4LB
(Wandsworth)
T (020) 8871 9752   slybeastbrewing.com
First sold beer: October 2019, ¶(informal)
🕐 *We-Th* 12.00-23.00, *Fr-Sa* 12.00-24.00,
   Su 12.00-22.30.
4 cask, 4 keg, 4-5 bottles, tequila.
¶ Enhanced pub grub, lunchtime sandwiches
££, ♿
*Tastings, food matching, big screen sport,
shuffleboard, vintage arcade games*

≥ Wandsworth Town   ⛴ Wandsworth Riverside
🚌 Southside Shopping Centre   🚲 NCN20, C8
🚶 Wandle Trail, link to Thames Path

Ram Inn

Commercial brewing returned to the historic
Ram site in central Wandsworth in October
2019 with the reopening of the landmark
Ram Inn as a brewpub, soon to be joined by
Sambrook's around the corner (below). Head
brewer Alex Leclere presides over a 10hl
brewhouse behind glass in one corner, making
SlyBeast beers named after two dogs belonging to the sister of one of the licensees: their
stylised profiles appear on the logo. Besides
the house beers and familiar Young's brands,
you'll find guests from other locals including
Sambrook's and Wimbledon. The big pub has
been indulgently refurbished: the ground floor
bar is traditionally styled with plenty of wood,
stained glass and a ram emblem rescued from
an upstairs room, while a generous upstairs
space, in sharp contrast, is playfully done out as
an indoor garden, with fake grass, multicoloured oil drums, shuffleboard, arcade games and
a taco truck open at busier times. The regular
menu might include T-bone steaks, beer
cheese fondue or spicy cauliflower wings. For
more on the long story of brewing on the site,
see the Ram Resurgent (below).

BEERS are in keg and cask, sold in the pub and
in some other Young's outlets. The flagship is
1533 Session IPA (4.2%), named after the
earliest record of an inn on the site, with
changing specials and seasonals.

Rose and Crown 26

Contemporary pub
140 Tooting Bec Road SW17 8BH
T (020) 8767 1589   frontierpubs.co.uk
🕐 *Mo-Th* 12.00-23.00, *Fr-Sa* 12.00-24.00,
   Su 12.00-22.30. Children until 19.00.
2 cask, 10 keg, 30 bottles/cans, cider/perry, gins.
¶ Pizzas and salads **££**, ☂ Small rear garden, ♿
*Occasional small beer festivals, food promotions,
big screen sports, family days, board games*

⊖ Tooting Bec   🚲 Link to C5, C57   🚶 Link to Capital Ring

Rejigged by Frontier in February 2017, this
bulky corner pub by Tooting Bec Common is a
particularly noteworthy member of the group.
A generous interior wrapped round the bar
has half-height panelling and some attractive
window seats. Five Points and Sambrook's are
fixtures on cask and a good few of the kegs are
from bigger suppliers like Beavertown, Brixton
and Camden Town, but enthusiastic and
knowledgeable staff ensure a rotation of
guests from breweries like BBNo, Belleville,
By the Horns, Harbour and Villages, all available
in tasting flights. There's a regular Battle of
the Breweries where customers vote on their
favourite and the winner is listed for a month.
Draught darker options can be scarce but
there's plenty in the fridges including some
rarities. As always with this chain, food is
freshly baked pizza with toppings like *nduja*
(spicy, spreadable salami), wild mushrooms or
burrata cheese, with vegan options too.

Sambrook's Brewery ㉗ (Ram Brewery)

Brewery, taproom

1 Bellwether Lane SW18 1UD (Wandsworth)
T (020) 7228 0598 **sambrooksbrewery.co.uk**
First sold beer: 1533 (Ram Brewery), November
2008 (Sambrook's at original site), 🍴

🕐 *Taproom*: *Daily* 12.00-24.00. Heritage centre:
Tu-Sa 11.00-19.00 or by appointment.
Children welcome.

4 cask, 10 keg, 10+ bottles/cans, growlers,
minicasks, bag-in-box. 🍷

🍴 Pizzas, light bites **£-££**, 🪑 Tables on historic
brewery yard, ♿

*Brewery museum, brewing sessions, beer festivals,
tastings, beer launches, comedy, seasonal events,
functions*

🚆 Wandsworth Town ⛴ Wandsworth Riverside
🚌 Southside Shopping Centre 🚲 NCN20, C8
🚶 Wandle Trail, link to Thames Path

Founded in Battersea, London's fifth-oldest
brewery now occupies part of London's, and
likely Britain's, oldest brewing site, in a row of
listed 1880s buildings in the redeveloped
former Young's Ram brewery in Wandsworth.
A large taproom occupies a high-ceilinged
former engine house lit by four imposingly tall
arched windows, laid out with beer hall-style
tables and benches, with cosier booths around
the edges. A kitchen in one corner, operated
by the highly regarded Crust Brothers, specialises in Neapolitan pizzas, including vegan,
white and personalised options, plus salads
and sides. There's more upstairs, including an
events space where you can admire the base
of the brick chimney that dominates the site.
The old brewhouse to the south, disused since
the 1980s, is now the shop and entrance to the
heritage centre, with displays on the history of
brewing and of the site and views of preserved
equipment including two tall coppers. Take a
tour and there's a good chance it'll be led by
the legendary John Hatch, the former Young's
employee who continued to brew onsite during
the redevelopment. Tours include a visit to the
current brewhouse in the building to the north,
where the new 20 hl automated brewhouse
had to be manoeuvred in around low Victorian

beams. It's taken a while, but this is a delightful
outcome to what could have been a serious
loss of brewing heritage. For more on the
story, see The Ram Resurgent (below).

BEERS are in cask (still the core of the business),
keg, can and bottle, the last two packaged at
SEB (South East Bottling) in Broadstairs which
the brewery jointly owns with two Kent breweries, Gadds and Westerham. Styles have a more
traditional slant than typical among the capital's
breweries. The flagship is bitter **Wandle Ale***
(3.8%), its name now particularly appropriate
as the like-named river runs only metres away.
Other core beers include light but hoppy
Session Pale Ale (4% keg, 3.4% cask); **Pump-
house Pale Ale** (4.2%); modern red rye ale
Battersea Rye* (4.5% cask, 5.8% bottle/ keg);
special bitter **Junction*** (4.5%); **London Pale
Ale** (4.5%, not cask); **Powerhouse Porter**
(4.9%); and **Battersea IPA** (6.2%, not cask).
Seasonals include popular **Lavender Hill** pale

ale with lavender honey (4.5%), **Black IPA** (6.9%) and **Imperial Stout*** (10.4%). A new lager range in keg and can, facilitated by the addition of horizontal conditioning tanks during the move, launched in 2021 with **Pagoda Pils** (4.5%). John Hatch's Ram nanobrewery is also now in the Sambrook's precincts and still producing beers like **QA** (Quaffing Ale, 3.9%), an ordinary bitter, and best bitter **Wandsworth Phoenix*** (4.3%) plus bespoke brews and specials, using a descendant of the Young's yeast.

SlyBeast Brewing
See Ram Inn

We Brought Beer

17B Tooting Market, 21 Tooting High Street SW17 0SN

T (020) 8673 9324   webroughtbeer.co.uk

🕐 *Tu-We* 14.00-19.00, *Th-Fr* 14.00-21.00, *Sa* 12.00-20.00, *Su* 12.00-18.00. Children welcome.

3 keg, 200 bottles, growlers, brewing kits, specialist gin and wine at nearby stalls.

🍴 Various from neighbouring traders,

♿ (in market)

Occasional joint events with neighbours

🚆🚌Ⓤ Balham   ♿ CS7   🚶 Link to Capital Ring

Resplendent in clean white tiles, this little bar is a welcome attraction in covered Tooting Market (not to be confused with Tooting Broadway Market nearby, home to Craft Tooting above). Kegs tend to be light, refreshing and mainly British, though one line often dispenses something stronger and more unusual. Bottles and cans include a good range from London and the UK – for example Burnt Mill, Partizan, Weird Beard or Wylam – and some craft imports like Dugges or Naparbier. There's a cluster of communal tables nearby, and local deliveries too. The original parent shop in Balham is now a Clapton Craft.

TRY ALSO

Antelope 76 Mitcham Road SW17 9NG theantelopepub.com: Longstanding good bet for beer close to Tooting Broadway Tube station, an Antic pub since 2009. Seven well-kept casks, six interesting kegs and a handful of bottles/cans. Comprises two spacious rooms with candles and a real fire behind an unusual three-arched façade.

Clapton Craft SW12 28 Hildreth Street SW12 9RQ claptoncraft.co.uk: At the end of an attractive pedestrianised street of independent shops, this began as the original We Brought Beer. It transferred to Clapton Craft in September 2020 and stocks their usual exemplary range (p179), available to take away or drink in.

Duke of Battersea 74 Battersea Bridge Road SW11 3AG brewdog.com: The inaugural Draft House, opened in 2007 on a corner site just south of Battersea Bridge and rebranded as a BrewDog pub in 2021. Two cask, 14 keg and 45 bottles/cans including a few more US and Scandinavian imports than usual in a pleasantly pubby environment.

Firefly 3 Station Parade, Balham High Road SW12 9AZ fireflybar.co.uk: Lively and popular combination of beer bar and Thai restaurant close to Balham station. One cask, 14 keg and 15 bottles/cans including locals Belleville, Gipsy Hill and Kernel, Belgian and German imports and interesting guests.

Hagen and Hyde 157 Balham High Road SW12 9AU hagenandhyde.com: Cavernous but curiously cosy Antic venue, handy for Balham station, with a split-level beer garden and more of interest than average, often featuring local guests in unusual styles among five cask, nine keg and around 20 bottles/cans.

Northcote Arms 94 Northcote Road SW11 6QW brewdog.com: This was the second and one of the smaller Draft Houses, since rebranded as a BrewDog pub. Among boutique shops not far from the Eagle (above), it has a relaxed local vibe. Three cask, 15 keg and around 60 bottles/cans.

LONDON'S BREWING | The Ram resurgent

The Ram brewery, at Wandsworth near the mouth of Thames tributary the Wandle, can justifiably claim to be the oldest continuous brewing site in Britain, and certainly in London. Shepherd Neame in Faversham, Kent, claims to be Britain's oldest *brewer* as it's the successor of a business founded in 1698. But there's evidence of brewing at the Ram more than a century before that, and likely beyond.

Back in 1512, when Henry VIII's navy is recorded as sourcing beer supplies from the vicinity, Wandsworth was a small but prosperous village at the point where the road from London to Kingston upon Thames crossed the Wandle. We don't know where that early brewery was, but we do know an inn with the sign of a ram stood on the site of the present Ram Inn at the corner of the High Street and Ram Street, just east of the river, from at least 1533. A hostelry servicing traffic on such a busy road would undoubtedly have its own brewhouse, and by 1581, it was certainly occupied by a brewer, Humphrey Langridge. By the late 18th century, the Ram had developed into a successful porter brewery which had already expanded into adjacent buildings and begun to build an estate of pubs under the ownership of the Tritton family.

Future owners the Youngs were initially involved in the industry as prominent manufacturers of brewing vessels based in Southwark: it was a Young's porter tun that triggered the Great Beer Flood of 1814 (p82). Charles Allen Young bought the Ram in 1831, initially in partnership with Anthony Bainbridge: the partnership was dissolved abruptly in 1883 when Anthony's son Herbert was discovered pursuing an adulterous affair in Paris with the wife of Charles's son, Charles Florance. Now simply known as Young & Co, the brewery had successfully shifted its focus from porter towards the lighter, more sparkling beers for which the Young's name would become famous. The site, which gradually expanded west to the Wandle and some way north to occupy almost 2ha, was rebuilt several times: much of what's visible today was erected in the years following a major fire in 1882. The oldest surviving building is the 1724 brewer's house on the High Street.

The beer consumer movement of the 1970s and 1980s knew Young's as a fiercely independent fortress of brewing tradition. It always kept the faith with traditional cask ales, retained wooden casks years after most of the industry had converted to metal, kept a live ram on the site as a mascot and delivered locally using horse-drawn drays to the end. It retired its steam engines as late as 1976, and even invited the Queen Mother to pull its pints.

After decades of resolutely defending the company's independence and repulsing approaches from major brewers during the years of merger mania, it was therefore a shock to many when, in 2006, chairman John Young admitted he'd let his head rule his heart as he announced Young's was partnering with Charles Wells and relocating all production to the latter's big 1970s plant in Bedford. Rocketing property values and the challenges of modernising the cramped old site had finally undermined the case against change. In a poignant twist, John, a great-great-grandson of Charles Allen Young, died aged 85 the very week his company brewed its last beer at the Ram.

The day after the closure announcement, two Young's staff, John Hatch and ex-Truman brewer Derek Prentice, contacted the London Borough of Wandsworth to see what could be done about maintaining brewing on the site. The council couldn't stop the sale but resolved to make the provision of a microbrewery one of the conditions of planning permission for future redevelopment. While Derek got a new job at Fuller's, John, a former homebrewer who had joined Young's in 1988 as a biochemist before becoming brewhouse manager and health and safety supervisor, approached new owners Minerva with a stopgap plan. 'I told them, look,' recalls John, 'isn't it a shame that you've got the world's oldest brewery, but then there'll be a gap and you'll have the world's newest brewery. I can build you a nanobrewery and keep things going so you'll have a USP for the

John Hatch and his legendary nanobrewery

site. Not only did they say yes, so long as I cleared it with Young's, they also offered me the job of site manager. I was delighted, but I only expected it to be for two or three years.' Young's agreed too, but only on condition John didn't sell the beer he brewed.

One final gyle from the old brewhouse was used to fill bottles with a year's supply of wort, keeping fermentation going while John cobbled together a tiny 50 litre kit from bits and pieces found around the site. The cold liquor tank was a cloakroom water tank, the hot liquor tanks immersion heaters from mess rooms and the mash tun a waste receptacle from the bottling line, adapted with some of the insulation from the main mash tun. In place of a sparge arm, John ingeniously rigged up a device that sprayed hot liquor onto a tiny electrically powered plastic propeller. A tea urn was repurposed as a copper and two filtration tanks were turned upside down and fitted with cooling coils to serve as fermentation vessels. He used the Young's house yeast, and

with no lab facilities has simply kept repitching it: almost 1,000 fermentations later, it's developed something of an individual character. He also salvaged other items from around the site, from brewing logs to bottles and pub signs, to create an unparalleled collection of Young's-related material.

While the new brewhouse was assembled from scrap at negligible cost, buying ingredients and other supplies was more of a problem given the ban on commercial sales. But then a running club which had missed visiting the old brewery asked John if he could host a tour. He brewed a special beer for them and soon found his honesty box stuffed full. Offering beer to guests on private tours in exchange for voluntary donations proved a vital way of sustaining the project, alongside catering to film and TV crews seeking an atmospheric location: 'If there's been a grisly murder on TV in recent years, it's probably been here,' says John. Meanwhile, the redevelopment became increasingly delayed by planning and funding issues. Finally, a new owner, Greenland, owned by the Chinese government, bought the site from Minerva and started construction in 2014. This put a stop to the tours and necessitated a move to the old stable block, but by now the honesty box had a new source of income from monthly comedy nights.

Elsewhere, the closure of Young's had helped spur others to enter the industry. City accountant Duncan Sambrook opened Sambrook's, not far from Wandsworth, in what was then one of the less sought-after parts of Battersea in 2008. With the help of veteran microbrewer David

Welsh, formerly of Ringwood brewery in Hampshire, he installed a 33hl Canadian-built brewhouse in a former photography studio not far from the Thames on Yelverton Road. While Sambrook's earliest beers, Wandle and Junction, were by no means clones of Young's brand leaders Bitter and Special, they settled into a similar niche, and with some irony were soon appearing in Young's pubs in response to the local loyalties of customers. Such demand prompted expansion into two neighbouring units.

There was a certain poetry to the announcement in 2019 that, with redevelopment almost complete, Sambrook's would be satisfying the requirement for an onsite brewery by relocating to the Ram. Even more pleasingly, John Hatch, whose three-year stopgap was eventually lengthened to 15 years, was joining the Sambrook's team, bringing his brewing kit and collection with him. Following some inevitable Covid-related delay, during which John distributed free beer in polypins to the locked-down local residents, the first Sambrook's beer was produced on the site in April 2021: appropriately, it was a batch of the flagship Wandle Ale, now brewed within 100 m or so of the river itself. The taproom opened in July, with the heritage centre following in the autumn. The complex takes up a range of 1883 Grade II*-listed brewery buildings along Ram Street, including an engine house, chimney, porter tun room and pre-1980s brewhouse still complete with its domed Victorian coppers.

While Sambrook's is the inheritor of the continuous

cont.

cont.

LONDON'S BREWING | The Ram resurgent

brewing tradition through its connection with John, another surprise was the appearance in 2019 of a second brewery on the site, back at the Ram Inn where it all began. The pub, rebuilt in 1885 after the fire, was renamed the Brewery Tap in 1974. Though closed with the brewery in 2006, it was the one part of the site retained by Young's, which remains in business as a pub company (Brewers without breweries p324). It's been leased to well-known local licensees Keris and Lee De Villiers, who have reopened it under its old name (above), complete with a small brewhouse operating under the name Sly Beast. Its flagship beer, appropriately enough, is named 1533.

Meanwhile, the rest of the Ram has become one of London's most prestigious new neighbourhoods, where one-bedroom flats sell for over £700,000. But everyone can now wander unhindered through the brewery yard and admire the preserved historic buildings, including views previously obscured by less attractive late 20th century additions. Even the horse stalls in the stables, each complete with a nameplate for its former occupant, will still be in place when the building (not part of the Sambrook's project) reopens in 2022, likely as a restaurant. And with no less than two working breweries, the Ram can add to its long list of records as being possibly the best-preserved piece of London brewing heritage you could hope to find.

Outer Southwest London

7000 Jars of Beer

Shop, bar

1 Crown Passage, Kingston upon Thames KT1 1JB
T (020) 8549 4000   **7000jarsofbeer.co.uk**
🕐 *Tu-We* 12.00-20.00, *Th-Fr* 12.00-21.00,
　 Sa 11.00-21.00, *Su* 11.00-18.00.
　 Children welcome.
4 keg, 200-250 bottles/cans, growlers, gins,
　 wines from small producers. 🍴
🍴 BYO
Tutored tastings, tap takeovers

🚆 Kingston   🚢 Kingston Turks Pier   🚲 NCN4, link to
C28, C29   🚶 London Loop, Thames Down Link, Thames Path

Much care and thought is evident in this smart
bottle shop and bar, in everything from the
simple but tasteful décor to the varied and
helpfully-categorised range. 'It was by country,'
owner Susie Statham (ex-Partizan) told me,
'but we found that didn't make things easier
for people just getting into beer.' Opened in
September 2017 in an alley off Kingston's
historic market place, it regularly offers London
beers on keg and across the shelves, including
very local Park, Twickenham and tiny Anomaly,
plus Burnt Mill, First Chop, Time and Tide and
Tynt Meadow, with numerous reduced alcohol
and gluten-free options. Imports could include
Cyclic Beer Farm from Barcelona alongside
Boulevard, Half Acre, Modern Times, Põhjala
and familiar Belgian names. Tutored tastings
are a regular feature, including a popular
'introduction to craft beer'.

Visitor note *Before he was the sun in the sky, the Egyptian*
god Ra was a king on earth, and became angry with
malcontents plotting against him. His anger transformed his
gentle daughter Hathor into her ferocious alter-ego Sekhmet,
who after hunting down the rebels got bloodthirsty and
started killing people indiscriminately. So Ra had his servants
brew 7,000 jars of beer, dye it red and flood the killing fields
with it to the depth of three palms. Sekhmet, mistaking the
beer for blood, drank it and became drunkenly pacified,
averting the threat to humanity.

Albion

Contemporary pub
45 Fairfield Road, Kingston upon Thames KT1 2PY

T (020) 8541 1691   **thealbionkingston.com**
⏱ *Mo-Th* 12.00-23.00, *Fr-Sa* 12.00-23.30, *Su* 12.00-22.30. Children welcome.
10 cask, 19 keg, 35+ bottles/cans, 5 ciders/ perries, whiskies and other spirits.
🍴 Imaginative comfort food **£-££**,
🌳 Rear garden, ♿
Quiz (Su), food promotions

🚆 Kingston   🚲 C29, link to NCN4   🚶 Link to Thames Path

This solid corner pub overlooking the greenery of Kingston's Fairfield was reopened in October 2016 by the Sussex Arms (p312) owners on a long lease from Greene King. It offers some of the best beer in the area in the comfortable surrounds of a proper pub, with wood panelling, decorated ceilings, and keg taps emerging from smart tiling behind the bar. Besides house Big Smoke, the casks might be from Arbor, Burning Sky, Gloucester, Marble, West Berkshire or Wiper & True, with contributors to the keg range stretching to Harbour or Partizan, including stronger and darker options. Classics like Früh Kölsch and Bavarian Dunkelweizen associate in the fridges with BBNo and Cloudwater. A menu of decent comfort food might include homemade chicken curry, herb-crusted fish pie or vegan chilli, with good value sandwiches at lunchtime. Included in the pub group's Big Smoke loyalty card scheme.

Anomaly Brewing

Brewery, no visitors please
New Malden KT3 (Kingston upon Thames)
anomalybrewing.co.uk
First sold beer: October 2018

Graphic designer Adam Sutton began home-brewing in 2017 and became a part-time professional a little over a year later, working on a small scale using a 1.5hl direct-fired kit in a converted garage at his New Malden home. Following the success of his beers locally, he's planning to go full-time and may expand operations.

BEERS depart from the well-worn hoppy pale ale norm of most new startups, drawing inspiration instead from Belgian, French and older British styles. The flagship is **Luna-Tic** (7.1%), a dry-hopped take on a bière de garde, since joined by **Witch Doctor*** (4.6%), a coffee porter with a Belgian twist. Most beer is bottled, with keg recently added.

CTZN Brew ③②

Brewery, no visitors please
477 Upper Richmond Road West SW14 7PU (Richmond upon Thames)   **ctznbrew.com**
First sold beer (as Kew Brewery): June 2015.
🚚 (local deliveries only).

This little 10hl brewhouse in a former shop unit in East Sheen was founded as Kew Brewery by ex-Weird Beard brewer Dave Scott and his wife Rachel and sold in December 2018 to Jana Gray, formerly at the Amsterdam Brewery in Toronto, and her partner Jon. After struggling with lack of taproom space, during the 2020 lockdowns the partners rethought the project and relaunched in May 2021 with a new brand and a more spacious and accessible high street outlet in Twickenham (p309), though the beer is still brewed here for the time being. The new brand stresses the social and environmental concerns which have always been part of the brewery's DNA, with an ambition to include sustainable ingredients from Africa in the recipes.

BEERS are mainly bottle conditioned and keg. Among the core range are flavoured pale **Botanic** (3.8%); **Porter*** (4%); **Rye Pale Ale** (4.3%); and a flagship **IPA** (5.5%).

Drop Project Brewing Co ㉝

Brewery, taproom
8 Willow Business Centre, 17 Willow Lane,
Mitcham CR4 4NX
First sold beer: March 2021 ‼
⊕ *Fr* 15.00-22.00, *Sa-Su* 12.00-22.00. Children
    until 19.00.
Occasional cask, 6-12 keg, 12+ cans. ⌁.
⊪ Occasional food trucks, ⊓ Tables on
loading bay, ⌂
*Tastings, beer launches, meet the brewer, live
music, art exhibitions, cycle club.*

⇌ ⊖ Mitcham Junction ⅍ Link to NCN20 ⅋ Link to
Wandle Trail

Two former members of the Gipsy Hill team,
John 'JT' Taylor and Joe Simo, got together
with friend Will Skipsey to launch this eco-
conscious enterprise in October 2019, originally
cuckoo brewing at Missing Link in West Sussex
before commissioning their own brewhouse
on a Mitcham industrial estate. As much as
possible is recycled and they've committed to
planting a tree for every brew and for every
100 pints sold on site. A basic taproom with
views of the impressive 30 hl brewhouse
should be open by the time you read this,
soon expanding to accommodate additional
lines for independent guests and fridges of
stuff that the brewers like to drink from
Europe and the UK. The name refers equally
to liquids, brewing, board sports and music:
'when something drops it makes a splash,'
comments JT. It's an easy walk from Mitcham
Junction station, in turn only two tram stops
away from Therapia Lane, for Anspach &
Hobday (p242) and Signal (p250).

BEERS in keg and can include DDH New
England pale ale **Shifty** (5.2%); 'West Coast
pilsner' **Crispy*** (5.3%) with fruity US hops;
and a changing range of specials in varied
styles from lagers to sours.

Dysart ㉞

Restaurant
135 Petersham Road, Richmond TW10 7AA
T (020) 8940 8005
thedysartpetersham.co.uk
⊕ *Th-Fr* 12.00-14.45, 18.00-21.15, *Sa* 12.00-15.15,
    18.30-21.15, *Su* 12.00-15.30. Children until
    20.00.
17 bottles/cans, wines, specialist spirits.
⊪ Modern European gastro menu, tasting
menu with beer matching **£££**, ⊓ Front
garden, ⌂
Live classical and jazz music, functions

⇌ ⊖ Richmond ⊟ The Dysart ⅍ Link to Tamsin Trail
⅋ Capital Ring, link to Tamsin Trail, Thames Path

Winning its first Michelin star in 2019, the
Dysart is one of the few in its sector to make a
point of offering beer with food. It's idyllically
situated in the village-like and astronomically
expensive surroundings of Petersham, right
next to Richmond Park: the 1904 Arts and
Crafts building was once a landmark pub and
still has a bus stop named after it. Current
owner Barny Taylor leased it in 2004, ultimately
buying the freehold and dropping the pub to
concentrate on the gastro with the help of
Irish-born head chef and former Roux scholar
Kenneth Culhane. An inventive, regularly
changing menu with plentiful vegetarian
options makes use of unusual pickles from
local ingredients, and might include truffled
Jerusalem artichoke velouté, Yorkshire grouse
with apple and cabbage, steamed cod with
bacon and chanterelles or roasted cauliflower
tortellini, with Valrhona chocolate and praline
for dessert. A well-chosen UK beer list
encompasses locals like Park and Twickenham,
alongside Bristol Beer Factory, Harviestoun
and Meantime. There's a dazzling wine list too,
but the gourmet tasting menu also offers a
(much cheaper) beer matching route. Barny
reports that while most customers ultimately
go for the wine, the beer options spark conversations and prompt people to think about beer
with food perhaps for the first time. A smart and
airy interior has flagstone floors and a grand
piano in an alcove. The experience doesn't come
cheap, but the affordable lunchtime set menu
offers excellent value. Booking recommended.

Hand in Hand ㉟
Traditional pub
6 Crooked Billet SW19 4RQ **T** (020) 8946 5720
thehandinhandwimbledon.co.uk
🕐 *Su-Mo* 11.00-23.00, *Tu-Th* 10.00-23.00, *Fr-Sa*
10.00-24.00. Children very welcome (but
no very young children in bar area).
8 cask, 5 keg, 12 bottles, 1 cider/perry, 15-20
malts, some wines.
🍴 Pies, enhanced pub grub/gastro **££-£££**,
🎋 Front terrace, adjacent common, ♿
*Occasional beer festivals, cellar masterclasses, ale
supper club, tastings, meet the brewer, occasional
quizzes, dog walking events, fundraising, major big
screen sport*

🚆 Raynes Park, Wimbledon   ⊖⊕ Wimbledon   🚌 Edge Hill
🚲 Link to NCN208   🚶 Wimbledon Common paths

This picturesque pub with its poignant sign
commanding a triangle of green on the edge of
Wimbledon Common might not have the biggest range in the world but certainly takes its
beer seriously. Longstanding manager Andrew
Forde is, I believe, the only one in London to
invite the public into his cellar for regular cask ale
workshops, now supplemented by an 'ale supper
club' often with guest brewers. The handpumped
beers – Wells-brewed Young's bitter, Special and
Courage Directors, seasonals, St Austell Proper
Job and guests from locals like Twickenham,
Wimbledon and Surrey Hills – are reliably
immaculate. Food majors on pies, including
veggie options, and main courses like mussels
with chorizo, pork steaks and imaginative
salads. A 2019 refurbishment hasn't detracted
from its ability to provide a welcoming retreat
after an energetic stride across the common.

Visitor note. *The building originated as a bakehouse in 1831
and has been a Young's pub since 1974.*

Hand in Hand

Hope 🏅 ㊱
Traditional pub
48 West Street, Carshalton SM5 2PR
T (020) 8240 1255   **hopecarshalton.co.uk**
🕐 *Mo-Sa* 12.00-23.00, *Su* 12.00-22.30. Children
very welcome until 19.00 but not in front bar.
7 cask, 9 keg, 50 bottles, 4 ciders/perries,
mead, English country wines.
🍴 Pot meals, rolls **£**, 🎋 Large rear garden, ♿
*Near-monthly beer festivals, occasional meet the
brewer, tap takeovers, monthly jam session, mead
moot, morris dancing, pagan events, bar billiards,
board games, beer books*

🚆 Carshalton   🚲 Link to NCN20   🚶 Link to Wandle Trail

When the regulars heard that landlords
Punch were intent on selling their pub off as a
restaurant, they literally didn't give up Hope.
A group of them negotiated a 20-year lease
and reopened the place in 2010 as a beer-
friendly free house. Downton New Forest Ale
and Windsor & Eton Knight of the Garter are
regulars, with cask guests chosen by style
from breweries like Arbor, Kissingate, Siren,
Vibrant Forest and Weird Beard, usually with
two dark beers, one session beer, one stronger
pale and one traditional bitter. Keg taps dispense
beers from Kernel, Magic Rock, Mondo, Partizan
and the like alongside decent imported lagers,
while the changing bottled range could include
Mad Squirrel and Redchurch alongside
Mikkeller and 3 Fonteinen lambics. Typically
hearty pot-based meals are sweet and sour
vegetable noodles, pork *bigos* or *bœuf
bourgoignon* served with doorstep bread
slices. The front section is woody and
traditional, opening into a cheerful recently

added rear extension with much more space. There's a permanent marquee in the fine garden for the beer festivals, which include one dedicated to the dark stuff. All-in-all, it's an irresistible combination.

Visitor note: Though the pub is community-owned, the real boss is Pubcat, who turned up one day to claim the place and has since become something of a celebrity in her own right.

Jeffersons Brewery

Brewery, no visitors please
Richmond TW9 (Richmond upon Thames)
T 07960 597311   jeffersonsbrewery.co.uk
First sold beer: July 2017,

One of London's smaller commercial breweries, Jeffersons derives its name from homebrewing brothers Freddie and George Jefferies, who first sold their beer at the Barnes Fair in 2017 after two years of planning and preparation. Double and triple brew days are common on the custom-built 3hl kit thanks to rising demand. The site isn't suitable for visitors but a local taproom is planned.

BEERS are either in keykeg or bottle conditioned in 330ml bottles. Core beers (not tasted) are **Thirsty Eagle** American blonde (4.2%), **Across the Pond** session IPA (4.5%) and IPA **Big Ocean** (6%).

Micro Beers

Shop, bar
335 Upper Richmond Road West SW14 8QR
T (020) 8392 9333   micro-beers.co.uk
Mo-Tu 15.00-21.00, We-Th 14.00-21.00, Fr 12.00-21.00, Sa 11.00-21.00, Su 12.00-19.00. Children welcome.
4 keg, 150-200 bottles/cans, growlers, organic and natural wines.
Occasional popups
Meet the brewer, tap takeover, tutored tastings, beer books

≈ Mortlake   St East Sheen

This modern bottle shop-bar in East Sheen opened in November 2016 under the expert eye of South African-born owner Seán Looney, who previously ran a 'craft beer hotel' in

Norway then worked for We Brought Beer (p275). The Nordic connection helps explain the occasional presence of brewers like Amundsen and Lindheim, though there are also plenty of London and UK names – Gipsy Hill, Jeffersons, Kernel, North, Partizan, Verdant and Wylam among them. Traditional Belgian and German treats include Andechs, Rodenbach and St Bernardus. The draught taps draw on similar sources but avoid replicating bottles and cans and usually include sours and strong stouts as well as pales. A scattering of tables invites drinking in.

Mitre

Contemporary pub
20 St Marys Grove, Richmond TW9 1UY
T (020) 8940 1336   themitretw9.co.uk
Mo-Fr 15.00-23.00, Sa 12.00-23.00, Su 12.00-20.30. Children until 21.00.
7-8 cask, 6 keg, 6+ cans, some wines.
Order-in pizzas, Front terrace, rear garden
Live music (Su), bar billiards, board games, major big screen sports

≈ North Sheen   Richmond   St Mary's Grove

You have to work hard to attract custom on this quiet side street between Richmond and East Sheen, but the Mitre manages it. The former Young's house was refurbished and

Mitre

reopened in 2015 by Chris French, who focuses on keeping a wide choice of quality cask. Beers are usually sourced from outside the M25 and otherwise not readily available locally: Taylor Landlord is the only constant, with breweries like 360°, Bristol, Clouded Minds, Gadds and Summer Wine regularly favoured. Kegs and cans are from the likes of Burning Sky, Tiny Rebel and Wild. There's a beer-themed original work by graffiti artist Angry Dan in the pretty garden but otherwise the half-height wall panelling and antique pub mirrors create a traditional look. A scattering of music-related items reflects another of Chris's passions, while resident dog Rudi was named the cutest pub dog in Britain in a 2017 book.

Visitor note *The freehold is held by the Richmond Charities, which also owns the almshouses diagonally opposite and other properties nearby. Its roots go back to a 14th-century church charity, thus the pub's ecclesiastical name: look for the stained glass window at the front depicting a bishop's mitre.*

Park Brewery (The)
Brewery, taproom
7 Hampden Road, Kingston upon Thames KT1 3LG (Kingston upon Thames)
T 07949 574618   theparkbrewery.com
First sold beer: March 2014, ⑪(informal)
⊕ *Taproom:* Fr-Sa 17.00-21.00, Children welcome.
   Shop: Mo-Fr 09.00-17.00, Sa 15.00-18.00, by arrangement only.
2 cask, 5 keg, 6+ cans. ⌁
⑪ Pies, popups **£**
Functions

⇌ Norbiton   🚌 Waters Road

Husband and wife team Josh and Frankie Kearns started Park on a modest scale, brewing bottled beers in 1.5hl batches for a small pub group. Their activities soon expanded and diversified on a 6hl kit. Problems with premises interrupted production in March 2018 and for a while the beer was made elsewhere. A crowd-funding campaign allowed a move to the current, larger site on a small industrial estate, where brewing restarted in February 2019 on a 25hl custom-made brewhouse, with space to expand further. Head brewer is Phil Banks, formerly at Battersea Brewery. Note the paper

sculpture of the brewery's trademark stag's head in the pleasant upstairs taproom as a witty alternative to an actual stuffed beast.

BEERS in keg, cask and can carry branding reflecting the proximity of nearby Richmond Park and the names usually have a connection. Regulars include flagship pale ale **Killcat** (3.9%); **Phantom*** (4.2%), a golden ale made with a Kölsch yeast; darker, stronger pale **Gallows** (4.5%); coffee porter **Rituals at Dawn** (5%); and **Spankers IPA** (6%). There are numerous seasonals.

Richmond Vault
Bar, restaurant
5 Hill Street, Richmond TW9 1SX
T (020) 8332 0055   richmondvault.co.uk
⊕ Tu-Th 16.00-24.00, Fr-Sa 12.00-01.00,
   Su 12.00-22.00. Children until 21.00.
1 cask, 10 keg, 90+ bottles, gins, whiskies, cocktails.
⑪ Mediterranean menu, burgers, pizzas **££**
Occasional live music and magic shows

⇌ ⊖ Richmond   🚢 Richmond St Helena   🏃 Capital Ring, Thames Path

---

Originally a Belgian-themed place and then a showcase for distributors Pigs Ear, this Richmond town centre cellar bar reinvented itself again in April 2016 under new owners as a self-proclaimed 'secret grotto of amazing beers'. Changing casks might be from Kirkstall or Salopian, while the keg taps dispense locals as well as the likes of Bristol, Burnt Mill and Mad Squirrel. A good few Belgians remain in the fridges – Rochefort and de la Senne among them – besides options from high-achieving UK breweries (Cloudwater, Double-Barrelled, Wylam) and the occasional import from elsewhere. Mussels are still on the menu too, but other dishes take a Mediterranean turn: chicken *taouk* and veggie moussaka, for example, plus beer and pizza deals available on certain days. The rear has been opened up to reveal a cheerful skylight, but the place retains its vaulted, intimate feel, bolstered by beer-related displays in alcoves.

Sultan

Traditional pub

78 Norman Road SW19 1BT

T (020) 8542 4532   hopback.co.uk

🕐 *Mo-We* 15.00-23.00, *Th* 12.00-23.00,
  Fr-Sa 12.00-24.00, *Su* 12.00-23.00.
  Children until early evening.

5-6 cask, 8+ bottles, growlers, polypins,
  6+ ciders/perries.

🍴 Pies, toasties, cheeseboards **£**,

🌳 Rear garden, ♿

3 annual beer festivals, quiz, acoustic music,
open mic, beer club (We/Fr), morris dancing, darts,
board games, functions

⊖ Colliers Wood, South Wimbledon   🚌 Quicks Road
♿ NCN20, link to CS7, Q4   🚶 Wandle Trail

Despite management changes in recent years,
this backstreet pub in South Wimbledon
remains largely unchanged both as a well-run
community local and the only London
showcase for Salisbury's Hop Back brewery.
Most beers are from the owners or the
associated Downton brewery – the famous
Summer Lightning and excellent Entire Stout
are regularly on cask. There's a full range of
bottles including gluten-free options and
possibly a guest from Wimbledon just down
the road, or the likes of Acorn or Thornbridge.
Food is limited to toasties and cheeseboards
and the work of renowned pie-maker Richard
Barrick. The pub, named after a racehorse
rather than a middle eastern potentate, has a
rather plain and bulky 1930s red-brick
exterior, but inside is bright and cosy, with
two bars, open fires, stripped wood tables, a
conservatory and an attractive outdoor patio.
The microbrewery project reported in the last
edition of this book was subsequently
abandoned.

Tap Tavern 43

Bar

Princes Street, Richmond TW9 1ED

T (020) 8940 2118   taptavern.co.uk

🕐 *Mo-We* 12.00-23.30, *Th-Sa* 12.00-01.00,
  Su 12.00-22.45. Children until 19.30.

3 cask, 16 keg, 100+ bottles, 30 gins, other
  specialist spirits.

🍴 Imaginative pub grub **££**, 🌳 Front terrace, ♿

Tap takeovers, tastings

⇌ ⊖ Richmond   ⛴ Richmond St Helena
🚶 Capital Ring, Thames Path

Until April 2016, the red-brick Richmond Arms,
tucked away in a narrow street in the heart of
Richmond, was the last traditional gay pub in
southwest London. It reopened in August 2017
as a tastefully contemporary craft beer and gin
bar with a jungle of potted plants and a pleasant
front terrace. The cask range rotates brewers
like By the Horns, Pig and Porter, Twickenham
and Wimbledon, with kegs in a range of styles
and strengths, though nearly all pale when I
looked, perhaps from Arbor, London Beer
Factory, Siren or abroad. Bottles and cans mix
familiar names with rarer ones like Dig, Heavy
Industries, imports from Cigar City, De Molen
or Wicked Weed and Boon lambic. Among the
kitchen offerings are 'beer bites' like truffle
macaroni cheese croquettes or pig's cheek
'scrumpets' with IPA mustard. Staff recommend
a daily four-third tasting flight though irritatingly
there's a rule against serving thirds of cask.

Willoughby Arms

Traditional pub
47 Willoughby Road, Kingston upon Thames
KT2 6LN
T (020) 8546 4236 **thewilloughbyarms.com**
🕐 *Mo-Sa* 10.30-24.00, *Su* 12.00-24.00.
Children until early evening.
7 cask.
🍴 Pizzas, pies **£**, 🪑 Rear garden, front seating, ♿
*2 annual beer festivals, live folk (Mo), quiz (Su),
twice monthly acoustic open mic, big screen sports,
darts, pool, table football*

🚃 Kingston 🚋 Kingston Turks 🚌 Shortlands Road
🚲 Link to NCN4 🥾 Link to Thames Path

This rather clunky-looking 1892 backstreet
pub was in apparently terminal decline in 1997
when Rick and Lysa Robinson turned it round,
not by going gastro but by concentrating on
community appeal, sport and cask ale, a
mission further boosted since the last edition
of this book as the pub is now free of tie. Rick
is a member of the Society for the Preservation
of Beers from the Wood, which meets here.
The handpumps dispense solidly traditional
and immaculately cellared offerings like Weltons
Horsham Pale and Twickenham Grandstand
besides beers from breweries like Exeter,
Harvey's, Oakham, Pig and Porter and Windsor
& Eton, often including darker options. Check
out the free film and sport exhibition on the
walls, with a still from *Escape to Victory* to mark
the transition, or escape the big screen TVs in
the unspoilt, wood-panelled saloon bar while
recalling that the Yardbirds once rehearsed in
an upstairs room. It was a local CAMRA pub of
the year in 2020.

Wimbledon Brewery

Brewery, taproom
8 College Fields, Prince Georges Road
SW19 2PT (Merton)
T (020) 3674 9786 **wimbledonbrewery.com**
First sold beer: June 2015. 🍴
Shop 🕐 *Mo-Th* 09.00-17.00, *Fr* 09.00-16.00.
7 bottles/cans, minikegs, bag-in-box, limited
keg for growlers or drinking in. 🍺
Taproom 🕐 *Fr* 16.00-19.00, *Sa* 11.00-16.00.
Children welcome.
2 cask, 3 keg, 7 bottles/cans, growlers,
minikegs, bag-in-box.
🪑 Outside yard, ♿

🔵 Colliers Wood 🚌 Runnymede 🚲 Link to NCN20, CS7
🥾 Link to Wandle Trail

The original Wimbledon Brewery, and the last
in the area for over a century, stood in the
High Street between 1832 and 1889, when it
burned down: ironically, a fire station was
built on the site, since converted to shops and
flats. The brewery's legacy was reclaimed at
the 2015 AFC Wimbledon beer festival when
beers bearing the phoenix logo of a new
Wimbledon brewery went on sale. This was
the brainchild of Mark Gordon and Richard
Coultart, created with the help of veteran
London brewer Derek Prentice, formerly of
the old Truman's, Young's and Fuller's. Derek
devised the initial recipes and specified the
new 50hl brewhouse, installed in a sizeable
industrial unit near Merton Abbey Mills. The
land once belonged to the abbey, which like
similar institutions maintained its own brewhouse until it was dissolved in 1538. Since the
launch in 2015 fermentation capacity has more

than doubled, with space for further growth, and Derek's son Michael has become joint head brewer. A well-presented bar is squeezed beneath a staircase, with casks kept in the adjacent coldroom: takeaway is always available during working hours, and perhaps a draught option, with tables and chairs appearing during weekend taproom hours when the cask and keg choice widens considerably.

BEERS are mainly in cask, with around a third of the remaining production split between keg, bottles (filtered and reseeded with conditioning yeast) and cans (unfiltered and unpasteurised), packaged off-site. The focus is on well-balanced beers with good drinkability under locally inspired names. Core casks include **Common Pale Ale** (3.7%); **Copper Leaf Red Ale*** (4%, 4.5% in cans); **Phoenix London Porter** (4.8%); and English-style IPA, **Quartermaine** (5.8%, also bottled), named after an owner of the old brewery. Kegs/cans include **Gold Lager*** (4.8%), lagered for five weeks; and West Coast-style pale **Bravo*** (5.5%). Traditional milds and old ales are released seasonally, including **XX** (3.5%), **XXK*** (4.8%) and **XXXK*** (10%).

Workshy Brewing
Brewery, no visitors please
Richmond TW9 (Richmond upon Thames)
workshybrewing.co.uk
First sold beer: September 2021. 🖱️.

Active commercially since 2018, originally at Ubrew, this nonconformist Australian duo subsequently cuckoo-brewed at Portobello and elsewhere. By autumn 2021 they should also be producing small runs commercially on a home-based 2hl kit, with a larger space with taproom planned for 2022.

BEERS (not tasted) in keg, can and bottle, mainly in contemporary style, are sold through local outlets.

TRY ALSO

Antelope 87 Maple Road, Surbiton KT6 4AW theantelope.co.uk: The original home of now-relocated Big Smoke (p318), still a friendly,

characterful place in the Sussex Arms group with a pretty garden and customarily excellent beer: 10 cask, 13 keg and 35+ bottles/cans.
Beer and Beyond 73 Ridgway SW19 4SS beerandbeyond.co.uk: Small, friendly local bottle shop with chilled drink-in space on the edge of Wimbledon Village: three keg (with growler fills), around 180 bottles/cans, mainly London/UK independents and German classics. Closed Monday.
Lamb 73 Brighton Road, Surbiton KT6 5NF lambsurbiton.co.uk: Charming, comfortable, slightly bohemian family-friendly free house with extensive garden and a specialist range of British cheeses to enjoy alongside a small but perfectly formed selection of four casks from top independents, including Surrey Hills.
Red Lion 2 Castelnau SW13 9RU red-lion-barnes. co.uk: Handsome Fuller's pub in upmarket Barnes, close to the London Wetland Centre and the former Olympic recording studios, long managed by a multiple Cellarman of the Year winner who ensures his five cask beers are reliably excellent, alongside nine keg and 10+ bottles with a few interesting guests.
Roebuck 130 Richmond Hill, Richmond TW10 6RN greeneking-pubs.co.uk: Spectacularly-sited pub atop Richmond Hill with views once admired by Wordsworth and Turner. It's a local CAMRA favourite and longtime champion of multiple SIBA-sourced guest casks, including from nearby Wimbledon, which feature alongside Greene King staples across eight pumps.
Watermans Arms 375 Lonsdale Road SW13 9PY thewatermansbarnes.co.uk: Barnes riverside landmark, now pleasingly a pub again after decades as a restaurant thanks to the Big Smoke/Sussex Arms (p312) crew, who have applied their usual high standards to a diverse range of at least seven casks, 13 kegs and over 25 bottles/cans. Great river view from the upstairs balcony.
Woodys 5 Rams Passage, Kingston upon Thames KT1 1HH woodyspubco.com: Quirky retreat standing out among the chain venues of Kingston's riverfront with skateboard art and sofas made from bathtubs. Interesting food including vegan options, one or two casks and plenty of keg, bottles and cans including from locals and interesting independents.

Ghost Whale

LONDON DRINKERS | Keith Flett

A familiar name to readers of the letter columns of certain newspapers and magazines, Keith Flett (@kmflett on Twitter) is a trade union official, beard wearer and beer blogger based in north London. He's been a CAMRA member since 1975.

How do you rate London as a beer city, on a world scale?
Not sure I'm competent to rate it on a world scale but for cask, it's up there and for other craft beers, it's getting there.

What's the single most exciting thing about beer in London right now?
The range of beer styles now so easily available.

What single thing would make things even better?
More of the leading craft beers available in more of the 'mainstream' pubs.

What are your top London beers right now?
Redemption Big Chief, Five Points Pale and Best, Pressure Drop Pale Fire, Howling Hops House IPA.

What's your top great beer night out?
It's a reflection of the scene's progress than I'm now very happy with a couple of pints at my local craft bar the High Cross in Tottenham (p118), five minutes' walk from my flat. Otherwise a night in the Cock in Hackney (p136) is usually unforgettable.

Who's your London beer hero?
Andy Moffat at Redemption. One of the original new wave pioneers, still producing great beer 10 years on.

Who will we be hearing a lot more from in future?
I'm expecting interesting and possibly great things from Exale. I'm increasingly impressed by Wild Card, Hackney and Howling Hops too.

Which are your other top beer cities?
I don't get (let) out much due to working, so I'll have to stick to the UK and say Bristol and Manchester.

WEST
LONDON

WEST LONDON

This section covers the W and SW post-codes outside the central area and north of the Thames, with a couple of exceptions. A handful of listings immediately west and northwest of Central London didn't fit neatly anywhere else, so I've grouped them as **Maida Vale to Dollis Hill**. They include places on the fringes of the City of Westminster, the borough of Kensington and Chelsea and beyond into Brent, including some with NW postcodes.

My **Hammersmith and Fulham** section is equivalent to the borough of the same name, which also takes in Shepherds Bush. The beer choice has significantly expanded here recently, especially around the major centre of Hammersmith.

Rising levels of beer interest are also evident further west, partly inspired by the presence of a very good but, until recently, isolated 21st-century brewery, Weird Beard in Hanwell. Besides the borough of Ealing, which encompasses Acton and Greenford, the **Ealing and Chiswick** section extends into the eastern part of Hounslow borough to take in Brentford and Chiswick, the latter home to London's biggest and oldest continuously operating commercial brewery, the world-famous Fuller's.

Outer West London wraps up the rest, including a notable cluster of recommendations around Twickenham and an important brewery. For the southern part of Richmond borough on the other side of the Thames, see Outer Southwest London (p279).

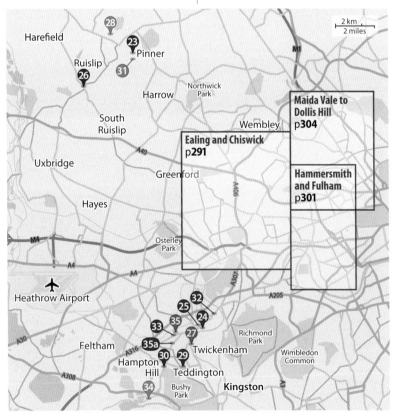

Ealing and Chiswick

BeerKat ❶

Bar, shop
38 The Broadway W5 2NP
T (020) 8161 0519 **beerkat.pub**
🕐 *Mo-Th* 12.00-23.00, *Fr-Sa* 12.00-24.00,
 Su 12.00-22.00. Children until 19.00.
11 keg, 150+ bottles/cans. 🍷.
🍴 Pizza menu **££**, 🪑 Front terrace
Tap takeovers, seasonal events

🚆 ⊖ Ealing Broadway

Opened in January 2020 opposite Ealing Broadway station, this cheerful bottle shop-bar is a new departure for pub operators (and brewers) Laine's in a busy area where similar venues are sparse. Its origin as two separate shop units is obvious: the one on the left is smaller and cosier, though it's all fairly simple and basic, enlivened by quirky art and plants in tin baths. A small outdoor terrace fronts on to the busy street. Besides Laine's beers on keg there are rotating guest choices mainly from London brewers, with a good showing for locals Weird Beard, including an imperial stout when I called. The fridges stretch further out – Burnt Mill, Double-Barrelled, smaller Londoners like Three Sods and a few imports from the likes of Saugutuck. A pizza oven behind the bar provides the food.

Black Dog (Fearless Nomad) ➋

Brewpub, contemporary pub
17 Albany Road, Brentford TW8 0NF (Hounslow)
T (020) 8568 5688 **blackdogbeerhouse.co.uk**
First sold beer: January 2020, ⑂(informal)
🕐 *Mo* 12.00-23.00, *We-Sa* 12.00-23.00,
  Su 12.00-22.30. Children until 20.30.
7 cask, 13 keg, 60+ bottles/cans, 5 ciders/
  perries, some wines and specialist spirits.
🍴 Inventive enhanced pub grub **££-£££**,
☂ Back garden ❀
Tap takeovers, occasional live music, board games

🚆 Brentford 🚌 Albany Road Brentford 🚶 Thames Path,
link to Brent River Park Walk, Capital Ring, Grand Union Canal Walk

Opened in October 2018 in a Brentford backstreet conservation area, this is a thoughtful reinvention of the Albany Arms, a once-troubled former Royal Brewery pub rebuilt in 1901. After many years setting up and operating beer-friendly pubs for other companies, Ash Zobell and brothers

Pete and James Brew created this highly attractive and civilised refuge which rightly picked up a local CAMRA award in 2020. A 1.6hl kit in a well-equipped shed in the back garden went into production under Pete's supervision late in 2019, but the selection is drawn from numerous other quality independents too, including some rarely seen in London, in styles that range from traditional bitters to strong stouts and exotic sours: a recent sampling yielded Attic Brew, Mobberley, Odyssey, Phantom and Surrey Hills among others, plus US, German, Dutch and Scandinavian imports in keg, bottle and can. The food menu surprises with a large range of tinned seafood including sardines from small producers and calamari in squid ink, served with sourdough bread, as well as dishes like fresh potato gnocchi with peas and broccoli, crusted baked hake and braised chorizo, steamed mussels and gourmet cheeseboards. The living room-like interior with its fireplaces and pot plants preserves some original stained glass.

BEERS in keg and cask are currently changing specials exclusively sold in the pub, though there are expansion plans for 2022. Styles tend towards the adventurous and unusual, like Belgian strong stout **Muscles from Brussels*** (9.5%).

Dodo ③
Micropub
52 Boston Road W7 3TR
T (020) 8567 5959 thedodomicropub.com
Tu 17.00-22.00, We-Th 12.00-14.00, 17.00-22.00, Fr-Sa 12.00-22.30, Su 12.00-17.00 (restricted opening Jan-Feb, please check). Children until 19.00.
5 cask, 20 bottles/cans, growlers, 4 ciders/ perries, natural and organic wines.
🍴 Pies, charcuterie plates, snacks, monthly free cheeseboard, occasional popups or BYO from local chippy £
Meet the brewer, tap takeovers, occasional silent disco, monthly adult colouring, board games

🚇 Hanwell 🚌 Lower Boston Road, Rosebank Road 🚶 Link to Brent River Park Walk, Capital Ring, Grand Union Canal Walk

---

Opened in February 2017 by former marketing specialist Lucy Do (thus the name, although the extinct bird features heavily in the clean white and pastel-green décor), this shopfront site a short walk from Hanwell Broadway is surely one of the most conscientious and best-run micropubs in London. A changing range of cask from brewers like Cocksure, Park, Wild or locals Weird Beard, usually including darker and stronger as well as session options, is fetched from the rear stillage in traditional micropub style. A couple of keg options are similarly sourced, and a shortish but immaculately picked bottle and can list includes Belgians, great London and UK choices like Partizan and gluten-free and low alcohol treats. Besides the exemplary beer offer, knowledgeable, friendly and efficient service and nice touches like a monthly free cheeseboard have attracted a loyal local following and secured several awards.

Ealing Brewing ④
Brewery, taproom: 2 The Ham, Brentford TW8 8EX (Hounslow)
T (020) 8568 9906 ealingbrewing.com
First sold beer: December 2016 (as Marko Paulo at original site)
Sa-Su 13.00-21.00. Children welcome.
4 cask, 4 keg, bottles, minicasks. 🍷
🍴 Occasional food truck

🚆 Brentford 🚌 Brent Lea 🚲 C9 🚶 Grand Union Canal Walk, Thames Path, link to Brent River Park Walk, Capital Ring

Owl and the Pussycat ④a
Micropub: 106 Northfield Avenue W13 9RT (Ealing) markopaulo.co.uk
Mo-Th 16.00-22.00, Fr-Sa 13.00-22.30.
8 cask, 6 keg, bottles, growlers, minicasks, 6+ ciders/perries.
🍴 Retro snacks
Tastings, board games, community library

🚇 Northfields

The Owl and the Pussycat opened in December 2016 complete with a tiny brewery named Marko Paulo after its founders, former teachers Paul Nock and head brewer Mark Yarnell. Its success exceeded expectations, and in summer 2019, the operation expanded to an industrial unit in Brentford with a 6hl kit under the Ealing Brewing name, with a taproom opening in November. Production at the pub had ceased by September 2021, but it remains a quiet and civilised drinking retreat in classic micropub style, decorated with several paintings depicting the titular characters from Edward Lear's poem. The beer range focuses on house lines in cask and keg, with much attention paid to correct serving temperatures.

BEERS in cask, keg, bottle, minicask and bag-in-box cover one of the widest style ranges in London. There's usually some variant on a bitter, mild, porter/stout and lager, plus a varying well-hopped golden ale named after Niagara Falls barrel surfer Charles Blondin, who once lived locally (usually 4-4.5%). Specialities have included Flemish-style sour reds and Lithuanian-style farmhouse ale. Quality is generally high, with **Mild*** (3.6%), **Burton Ale*** (5.5%) and **Foreign Extra Stout*** (6.6%) particularly noteworthy.

Fearless Nomad

See Black Dog

Fuller's Griffin Brewery ⑤

Brewery, taproom (Asahi)
Chiswick Lane South W4 2QB (Hounslow)
T (020) 8996 2000   **fullersbrewery.co.uk**
First sold beer: 1650, **⁈**
🕐 *Tu-We* 10.00-18.00, *Th-Sa* 10.00-20.00,
   Su 12.30-18.00
3-5 cask, 5-7 keg, 50+ bottles/cans, growlers,
   minikegs, wines, merchandise ⌂
🍴Tables planned for brewery yard evenings
and weekends, ♿
Tastings, functions

⊖ Stamford Brook, Turnham Green   🚌 Hogarth Roundabout
🚶 Thames Path

As London's only continuously operating
historic brewery (see panel below) as well
as its biggest, Fuller's shouldn't be missed.
Book in advance for frequent tours led by
well-informed guides which feature much
of interest, including the former brewhouse
still containing an 1863 mash tun with an
unusual 'Chinese hat' lid and the 1830s
London Copper, the oldest vessel on the site.

You'll finish with tastings at the atmospheric
Hock Cellar where there are extensive
historical displays. Passers-by don't need a
tour ticket to view the brewery yard with its
famous wisteria and planters of flowering
London Pride. The visitor centre building
was refurbished and expanded in July 2018,
with a new bar stocking specials from the
pilot brewery, visible behind glass at the
back, besides the core range, bottled rarities
and merchandise. Drink-in facilities added in
2021 partially make up for the sad loss of the
Mawson Arms, the historic brewery tap round
the corner, which closed for good during the
2020 lockdown.

*Visitor note. The site is between the River Thames and the
A4 Hogarth roundabout, next to pretty Chiswick village and
close to visitor attractions Chiswick House and Hogarth House,
the latter of which is the former residence of the artist and
engraver who famously depicted Gin Lane and Beer Street.*

BEERS are in cask, keg, can, bottle conditioned
and in filtered bottles, with some minikegs.
Several of the core brands are related through
the technique of 'parti-gyling', taking multiple
runnings at different gravities from the same
basic mash and tweaking the hop additions.
All Fuller's-branded beers are fermented using
a longstanding house yeast, while Gales and
Dark Star beers, from breweries acquired by

Fuller's pilot brewhouse

Fuller's, use different yeasts. Regulars include flagship **London Pride** (4.1% cask, 4.7% bottle/can); **Frontier** (4.5%), labelled a lager but really a Kölsch style, fermented with house yeast then properly lagered; **London Porter*** (5.4%); style-defining **ESB**** (Extra Special Bitter, 5.5% cask, 5.9% bottle); bottle-conditioned historic pale ale **1845*** (6.3%); and bottled barley wine **Golden Pride*** (8.5%). Classic ordinary bitter **Chiswick**** (3.5%) is sadly no longer part of the regular range but occasionally returns as a special. Beers under other brand names include influential **Dark Star Hophead*** (3.8%), a light cask pale ale that introduced US Cascade hops to many British drinkers; golden ale **Gales Seafarers** (3.6%); and unusual dark bitter **Gales HSB*** (4.8%). There are numerous specials and seasonals including **Vintage Ale**** (8.5%), an annually produced bottle-conditioned version of Golden Pride and one of the classic beers for cellar ageing. The brewery has custodianship of another legendary beer, mixed fermentation stock ale **Gales Prize Old Ale** (9%): some of the last batch brewed at Gale's is kept at Dark Star and occasionally emerges in blends, most recently in a 2018 barrel-aged edition (**) in collaboration with Marble in Manchester.

George and Dragon

Contemporary pub
183 High Street W3 9DJ
T (020) 8992 3712
georgeanddragonacton.co.uk
🕐 *Mo-We* 16.00-23.00, *Th* 16.00-24.00, *Fr* 16.00-01.00, *Sa* 12.00-01.00, *Su* 12.00-23.00.
  Children in front area only.
4 cask, 9 keg, 20+ bottles, 2 ciders.
🍴 Thai menu **££**, 🪑 Side yard, ♿
Live jazz (Th), open mic (Su), monthly acoustic night, weekend live music

⊖ Acton Central 🚃 King Street

Unusually, you'll need to walk through the wood-panelled front section of this sprawling and lively pub in central Acton to find the main bar in a barn-like space at the back, dominated by a gleaming microbrewery installed by owners Remarkable Restaurants in 2014, though currently disused. Nonetheless the place

retains a beer focus, with cask from Clouded Minds, Portobello and other independents, keg from the likes of Arbor, Magic Rock, Saltaire and Czech brewers Litovel, which the owners import, and an impressive fridge with Belgian Trappists and lambics alongside Schneider Weisse and UK stars like Siren. The Thai menu includes unusual specials like crispy tofu and nam tok moo pork.

Visitor note. The George began as one of several inns in what was once a bustling market town alongside the road from London to Oxford. It was likely created by knocking two 17th-century houses together, and escaped the pub rebuilding mania of the late 19th century to survive as Acton's oldest building. Once a Courage house, it was restored in 2006, uncovering an original fireplace and much of the interwar panelling. Look out for the embossed list of licensees stretching back to 1759, in the solemn style usually reserved for Rectors of this Parish.

Owl and the Pussycat
See Ealing Brewing

Parakeet City Brewing
Brewery, no visitors please
Ealing W5
parakeetcitybrewing.com
First sold beer: October 2020

Brewers Thomas and Martin, who grew up locally, are proud to take responsibility for every aspect of the brewing process at this small home-based operation, working as sustainably as possible with a 2.5hl kit. Motivated partly by the relative paucity of breweries in west London, they were eagerly welcomed by local drinkers and are now planning to expand to a bigger site with taproom, perhaps in 2022. The origin of the name will be obvious to anyone who has noted the bird life in the average London park recently.

BEERS, currently only in can and sold through local outlets, focus on easy-drinking contemporary styles, led by a **Session IPA** (4.7%, not tasted).

Perivale Brewery

Brewery, taproom
Horsenden Farm, Horsenden Lane North, Greenford UB6 7PQ (Ealing)   perivale.beer
First sold beer: December 2018, 🍴(informal)
🕐 *Monthly Sa* 11.00-19.00, earlier in winter, twice monthly in summer. Children very welcome.
4 keg, 5-6 bottles. 🖐
🍴Pizza truck, 🪑All outdoors, ♿
Occasional music

🚇 Perivale   🚌 Perivale Community Centre   🚲Q16
🚶Capital Ring, Grand Union Canal Walk

Perivale is London's only farm brewery, located in outbuildings little bigger than cupboards next to a Victorian farmhouse and verdant herb garden draped with hops beneath Horsenden Hill, a rural oasis in deep suburbia. Lead brewer Mike Siddell, who founded it with two friends, is a homebrewer, former London Fields team member and violinist with rock band the Leisure Society. Living on a boat at Southall, just along the nearby towpath, he was alerted to the vacant space, formerly used by a woodworker, and installed a 1.2hl kit there himself. Operations expanded in 2021 into an adjoining shed with a 4.5hl kit. The regular 'tap days' are surely one of London's prettiest outdoor taproom experiences.

Visitor note. Horsenden Hill is a 100ha patchwork of old hay meadows and woodland preserved as a public space when the surrounding area was undergoing rapid development in 1933, incorporating the buried remains of an Iron Age settlement which is now a Scheduled Ancient Monument. The Paddington Arm of the Grand Union Canal snakes to the south, and a branch of the Capital Ring walking trail runs right past the brewery on its way up the hill, which affords wide views from its 85m summit.

BEERS are filled into keykeg and hand-bottled, usually only available from the brewery. Regulars include pale ale **VeriPale*** (5.3%)

and generously dry-hopped **VeriHazy** (6%) alongside beers with locally foraged ingredients like a nettle pils and a wild herb gruitbier.

Pint of Hops (A) ⑨

Shop, bar
73 Churchfield Road W3 9AX
a-pint-of-hops.business.site
🕐 *Mo* 15.00-21.00, *Tu-Sa* 12.00-21.00, *Su* 12.00-17.00. Children welcome. Cash-free. Occasional cask, 4 keg, 150 bottles/cans.
🍴 Snacks, BYO, 🪑 Standing at front
Meet the brewer, tap takeovers, tastings

🚇 Acton Central

In a row of independent shops between Acton High Street and Acton Central station, this friendly little place opened in April 2019 in a former wine merchant's. It's primarily a bottle shop with a few seats for drinking in under some impressive murals. Kegs cover a range of contemporary styles, sometimes supplemented in the cooler months with more traditional options in polypins from brewers like Twickenham. There's the expected range of locals (By the Horns, Pressure Drop, Wild Card), renowned contemporary Brits (Cloudwater, North, Northern Monk, Verdant), Belgian and German mainstays and plenty of highlights like big bottles from Kernel and rarities like Ireland's O Brother.

Tabard ⑩

Traditional pub
2 Bath Road W4 1LN
T (020) 3582 2479   greeneking-pubs.co.uk
🕐 *Su-Th* 12.00-23.00, *Fr-Sa* 12.00-24.00.
 Children until 21.00.
8 cask, 7 keg, 7 bottles, 2 ciders, some malts
 and gins.
🍴Pub grub **££**, 🎍 Front/side terrace, ♿
*2 annual beer festivals, food promotions, live music
(Sa), monthly pianist, quiz (We), shuffleboard, board
games, functions, theatre/comedy venue upstairs*

⊖ Turnham Green

'We're the best real ale pub in west London,'
a Tabard staff member once told me with
admirable loyalty. While that claim may be
debatable, this large place almost next door
to Turnham Green Tube station is among
the best of London's Greene King outlets,
thanks to the commitment of successive
managers. The owner's Abbot and IPA are
now obligatory but there are plenty of varied
cask guests from suppliers like Mad Squirrel,
Titanic, Truman's and Wild. You may find Left
Handed Giant, Northern Monk, Portobello
and Tiny Rebel among the kegs, bottles and
cans. The pub grub menu is comprehensive
if a little corporate, including sandwiches,
jacket potatoes, steak and ale pie and veggie
options like chickpea and red pepper burgers.
The pub is close to Acton Green and Chiswick
commons, with a separately managed
upstairs theatre that's played host to Russell
Brand and Al Murray.

*Visitor note. Built in 1880 as part of London's first garden
suburb, Bedford Park, the Grade II* listed pub has a handsome
Arts and Crafts exterior and some exquisite internal tiling by
William de Morgan and Walter Crane, including a fireplace
surround depicting Little Bo Peep. The original sign was
uncovered during a recent refurbishment and may be restored.*

Weird Beard Brew Co ⑪

Brewery, shop
9 Boston Business Park,
Trumpers Way W7 2QA (Ealing)
T (020) 3645 2711   weirdbeardbrewco.com
First sold beer: March 2013, 💬 (informal)
🕐 **Shop** *(pre-ordered click and collect)*: *Mo-Fr* 12.00-17.00.
 Near-monthly open days *(usually Sa)*, please
 check. Children welcome.
1-3 cask, 10 keg, 15-20 cans. 🍺
🍴Food truck **£**, 🎍Tables in front yard, ♿
Occasional DJs, bands

⊖ Boston Manor 🚌 Elthorne Park Road 🚶 Brent River
Park Walk, Capital Ring, Grand Union Canal Walk

After meeting each other at an IPA tasting in
2011, three award-winning homebrewers and
London Amateur Brewers members set up
two separate companies with the intention
of pooling their resources: Weird Beard,
founded by Gregg Irwin and Bryan Spooner,
and Ellenberg's, run by Mike Ellenberg. After
various delays, they began work on a 16hl kit
in an industrial unit by the Grand Union Canal
in Hanwell early in 2013. Weird Beard turned
out to be the more successful of the pair, and
early in 2014 bought out Ellenberg's share.
Operations subsequently expanded into two
nearby units, with additional fermentation
capacity, a bottling line and a barrel vault.
Gregg moved on early in 2017, but Bryan
continues to direct brewing operations, as
well as retaining facial grooming practices
appropriate to the brewery's name. Public
opening is restricted to near-monthly well-
attended open days: a permanent off-site
taproom is a long-term ambition, though in
the meantime a vintage Volkswagen Type II
camper van is being converted into a mobile
bar for events. An isolated presence in this
part of London until very recently, Weird
Beard has become one of the capital's most
distinctive and interesting brewers.

BEERS are mainly in keg and can, with some
cask and occasional bottled specials. Regulars
include **Black Perle*** (3.8%) coffee milk stout;
session IPA **Little Things That Kill*** (3.9%);
lager **Kill Pils*** (5%); **Mariana Trench*** (5.3%)
transpacific pale; and West Coast-style IPA
Five O'Clock Shadow (7%). Notable among
a wide range of specials and occasional beers

LONDON'S BREWING

Fuller's faces the future

Followers of the London beer scene are now used to shock announcements involving multinational acquisitions, but few could not have been jolted on 25 January 2019 when Fuller's, London's biggest and arguably its oldest brewery, released news of its deal with Tokyo-based Asahi. Following in the footsteps of fellow historic London independent Young's and many other UK family brewers, the company was ditching brewing to concentrate on its pub estate, where 87% of its profit was generated. Asahi was buying the beer business, including the historic Griffin brewery, for £250 million, its second London acquisition after Meantime.

Though Asahi has undertaken to continue production at Fuller's traditional home, the deal has raised concerns for the long-term future of what's now London's last continuously operating historic commercial brewery and the only one not founded in the 21st century. The Griffin on Chiswick Mall, between the river Thames and the main A4 road, can trace its history back to the 1650s, when it was a domestic brewhouse in the garden of stately home Bedford House. Thomas Mawson turned it into a commercial operation in 1701, and the Fuller family became involved in 1829. The currently quoted founding date of 1845 is when a new partnership took over, involving John Bird Fuller, Henry Smith (formerly of Ind & Smith in Romford: see Beyond the marshes p168), and John Turner. Fuller Smith & Turner became a limited company in 1929, though descendants of the initial partners have remained

involved and are still represented on the board of the successor pub group.

As one of two remaining independent family brewers in London by the early 1970s, Fuller's was already stripping handpumps from pubs and about to convert production entirely to pasteurised keg beers. In retrospect, it's highly likely this would have resulted in the firm's demise as it struggled against larger and more efficient competitors. Instead it was persuaded by the growing real ale revival to switch the emphasis back to cask, and its reputation and business steadily grew. In the early 1980s, it was producing around 100,000hl a year and owned around 100 pubs, mainly clustered close to home. By 2019, its output was over 550,000hl and its 400-strong pub estate stretched from Bath to Birmingham. Its flagship beer London Pride is the UK's third biggest-selling cask ale brand and strong bitter ESB has become the benchmark of a recognised international style. Rather than

reacting with suspicion and hostility as some old-established firms might have done, Fuller's embraced the London brewing renaissance from the start, playing a full role in the London Brewers Alliance and acting as friendly mentor as well as inspiration to many of the newcomers.

The site retains a fine collection of historic brewery buildings around a traditional yard: the wisteria that adorns the walls of the former head brewer's house was grown from the earliest cutting to arrive in Britain from China in 1816. Inside, though some historic vessels have been retained as display items, the current brewhouse is a modern installation from the mid-1990s, with a 540hl twin mash tun system and fermentation entirely in cylindroconical tanks. A16hl pilot brewery was added when the visitor centre was refurbished in 2018. The practice of parti-gyling - making two different beers at different strengths from the same mash - is retained for several of the beers, which are also linked in flavour profile through a distinctive, and closely guarded, house yeast.

In 2005, Fuller's bought another old-established family brewer, Gales in Horndeam, Hampshire, and closed it the following year, transferring the yeast and some of the brands to Chiswick. In February 2018, the company bought the revered Dark Star in Partridge Green near Horsham, West Sussex, the descendant of a pioneering London microbrewery (as explained in From Black Eagle to Dark Star p114) that became one

cor

LONDON'S BREWING | Fuller's faces the future *cont.*

of the leading early champions of hop-forward US styles in the UK. Subsequently part of the package sold to Asahi, it still operates as a separate brewery, though some Dark Star brands now emerge from the Griffin.

Under the new arrangement, Fuller's brewery is still supplying beers to Fuller's pubs, while Asahi is free to use the trademarks to market the beer elsewhere. The new owner has gone to great lengths to reassure drinkers it respects the brands and their

heritage and is committed to keep brewing them at the Griffin. But the redevelopment value of this large site, right next to the river and one of London's prettiest 'villages', can't have escaped notice.

And there are other issues too. As an integrated brewing and pub company which was strongly brewer-led, Fuller's put considerable efforts into ensuring the quality of beer in its pubs. Now that the two sides have separated, maintaining

those standards will become more complicated. The brewing team who secured Fuller's place in world class ranks in recent decades, including John Keeling, Derek Prentice and Georgina Young, have moved on or retired. Beer lovers across the world are watching with interest and concern as London's most venerable brewing institution enters a new phase of its long history.

---

are rich **Sharp Dressed Stout*** (6%); dark lager **Faithless Spreadsheet Ninja*** (5.5%), so-named as I once mistyped the original name of the pils, Fearless Spreadsheet Ninja, as 'faithless', and they thought the name was so cool they brewed a beer to match; and imperial stout 貞子*・** (Sadako, 9.5%), also available in limited barrel-aged editions.

TRY ALSO

BrewDog Ealing 19 Dickens Yard W5 2TD brewdog.com: BrewDog's westernmost London bar, with a largish front terrace on central Ealing's Dickens Yard development, with the usual mix of own brand and guests across 30 keg and 70 bottles/cans.

Express 56 Kew Bridge Road, Brentford TW8 0EW expresstavern.co.uk: Handsome landmark pub at the northern end of Kew Bridge, now part of the Sussex Arms (p312) group, with 10 cask, 12 keg and 20 bottles/cans including Draught Bass as promised by a vintage illuminated red triangle outside. Regional heritage features include a fine clock above the landlord's parlour behind the bar.

Fox Green Lane W7 2PJ thefoxpub.co.uk: Handsome, friendly 1848 pub with well-preserved heritage interior and a surprisingly rural feel next to the famous Hanwell Flight of locks on the Grand Union Canal. Longstanding real ale favourite maintaining the standards

under new ownership with four decent casks and a smattering of kegs including locals.

Grove 1 Ealing Green W5 5QX thegrovew5. co.uk: Elegant pub with a delightful terrace overlooking Ealing Green, part of Greene King's Metro chain, with well-regarded food and a creditable beer range, including plenty from locals and UK independents. At least four cask, around 10 keg and a dozen bottles/cans.

Kings Arms 110 Uxbridge Road W7 3SU frontierpubs.co.uk: One of the more beer-friendly Frontier outlets, a handsome ex-Mann's 1930s high street pub with a big back garden in Hanwell, stocking up to two cask, 13 keg and a few bottles and cans including local and unusual choices.

Northumberland Arms 11 London Road, Brentford TW8 8JB facebook.com/ northumberlandarmsbrentford: Smallish traditional pub opposite Brentford Lock linked to Tiny Vessel brewery (p313), stocking their beers alongside a scattering of other interesting cask and keg options.

Old Pack Horse 434 Chiswick High Road W4 5TF oldpackhorsechiswick.co.uk: Handsome 1910 heritage pub overlooking Turnham Green, the work of the renowned TH Nowell Parr, now a crafty Fuller's with a Thai restaurant and up to five cask, 12 keg and 15 bottles/cans including locals and unusual imports, looked after by an enthusiastic manager.

Hammersmith and Fulham

BrewDog Shepherds Bush

Bar

15 Goldhawk Road W12 8QQ

T (020) 8749 8094   **brewdog.com**

🕐 *Mo-Fr* 12.00-24.00, *Sa* 11.00-24.00,
Su 11.00-22.30. Children until 20.00.
38 keg, 80+ bottles, specialist spirits. ⌕
🍴 Burgers, salads **££**, 🪑 Tables on street, ♿
*Meet the brewer, tap takeovers, quiz (Tu), retro
gaming (Su), seasonal events, pinball, board games*

⊖ Goldhawk Road

The BrewDog with the biggest draught range
in London opened in late 2013 in a former DJ
and comedy bar just off the southwestern tip
of Shepherds Bush Green. It's a large space
decorated in standard minimalist industrial
fast food bar chic, but with plenty of squishy
banquettes, big windows with street views
and a hidden snug if you can nab it. The owner's
beers only take up half the taps on the corru-
gated concrete bar, with others in a varied
selection of styles and strengths perhaps from
Brits Buxton, Hammerton, Harbour, Marble or
Bearded Iris and Pipeworks in the US. Big
bottles from 3 Fonteinen and Crooked Stave
are in the fridges alongside plenty of BrewDog

specials and mixed fermentation OverWorks
releases. Food is the regular burger, hot dog
and wings offer with plenty of veggie and
vegan choices. Staff dispense tasters and
third pint measures with evangelical zeal.

Concrete Island Brewery

Brewery, no visitors please
Wood Lane W12 (Hammersmith & Fulham)
concreteislandbrewery.co.uk
First sold beer: September 2017

Originally known as the Small Beer Brewery
but sensibly renamed to avoid confusion with
the unrelated Bermondsey brewery, this is
one of London's very smallest commercial
producers. It's run by Steve Smith, an award-
winning London Amateur Brewers member
who produces 2.5hl a year on a home-based
25 litre kit.

BEERS (not tasted) are bottled and include a
core pils, pale ale and porter plus one-offs and
seasonals. The brewery can create bespoke
labels for events or as gifts and has been
known to brew specific beers on request.

a brewery like Anarchy or Beatnikz Republic, and a keg cellar with reserved places for stouts, porters, sours and amber ales, including strong options, alongside changing Kernel pales and London lagers from Hackney and Pillars. The fridges may reveal Box Social, Loka Polly, Padstow, Westbrook from the US, lambic from Hanssens and Tilquin and San Diego's Alesmith with its legendary Speedway Stout. There's a burger kitchen offering several variations, and a surprisingly green and pleasant outside yard just across two lanes of traffic from the Rik Mayall Memorial Bench. The Eventim Apollo, formerly known as the Hammersmith Odeon, and the Lyric theatre are nearby.

Duke of Hammersmith ⑮

Contemporary pub
238 Shepherds Bush Road W6 7NL
T (020) 7042 5109 **brewdog.com**
🕐 *Su-We* 12.00-23.00, *Th* 12.00-24.00, *Fr-Sa*
  12.00-01.00. Children until 22.00.
2-3 cask, 15 keg, 60 bottles, specialist spirits.
🍴 Burgers, pub grub, sharing plates **££**,
🍽 Tables at front, two rear yards, ♿
Tastings, tap takeovers, quiz (Tu)

⊖ Hammersmith   CS9   🏃 Link to Thames Path

Well-placed for the Lyric theatre and other entertainment and shopping venues, the former Laurie Arms received the Draft House treatment in February 2015, complete with an airy conservatory known as the Tramshed extending the drinking area. Since rebranded as a BrewDog pub, it still has one of the better beer ranges in the chain, with casks often featuring Purity and Siren, the usual exclusive house kegs from highly rated suppliers, and Bohem, Buxton, One Mile End and Siren likely to appear on other taps, all available in thirds and tasting paddles. Among the more unusual labels in the fridge when I last looked in were Farmageddon from County Down, Japan's Hitachino Nest, Schneider specials and several lower alcohol choices. Wings, fish and chips, chilli, pies and dishes like sweet potato and falafel salad ensure you won't go hungry.

Visitor note. Look for the collection of memorabilia from the Hammersmith Palais, which once surrounded the building on three sides.

Craft Beer Co Hammersmith ⑭

Bar
17 Broadway Shopping Centre W6 9YD
T (020) 8748 7033 **craftbeerco.com**
🕐 *Su-We* 12.00-23.00, *Th-Sa* 12.00-24.00.
  Children until 20.00.
6 cask, 18 keg, 50+ bottles/cans, specialist spirits.
🍴 Burgers, salads, sharing plates **££**,
🍽 Front yard, ♿
Meet the brewer, tap takeovers, occasional live music

⊖ Hammersmith   🏃 Link to Thames Path

It may be a long way from a traditional boozer, but this latest Craft Beer Co, opened in May 2019, looks fabulous. Shiny wood veneers, pale green and pink tiles, geometric flooring and a battery of TARDIS-like hexagonal mirrored panels dazzle the drinker, like a modern version of the most extravagant Victorian 'gin palace'. Not bad for what was previously a dowdy pub in the grim early 1990s Broadway Shopping Centre. The beer lives up to the surroundings, with cask guests, often several at a time from

Kings Arms

Contemporary pub
452 New Kings Road SW6 4RN
T (020) 7371 9585 **kingsarms-fulham.co.uk**
🕐 *Mo-Sa* 11.00-23.00, *Su* 12.00-22.30.
  Children until early evening.
5 cask, 4 keg, some specialist spirits.
🍴 Enhanced pub grub, stone-baked pizzas,
lunchtime sandwiches **£-££**
🪑 Sheltered side terrace, ♿
Monthly karaoke, occasional live music, functions

⊖ Putney Bridge 🚲 NCN4 🚶 Thames Path

This substantial 1888 corner pub near Putney
Bridge Tube station became a first London outlet for independent family brewer Wadworth,
based in Devizes, Wiltshire, in August 2018.
A comfortable interior replete with bare floorboards, glazed tiling, pillars and stained glass
remnants creates a good atmosphere in which
to sample a range of the brewery's traditional
casks, including rum-infused Swordfish and
seasonals besides the famous 6X. The odd
guest might be from Black Sheep, Elgoods
or White Horse. There's a bit more from
Wadworth in keg and bottle besides a few
familiar names from elsewhere. Lunchtime
ciabattas, unusual salads and options like
haddock and Applewood cheese fishcake
join the usual pub grub fare on the menu.

Visitor note. *Look out for the now-gated arch decorated
with astonishingly elaborate terracotta leading into an
outdoor courtyard on the Fulham High Street side.*

Macintosh Ales

Brewery, no visitors please
Stamford Brook W6   **macintoshales.com**
First sold beer: January 2018. 🍺

Founded by Charlie Macintosh to make 'modern,
balanced ales that respect the ingredients and
tradition', this home-based operation uses a
self-built 2hl kit in a converted garage for small
runs and cuckoo brews longer runs at other
London breweries. Charlie hopes to move to
a bigger site and taproom at a later stage.

BEERS in cask- and bottle-conditioned form
are made with home-crushed malt and whole
leaf hops, sold in cask or hand-bottled and
bottle-conditioned, including a traditional
Best Bitter* (4.6%).

White Horse 🔟

Contemporary pub
1 Parsons Green SW6 4UL
T (020) 7736 2115   **whitehorsesw6.com**
🕐 *Su-We* 12.00-23.30, *Th-Sa* 12.00-24.00.
  Children welcome.
6 cask, 1 tank, 13 keg, 100 bottles/cans, malts,
  gins, wine.
🍴 Gastro/enhanced pub grub menu **££-£££**,
🪑 Front terrace, ♿
*4 annual beer festivals, occasional open mic, meet
the brewer, tap takeovers, functions*

⊖ Parsons Green

Although now part of the M&B Castle chain,
this longstanding beer exhibition overlooking
dappled Parsons Green makes full use of its
dispensation to order from far and wide.
Guests like Greytrees, Gun, Heavy Industry
and Saltaire keep things interesting alongside
Harvey's Best and Oakham Citra on the cask
pumps, while kegs could be from the UK (Deya,
Time and Tide), mainland Europe (Huyghe,
Lervig) or the US (Firestone Walker). There's
even a heading for barley wines on a bottle
list which includes White Shield, numerous
Trappist and Belgian abbey beers, excellent
lambics and big bottles from the UK and US.
Besides upmarket versions of pub grub
staples, the kitchen offers dishes like trout
and king prawn in brown butter or spiced
tofu, chickpea and tomato stew. Thanks to its
prize location in an area of Chelsea overspill,
the pub is known rather unkindly to some as
the 'Sloaney Pony' and there's still a certain
colonial poshness about its leather sofas,
ceiling fans and wooden Venetian blinds.
But customers are generally a genial mix and
staff remain polite and informative even
when, as often, they're run off their feet.

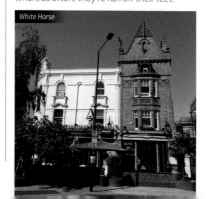
White Horse

Visitor note. *The pub, a former coaching inn, has been a specialist beer champion for 40 years. In 1981, postgraduate student Mark Dorber took a holiday job here and soon found himself hooked. Inspired by the writings of Michael Jackson, he started his own beer hunts, ran festivals celebrating rare styles and eventually became manager. By the 1990s the place was renowned for its lengthy bottled list and celebrated beer and food dinners sometimes presided over by Michael himself. Mark eventually moved on in 2007 but subsequent managers have maintained his beery legacy.*

TRY ALSO

Prairie Fire at the Wood Lane Arches 88 Wood Lane Archways, Wood Lane W12 7LH prairiefirebbq.com: Barbecue restaurant run by US expats in railway arches close to Wood Lane, Westfield and the old Television Centre. Attached taproom also open to non-diners pours a decent range of 16 kegs and up to 20 bottles/cans including numerous Londoners. **Prince of Wales Townhouse** 73 Dalling Road W6 0JD princeofwales-townhouse.co.uk:

Big Brewer's Tudor pub near Ravenscourt Park station refurbed 2021 by Big Smoke (see Sussex Arms p312) to the usual high standards, with five cask and 20 keg across a range of styles and real ciders, plus beer garden, workspace facilities and B&B rooms. Open for breakfast daily.

HERITAGE PUB

Dove 19 Upper Mall W6 9TA dovehammersmith.co.uk: Picturesque and characterful pre-1750 riverside pub on Hammersmith Mall, retaining 18th-century woodwork features thought to be among the oldest purpose-made pub fittings still in use, and the smallest public bar in Britain, a tiny panelled snug likely created due to a misunderstanding about a new licensing law in the 1910s. Now a Fuller's pub within sight of the brewery chimney a little upstream, it offers a limited but well-kept range.

LONDON DRINKERS — Lucy Do

After over 14 years in marketing, Lucy shifted careers to open the Dodo in Hanwell (p293), one of the first micropubs in west London, in January 2017. 'We champion independent beer, which mostly means cask ale, as well as community and conversation,' she explains. Follow the pub on Instagram or Twitter @thedodomicropub.

How do you rate London as a beer city, on a world scale?
I'm 100% biased but there's a lot to love about London as a beer city and its pubs are beacons for hospitality and shared experiences. You can't beat the unpretentious, warming magic of a pub that cares about people and beer.

What's the single most exciting thing about beer in London right now?
Collaboration over competition. It's great to see breweries working with each other, artists, pubs, small businesses and their patrons. I've never been in an industry before where people work together as much as they do in beer.

What single thing would make things even better?
Even more people drinking beer and enjoying beer spaces to keep the industry alive.

What are your top London beers right now?
I have to say the Dodo, a beer we created with our local brewery Weird Beard. This isn't just a shameless plug: it sells out super-fast and it's done well for the brewery in other outlets too. My others would be Canopy Sunray Pale, Kernel Bière de saison Damson, BBNo 65 DDH IPA No 5, By the Horns Lambeth Walk, Five Points Pale and Railway Porter and Weird Beard Black Perle.

What's your top great beer night out?
A friendly micropub, independent pub or brewery taproom: my most recent great beer outings of note were to Cloudwater (p209) and the Sutton Arms (p99).

Who's your London beer hero?
I've been inspired by so many women in beer I couldn't possibly pick just one. Jaega Wise, Melissa Cole, Natalya Watson, Lotte Peplow, Estelle Theobalds and Jane Barnes all spring to mind.

Who will we be hearing a lot more from in future?
All of the above! From a brewery perspective, hopefully there will be more coming out of west London.

Which are your other top beer cities?
Brussels, Ghent and, surprisingly, Bologna: although it's very wine heavy, we found a few independent beer options and lots of cool, laid back drinking spaces.

Maida Vale to Dollis Hill

Beer + Burger Willesden ⑲

Bar, restaurant, shop
88 Walm Lane NW2 4QY
T (020) 3019 7575 beerandburgerstore.com
🕐 *Mo-Th* 12.00-23.00, *Fr-Sa* 12.00-24.00,
Su 12.00-22.30. Children until 19.00.
19 keg, around 350 bottles, bottled ciders
and perries.
🍴 Gourmet burgers and sides **££**, ♿
*Running club, bottle club, tap takeovers, food
promotions*

⊖ Willesden Green   🚲 Q3

Opened late in 2016 in a former Irish bar as the
founding branch of what's now a small chain,
this buzzing place opposite Willesden Green
station boasts a parade of fridges that would
do the average bottle shop proud. And that's
before you get to the slew of keg taps pouring
a range of contemporary styles and a well-
reputed gourmet burger menu including tasty
vegan options and sides like 'mac balls' and
deep-fried jalapeños. Look out for Londoners
like Affinity, Gipsy Hill and Howling Hops,
other UK stars like Buxton, Dry & Bitter and
Wiper & True, and house exclusives and
collabs. Bottles and cans expand into Belgian
and German classics and a few rarities in big
bottles. You don't have to eat, but the bare
wood décor of this long and narrow site leans
more towards fast food turnover than lengthy
sampling sessions. Both food and drink are
sent out locally via Deliveroo.

Parlour ㉑

Bar, restaurant
5 Regent Street NW10 5LG
T (020) 8969 2184   parlourkensal.com
🕐 *Tu-Su* 10.00-24.00. Children until early
evening.
9 keg, 18 bottles, cocktails, specialist spirits,
wines.
🍴 Modern British, cooked bar snacks **££-£££**,
🌳 Rear garden 🐾
*Tastings, quizzes, films, guest chefs, cocktail
masterclasses, functions*

⊖ Kensal Rise, Kensal Green   🚃 Harrow Road Kilburn Lane
🚲 Link to Q16   🚶 Link to Grand Union Canal Walk

Originally a Truman's pub called the Grey Horse on a side street near Kensal Green Cemetery, this long-neglected building was refitted in November 2012 as a welcoming white-tiled bar-restaurant. There's a leafy little garden centred on a tree and Cocteausque ironwork sculptures wrought by a relative of one of the owners. The ongoing intention to install cask lines hasn't yet been realised but there are plenty of good UK choices from keg, bottle and can including Londoners like 40FT, Meantime and Sambrook's, Braybrooke lager and more traditional beers from Hook Norton and Timothy Taylor. A varied menu offers all day breakfasts, snacks and tapas (raw vegetable ravioli, duck liver profiteroles), main courses like cauliflower steak or fillet of sea bream with asparagus and retro desserts like arctic roll. Subscribers to a local organic veg box scheme can pick up their shopping here too.

Portobello Brewing Co (22)

Brewery
6 Mitre Bridge Industrial Park,
Mitre Way W10 6AU
T (020) 8969 2269 portobellobrewing.com
First sold beer: December 2012,
‼ Pre-arranged for groups only.
🕑 Currently no regular hours, though taproom planned.
Cask, keg, bottles/cans vary. 🍺
♿ Flat access only

 White City 🚌 Mitre Way Wormwood Scrubs

While most recent brewery start-ups in London are the work of enterprising homebrewers, Portobello was an initiative from the established industry. Back in 2006, Rob Jenkins, formerly at Whitbread, Brakspear, Young's and Wells, planned with other now-redundant Young's employees John Hatch and Derek Prentice to create a successor to the Wandsworth brewery. Ultimately all three went their own way, and Rob established Portobello with head brewer Farooq Khalid. In 2013, they were joined by Joe Laventure, previously with Whitbread and Budvar UK. The original relatively capacious 30hl kit was upgraded in 2014 to a 50hl brewhouse. An arrangement in 2018 with Remarkable Pubs to take over the microbrewery at the George and Dragon in Acton was abandoned soon after it launched, but in 2019 the company added its own first pub by buying the King and Co in Clapham (p263). A deal struck late in 2020 to take on numerous pubs previously run by Antic expanded the retail side to 15 sites. The brewery, on an industrial estate between Wormwood Scrubs and Eurostar's North Pole rail depot, expanded into a neighbouring unit during 2021, with plans to increase annual production to 10,000hl and to open a long-desired taproom in 2022.

BEERS 'brewed the West Way' are in cask, keg, can and bottle, widely sold through pub chains and supermarkets. The original vision was to produce mainly cask, but although still important this is now only 30% of the business, with 60% craft lager in keg and can. The brewery cans and bottles offsite, mainly at Marston's in Burton upon Trent. Core beers include **Notting Helles*** (4%) pale lager; straw-coloured **VPA** (Very Pale Ale, 4%); **Westway Pale Ale** (4%); amber ale **Portobello Star** (4.3%); **London Pilsner** (4.6%); and **Market Porter*** (4.6%). **The Big O** (0%) alcohol-free lager is a recent addition. There are also seasonals and specials, with some beers now in supermarkets.

TRY ALSO

Elgin 255 Elgin Avenue W9 1NJ theelgin.com:
Stylish contemporary recast of an old pub in a
select area by Maida Vale Tube station from
the people behind Heist Bank (p122): nine kegs
and 15+ bottles/cans, mainly from the UK,
cover a wide range to match an eclectic and
imaginative menu, from breakfast onwards.

Real Drinks Little Venice 4 Formosa Street
W9 1EE realdrinks.co.uk: Smallish branch of
the Twickenham-based chain (p312) near Little
Venice and Warwick Avenue Tube station and
opposite the Prince Alfred (Heritage pubs
below). An excellent range of eight kegs and
150 bottles/cans, with a few smart wooden
tables for drinking in. Lists on Untappd.

Real Drinks Notting Hill 97 Golborne Road
W10 5NL realdrinks.co.uk: Perhaps the best-
looking branch of the Twickenham-based
chain (p312), on two levels with plenty of drink-
in space including a small yard, a little north of
the Westway, with a mouthwatering choice of
six keg and up to 350 bottles/cans. Lists on
Untappd.

Union Tavern 45 Woodfield Road W9 2BA
union-tavern.co.uk: Fuller's crafty pub beside
the Grand Union Canal Paddington Arm at
Westbourne Park, with free moorings for
boaters. The beer offer is recovering after a
dip, with three cask, nine keg and around 18
bottles/cans mainly from excellent UK suppliers.

Wolfpack 53 Lonsdale Road NW6 6RA
wolfpacklager.com: Former mechanic's
workshop that's now a lively bare brick bar in
a picturesque mews close to Queens Park
station, a shop window for cuckoo-brewed
Wolfpack lager (p324) among a small but
choice range of seven kegs that includes
Belgian classics and craft imports. There are
now similar branches in Fulham and West
Hampstead.

HERITAGE PUB

Prince Alfred 5A Formosa Street W9 1EE
theprincealfred.com: Handsome 1865
Italianate pub near Little Venice, retaining the
carved wood and frosted glass partitions, one
with snob screens, that in 1898 divided it into
five small and separate rooms around a peninsula bar. Alongside the Princess Louise (Heritage
pubs p105), it's London's best surviving demonstration of this favoured late Victorian layout.
Now a Young's pub with the regular range.

Prince Alfred

HOP HISTORIES | Toucan gestures

Accounts of big brewing in the early 1970s often mention the Big Six, but a more accurate term would be the Big Seven. The seventh brewer was Guinness, which between 1937 and 2005 operated a subsidiary brewery at Park Royal in West London. The reason for the discrepancy is that, although Guinness and the other six between them were responsible for the vast majority of beer drunk in the UK, the Irish giant uniquely owned no pubs, instead using its strong brand and a network of wholesaling and bottling deals to ensure its ubiquity in almost every pub.

Even before it built Park Royal, Guinness's history, and the history of Irish brewing in general, was intertwined with London brewing. Back in 1759, when Arthur Guinness first set up on his own at St James's Gate in Dublin, the whole of Ireland was ruled from London. Guinness first brewed ales in the local style but in 1778 attempted porter for the first time, copying the London-brewed beers which by then were becoming increasingly fashionable in the Irish capital. His was likely not the first Irish brewery to do this but ultimately the most successful.

By the mid-19th century, Guinness was one of the biggest brewers in the British Isles, successfully transforming porter and stout into something charac-teristically Irish. The fame of Irish stout, and of Guinness in

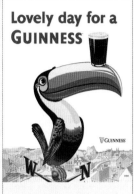

Lovely day for a **GUINNESS**

particular, spread across the world with the Irish diaspora, making it one of the first global brands, and by 1914 St James's Gate was producing an astonish-ing 4.34 million hl a year.

Quite why Irish porter and stout retained their popularity while their English parent styles declined has not yet been satisfactorily explained but by the 1930s, with Dublin now the capital of an independent state and English porter heading inexorably towards extinction, mainland Britain was one of Guinness's most important export markets. The beer's appeal spread far beyond the Irish community thanks in part to the brewery's well-known flair for clever advertising, with still-quoted tag lines like 'Guinness is good for you' and memorable characters such as the iconic toucans. While important markets in the northwest and Scotland were easily reached by ship from Dublin, the south of

England was less accessible, so Guinness decided to build a satellite brewery in London.

The site chosen was Park Royal in Willesden, a former Royal Agricultural Society showground in the western suburbs on the A40 trunk road which was then being redeveloped as an indust-rial zone. The company built a massive state-of-the-art facility, designed in art deco style by George Gilbert Scott, which when it opened in 1937 for a while restored to London the long-lost distinction of being home to the biggest brewery in the world. It turned out to be last new brewery in the capital before the arrival of modern microbrewing in the late 1970s. Park Royal was pasteurising and pressurising its draught beer by the 1950s, but its standard bottled stout was bottle condi-tioned until 1994.

In 1997, Guinness merged with former Watney owner Grand Metropolitan to form Diageo, one of the biggest drinks companies in the world. In 2005, following an increase in capacity in Dublin, the London plant was deemed surplus to requirements and closed. Despite its importance, the brewery building was rejected for listing by English Heritage and demolished, among some controversy, in 2006. Diageo's offices are still based on part of the site (Lakeside Drive NW10 7HQ), while the rest is now used as homes, business parks and green space.

Outer West London

Beer Asylum ㉓

Bar, shop
1 Red Lion Parade, Bridge Street, Pinner HA5 3JD
T (020) 8429 2400   beerasylum.com
🕐 *Tu-We* 12.00-21.00, *Th-Sa* 12.00-22.00, *Su* 12.00-17.00. Children welcome.
5-6 keg, 200+ bottles, growlers, some gins.
♿
Frequent tastings, beer and food matching, meet the brewer

⊖ Pinner   🏃 Celandine Route

A labour of love by a true enthusiast, ex-Fuller's and Young's licensee Jason Carroll, in an area relatively lacking in beer choices, this suburban high street treasurehouse has been reconfigured several times since opening in June 2016, emerging as a pleasing blend of bottle shop and micropub. An attractively tiled bar commands a roomful of seating at high wooden tables recycled from former beer shelves, and well-stocked fridges offer unusual bounty: 'if it's in the supermarkets, we delist it,' says Jason. There's good representation from London brewers including Kernel, Partizan and locals

Mad Yank. Cloudwater, Paradigm, Popes Yard and Ireland's White Hag might also be spotted, alongside plenty of classy, expertly-picked Belgian and German choices including good lambics. Everything is available to drink in and take out, with growlers filled from the well-chosen keg selection if required. Renowned food matching events regularly pack the place out.

Brewery Market ㉔

Bar, shop
48 Church Street, Twickenham TW1 3NR
T (020) 3601 9494   brewerymarket.co.uk
🕐 *We-Th* 15.00-21.00, *Fr-Su* 13.00-22.00. Children welcome.
12 keg, 200+ bottles/cans, growlers
Tap takeovers, meet the brewer, mini-beer festivals, tastings, functions

🚆 Twickenham   🚌 York Street Twickenham   🏃 Thames Path

This small but energetic beer hub opened in October 2018 in former offices on Twickenham's most attractive and historic street. Bottles and cans are all kept in fridges: wider UK producers like Beak, Burnt Mill, Double-Barrelled, Cloudwater and Polly's line up alongside locals like Jawbone and Jeffersons, rare US imports and Belgian and German classics. Keg lines include dark and sour options across a notably wide range of strengths. The long room with its simple furniture isn't London's most inviting space when quiet, but the enthusiasm and knowledge of founder Linda Birch is reflected not just in the choice but in the busy and imaginative programme of tastings, food matching and themed events.

CTZN Brewhouse ㉕

Bar, planned brewpub
29 York Street, Twickenham TW1 3JZ
ctznbrew.com
🕐 *We-Sa* 11.00-23.00, *Su* 12.00-21.00.
    Children welcome.
12 keg, 5+ bottles/cans, minikegs, specialist
cider, coffee
🍴 Burgers, pizza, ♿
Tastings, food matching, live music, quiz

🚆 Twickenham   🚶 Link to Thames Path

Opened in 2021 in central Twickenham, this
is the showcase for CTZN Brew (formerly
Kew Brewery). The main brewery is in East
Sheen (p280) but there are plans for an
additional pilot kit here for small-batch
experimental beers, public brewing days
and a brew school, hopefully by the end
of 2021. It's a spacious high street site with
a comfortably distressed look, stocking
guests from other locals like Jawbone,
Twickenham and Workshy alongside
CTZN brews.
Gourmet comfort
food like smashed
burgers and loaded
chips hints at the
Canadian links
of the owners.
See the brewery
entry for more
about the beers.

Hop and Vine ㉖

Micropub
18 High Street, Ruislip HA4 7AN
facebook.com/hopandvinebar
🕐 *Tu-Th* 17.00-22.00, *Fr-Sa* 12.00-23.00, *Su* 12.00-
    18.00. Children until early evening.
4-7 cask, 1-2 keg, 50 bottles/cans, growlers, cider,
    some organic wines and specialist spirits.
🍴 Cheese and charcuterie plates **££**,
⛩ Back garden, ♿
Occasional tastings, food matching

🚇 Ruislip   🚌 The Oaks

Opened in December 2016 by Em Jennison
and Ricky Ives in a former café at one end of a
lengthy interwar high street, this is a beacon
of beery excellence in the far-flung tropic of
Ruislip. The half-panelling, old wooden barrels
and rear stillage suggest a micropub, but
there's a decent-sized bar counter, with keg
and packaged options, a takeaway trade that
includes growlers, and drinking water on
every table. The Paradigm brewery, outside
London at Sarratt in
Hertfordshire but just
down the road from
here, is a favoured
supplier, and once a
year brews a special
pale ale from hops
grown in the pub's
pretty back garden
and associated
allotment. Arbor,
Cloudwater, Lost &
Grounded, Moor,
Tempest, Vibrant

Em Jennison of the Hop and Vine

Forest and Wylam may also feature, with at least one dark choice on, and the bottle fridge is a roll-call of high-achieving London and UK brewers.

Jawbone Brewing

Brewery, taproom
Unit C, 1 Strawberry Vale, Twickenham TW1 4RY (Richmond upon Thames)
jawbonebrewing.com
First sold beer: December 2020 ‼
🕐 *Taproom: Th* 18.00-21.00, *Fr* 17.00-21.00, *Sa* 12.00-21.00. Children welcome.
🕐 *Shop:* Taproom hours plus *Mo-We* 16.00-18.00, *Th-Fr* from 16.00 (pre-arranged pickup only when taproom is closed).
2 cask, 7 keg, 6+ cans, growlers. 🍴
🍴 Order in from neighbouring café, ♿
Tastings, pub games

🚆 Strawberry Hill   🚍 Michelham Gardens   🚶 Thames Path

Energetic former Weird Beard brewer Ben Hughes has found a characterful and attractive location for this solo project, in a working boatyard on the Thames by Swan Island in Twickenham, next to riverside Radnor Gardens. The brewery even occasionally dispatches beer by boat. Packaging uses contemporary views of the surroundings while the décor in the atmospheric taproom suggests both the

Jawbone Brewing

industrial heritage and the building's immediate past as an artist's studio. The generously sized, steam-heated 30hl brewhouse was formerly at Wylam and Mad Hatter. There's no outdoor space but the park café in adjoining Radnor Gardens also serves the beer. Other interesting collaborations include beer truffles made by fine chocolatier William Curley, also based on the site.

BEERS are in keg and 440ml can, with some cask, covering a range of styles while aiming to stay modern, flavourful and approachable. The core range includes pale ale **Bone Idle*** (4.6%), which rapidly became a local takeaway favourite during the lockdowns; and IPA **Longshore Gang*** (5.7%). Specials include **Boatyard Blues** (4.4%), an unusual 'raw' pale ale made without boiling, with a kveik yeast.

Mad Yank Brewery

Brewery, no visitors please
Pinner HA5 (Hillingdon)   **madyank.com**
First sold beer: February 2019
Offsite taproom planned. 🍴

German-born former marketing specialist Larissa Graeber and her husband Grant, who came to the UK as an officer with the US Navy based in Northwood, originally planned a brewery in central London with a 16hl kit. When this fell through, they decided to convert their garden 'summerhouse' in London's far-flung northwest into a 2.5hl facility. Expansion plans were slowed due to the lockdown but are now back on track: brewery capacity should double by the end of 2021 and two possible taproom sites are under development.

BEERS in keg and bottle are sold locally, often at Beer Asylum (above). The range regularly changes, covering a variety of styles and aiming to offer alternatives to beers commonly available from others, for example by avoiding popular hops. Among the recurring successes are strong wheat beer **Sunset Cliffs** (7%); milk stout **Monaco*** (7.3%); and **Brutify'd*** (8.8%), an imperial stout aged on rum barrel chips with cocoa and almond.

Masons Arms

the keg taps, while bottled options include Hogs Back and Shepherd Neame. The spotless and decidedly traditional interior is arranged around a horseshoe bar, with fresh flowers offsetting an astonishing collection of beer-related ephemera and breweriana. Then there's the well-tended garden, in which old urinals have been recycled as planters.

Visitor note. The modestly handsome building, with a fine tiled frontage now restored to its former glory, was once tied to the local Isleworth Brewery. Both Bushy Park, one of London's lesser known royal parks, and Teddington Lock, the upper limit of the tidal Thames, are within relatively easy walking distance.

Noble Green Wines   30

Shop

153 High Street, Hampton Hill TW12 1NL

T (020) 8979 1113   noblegreenwines.co.uk

⏱ *Mo-Fr* 11.00-20.00, *Sa* 10.00-20.00, *Su* 11.00-18.00.

3-4 cask, 400 bottles/cans, growlers, cask and bottled ciders and perries, wines, specialist spirits.

⇌ Fulwell   🚍 Parkside   🏃 Bushy Park Paths, Link to London Loop

Masons Arms   29

Traditional pub

51 Walpole Road, Teddington TW11 8PJ

T (020) 8977 6521   the-masons-arms.co.uk

⏱ *Mo-Th* 12.00-23.00, *Fr-Sa* 12.00-23.30, *Su* 12.00-22.30. Children in garden only.

4 cask, 3 keg, 8 bottles, 1 cider/perry.

🍴 Lunchtime rolls, cheeseboard *(Su)* **£**,

🎍 Small rear garden ☺, ♿

Occasional live music, darts, rings, skittles, board games

⇌ Teddington   🚍 Teddington Memorial Hospital
🚲 Link to NCN4   🏃 Link to London Loop, Thames Path

Licensee Rae Williams had been working at this small corner pub in a residential street behind Teddington High Street for many years when she bought the freehold with a business partner in May 2010, turning it into a real ale showcase that will amply reward a visit. The handpumps dispense Hop Back Citra and Sambrook's Junction, plus a good range of guests from breweries like Andwells, Coastal or Pig and Porter, usually including a dark choice. Gipsy Hill and Thornbridge feature on

This shop opposite the Hampton Hill Theatre was opened as a wine merchant with a sideline in beer. Thanks to customer demand and enthusiastic and knowledgeable buyers, the sideline has grown year on year, pushing out some of the wines. Cask beers are poured on gravity into takeaway vessels of various sizes, with whole firkins available to order, often from local or regional suppliers like Burning Sky, Dark Star, Surrey Hills, Twickenham and Windsor & Eton. An impressive selection of London bottles and cans – Brick, By the Horns, Gipsy Hill, Mondo, Park, Wimbledon – lines up beside unusual choices from elsewhere in the UK and a comprehensive range of Harvey's bottles. Well-established Belgian and German bottles including several Trappists, alongside newer Scandinavian arrivals (Beerbliothek, Egir) and directly-imported Americans (Hardywood, Port City). The shop is spacious, easy to browse, and well worth a special shopping trip, though there are no drink-in facilities.

Pinnora Brewing (31)

Brewery, no visitors please
2 Jubilee Parade (rear), West End Avenue,
Pinner HA5 1BB (Harrow)
pinnorabrewing.com
First sold beer: March 2019.

Labelling itself with the first recorded name
for Pinner in the 13th century, Pinnora was set
up by two local brothers, Gareth and Gawain
Cox. Both have been involved in commercial
brewing for others since 2016, inspired by
their late father, a keen real ale fan. In 2018
they moved into a very small commercial unit
near the village centre and a few months later
began brewing in their own right on a 2hl kit.
Restrictions on their current space prevent
them from welcoming visitors but expansion
to additional units is planned.

BEERS in keg, bottle and can include a Spring
Ekuanot pale ale (not tasted), an official beer
for the Chelsea Pensioners and 'Transitory
Sequence' seasonals with names drawn from
local history.

Real Drinks (32)

Shop, bar
371 Richmond Road, Twickenham TW1 2EF
T (020) 8892 3710   **realdrinks.co.uk**
Su-Mo 12.00-20.00, *Tu-Sa* 10.00-21.00.
  Children welcome.
4+ keg, 350 bottles/cans, growlers, specialist
  cider/perry, natural and other wine,
  specialist spirits.
Tap takeovers, occasional tutored tastings

≥ St Margarets Richmond Landing Stage, Richmond St
Helena First Creswell Road Thames Path, link to Capital Ring

Opened in 2005 under the name realale.com
as a shop window for a thriving online
business, this well-stocked and pleasantly
appointed corner store just across Richmond
Bridge has always focused largely on small
British producers: founder Nick Dolan is also a
director of Norfolk's renowned Woodfordes
brewery. It has therefore been well-placed to
evolve with the changing times as UK brewing
has expanded and flourished: 'We used to
have a wall full of bitters,' a youthful staff
member once told me, 'but it's a different

market now.' There are still a few more
traditional beers, including some from
Woodforde's, but most space is given over to
newer arrivals from London and elsewhere like
Arbor, Beatnikz Republic, Brick, Burning Sky,
Fallen, Park, Pressure Drop, Villages and Wild,
alongside reliable names from Belgium and
Germany and a handful from the US. Keg taps,
also largely UK-slanted, originally provided
growlers, but drink-in facilities added late in
2019 bring this pioneering outlet into line
with more recently opened branches
(Try also p306). Full lists are on Untappd.

Rifleman

See Twickenham Fine Ales

Sussex Arms   (33)

Contemporary pub
15 Staines Road, Twickenham TW2 5BG
T (020) 8894 7468
thesussexarmstwickenham.co.uk
Mo-Th 12.00-23.00, *Fr-Sa* 12.00-23.30,
  Su 12.00-22.30. Children until 20.00.
15 cask, 14 keg, 30+ bottles, 6 ciders/perries.
Enhanced pub grub, pies, burgers, pizzas
££, Large rear garden, front terrace
*Two annual beer festivals, quiz (We), occasional live
music, seasonal events*

≥ Strawberry Hill First Cross Road Link to River
Crane Walk

The successful transformation, in July 2011, of
this big Brewer's Tudor roadhouse just west
of Twickenham Green from a sink boozer ('it
wasn't a nice place,' a customer once delicately
told me) into a flourishing beer and cider
specialist inspired the creation of what's
now a significant group of well-run and beer-
friendly London pubs. A mouth-watering
bank of handpumps focuses on small
producers, including associated brewery
Big Smoke (p318) and nearby Thames Side
and Twickenham. Others, in a range of
styles and strengths, might include Andwell,
Arbor, Flying Monk, Mad Squirrel and Siren.
Originally the keg lines remained tied but
have since been freed to dispense the likes of
BBNo, Cloudwater, Loka Polly, Pressure Drop

Sussex Arms

or Ireland's White Hag, with bottled Schneider Weisse and Rochefort Trappists in the fridges. The main bar has original dark wood and restored leaded windows, with a delightfully tiled little room further back and a massive beer garden. The shortish menu highlights pies – the first chef was a specialist baker and pastry chef – alongside burgers, salads, pizzas, vegan options and dishes like seafood linguine. The formula attracts enough of a crowd to keep even a pub of this size busy. Note the loyalty card scheme shared with other outlets in the group.

Sussex Arms

Tiny Vessel Brewing Co

Brewery, no visitors please
505 Platts Eyot, Hampton TW12 2HF
(Richmond upon Thames) **tinyvessel.co.uk**
First sold beer: December 2016

One of London's most unusually located breweries as well as one of its smallest, Tiny Vessel is in a workshop on Platts Eyot, a privately-owned island in the Thames at Hampton on the edge of the capital. The only link to the mainland is a suspension footbridge so anything substantial has to be moved by boat. The project is the brainchild of Ivailo Penev, a Bulgarian-born brewer who had been cuckoo-brewing botanically-flavoured beers under the name Rose Brew since 2014, and business partner Neal Durrant. Ivailo also runs Brentford pub the Northumberland Arms (Try also p299).

BEERS (not tasted) are in keg and bottle. Recipes change, but two award-winning beers, **Dark Matter** carob porter (4.5%) and coriander-infused English IPA **Summit Else** (5.2%), regularly recur.

Twickenham Fine Ales ㉟

Brewery, taproom: 18 Mereway Road,
Twickenham TW2 6RG (Richmond upon Thames)
T (020) 8241 1825 **twickenham-fine-ales.co.uk**
First sold beer: November 2004. 🍴🍴
Shop 🕐: Mo-Fr 11.00-17.00, Sa 10.00-13.00.
Taproom 🕐: Events and rugby match days only:
check website as times vary. Children
welcome.
2 cask, 1 keg, 6 bottles, growlers, bag-in-box.
🍴 Barbecue on rugby match days **£**,
🪑 Benches at rear
Monthly comedy

🚆 Whitton, Twickenham   🚌 First Cross Road
🚶 River Crane Walk

Rifleman ㉟ₐ

Traditional pub: 7 Fourth Cross Road,
Twickenham TW2 5EL
T (020) 8255 0205
🕐 Mo-Th 16.00-23.00, Fr 14.00-23.00, Sa 12.00-
23.00, Su 12.00-22.30. Children until 20.00.
6 cask, 4 keg, 10+ bottles/cans, some wines,
gins, specialist spirits.
🍴 Pies and cold plates **£-££**,
🪑 Front terrace, rear garden
Tastings, open mic (Th), big screen sport, darts

🚆 Fulwell   🚌 Trafalgar Road Prince of Wales
🚶 Link to London Loop

Now something of a London veteran,
Twickenham Fine Ales is the fourth oldest of all
the London breweries and the oldest independent standalone brewery in the capital. When
opened on redundancy money by former
IT professional Steve Brown in 2004, it was
the first brewery in Twickenham since Cole &
Burrows closed in 1906, but passed under the
radar of all but a few drinkers by selling only to
very local outlets. All that changed late in 2012
following a major expansion to long-sought
new premises near Twickenham Green with a
40hl kit. Though the beers are now sold widely,
the brewery retains a strong local base, and
Steve is determined to stay in Twickenham
when further expansion becomes inevitable.

Much is made of the locality's association
with rugby union, a sport where real ale is the
traditional tipple of choice. The taproom opens
before matches at the main Twickenham
stadium or at local team Harlequins' Stoop

ground nearby, and sometimes during major
rugby tournaments: these busy occasions,
when visitors drink among the brewing vessels
and in the outside yard, have become a local
institution. In August 2019, the company
realised a long-held ambition by taking on the
Rifleman, a corner pub only a few streets away.
This small but handsome place with its pretty
front terrace and cheerful single bar has undergone several changes of ownership in recent
years, with varying degrees of beer-friendliness,
but is now a fine showcase for its new owner's
cask, keg and bottled beers alongside Young's
bitter and traditional-leaning guests from
brewers like Adnams, Butcombe and Oakham.

*Visitor note. The Rifleman sign depicts local resident Frank
Edwards, known as the Footballer of Loos, a rifleman who
dribbled a football across enemy lines during the Battle of
Loos in 1915.*

BEERS tend towards the traditional with a
modern twist, with cask still an important part
of the business, alongside keg and off-site
bottling and canning. Cask regulars include
traditional bitter **Grandstand*** (3.8%); flagship
golden ale **Naked Ladies*** (4.4%), named after
statues in the gardens of nearby York House;
and **Red Sky** (4.1%), a red ale with southern
hemisphere hops. Keg and canned beers
include a session IPA There are numerous
seasonals and specials including honey-infused
dark mild **Honey Dark*** (4.8%), available
year-round in bottle and sometimes seen
barrel-aged, and old ale **Winter Star*** (4.4%).

TRY ALSO

Brouge (Old Goat) 241 Hampton Road, Twickenham TW2 5NG **brouge.co.uk**: Roadside pub converted in 2003 into a pleasant, airy Belgian-inspired bar-restaurant, with a Twickenham cask beer and decent kegs from bigger breweries. Plus a 40-strong list of mainly Belgian bottles, solid but less adventurous than it once was, to wash down mussels and *waterzooi*.

Jolly Coopers 16 High Street, Hampton TW12 2SJ: Excellent traditional community free house in a village setting a step from the Hampton ferry. Well-kept by the same owners for over 30 years, with several good cask options, often including the local Park brewery.

London Apprentice 62 Church Street, Isleworth TW7 6BG **greeneking-pubs.co.uk**: Famous 18th century Grade II*-listed riverside pub in picturesque setting on Thames Path in Old Isleworth, a few steps from Syon Park. Five cared-for traditional leaning, sometimes local, casks and a couple of better-known 'craft keg' options.

Queens Head 54 Windsor Street, Uxbridge UB8 1AB **greeneking-pubs.co.uk**: Old school sporty town centre pub in attractively saggy early 19th century building close to station, with keen licensee offering locals like Twickenham besides Greene King across five cask lines sufficiently well-kept to bag a local CAMRA award in 2020.

Ricardo's Cellar 44 Church Street, Twickenham TW1 3NT **ricardoscellar.com**. Independent off licence and deli sharing space with a record dealer a few doors from Brewery Market (above): 50+ bottles/cans for takeaway only with lots of locals and own brand exclusives commissioned by an enthusiastic owner (Brewers without breweries p322).

Roebuck 72 Hampton Road, Hampton Hill TW12 1JN **roebuck-hamptonhill.co.uk**:

Salmon-pink painted Hampton Hill landmark with eccentric bric-a-brac collection (including life-size basketwork motorbike) and five cask ales, including Sambrook's and locals like Park, from an exemplary cellar. Short walk from Noble Green Wines (above) and Bushy Park.

LONDON HEATHROW AIRPORT

Heathrow is one of the world's biggest airports serving one of its best beer cities, but its catering outlets are not quite the ambassadors they should be for the world's greatest long drink, especially compared to some of the US terminals at the other end of the westbound flight paths. Things are improving slowly, particularly at Terminal 2, which since May 2021 has hosted the **Big Smoke Taphouse and Kitchen** by Gate A20 on airside level 4, run by the team behind the Esher brewery and numerous great London pubs like the Sussex Arms (p312). No cask, sadly, but five of the brewery's beers on keg and several more in cans, including an airport exclusive. On the main departure concourse, by gates A1 and A2, is Fuller's only airport bar, **London's Pride**, a smart white-tiled place presenting a good range of the brewery's beer in cask, keg, can and bottle, plus a few London guests. One end of the main departure hall, before security, is occupied by Wetherspoon outlet the **Flying Chariot**, with two floors, its own observation tower and the usual reasonable range of cask, keg and bottled/canned beers, including rotating local guests. Over at Terminal 5 airside is another Wetherspoon of note, the large and busy **Crown Rivers**, split between two sides of a public walkway downstairs from security by domestic gate A7. This also features Windsor & Eton, and often has stronger-than-average cask beers: apparently drinkers tend towards these when contemplating a lengthy flight.

Hop and Vine

LONDON DRINKERS | Lily Waite

A beer writer (lilywaite.net), photographer and ceramicist (lilywaiteceramics.com), Lily is also the founder of LGBTQ-focused non-profit brewing initiative the Queer Brewing Project. She's lived in London for five years, working in bars and bottle shops across the city. Follow her @lilywaite.

How do you rate London as a beer city, on a world scale?
It's one of the world leaders, steeped in incredibly rich brewing history with innumerable world-class bars, shops and breweries covering every base, and a drinking culture that's incredibly exciting.

What's the single most exciting thing about beer in London right now?
The beers emerging from the Kernel's foeder-ageing programme. Their new taproom is oh-so-cosy, too, and I'll be spending a lot of time there.

What single thing would make things even better?
DEYA's Steady Rolling Man as a permanent fixture in my local, the Jolly Butchers. And a few more soft furnishings in taprooms.

What are your top London beers right now?
My all-time favourite is the Kernel Table Beer, a hoppy low-ABV Pale Ale that's simultaneously complex, refreshing, quaffable and friendly. Pressure Drop's Pale Fire is a classic, and Boxcar's Dark Mild is fantastic for the colder months.

What's your top great beer night out?
Much as I love hopping from taproom to taproom, spending an evening sinking pints of well-kept cask in a pub like the Southampton Arms (p175) is always great fun. Or pulling sharing bottles out of the fridge in a great bottle shop and enjoying them with friends.

Who's your London beer hero?
My dear friend Melissa Cole springs to mind, as does Matthew

Curtis, both talented writers and organisers of unmissable events. Duration Brewing may now be based in Norfolk, but they started in south London, so co-founders Derek Bates and Miranda Hudson still count.

Who will we be hearing a lot more from in future?
Sam Dickison is making some amazing beers at Boxcar. He's not unknown by any means but I'm so excited to see what he does when he really hits his stride.

Which are your other top beer cities?
Berlin's probably my favourite city in the world, and is excellent for beer, with outstanding craft breweries and brewers reviving lost styles as well as quality mass-produced lager if you're looking for a quick, easy-thinking pint. Denver has a brightly coloured, fun scene and great breweries.

THE
REST

Breweries outside London

When the London Brewers Alliance (LBA) started in 2010, there were so few potential members that the geographical boundary was stretched to accommodate as many of them as possible. It was later fixed to 'within the M25 motorway', including some territory out of the bounds of this book, which covers Greater London as recognised by the Greater London Authority. I'm waiting to see what will happen when someone sets up a brewery in the small square of the London Borough of Havering protruding beyond the M25 and then applies to join the LBA, but in the meantime here are some LBA members outside London that you should know about.

Big Smoke Brew Co

Unit D3 Sandown Industrial Estate, Esher KT10 8BL (Elmbridge, Surrey)
T (01372) 469606   **bigsmokebrew.co.uk**
First sold beer (at original site): September 2014

As its name suggests, Big Smoke was originally a London brewery, with an 8hl setup in an outhouse behind the Antelope in Surbiton (Try also p287), under the same ownership as the Sussex Arms (p312) and several other excellent pubs. Demand grew to the extent that it was forced to contract-brew some of its beers, and in April 2019 it relocated just outside London to its current dedicated production site, with a 33hl kit, a canning line and a taproom (*Fr-Su*). Beers in cask, keg and can are widely available not only in the linked pubs but in many other outlets throughout the capital, so it remains a London brewer in spirit. Award-winning **Underworld Milk Stout*** (5%) is particularly recommended.

Brightwater Brewery

37B The Parade, Claygate, Esher KT10 0PD (Elmbridge, Surrey)
T (01372) 462334   **brightbrew.co.uk**
First sold beer: February 2013

Founded by Alex Coomes and Susan Harding, this is a small operation mainly producing cask and bottle-conditioned beer. It gained its own outlet next to Claygate station in 2015: Platform 3, a micropub in the true sense of the word as it's one of the smallest in the country (*Th-Su*). The address above is for the pub; beers (not tasted) are brewed elsewhere in the village.

Creative Juices Brewing Company

Woodoaks Farm, Denham Way, Rickmansworth WD3 9XQ (Three Rivers, Hertfordshire)
T (01923) 771779
creativejuicesbrewingcompany.com
First sold beer: November 2019

The brainchild of former marketing executive Ben Janaway, this brewery makes use of its rural location in a refurbished disused milking shed and grainstore on a dairy farm just northwest of London with a taproom and rustic beer garden (*We-Su*). Beers in can and keg take a contemporary look at traditional styles, including a best bitter, **Of Course I Still Love You** (4.4%, not tasted).

Thames Side Brewery

Bridge Street, Staines upon Thames TW18 4TG
(Spelthorne, Surrey)
T 07749 204242 **thamessidebrewery.co.uk**
First sold beer: August 2015

Literally beside the Thames, this 6.5hl outfit
was founded by Andy Hayward as the first
brewery in Staines for 80 years. Originally,
it was in an old boatyard but moved a short
distance in 2019 to a building once used by
sea cadets, adding a taproom with fine river
views (*We-Su limited hours, please check*). Most beer
is cask (not tasted), with some keg, and a
wide variety of styles, some made on a 1.5hl
pilot kit.

Windsor & Eton Brewery

1 Vansittart Estate, Duke Street, Windsor
SL4 1SE (Windsor and Maidenhead)
T (01753 854075) **webrew.co.uk**
First sold beer: May 2010

Though in Windsor some way west of the
M25, Windsor & Eton was one of the
founders of the LBA and makes good use of
its grandfather rights today as an active
member, its excellent beers widely on sale in
the capital. Co-founder Paddy Johnson has
impeccable London brewing credentials: he
began his career at Courage in Horsleydown
before working in other parts of the UK for
Bass and Scottish & Newcastle. Co-founder
Will Calvert is another ex-Courage employee.
The brewery uses a 28hl bespoke kit to
produce a range of beers in cask, keg, bottle
and can, with more contemporary styles
under the sub-brand **Uprising** overseen by
Paddy's son Kieran. There's a shop and
taproom at the brewery (*closed Su*) and the
Rose and Olive Branch in nearby Virginia
Water became the first pub in 2020.
I particularly recommend pale ale
Windsor Knot* (4%), inaugural best bitter
Guardsman (4.2%), Czech-style lager
Republika* (4.8%) and black IPA
Conqueror* (5%).

Titsey Brewing Co

Botley Hill Farm, Limpsfield Road,
Warlingham CR6 9QH (Tandridge, Surrey)
T (01959) 528535   **titseybrewingco.com**
First sold beer: August 2017. 🍺.

South African-born Craig Vroom started
brewing one cask at a time in the idyllic setting
of a 16th century listed farmhouse on the
Titsey Estate, at the highest point on the
North Downs Way National Trail atop the chalk
ridge just south of London. The operation was
upgraded in 2019 to an 8hl kit in a neighbouring
unit, but the Botley Hill Farmhouse, which is
open as a pub and restaurant, still sells the
beers. Further expansion to a barn and
taproom elsewhere on the estate is planned.
Beers (not tasted) in cask, keg, bottle and
bag-in-box are at session strength, the better
to refresh thirsty walkers and cyclists, and
are named after families connected with the
estate: they include **Green and Gold**, a wet
hop seasonal pale ale (4.2%).

Brewers without breweries

You don't need to have your own brewing equipment to market your own beer brands: you can simply use someone else's. Businesses who do this have long been known as contract breweries. Some say this term doesn't adequately reflect their engagement in production, and prefer to be known as cuckoo brewers if they work mainly in one location, or as gypsy brewers if they regularly change locations, though this last term is increasingly being replaced by 'nomad' to avoid any potential ethnic insult. I've used the term 'beer firm' as a more general description.

Such arrangements have traditionally been viewed with suspicion in the UK, although they're common in many other countries and there are good arguments for them. Brewing equipment and premises are expensive, yet few London brewhouses are used daily. Renting them out is a way of making use of spare capacity while giving keen brewers who lack resources a way into the industry at minimal expense, helping them build enough interest, sales and investor support to graduate to their own kit. Several of the excellent breweries now enriching London's beer culture began by using other people's facilities, including Ora, Truman's and Wild Card. And while some experienced brewers believe they couldn't truly shine without mastering the idiosyncrasies of their own equipment, much as virtuoso musicians get the best out of a favourite instrument, other very successful cuckoos say they are happy to remain so. Problems arise when brewers are less than honest about where the beer comes from: consumers increasingly care about provenance, and labelling something brewed in Bedford, Kortrijk or Munich as a London beer is deceitful.

The extent to which brewers without breweries contribute to the creation of the beer they sell varies hugely. At one extreme are those who get involved in every stage of the brewing process, buying ingredients, occupying someone else's brewhouse for the day to do the actual work themselves, and supervising fermentation and packaging. At the other are those who sketch out ideas for beers and leave it to the professionals to come up with the finished product, perhaps providing feedback during the development process. In between is a whole spectrum of collaboration between beer firm and host brewery.

The situation is complicated further by breweries who have their own kit but also use other people's. It's a common practice for established firms to contract out some of their production to others on a temporary basis, in response either to demand unexpectedly exceeding capacity or a technical problem. Beavertown and Camden Town have both used the services of mainland European breweries in recent years to help them cope with their success. At the other end of the scale are an increasing number of commercially licensed London breweries who do indeed sell beer made on their own kits in very small batches of 100 litres or less but call on others to help with larger orders. Given the difficulties of pinning down exactly how much of their output they make themselves, I've accepted all of these as breweries in their own right and you'll find them in the main listings, but for some of them, own-brewed products are a minimal part of the business.

You'll also encounter beers under unfamiliar brands brewed as bespoke recipes either for individual pubs, bars and shops or for chains, sometimes with staff from the client helping develop the recipe and even participate in the actual brewing. I can't keep track of all of these, but a few particularly interesting ones are mentioned in the main listings. It's also not unknown for companies without any brewing expertise simply to slap another label on a standard beer bought in from someone else, known as 'rebadging', but I don't regard such antics as brewing in any sense so haven't bothered about them here.

Even with the best of intentions, beer firms pose problems for anyone trying to keep close track of the industry, and not just because of their proliferation. They tend to be much less stable and harder to pin down geographically. They can easily shift locations from brew to brew, take extended breaks from brewing with little need to service debts and rent, and wrap things up easily if sales don't meet expectations. Producing a definitive list would be impossible, but below I've tried to cover the most prominent players that do at least most of their brewing in London or have other clear London links.

Better World. Currently based in Borehamwood, just outside London, but cuckoo brewing at Pretty Decent, this firm, originally known as No Heroes, is as socially conscious as its host and is promising to plant a tree for every sale. It plans a brewery and taproom in Southwark in 2021. Beers not tasted. betterworldbrewing.co.uk

Big Hug. Though a few early brews in 2014 were on a pilot kit under the name Bear Hug, this trio of friends reconciled themselves to hobo brewer status after a fruitless search for sites. Beers (not tasted) are from a variety of facilities including Brewhouse & Kitchen, Portobello, Gadds in Ramsgate and the Great Yorkshire Brewery. It's a keen supporter of homeless charities. bighugbrewing.com

Bloomsbury. A brand name increasingly used for the house beers at the Euston Tap (p78) and its sister pubs owned by the Bloomsbury Leisure Group, custom-brewed in the UK and Germany including at Five Points. Not be confused with the similar brand sometimes used for house beers commissioned by former brewpub the Perseverance (see Gone below).

BritHop. Stuart Holland started this Bexley-based part-time enterprise in September

2017, cuckoo-brewing for cask, keg and can at Franklins in Sussex, with brands inspired by the indie music of the 1990s. A local brewhouse and taproom may well follow in 2022. Beers include **Pit*** (3.8%), a pale ale exclusively for the Cockpit micropub (p244); and award-winning **Shakermaker** oatmeal pale ale (4.8%, not tasted). brithopbeer.com

Brodie's Fabulous Beers. James and Lizzie Brodie launched this important early contributor to the London brewing revival in August 2008 in a former stable behind the family's pub, the King William IV, in Leyton. The 8hl kit was originally sourced in 2000 from Pitfield's and Dark Star founder Rob Jones as part of a partnership with an outside brewer but had been untouched since 2005. A seemingly endless stream of inventive and always interesting beers flowed thereafter, but personal issues forced the sale of the William and the closure of the brewery early in 2018, one of the most regrettable losses between the last edition and this one. Subsequently, some Brodie's beers have been cuckoo-brewed at Wobbly in Hereford, Rhymney in Blaenavon, South Wales and most recently at Battersea Brewery (p267) where former Brodie's head brewer Tom Barlow now works. The Brodie family still leases two central London pubs, the Cross Keys (31 Endell Street WC2H 9BA) and the Old Coffee House (49 Beak Street W1F 9SP), where the beers have been known to appear intermittently; Tom currently owns the brand and recipes, and although production has dwindled due to time and capacity constraints, he's keen to revive them should the opportunity arise.

Coalition Brewing Co. Launched in 2017 by three locals based in Purley and initially brewing at Hepworth in Pulborough, West Sussex, Coalition planned to open a brewpub in central Croydon during 2019 but the site fell through thanks to a regeneration scheme. An alternative south London site has since been found and should be operational by the end of 2021. The flagship is **Unity Lager** (4.5%, not tasted). coalitionbrewing.co.uk

Common Rioters. see Standing by (below).

Days Brewing. Launched by London-based Scots Duncan Keith and Mike Gammell in September 2020, this is another contributor to the expanding choice of decent low and no alcohol beers. A lager and a pale ale (not tasted) are brewed in Scotland using a special technique of fermentation control to achieve 0% ABV. daysbrewing.com

Eko Brewery. Anthony and Helena Adedipe's project, borrowing the Yoruba name for Lagos, gives an African twist to contemporary style brews, using ingredients like palm sugar and South African hops. Beers in bottle and can were first sold in 2019 and have mainly been brewed outside London so far, though the office is based here. ekobrewery.com

Hiver Beers. Founded by Hannah Rhodes, formerly at Meantime, in 2013, Hiver specialises in honey beers, made partly with London honey but brewed at Hepworth in West Sussex. The Bermondsey HQ doubles as a weekend bar (Try also p216) where you can taste flagship **The Honey Beer*** (4.5%) and its stablemates, amber ale **The Honey Ale** (4.5%) and **The Honey IPA** (4.9%). In 2020, it added a honey-free range under the name **Fabal** (not tasted). hiverbeers.com

Hop King. Ben Hopkinson, formerly at Late Knights, and his brother Ludi combined their enthusiasms for both beer and skateboarding by producing their own beer for their indoor skate park Hop Kingdom and Ben's Beer Rebellion bar from 2017. It's since been distributed elsewhere and is brewed at various locations including Fourpure. **Pale Ale** (4.2%) is also available in a version with legal cannabis derivative CBD (not tasted). hopking.org

Infinite Session. Based on the edge of the Olympic Park, this is another low alcohol specialist. Beers, including an award-winning **American Pale Ale** (0.5%, not tasted), are widely available in can and bottle. infinitesession.com

Jiddler's Tipple Craft Beer, North London-based vintage shirt fan Jacob Liddle brewed his first commercial batches of session pale ale **Everyday** (3.8%, not tasted) at Brum brewery in Birmingham in October 2019. The award-winning beer has since been joined by two more of similarly forgiving strength, now produced at By the Horns. A standalone brewery remains an aspiration for now. jiddlerstipple.com

Jubel. Founded by Jesse Wilson, a descendant of brewers and publicans, in 2018, Jubel markets a range of keg and canned gluten-free, vegan-friendly 'craft' lagers cut with fruit'. Currently there are three varieties, with elderflower, grapefruit and peach (all 4%, not tasted), brewed at Camerons, Hartlepool. jubelbeer.com

Little Faith Beer. This side project of a Kernel brewer supplies its own excellent bar in Deptford (p233). Beers in keg and can, brewed at London Brewing and Franklins in Sussex, include pale ale **New Colours** (4.3%) and coffee oatmeal stout **Americano Dream*** (4.8%). littlefaithbeer.com

Mothership Beer. This all-female beer collective led by Jane and Zoe began working commercially in 2018, cuckoo-brewing in various locations like By the Horns and Missing Link. They're currently working on plans for their own brewery and taproom. A variety of styles changes seasonally: past brews have included a **Watermelon Gose** (4.2%), **Brut IPA** (4.5%) with Champagne yeast and an **APA** (5.5%). mothership.beer

Queer Brewing Project. Led by London-based beer writer and educator Lily Waite since 2018, this is a collaborative project to promote greater diversity, acceptance, and visibility of LGBTQ+ people in the beer and brewing industries, and to raise money for relevant charities. There have been numerous collaborations with brewers in London, the rest of the UK and abroad, and I've enjoyed every one I've tried. thequeerbrewingproject.com

Ricardo's Cellar. This Twickenham shop (Try also p315) once hosted the Eel Pie brewing school, since wound up, but still commissions exclusive own brand bottled beers from Hepworth in Sussex, currently

Sovereign Lager (4.7%) plus a pale ale and an IPA. ricardoscellar.com

---

Roaring Four Brewing Co. Started by four homebrewing friends, one British and the others from New Zealand, this first brewed at London Beer Lab in 2015 and has also used the facilities at Altarnun in Cornwall. One of the four, Nick Thomas, owns Craft Beer Cabin (p245) which is a good source of the beers, mainly single hop pale ales and IPAs (not tasted). roaringfour.com

---

Rock Leopard Brewing Co. Based in southeast London, this firm has been brewing contemporary-style beers commercially since 2018, and currently cuckoo brews at Drop Project and Villages as well as Cloudwater in Manchester, the latter the source of tasty stout **Step Up*** (5%). A brewhouse and taproom is planned in Thamesmead, perhaps during 2022. rockleopardbrewing.com

---

Seven Sisters Brewery. With its spiritual home at Woodberry Down, Haringey, just off the Seven Sisters Road, this was started at Ubrew as a part-time project by maths teachers Chris Martin and Tristan Bradley and retail professional Julio Santoyo in 2016. It's since worked at Bianca Road and various Brewhouse & Kitchens before largely settling at Hambledon Ales in Yorkshire, though the beers are easy to find in north London, and it's also organised beer festivals in Stoke Newington. Products include a good **Table Beer** (2.8%) and the popular **End of Thyme** (5.3%, not tasted), a saison with thyme and honey. sevensisbrew.com

---

So What Brewing Co. Bullfinch (p219) head brewer Jon's side project, produced on the nanobrewery at the Bull and Finch, Gipsy Hill.

Soho Beer. Licensed trade veteran Michael Breen began planning a Soho brewpub in 2013 but the project was held up by unexpected difficulties. He finally launched **Soho Lager** (4.5%) in December 2019 in keg and bottle, devised by former Guinness master brewery Fergal Murray and initially brewed at Hepworth in Sussex. Success in various central London pubs rapidly followed before lockdown struck. Two sister beers are planned, and the brewpub is still on the long-term agenda.

Tankleys Brewery. Cuckoo brewing since 2015, Glenn Heinzel (see also Beerblefish p144) and Martin Hemmings are now perhaps best known for **Hawaiian Pizza Beer** (5.5%, not tasted), besides numerous small batch brews inspired by traditional English, Belgian and German styles, including a notable cask **English Strong Golden Ale** (5.7%). Most likely found in southeast and north London. tankleysbrewery.com

---

Three Hounds. Matt Walden, formerly at Brockley, began cuckoo brewing for sale on a market stall in 2016, and continued to offer own-brewed brands at his bottle shop and bar in Clock House, Beckenham, opened the following year (p252). He currently uses the facilities at By the Horns and Dogs Grandad, but plans to install his own 1hl brewhouse, perhaps during 2022. Beers, also sold through other outlets, include a popular session IPA, **Pendulum** (4.6%), named with a nod to the location. They're in keg and occasional can, with plans for cask once the brewhouse is up and running. threehoundsbeerco.com

---

Toast Ale. Based in Southwark, Toast was launched in 2016 by Tristram Stuart, founder of food waste charity Feedback, with the aim of recycling waste bread into beer, a process Tristram first saw in action at Brussels Beer Project. Income from sales helps support the charity. Most of the bread used is in the form of crusts from the sandwich industry and surplus loaves from large bakeries, typically replacing a third of the grist. The first brew was at Hackney brewery, but the core beers are now produced at SEB in Broadstairs, Kent, alongside one-off collaborations with brewers around the country and the world. The project has since expanded to New York City, working with local brewers. The flagship is a contemporary **Pale Ale** (5%). toastale.com

---

Watneys Beer. Generations of drinkers must have thought they'd seen the back of this once-notorious London brand (Roll out the Red Barrel p126). But in this postmodern world anything is possible and in 2016 it was back, licensed by Nick Whitehurst of Brands Reunited from Heineken. The recipes are new, with the brewing contracted and no intention of opening a physical facility. Last seen marketing a minikeg version of the once ubiquitous Party Seven giant can early in 2021 but I've been unable to confirm if more will follow. watneys-beer.com

Wolfpack Lager. Founded in 2014 by retired Saracens rugby players Alistair Hargreaves and Chris Wyles in a quest for better but still accessible lager, Wolfpack currently brews at Greene King in Bury St Edmunds. The beer (not tasted) is widely available, including from the duo's bar at Queens Park (Try also p306) and elsewhere and from a double decker bus parked outside the ground at Saracens games. wolfpacklager.com

Yeastie Boys. A pioneer of the now-flourishing New Zealand craft scene, this punningly named outfit was founded in Wellington in 2008 by Stu McKinlay and Sam Possenniskie. It has always cuckoo brewed even in its home territory, and in 2015 Stu relocated to London to extend the brand. He's since become a familiar and influential figure on the local scene, and now claims to lead 'the world's smallest multinational' with a similar operation in Australia. A popup Bermondsey taproom (Secret Goldmine, try also p216) began late in 2019 and there are plans for a more substantial dedicated outlet. The beers, now brewed at Utopian in Devon, are widely available: they include flagship **Digital IPA** (5.7%), **Pot Kettle Black*** (6%) porter with New Zealand hops, **Gunnamatta*** (6.5%) IPA with Earl Grey tea and interesting specials. yeastieboys.co.nz

Young & Co's Brewery. When Young's closed the historic Ram brewery in Wandsworth in 2006 (The Ram Resurgent p276), the original deal with Charles Wells in Bedford involved setting up a joint venture known as Wells & Young's, 40% owned by the latter, to continue brewing the brands. Young's sold its shares in this to Wells in 2011 and is now just a pub company, while Wells itself was bought by national brewer Marston's in 2017, which in turn merged its brewing interests into Carlsberg UK in 2020 to create CMBC (Carlsberg Marston's Brewing Company). CMBC still has the rights to the Young's brands, supplied to Young's pubs on a rolling contract. Wells downsized to a new site, Brewpoint, on the outskirts of Bedford, in 2020, so it's possible the Young's beers will move elsewhere in the group. The core beers were rebranded, in my view rather misleadingly, in 2019, though in top condition on cask they're still well worth trying. They include ordinary bitter **London Original*** (3.7%, formerly simply Bitter and known locally as Ordinary, much to the irritation of the late John Young); special bitter **London Special*** (4.3%); and a rare surviving Burton ale, seasonal **Winter Warmer**** (5%).

Been, gone and standing by

Gone

Perhaps the most missed brewery listed in the 2015 edition is **Brodie's**, now counted as a brewer without a brewery (p321). **AB InBev** finally closed the Stag in Mortlake in December 2015, a sad end for the last remnant of big brewing in the capital (Roll out the Red Barrel p126), though ABI now has a presence in London via Camden Town (p197). **Big Smoke** has moved just outside the London boundary: see Breweries outside London (p318). Nanobrewery **Left Bank**, founded in 2014 in Walthamstow, ceased by the end of 2016: it was a cuckoo for a while and then relocated to Wales. **Moncada**, founded in North Kensington in 2011 and the newest brewery listed in the first edition of this guide, expanded north to an industrial site near Staples Corner in Brent in 2017 but sadly ceased brewing in summer 2021, having struggled during the lockdowns. **Rocky Head**, founded in 2012 and always a part-time business despite the quality of its beers, stopped at the end of 2017. **Strawman**, which operated in Hackney and the Old Kent Road from 2013, ceased trading early in 2015.

Hop Stuff began on a small scale at the redeveloped Royal Arsenal site in Woolwich in 2013 and grew through several crowdfunding rounds to own three bars in southeast London and Kent and a sizeable production facility with an annual capacity of 15,000hl on former arsenal land in West Thamesmead, opened in 2017. Things began to unravel in April 2019 when the landlord locked staff out due to unpaid rent. In July, the brewery agreed a pre-packaged administration deal with US-Canadian group Molson Coors, owner of Carling and Sharp's, unfortunately with the loss of over £1.5 million to around 1,000 crowdfunding investors. Moves to restart production were put on hold during the lockdowns and at the time of writing the brewery is closed and up for sale, though Molson Coors is retaining the brands and brewing them elsewhere. The brewery may yet reopen under a new name and owner.

Bermondsey's shared brewing facility **Ubrew**, host to multiple cuckoos since opening in February 2015 as well as marketing its own brands, closed in 2019 after management and hygiene troubles. It's regrettable they didn't manage to sort these out as many in London's brewing community agree that the concept was a sound one. At its height, the project successfully brought together enthusiastic homebrewers and actual and potential commercial operators, facilitated much sharing of information and skills and gave some notable producers an early start. The unrelated Mash Paddle aims to fill the gap by the end of 2021 (p212).

Redchurch, founded by Gary Ward in September 2011 under railway arches near Cambridge Heath station, expanded to a production site outside London in Harlow in 2017 though kept its original site as a taproom and wild and mixed fermentation specialist under the sub-brand **Urban Farmhouse**. The company went into pre-pack administration in May 2019, with the brands and Harlow site sold on to new owners and almost £900,000 of crowdfunding investment lost. Gary retained the arches which he reopened as a bar called **Sundays** and there was talk of reviving the production of wild and mixed fermentation beers, but later in the year some of the brewing equipment was for sale on eBay and the site didn't reopen following the lockdowns.

The **Florence** pub in Herne Hill (133 Dulwich Road SE24 0NG) was one of the earliest of the new wave of London brewpubs, brewing since September 2007 when it was owned by Firkin founder David Bruce. Well-established brewer and beer writer Peter Haydon, who had been involved in setting up Meantime, took over brewing in February 2011, also producing his own beers based on historic recipes under the name **A Head in a Hat**. Peter retired at the end of 2015, and during 2017 and 2018 the brewery was used as a training facility by current owners Greene King under the name **Craft Academy**, with some beers sold at the bar. This had ceased by 2019 and the brewhouse left unused, although they've been looking for a new brewer so it may be revived.

Hops and Glory (382 Essex Road N1 3PF), the Canonbury pub where Solvay Society (p152) was based until it expanded to a new site in 2016, continued to brew intermittently under its own name. This stopped in 2017 when the brewer left and hasn't restarted since the pub reopened under new ownership as the Seveney in 2018.

Brewing activity at pubs tends to peter out as the owners discover making consistently saleable beer is more of a challenge than they expected. Unused brewhouses are currently gathering dust in various pubs around London, last fired up by a keen brewer who then moved on, likely to a more attractive job with a production brewery, whereupon the management found buying from others was the path of least resistance. Casualties since the last edition are: **Bloomsbury** at the Perseverance in Lambs Conduit Street, 2015–16, though cuckoo brewing persisted for some time after this; **Dragonfly** at the George & Dragon, Acton (p295) 2014–17, with an attempt to revive brewing in partnership with Portobello abandoned by early 2019; **Earl's** at the Earl of Essex, Islington (p78), in action from 2013 until late 2014 when the brewer left; **Laine Brewing (Acton)** at the Aeronaut, from 2013 until a serious fire in the early hours of New Year's Day 2017, after which the brewhouse was never replaced; **Laine Brewing (Battersea)** at the Four Thieves, which lost its brewhouse by the end of 2019, though the pub owner continues brewing at the Peoples Park Tavern (p139); and the **Old Brewery Greenwich**, operated by Meantime since 2010 but with no more

brewing after the pub was sold to Young's in 2016. Brewing at the **Sultan** in Wimbledon (p285) lasted a mere six months in 2015 before being abandoned. The **Still and Star** in Aldgate gave up on its Truebrew kit by summer 2015 (see Been and gone below) and the pub has since closed.

Michaela Charles (formerly White) has been so busy at other breweries that her **Upstairs** project has lapsed. She was head brewer at Alphabeta (Been and gone below), then at Enefeld and now at Beerblefish. In 2018, she worked with the British Museum on a fascinating project to recreate an ancient Egyptian beer.

Changed

The **Bull** (p186), host pub of **London Brewing (Highgate)**, was sold to new owners in 2016 and the brewing operation was eventually renamed **Gorgeous** (London Brewing continues to operate at the Bohemia p197). The brewing operation at the **Ealing Park Tavern** was renamed **Long Arm** and relocated to a like-named brewpub in Shoreditch (p109) in 2017. **Late Knights** collapsed in 2016, with the brewery reincarnated as **Southey** (p251). Brewing stopped at Kings Cross pub the **Queens Head** (p81) in 2017 but subsequently evolved into the standalone **Old Street** brewery (p138). Listed in 2015 as a cuckoo with aspirations for a physical brewery, **Soul Rebel** eventually emerged as **Hale** in 2018, which mutated to **Exale** (p146) in 2019.

Tankley's was listed as a future brewery in 2015 but has remained a cuckoo (see Brewers without breweries p323). And **Ha'penny** was reported closed in 2015 but its former site was later reinvigorated by **Solvay Society** (p152).

Been and gone

These breweries appeared and disappeared in the gap between the last edition and this one.

°**Plato** (2014–16). Tiny brewery attached to a homebrew supplies stall in Hackney's Netil Market.

Alphabeta (2016–19). House brewery in the PittCue restaurant in the City, closed when the company went into liquidation. The business's founder, who had sold the brand, has bought it back and is planning a new restaurant, but with no news yet as to whether it might also brew.

Brewery Below (2017–18). Small brewery in the cellar of Borough Wines, Islington: the branch has since closed.

Burlington Arms (2015–17). This West End pub was the second after the Still and Star (Gone, above) to install a Truebrew automated 100 litre 'technobrewery' with pre-programmed recipes, marketed to pubs as a hassle-free way of brewing house beer. It produced various beers under the **W1** brand, but this eventually petered out and by the time the pub was sold to new owners in 2017, only bought-in products were appearing on the bar. It seems these devices were unable to substitute for the skills of an experienced brewer: the products I sampled at the Still and Star were less than impressive. That pub's Truebrew had a second chance at the George and Dragon (below) but is also no longer in use and the manufacturer seems to have vanished too.

Cellar Boys (2017–18). Briefly brewing, initially under the name Paddies with Attitude, on a tiny kit in the cellar of the White Hart in New Cross (since closed). Cuckoo brewing followed but this too seems to have ceased.

Cricklewood (2017). Home-based brewery that briefly brewed commercially.

Eel Pie Brew School (2018–20). For a while this was arguably London's smallest commercial brewery, a 20 litre setup in Twickenham shop Ricardo's Cellar, primarily used for brewing courses taught by retired Heineken employee Guy Hutchinson but with some of the results sold in the shop. Activities had to stop during the lockdown and are unlikely to resume as Guy has since moved out of London, though the shop commissions its own beers (Brewers without breweries p322).

Gan Yam (2019). London-based cuckoo that briefly worked commercially on a home kit before relocating to Cumbria.

George and Dragon W1 (2016–17). The Truebrew kit originally at the Still and Star (Gone, above) subsequently operated at this Fitzrovia pub under the name **BrewIt** but with no more longevity than before. The pub has since changed owners.

Hill Brothers (2017–18). Short-lived home-based brewery in Camden Town.

Load of Hay (2016–17). Haverstock Hill pub that was briefly a brewpub, using the **Haverstock** brand. It reopened under new ownership as the **Belrose** in 2018 with the intention of continuing to produce house beers under the new name, but the brewery was abandoned due to temperature control problems and the beers commissioned instead from London Beer Lab. The pub changed hands again in 2019 and is now known as the Haverstock Tavern.

Lonesome (2016–17). Home-based brewer in Streatham.

Maregade (2015–19). Began by taking over the kit in the Cock Tavern, Hackney (p136) when Howling Hops expanded to Hackney Wick. Relocated to a Homerton railway arch in 2018 but forced to close due to licensing issues.

Mellor's (2021). A rather good contemporary cask specialist which brewed commercially at a private home in Haringey for a mere few weeks before relocating to Suffolk though at the time of writing still has a monthly stall at a Finsbury Park farmer's market. mellorsbrewing.co.uk

Montague Arms (2015). Very short-lived brewery in a big roadside Peckham/New Cross pub, operating under the name **Monkey Chews**.

Prince (2017–19). Wood Green pub (p191) equipped with a brewery when it reopened in 2017, initially operating under the name **House**. The brewer left in 2018 and the kit was subsequently used by the Goodness (p187) while its own plant was being installed elsewhere. It's since been removed and the area repurposed.

Project 88 (2017–18). Began as a nanobrewery at the inaugural Willesden branch of the Beer + Burger chain (p304) but became a cuckoo brewer in response to growing demand. The brand is no longer used but the outlets still stock collabs and exclusives brewed elsewhere.

Railway (2016–18). Small brewery operating as **Streatham** in an outhouse at the rear of this pub by Streatham Common station, under separate ownership from the pub itself.

Reunion Ales (2015–20). Opened by former homebrewer and financial professional Francis Smedley on an industrial estate in Feltham on London's western fringes, Reunion just missed the press date of the last edition of this book. A relatively substantial and highly professional operation with a notable product range including cask and gluten-free beers, it sadly became the first major London brewing casualty of the lockdowns, closing in August 2020.

Second Wave. Briefly operated a small brewery and taproom in West Norwood during 2019. This had to close, and they'd ceased trading by the end of the year.

Two Finches (2015–18). Very small brewery in an ancillary building at Finchley Cricket Club, selling through the club bar.

Standing by

Common Rioters is the brainchild of ex-Brewhouse and Kitchen brewer Stephen O'Connor and his beer sommelier wife Maryann. They've been active as cuckoo brewers in southeast London since June 2019, selling their beers, usually modern twists on traditional European styles including in cask, alongside others from stalls at various local venues and events. I particularly enjoyed **Sticky Stick*** (3.8%), a mild with shades of an Altbier. They're planning a brewpub in Blackheath, to be known as the Green Goddess, by the end of 2021, listed as a Try also (p240). The name refers to the successful 1876 protests opposing threatened further development of Plumstead Common. commonriotersbeer.co.uk

Earth Station HQ is a project led by award-winning brewer Jenn Merrick, which also aims to widen diversity in the industry by providing training and apprenticeships for local people. The original plan was for a brewery in an old fire station in North Woolwich, though this was delayed by construction work on the long-awaited Elizabeth Line (formerly Crossrail) and now may not go ahead. Another site isn't ruled out – meanwhile look out for Jenn's collaboration brews.

Kentish Town, a home-based brewery active since 2017 which contracts out larger runs, has been on hold since 2019 as the brewer had to leave the country for family reasons and then couldn't return due to the lockdown, so isn't in the main listings, but the intention is to resume production on his return. kentishtownbrewery.com

Mechanic is an excellent small brewery offering inventive beers rooted in both English and German brewing traditions, including in cask. The brainchild of Olga Zubrzycka, it began as a cuckoo in 2017 but graduated to its own kit in a Bethnal Green railway arch in January 2019. Sadly, a combination of Covid issues and spiralling rents forced Olga to give up the site early in 2021. At the time of writing, she was working on a brewing project in Poland but fully intending to return to London and revive Mechanic at a new site, perhaps as a brewpub, in 2021 or 2022. Beers have included **Green Diesel*** lime-flavoured stout (4.9%) and **Downtime Bock*** (5.2%).

Pubs and bars planning to add production facilities include the **Plum Tree** (p235) and **Three Hounds** (p252).

Current cuckoo brewers (Brewers without breweries p320) planning their own facilities are **Better World**, **Brithop**, **Coalition**, **Rock Leopard** and **Seven Sisters**.

Chains, pubcos and brewery pubs

Most London pubs are ultimately owned by big companies, often either breweries or pub companies (pubcos) that are successors to breweries (From alehouses to micropubs p25). These divide broadly into two groups. Managed houses are branches of the owning company, their staff on the company payroll. Leaseholds, sometimes called tenancies, are leased to independent businesses, in most cases at a lower-than-market rent in return for a contractual obligation to buy beer and sometimes other drinks from the owning company.

Managed houses are more likely to have obvious similarities to each other, and some-times a strong common brand, though a few are deliberately unbranded and left to develop their own identity within a general framework. Leaseholds are much more varied. Brewery-owned ones will likely be brewery-branded and mainly feature the brewery's beer, perhaps with an occasional guest or two sourced through the brewery. Pubco ones will likely stock a range sourced by the pubco from several different breweries, which usually means better-known brands from bigger independents who can meet expectations on price and quantity.

Increasingly, the keener pubco leasehold-ers source beers from smaller and more local breweries through the direct delivery scheme facilitated by the small brewers' trade organis-ation SIBA. Some licensees in managed chains have special dispensation to buy directly too and there are several examples in this book. An increasing number of licensees have leases that are wholly or partly free of tie in exchange for a higher 'market' rent. A recent phenomen-on is the 'managed expert partnership', where a pubco works more closely with a company leasing a number of pubs to create a mini-chain.

A minority of licensed outlets, though a high proportion of those in this book, are 'free houses'. These may be purpose-built pubs that never belonged to breweries, or have been abandoned by a brewery or pubco and sold on the open market, or buildings that weren't originally pubs. Some of them are genuinely independent while others belong to chains. The situation is further complicated by certain companies that manage small chains of pubs, some of them tied and some of them not.

There are far fewer branches of main-stream chains in this book than in previous editions. This may seem a little harsh on staff who have worked hard to offer a small range of good beers for many years in environments more appealing to a wider range of drinkers than most more specialist outlets. But besides the fact that the independent sector is now so far ahead in terms of variety, I've learned by experience that making sustainable recom-mendations for chain pubs is hazardous. A better-than-average beer offer is usually down to a particularly keen manager pushing the envelope. Such people tend to get moved on by head office, quite likely to turn around a poorly performing pub elsewhere, with no guarantee their successors will maintain the enthusiasm.

Below I list the main pubcos, brewery-owned pub groups and managed chains in London of interest to connoisseurs. Many offer something worth drinking in all or most of their outlets: chains like Antic, Frontier, Nicholson's, Portobello and Wetherspoon, for example, are usually reliable standbys for a decent beer in areas where there's little else. Numbers of outlets apply to Greater London only.

Antic

anticlondon.com (31 outlets)

Founded by Anthony Thomas with a single pub, the East Dulwich Tavern, in 2000, Antic has become an important presence, particularly in South London, turning numerous neglected pubs and abandoned public buildings into valued community assets. It terms itself a 'pub collective' and there is no branding, but the venues are usually easily recognisable: large, decorated in shabby-chic style with eccentric collections of junk, a youthful but inclusive ambience, short but imaginative menus and at least a few interesting local cask and keg beers and tasty bottles. A few are tied and more limited in range. The estate shrunk significantly in November 2020 when 13 pubs shifted to Portobello (below) following a decision by one of Antic's long-term financial partners which, judging by statements online, took the company by surprise.
See Leyton Technical (p148), Red Lion (p151); *try also* Antelope SW17, Hagen and Hyde (p275).

Barworks

barworks.com (16 outlets)

Beginning with a spirits-led cocktail bar in the 1990s, Barworks has matured gracefully to yield some of London's best new beer-friendly bars, adept at promoting quality beer to new audiences: nearly all have a long list including imported rarities. Venues are varied and unbranded, though several boast a slightly unsettling fondness for surreal art. The company was one of the original investors in Camden Town but there's no longer a formal connection. See also Graceland below.
See Commercial Tavern (p108), Exmouth Arms (p98); *try also* Crown and Castle (p141), Duke of York (p182), Fountain and Ink (p89), Griffin, Singer Tavern (p116), Three Johns (p81), Well and Bucket (p116).

Beer + Burger Store

beerandburgerstore.com (5 outlets)

Created by the family business that operates the Stag in Hampstead and the Mall Tavern in Notting Hill, these venues fuse gourmet burger bar with specialist beer dispensary as the name suggests. They stock a wide range of kegs and usually a hefty bottle and can range too. The original Willesden branch (p304) is typical; the rest are listed as Try alsos.

Big Smoke / Twickenham Green Taverns

(10 outlets)

Two related companies with a growing collection of friendly, well-run pubs stocking products from the very good associated brewery in Esher (Breweries outside London p318) alongside a range of other well-kept cask, keg and bottled/canned beer mainly from independents. A popular loyalty card scheme operates across all the outlets.
See Albion (p280), Lyric (p117), Sussex Arms (p312); *try also* Antelope KT6 (p287), Express (p299), Magdala (p177), Old Wheatsheaf (p199), Prince of Wales Townhouse (p303), Watermans Arms (p287) and Big Smoke Taphouse at London Heathrow Airport (p315).

Bloomsbury/Pivovar

(10 outlets)

A collection of informal, well-run, beer-focused free houses that ranges from major specialists with a huge range to smaller places with a limited but well-chosen selection of cask and keg. They're also noted for good Czech and German imports.
See Euston Tap (p78), Waterloo Tap (p88); *try also* Pelt Trader (p95).

Bottle Apostle

bottleapostle.com (4 outlets)

This small, enthusiastic wine shop chain has a fair range of beer, usually with approaching 100 bottles and cans and good representation for local producers, for takeaway only. Branches in Clapham and Crouch End are listed as Try alsos.

BrewDog

brewdog.com (25 outlets)

The provocative and successful Scottish-turned-multinational brewer is now one of London's major specialist beer retailers. Most venues are branded as BrewDog bars and simply named after their location: expect evangelical and knowledgeable staff, funky modern design and upmarket fast food menus with plenty of veggie and vegan options. Around half the keg taps are normally allocated to the owner's beer, the remainder will be guests from London and elsewhere, and most bars also have a good 50-100 bottles and cans. Eight venues are classified as BrewDog pubs rather than bars and have individual pub-style names. These are all former members of the Draft House chain, founded by pioneer London beer entrepreneur and early champion of third-pint measures Charlie McVeigh, who set out to place a more contemporary and populist spin on specialist beer back in 2007 with his first venue in Battersea. BrewDog bought the business in 2018 and initially retained its separate identity. As the designation suggests, these venues are a bit more pubby than the bars and still offer traditional cask on handpump as well as a range of keg, bottle and can options. *See* BrewDog Clapham Junction (p269), BrewDog Outpost Tower Hill (p92), BrewDog Shepherds Bush (p300), Duke of Hammersmith (p301); others listed as Try alsos.

Castle

mbplc.com/ourbrands/castle (100+ outlets)

Mitchells & Butlers' unbranded chain includes numerous well-run and attractive pubs, usually with a more contemporary and individual ambience than its Nicholson's-branded outlets, but the beer range hasn't kept up as well as it should have done. They usually have a few casks and kegs from small independents, but otherwise lean too far towards bigger brewers and more mainstream brands, with little local identity. The ones listed here are exceptions. *See* Bolton (p120), De Hems (p117), White Horse (p302); *try also* Queens Arms (p125), Windsor Castle (p125).

City Pubs

citypubcompany.com (18 outlets)

An expanding group of mainly free-of-tie pubs which are usually smart and slightly upmarket with at least some food but remain essentially drinking rather than dining venues. One of them, the Temple Brewhouse (p105), is a brewpub which also supplies some of the others; otherwise there's usually at least some interesting cask and keg.

Clapton Craft

claptoncraft.co.uk (7 outlets)

Founded by New Zealander William Jack in 2014, this is now one of London's leading specialist bottle shops, with a growing sideline in natural and organic wines. Until recently they were all takeaway only, but a tasting room added to the Finsbury Park branch in 2019 (p179) has been a great success and the formula has since been repeated elsewhere. Other branches are listed as Try alsos.

Craft Beer Co

thecraftbeerco.com (6 outlets)

Surely London's leading chain of specialist beer bars, with an impressive range across the formats in all outlets. They always stock cask, with a habit of offering several beers from the same brewery, usually a more unusual one from outside London, on a rotational basis. Keg choices include both local and international producers, with interesting contributions from Belgium and the US among the bottles and cans. The roots of the group are at the Cask in Pimlico (p122), opened by Martin Hayes in 2009 and still technically under separate ownership arrangements: the first Craft Beer Co proper followed in 2011 in partnership with Peter Slezak. *See* Craft Beer Cos Clerkenwell (p97), Covent Garden (p102), Hammersmith (p301); all others listed as Try alsos.

Craft Pubs

See Stonegate.

Draft House

See BrewDog.

ei (Enterprise)

See Stonegate.

Electric Star

electricstarpubs.co.uk (7 outlets)

A small independently owned chain of contemporary London pubs that usually offer entertainment such as music and DJs alongside food and a good few locally sourced beers.

ETM Group
etmgroup.co.uk (14 outlets)

Founded by brothers Ed and Tom Martin in 2000, this is now an eclectic collection of mainly upmarket venues, from sports bars through gastropubs to fine dining restaurants. One, the Long Arm (p109), has its own brewery which also supplies other outlets in the group.

Frontier
frontierpubs.co.uk (10 outlets)

Launched in 2016, this is the most interesting for our purposes of Stonegate's expert managed partnerships: a small chain of lively, youthful pubs with an offer combining 'craft beer' and gourmet pizzas baked in an open kitchen. The beer range, which usually includes at least some cask and local options, ranges from good to excellent, and staff are better informed than typical in mainstream chains. *See* Rose and Crown SW17 (p273); *try also*, Kings Arms W7 (p299).

Fuller's
fullers.co.uk (around 200 outlets)

Until 2019, Fuller's was London's last surviving traditional vertically integrated brewery and pub operator, but now it's simply a pub operating company, with the brewing operation sold to Asahi (Fuller's Griffin Brewery p294), though the pubs still stock the beer brands. The estate includes both managed pubs and leaseholds, with the balance shifting more towards the former. Recent openings are mainly big, smart places with an extensive food menu and a decent beer offer including guests from other London brewers, and a few have a 'crafty' focus with an even wider range of interesting beers. Fuller's cask beer is in nearly all the pubs and usually kept to at least an acceptable standard. For background see Fuller's faces the future (p298). *See* Great Northern Railway Tavern (p188), Harp (p102), Olde Mitre (p104), Star Tavern (p124); *try also* Barrel and Horn (p253), Hercules (p89), Hydrant (p95), Old Pack Horse (p299), Parcel Yard (p81), Red Lion SW13 (p287), Union Tavern (p306); *heritage pubs* Churchill Arms (p125), Dove W6 (p303), Viaduct Tavern (p95), Victoria (p125).

Graceland
(5 outlets)

An offshoot of Barworks (above) with an obviously similar formula, although Graceland venues are overall even more beer-friendly and a bit more like pubs than bars. *See* Earl of Essex (p78), Kings Arms E2 (p160); *try also* Axe (p182), Bethnal Green Tavern (p162), Red Hand (p182).

Greene King
greeneking.co.uk/pub-finder (200+ outlets)

Based in Bury St Edmunds, Suffolk, with a history dating back at least to 1799, Greene King was once a real ale icon. It emerged from the takeover wars of the 1990s a claimant to the title of Britain's biggest non-multinational brewery, achieved through ruthlessly buying up and closing several well-loved family brewers, taking over their pubs and cherry-picking their brands for approximation in Bury. More recently, it's acquired several managed pub chains which have either been absorbed into its core brand or the Metropolitan chain (below). Unlike its predecessor national breweries, it's still committed to cask ale: its bestseller, IPA, has an historical right to the name but is now essentially a light and inoffensive bitter. It was bought in August 2019 for £2.7 billion by Hong Kong-based conglomerate CKA but has so far continued to operate as a traditional integrated brewery and pub company. A good few of its London pubs stock a range of guest beers. *See* Tabard (p297); *try also* London Apprentice (p315), Prospect of Whitby (p162), Red Lion BR1 (p253), Roebuck TW10 (p287), Queens Head UB8 (p315); *heritage pubs* George (p89), Salisbury (p106).

Hall & Woodhouse
hall-woodhouse.co.uk (8 outlets)

Founded in 1777, this brewery in Blandford Forum, Dorset, is also known as Badger after its trademark. It owns a handful of London pubs, mainly traditionally styled and serving its straight-ahead cask and keg beers and filtered bottles. I've not found one strong enough on beer for a full recommendation, but the Ship and Shovell (1 Craven Passage WC2N 5PH) and St Stephens Tavern (10 Bridge Street SW1A 2JR) are both in interesting, centrally located buildings.

Heineken

See Star.

Hippo Inns

hippoinns.com (12 outlets)

Another Stonegate expert managed partnership, in similar contemporary style to Frontier (above) but with less of a beer focus. There's usually a handful of decent options on draught and the Eagle (250 Ladbroke Grove W10 5LP) sells Truman's lager from tank.

Laine

laine.co.uk (21 outlets)

This group originated in Brighton, taking its name from the celebrated North Laine neighbourhood, but now has a significant London collection of mainly big and characterful pubs, including a brewpub. Outlets usually stock at least a few casks and kegs from the brewpub and a production brewery in West Sussex shared with Hepworth, plus varying numbers of guests including bottles and cans. The group was bought in 2018 by Vine Acquisitions, the company that also owns Punch (below), but still operates with its own identity.
See BeerKat (p291), Peoples Park Tavern (p139); try also Watsons General Telegraph (p227).

Marston's

marstons.co.uk (15 outlets)

Following the sale of Greene King to CKA in 2019, Marston's was briefly the biggest British-owned brewing group. That ended in October 2020 when, following several years of financial difficulties, the company merged its brewing operations into a joint venture with Carlsberg of Copenhagen to form Carlsberg Marston's Brewing Company (CMBC). The core brewery in Burton upon Trent is well-known for Pedigree, the only UK beer still brewed using the historic Burton Union fermentation system, but the wider group encompasses five other brewing sites and brands that include former London speciality Mann's Brown as well as Banks's, Brakspear, Jennings, Ringwood, Wells, Wychwood and Young's. The old Marston's is now just a pub company with around 1,400 sites across the UK. Only a handful are in London, none of them an adequate showcase for such an impressive portfolio.

McMullen

mcmullens.co.uk (20 outlets)

Established in Hertford in 1827, 'Macs', as it's known locally, is now the oldest brewery in Hertfordshire, though it downsized from a Victorian tower brewery to a modern micro in 2006 to qualify for duty relief. It brews several traditional though not especially distinctive cask beers. Its London pubs are largely in the north and northeast, but it also has a few in central London. The Spice of Life (6 Moor Street W1D 5NA) is dead central and stocks a relatively comprehensive range.

Metropolitan

metropolitanpubcompany.com (50+ outlets)

This is Greene King's unbranded chain, originating in two groups of upmarket, largely food-led pubs the Bury brewer bought in 2011: one of these, the Capital Pub Company, had been founded by David Bruce of Firkin fame. For a while, the new owner's own beers were hard to spot. Today, the core cask brands are usually on alongside GK 'craft' beers and some from its Scottish subsidiary Belhaven, plus at least a few local guests and other independently brewed options. Some outlets make a point of stocking an impressive range.
See Williams Ale and Cider House (p94), try also Grove (p299), Hare and Billet (p240).

Mitchells & Butlers

mbplc.com

Britain's biggest managed pub company, with 1,700 properties, is another Bass successor: it revives the name of a Birmingham brewery taken over by Bass in 1961 and closed in 2002 when the remains of the Burton giant were carved up between the companies that are now AB InBev and Molson Coors. Its pubs are segmented into brands, including household names like All Bar One and O'Neill's. The ones of most interest to readers of this book are Castle and Nicholson's, which have separate entries, but Ember Inns (emberinns.co.uk), usually big, food-centred places in suburbia, are sometimes worth a look too.

Mosaic
mosaicpubanddining.com (14 outlets)

Created in 2015 by former executives of the Capital (now Metropolitan) and City pub groups, this has grown into a similar collection of upmarket food-led pubs and bars. It includes several characterful venues where you'll usually find at least a few beers of interest, including brands originating at the linked Battersea brewery (p267).

Mother Kelly's
motherkellys.co.uk (7 outlets)

The original Mother Kelly's in Bethnal Green, with its wall of help-yourself bottle fridges supplementing an array of keg taps, changed perceptions about specialist beer bars in London and helped inspire the current wave of bottle-shop bars. Several others have appeared since, tilted at various angles towards bottle shop or bar depending on the available space. The two more traditional pubs that first experimented with widening the beer range are still around too. Expect an impressive range served by well-informed staff, and simple but good quality cold plate-style food.
See Mother Kelly's Bethnal Green/E2 (p161), Vauxhall/SE11 (p85) and Queens Head (p81); *try also* Mother Kelly's Church Street/ N16 (p183), Stratford E20 (p156) and Simon the Tanner (p89).

Nicholson's
nicholsonspubs.co.uk (43 outlets)

The most cask-friendly of the Mitchells & Butlers brands, used for traditionally styled and centrally located pubs, often in heritage buildings with separate dining rooms. Most have at least six cask choices, with a house pale ale commissioned from St Austell in Cornwall, the ubiquitous Doom Bar and rotating guests from a seasonally refreshed list. Quality is usually reliable, with each pub allocated a specially trained 'cask master', though the selection seems to have become less adventurous in recent years. In addition, you'll find a handful of kegs, cans and bottles, a good few gins and a solid but rather corporate pub grub menu.
See Magpie (p93); *heritage pubs* Argyll Arms (p119), Blackfriar (p95), Dog and Duck (p119).

Portobello
portobellobrewing.com (15 outlets)

This ambitious West London brewery (p305), founded in 2012, dipped its toe into the pubs sector in 2019 with the acquisition of two sites, then rapidly became a significant player when it took control of 13 former Antic pubs in a surprise deal in November 2020. All now stock beers from the owning brewery and other independent producers, including cask.
See King and Co (p263), Royal Albert (p236), Westow House (p226).

PubLove
publove.co.uk (7 outlets)

Combining the function of pubs and independent youth hostels, these venues tend to gravitate towards main stations for understandable reasons though the bars are open to all. Pleasingly, they also make a point of offering a few decent local beers in cask, keg, bottle and can. The brand has been around for a few years but has recently become another Stonegate expert partnership. The Exmouth Arms near Euston (p81) is a Try also.

Punch
punchpubs.com

Punch was Britain's other big leasehold pub owner alongside Enterprise (ei), originating in 1997 with large tranches of former Bass and Allied Breweries pubs, both managed and leasehold, though the managed pubs were eventually separated off and ended up with Greene King. Following several years of financial troubles, Punch now only has around 1,300 pubs across Britain after being carved up in 2017 between Heineken (see Star below) and two private equity firms acting as Vine Acquisitions, which also now owns Laine (above). As with Stonegate, Punch leaseholders are individual businesses, so I haven't indexed them here.

Ram Pub Company
See Young's.

Remarkable

remarkablepubs.co.uk (16 outlets)

This small group founded in 1985 by Jean and Robert Thomas includes some beautiful heritage pubs and other handsome traditional venues. Most serve a least a few good casks, kegs, bottles and cans, always including Litovel lager which the group imports from the Czech Republic.

See George and Dragon (p295); *try also* Salisbury Hotel (p193), Shaftesbury Tavern (p183).

Samuel Smith

samuelsmithsbrewery.co.uk (38 outlets)

Founded in 1758 in Tadcaster, this is the oldest brewery in Yorkshire, though arguably not the most popular one: eccentric chairman Humphrey Smith has been in the news several times over the past few years for, among other things, frustrating his neighbours by refusing the construction of a temporary bridge in the town when the main one was damaged in floods; being prosecuted by the pensions regulator and fined after ignoring 'tiresome' requests to hand over documents; and enforcing bans on swearing and mobile phones by clearing whole pubs of customers and sacking staff on the spot. His brewery owns a surprisingly large number of London pubs, including several meticulously cared-for heritage gems, known for their traditional atmosphere and cheap prices. Everything on sale is own brand: not just the single cask ale, Old Brewery Bitter, and the rather better specialist bottles, but the wines, spirits and soft drinks too. The company finally has a website but, typically, it doesn't bother to list the pubs. You'll find them on Google, but it may be wise to step outside before looking the next one up on your phone, just in case Humphrey's about.

See Olde Cheshire Cheese (p104); *heritage pubs* Cittie of Yorke, Princess Louise (p105).

Shepherd Neame

shepherdneame.co.uk/pubs (52 outlets)

This family brewery on the edge of historic hop country in Faversham, Kent, claims to be Britain's oldest brewing firm, with a documented company history from 1698. It began

buying into London in the 1980s and now has an extensive estate of both managed pubs and leaseholds. All sell its traditional cask ales and a growing number of 'craft' kegs; the better ones sell its bottled beers including rather good historic recreations. My favourite is the Eleanor Arms (p159).

Star (Heineken)

starpubs.co.uk

Heineken is the only still-brewing successor to the Big Six brewers that retains substantial numbers of pubs, a position it strengthened in 2017 by buying a sizeable chunk of Punch to add to the estate it inherited from Scottish and Newcastle. It now owns almost 3,000 leasehold pubs across Britain. Much of the cask it supplies to these is from Edinburgh subsidiary Caledonian, Yorkshire brewer Theakston, which S&N once owned, and other larger producers. You may also spot kegs and cans from the widening portfolio of 'craft' brands in which it has an interest, including Beavertown and Brixton in London and Lagunitas in the US. As with other leasehold landlords, the individual pubs are separate businesses with their own identity.

Stonegate

stonegategroup.co.uk

Founded in 2010 with a tranche of pubs bought from M&B, Stonegate was still only a medium-sized operator with around 650 managed houses across the country when it bought out the much bigger, and mainly leasehold, ei in 2019, multiplying its estate overnight by a factor of 10. Its new acquisition had begun as Enterprise Inns, founded by controversial industry figure Ted Tuppen in 1991, and at one point was Britain's biggest pub owner, with a massive portfolio of tied leaseholds largely acquired by a variety of routes from the old Bass, Courage, Watney and Whitbread estates. One of the main targets of criticism of the pubco model, it was plagued with debt and financial problems and had already been shedding assets before the merger. Besides traditional leaseholds, Stonegate maintains 'expert partnerships' with other companies comprising small chains of branded pubs: of these, Frontier, Hippo and PubLove have separate entries above. Its managed pubs are organised into 'formats', including household name theme bars like Slug and Lettuce. Some managed outlets branded as Craft Pubs, like the Green Dragon (p247) and the Marquis of Wellington (Try also p216) have special dispensation to source widely.

Tonkotsu
tonkotsu.co.uk (12 outlets)

Small noodle bar chain with small but thoughtful beer range: see Try also p141.

Twickenham Green Taverns
See Big Smoke.

Urban Leisure
ulg.co.uk (8 outlets)

This small chain of eclectic contemporary bar-restaurants admirably favours more unusual local brews in the beer sections of its menus. *See* Heist Bank (p122); *try also* Elgin (p306).

J D Wetherspoon
jdwetherspoon.com (120 outlets)

The only national pub group with no roots in the old brewery tied-house system, Wetherspoon was founded in 1979 with a single North London pub by chairman Tim Martin, who named it after one of his former schoolteachers. The company now owns 900 outlets in the UK and Ireland, all of them managed and free of tie, often in buildings not previously used as pubs. There's a set formula, with low prices, standard menus of pre-cooked food and identikit furniture, though the interior decorations have been getting more adventurous and individual recently. Branches usually offer at least half a dozen cask choices and often

more, with due attention given to the cellar, guests that are often from local independents and a small range of noteworthy keg, bottled and canned beer. Cross-venue beer festivals include cask specials made in the UK by visiting international brewers. Branches are devoid of piped music, accessible, inclusive, family friendly, and sell food of consistently edible, though certainly not gourmet, quality from breakfast until late at night. I've featured flagship branch the Cross Keys, which has an exceptionally large cask range (p93).

While sneering at the chain's downmarket image is simple snobbery, it's true few of the venues could be appreciated for their character. More serious criticisms are around the aggressive pricing policy on specialist beer, which is challenging for many brewers and undersells a quality product; low wages which undervalue staff, provoking a strike in 2018 that darkened a previously good reputation as an employer; and the chairman's habit of using his business as a platform for his political views, including his staunch support of Brexit.

Young's
youngs.co.uk (around 100 outlets)

Like most pub-owning successors of old breweries, Young's inherited both managed and leasehold pubs, and had long concentrated on the former rather than the latter, particularly the large and lucrative food-led ones on good sites. In July 2021, it ditched nearly all its leasehold pubs, selling them to Punch. In those that remain, you'll frequently find beers from London brewers, often local to the pub, besides Young's beers brewed by CMBC (see Marston's above). For more background see The Ram Resurgent (p276) and the entry under Brewers without breweries (p324).
See Buckingham Arms (p120), Hand in Hand (p282), Ram Inn (p273); *heritage pubs* Lamb W1 (p82), Prince Alfred (p306).

Mail order and subscription boxes

Numerous breweries, bottle shops and other suppliers in the main listings offer online sales, identified with ⌐🖱. Many that didn't offer this facility before the lockdowns have since added it. Besides the traditional option of picking from a perhaps bewildering array of individual beers, many retailers now offer mixed cases, as well as subscription box schemes with beer chosen by them, perhaps in line with your general preferences.

Those offering a good range of London beer by mail order include **Beer Hawk** (p83), **Beer Merchants** (p130), **Caps and Taps** (p173), **Clapton Craft** (p179), **Craft Metropolis** (p246), **EeBria** (p210), **Ghost Whale** (p260), **Hop Burns and Black** (p222), **Indiebeer** (p181), **Noble Green Wines** (p311) and **waterintobeer** (p238).

Other suppliers of note without a walk-up London site are:

Borough Box. A good selection from Crate, Forest Road, Hiver, Jiddlers Tipple, Two Tribes and others, alongside an extensive collection of other drinks and food from independent artisan producers, with same day delivery in central London. boroughbox.com

Hoppily. Has a bottle shop-bar outside London in Leigh-on-Sea, Essex, but also offers a comprehensive mail order and subscription box service featuring 15-20 London brewers among other producers. Also collaborates on bespoke brews. hoppily.co.uk

Honest Brew. A pioneer of subscription boxes, this has since grown into a major online retailer for pick-your-own beers too, with around a dozen London breweries among a wide selection from across the UK and the world, including exclusive house collaborations. A membership scheme gets you discounts and other perks. honestbrew.co.uk

Six Pack Beer Club. Online retailer that rose from the ashes of a rather good small Hackney bottle shop, Craftndraft, forced to close during the lockdowns. Several Londoners and London-based cuckoos among a well-selected range mainly from contemporary UK brewers. In line with the name, the subscription box contains six rather than 12 beers: they claim it's 'the best one you will get in the UK'. sixpackbeer.club

All the above ship anywhere within mainland UK and most also serve outlying islands and Northern Ireland, usually at a higher delivery charge. The few that also shipped outside the UK suspended this facility when the country's exit from the EU made things much more complicated: at the time of writing, the only listed supplier I know to have resumed international shipping is Ghost Whale.

Festivals and events

Before the lockdowns, London boasted a huge range of beer-related events, from giant festivals like the annual Great British Beer Festival (GBBF) to 'meet the brewer' nights in pubs. All these were put on hold during the pandemic, with the occasional virtual substitute, so compiling the list this time has involved some guesswork. Please check well in advance before making any travel arrangements and bear in mind that demand for reinstated events is likely to be high, so it may be wise to make use of pre-booking facilities if available.

Beer festivals fall into two broad types: freestanding events in big venues not normally associated with selling specialist beer, and events in pubs and bars enhancing their regular range. Venues with regular beer festivals are noted in the main listings: there's no room to repeat them all here.

The biggest organiser of freestanding festivals is CAMRA: as well as the national GBBF, many London branches run their own festivals, and all are organised and staffed by volunteers. You pay an admission charge, reduced or sometimes free for CAMRA and EBCU members, and then pay for the beer as you go, at good value but not heavily discounted prices. Beer is mainly in cask though some events are now offering a small selection of keykeg beer alongside bottles and cans, imported beers and real cider and perry. Current details of CAMRA festivals throughout the UK are posted at **camra.org.uk/events**.

Increasingly, though, the beer enthusiast's calendar is filling with events organised by others, often inviting direct participation by breweries. Some of these are essentially commercial enterprises though there are not-for-profit and fundraising events too. Formats vary:

there may be a higher admission charge which includes at least some beer, or even unlimited tasting measures.

There's no entirely comprehensive source for events information, other than judicious use of social media, but the diary at **aletalk.co.uk** is better than most.

January

Tryanuary *all month*. Breweries and pubs traditionally struggle in January as people cut down on their consumption, a trend intensified by public health initiatives like Dry January. Thus this national campaign to support independent local businesses by encouraging people to try new beers, including lower alcohol ones, and collectively promoting a host of locally organised activities. tryanuary.com

February

South Norwood Beer Festival *1st week*. Over 25 cask beers plus ciders and perries are on offer at this small festival organised by Croydon & Sutton CAMRA at the Stanley Halls since 2016. croydon.camra.org.uk

Love Beer London *2nd weekend*. A charity fundraising collaboration between Craft Beer Cares, London Brewers Alliance and SIBA, this keg beer festival took place in Tottenham in 2020, attracting almost 100 breweries, most of them from London. The organisers are keen to repeat the event but date and venue may change. lovebeerlondon.co.uk

Cask *3rd weekend*. Founded by Affinity Brew Co in 2018, this unexpectedly popular event has helped revive interest in cask among a younger generation of drinkers, moving year on year to bigger venues, most recently

Copeland Park in Peckham. Among other things it's a chance to try cask beers from breweries who don't normally make them alongside established producers. **affinitybrewco.com**

March

Wandsworth Common Spring Beer Festival *last week*. Organised by Le Gothique bar at the landmark Royal Victoria Patriotic Building on Wandsworth Common, this family-friendly festival offers over 100 cask beers. **le-gothique.co.uk/beer-festivals**.

April

Rosslyn Park Beer Festival *1st weekend*. A longstanding annual fundraiser for the Slingbacks women's rugby team, this small but well-regarded cask festival takes place at their Rosslyn Park ground. **facebook.com/ TheSlingbacks**

May

Mild Month *all month*. CAMRA's designated month to support and promote mild ales is a good time to find examples on sale, with many breweries who don't regularly make them timing seasonal releases to suit.

Bexley Beer Festival *2nd week*. 100+ mainly cask beers plus ciders and perries are available at this festival organised by Bexley CAMRA since 2005, these days usually at the Old Dartfordians sports club. **bexley.camra.org.uk**

Kingston Beer Festival *3rd week*. 60+ cask beers, including many local options, plus ciders and perries are on offer at this festival organised by Kingston & Leatherhead CAMRA since 1999. It's usually at Kingston Workmen's Club, behind the famous cascading phone box sculpture. **surrey.camra.org.uk**

Crystal Palace FC Beer Festival *3rd weekend*. Held at the football club's Selhurst Park ground since 2010, this event featured 200 beers from independent breweries in 2019, as well as charity football matches. **cpfc.co.uk**

Kidbrooke Beer Festival *4th week*. A welcome event in beer-friendly southeast London, organised by South East London CAMRA

since 2013. 50+ cask beers mainly from local breweries plus ciders and perries, usually held at Charlton Park rugby club. **sel.camra.org.uk**

Ruislip Beer Festival *last weekend, or first weekend of June*. Small festival with 30+ cask beers, organised by Ruislip Rugby Club with the support of West Middlesex CAMRA since 2010. **ruislipbeerfestival.camra.org.uk**.

June

Ruislip Beer Festival. See May.

Beer Day Britain *15 June*. A national celebration of beer which includes numerous local events and a nationwide 'cheers to beer'. Founded by beer writer and educator Jane Peyton and supported by the British Beer and Pubs Association, CAMRA and SIBA. **beerdaybritain.co.uk**

Naturist Foundation Jazz and Real Ale Festival *last weekend*. A four-day festival with over 20 beers on offer besides a busy programme of jazz and blues performances, camping space on the Foundation's woodland site at Brockenhurst near Orpington, and clothing optional. **naturistfoundation.org**

LBA Beer Festival *Dates TBC*. An increasingly important event in the capital's beer calendar bringing together most of the members of the London Brewers Alliance: the last two have been held in the historic brewery yard at Fuller's. **londonbrewers.org/events**

July

City Beerfest *1st Thursday*. Jointly organised since 2013 by the City of London and the Worshipful Company of Brewers to raise money for the Lord Mayor's Charity Appeal, this event at the Guildhall features around 15 brewers, mainly larger independents. **citybeerfest.org**

Ealing Beer Festival *2nd week*. This big open-air event organised by West Middlesex CAMRA in Walpole Park, now in its fourth decade, is an excellent prelude to GBBF, particularly in good weather. 500+ cask beers, imported beers, cider and perry. **ebf.camra.org.uk**

Epping Ongar Railway Beer Festival *3rd weekend*. Not precisely in London but organised since 2012 by a heritage railway which used to be part of the London Underground and is easily reached via the Central Line and a vintage bus service. 80 mainly local cask beers served not only from static bars at the stations but on steam-hauled trains. eorailway.co.uk

Indie Beer Shop Day *3rd Saturday*. Modelled on the long-running and successful Record Store Day, this ran for the first time in 2021 and will hopefully become a recurring diary entry. Look out for events and special beer releases in participating shops. indiebeershopday.uk

Beckenham Beer and Cider Festival *4th week*. Around 60 beers, mainly cask with some keykeg including plentiful local options, plus ciders and perries, are sold at this festival organised by Bromley CAMRA at Beckenham Rugby Club since 2013. bromley. camra.org.uk

Brew//LDN *4th weekend*. Organised by the founders of the Craft Beer Rising festival (which has since been sold on and appears to have been mothballed), this is a commercial event involving both independent brewers and multinationals, but nonetheless varied and enthusiastic, with over 70 breweries represented from London, the UK and elsewhere. In 2021 it was held at the Surrey Quays Printworks. brewldn.com

August

Great British Beer Festival (GBBF) *2nd week*. CAMRA's flagship national event was established in 1977 and is now one of the biggest of its kind in the world, with over 1,000 beers, ciders and perries on sale. Held at Olympia in recent years, it's a must for every beer connoisseur, particularly following long-awaited improvements in 2019 such as glass rinsing stations, readily available drinking water and beer education exhibits. Cask is quite rightly still the main emphasis, but now alongside UK keykeg. It's also noted for a fabulous range of imported beers under the *Bières sans frontières* banner. Tutored tastings, author signings at the large bookstall, breweriana auctions and various other activities round things out. gbbf.org.uk

Great British Beer Festival (GBBF)

London Craft Beer Festival (LCBF) *2nd weekend*. Independently organised since 2014, this more contemporary-focused, brewer-supported event is a valuable complement to GBBF, featuring over 90 breweries dispensing mainly in keg but with some cask, and talks and tastings too. Recently it's been in the atmospheric though labyrinthine surrounds of Tobacco Dock. londoncraftbeerfestival.co.uk

Mindful Drinking Festival *3rd weekend*. Free event run by Club Soda, a social business that supports people to control their drinking, with a wide range of low and no alcohol drinks including beer as well as stalls and workshops. Venues have varied. mindfuldrinkingfestival.com

September

Nicholson's Cask Ale Festival *mid-September and all of October*. A more varied cask range than usual across the Nicholson's chain, though fewer brewers are participating these days. nicholsonspubs.co.uk

Hampton Beer Festival *3rd weekend*. A small, family-friendly cask festival in a scout hut which has been raising money for charity since 2014, heavily featuring local producers. hamptonbeerfestival.co.uk

Oktoberfest *from 3rd week into October*. The Munich Oktoberfest traditionally runs from mid-September to early October; British tie-ins tend to take place later to avoid confusion. Most of these are more about the quantity than the quality (see **london-oktoberfest.co.uk**), but some London bars and breweries use the occasion to explore a more interesting range of German styles. There's even a vegan version: see **vegtoberfest.co.uk**.

Cask Ale Week *last week, continues into October*. A national campaign supported by CAMRA and Cask Marque, with numerous promotions and events taking place particularly in Cask Marque-accredited venues. caskaleweek.co.uk

Wet Hop Season *last week, continues into October*. The increasing interest in wet, or if you prefer, green hop beers is making this a particularly exciting time of year. Kent Green Hop Fortnight (**kentgreenhopbeer.com**), starting at the very end of the month and continuing into the next, has been encouraging Kent brewers to make the most of the local harvest for several years now and, given their proximity, some of these brews find their way to London. London brewers are increasingly following suit, either by working with commercial growers outside London or with various hop growing collectives across the capital that consolidate the produce of private gardens and allotments: look out on social media for beer launches and other events.

October

Cask Ale Week, Nicholson's Cask Ale Festival, Oktoberfest, Wet Hop Season. See September.
Brew Con *Dates TBC*. London's homebrewing conference, founded in 2017 by the Beer Boars club, includes talks and workshops, exhibitor stands, a competition and of course bars. It was hosted at Beavertown in 2019. brew-con.co.uk

Wetherspoon World's Biggest Real Ale Festival *second and third weeks*. This event sees a much wider range of cask beers than normal sold across the Wetherspoon estate, with some pubs adding extra stillages and all offering tasting flights of thirds. The choice includes numerous specials and beers created in the UK by invited international brewers. jdwetherspoon.com

Peckham Levels Beer Festival *3rd weekend*. A small festival featuring mainly local breweries in a repurposed multi-storey car park that now houses a variety of creative businesses and startups. peckhamlevels.org

Twickenham Beer and Cider Festival *4th week*. Over 60 cask beers including various award winners, plus ciders and perries, are available at this friendly festival organised by Richmond and Hounslow CAMRA since 2000. The regular venue is York House. rhcamra.org.uk

Wandsworth Common Halloween Beer Festival *last weekend*. The rather creepy Gothic-meets-French-château architecture and forbidding reputation of the Royal Victoria Patriotic Building on Wandsworth Common adds to the atmosphere of this family-friendly seasonal event, now one of London's biggest independent festivals with over 100 cask beers. le-gothique.co.uk/beer-festivals.

December

Pigs Ear Beer Festival *1st week*. Organised by East London and City CAMRA since the 1980s, this well-run event brightens the darkening evenings with well over 200 cask beers plus keykeg, imports, cider and perry, in the characterful surroundings of Hackney's Round Chapel. Always with a good selection of dark beers, winter ales and the products of east London brewers. pigsear.org.uk

Also

London Brewers Market. Organised by Five Points but showcasing many other London brewers, this event doesn't have a regular schedule, in recent years piggybacking on various music festivals and other activities: *see* londonbrewersmarket.com for the latest information.

Beer tourism

It's a sign of the rehabilitation of London's status as a brewing city that international beer tourism operators from other parts of the globe are now stopping off rather than skipping straight on to Belgium or Germany. There are also a growing number of local tours and other facilitated activities suitable for Londoners and day trippers as well as travellers from further afield. All these were of course suspended during the pandemic due to social distancing and travel restrictions, but demand remains high so they should return as such problems ease.

I've summarised all the ones I know about below, besides tours and tastings provided by individual breweries, which are highlighted in the main entries with a ‼ symbol: see Brewery details (p67) and my favourite brewery experiences under London's Very Best Beer (p72). As well as scheduled tours, most providers (including breweries) can arrange private bespoke tours for groups, or even individuals who can afford it. Many also sell gift vouchers, enabling the lucky recipient to choose their own date and time.

I should declare an interest: I offer my own tours, work regularly for UK Brewery Tours and lead intermittently for Bier Akademie, Bon Beer Voyage and Context Travel. I've therefore tried to keep the listings informative and comprehensive, and suggest you refer to sources like TripAdvisor for independent opinions.

Ale Hunters Brewery Tours. Afternoon pub walks and beer tastings in Belgravia, the City and the West End and Bermondsey brewery tours with an accredited beer sommelier and former Fuller's tour guide. Longer trips to Belgium too. **alehunters.co.uk**

Bier Akademie. Led by a German beer sommelier and writer based in the beer heartland of Bamberg, with bespoke trips for groups to a variety of global destinations including London as well as beer education activities. **bierakademie.net**

Bon Beer Voyage. Florida-based beer travel company run by enthusiasts, regularly taking groups to Europe including London, though their canal cruise from Amsterdam to Bruges visiting breweries along the way sounds cool too. **bonbeer.com**

Brewtopia Beer Excursions. Atlanta, Georgia-based beer writer Owen Ogletree knows London better than some Londoners, organising regular trips pairing the GBBF and LCBF with brewery and pub visits. **classiccitybrew.com/brewtopiatrips.html**

Ciao! Travel. San Diego, California-based business organising various beer trips combining London with destinations in Belgium, Switzerland and elsewhere in Europe, as well as visits to major jazz festivals. **ciaotravel.com**

Context Travel. US-based agency offering expertly led afternoon tours of Bermondsey and Southwark taking in brewing heritage, pub culture and a brewery visit, besides a vast portfolio of activities on other themes in cities across the globe. **contexttravel.com**

Des de Moor Beer Tours. Short morning and evening brewery heritage walks with your author in Southwark and the East End, including a brewery visit, plus afternoon historic pub tours and beer tastings in Holborn and the City. **desdemoor.co.uk/beer-tours**

Dragon and Flagon Pub Tours. Walking tours in various parts of central London each taking in five or six pubs including many historic and hidden gems, in the company of the redoubtable Vic Norman. Self-guided tours too. londonpubtours.weebly.com

Fat Tire Tours. Guided afternoon cycling tours of the West End's hidden pub gems, including a tutored beer tasting, and afternoon and evening riverside options with a similarly beery angle, plus numerous tours on other themes. fattiretours.com/london

Jane Peyton London Pub Tours. Walking tours for private groups led by a well-known accredited beer sommelier and educator, with beers in several historic Holborn and City pubs and history along the way. jane-peyton.com/tour-guide

Liquid History. Afternoon walking tours around the hidden alleys and courtyards of Fleet Street and St Paul's, visiting several historic pubs in the company of brewers and history experts. Beers not included but guides will recommend. liquidhistorytours.com

London Craft Beer Cruise. A 'floating beer festival' presenting a range of London-brewed beers on a scenic cruise along the Thames in the company of a beer sommelier, monthly from May to September. londoncraftbeercruise.co.uk

Secret Beer Tours. Afternoon walking tours around Shoreditch with a more contemporary focus than some and a wide range of beers to try, ending at a more traditional tucked-away City pub. Food and gin tours too. secretfoodtours.com/london

UK Brewery Tours. Wide range of highly rated walking tours, tastings and food pairing activities on the Bermondsey 'mile' and in the East End, plus a Peckham craft beer and street art tour, mainly held on Saturday daytimes but some weekday evenings too. Also in other UK cities. ukbrewerytours.com

Days out. As a good Londoner, I of course agree with Samuel Johnson that one should never tire of the place, but it also happens to be the UK's best-connected transport hub. Frequent trains go to several other excellent beer cities: Bristol, Brussels, Leeds, Manchester, Norwich and Sheffield are all around two hours away or less, manageable for a well-planned day trip and rewarding for a longer stay. Book in advance for the best fares. nationalrail.co.uk, eurostar.com

Other recommendations

I'm by no means the only chronicler of good beer, pubs and bars in London. For alternative recommendations, and a second opinion on some of the places listed here, consult the following sources.

Websites and magazines

Local CAMRA recommendations.
The UK-wide database at whatpub.com is a comprehensive resource covering pubs, bars and other outlets, regularly updated by local CAMRA volunteers. The London CAMRA branches support the **LocAle** scheme accrediting pubs that regularly stock at least one cask beer brewed within 30 miles (48km), a radius which takes in quite a few breweries outside London too: you can find the current list at london.camra.org.uk. Free bimonthly magazine *London Drinker* (londondrinker. camra.org.uk) is a good source of news on openings and closures, new breweries and forthcoming events. It went online-only during the pandemic but the editor plans to return to publishing a parallel print edition with stocks distributed to numerous beer-friendly pubs. Some CAMRA branches have list of recommended pubs on their websites: see Organisations (p350).

A London Beer and Pub Guide.
An independently maintained and unapologetically personal online take on the London scene from self-confessed beer geeks Jezza and Steve. It's become an essential resource, assiduously up to the minute on London breweries, particularly those with regular taprooms, as well as specialist pubs and bars. It made a heroic effort to publicise outlets offering local delivery services during the lockdowns. Also available as an app. beerguideldn.com

Untappd. Hardly anyone had heard of Untappd when the last edition of this book was published but it's rapidly become the beer geek's favourite social networking resource. It's not straightforward to find venues but easy to search for a beer and find out who is stocking it. Numerous places listed in this book now use it to host their beer lists. Also available as an app. untappd.com

Ratebeer. This crowd-sourced veteran has been a little eclipsed by Untappd – the fact that it's now owned by AB InBev hasn't helped – but still numbers numerous serious-minded reviewers among its contributors. The Places section has extensive listings for London. ratebeer.com

Londonist Best Pubs in London. A neatly mapped selection based on regular polls of readers and contributors to this useful alternative news and blogging site, which also regularly covers beer topics. londonist.com/pubs

Time Out. London's long-running weekly events and attractions guide is now a free publication, and widely distributed. Its annual pubs and bars guidebook was discontinued several years ago, but there are numerous searchable reviews and recommendations on its website. timeout.com/london

Cask Marque/Beer Marque. This is an industry-backed scheme for accrediting pubs on their beer quality, based on regular inspection visits. A specific accreditation for cask beer has been awarded since 1998, and the extended Beer Marque, which assesses the quality of all draught beer, was added in 2019. There's a fee to participate, so plenty of pubs with first rate cellars aren't accredited, including many smaller and independent operators. But it can be a useful way of finding reliable beer in an unfamiliar area, and there's an app too. cask-marque.co.uk

Heritage pubs. See p71.

Books

Good Beer Guide. Published annually, this essential guide contains recommendations of top cask beer pubs across the UK as well as London, chosen by local CAMRA branches. It aims for a good spread of outlets so will usually have suggestions in places where I don't. It's also available as a mobile app and a POI file. camra.org.uk/gbg

Camra's London Pub Walks. My colleague Bob Steel sadly died in August 2020, but this delightful book, last revised in 2016, is a worthy legacy. It covers not just the well-known tourist areas but several more obscure but rewarding locations, highlighting several cask beer outlets on each route.

The London Craft Beer Guide. Craft Beer Channel duo Jonny Garrett and Brad Evans have chosen just 42 of 'the best breweries, pubs and taprooms for the best artisan brews' to feature in this handsome book published in 2018, telling the stories behind them in admirable depth with the help of great photography. I've covered all their picks, except for one or two now closed, in the listings section, but inevitably in more cursory fashion. thecraftbeerchannel.com

An Opinionated Guide to London Pubs. Matthew Curtis, founder of online magazine *Pellicle* and one of our most forthright and influential contemporary beer writers, reveals a deep appreciation of traditional pubs in this attractive little book published in 2021 by

LONDON DRINKERS | John Keeling

Originally from Manchester, John (@fullersjohn) joined Fuller's as a junior brewer in 1981 and became Brewing Director in 1999. As well as being responsible for much of the great beer to emerge from Chiswick, he's become an inspiration and support to a new generation of London brewers and an internationally respected beer judge. He's now happily retired but, he says, 'available to bore people with tales of London brewing in exchange for free beer'. John has a strong belief that 'popular beer doesn't have to be bland. The only reason bland beers are popular is that they're propped up with massive marketing campaigns. But I grew up drinking Draught Bass and Boddingtons, which in those days were flavourful, distinctive beers, and everybody drank them.'

How do you rate London as a beer city, on a world scale?
It's near the top: the current scene is in flux and still developing but that has been the case forever. London has a vast history of brewing with an influence on the industry throughout the world, and it's a great city to visit in other ways.

What's the single most exciting thing about beer in London right now?
The great diversity, with Fuller's representing the old guard and new breweries and tap rooms appearing all the time. Where else will you find a story like the Ram Brewery and John Hatch? (The Ram Resurgent p276).

What single thing would make things even better?
Less experimentation and more consistency. Brewers need the science as well as the art.

What are your top London beers right now?
I always have a soft spot for Redemption who are great

brewers. Boxcar are jolly good too. I'm delighted that we can have a brewery like Camden Town and then someone like Boxcar and we all get along.

What's your top great beer night out?
Great cask beer erring on the traditional side, local pub so not far to walk home. Good friends for good chat.

Who's your London beer hero?
John Hatch and Derek Prentice. Londoners through and through.

Who will we be hearing a lot more from in future?
The London Brewers Alliance, showing that brewers are friends and able to help and encourage each other.

Which are your other top beer cities?
Melbourne has a great beer scene. I love Chicago and Boston too.

Hoxton Minipresss. It covers 52 characterful venues, including numerous beer champions, in succinct paragraphs accompanied by gorgeous photos by Harry Adès.

Great Pubs of London. George Dailey's 2019 tribute to 25 'historically and architecturally significant' London pubs comes in both a pocket edition and a coffee table version which makes even more lavish use of his daughter Charlie's excellent photographs. Anyone with an interest in London pubs should be familiar with his choices, some of which I've listed too, particularly as heritage pubs. Sadly the text indulges in far too much romantic flimflam of dubious reliability and fails to provide sufficient historical context to explain why these beautiful buildings look like they do.

London's Best Pubs. This handsome book by Peter Haydon and Tim Hampson features mainly traditional pubs, including heritage gems and other notable hostelries. Most of them serve at least some decent beer but the focus is mainly on appearance, atmosphere, siting and history. It was revised in 2015, and supplemented in 2016 by Tim's *London's Riverside Pubs*. Both are now a little out of date, but these sorts of places don't change very much.

Lunchtime at the Cockpit p244

APPENDICES

Bibliography and more information

London

There are numerous histories of London. I've found these useful:

Peter Ackroyd, *London: the Biography*, Vintage 1991
Roy Porter, *London: a Social History*, Penguin 2000
Francis Sheppard, *London: a History*, Oxford University Press 1998

An essential visit for anyone interested in the city's history is the **Museum of London** which as well as displays and events has an excellent bookshop. It's long been based at the Barbican (150 London Wall EC2Y 5HN, **museumoflondon.org.uk**), though plans to move to a bigger site in the historic buildings of Smithfield Market by 2025.

Most big London bookshops have a range of guidebooks to contemporary London, including more specialist books on quirky and hidden features, and numerous walking guides. For a general guide, I'd recommend *Time Out London* or *Lonely Planet: London*, both of which are regularly updated. The official visitor website at **visitlondon.com** is also useful and has lists of walk-in visitor information centres.

For what's on information and latest news, pick up a free copy of *Time Out*, check out **timeout.com/london**, or peruse **londonist.com**. There are an increasing number of interesting local magazines, often distributed free through independent retailers, and a wealth of neighbourhood blogs, too numerous to list here.

Beer and brewing

For **useful general reading** on beer, I'd recommend:

Pete Brown, *Miracle Brew: Adventures in the nature of beer*, Unbound 2017: An informative investigation of the main ingredients of beer from a non-technical viewpoint.
Randy Mosher, *Tasting Beer* 2nd edition, Storey Publishing 2017: A fascinating exploration of beer flavour from a renowned US author and homebrewing guru.
Garrett Oliver (ed), *Oxford Companion to Beer*, Oxford University Press 2011: An encyclopaedic reference for the enthusiast, now a little old and not flawless but still useful.
Tim Webb and Stephen Beaumont, *World Atlas of Beer* 3rd edition, Mitchell Beazley 2020: Authoritative and unafraid to challenge received opinion.

On **beer and food pairing**, see:

Claire Bullen and Jen Ferguson, *The Beer Lover's Table: Seasonal recipes and modern beer pairings*, Dog 'n' Bone 2019. Contemporary recipes with pairing suggestions and much background information and advice, from top London bottle shop Hop Burns and Black.
Melissa Cole, *The Beer Kitchen: The art and science of cooking and pairing with beer*, Hardie Grant 2018. Comprehensive guide from one of our London drinkers, including a non-specialist explanation of the science and 70 recipes.
Mark Dredge, *Beer and Food Matching: Bringing together the finest food and best craft beers in the world*, Dog 'n' Bone 2018 (originally published 2014). A useful practic al guide from an award-winning London-based beer writer.

Garrett Oliver, *The Brewmaster's Table*, HarperPerennial 2005: The breakthrough guide to beer and food, now over 15 years old but still essential.

For **historical background** on beer, brewing and pub culture in London from the distant to the very recent past, I'm indebted to the following sources:

Norman Barber, Mike Brown and Ken Smith, *Century Plus Plus of British Brewers 1890–2012*, Brewery History Society 2013

Jessica Boak and Ray Bailey, *20th Century Pub: From beer house to booze bunker*, Homewood Press 2017

Jessica Boak and Ray Bailey, *Brew Britannia: The strange rebirth of British beer*, Aurum 2014

Jessica Boak and Ray Bailey, *Gambrinus Waltz: German lager beer in Victorian and Edwardian London*, self-published 2014

Geoff Brandwood and Jane Jephcote, *London Heritage Pubs: An inside story*, CAMRA Books 2008

Mike Brown, *London Brewed: A historical directory of the commercial breweries of London from circa 1650*, Brewery History Society 2015

Pete Brown, *Hops and Glory: One man's search for the beer that built the British Empire*, Macmillan 2010

Martyn Cornell, *Amber Gold & Black: The history of Britain's great beers*, History Press 2010

Martyn Cornell, *Beer: The story of the pint*, Headline 2003

Jonny Garrett and Brad Evans, *The London Craft Beer Guide: The best breweries, pubs and tap rooms for the best artisan brews*, Ebury 2018

T R Gourvish and R G Wilson, *The British Brewing Industry 1830-1980*, Cambridge University Press 1994

Peter Haydon, *The English Pub: A history*, Robert Hale 1995

Peter Haydon and Tim Hampson, *London's Best Pubs* 3rd edition, IMM Lifestyle 2015

Ian Mackey, *Twenty Five Years of New British Breweries*, self-published 1998

Helen Osborn, *Britain's Oldest Brewery: The story behind the success of Young's of Wandsworth*, Young's 1999

William Page (ed), 'Industries: Brewing' in *A History of the County of Middlesex*, 1911, accessed at british-history.ac.uk

Ronald Pattinson, *London!*, barclayperkins.blogspot.com 2010

Roger Protz and Adrian Tierney-Jones, *Britain's Beer Revolution*, CAMRA Books 2014

John Spicer, Chris Thurman, John Walters and Simon Ward, *Intervention in the Modern UK Brewing Industry*, Palgrave Macmillan 2012

Adrian Tierney-Jones, *Crafting a Company: How Fuller, Smith & Turner became London's iconic brewery*, Fuller's 2015

I've also made use of the official records of listed buildings at **historicengland.org.uk/listings**; the inventories of heritage pub interiors at **pubheritage.camra.org.uk**; the independent database of British brewers at **quaffale.org.uk**; and numerous pieces on Martyn Cornell's Zythophile blog at **zythophile.co.uk**; and Jessica Boak and Ray Bailey's blog at **boakandbailey.com**

Organisations

Beer and Cider Academy. The beer and cider education arm of the Institute of Brewing and Distilling (IBD), delivering numerous courses and taste training sessions at its Bermondsey base for professionals, homebrewers and interested amateurs, and accrediting beer sommeliers and pommeliers. **beerandcideracademy.org**

Beer Passport. London brewery discount scheme founded in 2020 as a commercial enterprise by two keen beer fans, currently covering 23 breweries. **beerpassport.co.uk**

Brewery History Society. Membership organisation which promotes research into all aspects of the brewing industry, encourages interchange of information about breweries and brewing and collects archival material. UK-based but international in scope, it organises various activities and visits and publishes an excellent journal, essential for anyone with a special interest in the subject. **breweryhistory.com**

CAMRA (Campaign for Real Ale). Founded in 1971 and now one of the world's biggest and most successful independent consumer membership organisations, CAMRA advocates for the production, availability and consumption of quality real ale, cider and perry; pubs and clubs as social centres and part of the UK's cultural heritage; and the benefits of responsible social drinking. 14 branches in London organise activities such as pub and brewery visits, talks, tastings, beer festivals, pub and brewery research, campaigning around local planning and pub closures, publishing *London Drinker* magazine and beer quality rating, all entirely coordinated by volunteers. For details of local branches and London-wide activities see **london.camra.org.uk**; for national information and to join see **camra.org.uk**. See also Websites and magazines p344.

Craft Beer Cares. A collective of craft beer fans, many in London, who want to do good and have fun, organising various beer-related events to raise money for charity and promote social causes within the industry. They've found that drinking excellent beer while supporting an excellent cause is a good way to avoid nihilistic hangovers. **facebook.com/CraftBeerCares**.

London Amateur Brewers (LAB). An informal group of homebrewers who share skills, knowledge and beer to widen their appreciation of the world's finest drink and improve the beer they make themselves. Founded in 2007 by the late Ant Hayes, it's made a major contribution to beer culture in London and nurtured various now-professional talents. **londonamateurbrewers.co.uk**

London Brewers Alliance (LBA). Founded in 2010, this is the trade organisation for breweries in London and has undoubtedly played a major role in the recent resurgence of brewing. Full members must be commercial breweries operating within the M25. Its main object is to promote excellence in all aspects of brewing within London, by promoting its members and their beer and supporting the improvement of brewing skills among them. It also hopes to unite those who make local beer with those who love it. More information and a full list of member breweries at **londonbrewers.org**.

SIBA (Society of Independent Brewers). The trade organisation representing around 830 independent brewers across Britain, SIBA lobbies and campaigns for its members' interests, runs regional and national competitions and the BeerX trade event (outside London) and awards the Assured Independent British Craft Brewer accreditation. **siba.co.uk**

Society for the Preservation of Beers from the Wood (SPBW). A consumer campaign that predates CAMRA by almost a decade, the SPBW began in 1963 by arguing for the retention of wooden casks. It's since dropped that insistence, though still highlights the use of wood; otherwise, it's largely a social organisation for cask beer fans, organising brewery visits and pub crawls. There are six branches in London. **spbw.beer**

Places by theme

Breweries

Breweries with taprooms

These breweries have a taproom or similar facility on site or close by, open at least weekly.

40FT 129
Anspach and Hobday 242
Battersea Brewery 267
Beavertown (Tottenham Hale, part-Heineken) 184
BBNo (Brew by Numbers) SE16 107
BBNo (Brew by Numbers) SE10 228
Beerblefish Brewing Co 144
Belleville Brewing 268
Bexley Brewery 244
Bianca Road Brew Co 208
Bohem Brewery 185
Boxcar Brewery 158
Br3wery 244
Brixton Brewery Taproom (Heineken) 258
Brockley Brewery (Brockley) 230
Brockley Brewery (Hither Green) 230
Bullfinch Brewery 219
By the Horns Brewing 270
Camden Town Beer Hall (AB InBev) 172
Canopy Beer Co 220
Clarkshaws Brewing 258
Deviant and Dandy 132
Distortion Brewing 271
Dogs Grandad 259
Drop Project Brewing Co 281
Ealing Brewing 293
Exale Brewing 146
Five Points Brewing Co 134
Forest Road Brewing Co 231
Fourpure Brewing (Lion/Kirin) 210
Friendship Adventure 260
Fuller's Griffin Brewery (Asahi) 294
Gipsy Hill Brewing 221
Goodness Brewing Company 187
Gravity Well Brewing Co 146
Hackney Brewery 147
Hammerton Brewery 180
Howling Hops Brewery 135
Husk Brewing 166
Ignition Brewery 232
Jawbone Brewing 310
Kanpai London Craft Sake 223
Kernel Brewery 211
London Beer Lab 263
London Fields Brewery (Carlsberg) 137
Meantime Brewing (Asahi) 234
Mondo Brewing 272
Muswell Hillbilly 189
Neckstamper Brewing 149
Old Street Brewery 138
ORA Beer 190
Orbit Beers 225
Park Brewery 284
Partizan Brewing 212
Pillars Brewery 150
Pressure Drop Brewing 190
Pretty Decent Beer Co 150
Redemption Brewing 192
Sambrook's Brewery 274
Signal Brewery 250
Signature Brew 151
Solvay Society 152
Southey Brewing Co 251
Southwark Brewing 214
Spartan Brewery 215
Three Hills Brewing 215
Three Sods Brewery 140
Twickenham Fine Ales 314
Two Tribes Brewing 181
Villages Brewery 237
Werewolf Beer 176
Wild Card Brewery 155
Wimbledon Brewery 286

Brewpubs

Sometimes the brewery operates under a different name from the pub. I've shown brewery names first below, but pub names in the main entries.

Affinity Brewing Co (Grosvenor Arms) 261
Barnet Brewery (Black Horse) 196
Battersea Brewery 267

Beavertown Tottenham Hotspur
  (part-Heineken) 184
Block Brewery (Wenlock Arms) 113
BrewDog Outpost Tower Hill 92
Brewhouse and Kitchen Highbury 178
Brewhouse and Kitchen Hoxton 108
Brewhouse and Kitchen Islington 77
Broken Drum 244
Bullfinch Brewery (Bull and Finch) 219
Common Rioters (Green Goddess) Try also 240
Crate Brewery 131
E5 Poplar Bakehouse 159
Essex Street Brewing (Temple Brewhouse) 105
Fearless Nomad (Black Dog) 292
German Kraft (Kraft Dalston) 136
German Kraft (Mercato Metropolitano
  Elephant) 84
German Kraft (Mercato Metropolitano Mayfair)
  123
Goose Island Brewpub (AB InBev) 108
Gorgeous Brewery (Bull) 186
Hackney Church Brew Co 135
Laine's Beer Lab (Peoples Park Tavern) 139
Little Creatures Regents Canal (Lion/Kirin) 79
London Brewing (Bohemia) 197
Long Arm Brewery 109
Mikkeller Brewpub London 99
Old Fountain Brewhouse 111
St Felix Place 87
SlyBeast Brewing (Ram Inn) 273
Tap East 153
Up the Creek 237
Zerodegrees Blackheath 239

Other London breweries
These breweries either don't have a taproom
on site or open less frequently than weekly, but
those marked * have a dedicated taproom at
another location. See entries for details.

Anomaly Brewing 280
Brick Brewery* 229
Brixton Brewery (Heineken)* 218
Camden Town Brewery (AB InBev)* 197
Concrete Island Brewery 300
Cronx Brewery* 131
CTZN Brew* 280
Earth Ale* 186
East London Brewing 145
East Side Brewery 165
Enefeld Brewery 198
Greater Good Fresh Brewing Co 147
Greywood Brewery 188

Inkspot Brewery* 262
Jeffersons Brewery 283
London Beer Factory* 223
London Beer Lab (Loughborough Junction)* 263
Macintosh Ales 302
Mad Yank Brewery 310
Magic Spells 149
Mammoth Beer 137
Marlix Brewing Co 248
Mutineers Brewery 248
Oddly Beer 199
Old Kent Road Brewery 235
One Mile End* 189
Parakeet City Brewing 295
Perivale Brewery 296
Pinnora Brewing 312
Portobello Brewing Co 305
Small Beer Brew Co 213
St Mary's Brewery 175
Tiny Vessel Brewing Co* 313
Truman's Beer* 140
Urban Alchemy Brewing Co 199
Volden Brewing 238
Weird Beard Brew Co 297
WorkShy Brewing 287
Wrong Side of the Tracks 239

Other brewery outlets
These breweries are located outside London
but have featured outlets in this book.

Baladin (Piozzo, Piemonte, Italy): Baladin Camden 17
Big Smoke (Esher, Surrey) 330
BrewDog (Ellon, Aberdeenshire, Scotland) 330
Cloudwater (Manchester): Cloudwater Taproom 20
Goose Island (AB InBev; Chicago, Illinois, USA):
  Goose Island Brewpub 108
Greene King (Bury St Edmunds, Suffolk) 332
Hall & Woodhouse (Blandford Forum, Dorset) 332
Harvey's (Lewes, East Sussex): Royal Oak 86
Hop Back (Salisbury, Wiltshire): Sultan 285
Lagunitas (Heineken; Petaluma, California and
  Chicago, Illinois, USA): St Felix Place 87
Laine (Horsham, West Sussex) 333
Little Creatures (Lion/Kirin; Fremantle, Western
  Australia): Little Creatures Regents Canal 79
McMullen (Hertford, Hertfordshire) 333
Mikkeller (Copenhagen, Denmark): Mikkeller Bar
  London 110, Mikkeller Brewpub London 99
Moor Beer (Bristol): Moor Vaults 212
Oakham (Peterborough): Oaka London 224
Porterhouse (Dublin, Ireland): Porterhouse 105
St Peter's (Bungay, Suffolk): Jerusalem Tavern 98

Samuel Smith (Tadcaster, North Yorkshire): Olde Cheshire Cheese 104

Shepherd Neame (Faversham, Kent) Eleanor Arms 159

Verdant (Falmouth, Cornwall): Experiment 133

Wadworth (Devizes, Wiltshire): Kings Arms SW6 302

West Berkshire (Yattendon, West Berkshire): Oxford Tavern 173

Inside and out

Heritage pubs

All these pubs are on the National Inventory of Historic Pub Interiors except those marked (R) which are in the Regional Inventory, or as shown. Pubs included in the separate Heritage pubs listings rather than as main entries or Try alsos are indicated by*. For more background see p71.

Argyll Arms* 119
Blackfriar* 95
Blythe Hill Tavern 229
Churchill Arms (R)* 125
Cittie of Yorke* 105
Dog and Duck* 119
Dove W6 (R)* 303
Express (R) Try also 299
Fox (some regional importance) Try also 299
George* 89
Great Northern Railway Tavern (R) 188
Ivy House (R) 222
Kings Arms SE1 (R) 160
Lamb WC1 (R)* 82
Mayflower (some regional importance)* 216
Old Pack Horse (R) Try also 299
Olde Cheshire Cheese 104
Olde Mitre 104
Pineapple (R) 174
Prince Alfred* 306
Princess Louise* 105
Queens* 193
Salisbury* 106
Salisbury Hotel Try also 193
Shaftesbury Tavern (R) Try also 183
Tabard (R) 297
Viaduct Tavern* 95
Victoria* 125
Windsor Castle Try also 125

Interesting buildings

BBNo SE10 228
Bohemia 197
Cock Tavern 136
Commercial Tavern 108
Crosse Keys 93
Earth Tap 186
Euston Tap 78
Exmouth Arms 98
Fuller's Griffin Brewery 294
George and Dragon 295
Jerusalem Tavern 98
Muswell Hillbilly 189
Perivale Brewery 296
Porterhouse 105
Ram Inn 273
Sambrook's Brewery 274
Star and Garter 251
Truman's Social Club 154
Two Tribes 181

Great gardens

Bird and Barrel 243
Black Dog 292
Blythe Hill Tavern 229
Brick Tap Room 218
Chesham Arms 131
Cockpit 244
Dog and Bell 231
Earl of Essex 78
Masons Arms 311
Parlour 304
Peoples Park Tavern 139
Pineapple 174
Smokehouse 181
Star and Garter 251
Strongroom 112
Sussex Arms 312

On offer

Accommodation

Note that at several of these venues, bedrooms are in the same building but operated separately from the pub.

Alma 76
Bull and Last Try also 177
Exmouth Arms NW1 Try also 81
Long Arm Brewery 109
Prince of Wales Townhouse Try also 303
Red Lion 151
Singer Tavern Try also 116
Westow House 226

Food (exceptional)

German

Homebrewing and brew schools

Italian

Japanese

Micropubs

Music

Polish

Theatre and comedy

Nearby

AFC Wimbledon Stadium

Alexandra Palace and Park

Almond Road beer venues and Bermondsey Blue Market

WELCOME BACK TO
THE DOG AND BELL!
AS WE WERE
SAYING,
BEFORE WE
WERE SO
RUDELY
INTERRUPTED
TEA & Freshly Ground COFFEE

Beer venues A-Z

Acknowledgements

Many, many people participated in various ways in the making of this book, both wittingly and unwittingly.

First and foremost, I'd like to thank the owners, managers and staff of all the outlets listed, not only for contributing to London's burgeoning beer culture but for being so courteous and helpful when I turned up unexpectedly with damn fool questions when they had customers to serve. Equally, I'm extremely appreciative of the owners, managers and staff of all the London breweries, both for making great beer and for taking time out from doing so to share their stories, views and, in many cases, beers with me. Thanks also to the London Brewers' Alliance and John Cryne, Paddy Johnson and Steve Williams in particular.

Geoff Strawbridge, Roy Tunstall, *London Drinker* editor Tony Hedger, CAMRA's London Liaison Group and local branches have been extremely helpful in getting the word out there and keeping me in touch. The branches also deserve to be thanked for all the great work they've done over the years in protecting and promoting London's beer culture. Without them I suspect we wouldn't be enjoying the current abundance. John Paul Adams and Jeremy Gray deserve special thanks for their tireless chronicling of the London brewing scene, from which I have unashamedly and repeatedly cribbed.

The following provided helpful additional suggestions and invaluable intelligence for this and previous editions: Mitch Adams, Rachel Alcock, Paul Anspach, Ray Bailey, Dominic Bates, Stephen Beaumont, Ruth Berman, Andrew Birkby, Ted Blair, Jessica Boak, Anna Borrelli, John Bratley, Ric Brown, Ben Butler, Martin Butler, Mark Chant, Michaela Charles, Paul Charlton, Matt Chinnery, Ian Collinson, Jo Copestick, Martyn Cornell, Colin Coyne, Liz Cronin, Simon Croome, Jasper Cuppaidge, Matthew Curtis, Lorenzo Dabove, Glynn Davis, the Deptford Dame, Mark Dredge, Ben Duckworth, Karl Durand O'Connor, Stephen Eastwood, John Elkins, Phil Emond, Jen Ferguson, Charlie Gallagher, Des Garrahan, Eddie Gershon, George Gimber, Laura Goodman, Nick Goodwin, Steve Grae, John Gray, John Hatch, Will Hawkes, Glenn Heinzel (who also provided a very welcome couple of lifts), Joakim Hellborg, Mike Hill, Jack Hobday, Tim Holt, Chris Hooper, David Hope, HuishHugh, Stephen Jackson, Rob Jones, Bob Keaveney, John Keeling, Teresa Langston, Richard Larkin, Alec Latham, Anita Le Roy, Shea Luke, Graham McAteer, Thomas Marshall, Phil Marson, Tim Martin, Jenn Merrick, James Morgan, Nathan Nolan, Nicos, Evin O'Riordain, Owen Ogletree, Charles Owens, the late and sadly missed Glenn Payne, Simon Pipola, Ron Pattinson, Rick Pickup, Dominic Pinto, Logan Plant, Derek Prentice, Roger Protz, Evan Rail, Markus Raupach, Glyn Roberts, Tony Roome, James Rylance, Duncan Sambrook, Steve Shapiro, Holly Simpson, Tim Skelton, Nigel Slater, Andy Smith, Nathanial Southwood, the late and sadly missed Bob Steel, Julian Stone, Emma Stump, Clare Wadd, Fred Waltman, Rex Ward, Roger Warhurst, Emma Watts, Tim Webb, Peter Wells, Ian White, Gail Ann Williams, Glenn Williams, Helen Wilson and Jaega Wise. I raise a glass of Southwark ale to them all.

I'm further grateful to all the London Drinkers, the team at Taps and Tapas and other contributors named in the text; to managing editor Katie Hunt, acting editor Alan Murphy, project manager Julie Hudson and marketing whizz Toby Langdon at CAMRA Books; designer Dale Tomlinson and cartographer James Hall; Simon Hall, who commissioned the book in the first place and worked on the previous editions; Emma Haines, Katie Hunt and Ian Midson who also worked on the previous editions; Tim Hampson at *BEER* magazine who was forgiving beyond the call of duty with deadlines for other stuff I was supposed to be writing for him; Hannah Colebourn, Julia Crear and Tricia Edeam at Living Streets for helping me schedule around the other work they needed me to do; Dom Bowcutt and Paul Davies at UK Brewery Tours for swapping Saturdays and some valuable suggestions too; colleagues at the Ramblers who gave me the flexibility to create the first two editions; and the amazing teams at Moorfields Eye Hospital and St Bartholomew's Hospital, without whom…

As the original edition was my first book, I want to express my gratitude to the following: Tom and Jasper who first published my beer reviews on the Oxford Bottled Beer Database; Ted Bruning who gave me my first paid gig as a beer writer; and Sally Toms, Dominic Bates, Adrian Tierney-Jones and Tom Stainer who all supported my writing. Love and thanks too to my sister Adèle de Moor and my nephew Sunny de Moor, also now a beer expert in his own right and a welcome source of ideas and recommendations. My mother Phyllis de Moor always encouraged me in my creative endeavours and was proud to see the first two editions. She's sadly no longer around to read this, but still deserves perhaps the biggest thanks of all.

Second only to Phyllis in deserving my gratitude is my partner, Ian Harris, who as previously has been unfailingly patient and supportive despite being the exception that proves the 'it's not that you don't like beer, it's just that you haven't found a beer you like yet' rule. I've written yet another edition of the bloody book, Ian. Bloody, bloody book.

CAMRA Books

Modern British Beer
MATTHEW CURTIS

This book is about why modern British beer is important. Over the course of the past two decades the British beer scene as we know it has changed, forever. Matthew Curtis gives a personal insight into the eclectic and exciting world of modern British beer from a choice of 86 influential brews; from how they taste, how their ingredients are sourced, to the engaging stories of the people behind the scenes working hard to bring exciting beer to drinkers all over Britain. This book is a fantastic starting point to explore British beer with an exciting location closer than you think.

RRP **£15.99**   ISBN 978-1-85249-370-7

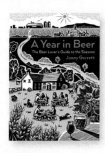

A Year in Beer
JONNY GARRETT

Chefs have been telling us to eat seasonally for decades, yet, when it comes to drink, we tend to reach for the same thing, whatever time of year. But beer is inextricably linked to the seasons, and thinking about it all seasonally opens the door to even greater beer experiences. *A Year in Beer* is an exploration of how our ingredients and tastes change with the seasons, and how Britain's rich brewing history still influences us today. Discover the best UK beer experiences, from summer beer festivals to the autumn hop and apple harvests – taking in the glory of the seasons that make them all possible.

RRP **£15.99**   ISBN 978-1-85249-372-1

World Beer Guide
ROGER PROTZ

The world of beer is on fire. Traditional brewing countries are witnessing a spectacular growth in the number of beer makers while drinkers in such unlikely nations as France and Italy are moving from the grape to the grain. Drawing on decades of experience, Roger Protz takes readers on a journey of discovery around the world's favourite alcoholic drink – uncovering the interlinked stories behind the best breweries and beers across every continent in the world.

RRP **£30**   ISBN 978-1-85249-373-8

Order these and other CAMRA Books from **shop.camra.org.uk**